GLOBAL CAPITALISM

ALSO BY JEFFRY A. FRIEDEN

DEBT, DEVELOPMENT, AND DEMOCRACY: MODERN POLITICAL ECONOMY AND LATIN AMERICA, 1965–1985

BANKING ON THE WORLD: THE POLITICS OF AMERICAN INTERNATIONAL FINANCE

W · W · NORTON & COMPANY · NEW YORK · LONDON

GLOBAL CAPITALISM

ITS FALL AND RISE IN
THE TWENTIETH CENTURY

JEFFRY A. FRIEDEN

For information about permission to reproduce selections from this book, write to Permissions,
W. W. Norton & Company, Inc., 500 Fifth Avenue, New York, NY 10110

Manufacturing by Courier Westford
Production manager: Julia Druskin

Library of Congress Cataloging-in-Publication Data

Frieden, Jeffry A.
Global capitalism : its fall and rise in the twentieth century / Jeffry Frieden. — 1st ed.
p. cm.
Includes bibliographical references and index.
ISBN 0-393-05808-5 (hardcover)
1. International economic relations—History—20th century. 2. Capitalism—History—
20th century. 3. Globalization—Economic aspects—History—20th century. 4. International
finance—History—20th century. 5. Economic history—20th century. I. Title.
HF1359.F735 2006
337'.09'04—dc22

2005024357

ISBN 978-0-393-32981-0 pbk.

W. W. Norton & Company, Inc., 500 Fifth Avenue, New York, N.Y. 10110
www.wwnorton.com

W. W. Norton & Company Ltd., Castle House, 75/76 Wells Street, London W1T 3QT

4 5 6 7 8 9 0

Contents

7. The World of Tomorrow   155

8. The Established Order Collapses   173

9. The Turn to Autarky   195

10. Building a Social Democracy   229

III. TOGETHER AGAIN, 1939–1973

15. The End of Bretton Woods   339

IV. GLOBALIZATION, 1973–2000

16. Crisis and Change   363

17. Globalizers Victorious   392

18. Countries Catch Up   413

Foreword by *Paul Kennedy*

Of all the ways in which the twentieth century makes its claim to a special place in history, few can equal in importance the enormous transformation of economic life. Were a farmer in Illinois or a peasant in Bangalore, both struggling to make ends meet around 1900, brought back to our planet today, he would be astounded at its transformation. The massive increases in productivity and wealth, the mind-boggling new technologies, and the improvements in material comforts would have made him speechless. Astonished though he would be, he would not of course have guessed at the many convulsions and setbacks that had occurred to the world economy in the hundred-year interval.

Recording that tale is the task that Professor Jeffry A. Frieden sets himself, with insight and poise and vast learning, in *Global Capitalism*. This work has a powerful theme that runs right through, thus helping the reader to make sense of the whole; this is not your standard economic history textbook, though it surely will be used in many classes. That theme is captured well in the subtle combination of the title and subtitle of Professor Frieden's book: "fall and rise," and "global capitalism."

At the core lie the "creative gales" of modern world capitalism (to borrow Joseph Schumpeter's famous phrase). Already by the late nineteenth century those gales were blowing across the globe, creating new structures of production, trade, and finance, and battering their predecessors into the ground. They coexisted with contemporary forces of nationalism and militarism that were in their way equally rampant and pervasive. This was an explosive mix, producing in turn the death and destruction of World War One, and the calamitous economic and political reverberations of the succeeding two decades.

It is hard to suggest a single part of Professor Frieden's impressive book for special attention, but it seems to me that his discussion of political economies between the two world wars is really wonderful. Here he shows how troubled the capitalist system of free markets and laissez-faire had become, not simply because of its failure to provide sufficient wealth and jobs but also because of the reactions against liberal capitalism in the political realm. With the USSR pushing for "socialism in one country," the fascist states practicing a mixture of economic autarky and external aggression, and the United States (by now the world's greatest power) retreating to the wings of the world's stage, the old system could not survive. Things fell apart.

They were put together again by the remarkable turnaround in America's commitment to world affairs following Pearl Harbor, a commitment that was to last throughout the Cold War that followed, and that was of a strongly coeval nature: global capitalism could not survive without the military power and political will of the West, and the latter's capacities could only be sustained by the productive successes of the capitalistic system. This time, things held together.

Professor Frieden's story is by no means triumphalist, like the accounts offered by conservative, free-market economists of our present day. He is all too aware—as were Marx, Schumpeter, and Keynes before him—that capitalism, by its very nature, creates losers as well as winners. His account of the mass unemployment of the 1930s is very sobering, and his analysis (see Chapter 19) of "the African catastrophe" of our current times is profoundly depressing. Moreover, he is wise enough to conclude this great survey, not on any supremely confident note, but by asking a number of serious questions about our world economy as it lurches through the first decade of the twenty-first century. In consequence, the reader comes away from this book not only impressed by its display of knowledge and judgment but also somewhat disturbed by the prospects for the world of commerce, finance, and markets that lie ahead. And it is surely right for us to put down this text in a mood of deep reflection. Schumpeter's creative gales are not yet finished, and it is the merit of *Global Capitalism* to have reminded us that our system of economic exchange comes with its perils as well as its manifold benefits.

Preface

National economies are more open to one another than ever before. With international trade at an unprecedented level, much of what people consume is imported and much of what they produce is exported. Businesses send huge quantities of capital to other nations; in some countries as much as half of all investment is made abroad. Millions of people migrate yearly in search of jobs. Manufacturers, farmers, miners, bankers, and traders must think globally about every economic decision they face. Technologies, artistic movements, business practices, musical trends, and fads and fashions reach all corners of the developed world almost instantaneously. Global economy and culture form a nearly seamless web in which national boundaries are increasingly irrelevant to trade, investment, finance, and other economic activity.

Many people now regard globalization as inevitable and irreversible. After decades of international economic integration, people in the world's economic centers think of global capitalism as the normal state of things, certain to continue into the foreseeable future and perhaps forever.

The situation at the turn of the twentieth century looked remarkably similar. In the early 1900s international economic integration was largely taken for granted. It had been the norm for the world's economic leader, the United Kingdom, for sixty years, and for the world's other major industrial and agricultural nations for about forty years. Open

trade relations, international finance, untrammeled international investment and immigration, and a common monetary order under the gold
standard had been the central organizing principles of the modern
world for generations.

But it took only a few months for the entire edifice of globalization to
collapse. World War One broke out in August 1914 and swept away the
foundations of the preexisting global economic order. For years world
economic and political leaders attempted, without success, to restore
the pre-1914 international economy. The international order disintegrated and imploded brutally into the Great Depression of the 1930s
and World War Two.

Globalization was a choice, not a fact. For decades global capitalism
had seemed unchanging in its basic outlines, but World War One
showed it to be a series of points in a long and tortuous trajectory.
Globalization unraveled so quickly that participants never had a chance
to stop the collapse. An international order whose economic, political,
social, and cultural components had defined the world for decades
before 1914 disappeared completely.

For eighty years after 1914 global economic integration existed only in
the imagination of theorists and historians. Into the 1920s attempts to
rebuild the previous world economy failed repeatedly; in the 1930s the
nations of the world turned away from international economic connections and sought self-sufficiency. After World War Two, the Communist
world rejected global capitalism on principle, while the developing
world rejected it in practice. Over the course of the 1950s and 1960s the
industrial nations of Western Europe, North America, and Japan edged
toward greater economic ties, but their governments continued to control most trade, investment, and immigration. Only after two decades of
crisis and turmoil, in the early 1990s the developing nations turned outward, the Communist nations abandoned central planning for international markets, and the industrialized world dropped most of its prior
controls on world economic ties. Globalization had returned
triumphant.

As was the case a hundred years ago, many people now take an integrated world economy for granted, regard it as the natural state of
things, and expect that it will last forever. Yet the bases on which global
capitalism rests today are not very different from what they were in
1900, and the potential for their disruption is as present today as then.

Globalization is still a choice, not a fact. It is a choice made by governments that consciously decide to reduce barriers to trade and

investment, adopt new policies toward international money and finance, and chart fresh economic courses. Decisions made by each government are interconnected; international finance, international trade, and international monetary relations depend on the joint actions of national governments around the world. National policies and relations among national governments are the sources of globalization and determine its staying power.

Globalization needs supportive governments, and supportive governments need domestic political support. International economic affairs depend on political backing from powerful countries and from powerful groups in those countries. The integrated world economy before 1914 rested on government actions to sustain it; when these policies became unpopular, they could not be maintained, and with them fell the international economic order. Today's global economy also depends on the domestic political underpinnings of national policies.

What is to be done about the world economy? Is contemporary globalization inevitable? Is it desirable? Will it last forever? We now know that the 1900 image of global capitalism was misleading. The apparent stability of the early 1900s was followed by decades of conflicts and upheavals. Today's international economic order also seems secure, but in historical perspective it may be only a brief interlude. The historical forces that shaped the world economy in the twentieth century continue to determine today's version of globalization and will decide its fate.

Prologue: Into the Twentieth Century

In June 1815 three hundred thousand troops converged near Brussels for the battle that was to end the Napoleonic Wars. The forces of Britain, Prussia, Austria, Russia, and the Netherlands gathered against the French, to determine which great power would control the world. By midnight on June 18 the French defeat was clear. Across the Channel two and a half days later news of Wellington's victory reached the cabinet meeting in London, two hundred miles from the battlefield. Napoleon was defeated, and the age of British supremacy began.

The British and Allied victory in the Napoleonic Wars was the culmination of three hundred years of absolutist monarchy and of the economic order that supported it. Europe's great powers organized themselves to battle over territory and subjects, sending their armies into round after round of dynastic wars. The region's rulers supported their military machines with an economic system called mercantilism, which they used to manipulate their economies for military advantage. Political and diplomatic concerns were primary; economic relations were tools to enforce or reinforce dynastic power, and private fortunes depended on favored ties to royal families. The French revolutionary challenge to this political and economic order was defeated in 1815 on the outskirts of Brussels.

After 1815 the combination of British supremacy, French defeat, and a power balance in Europe calmed the continent's incessant conflict.

The subsequent period has gone down in history as the Hundred Years' Peace, for great power wars nearly ceased. But as the dynastic order stabilized, its economic underpinnings fell apart. In the century between the end of the Napoleonic Wars and the beginning of World War One, the relationship between monarchs and markets was turned on its head.

From mercantilism to free trade

The absolute monarchs who ruled Europe and the world before 1800 were concerned with geopolitical alliances, colonial extraction, and the size and power of their national states. They managed their economies as part of the military and diplomatic vicissitudes of dynastic politics, manipulating their trade by military means.

Europe's sovereigns used a system of economic control known as mercantilism to exploit colonial markets and strengthen royal dominance. Sometimes the crown's own armies oversaw the extraction of natural resources—gold and silver from the mines of South America, for example. Most of the time crown princes worked with merchant princes— royally chartered monopolies, such as the British and Dutch East India companies—to squeeze profits out of captive colonial markets. Mercantilism enriched the crown, which then used those riches to build up military force. "Wealth is power," wrote the English philosopher Thomas Hobbes, "and power is wealth." One of his fellow mercantilist thinkers drew out the connections: "Foreign trade produces riches, riches power, power preserves our trade and religion."[1]

Under mercantilism, the colonial power forced its colonies to trade with the mother country, to enrich the government and its supporters. The mercantilists compelled their subjects to sell many goods only to them, paying the colonies less than world market prices for crops and raw materials: Virginia tobacco in London; Cuban sugar in Madrid. Mercantilist policy also required the colonies to buy many products from the mother country, ensuring that the homeland could sell to its subjects at above world market prices.

The mercantilist system opened much of the world to commerce, but that commerce was regulated by military might for the benefit of the mighty. The system's intellectual supporters could justify the exploitative economics of the system because rulers used some of the accumulated riches to protect their subjects. And many colonial subjects did appreciate the protection; in North America, for example, British military force shielded settlers from the French and Spanish and their Native American allies. Some North American colonists, especially the Virginia planters and New England merchants whose businesses were most directly affected by British mercantilist controls, complained. But to many it seemed a fair trade: Military power allowed economic growth, and economic growth under mercantilist control financed military power.

At the time of the Napoleonic Wars, mercantilism was already beginning to weaken. British industrialists introduced a flurry of technological innovations that revolutionized production starting around 1750. Employers brought dozens, even hundreds of workers together in large factories to use new machinery, new energy sources, and new forms of organization. Power looms and mechanical spinners transformed the textile industry. Improvements in the use of waterpower and eventually the development of steam power made the machinery more powerful still. By the 1820s British factories could undercut competitors in virtually every market. The economic interests created by Britain's Industrial Revolution saw mercantilism as irrelevant or harmful.

British manufacturers wanted to eliminate the country's trade barriers. Allowing foreigners to sell their products to Britain promised several positive effects. British manufacturers could lower their costs directly by importing cheaper raw materials, and indirectly because cheaper imported food would allow factory owners to pay lower wages without reducing workers' standard of living. At the same time, if foreigners earned more by selling to Britain, they would be able to buy more British goods. British industrialists also realized that if foreigners could buy all the manufactures they needed from low-cost British producers, they would have less need to develop their own industries. For these reasons, Britain's manufacturing classes and regions developed an antipathy to mercantilism and a strong desire for free trade.

As the City of London became the world's financial center, it added its influence to that of other free trade interests. Britain's international bankers had a powerful reason to open up the British market to foreigners: The foreigners were their customers. American or Argentine access to the thriving British market would make it easier for Americans and Argentines to pay their debts to London. The industrial and financial interests mounted a concerted attack on what antimercantilist crusader Adam Smith called "the mean and malignant expedients of the mercantile system."[2] By the 1820s those "malignant" mercantilist expedients were under constant challenge. The opponents of mercantilism focused on the Corn Laws, the taxes imposed during the Napoleonic Wars on imports of grain (corn, in British parlance), which served to increase the domestic price of grain substantially.

British farmers, however, were eager to maintain restrictions on agricultural imports. They relied on the Corn Laws' very high tariffs on imported grain and argued that repeal of the laws would doom British farming. Supporters of the laws invoked the desirability of self-sufficiency in food, the importance of farming to the British way of life, and the painful adjustment that a flood of cheap grain would impose. Free traders focused on the benefits of access to inexpensive goods, especially the cheap food that repeal of the Corn Laws would bring. Protectionist farmers battled free-trading manufacturers and bankers.

The free traders won, but only after a protracted and bitter struggle. The defeat of mercantilism required a major reform of British political institutions, a changed electoral system that reduced the power of farm constituencies and increased that of the cities and their middle-class residents. Even with the electoral reforms in place, the final votes in 1846 and 1847 were extremely close and tore the Conservative Party apart. A few years later Parliament repealed the last vestiges of British mercantile controls on foreign trade.

Once Britain, the world's most important economy, discarded mercantilism, other countries faced new choices. The policy problems of the mercantilist era—military alliances and monopolies—gave way to the great debates of the nineteenth century about whether and how countries should join the global market. As Britain liberalized trade, many of its customers and suppliers followed suit.

In 1860 France joined Britain in a sweeping commercial treaty that freed trade between them and drew most of the rest of Europe in this direction. As the German states moved toward unification in 1871, they created a free trade area among themselves, then opened trade with the rest of the world. Many New World governments also liberalized trade, as did the remaining colonial possessions of the free-trading European powers. Mercantilism was dead, and integration into world markets was the order of the day. Over the course of the 1800s the trade of the advanced countries grew twice to three times as fast as their economies; by the end of the century trade was seven or eight times as large a share of the world's economy as it had been at the beginning of the century.[3]

Transportation and communications advanced dramatically too. At the time of the Battle of Waterloo, long-distance travel, transportation, and communications were extremely expensive and exceedingly slow, whatever the price. By the late 1800s telegraphs, telephones, steamships, and railroads had replaced horses, carrier pigeons, couriers, and sails. The railroad, the most significant advance in land transportation since the time of the Greeks, fundamentally changed the speed and cost of carrying cargo overland. The steamship revolutionized oceangoing shipping, reducing the Atlantic crossing from over a month in 1816 to less than a week in 1896. Also, steamships could go faster, hold more, and operate more cheaply than sailing ships.

The new technologies expanded the effective market for most goods from the radius of a few days' walk to the entire modern world. In 1830 it cost more than thirty dollars to move a ton of cargo three hundred miles overland—from central Pennsylvania to New York, Berlin to Bonn, or Lyons to Paris—and another ten dollars to ship it across the Atlantic. This was a prohibitive expense for such heavy goods as wheat or iron bar; it cost about the same forty dollars to buy a ton of each as it did to ship a ton over land and sea. Thus before the mid-1800s most goods traded internationally were valuable, light, and not perishable: spices; fancy textiles; precious metals; crops with a high cost-to-weight ratio, such as cotton and tobacco. By 1900 the railroad had reduced the cost of land transportation by more than four-fifths, the steamship by more than two-thirds. To ship a ton of cargo the same three hundred miles overland now cost five dollars instead of thirty, across the Atlantic three dollars instead of ten. The overall price of bringing this ton of goods from the American interior to England had dropped from forty to eight dollars, from roughly the same as the price of the ton of wheat or iron bar to one-fifth the price of the good.

The transportation revolution led to a twentyfold increase in the world's shipping capacity during the nineteenth century.[4] Europe flooded the world with its manufactures and was in turn flooded with farm products and raw materials from the prairies and the pampas, the Amazon and Australia.

With the new transportation technologies and the triumph of free trade in Britain, the world of militarized national mercantilisms gave way to a truly international market. The old order preserved by force of arms at Waterloo was gone and replaced by a new global capitalism. Markets, not monarchs, were the dominant force. News raced around the world by telegraph and telephone in minutes, not weeks or months. Investors from London and Paris to New York, Buenos Aires, and Tokyo wove a nearly seamless web of global capital. The world had changed from the era of Waterloo in every dimension, political, technological, financial, and diplomatic.

From silver to gold

The gold standard became the most powerful organizing principle of global capitalism during the nineteenth century. For centuries before 1800 most countries used gold and silver money interchangeably. Merchants preferred silver, copper, and other cheaper metals for local business and reserved the more valuable gold for international transactions. But in 1717 Sir Isaac Newton, master of the mint, standardized the English currency and put the country on a gold standard in practice (if not in theory; silver continued to be legal tender although it was not used). The United Kingdom was virtually alone as a gold monometallic country; it deviated from the gold standard only once, temporarily, during the Napoleonic Wars. Almost all other countries were bimetallic, using both gold and silver.

Centuries of shared gold and silver money came to an abrupt end in the 1870s. New silver discoveries drove down the price of silver and made the existing rate of exchange between the two metals unstable, so governments either had to change the rate or had to choose between gold and silver. Meanwhile, as international trade and investment grew, gold, the traditional international medium of exchange, became more attractive than domestic silver. Finally, Great Britain's status as the global market leader attracted other countries to use the same monetary system.

In the 1870s most major industrial countries joined the gold standard. When a country's government went on gold, it promised to exchange its currency for gold at a preestablished rate. The country's currency became equivalent to gold, interchangeable at a fixed rate with the money of any other gold standard country. Germany went on gold in 1872, Scandinavia in 1873, the Netherlands in 1875, Belgium, France, and Switzerland in 1878, the United States in 1879. Whereas in 1871 only Britain and some of its colonies (and its ally Portugal) were on gold, by 1879 most of the industrial world had adopted the gold standard.

With all major currencies directly convertible into gold at fixed rates, the industrial world essentially shared one international currency. In effect, gold was a common global money for all countries on the gold standard, but under different names—marks, francs, pounds, dollars—in different countries. Gold-backed money invested by Germans in Japan, or Belgians in Canada, would be paid back in equivalent amounts of gold-backed money. Contracted prices would not fluctuate, for exchange rates did not move. The gold standard rates of exchange between the pound and the mark, the franc and the dollar, and other currencies were so fixed for so long that, it is said, schoolchildren learned them by rote because they seemed as stable as the multiplication tables. The predictability of the gold standard facilitated world trade, lending, investment, migration, and payments. Bankers and investors could be certain about debts being paid in gold equivalents or about earning profits in gold-backed currencies.

Other forces also facilitated international finance. With the development of worldwide telegraphy, information could be transmitted instantaneously from any developed area to investors in London, Paris, and Berlin. Financial journalism became international, with stories filed in New York or Buenos Aires appearing in the following day's London and Paris newpapers.

International investment soared. Citizens of rich countries invested huge portions of their savings abroad. Foreign investments, largely in bonds and stocks, accounted for about one-third of the savings of the United Kingdom, one-quarter of France, one-tenth of Germany.[5] World markets for goods and capital were linked more tightly than they had ever been by free trade, the gold standard, and the new technologies of transportation and communications.

Threats to the global order

Not everyone welcomed economic integration. With the opening of the world economy and the application of new transportation technologies, cheap New World grain flooded the world market. The dramatic fall in farm prices devastated many rural areas in the Old World and caused near-starvation conditions from Scandinavia to Sicily.

Nor was technological change an unmitigated good. New factory techniques made craftsmen obsolete, and advances in agricultural productivity made farmers redundant. Technological change allowed remarkable increases in the productivity of just about everything, but the benefits of these advances were not evenly distributed. When a machine and five men could do the work of a hundred, the social good was plain to see, but even if a few of the other ninety-five were employed making the machine, most would have to abandon their accustomed lives and find other ways to support themselves. The trade and technologies that increased aggregate income could also ruin millions of farmers and workers.

The new world economy also had a mixed impact on the poor countries. Some underdeveloped regions grew rapidly. But others in Africa, Asia, and Latin America—or on the rapidly shrinking frontiers of such "areas of recent settlement" as North America—would have appreciated a world without the Gatling guns, steamships, and railroads that gave Europeans such an advantage in establishing their dominion. Indeed, some of the most striking technical advances were in the weapons of mass destruction whose potency would fully be demonstrated only after 1913. The technological and industrial gap that opened ever wider between rich and poor nations led to a new round of colonial conquest.

A macroeconomic phenomenon that has gone down in economic history as the Great Depression of 1873–1896 contributed to dissatisfaction with free trade and the gold standard. The name may be misleading, because that depression was not an economic collapse but a gradual and continual decline in world prices. From 1873 until 1896 prices dropped by 22 percent in the United Kingdom, 32 percent in the United States, more elsewhere.[6] This depression of prices that gave the episode its name caused serious problems. Prices and earnings declined, but debt burdens remained constant. Expectations of further price declines caused uncertainty and pessimism. More important, the price declines were not across the board. The prices of goods that entered readily into world trade fell particularly rapidly, such raw materials as wheat, cotton, and coal by 59, 58, and 57 percent respectively. But the prices of other goods and services fell more slowly or not at all. For example, American farm prices declined by more than a third, mining prices by nearly half, but construction costs stayed constant.[7] The price changes sparked social protests throughout the world's farming and mining regions.

Producers faced with declining prices sought relief by protection from imports. Farmers and manufacturers demanded and often received protective tariffs that reversed the previous trend toward freer trade.

France and Italy engaged in a bitter trade war. The world's largest economy, the United States, raised protectionist walls around its domestic market, and the world's second-largest economy, Germany, increased tariffs on many goods. Great Britain and the Low Countries almost alone continued to stand for free trade, and there too manufacturers were beginnning to clamor for government to defend them against cheap imports from low-wage producers from the Continent and North America.

For those that thought they were on the losing side of the world economy, the gold standard became a potent symbol of the hated economic Pax Britannica.[8] American opponents of gold insisted: "A vast conspiracy against mankind has been organized on two continents, and it is rapidly taking possession of the world."[9] According to American antigold orator Mary Elizabeth Lease, gold supporters were stooges of this conspiracy: "Wall Street owns the country. . . . Money rules, and our Vice President is a London banker."[10]

As prices fell particularly steeply in the early 1890s, complaints about the gold standard gathered strength. Farmers and miners believed that going off gold would enable their governments to push prices of their goods higher. In America antigold activists won election after election in the country's farming and mining regions. In Latin America and Asia the gold standard was so unpopular that it was rarely adhered to. Italy, Spain, and Portugal went off gold; the Russian and Austro-Hungarian empires resisted going on it. The gold standard glue that held global capitalism together seemed to be weakening.

As the gold standard trembled, the international financial system began to show signs of strain. The Great Depression hit debtor nations particularly hard, impeding their ability to pay their creditors. South America's finances weakened, and in 1890 the threat that Argentina might default on its debts caused the collapse of one of the world's great investment houses, Baring Brothers of London. A financial panic swept the United States in 1893, and foreign investors shied away from the world's most important borrower. After nearly thirty years of uninterrupted growth, financial flows slowed.

The Great Depression created greater frictions among the great powers than had existed for decades. For most of the nineteenth century the striving for external markets had largely been restricted to commercial competition, and the European colonial empires had contracted substantially. But during the last decades of the century a new round of colonial expansion began in Africa, the Middle East, and Asia. At least some of its roots can be found in the desperate search for markets by rich-country producers faced with macroeconomic distress. Eventually these rekindled colonial aspirations fed into other geopolitical trends to exacerbate long-dormant frictions among the great powers.[11]

By the 1890s war clouds seemed everywhere. French troops marched across the Sudan to Fashoda, claiming territory the British regarded as theirs. British adventurer L. Starr Jameson led a raid on the Transvaal, lighting the spark that led to the Boer War. Italian and Ethiopian troops fought bitterly in the Ethiopian highlands, as did British and Ashanti soldiers in West Africa. Japan, Russia, and the European powers jockeyed for position in the Far East, while insurgents in the Spanish Philippines and the Dutch East Indies fought for their island nations' independence. In the Western Hemisphere, the activities of U.S.-based Cuban freedom fighters raised the specter of political turmoil in the Caribbean and aggravated already tense Spanish-American relations.

As the nineteenth century closed, events seemed to threaten global capitalism's essence. Free trade, the gold standard, international finance, and even peace among the great powers all were called into question. Voices everywhere were raised in favor of trade protection, against gold, against global economic integration. Every new crisis caused virulent conflicts of interests and ideas.

PART I

LAST BEST YEARS
OF THE GOLDEN AGE,
1896–1914

1

Global Capitalism Triumphant

As the spring of 1896 came to the American Great Plains, farmers faced the planting season with dread. Farm prices continued to decline. The price of wheat, which had hovered around a dollar a bushel for decades, closed out 1892 under ninety cents, 1893 around seventy-five cents, 1894 barely sixty cents. In the dead of the winter of 1895–1896, the price went below fifty cents a bushel. In the Dakotas and other remote regions this translated into prices paid to farmers of about thirty cents, barely one-third what they had come to expect.

While farm prices dropped, the things farmers needed were as expensive as ever. Prices of farm equipment, tools, and fertilizer remained high. Railroad shipping costs held steady and even rose. And mortgage payments stayed where they were, showing no mercy to farmers who were earning one-half or one-third of what they had when they borrowed the money.

Faced with destitution, American farmers organized themselves into the country's first real mass movement. The Populist movement and its People's Party elected hundreds of state legislators and dozens of national senators and congressmen all over the country's southern and western agricultural regions. In 1892 the party's presidential candidate got more than a million votes.

The Populist program demanded, first and foremost, that the United States go off the gold standard. Under the gold standard, the party's platform charged, "the supply of currency is purposely abridged to fatten usurers, bankrupt enterprise, and enslave industry."[1] The solution to what the Populists called "The Money Question" was to free the country from this British-led scheme to enrich international bankers, investors, and traders at the expense of farmers and miners. Instead, America should go off gold and on silver, at a depreciated exchange rate that would raise farm prices and lower interest rates.

As farm conditions worsened, America's farmers heeded Populist orator Mary Elizabeth Lease's injunction to "raise less corn and more hell." Farmers blazed with anger at the gold supporters whose insistence on a global standard was destroying their livelihood. Millions rallied for the alternative silver standard, the salvation of farmers and miners.

The country's ruling Democratic Party could not ignore the Populist competition. President Grover Cleveland had been a reliable backer of the gold standard, but now his Democratic Party was being overtaken by bitter opponents of gold who saw him and other party leaders as traitors to their interests. In July, as farm prices stayed low, the Democratic National Convention convened in Chicago. All talk was about how the Populists and their supporters were turning the 1896 campaign for the presidency into an epochal "battle of the standards."

Antigold activists took the convention, and the Democratic Party, by storm. A young congressman from Nebraska galvanized the delegates and the country with a stirring call to arms. William Jennings Bryan dismissed the pleading of the party's financial leaders: "You come to us and tell us that the great cities are in favor of the gold standard; we reply that the great cities rest upon our broad and fertile prairies. Burn down your cities and leave our farms, and your cities will spring up again as if by magic; but destroy our farms and the grass will grow in the streets of every city in the country." Speaking for the party's majority, Bryan challenged gold backers at home and abroad: "You shall not press down upon the brow of labor this crown of thorns, you shall not crucify mankind upon a cross of gold."

Bryan's unyielding opposition to the gold standard and to international finance won him the Democratic presidential nomination. His triumph was a stunning repudiation of the country's northeastern business elite. The *Times* of London reported from Chicago: "It is no longer a convention, but a political insurrection, which is in progress at Chicago. The Democratic party . . . is henceforth to be governed, as

Bismarck said the world could not be governed, from below. There has been an upheaval of the political crust, and strange creatures have come forth."[2]

The financial leaders of Europe and the world watched in shock as the assault on the gold standard challenged the very structure of the international economic order. The United States was the world's largest economy, biggest borrower, and most important international destination for capital and people alike. Now it posed the greatest threat to the global economic order. "The issue," wrote the *Times*' reporter, "is no longer between Silver and Gold only, but between society and a very crude form of Socialism."[3] The new Democratic Party platform was, the British correspondent seethed, "a creed of repudiation, public and private, of lawlessness, of warfare on property and on public and private rights."[4] The language might have been exaggerated, but the concern was real: If the Democrats won and implemented their platform, the gold standard everywhere would be in peril.

As the political frenzy peaked, mundane trends started to undermine it. New gold discoveries brought more of the precious metal onto the market. As the supply of gold grew, prices rose. At the end of August 1896 wheat prices began to increase, first slowly and then more rapidly. By the end of October, as the American election came near, the price of wheat was nearly 50 percent higher than it had been over the summer.

On November 3 American voters narrowly defeated the Democrats and their assault on the gold standard. Supporters of gold had organized massively, with northeastern businesses contributing fortunes to the campaign of the Republican presidential candidate, William McKinley. The rise in farm prices helped take the edge off discontent, especially in districts wavering between the Democrat-Populists and the Republicans. In the end the margin was slim, but the *Times* hoped it would "suffice to bury Bryanism, Silverism, Socialism, and all the revolutionary proposals of the Chicago platform beyond hope of resurrection in this generation." The *Times* correspondent reported from the nation's financial capital: "The scene in New York passes all description. Vast multitudes still at midnight fill all her streets. . . . Bands are playing, flags waving, lights flashing, hearts beating, the sky is filled with illuminations, and in every quarter of the heavens electric beams are streaming out with the glad tidings of great joy that this Republic is again—I use Lincoln's phrase—to live and not to die! For that is the meaning of the Republican triumph of to-day."[5]

So ended the Great Depression of 1873–1896. In its place arose the crowning achievement of the golden age, two decades of growth and globalization.

The gold standard reaffirmed

The years from 1896 to 1914 were the high point of international economic integration. The 1873–1896 deflation halted and threats to global capitalism dissipated. For the first time in twenty years prices rose continually: between 1896 and 1913 by 16 percent in Britain, by 41 percent in America. Prices of raw materials and agricultural goods rose particularly fast. American farm prices, which had dropped 38 percent between 1873 and 1896, rose 78 percent from their 1896 trough to 1913. The all-important American price of wheat dropped below fifty cents a bushel in 1896 but was back above a dollar ten years later. Farmers and miners could concentrate, to turn the Populist plea around, on raising more corn and less hell.

As the tension of the early and middle 1890s eased, governments enthusiastically engaged their economies with world markets. As international trade grew, trade conflicts faded. International lending and investment picked up, so that in the years before World War One Britain exported more than half of all its capital. Hostility to the gold standard, to international finance, to the world economy generally became muted. Even military and political conflict among the great powers eased.

The opening years of the twentieth century were the closest thing the world had ever seen to a free world market for goods, capital, and labor. It would be a hundred years before the world returned to that level of globalization. In addition, this integrated international economy grew at its most rapid rate in recorded history. Output and incomes rose, and not just in rich nations: Many relatively underdeveloped countries also grew dramatically. The economies of Canada and Argentina more than tripled, and their output per person nearly doubled.[6] In less than twenty years these two nations changed from being much poorer to much richer than France and Germany.

The turnaround in prices that blunted the attack on gold was driven in part by the operation of the gold standard itself. In a world whose major currencies were based on gold, a decline in goods prices was the same as a rise in the price of gold. When the price of a bushel of wheat fell from one gold dollar to half a gold dollar, the same gold dollar could buy twice as much wheat. Low goods prices meant high gold prices, and high gold prices meant powerful reasons to find more gold. Prospectors scoured the earth and started making important new discoveries in the late 1880s. Gold rush followed gold rush, from South Africa and Australia to the Yukon and the American West, and by the late 1890s the world's new gold supply was double what it had been ten years earlier. As new gold flowed into the money supply, the value of gold declined. Since gold was money, a decline in the price of gold was the same as a rise in the price of goods; a reduction by half in the price of the gold that constituted the gold mark meant a doubling in the prices of goods in terms of gold marks. And so the new gold supplies led to a generalized rise in prices.

As prices rose after 1896, gold became less politically contentious, and countries that had avoided the gold standard flocked to it: Japan and Russia in 1897, Argentina in 1899, Austria-Hungary in 1902, Mexico in 1905, Brazil in 1906, Thailand in 1908. Even India, on silver for centuries, was pushed onto a modifed gold standard by the British, a complicated process that inspired the passage in Oscar Wilde's 1895 *The Importance of Being Earnest* in which a prudish Miss Prism instructs her charge Cecily, "The chapter on the Fall of the Rupee you may omit. It is somewhat too sensational. Even these metallic problems have their melodramatic side."[7] By 1908 China and Persia were the only countries of any import not on gold.

The gold standard was central to the golden age of international economic integration. It brought a stability and predictability that greatly facilitated international trade, investment, finance, migration, and travel. Businessmen, investors, and immigrants did not have to worry about changes in exchange rates, about controls on currencies, about any real impediments to moving money around the world. The impact on trade was substantial; being on gold in this period is variously estimated to have raised trade between two countries by between 30 and 70 percent.[8]

The gold standard was more important for international finance than it was for trade. International financiers regarded being on gold as an obligation of well-behaved members of the classical world economy, a signal of a country's economic reliability.[9] Investors had good reasons to focus on government commitments to the gold standard. Hewing to gold could be difficult and might require overriding political resistance. Investors knew that a government willing and able to overcome opposition to gold was also likely to honor its foreign debts even in the face of domestic protests. Just as in later years British or American financial experts, or the International Monetary Fund, reassured lenders by approving of a government's policies, so membership in the gold club conferred a sort of blessing on its initiates.

The gold standard symbolized financial rectitude because it required governments to fit their economic policies to global economic pressures. Adherence to gold forced national economies to adjust when they spent beyond their means. If a nation ran a trade deficit, importing more than it exported, it spent more money—that is, gold—to pay for imports than it earned for its foreign sales. As gold left the country, the domestic supply of money declined, and the nation's purchasing power also declined. This reduced demand and made it hard for national producers to sell their goods. Producers had to cut prices and force wages down. So by the inherent working of the gold standard, a country spending more than it earned was compelled to reduce wages and prices, spend less and produce more cheaply. If the process ran smoothly, the economy would soon rebound. As local wages and prices dropped, foreigners would buy more of the country's goods and nationals would buy fewer imports. Thus imports would drop and exports would rise, returning the country to balance.

The gold standard acted as a metallic regulator to impose wage and price restraint. The Scottish philosopher David Hume identified this regulatory process in the 1750s, and it was called the price-specie flow mechanism, because changes in prices led to specie (gold) flows that tended to force prices and economies to return to balance. Any gold standard country that spent more than it earned (or could borrow) would be forced by the operation of the gold standard to reverse course, reduce wages and spending, and move back toward equilibrium. Governments on gold had to privilege international ties over domestic demands, imposing austerity and wage cuts on unwilling populations in order to adhere to gold. This made the gold standard a litmus test that international investors used to judge the financial reliability of national governments.[10]

The gold standard's stimulus to international trade, investment, and migration was assisted by advances in transportation and communications technologies, by generally favorable macroeconomic conditions, and by the atmosphere of peace among the great powers. All these factors permitted the world's economies to become more and more tightly integrated as the golden age progressed.

The use of the railroad and steamship, both in place by 1870, expanded much more rapidly thereafter. There was an extraordinary rush of railroad building in underdeveloped regions in the decades before 1914. In 1870 the *combined* vast expanses of Latin America, Russia, Canada, Australia, South Africa, and India had barely as much railroad mileage as in Great Britain. By 1913 these regions had ten times Britain's railroad mileage. Argentina alone went from a few hundred miles of rail in 1870 to a system more extensive than Britain's.[11] The development of steam turbines in the 1890s increased the speed of steamships, and eventually new oil-fueled ships with diesel engines competed with steam power. And the invention of refrigeration made the transportation of perishable products possible for the first time, allowing Argentina to export chilled beef and Honduras to export bananas. All these developments dramatically reduced the time and expense to get goods to market. In the twenty years before 1914 the cost of oceangoing shipping to Britain dropped by one-third, while the prices of goods shipped rose by one-third on average.

Spurred by these advances in transportation, world trade went from under $8 billion in 1896 to over $18 billion in 1913; even corrected for inflation, this was nearly a doubling. There was something close to an integrated world market for most goods, so that their prices became more similar as time went by—even among countries thousands of miles apart. Wheat and iron are exemplary. In 1870 these two goods were almost prohibitively expensive to trade, resulting in major price differences across countries. Wheat that cost $100 in Chicago cost $158 in Liverpool. Similarly, pig iron in Philadelphia cost 85 percent more than it did in London. By 1913 improved technologies had reduced transport costs and brought prices together; now wheat cost only 16 percent more in Liverpool than in Chicago, and pig iron cost just 19 percent more in Philadelphia than in London. Prices of the world's most important commodities moved together in Sydney and Chicago, Odessa and Buenos Aires.[12]

In an earlier era, when foreign trade was expensive and uncertain, not participating in it had small costs. It was easy to forgo foreign commercial opportunities that were risky and marginal. But as international transportation shifted from barges and sailing ships to railroads and steamships, producers had greater incentives to export and consumers greater incentives to import. The costs of closure rose as the opportunities of openness expanded.

Meanwhile worldwide telegraphy meant that information could be transmitted instantaneously from any reasonably developed area to investment houses and traders in London, Paris, and Berlin. The development of the telephone greatly facilitated telecommunications, in a much more convenient form than the telegraph. Investors developed completely global interests, and international investment grew even more rapidly than world trade, to forty-four billion dollars on the eve of World War One. Foreign investors financed much of the rapid growth of developing regions like the United States and Australia. Foreigners accounted for more than one-third of Canadian investment and as much as three-quarters of the investment in some Latin American countries. By 1913 overseas investors owned one-fifth of the Australian economy and fully one-half of the Argentine. The flood of money from abroad was not only important to the rapidly growing countries that were using the capital but central to the European economies that were investing it. By the early 1900s investment abroad accounted for one-quarter to one-third of the wealth of the major powers.[13]

International immigration also soared. Millions of people looked to the dynamic regions in the New World and elsewhere and left the poor parts of Europe and Asia. In the first decade of the century outmigration amounted to 3 percent of the populations of Great Britain, Italy, and Sweden, 5 percent of Spain's, and 7 percent of Portugal's. On the receiving side, immigrants in this decade were equal to 6 percent of the American population, 13 percent of Canada's, and an amazing 43 percent of Argentina's. On the eve of World War One, huge shares of the population of the world's most rapidly growing economies were immigrants; indeed, half the 1.3 million people of Buenos Aires were foreign-born.[14]

Almost as many people left their native lands in Asia as left Europe. Most were Chinese and went to Southeast Asia and the New World. Indians went largely to African and Asian lands along the Indian Ocean and to the Caribbean. Many Asian migrants were indentured, bound to work—usually on plantations—at their destinations. A large proportion of the Asian migrants returned to their homelands. In part this was due to the terms of the indentures, in part because living conditions in Trinidad or the Philippines were less appealing than in San Francisco and Sydney. But many stayed and established substantial Chinese, Indian, and other Asian communities from Lima to Cape Town, from Singapore to Hawaii.

The reversal of the great deflation of 1873–1896, technological development, and general macroeconomic stability all contributed to the rapid pace of global economic integration before 1914. The gold standard, world trade, and international finance knitted the world economy together as never before.

Specialization and growth

Countries that joined this golden age global economy remade themselves in line with their newfound positions in the world market. Each region specialized in what it did best. Britain managed investments, ran the world's banking and trading systems, and supervised and insured world shipping and communications. Germany produced iron and steel, chemicals, and heavy equipment for railroads, mines, plantations, and shipping lines. Argentina, South Africa, and Australia used British capital and German machinery to open new farms and mines and sent the minerals back to Germany to be worked into machinery and some of the earnings back to Britain as interest on its investments.

Countries, and groups and regions within countries, became increasingly specialized. People, companies, regions, and countries cut back on economic activities they were less good at to concentrate on those at which they were particularly good. In earlier eras countries had tried to be self-sufficient, but now they focused on producing and exporting what they did best and trading for the rest.

The industries of Western Europe flooded the world with machinery and equipment to work farms and run mines, to build railroads and ports to get products to market. European investors provided capital to finance the massive construction projects in which this equipment was deployed. Resource-rich regions of the New World, Asia, and Africa concentrated on bringing their agricultural and mineral bounty to market. The hinterlands of Europe and Asia sent their redundant workers and farmers to help staff the new mines, plantations, and mills. And as the pampas and the Great Plains, the Yukon and Witwatersrand, Trinidad and Sumatra yielded up their riches, the industrialists and investors and immigrants got paid in the profits of their endeavors.

Global capitalism made specialization possible. Countries, manufacturers, farmers, and miners could focus single-mindedly on producing their best goods and services if they had access to markets large enough to sell what they produced and to buy what they consumed. Now, for the first time, they did. The gold standard, free trade, and new transportation and communications technologies created a convenient, accessible, and predictable global market. Grains, copper and iron ore, coal, even beef and bananas could be sent by rail and ship halfway around the world at little expense. Investors could buy the stocks and bonds of distant corporations and governments and monitor their progress with ease. Europeans could buy cheap food from the New World and concentrate their productive efforts on the industrial techniques they had innovated and mastered. Argentines could focus on working the world's most fertile plains for their grain and cattle, using the profits to import manufactured goods from Europe.

Farmers and miners in the newly specializing regions expanded production at an extraordinary pace. In the twenty years before World War One, the amount of land planted to wheat in Argentina and Canada went from three or four million acres in each to about sixteen million acres in each. As farmers opened up new lands and intensified the farming of others, world wheat, coffee, tea, and cotton production more than doubled from 1870 to 1913.[15] Producers of other newly marketable goods in the developing world moved even faster. In less than fifteen years, from the turn of the century to World War One, the mining output of the developing regions grew nearly threefold. Between 1880 and 1910 the world's output of bananas rose from 30,000 to 1.8 million tons, of sugarcane from 1.9 to 6.3 million tons, of cocoa from 60,000 to 227,000 tons, of rubber from 11,000 to 87,000 tons.[16]

The classical economic theorists of the day could look with approval on the process. Adam Smith, in his 1776 founding text of classical economics, *The Wealth of Nations*, made specialization—the division of labor—the centerpiece of his argument. He and his fellow economic liberals argued, against the mercantilists, that self-sufficiency was foolish, that a greater division of labor made societies wealthier. In a famous example, Smith pointed out that an individual pin maker working alone could make at best twenty pins a day. However, in the manufactories of the day, pin making was divided into about eighteen different steps, each done by one or two specialized workers. In this way a pin factory with ten workers produced forty-eight thousand pins a day, making each individual some 240 times as productive as he would be if working alone.[17] Specialization increased productivity, and productivity fed economic growth.

Productivity in this context is not the term used by managers to insist that workers work longer hours. It refers to the amount produced by one unit of labor with the other factors of production—especially land and capital—at its disposal. In farming, for example, the same amount of labor is more productive on good soil than on poor, with machinery and fertilizer and irrigation than without. This is true even if the farm labor in question is identical. German grain farmers in 1900 were not as productive as Canadian grain farmers, not because they worked less, or were less skilled, but because German land was not as suited to grain farming. By the same token, the fact that American labor productivity in 1913 was two and a half times Italian levels does not mean that the average American worked more than twice as hard as the average Italian; if this had been the case, why did millions of Italians come to the United States to work? It means that the average American worker produced two and a half times as much in an hour as the average Italian worker because of the far greater amount of capital available to each worker. In fact there was more than three times as much machinery per American worker in 1913 as per worker even in Britain, the world's industrial leader.[18]

The classical economists emphasized that specialization required access to large markets. Adam Smith and his colleagues argued that restricting market size retarded economic growth, thus challenging mercantilist thought, which tried to limit access to markets. A village cut off from the rest of the world and forced into self-sufficiency has to produce everything it needs, but if that village is part of a larger national or global market, it can specialize in what it does best. Producers need ample markets to specialize; the division of labor depends on the size of the market.

Global markets led to global specialization. Smith would have been reassured to see that as countries tied themselves to the world economy and gained access to world markets, they immediately began to specialize. His views were confirmed by the experience of dozens of regions. Countries with access to more extensive markets specialized; as they specialized, their productivity rose, and so did the growth and development of their economies.

The international division of labor of the decades before World War One transformed whole continents. Extraordinary new agricultural and mineral areas were drawn into world markets, flooding Europe with cheap food and raw materials. Inexpensive and innovative industrial goods poured out of Europe's factories and into parts of the world that had always relied on handicrafts. Countries that had grown all their own food began importing much of it, at much lower prices. Regions whose people had worn locally handcrafted clothing and used handmade tools switched to cheaper machine-made cotton textiles and manufactured gear. Whole towns and regions focused their efforts on iron mining, textile manufacturing, rice cultivation, or rail production, sending their goods around the world in search of markets.

Viewed from a global standpoint, the process worked beautifully. Labor and capital moved around the world from where they produced less to where they produced more. Unproductive Polish or Portuguese peasants who could not compete with Canadian and Argentine grain farmers became productive urban workers in Warsaw and Lisbon or emigrated to become productive factory workers in Toronto or farmworkers on the pampas. Capitalists searched out areas where their money could be more profitable, eschewing one more railroad line or power plant in England for a bold new project in Kenya. The same effect could be had even without movements of people and money, simply by way of trade. A country with excess labor could send emigrants to areas of recent settlement, or it could employ the cheap labor in factories to produce manufactures to send to these areas. Sending labor from Italy to Australia had effects similar to sending labor-intensive manufactures: Italian workers were more productively employed, and Australia got access to cheaper labor either directly or indirectly.

Specialization was neither easy nor costless. It remade economies and societies and often destroyed traditional ways of life. Agricultural specialization—the opening of the pampas and the prairies that inundated world markets with cheap grain—drove European agriculture into crisis. Displaced European farmers poured into the cities to work in grimy factories. Others moved precisely to the regions that had caused the problems in the first place, in the New World and other areas of recent settlement. Farmers who could not subsist in Italy or Sweden could try their luck in the states of São Paulo or Minnesota. The tens of millions of farmers forced off the land into cities, or across oceans to new lands, often found poverty, discrimination, disease, and isolation rather than the hoped-for prosperity. The new international division of labor divided families, villages, and countries, forcing tight-knit traditional societies apart.

Wrenching though this was, economic integration and specialization made both the Old World and the New more efficient. European farmers who could not compete went into more productive activities. They were more productive in Europe's factories than on its relatively poor land; if they stayed in farming, they were more productive in the New

World than in the Old. Displaced farmers and workers on all continents suffered, but overall they, or at least their children and grandchildren, were likely to be better off.

This global division of labor raised productivity at both the international and national levels. It could hardly have been otherwise: Shifting labor and capital from less to more productive uses had, by definition, to increase their productivity. Hardscrabble farmers of eastern Germany and southern Italy moved to modern factories in Berlin and Chicago. The backwoods of Argentina and Canada, newly accessible to world markets, were turned from indigenous hunting grounds into the world's best wheat fields. The people, factories, and land produced more, incomes rose, and economies grew.

Golden age gains from international economic exchange made possible golden age gains from specialization. Without access to migration across countries and oceans, farmers would have been stuck on untenable farms. Without access to a world market for their products, South African miners and Australian ranchers would have had no place to sell their gold and meat. Without international trade and finance to ship, insure, bankroll, and manage, London would have been the economic nerve center of only a small island rather than the whole world. The world exchanged machine tools for food, copper for clothing, and foreign bonds for steel, and the producers and sellers of machine tools, food, copper, clothing, bonds, and steel all profited.

Globalism and its discontents

The golden age's abandonment of mercantilism seemed amply justified. A profound rejection of the previous era's pervasive government control of the economy brought significant success. Free trade, capital movements, and immigration reduced state control. The gold standard presupposed that governments would allow the free conversion of money into gold and back and would permit rather than impede domestic economic adjustment. Certainly governments stepped in, frequently and forcefully, to enforce the private property rights of investors and traders. But the order and ideology of the day presumed a government that did little but safeguard the operation of markets.

Yet there were stresses and strains under the surface of pre-1914 global capitalism. One source of tension was the subjugation of poor nations and peoples. For even as governments in Europe, America, and Japan celebrated market forces, they were using forces of a different kind—artillery, gunboats, infantry—to subordinate hundreds of millions of new colonial subjects in Africa, Asia, and Latin America.

Another problem was that not everyone benefited from global economic integration. Many traditional societies stagnated or fell apart. Even in the rapidly growing regions of the world, the fruits of growth were not distributed evenly. Societies that abandoned less productive economic activities often also abandoned those trapped in them. It is easy to see the logic in giving up wheat farming on mediocre land once the fruited plains of North America and the pampas opened or of closing down inefficient handicraft weaving once cheaper and better machine-made textiles were available. But what of the farmers and artisans whose land and skills were no longer valuable, whose traditional livelihoods were no longer available?

Economic integration put enormous pressure on those whose goods were not able to compete with the new world leaders. Consumers no longer needed European grain farmers, Latin American moneylenders, Chinese artisans, and Indian weavers. Whole industries, regions, and classes were made redundant, and those on the losing side of specialization and economic integration were less willing to accept a hands-off government that did nothing to ease their suffering.

Enthusiasm for the golden age was not universal. Opening markets, paying back debts to foreigners, and following the gold standard all involved sacrifices, often by the poor and weak. These sacrifices were rarely made willingly. Even in countries that were growing, there was a residue of social and political conflict over the national requisites and perquisites of economic integration. There were also whole countries that took a guarded or hostile attitude toward international economic ties, governments that restricted and closely regulated international trade and investment.

The global capitalism of the late nineteenth and early twentieth centuries was almost certainly good for global growth, for the economies of most countries, and even for the incomes of most people. It was not equally good for everyone and was bad for many. Nonetheless, the successes of these decades seemed to bear out the arguments of supporters of international economic integration, in favor of international finance, free trade, and the gold standard. They also appeared to support the classical liberal idea that favored limited government intervention in the market, just enough to ensure full participation in the global economy. To many of the world's people, especially those in the world's leading economies, the decades preceding World War One provided evidence that the market and the international economy were powerful engines of prosperity and even of peace.

2

Defenders of the Global Economy

In 1919, as veterans straggled back from the bloody battlefields of World War One, John Maynard Keynes wrote nostalgically of a bygone era of economic good feeling:

> What an extraordinary episode in the economic progress of man that age was which came to an end in August, 1914. . . . The inhabitant of London could order by telephone, sipping his morning tea in bed, the various products of the whole earth, in such quantity as he might see fit, and reasonably expect their early delivery upon his doorstep; he could at the same moment and by the same means adventure his wealth in the natural resources and new enterprises of any quarter of the world, and share, without exertion or even trouble, in their prospective fruits and advantages; or he could decide to couple the security of his fortunes with the good faith of the townspeople of any substantial municipality in any continent that fancy or information might recommend. He could secure forthwith, if he wished it, cheap and comfortable means of transit to any country or climate without passport or other formality, could despatch his servant to the neighboring office of a bank for such supply of the precious metals as might seem convenient, and could proceed abroad to foreign quarters, without knowledge of their religion, language, or customs, bearing coined wealth upon his person, and would consider himself greatly

aggrieved and much surprised at the least interference. But, most important of all, he regarded this state of affairs as normal, certain, and permanent, except in the direction of further improvement, and any deviation from it as aberrant, scandalous, and avoidable.[1]

Never mind that Keynes's "inhabitant of London" with a telephone, a servant, and the luxury to sip morning tea in bed formed a tiny portion of the population. Never mind that the opportunities Keynes associated with this wondrous global capitalism were irrelevant to the impoverished people of Asia and Africa. Never mind that Keynes's nostalgia was not shared by the millions who gravitated toward socialist and other radical movements in response to the social dislocations of the era.

Keynes's observation that "social and economic life" had experienced an "internationalization . . . which was nearly complete in practice"[2] does capture the essence of global capitalism before World War One. For decades the world economy was essentially open to the movement of people, money, capital, and goods. The leading businessmen, politicians, and thinkers of the day regarded an open world economy as the normal state of affairs. They assumed that people and money would flow around the world with few or no restrictions. Trade protection, although common, was seen as an acceptable departure from the norm, driven by the exigencies of short-term domestic or international politics. Capitalism was global, and the globe was capitalist.

The international economic system of the golden age ran like a London gentleman's club. Members supported one another when necessary to keep the club running smoothly and inducted new applicants if they met the club's standards. The standards were high: a commitment to economic openness, to the protection of property across borders, to the gold standard, and to limited government intervention in the macroeconomy. Countries that met these standards enjoyed the benefits of club membership. And countries most of the time seemed eager to qualify for membership.

Many Europeans assumed that there would always be broad economic, political, and intellectual support for international economic integration. But with the aid of hindsight we know that this golden age of globalization was not the new natural order of things. The demands of membership in the club of globalizers turned out to be too taxing for most nations, including some of its founding members. How, then, was this era of economic integration sustained for so long?

Intellectual support for the golden age

Before 1914 almost everyone who mattered politically, in all the countries that mattered economically, agreed that governments should privilege their international economic ties. Foreign economic commitments were more important government tasks than dealing with industrial unemployment or farm distress. Few political leaders believed that government could or should do much about the domestic business cycle, joblessness, or poverty. In fact most orthodox supporters of the system argued that substantial state intervention in the market would interfere with the natural operation of the gold standard. They believed that unemployment compensation, aid to troubled farmers, and extensive social programs for the poor would impede the adjustments required by the gold standard; such programs would keep wages and prices from falling as necessary to keep economies in balance.

Governments were important, though, because they controlled the nation's currency, trade, and international financial relations. Governments also enforced property rights at home and abroad and otherwise secured the benefits of the global economy to their citizens. The governing classes of industrialized and poor nations alike did everything feasible to prove their international economic integrity but little to manage the domestic economy.

Proponents of golden age globalism often ascribed their success to their enlightened ideas—rather like members of an exclusive club who attribute the club's attractiveness to the character of its members rather than the material benefits of membership. To be sure, the new policies of economic openness followed the precepts of economic liberalism, as espoused by Britain's classical economists. Adam Smith's successors extended his argument about the benefits of specialization to the international economy and elaborated on his case against mercantilism.

David Ricardo, the most influential classical theorist of international trade, was a London banker who focused on the comparative cost of goods within and across countries. He gave a famous example drawn from Anglo-Portuguese economic relations. Ricardo's illustration starts in a world with no trade. If England produces cloth more efficiently than it produces wine, then English cloth will be cheap relative to English wine. If Portugal produces wine more efficiently than cloth, then Portuguese wine will be cheap relative to Portuguese cloth. If the two countries open up to trade, they will buy abroad what is cheaper abroad: The English will buy wine from Portugal, and the Portuguese will buy cloth from England. Ricardo pointed out that England should buy all its wine from Portugal and Portugal all its cloth from England, so that each country could focus on making what it could make most cheaply.

This Ricardian comparative advantage implies that countries should do what they do best—not in comparison with other countries, but rather what they do best relative to other things they do. Even if England produces both cloth and wine better than Portugal, it should still produce only cloth and buy all its wine from Portugal. The comparison implied by the term compares activities within one nation (British farming and British manufacturing), not between one nation and another (British farming and Portuguese farming).

Comparative advantage applies the principle of specialization to countries: Like people, nations should do what they do best, regardless of how well others do these things. To say that an individual should specialize in what he does best says nothing about how the individual's skills compare with others' skills. An outstanding chef who is a good dishwasher should still hire a dishwasher, even a mediocre one, for the chef's time is better spent cooking than washing dishes. A master carpenter should hire a less skilled laborer to do simple cutting and sanding even if the carpenter is better at cutting and sanding. The same is true of regions: If Iowa land is better for corn farming than dairy farming, and Wisconsin land is better for dairy than corn, then Iowa farmers should specialize in corn and Wisconsin farmers in dairy. Similarly, nations gain most by exporting what they produce most efficiently in order to pay for imports of the best products of other countries.

The law of comparative advantage has clear free trade implications. Since a country always gains from following its comparative advantage, and barriers to trade impede its ability to do so, trade protection is never beneficial to the economy as a whole. Government policies that keep out imports simply force the country to produce goods that are not its comparative advantage to produce. Trade protection raises the price of imports and lowers the efficiency of domestic production.

The classical political economists reversed earlier mercantilist thinking. The mercantilists wanted to restrict imports and encourage exports in order to stimulate the national economy. The classical economists insisted otherwise: Imports are the gains from trade, while exports are its costs. Importing goods allows the nation to focus its productive energies on making goods that it produces best. There is a clear parallel to a household. A farm family "exports" (sells its crops) in order to "import" (buy the goods and services it wants). The farm family wants to maximize the imports it buys and thus needs to earn more, and the best way to earn more is to produce what it produces most efficiently. The classical economists showed that just as farmers, workers, and firms gain by specializing and trading as much as possible, so do countries. Free trade induces a country to follow its comparative advantage and is the best possible policy—even if pursued unilaterally.

By the 1850s Great Britain, the breeding ground for classical economic theory, had enthusiastically embraced free trade, the gold standard, free capital movements, and free migration. The rest of the world followed suit over the next sixty years, with varying degrees of enthusiasm. The classical political economists had won the day intellectually.

The classical ideas alone were not the cause of the era's global economic openness. After all, arguments against government intervention in cross-border trade and investment are very old. Adam Smith demolished mercantilist thinking in 1776; David Ricardo, along with James Mill and and Robert Torrens, fully stated the doctrine of comparative advantage before 1820.[3] Yet it was not until 1846 that the British Parliament repealed the country's major agricultural tariffs, the Corn Laws. Other countries followed suit only gradually and partially. The heyday of European free trade came a hundred years after Smith had demonstrated its desirability.

In fact countries did not follow classical economic principles very closely, and the strongest intellectual arguments were the least obeyed. The theoretical case for free trade was overwhelming, yet only Britain and the Low Countries actually pursued free trade; all governments were protectionist to one degree or another.[4] On the other hand, almost every country adhered to the gold standard or aspired to do so, despite the weakness of the intellectual argument for gold. Indeed, many classical economists regarded the commitment to gold as little more than a precious metal fetish.

The theoretical power of classical ideas did not ensure the adoption of classical policies. Also, despite the triumph of classical theories, the policies of the golden age did not persist. The golden age was followed by thirty years during which governments did not resume past levels of economic integration. Governments and people cannot have chosen openness simply because they understood its superiority and the intellectual power of its theories unless their retreat from it was due to a fit of collective amnesia. Classical economics, like neoclassical economics after it and until today, argues powerfully against restrictions on the international movement of goods, capital, and people. Countries followed, and still follow, these principles to very different degrees, and the world has varied tremendously in its overall orientation toward economic integration. Something other than the ideas themselves was at work.

Nathan Mayer Rothschild, 1840–1915

Powerful people defending their interests drove the opening of country after country to the world economy. Nathan Mayer Rothschild was economically and politically central to the era.[5] His life encompassed the golden age: Born in 1840, a few years before the repeal of the Corn Laws, he died in 1915, as the world economy fragmented under the weight of World War One.

Amschel Mayer Rothschild founded the House of Rothschild in Frankfurt in the late 1700s, then sent his five sons to other European capitals; soon the bank was established in Vienna, Naples, Paris, and London. As with many other Jewish businessmen in this period, the combination of early financial and commercial experience and pan-European family connections positioned the Rothschilds well. Amschel Mayer's third son, Nathan Mayer, ran the London office. During the Napoleonic Wars, like many other London bankers, Rothschild provided financial services to the British crown, lending it money and transferring soldiers' pay to the Continent. At the time of the Battle of Waterloo, Nathan Mayer was so concerned about the financial implications of the conflict that he arranged a private relay of couriers to bring him the latest military news. The banker's relay covered the two hundred miles from Brussels to London with unprecedented speed and gave Rothschild the news within twenty-four hours—so quickly that the government was not inclined to believe him when he passed on the information the next morning.

His exploits during the Napoleonic Wars helped confirm Rothschild's leadership in the City of London. Nathan Mayer's eldest son, Lionel Nathan Rothschild, continued the firm's trajectory toward the center of London finance and international politics. *His* son was also named

Nathan Mayer, and by the time the second Nathan Mayer (called Natty) took over from his father, in 1879, the Rothschild name was synonymous with wealth, global connections, and diplomatic influence. The firm had representatives in every financial capital and could mobilize funds so quickly and effectively that governments could not afford to alienate the powerful family.

The Rothschilds became the paragon of the successful Jewish international banker. The Austrian Hapsburgs elevated the family to the nobility, with the title of baron. In 1858 Nathan's father, Lionel, became the first Jewish member of the British Parliament. The next year Nathan was one of the first Jews to attend Cambridge University, and in 1885 he became the first Jewish peer in British history. Despite the persistence of crude anti-Semitic attacks, Lord Nathan Mayer Rothschild was a powerful member of the City of London and the world's financial community and was passionately involved in politics. Family ties, especially to the prominent French branch, and the firm's broader financial network made Rothschild influence powerful all over the Continent.

Nathan Rothschild used his position to reinforce the three major pillars of the golden age international economy: international finance (his own business), the gold standard, and free trade. Nathan's banking activities were particularly closely connected to the global gold standard. Like other international bankers, Rothschild regarded the gold standard as central to global capitalism. International investors lent money to countries on gold, and denied it to countries not on gold, and used their financial and political influence to encourage countries to go onto gold.

The Rothschilds paid close attention to the United States, the world's most important borrower in the nineteenth and early twentieth centuries. In the 1830s, as the United States grew in economic importance, the Rothschilds dispatched a Frankfurt employee to the other side of the Atlantic. When August Schönberg entered the United States, he changed his name from the German/Yiddish for "beautiful mountain" to the French, Belmont. Much to his patrons' displeasure, August Belmont also converted to Christianity. He became enormously influential in economic, political, and social circles and married the daughter of Commodore Matthew Perry, whose visit to Japan in 1854 is said to have "opened" the country to the world economy. By the 1860s Belmont was one of the nation's leading businessmen, in large part because of his Rothschild connection.

The Rothschilds and their agent, August Belmont, tenaciously supported opening the United States to the rest of the world economy.

They expended much effort trying to influence the American debates over gold. The gold standard was central to the security of the Rothschilds' overseas investments; a borrowing country not on gold was regarded as unreliable. However, during the Civil War the United States went off gold and stayed on paper money, greenbacks, even after the war. Many American business and political leaders believed that gold was not suited to the economic needs of a rapidly growing economy.

In the mid-1870s Belmont and the Rothschilds pushed relentlessly to convince the United States to join the gold standard club. The measure was controversial, and Congress defeated many attempts to get the country onto gold. But Belmont argued that "sound financial policy and love of our country's fair name alike" demanded that the administration of President Ulysses Grant demonstrate "uncompromising hostility to the blind and dishonest frenzy which has taken hold of Congress." [6] Grant eventually agreed and prevailed on a lame-duck Congress to approve the country's adoption of the gold standard; when the time came, Belmont and the Rothschilds provided more than half the money the government needed to accumulate enough reserves to put the dollar onto gold.

But the American commitment to gold remained weak and was challenged again by the Populist assault of the 1890s. After 1893, as the antigold movement swept the country, foreign investors started selling off dollars to guard against the threat of devaluation. The U.S. government was running out of gold, and in February 1895 it turned once more to Nathan Rothschild and his American representative, now August Belmont, Jr. Belmont and a rising American financier, J. P. Morgan, formed a syndicate to provide the Treasury with all the gold it needed for the next year and a half, until the presidential election. When the gold opponents were defeated in 1896, the dollar stabilized, but the U.S. currency almost certainly could not have been defended without Rothschild's support.

Elsewhere in the New World, Nathan Rothschild also defended and bankrolled economic openness. The Rothschilds had long been official banker to Brazil and had great influence in Chile as well. In Argentina their competitors at Baring Brothers were originally predominant, but such competition did not weaken the Rothschild commitment to international financial stability. Thus in 1890, when an Argentine default bankrupted Baring Brothers and threatened a broader financial panic, Nathan Rothschild stepped in. Although he regarded Baring's problems as largely a result of its own improvidence, he energetically rallied other private bankers and the British government behind a massive rescue effort. As Rothschild put it, without such an effort "most of the great London houses would have fallen with them,"[7] so Barings was bailed out, and the crisis resolved. Rothschild chaired the committee that oversaw the renegotiation of the Argentine debt and its return to the London financial markets several years later.

The serious crisis of 1907 demonstrated how the Rothschilds could draw on their financial resources and international network to encourage cooperation among major financial powers. The crisis started as a financial panic in the United States but quickly turned into a broader loss of confidence. The American bank run scared investors everywhere. The Berlin correspondent for the *Economist* reported: "Quotations fluctuate, under the spell of the American cables, up and down, and when other influences come into play to lift prices somewhat, these are soon obliterated by renewed concern about the American situation."[8]

Nathan Mayer Rothschild was forthright in his view that American policy was to blame for the crisis, but as it deepened, this became irrelevant. Rothschild, who was a governor of the Bank of England, believed that the French and British authorities must cooperate to calm the markets. He reminded his French cousins "how intimately and of necessity all countries are bound together." It was crucial to ensure that "the Bank of France and others [act] generously on these occasions." Nathan Rothschild urged his brethren, one of whom was on the board of directors of the Bank of France, to encourage their government to join with the Bank of England to resolve the crisis. The French government did in fact lend tens of millions of francs to the Bank of England to help it weather the financial storm, as did the German authorities. The Rothschild web of economic interests helped guarantee that policy makers would mount such multicountry efforts to stabilize financial markets and sustain the gold standard.[9]

The Rothschilds were of course fervent supporters of world trade. Nathan's brother-in-law Alphonse across the Channel worried that France would "die from suffocation under protectionism" and pointed out to the country's increasingly powerful socialist politicians that "the best of socialisms is the free exchange of international production."[10] Toward the end of his life Nathan Rothschild's free trade orthodoxy softened a bit, not because of any conversion to the cause of protection but rather because of the intricacies of Conservative Party politics. Many Tory industrialists had by the early 1900s become sympathetic to some form of preferential trade relations with Britain's colonial empire. The plan for imperial preferences was championed by the Birmingham mayor Joseph Chamberlain, a former screw manufacturer and a powerful leader of the Conservative Party. As a lifelong Conservative, Rothschild had a strong interest in maintaining a united party, and he counseled for the party's adoption of some of Chamberlain's program. Nonetheless, Rothschild's fundamental commitment to economic integration continued to the end of his life.

Rothschild worked tirelessly in Europe and the New World to keep global financial markets accessible and stable; he also bankrolled ambitious ventures in southern Africa to bring new investments to world markets. The Rothschilds had long been interested in the mineral wealth of the region. Indeed, their interest in precious metals went well beyond support for the gold standard: The British and French Rothschilds had major investments in silver and mercury in Spain, rubies in Burma, gold in Venezuela, nickel in Australia and New Caledonia, copper in Mexico and Montana, and petroleum in Russia. South Africa promised to be the most lucrative underground prize of all.

As the price of gold rose relative to other goods during the Great Depression of 1873–1896, prospectors everywhere looked for new finds. No discoveries were as important as those in 1886 at Witwatersrand, South Africa, which turned out to be the most productive gold-producing region in the world. The findings in the Rand, as it was called, coupled with the development of new technologies to extract gold from unprecedented depths underground, made South Africa the world's greatest gold producer. Nathan Mayer Rothschild and his partners were involved from the very start, through their Exploration Company. At much the same time as they were amassing interests in the South African goldfields, the Rothschilds built a position in the region's lucrative diamond mining.[11]

Nathan Rothschild soon joined forces in the diamond business with one of the region's wealthiest mining magnates, Cecil Rhodes. Together the two were able to bring 98 percent of South African diamond production under the control of their De Beers Mining Company. Rothschild boasted to Rhodes that the history of their joint endeavor with De Beers was "simply a fairy tale" and marveled at their having achieved "a practical monopoly of the production of diamonds."[12] Rhodes had broader ambitions. Economically he coveted a larger share of the area's goldfields. Politically Rhodes, the prime minister of the Cape Colony after 1890, wanted to bring the gold-rich area of South Africa under British control. His obstacles were the governments of the Orange Free State and the Transvaal (in the northern part of what is now South Africa), two independent republics run by Afrikaaners, descendants of Dutch settlers who were hostile or indifferent to the concerns of British miners and others.

Nathan Mayer and the other Rothschilds found themselves in a difficult position in southern Africa. On the one hand, they had substantial interests in the goldfields of the Transvaal, an area controlled by the Afrikaaners, and wanted to maintain cordial ties with the local government. On the other hand, they would have preferred a more friendly government—even an extension of Britain's Cape Colony to the south—in control of their lucrative real estate. To make matters more complex, Rothschild was closely linked to Cecil Rhodes, who had clear designs on the two Afrikaaner republics. Like the Rothschilds, the British Foreign Office was forced into a combination of threats against the Afrikaaners and attempts to placate them.

Rothschild and his fellow investors preferred a cooperative solution, but the conflicts of interests and people in question made this impossible. British miners and other settlers were flooding into the Transvaal, and the Afrikaaner government felt itself besieged by hostile foreigners. Rhodes, governing the adjoining British colony, pursued his imperial dreams by fomenting conflict with the Afrikaaners. In the waning days of 1895, Rhodes's associate L. Starr Jameson led a small group of armed men in an attempt to overthrow the Transvaal government. The attack was an embarrassing failure, and Rhodes was forced to resign; but it set the British and Afrikaaners on a collision course that culminated in the Boer War in 1899. By 1902 half a million British troops had forced all of South Africa into the empire, but at a high price. The war was difficult and lengthy, British mistreatment of civilian Afrikaaners caused worldwide outrage, and the eventual settlement left the government of the Union of South Africa under the effective control of the country's Afrikaaner community.

Cecil Rhodes and Nathan Mayer Rothschild did not fulfill all their South African dreams. Rhodes died before the Boer War ended, and his plans for a Cape Town to Cairo railroad remained a fantasy. South Africa was now British, but Rhodes's Afrikaaner enemies controlled the government. Rothschild came closer to success, maintaining the family's gold and diamond interests intact. But the political fallout from the war was serious. Rothschild wrote to Rhodes: "Feeling in this country [is] running high at present over everything connected with the war and there is considerable inclination, on both sides of the House, to lay the blame for what has taken place on the shoulders of capitalists and those interested in South African Mining."[13] Popular distaste for the Boer War, for Joseph Chamberlain's involvement as colonial secretary, and for the intimations of a connection between the military adventure and financial gain all helped doom Nathan Rothschild's Conservative Party to a resounding defeat in the 1906 general elections.

A firm and a family so integral to the global economy and global politics had to expect setbacks. Yet the Rothschilds had come remarkably far. It was now the first family of international finance, and Nathan Mayer Rothschild had been arguably the single most powerful individual in the world for several decades. The Rothschilds used their fortunes and their political influence to support global economic integration, and they derived enormous financial benefits from the worldwide triumph of this commitment to economic openness. World trade, the gold standard, and international investment all went from strength to strength, and so did the Rothschilds.

The free traders

A powerful array of interests benefited, like the Rothschilds, from international economic relations and fought for greater freedom for international trade. Even David Ricardo, the great theorist of the comparative advantage argument for free trade, was a political activist in debates over British economic policy. Ricardo came, in fact, from the financial community, one of the most important free trade groups in the United Kingdom. Bankers and foreign investors wanted their country to be open to imports, to enable their debtors to earn money to repay their debts.

Producers of a country's exports constituted another influential group favorable to global integration. Producers for export supported trade liberalization, which made the cheapest goods available as inputs into production. This lowered exporters' costs and made them better able to compete in world markets. This was true whether the exports being produced were raw cotton from Louisiana or cotton textiles from Lancashire; export farmers wanted to be able to import cheap equipment, machinery, and fertilizer, while export manufacturers wanted to be able to import cheap cotton. Protectionist barriers to their inputs could only hurt the competitive positions of firms or farms fighting for world markets. Exporters also abhorred protection because trade barriers invited retaliation, exposing them to the risk of being frozen out of markets.

The free traders were typically those groups whose economic activities were closest to their countries' comparative advantage. London bankers, German manufacturers, Argentine cattle ranchers, and Indochinese rubber planters specialized in what their respective regions did best, and they shared an interest in an economic order that rewarded those who specialized in their nations' comparative advantages. Consumers also benefited from freer trade that reduced living costs, but consumers were poorly organized and represented. It was primarily the powerful free trade business groups that were effective in fighting to keep tariffs low before World War One.

But there were challengers to the political and intellectual supporters of free trade. Even those who believed in the abstract that free trade was a good idea for the economy as a whole might have quite other beliefs about its value to themselves. Comparative advantage deals with aggregate social welfare, the net benefits to society as a whole. This has to do with the well-being of the entire society, toting up greater efficiency as a plus and inefficiency as a minus. But the fruits of access to new markets might accrue to one segment of the society, while the costs of facing foreign competition might affect quite another. Net benefits count up the pluses and the minuses. Classical economists argued that free trade's greater efficiency could be distributed to compensate those on the losing side, leaving everybody better off. But taking from winners and giving to losers is not always politically feasible.

The economic appeal of openness may be clear in the abstract and the aggregate, but governments need to respond to constituents who are unlikely to be willing to sacrifice their region, class, company, or farm on the altar of long-term overall economic growth. The aggregate effects of freer trade may be positive, but its *distributional* impact divides groups and people into winners and losers. Liberalizing trade redistributes wealth and income, helping more efficient producers, but hurting less competitive ones.

Farmers in industrial countries and industrialists in farm countries wanted protection. These two broad groups were typical of those whose economic activities were not in their countries' comparative advantage. Relatively inefficient farmers, especially in Europe, were suffering at the expense of New World, Russian, and antipodean farm products.

Allowing the free import of wheat into Europe in 1900 would certainly have made economies more efficient, forcing the closure or conversion of inefficient farms. It would have suited the interests of the region's industrial exporters, avoiding retaliation and providing access to cheap inputs. It was important to European international bankers, who wanted Americans and Russians to export their way out of debt. Free grain trade would have lowered the cost of food, which is why socialist labor movements and many urban employers favored liberalizing trade in farm goods. But cheaper grain would have exacerbated difficult agricultural conditions and wreaked havoc with millions of European farmers and their tight-knit communities. All things considered, European farmers would have much preferred less imported grain and more ruined bankers.

Manufacturers in nations in the early stages of industrialization were a second large protectionist group. Especially in countries that were late developers, manufacturers insisted they could flourish only if they were sheltered from the established industrial powers, especially Great Britain. This cry for infant industry protection—tariffs for embryonic manufacturing sectors until they were big and strong enough to compete—was heard almost everywhere, even in some relatively rich countries. Industries demanded trade barriers most stridently in the countries where industry was battling to establish itself, such as in the New World, the areas of recent settlement, and more backward countries in southern and eastern Europe. All of them argued forcefully that national industry would grow slowly, if at all, if they had to compete with the British and Germans.

Protectionists succeeded in many instances. The protection provided to those distant from comparative advantage depended on the local political scene. The battle was typically among powerful special interests, for consumer groups from the middle and working classes had little representation anywhere, even where they (or their male halves) did have the vote. Concentrated banks and industries and big farmers tended to be the ones best represented in the debates and tended to get what they wanted, whether what they wanted was protection or free trade, depending on the country and its circumstances.[14]

Austria-Hungary, France, Germany, Italy, and other marginal grain producers had tariffs of around 40 percent on wheat on the eve of World War One. Governments also gave industrialists some protection, even in France and Germany—albeit only a fraction of what they gave their struggling farmers. To be sure, western European countries were only mildly protectionist; by one measure, the large Continental economies had average tariffs of between 12 and 18 percent in 1913.

Outside Europe, protection was widespread. Tariffs on manufactured imports into such countries as Brazil, Mexico, and Russia were two, three, or more times as high as in continental Europe. Trade protection in the United States and the other areas of recent European settlement—Oceania, Canada, much of Latin America—tended also to be very high. Tariffs too increased almost everywhere over the decades before 1914.[15]

The world's most populous country largely opted against full international economic integration. China's imperial rulers feared the disruptive effects of the world economy on their society and their place in that society and attempted to circumscribe carefully the activities of foreign traders and investors. By the turn of the century more and more Chinese, especially those who had had some contact with global economic possibilities and wanted more, were questioning the imperial system's insularity. However, it was not until the very eve of World War One—with the eruption of a nationalist revolution in 1911—that there appeared to be any real probability that the nation would turn toward economic integration.

The world's most populous democracy was hardly a paragon of globalization. Protectionists dominated American policy making. They were not extreme in their views: They were happy for American farmers and miners to sell what they could abroad and for foreigners to invest what they wanted in the United States, but they insisted on reserving most of the national market for manufactured goods to themselves. The option for closure did not go unchallenged. Export-oriented cotton and tobacco farmers from the South and Anglophilic bankers from the Northeast resisted the industrialists' trade protection, as did the Democratic Party. But as in China, it was not until the 1912 election, which brought Woodrow Wilson to the presidency, that the Democrats were able to prevail.

Despite exceptions, unprecedented liberalization characterized international trade in the golden age. Important groups of countries had freer trade relations than at any time before or since. Such countries included the traditional bastions of free trade, the United Kingdom, the Netherlands, and Belgium. The smaller industrial nations were more likely to avoid trade protection, as the benefits of free trade were greater for countries with limited home markets.

The very poorest developing countries also tended toward free trade.

Some of them were unable to resist the attempts of European and other powers to pry open their markets. Actually, many extremely poor nations had little to protect; they produced raw materials and agricultural goods for export and had little or no manufacturing. Siam and Persia, for example, were nearly as open to trade as Great Britain or the Netherlands.

Finally, the colonies usually had no choice about allowing free trade with the metropolitan country. The British and Dutch colonies were forced to follow British and Dutch free trade dictates. Here too there were exceptions. Britain's self-governing territories (less elegantly known as the White Dominions—Canada, Australia, New Zealand, and South Africa) had effective independence and pretty much determined their own trade stance. India agitated for, and eventually received, tariff autonomy. In all these cases the choice was for more protection than British free trade would have allowed. On the other hand, the major colonial powers agreed to free trade for the Congo Basin. And, ironically, German colonial policy was less protectionist than its policy toward the home market. The colonies were hardly advertisements for the free choice of free trade, but many nonetheless shared the global tendency toward commercial integration.

Political power was the key to the triumph of economic openness. Undoubtedly, openness was assisted by intellectual consistency, macroeconomic stability, and technological advancement, but its real source was the political power of those who stood to benefit from it. Free traders prevailed in domestic political battles, allowing international trade to grow much more rapidly than output, and country after country geared up to produce for export and consume imports. On the eve of World War One, world trade was nearly twice as important to the world economy as it had been forty years earlier.

Supporters of the golden pillars

Proponents of the international gold standard were as busy, and as committed, as the free traders. The international financial community relied on the reigning international monetary system to tie together lenders and borrowers, investors and their investments and to help safeguard contracts and property across borders. Joining the powerful financial interests were the firms that managed world trade, shipping, insurance, and allied activities. Most of the export-oriented manufacturers of Europe too were part of the global gold bloc, for a stable payments system permitted a flourishing world market for their goods.

Powerful interests outside the European monetary core also aligned with the gold standard to protect their interests. Borrowers and their bankers relied upon European capital and regarded gold as essential to keep funds flowing in. American bankers from August Belmont to J. P. Morgan adamantly supported gold, for they managed much of the investment by Europeans in the United States. Those in the areas of recent settlement, colonies, and the developing world generally whose living relied upon international trade, payments, shipping, and the like also defended the gold standard.

Yet supporters of alternative monetary systems—especially a silver-backed currency or a pure paper currency—launched continual attacks on the gold standard. Many important countries rotated on and off gold; only after prices began rising in 1896 did membership in the system became nearly universal. The costs of being on gold could be substantial. A government commited to a gold-backed currency could not use monetary policies, such as devaluing or lowering interest rates, to deal with domestic economic difficulties. The rules of the gold standard game—free convertibility of currency into gold, allowing domestic prices and wages to move freely up and down to maintain the gold value of the currency—required governments to give up active monetary policy, even when such a policy was justified by local conditions.

There could be great pressures to go off gold, especially in the face of bank panics, mass unemployment, and social unrest. Enemies of gold-backed money were legion, and their ranks increased in hard times. The principal adversaries of gold were those who would gain most from a devaluation, or from a relaxation of monetary conditions. In many cases, a devaluation could raise the prices of farm and mine products, reduce the real burden of debts, and bring down unemployment. But gold made a devaluation impossible.

Being on gold eased access to foreign markets, capital, and investment opportunities but restricted government's ability to react to national economic conditions. The benefits of currency predictability and access to foreign capital had to be weighed against the costs of giving up one of government's most powerful policy tools. It was difficult to evaluate gold's international economic advantages against its domestic economic sacrifices; even today scholars do not agree on whether the gold standard was a good thing. Supporters and opponents met on the political battleground, in a conflict made even more bitter because the principal beneficiaries of the gold standard were typically not those who paid the price of compliance. Keeping the United States, Russia, or Brazil on gold meant prosperity for some and distress for others, and it could not help being politically controversial.

Gold's supporters and opponents fought the "battle of the standards" all over the world. Typically, the battle pitted farmers and miners, who wanted a depreciated currency, against internationalist interests, which wanted stable gold-backed money. The outcome depended on the strength of the interests and their representation. Progold interests in developed countries were particularly important, given the powerful financial and commercial elites that stood behind gold, and even in democratic countries, farmers, miners, debtors, and workers were typically no match for gold backers. In the developing countries matters were different. Landowners and miners dominated many of these oligarchic nations, and given the interests of the primary sectors—agriculture and raw materials—so long as the Great Depression lasted, these countries were more often off gold than on. The two camps met with special ferocity on the highly politicized battlefields of the United States, which had powerful farmers and miners, on the one hand, and a powerful financial community, on the other—as well as a functioning electoral democracy.

Given the controversies over trade and the gold standard, it is remarkable that the international economy was so integrated for so many decades before 1914. World trade remained generally, and impressively, open in the face of protectionist pressures. This was true not just of extremely poor countries and colonies but also of some of the most powerful industrial nations in the world. And despite the difficulties of adherence to the gold standard, almost every major nation was on gold for decades before World War One.

Global networks for a global economy

Powerful economic, political, and social connections across borders and oceans tied together supporters of global economic integration in the golden age. Free traders and gold backers in many countries encouraged and supported each other. In trade policy, one country's imports had a clear relationship to another's exports. Britain's industrial exporters wanted South American cotton and copper, while South American farmers and miners wanted British farm and mining equipment. British trade with Argentina or Chile fostered Argentine or Chilean support for access to British goods. A shared concern about retaliation also allied European and South American free traders: European manufacturers hoped their country's trade policies would induce openness across the Atlantic, while South American export farmers and miners hoped for a liberalization of their trade that would curry favor with European customers and investors.

British free trade activists had long understood how important links among interest groups across borders could be. In the 1840s free traders trying to repeal the Corn Laws recognized the importance of trade policy in the United States, where sectional conflicts pitted the free trade exporting South against the protectionist manufacturing North. British free traders recognized that the Corn Laws were driving the pivotal midwestern grain-producing states into the arms of the protectionists. Richard Cobden, leader of Britain's free traders, complained that with protection "we offer them no inducement to spread themselves out from the cities—to abandon their premature manufactures—in order to delve, dig, and plow for us." One of Cobden's parliamentary allies argued: "We convert our natural and best customers, not only into commercial rivals, but into commercial enemies." Another noted during the parliamentary debates: "In the last election a great deal turned upon the question of the tariff; and in Congress there was a decided majority in favor of relaxation in commercial policy. There never was a moment in which it was more likely that if England relaxed her policy, she would meet with a corresponding relaxation in the United States."[16] The eventual change in British trade policy did cement a transatlantic free trade alliance: From the repeal of the Corn Laws until the Civil War, America's export farmers reliably opposed trade barriers on British manufactured goods, despite the objections of northern industry.

For decades dozens of countries repeated this pattern. Europe's free trade manufacturers and lenders found allies among the developing world's primary exporters and borrowers. British industrialists and investors had economic ties to Brazilian and Egyptian farmers, American bankers, and Australian miners. These ties were also often cultural and social, as demonstrated by the spread of English, of soccer football, and of British political economy and by the large and influential British and Anglophile communities from Buenos Aires to Shanghai. Every nation drawn into world trade soon had powerful interest groups pushing to consolidate commercial integration, typically in alliance with powerful interests abroad. Colombian coffee growers, Southeast Asian rubber planters, and Chilean nitrate and copper miners owed much of their national influence to their profitable links to the world's most important markets.

Great Britain was at the center of the free trade network. With its empire, it accounted for about one-third of all international trade. British policy was unremittingly committed to global economic integration, for fully one-tenth of British national income came from earnings on foreign investments, shipping, insurance, and other international services—and this does not even include export earnings.[17] Trade not directly linked with Britain was often part of a broader British-led trading system, which reinforced the free trade orientation of Britain's trading partners. For example, Denmark exported its dairy and pork products to the British market and bought manufactured goods elsewhere. In the early twentieth century Denmark's trade with Germany and the United States was unbalanced in the extreme; it imported three times as much as it exported. But the country made up for this with a countervailing unbalanced trade with the United Kingdom, to which Danes exported three times as much as they imported. This rewarding triangular trade depended on a generalized system of international free trade.[18]

The unwavering British commitment to free trade also meant similar policies in Belgium, the Netherlands, and other small European nations. A free trade Britain meant a free trade baseline for the commercial relations of the world's greatest empire, even if some of its members strayed. A free trade Britain drew Peru and Japan and Siam into its system of interlocking trade, investment, transportation, and communications ties.

Perhaps most important, the ready availability of the British market helped cement the internationalizing vocation of those who sold, traded, and borrowed there. Even if German policy was protectionist, Germany's exporters and bankers could grow richer—and, eventually, more politically influential—by trading with or through London. The same held for exporters, borrowers, and lenders everywhere; the very workings of the British economy relied upon and reinforced the desire of Britons and others to maintain an open trading system. And so the world's trade grew continually, drawing producers and consumers from dozens of countries into a thick, self-reinforcing network. Despite temptations for trade protection and some surrenders to these temptations, world trade was generally open.

Gold standard supporters also had many international connections. Financiers and central bankers of the world's principal monetary powers—Britain, France, Germany, the Netherlands, Belgium, and others—were in frequent contact and had shared interests in sustaining the global monetary order. In the borrowing countries too, powerful groups with strong international financial ties—plantation owners in Malaya, railroad men in Brazil, miners in South Africa, bankers in Peru—had every reason to safeguard a monetary and financial order that gave them access to Europe's capital. All those connected to the international financial and investing system saw the gold standard as central to its smooth functioning, and they shared a commitment to sustain it.

The gold standard rested on implicit or explicit cooperation among the major financial and monetary powers. In times of serious difficulty, such as the Panic of 1907, the monetary authorities of Great Britain, France, Germany, and sometimes others worked together to avoid too serious a dislocation of the system. It also rested on a strong relationship between Europe's international bankers and their clients in the developing world. Missions went forth from the major financial centers to Constantinople and Lima, Rio de Janeiro and Bangkok, providing advice on how to manage the debtors' economies, often by moving toward gold. When debts went sour, committees of creditors supervised orderly renegotiations, typically including plans for adherence to the gold standard.

A major source of the gold standard's staying power was, as with trade, the extraordinary position of the United Kingdom. Ludwig Bamberger, the banker and politician who helped guide Germany onto gold, said, "We chose gold, not because gold is gold, but because Britain is Britain."[19] Gold brought better access to Britain's financial connections, and London accounted for nearly half of all international investment at the turn of the century. Reliance on British capital gave developing nations around the world good reasons to follow the British lead. As the United Kingdom wove an international economy around London, it was natural for participants to gravitate toward Britain's gold-based currency system. The more countries were on gold, the greater the benefits to others of staying or going onto gold. It did little harm to be one among many countries that had bimetallic or paper money, but to be one of a handful of countries not on gold risked relegation to second-class citizenship in the global economy.

By the 1890s a virtuous circle was at work in international trade, money, and finance. As world trade grew, more exporting groups arose, and exports became more important for them. The more important foreign markets were to domestic producers, the more reluctant they were to see them endangered by retaliation to national tariffs. The wider and more attractive the variety of products available on international markets, the more insistent were demands for access to these fruits of trade. This was true even in highly protectionist countries. As American exports of raw materials and agricultural products grew, the hostility of southern and western farmers and miners to trade protection sharpened and deepened. Eventually even many manufacturers took advantage of the open world trading system: Between 1890 and 1910 the proportion of American manufacturers for whom exports were more than 5 percent of output rose dramatically from one-quarter to nearly two-thirds.[20] By 1910 there were powerful pressures to loosen the country's near embargo on manufactured imports. The shift was reflected in American politics, as the free trade Democrats gained strength and even the protectionist Republicans moderated their stance. When in 1912 the Democrats won the presidency and the Congress, one of their first steps was to reduce American tariffs dramatically. In the United States, as elsewhere, the rapid growth of trade weakened protectionists and strengthened free traders.

The virtuous circle operated with the gold standard too. The better established the gold standard became, the more reasons its supporters had to safeguard it. As the world financial system grew, more international investors had more at stake, and they provided greater domestic bases of support for enabling government policies. There was, after all, something to the antigold charges of an international gold conspiracy: Those who believed the reigning monetary order was desirable had many common interests and worked to protect them. Because the opponents of gold were primarily striving for national autonomy as opposed to international monetary harmonization, it was harder to establish any global coordination in this direction; going off gold meant precisely forgoing global coordination.

Global economic integration reinforced itself. The more countries were on gold, the higher the level of international trade, investment, lending, and migration. The more cross-border economic activity took place, the stronger was support for the gold standard as a guardian of predictability, macroeconomic balance, and creditworthiness. The broader and deeper were commitments to gold, the greater swelled the ranks of those whose livelihoods depended on the gold standard and its accoutrements. And so support for the pillars of the golden age grew in extent and intensity. Its network of defenders became more plentiful, and their resolve stiffened, as more and more countries went onto gold and as world trade and payments expanded.

The international migration of capital and people

While free trade and the gold standard were the two most obvious distinguishing marks of pre–World War One global capitalism, the movements of capital and people also influenced the economic order. Unlike in trade and money, however, there was no identifiable global system or policy standard toward which countries and groups converged. Instead there was a presumption that such movements would be essentially free, a presumption that was rarely questioned and even more rarely proved wrong.

Countries sending capital and people and countries receiving them had little interest in restricting such movements. Those who invested or moved overseas did so, one can be quite sure, with high expectations. They were generally right. The average rate of return on British investments abroad was 50 to 75 percent higher than at home. The difference was even more striking in the all-important railroad sector, which accounted for nearly half of all British foreign investment: British-owned foreign railroads earned about twice as much as those in the United Kingdom.[21] For the home countries of these great investors, the earnings on foreign endeavors could be tremendous. Britain, foremost among international investors, had by the turn of the century come to rely heavily on its overseas profits. Indeed, in the decade before 1914 Britain ran a trade deficit equal to 6 percent of gross domestic product (GDP), a formidable sum that was countered and more by net earnings on overseas investments of 7 percent of GDP.[22] This led supporters such as Winston Churchill, speaking during the 1910 election campaign, to wax enthusiastic about Britain's international investments: "Foreign investment and its returns are a powerful stimulus to the industrial system of Great Britain . . . they give to the capital of the country a share in the new wealth of the whole world which is gradually coming under the control of scientific development."[23]

By the same token, wages in the countries immigrants went to were dramatically higher than in the countries they came from. In 1910, for example, wages in the United States and Canada were about three times as high as in Italy and Spain, while in Argentina they were about twice as high. American and Canadian wages were about double those in Ireland and Sweden and nearly double those in Great Britain.[24] Although the lives of immigrants were rarely easy, their lives would almost certainly have been even harder had they stayed home. Their countries of origin had little reason to oppose their leaving since this reduced economic and social pressures on overcrowded lands. It also held out the hope of remittances from immigrants who sent money back to those they left behind.

Overseas investors and immigrants and their home countries certainly supported freedom of movement for themselves and their money. The countries in which they invested or settled had reasons to welcome them. Newly developing countries were starved for capital, then as now. As the comparable wage rates show, they were also typically regions with labor scarcities, in which willing new workers could make a major contribution to national development. The thirst for labor was so great in many of the immigrants' destinations that the government subsidized their relocation. In Brazil, after the abolition of slavery in 1888, coffee planters desperate for labor convinced the national and local governments to offer free passage to Europeans willing to come to Brazil to work. Over the next twenty years nearly three million Europeans flooded into southern Brazil, remaking the country's economy as well as its social structure.

Enthusiasm for international investment and migration was not, however, universal. There was some concern in countries from which capital was flowing that this was restricting the supply of funds to worthy businesses at home. Although subsequent economic analysis tends to be agnostic on this count,[25] certainly many businesses in Europe resented the huge loans proffered by European financiers to the tsar, or to the province of Buenos Aires, when they could not borrow. Joseph Chamberlain, a prominent British critic of foreign investment, railed against what he considered to be the neglect of industry by London's free trade foreign investing community: "Banking is not the creator of our prosperity, but is the creation of it. It is not the cause of our wealth, but it is the consequence of our wealth; and if the industrial energy and development which has been going on for so many years in this country were to be hindered or relaxed, then finance, and all that finance means, will follow trade to the countries that are more successful than ourselves."[26]

In borrowing countries also, there was concern in some quarters that reliance on foreign capital was misguided. Such nationalist sentiments were naturally most popular when it came time to repay loans. The concerns were not necessarily misguided: There was little economic justification for Chinese or Brazilian citizens to be forced to curtail consumption to repay debts that had gone to expand the personal fortunes of emperors, favored businessmen, or corrupt politicians.

But in most cases the export of capital was not very controversial. It tended to go from countries that had plenty of it to countries that were willing and able to pay for it. The principal recipients were not the very poor regions of Asia or Africa but the rapidly developing areas of recent European settlement. In 1914, in fact, three-quarters of British foreign investment was in the United States, Canada, Australia, South Africa, India, and Argentina.[27] In these countries most of the money was used for railroads, ports, power plants, and other projects crucial to development.

Immigration excited substantially more opposition. European or Asian laborers flooding into Sydney, Toronto, or San Francisco became direct competition for the workers already there. Then, as now, the bulk of immigrants clustered in the lower depths of the labor market, as unskilled laborers doing the hardest, least desirable work. Immigration did not in most instances have an appreciable impact on the wages of skilled workers, but it certainly lowered the wages of unskilled workers in direct competition with immigrants. One study of conditions around the turn of the century found that the greater an American city's foreign-born population, the lower were laborers' wages. While there was no impact on the wages of artisans, the effect on American unskilled workers was appreciable: Every percentage point increase in the foreign-born depressed laborers' wages by 1.6 percent.[28] More general analyses confirm the American results, for the obvious reason that immigration had a massive impact on the supply of labor in many receiving countries. Immigration from 1870 to 1910 had by the latter year made the Argentine labor force 75 percent larger than it would have been without immigration; Canada and Australia had more than one-third more labor than they would have otherwise, the United States one-fifth. The result of the increased labor supply was appreciably lower wages than would have prevailed without immigration, lower by one-third in Argentina, by one-quarter in Canada and Australia, by one-eighth in the United States.[29]

Workers thus had an incentive to try to restrict new immigration. New immigrants were often the greatest economic threat to those who had immediately preceded them and who now occupied the lowest rung on the local social ladder. In the United States the Irish turned on the Italians, who turned on the Jews, and all of them turned on the black internal migrants from the American South. But while laborers were wary of free immigration, employers had every reason to want it. They of course were the principal beneficiaries of the lower wages, especially if they were in industries relying on unskilled labor. While immigrants were one-fifth of the turn-of-the-century American male labor force, they were two-thirds of the clothing industry and more than half of all iron and steel foundry laborers.[30]

The result was, as with trade and the gold standard, a straightforward conflict of interests. Unskilled workers in the receiving country wanted to keep new unskilled workers out, while employers of unskilled labor wanted access to them. Recognizable ethnic, religious, or racial differences among groups exacerbated the conflicts. Where labor was particularly strong politically, it often obtained severe restrictions on immigration. Australia was perhaps the best example. Great shortages of labor there gave trade unions a power that was probably unrivaled anywhere in the world, and they used their power to press for severe restrictions on immigration. For racial and economic reasons, the principal target was immigrants from Asia; they were physically and culturally distinct, and as they were poorer than Europeans, they were usually willing to work for less. The result was a strict color bar—the "White Australia" policy—that was adopted with the Immigration Restriction Act of 1901. In the United States anti-immigrant sentiment was concentrated in the West. There, as in Australia, distance made labor scarce. There too, as in Australia, this labor scarcity meant high wages for those who arrived first and attempts to limit entry. Also as in Australia, the principal target was Asian immigration. The result was a series of restrictions on immigration from Japan and China that lasted for many decades.

There were many examples of immigration restrictions, yet in the global sense they were relatively rare. Labor was rarely strong enough to affect immigration policy and did so in only a few countries. Where, as in Argentina and Brazil, society and government were dominated by the interests of landowners and industrialists who wanted as much immigration as possible, governments tried actively to encourage increased supplies of labor. Even where some restrictions were imposed, as in Canada and the United States, borders remained essentially open to most immigrants, especially those from Europe. And like trade, the gold standard, and investment, immigration helped build further support for economic openness. Many of the immigrants hoped to return to their homelands permanently or to visit, to buy property at home, and to send money back to relatives. They appreciated open borders and the easy ability to transfer funds among gold-backed currencies. In turn they helped spur economic integration, by helping open new lands and establishing new industries in areas that otherwise would have been starved for labor.

Globalization

The global capitalism of the late nineteenth and early twentieth centuries came close to the classical ideal. International trade, investment, and migration all were relatively free and tied together by a firmly established gold standard. The owners of firms, mines, farms, and plantations on every continent produced for global markets, using capital and labor from around the globe. Those who prospered were a powerful, ever-increasing force for continued economic integration. In these conditions, the world economy grew more rapidly than ever before. Living standards shot upward, as country after country closed in on or surpassed the levels of development of the world's leading industrial nation, Great Britain.

Trade liberalization reinforced itself, the gold standard reinforced itself, and each reinforced the other. The gold standard increased the attractiveness of international trade and finance, while international trade and finance increased the attractiveness of being on gold. Global economic openness encouraged faster transport, better communications, more reliable currencies, freer trade policies, and more political stability, and these in turn encouraged more economic openness. The resulting virtuous circle or upward spiral of economic openness grew at an ever-increasing rate over the course of the late nineteenth and early twentieth centuries.

The gentleman's club that was golden age global capitalism was founded around a British and western European nucleus. But it was open to new members from the New World and elsewhere, and by the turn of the twentieth century countries like the United States, Australia, and Argentina had joined. Such other rapidly growing and globally integrated nations as Japan and Brazil were also members, although their status was certainly not that of the founding British, French, and Germans. Whether these countries were senior or junior members of the club, their rulers were supremely conscious of the need to maintain a standard of conduct consistent with their obligations: general economic openness, commitment to gold, minimal interference with the working of global or national market mechanisms. The club was prosperous and growing, and its members had few reasons to complain.

3

Success Stories of the Golden Age

The Paris International Exposition of 1900 was the largest the world had ever seen. It was the last of a series of seven French and British world fairs that started with London's Great Exhibition of 1851 at the Crystal Palace. The previous fairs showcased the industrial achievements of the past; the Paris exposition pointed toward the twentieth century.

Visitors to the 1900 fair could walk from the Trocadéro through the Eiffel Tower, which had been built for the Paris exposition in 1889. The exhibition's gates opened onto an international mix: "Flemish carillons mingle with medieval bells, Muezzin chants with the tinkle of Swiss cow-bells; the towns of Nuremberg and Louvain, Hungarian dwellings, Roumanian monasteries, Javanese palaces, the straw huts of Senegal, the castles of the Carpathians, form an astounding international medley beneath a grey Lenten sky."[1]

The new century's scientific and industrial advances filled the exhibition. To one Frenchman it seemed "The world revolves so fast that one is dizzy . . . whirled in a maelstrom of progress."[2] Visitors viewed the latest technologies: a wireless telegraph; the world's most powerful telescope; a Palace of Electricity. "Electricity!" wrote an enthusiastic viewer:

Born of Heaven like the true Kings! Electricity triumphed at the Exhibition, as morphia triumphed in the boudoirs of 1900. The public laughed at the words—Danger of death—on the pylons, for they knew that Electricity could cure all ills, even the neurosis which was so much in fashion; that it was progress, the poetry of rich and poor alike, the source of light, the great signal; it crushed acetylene as soon as it was born. . . . Electricity is accumulated, condensed, transformed, bottled, drawn into filaments, rolled upon spools, then discharged under water, in fountains, or set free on the house tops or let loose among the trees; it is the scourge and the religion of 1900.[3]

Visitors could arrive on the new Paris metro, take moving sidewalks from pavilion to pavilion, and ride the world's first escalator (only up, though) to startling new displays. "In the Pavilion of Optics, one may see—horrid sight—a drop of Seine water magnified ten thousand times and, a little further on, there is the moon, only a meter away. Doctor Doyen, a surgeon prone to self-advertisement, even uses a new invention, the cinematograph, to show himself in the act of performing an operation. . . . Elsewhere, they synchronize the voice from a phonograph, with moving pictures."[4]

A Scotsman marveled at the new technologies and their proponents: "the engineers and electricians among Siemens' or Lord Kelvin's patents, the ironmasters crowding to buy the colossal gas engine which utilizes the hitherto wasted energies of the blast furnace and literally wins the power of a thousand horses from what has been hitherto a useless pollution of the air . . . the show of automobiles, the latest telephotographic lenses, the rival typesetting machines, the best trained apple trees, the newest antiseptics and filters."[5]

Amid all the evidence of technological progress, the fair's fifty million visitors may have noted another reality: Industrial leadership was slipping away from Great Britain and its fellow early industrializers, France and Belgium. One Englishman thought the exposition presaged "the Americanization of the world." Overall, however, Germany dominated the exposition, "as if she had made herself mistress of all the machinery on earth. She insisted on the beauty of steel, and the Louis XV armchair was banished. She is going to crush and pulverize the world."[6]

"I heard my elders talking," wrote a French boy. "'Have you seen the Germans? They are amazing! They put air in bottles! They manufacture cold!' " Germany, a country barely thirty years old and long regarded as a backward land of simple farmers, shocked the visitors with its pavilion:

"Under its rustic aspect, beneath its green and yellow wooden towers, the Palace of the *Reich* conceals a veritable explosion of method, science, and labor resulting in an immense system of practical strategy, the greatest instance of commercial encirclement the world has ever seen."[7] The visiting Frenchman observed further: "No other race had yet succeeded in wresting such stupendous results from the earth by the sweat of man's brow. Well do I remember the great impression made on me by the huge Hélios dynamos of two-thousand horse-power from Cologne, hitched to steam-engines and those other generators from Berlin and Magdeburg and the crane that raised twenty-five tons, dominating all the gallery; beside these, the machines of other countries looked like toys."[8] French veterans of their nation's defeat thirty years earlier shook their heads sadly, recalling the decisive battle of the Franco-Prussian War: "The Exhibition is a commercial Sedan."[9] The Germans had, it was rumored, offered to supply all the electricity for the fair, but the French, humiliated by the symbolism of France's industrial subordination, had turned them down.

Even more astonishing was the economic emergence of an Asian island nation known for its exoticism, not its industry. "It begins the century well, this young victor," said one observer.[10] Another was uneasy, seeing shades of Germany, and of its military might, coming out of Asia: "Japan seems to be the Oriental echo of that great voice of the Rhine singing a hymn to labour, fatherland, and ennobling war. . . . What is the meaning of all this armor-plating, these tubular boilers, this adventurous policy, this commercial arrogance? Nagasaki and her lanterns, we know, but what of Kobé and her blast furnaces?"[11]

To many citizens of the first industrial nations, the exposition's revelation of economic advance elsewhere was troubling. "These nations who are making a new life for themselves," wrote a Frenchman, "who know nothing of politics and the neurotic, degenerate, fin-de-siècle attitude, against whom do they propose to try their strength?"[12] From central Europe to Australia, from Argentina to Japan, the world's former industrial core was being outperformed by a host of countries outside that core. A visitor to the 1900 Paris fair might well wonder how northwestern Europe had slipped from its unchallenged leadership of the world economy.

Britain overtaken

As economies integrated, modern manufacturing spread from its limited base in Britain and northwestern Europe to the European continent, to North America, even to Japan and Russia. In 1870 Britain, Belgium, and France together produced nearly half of the world's industrial output, but by 1913 they were producing barely one-fifth. German industrial output exceeded Britain's, and America's was substantially more than double Britain's.[13] In 1870 urban industrial areas were a rarity, even in Europe, but by 1913 they were the norm. By 1913 every country in western Europe, except Spain and Portugal, was industrialized. The Austrian and Czech lands of the Austro-Hungarian Empire, the United States and Canada, Australia and New Zealand, Argentina and Uruguay all had smaller shares of the population in agriculture than did France and Germany.[14] By 1913 it could truly be said—as it could not have been in 1870—that substantial parts of the world, from Chicago to Berlin and from Tokyo to Buenos Aires, were industrial.

Great Britain, the world's first manufacturing nation and longtime industrial leader, had been overtaken by several countries and stood near to being overtaken by still others. This was true by any measure. Living standards in the United States, Australia, and New Zealand were higher than in the United Kingdom, and Argentina and Canada were gaining fast. Manufacturers in Germany and the United States were producing much more than in Britain, especially in leading sectors: In 1870 British iron and steel production was greater than that of these two nations combined, while by 1913 Germany and the United States combined outproduced the UK roughly six to one. Britain had lost its technological edge also. Germans made significant advances in electrical engineering and chemicals, and Americans introduced revolutionary methods of mass production.[15] The homeland of the Industrial Revolution was being left behind.

The rapid industrializers varied. The United States and Germany, both wealthy to begin with, had productive agricultural and commercial economies and moved more or less smoothly into modern manufacturing. Other rapid industrializers, such as Italy, Austria-Hungary, Russia, and Japan, started out much poorer. They had backward agricultural economies (in the case of Russia and Japan, just a step away from feudalism) but developed dynamic manufacturing sectors in the early twentieth century. They remained largely rural, and often the rural economies lagged far behind the cities; but they did build impressive industrial bases.

The Russian and Japanese experiences were especially dramatic. Both had been poverty-stricken, their incomes per person in 1870 barely distinguishable from those of other poor countries in Asia and well below those of Latin America. But in the latter part of the nineteenth century both embarked on major industrialization drives. Their respective governments focused on expanding exports and attracting foreign capital to fuel industry.

Russia's tsarist autocracy sought industrial investment from abroad, exported raw materials and grain to earn foreign currency for industry, and protected domestic manufacturing with high trade barriers. The speed of Russian industrial growth was remarkable. Steel production sextupled from 1890 to 1900, then more than doubled from 1905 to 1913 (the early years of the century were disrupted by war with Japan and a failed democratic revolution). The production of coal and of pig iron increased sixfold from 1890 to 1913, and consumer goods industries grew nearly as rapidly. By 1914 Russia had two million modern industrial workers and some of the world's largest factories.[16] Most farming remained premodern, however. Russia industrialized rapidly, but in a highly distorted manner: An extraordinarily backward countryside surrounded a few islands of modernity.

Japan had a more balanced economic development. The Meiji restoration of 1868 overthrew military rule by the feudal lords of the shogunate. The new reformist imperial government aimed at economic modernization by way of full participation in the world economy. It avidly pursued foreign technology and capital, and within a few years the country was successfully exporting to European markets. Japanese agriculture was relatively efficient, unlike that of Russia, and industrial growth relied as much on broad economic development—including rising incomes in the countryside—as it did on foreign trade. Japan's early industrial growth was closely tied to its comparative advantage, especially in the silk trade. As late as 1914 one-third of all exports were of raw silk or silk products.[17] Assisted by the abundant, relatively well-educated Japanese labor force, the cotton goods industry also grew rapidly. Between 1890 and 1913 yarn output went from 42 to 672 million pounds. Exports of yarn rose from nothing in 1890 to 187 million pounds in 1913, and of cloth from nothing to 4.3 million square yards in 1913, when cotton textiles were over one-fifth of total Japanese exports.[18]

The Japanese demonstrated the broader fruits of their economic success when they defeated China in war in 1895, took Taiwan, increased their influence in Korea, and obtained a foothold in the struggle for spheres of influence in China. They made an even more striking statement in the war with Russia in 1904. Japan crushed the Russians, the first time in modern history that an Asian power had defeated a European. Europeans were especially shocked by the naval engagement in Tsushima Strait in May 1905. Japan's fleet proved faster, more modern, and better armed than Russia's, which it virtually destroyed.

German science, American technology, and Japanese military might dazzled the world's old industrial core. A range of countries that in the middle of the nineteenth century were well outside the circle of modern industrial society had, by the beginning of the twentieth, jumped into the center of the circle. They had become full members of the gentleman's club of the golden age world economy.

New technologies and the new industrialism

Changes in the very nature of manufacturing fostered the rapid spread of industrialization. The widespread use of electric power, cheaper techniques to produce steel, the development of a modern chemical industry, and other technical changes transformed industrial production. A flurry of inventions also brought forth novel products, such as typewriters, bicycles, phonographs, handheld cameras, and the "artificial silk" called rayon. Internal-combustion engines led to the invention of the motor vehicle and launched the most important industry of the twentieth century. Manufacturing in the middle 1800s had largely meant textiles, clothing, and footwear but by the end of the century focused on steel and chemicals, electrical machinery and automobiles.

Both mass production and mass consumption rose together. Earlier industrial products largely provided the basic necessities of life. As income per person in Europe, North America, and the areas of recent settlement doubled between 1870 and 1913, the demand for consumer goods other than food, clothes, and shelter more than doubled. Meanwhile new inventions made a new range of household machines possible. Now many families had electric lighting, sewing machines, telephones, phonographs, and eventually automobiles and radios. The United States led the trend to produce machinery for mass consumption, especially the new household appliances. North America was chronically short of labor, meaning that domestic servants were too expensive for the middle classes and that women were much more likely to work than in Europe. This created a thirst for gadgets to lessen the load of household chores and to free labor for other things.

The automobile was an archetypical industrial product that led to new production and consumption patterns. The "horseless carriage" met a demand for personal transportation that grew with incomes and available leisure time. The assembly line put the motorcar, originally an artisanal luxury item, within reach of the middle classes. The initial burst of energy in the industry came in the ten years before World War One. The phenomenon was essentially American; Europe did not join the automotive age in earnest until the 1920s. In 1905 there were about 160,000 motor vehicles in the world, half of them in the United States. By 1913 there were about 1.7 million cars on the world's roads, three-quarters in the United States. Meanwhile Henry Ford's innovations brought the price of a Model T down from $700 to $350 between 1910 and 1916—at a time when other prices rose 70 percent. Given the rise in wages over those years, this meant that it took the average American worker nearly a year and a half to earn enough to buy a Model T in 1910, but only six months in 1916. As productivity shot up, prices dropped, and demand increased, Ford output went from 34,000 cars in 1910 to 730,000 in 1916, when the country as a whole turned out over 1.5 million cars—three or four times as many as then *existed* in the rest of the world. The automobile had arrived, and modern industry would never be the same.[19]

The automobile was the most striking of these new consumer durables, as they were called to distinguish them from less permanent products, such as shoes and canned beef. Durable goods production used many more intermediate manufactured inputs—goods at a middle stage of finishing, such as steel, copper wire, and glass—than did the earlier consumer nondurables, which typically were just a few steps away from raw materials. They also involved more sophisticated machinery.

The new industries tended to give rise to much larger factories and corporations than the old. Before the 1890s most manufacturing could be done in small shops. Factories with forty or fifty workers could easily realize the advantages of specialization, modern machinery, and steam power. But the new techniques typically required larger agglomerations of people and equipment. Steel mills were primary examples: By 1907 three-quarters of the workers in the German iron and steel sector were laboring in factories with more than 1,000 workers; in 1914 the average American steelworks had 642 workers.[20] Average plant size grew dramatically in chemicals, machinery and engineering products, metalworking, and even such erstwhile strongholds of small enterprise as textiles. The typical factory changed from a small shop to a huge mill. Economies of scale were much more important in these complex manufactures than they had been in sectors typical of the first Industrial Revolution. Average plant size was much larger in automobiles and chemicals than in garments—as is still the case.

The new consumer durables were expensive products that people would buy to use for years, so that their reputations for reliability and service were important. Thus brand name recognition mattered, and it is no coincidence that modern advertising goes back to the early consumer durables. When name recognition, service, and other reputational factors are important, there is a natural tendency for a few very large firms to dominate the market. And so they did. Singer, Ford, General Electric, Siemens all came to the fore along with the rise of consumer durables industries.

The rapidly industrializing nations had the advantage of lateness. Germany and the United States, for example, were well positioned to adopt the new patterns of production and consumption that made factories bigger and firms larger. German, American, and other later developers could start with the most modern plant and equipment, in huge factories producing the latest inventions with the latest technologies. However, history weighed on British manufacturing, with its older industries, smaller factories, and firms slow to catch up with the huge scale of American and Continental companies. The second wave of industrializers used their very newness to beat the British at their own industrial game.[21]

The new industrializers relied heavily on an open world economy. The international diffusion of new technologies depended on global integration; most of the new industries also needed the scale of a global market rather than restricted national markets. London and other European capital markets stood ready to lend to any reasonable project.

Sweden, a great success story of this period, illustrates the central role of economic integration in the second wave of industrial development.[22] The country was one of western Europe's poorest in 1870, but rapid growth elsewhere increased demand for Sweden's exports, especially of lumber and simple wood products such as safety matches. The timber boom allowed Sweden to build new industries aimed at foreign markets for high-quality steel, machinery, and other goods. Industrialization in Sweden was also fueled by foreign loans, which financed some 90 percent of the government's borrowing; much of the foreign capital went, directly or indirectly, to build up the country's railroads, utilities, and port facilities. For Sweden, as for the other new industrializers, modern manufacturing went hand in hand with access to foreign markets, foreign technology, and foreign capital.

Protecting the infant industries

Although the challengers to British manufacturing prowess relied on access to overseas markets, suppliers, capital, and technology, they also tended to use trade barriers to protect their industries. Their business and political leaders generally favored foreign investment, international finance, and free immigration, and they saw trade as an important engine of growth, but many industrialists who regarded themselves as firm economic internationalists also strongly supported trade protection for their own industries. This was so to differing degrees—American manufacturers were much more protectionist than their German or Japanese counterparts—but almost all the industrializing countries protected industry to some extent. National manufacturers with protection from foreign competition could charge domestic prices above world levels and earn very high profits, which they could plow back into industry.

This artificially rapid industrialization was just what was expected, and desired, by those who believed that protection was a justifiable means to an industrial end. The best-known early theoretician of industrialization by protection was Friedrich List, a nineteenth-century German political economist and activist. List regarded free trade as an ultimate goal but argued that temporary trade protection was needed to equalize relations among the major powers: "In order to allow freedom of trade to operate naturally, the less advanced nations must first be raised by artificial means to that stage of cultivation to which the English nation has been artificially elevated."[23]

List and other supporters of protection focused on infant industry arguments and on the unique needs of modern industry for large-scale production: "The system of protection can be justified solely and only for the purpose of the *industrial development* of the nation."[24] They pointed out that one could not build a modern steel industry bit by bit but had to start with large integrated steel mills; initially, they argued, the mills might be inefficient, but over time they would become competitive, and protection could be removed. Protectionists pointed out that no country had industrialized without protective barriers; the United Kingdom had removed mercantilist controls on trade only *after* achieving industrial prowess. And, they often argued, national security demanded as much industrial self-sufficiency as could be made possible. List indeed regarded his argument as primarily relevant to large, relatively rich countries, where industry was crucial to national power and influence. Whatever short-term sacrifice protectionism implied, for these nations the longer-term benefits were worth the price: "The nation must sacrifice and give up a measure of material property in order to gain culture, skill, and powers of united production; it must sacrifice some present advantages in order to insure to itself future ones."[25]

The argument that early industries needed government support was even accepted, albeit cautiously, by such paragons of classical trade theory as John Stuart Mill, a contemporary of List's. So too was the infant industry argument generally acknowledged by many neoclassical economists in the early twentieth century. Mill and the neoclassicals, however, always thought of protection as a very temporary expedient more to be tolerated than embraced.

Whatever theory preached, in practical political terms manufacturers in most late-industrializing countries wanted protection and were powerful enough to get it. Virtually all the rapid industrializers, from the United States to Japan and from Italy to Russia, had relatively high industrial tariffs. The Russian government imposed some of the highest tariffs in modern history, 84 percent on manufactured goods (nearly double what were probably the second-highest such tariffs, an average of 44 percent in the United States).[26] Apart from high-speed industrial development, this gave rise to a peculiar industrial structure. The very high levels of protection tended to create and defend monopolies. High trade barriers also contributed to foreign ownership of industry, as European firms unable to export to the Russian market instead jumped tariff walls and set up shop inside the empire. Indeed, contemporaries often remarked on two distinguishing features of Russian industry, both of which were related to the pattern of industrialization the tsarist regime had pursued: large-scale and heavy foreign ownership. About 40 percent of industry was foreign-owned, and over 40 percent of all workers were in factories of more than a thousand employees. This unusually high proportion of the industrial labor force concentrated in very large plants undoubtedly facilitated the activities of the revolutionary groups that organized the Russian proletariat in the years before and during World War One.[27]

Japan had much more moderate trade barriers than Russia or the United States; by most estimates Japanese tariffs were roughly similar to those of continental Europe.[28] The country relied heavily on exports of simple manufactured products (silkens and cotton textiles) and had hitched its industrial wagon clearly to the international economy. Yet manufacturing was protected and subsidized by the government, and the economic results were striking, as the world witnessed during the Russo-Japanese War.

Trade protection had some troubling effects. The classical trade theorists had long pointed to two undesirable results of trade barriers. First, by raising prices, protection transferred income from consumers to producers. A tariff on shoes makes shoes more expensive, to the benefit of shoe manufacturers and the detriment of those who wear shoes. Second, protection deflected the economy from its comparative advantage: By making protected activities artificially profitable, trade protection diverted resources to inefficient uses. A shoe tariff leads a country to produce more shoes than it should, given its comparative advantage. The first effect is a distributional one, taxing consumers to benefit producers; the second effect reduces efficiency (or aggregate welfare), diverting resources from more to less productive uses.

In addition, tariffs were associated with cartels, informal or formal combinations among large corporations. Sometimes an existing cartel demanded trade protection. Cartel members agreed to limit supply and keep prices artificially high, and this could not be sustained if imports were let in; foreign producers outside the cartel would bid prices down. So cartel stability required protection from foreign competition. Sometimes the process went in reverse, and protection spawned cartels: As trade barriers protected local firms from foreign competition, national firms agreed not to compete against one another in order to keep prices high. Either way, the rise of trusts in the United States overlapped the spread of trade protection. In the United States the growth of the Sugar Trust, the Steel Trust, and other oligopolistic combines would have been impossible without America's high tariff barriers.

Heavily cartelized and strongly protected, Continental industries were similar. The German government, for example, restricted imports of iron and steel, even though German firms were among the world's most efficient. This allowed the biggest firms in the iron and steel industry to create formal, and fully legal, cartels to keep prices high. The cartels provided the large integrated German companies with hundreds of millions of marks' worth of extra profits but worked against the smaller companies that were not party to the arrangements and of course against consumers who had to pay higher cartel prices.[29]

The winners and losers from protection frequently fought bitter political battles. American farmers resisted a trade policy that forced them to sell their wheat and cotton at world prices but buy their fertilizer, machinery, and clothing at prices 40 percent above world levels. This amounted, they complained, to a tax on farmers. The situation was analogous in Europe, although here it was manufacturing workers who railed against high tariffs on imported grain and beef. The Belgian Workers' (Socialist) Party complained in 1913 that "the high cost of food has made itself felt everywhere, but the protectionist countries, including Belgium, have suffered the most. . . . The protectionist measures which have been taken in our country are to the advantage of the landowners alone and the closing of the frontiers against imports of foreign cattle also prevents the working classes from eating adequately."[30]

The contribution of trade protection to rapid industrialization in the late nineteenth and early twentieth centuries was controversial then, and the judgment of history remains ambiguous. Trade protection harmed consumers: Industries paid more for supplies, and households paid more for food, clothing, and other necessities. Production was diverted toward the protected industries regardless of their efficiency. Certainly industrial protection sped the development of protected industries; the cartel-tariff system was at least partly responsible for the doubling of German steel output every six or seven years for decades before 1913. Whether the costs outweighed the benefits for societies at large is an open question. Germany and the United States would certainly have industrialized without tariffs, and both countries might have been better off with less heavy industry; but this was not a popular option for either country's industrialists or for their foreign policy and military elites.

Overall, while infant industry protection was common in the decades before World War One, it did not fundamentally interfere with the overall openness of the international economy. Barriers to imports proliferated, but they were highly targeted rather than broadly applied. The rapidly industrializing nations that protected industry usually permitted the free or almost free entry of raw materials and agricultural goods that did not compete with home production and of intermediate inputs not locally available. Trade grew extremely rapidly in all countries, including the most protectionist; by 1913 all major nations were exporting far more of what they produced, and importing far more of what they consumed, than they had in 1870.[31] The rapid industrializers of the turn of the twentieth century were enthusiastic participants in world trade and investment, but they were willing to bend the rules of free trade if a quick profit and quick industrialization were available.

The areas of recent settlement

By the 1890s Europeans and others were opening up large areas of recent settlement to agriculture, mining, and other exploitation. These regions, previously barely participants in the global economy, grew with extraordinary rapidity. They held natural resources whose extraction did not become economically feasible until the recent exploration, migration, and technological change.

The pampas, Great Plains, and prairies had always existed, of course, as had the Australian outback and the mineral deposits of southern Africa. In some cases, Europeans had not known of them. In others, they could not be exploited until new technologies, such as refrigerated shipping to bring mutton or beef from the ends of the earth to Europe, were developed. Once the possibilities were clear, people rushed to turn the natural potential of these lands into hard cash. All or parts of Australia and New Zealand, Canada and the United States, South Africa, and the Southern Cone of Latin America (Argentina, Uruguay, Chile, southern Brazil) seethed with this new activity.

These countries grew rich from their natural resources; farming and mining fed broader economic development. Cattle ranching led to slaughterhouses, meatpacking plants, tanneries, and shoe factories. Wheat farming gave rise to granaries, shipyards, and railroads. Warehouse, railroad, and port workers had to be housed; the construction industry grew, and then brickyards, steel mills, and other producers of building materials. Ports and rail junctions required electric power plants and waterworks. Growing populations required clothing, telephones, lamps, and books, and soon local manufactures expanded widely. Where a manufacturing base already existed, as in North America, the resource booms quickened the process of industrial growth. Where there was little or no manufacturing, but a ready supply of know-how, capital, and enterprise, modern industry sprang up quickly.

The regions of recent settlement differed from the rest of the world. They were very sparsely populated; in some cases, the preexisting population had been expelled or exterminated. Their inhabitants were creating thriving modern economies—farms and mines, roads and railroads, towns and cities, factories and ports—where little economic activity had previously existed.[32] Few entrenched interests stood in the way of exploitation of the regions' primary (agricultural and mineral) resources or of commercial development.

Local institutions also assisted the economic development of these areas. Many were direct offshoots of British society and imported— along with millions of Britons—some variant of the British political and legal systems. This meant, most centrally, a tradition of respect for private property rights in both the legal and political realms. (These rights were of course restricted to the Europeans rather than to the indigenous populations, whose property was typically stolen with impunity.) Unlike many other developing areas, they were generally politically stable and legally predictable. Farmers who improved their land could be reasonably sure that their investments would not be seized arbitrarily by others or by the government. Political institutions that could incorporate new social groups also allowed important economic interests to rely on government to take their concerns seriously. Skepticism in this regard was common elsewhere in the developing world and tended to dampen development. But in the areas of recent settlement, wealth was a national fixation, and property nearly sacrosanct. The Southern Cone of Latin America had vestiges of colonial Iberian institutions, which were somewhat less suited to developmental purposes, but relative to regions that had never known stable property rights, this area too was quite advanced.[33]

The areas of recent settlement also had the advantages of temperate climates and fertile land well suited to temperate farming and ranching. The technologies developed in temperate agriculture, which had given western Europe its developmental edge for centuries, could be applied directly to these lands. Grain output per acre in temperate farming was two or three times as high as in other agricultural areas, and with mechanization, output per person was many times higher still.[34] This

European level of agricultural productivity allowed the areas of recent settlement to pay European-style wages and therefore attract European immigrants. In the tropics and subtropics the level of productivity of existing agricultural technology was much lower, as was the standard of living, so that Europeans would not move there as simple laborers or farmers.

It was the character of agricultural production, rather than something innate to Europeans, that made them more productive than others; in the few places where (as in parts of Latin America) the new lands were opened by Japanese or Chinese farmers, they were every bit as fruitful as Europeans. But European emigrants clustered in the high-productivity areas with living standards higher than in their countries of origin.

Waves of European immigrants flocked to the sparsely settled temperate regions to build new societies on the basis of extremely productive farming, ranching, and mining. In these open spaces they achieved levels of output and income per person that generally surpasssed those of Europe. High levels of income in turn provided a large home market for local goods. Initially, local production made the most sense in things that were hard or difficult to import—construction and other services, electric power, heavy building materials—and that is where local industry got its start. Over time, as Buenos Aires and Rio de Janeiro grew into cities of more than a million people, some of their inhabitants took advantage of local prosperity to set up manufacturing industries, especially in the processing of local primary products.

Uruguay's rolling plains were ideal for livestock and grain, and in the 1870s the country began growing very rapidly on the basis of farm and ranch exports to Europe. Hundreds of thousands of Spaniards, Italians, and other Europeans poured into Uruguay (which, although small by Latin American standards, is substantially larger than England). Soon the port of Montevideo was thriving, and the country's standard of living was as high as that of France and Germany. In the early years of the twentieth century Uruguay's political order was remade in line with its newfound wealth. José Batlle y Ordóñez led the reform effort, serving twice as president between 1903 and 1915. Batlle introduced free universal education, the eight-hour day and progressive labor regulation, public pensions and workers' compensation, a comprehensive public health system, legal divorce and extensive women's rights, and other policies that eventually came to characterize wealthy societies in the late twentieth century—so much so that Uruguay is sometimes considered the first modern welfare state. All this was made possible by the standard of living provided by the country's lucrative export farming and ranching economy.

Like Uruguay, the other areas of recent settlement grew because of their access to world markets, with economies organized to produce exports for European markets. They were peopled by millions of European immigrants. European capital fueled much of their growth, financing everything from railroads and power plants to slaughterhouses and factories.

The golden age world economy was the source of much of the prosperity realized by Argentines and Canadians, Australians and Uruguayans. The areas of recent settlement had the right domestic characteristics to take advantage of the opportunities presented by transportation and communications advances, and they turned in an extraordinary performance in the years before World War One. In 1896 Australia, Canada, and Argentina produced about 80 million bushels of wheat, barely one-sixth of western European production, but in 1913 these three countries combined produced 438 million bushels of wheat, more than all western Europe combined.[35] Their growth was not confined to farming: By 1913 Canada, Australia, and New Zealand produced more manufactured products per person than any European country but the United Kingdom; Argentina, more than Italy or Spain. And this does not even include the United States, large parts of which had many characteristics of the other recently settled regions. These areas as a whole—Australia and New Zealand; Argentina, Uruguay, Chile, and southern Brazil; North America west of the Mississippi—had a population of twelve million in 1870, equivalent to barely one-third the population of France. By 1913 their combined population was fifty million, one-quarter larger than that of France.

By any measure, these countries experienced a remarkable economic development. These achievements were the subject of many surprised and admiring travelers' reports. A British visitor to Buenos Aires on the eve of World War One wrote of visiting the city's Palermo district, "a combination of Hyde Park and the Bois de Boulogne—open sweeps and charming trees, a double boulevard with statues and commemorative marbles in the middle, well-cared-for gardens, radiant flowers and the band playing. A drive through Palermo at the fashionable hour causes one to gasp at the thought that one is six thousand miles from Europe. Nowhere in the world have I seen such a display of expensive motorcars, thousands of them." Summing up his impressions, the Briton said,

"[O]ne cannot go through the country and see its fecundity, go into the killing houses of La Plata and Buenos Aires, watch the ocean liners, with the Union Jack dangling over their stern, being loaded with many sides of beef, visit the grain elevators at the ports of Bahía Blanca and Rosario pouring streams of wheat destined for European consumption into the holds of liners, without the imagination being stimulated when standing on the threshold of this new land's possibilities."[36]

Growth in the tropics

Other resource-rich areas of the world also developed rapidly. They had promising natural endowments, like the areas of recent settlement, but much larger populations. These areas were typically tropical or semitropical and were already involved in international trade. Their exports, and economic activity more generally, received a strong push (or pull!) from technological advances and global growth.

Many parts of Latin America, Africa, and Asia participated in the rapidly growing international economy. The success stories have tended to be overshadowed in historical memory by the many and prominent failures, such as China. So too, positive economic developments have tended to take second place to the dramatic expansion of colonialism that took place at much the same time, in some of the same regions. Yet a careful look at what would now be called the Third World reveals some impressive economic trends.

The bulk of Latin America was, unlike the nearly empty Southern Cone and Amazon, rather densely populated. The region had long experience with world trade, dating back to Spanish and Portuguese colonialism. The trade expansion after 1870 had the most dramatic effects on Argentina and Uruguay, but other countries were not too far behind. Mexico's silver and copper mines poured their metals onto world markets. Dictator Porfirio Díaz, who ruled the country from 1876 to 1910, pursued the goal of opening its mineral wealth to foreign investment and accelerating its transit to foreign markets. The eventual discovery of oil created an accompanying bonanza on the Caribbean coast. By 1910 mining and petroleum were accounting for nearly one-tenth of national economic activity. But this was merely the spearhead to faster growth in Mexico. Modern agriculture expanded rapidly, especially on the large-scale farms (haciendas) that dominated production for export. The economy diversified into manufacturing, and by 1910 local industry was supplying 97 percent of domestic textiles consumption. In 1913 Mexico's output per capita was comparable to that of Portugal, Russia, or Japan—poor countries, to be sure, but countries on the path to development.[37]

Farther south, Brazil secured a stranglehold on the world's coffee market, producing four-fifths of the world's coffee exports by 1900. The government used sophisticated schemes to exploit its monopoly and keep the world price of coffee high, and massive coffee earnings poured into the southern state of São Paulo where growers concentrated. Half of the country's cultivated land was turned to coffee, and two-thirds of farm output was exported. The coffee exports—and the rubber boom in the Amazon that lasted until 1910—spurred broader economic development. São Paulo State became an important industrial center. Assisted by high tariffs, the state's 1915 industrial output included 122 million meters of cotton cloth, many millions more meters of silk, wool, and jute textiles, along with 5 million pairs of shoes and 2.7 million hats. Almost all this was up from nearly nothing twenty years earlier.[38] By this point more than half the industrial products Brazilians consumed were produced at home.

Colombians took advantage of Brazil's ability to keep coffee prices high by opening up their western highlands for coffee cultivation, increasing the country's production from 30 to 140 million pounds of coffee between 1890 and 1913.[39] Many of the smaller nations of Central America also participated in the coffee boom. Elsewhere in Latin America, the details were different, but the general outline was similar. Fortunes were made by people's developing a primary product and shipping it to Europe or North America. For Chile, it was nitrates and copper; for Cuba, sugar; for Peru, it was cotton and sugar on coastal plantations, silver and copper in the Andean highlands, rubber in the Amazon. Foreign capitalists provided loans and investments to help build the roads, railways, ports, and other necessary infrastructure. The profits were plowed back into further agricultural and mineral development and eventually into industrial ventures. By the eve of World War One the major countries of the region had begun to industrialize.

West Africa also turned its attentions to producing for world markets. The region's involvement in world trade went back to the fifteenth century. The slave trade had, for all the misery it caused, created an important indigenous merchant class that went into the "legitimate" import-export trade once slaving had been shut down. And of course there were powerful foreign trading enterprises in the region. West Africa's international economic ties were increased by the scramble among the European powers that left almost the entire region—indeed almost the entire continent—in colonial hands. It is a matter of continuing controversy how important foreign economic interests were in colonial expansion itself. Nonetheless, it seems clear that European expectations about the region's economic potential contributed to the British, French, and German policies that led those three countries to seize the region.[40]

In the aftermath of European appropriation, West Africa's trade grew rapidly; the region's exports quadrupled between 1897 and 1913.[41] The boom was concentrated in the four wealthiest and most important colonies: Britain's Nigeria and Gold Coast, France's Senegal and Ivory Coast. These regions already produced groundnuts (peanuts), palm oil, and related crops, products much in demand as the result of rapid industrial development and the expansion of working-class consumption in Europe and North America. Palm oil was used to lubricate machinery and in the tinplate industry; palm kernels were used in the manufacture of soap, candles, and the recently invented margarine. Groundnut oil was an inexpensive substitute for olive oil. As Europeans demanded more of these products, Africans turned from gathering the wild palm fruit to planting it and expanded the farming of groundnuts. Exports grew dramatically, especially as transportation improved. A railroad from the coast to Kano in northern Nigeria was completed in 1911. As traders and farmers realized how lucrative the European market for locally grown groundnuts could be, within two years the local price of groundnuts increased fivefold. In less than ten years Nigeria's total groundnuts exports had gone from a couple of million pounds to over 130 million pounds.[42]

As production of traditional goods expanded, exports of new (or newly emphasized) crops grew even more rapidly. Cocoa in the Gold Coast sprang from nowhere to dominate the world market; timber exports from the Ivory Coast sextupled in twenty years; coffee and some mineral production soared as well. The crops were typically grown by small-holding farmers and drew ever larger portions of the population into the modern economy. However, relatively little modern industry developed in western Africa. Manufacturing for the local market was less attractive than in Latin America, where income per person was two or three times as high and cities and other infrastructure were much larger and better

developed. Moreover, colonialism restricted the ability of local manufacturers to receive the trade protection that was common throughout
Latin America. Nonetheless, it appeared that the bases were in place for
sustained economic growth.

The successful areas of South and Southeast Asia also expanded existing farming or opened up new lands to capitalize on growing export
markets. Burma and Thailand were rice producers of long standing but
solely for local consumption until new political and economic conditions
allowed them to become exporting dynamos, supplying markets all over
the rest of Asia and elsewhere. Thailand's independent monarchy was
favorable to trade, if not enthusiastic about industry, and under its rule
the country's rice exports increased tenfold, from about a hundred thousand to a million tons in forty years; by the early 1900s half of the country's crop was being exported.[43] Farmers in Burma's Irrawaddy Delta
had also long grown rice, but not intensively, for the government prohibited its export. When Britain took over the region and forcibly opened it
to trade, people flooded into the coastal areas to grow rice, and soon rice
flooded out. In the words of one historian, Burma was remade "from an
undeveloped and sparsely populated backwater of the Konbaung
Empire into the world's leading rice-exporting area."[44] Under the com-
mercially minded French colonial regime in Indochina, Vietnamese
land devoted to rice expanded more than fivefold, and the colony
became the world's third-largest producer.

British Ceylon brought coconuts and tea to market; Malaya produced
more than half the world's tin. After 1900 both rapidly expanded rubber
production from almost nothing to become major players. The Dutch
East Indies also joined the race to supplant Amazonian rubber, supple-
menting its important coffee, tobacco, and sugar sales. The Philippines,
newly an American colony, expanded sugar production to tap the large
American market. Taiwan, then a Japanese colony, was developed by the
colonial authorities more or less explicitly to provide rice and sugar to
the homeland.

The impact of the export boom was broadly felt in many of these
cases. Rice was typically grown by small farmers, and the export-driven
prosperity of the early century raised incomes for wide swaths of the
populations of Thailand and Burma. So too was tea in Ceylon mostly a
small farmer's crop. Malayan tin was largely controlled by Chinese owners and mined by Chinese laborers, who flooded into Southeast Asia by
the millions. Even where—as in Indochina and the Dutch East Indies
and on Malayan rubber plantations—the most prosperous farms and

plantations were controlled by Europeans, the increased demand for labor spilled over into rising local incomes. As in western Africa, this did not lead to significant industrial development: Low local living standards meant small local markets for modern manufactures, and the colonial powers expressly or implicitly discouraged industrial development.

These poor, heavily populated regions threw themselves—or were thrown by new colonial rulers—into world markets and emerged with a great deal of prosperity. By the eve of World War One much of the population of a wide and growing band of tropical and semitropical countries and colonies—from Mexico and Brazil, through the Ivory Coast and Nigeria, to Burma and Indochina—was producing primary products for export. Coffee, peanuts, cocoa, rubber, palm oil, tin, copper, silver, and sugar poured out of these rapidly growing regions to Europe and North America, and money and manufactured goods poured back. Modernity had come to the tropics.

The elites that dominated government and society in all the rapidly developing regions, whether temperate areas of recent settlement or densely peopled semitropical zones, regarded involvement in the world economy as the key to prosperity and success. Why else go to the pampas or the prairies but to farm them for export markets? Many European, American, and Japanese imperialists argued that colonies were valuable primarily as sources of raw materials and agricultural products. Colonial regimes enthusiastically, even single-mindedly, pushed the new possessions to export primary products.

Local landowners, miners, and traders sensed the prospect of huge profits. Local governments foresaw new opportunities to sell off valuable new lands or tax profitable new export producers, all of which would enhance their power. The process was facilitated by the seemingly endless supply of capital pouring out of western Europe, capital that was desperately needed to open up the new lands, get the crops and minerals to market, build the new cities, and allow governments to satisfy the demands of their populations.

The hostile stereotype of a turn-of-the-century Latin American nation is of an oligarchic society dominated by exporting interests in league with European investors. The landed oligarchy, the agroexporters, the primary exporting sectors, the *vendepatrias* (country sellers): These later became the demonized enemies of nationalist leaders. There was something to the characterization, in its identification of the channels of power and influence that tied the countries together and into the world economy. They relied on primary exports, required access to European markets and capital, had a Europeanizing vision of the future, and certainly had little interest in sharing their wealth with the impoverished masses. What is missing, even in looking at the dictatorial thirty-five-year *Porfiriato* in Mexico, is that this export-oriented growth also made new economic opportunities broadly and deeply available to the local society, including to much of the middle classes, peasantry, and growing urban working class.

Ruling groups in many developing regions were firmly committed to taking their economies into the mainstream of the international economy. They permitted, encouraged, even forced farmers and others to sell their goods abroad. They invited in foreign investors, bankers, and traders; borrowed heavily in London, Paris, and Berlin; built railroads and ports; improved rivers; and created power and telephone systems, thus using the gains from world trade to enrich themselves. Where they were successful, generally, much of their society also did well—albeit not so well as the elites. In the areas of recent settlement, in Latin America and parts of Africa and Asia, the export-led expansion laid the basis of entry into modern economic growth.

Heckscher and Ohlin interpret the golden age

In 1919, after this global capitalism had been swept away by the Great War, the Swedish economist Eli Heckscher attempted to make economic sense of the remarkable pre-1914 experience. Along with his student Bertil Ohlin, Heckscher came up with a way of understanding different nations' involvement in world trade that revolutionized economic thinking and also serves to capture a complex reality. Heckscher and Ohlin believed in the law of comparative advantage—both as a prescription for what countries should do and as a description of what they generally did. Countries did in fact tend to export what they produced best and import what they produced less well. The problem was that the theory was nearly tautological: How could anyone know in advance what a country produced best unless by observing whether or not it was able to export it successfully?

So the two Swedes tried to explain national patterns of comparative advantage. Clearly comparative advantage was not simply a result of effort. Swedish farmers' difficulties were, they knew, not due to any lack of hard work on the part of the rural population. The problem was the country's land scarcity, not its people's laziness. Where land was in short supply and expensive, farming was costly; where it was plentiful and cheap, farming was low-cost. The point, they noted, was that countries differed in their endowments of the factors of production: Some were rich in land; others had abundant labor; still others were flush with capital. These endowments, they surmised, would determine national comparative advantage and in turn what different countries produced and exported. If there were two countries with identical populations and amounts of capital, the country with very little good farmland would be at a comparative disadvantage in farming, while the country with virtually unlimited supplies of farmland would have a comparative advantage.

The result was Heckscher-Ohlin trade theory, whose basic idea is simple: A country will export goods that make intensive use of the resources it has in abundance. Countries with lots of land will specialize in producing farm goods whose production requires lots of land. Countries rich in capital will focus on capital-intensive products, especially sophisticated manufactures. Regions with abundant labor will produce labor-intensive goods or crops. This pattern of specialization will lead to analogous trade patterns: Land-rich but capital-poor countries will export land-intensive agricultural products and import capital-intensive manufactured products. The Swedes' insights apply to movements of capital and people as well as to trade. They expected countries rich in capital to export capital and countries rich in labor to export labor (land of course cannot be traded across borders without changing the borders!).

The Heckscher-Ohlin approach does remarkably well at explaining the broad outlines of international trade, investment, and migration in this period.[45] Western Europe, capital-rich and land-poor, exported capital and capital-intensive manufactured goods to the rest of the world and imported land-intensive farm goods. Southern and eastern Europe, rich with labor, exported emigrants. Undeveloped temperate and tropical zones were rich in land and exported agricultural products; they were poor in capital and imported capital and capital-intensive manufactures. Within this category of rapidly developing countries rich in land, the Asian, African, and Latin American tropics had abundant labor and so exported more labor-intensive farm products than labor-poor North America, Australia, and Argentina. They all grew more than they ever had before; indeed, North America and South America were the fastest-growing regions in the world between 1870 and 1913.

Heckscher-Ohlin trade theory helps explain the success of countries that concentrated on using their abundant factors in the international division of labor. Land-rich countries that did whatever they could to develop agriculture prospered; so too did capital-rich countries that focused on foreign investments. The homelands of industrial capitalism flooded the world with capital-intensive manufactures. From the vast expanses of the pampas and prairies flowed grain and beef; tropical lowlands and highlands poured out palm products, groundnuts, rubber, tea, and coffee. International economic openness made it possible for industrializing and developing societies to catch up with the wealthy nations of northwestern Europe. The gap between rich countries and rapidly growing regions closed.

4

Failures of Development

Britain's consul to the colony known as the Congo Free State despaired of the fate of its oppressed inhabitants. "One asks oneself in vain," he wrote in 1908, "what benefits these people have gained from the boasted civilization of the Free State. One looks in vain for any attempt to benefit them or to recompense them in any way for the enormous wealth which they are helping to pour into the Treasury of the State. Their native industries are being destroyed, their freedom has been taken from them, and their numbers are decreasing."[1]

Despite the economic revolution of the golden age, most of the world remained grindingly poor. While rapidly developing regions climbed the ladder of industrial success, much of Asia, Africa, and the Middle East and even parts of Russia, eastern and southern Europe, and Latin America slipped to ever-lower rungs.

Almost every part of the world did grow, but there were great disparities in rates of growth. The differences in question—a percentage point here or there—may seem small, but the impact of slower growth is compounded over decades. For example, in 1870 China and India were about 20 percent poorer than Mexico on a per-person basis (a gap roughly equivalent to that between Western Europe and the United States in 2000). Over the next forty years the Asian giants' rates of growth averaged about one and a half percentage points less than Mexico's. By 1913 Mexico was three times as rich as the two Asian countries (a gap roughly equivalent to that between the United States and Mexico in 2000). [2] Overall, western Europe, the areas of recent settlement, and Latin America grew roughly four times as fast as Asia and half again as fast as southern and eastern Europe.

The ruling classes of those societies were principally responsible for their inability to take advantage of new economic opportunities. Many rulers were unable or unwilling to create conditions for sustained economic growth. Some of these rulers were foreign colonialists, who used venal and parasitical means to exploit local populations. The Congo was perhaps the most glaring example of a society shockingly abused by colonialists.

King Leopold and the Congo

William Sheppard was an African American missionary who went to central Africa to convert its people to Presbyterianism. Quite by accident, he found himself at the center of a global scandal that exposed one of the most murderous colonial regimes of modern times. [3]

Sheppard was born in Virginia, in the last few weeks of the American Civil War, to a family of free blacks. He was ordained a Presbyterian minister at the age of twenty-three and soon volunteered for African missionary work. In 1890 Sheppard and a white American minister, Samuel Lapsley, established a mission in Luebo, in the remote Kasai region of the central Congo Basin.

The young Americans' presence in this isolated region owed itself to the extraordinary designs and persistence of a European monarch fixated on the riches of Africa. By the time Sheppard reached Africa, King Leopold of Belgium had spent twenty years establishing a personal empire on the continent. Leopold knew that his Belgian homeland would never give him a colony—the country had no navy and no merchant fleet, and Leopold himself was practically the only prominent Belgian with imperial ambitions—so he presented himself as a benefactor who meant to bring Christianity to Africa's population. He railed especially against the continent's slave trade, which since the European powers suppressed the transatlantic slave trade in the 1840s was now largely an internal matter involving Arab and indigenous slavers. Leopold preached that the exploitation of "perfectly innocent beings who, brutally reduced to captivity, are condemned en masse to forced labor . . . makes our epoch blush."[4]

King Leopold began his African career as a patron of explorers, bankrolling the expedition of Henry Stanley that was the first to follow the Congo River from its source to the Atlantic. His credentials established, Leopold convinced the European powers to give him personal command of the entire Congo Basin, an area as large as western Europe and suspected to be the repository of enormous natural riches. His success in gaining control of the Congo was not a result of his abilities or Belgium's geopolitical influence, both of which were negligible. For the European powers that were dividing up all Africa, the new Congo Free State was a useful buffer separating French, British, German, and Portuguese colonies in the region. Leopold agreed to allow all foreigners equal access to the riches of the area, so there was no need for the Europeans to worry about the region's being sealed off to them.

Sheppard, Lapsley, and other Protestant American missionaries served Leopold's purposes. They countered the influence of Portuguese and French Catholic missionaries, whom Leopold suspected of favoring their homelands. As Americans they could build support in the United States for the Belgian's ambitions. The Protestants could also help open up areas in the Congolese interior for Leopold's free state, whose influence was limited by the vastness of the country. Leopold met with Lapsley as the two missionaries headed to Africa, and the ingenuous twenty-four-year-old was moved by the king's "apparent sympathy of my mission. . . . His expression is very kind, and his voice matches it. . . . I wonder now how God has so changed the times that a Catholic King, successor to Philip II, should talk Foreign Missions to an American boy and a Presbyterian."[5] Leopold urged Lapsley to go with Sheppard to the Kasai region; he said that his free state troops could protect them better there than elsewhere. In fact Leopold wanted the young Americans to go to Kasai because it was an area that the free state's authorities did not know or control well, and missions could help secure the influence and authority of Leopold's administration.

Sheppard took to Africa and its inhabitants from the start. He learned local languages and built up a network of friends and allies. When Lapsley died less than two years into the mission, Sheppard ran the new Presbyterian mission in Kasai by himself for five years. Sheppard studied indigenous societies with great interest and success, eventually gaining entry to the court of the king of the powerful and virtually unknown Kuba. He impressed audiences in Europe and North America with his reports and his collection of artifacts, and in 1893 Sheppard became the first African American, and one of the youngest people, to be elected a fellow of Britain's Royal Geographic Society, probably the most prestigious honor that could be bestowed on an explorer. The society also named a lake in the Kasai region after Sheppard, who had "discovered" it.

A contemporary discovery of a more mundane bookkeeping kind had a greater impact on the Congo. In the late 1890s Edmund Dene Morel worked for the British shipping line with the monopoly of the Congo's freight trade, visiting Antwerp often to check on business. Morel, a fervent believer in free trade and at the outset an enthusiastic supporter of Leopold's venture, eventually noted a suspicious fact. "The Congo," Morel wrote later, "was exporting increasing quantities of rubber and ivory for which, on the face of the import statistics, the natives were getting nothing or next to nothing. . . . Nothing was going in to pay for what was coming out." Almost all that the shipping line sent to the Congo from Antwerp was weaponry and ammunition for the free state troops. Nor could the trade be coming from elsewhere, for the line had a monopoly. Africans in the Congo were not allowed to use money, so if they were not being paid in goods, they were not being paid at all for supplying the ivory and rubber. Morel drew the inevitable conclusion: "Forced labour of a terrible and continuous kind could alone explain such unheard-of profits . . . forced labour in which the Congo Government was the immediate beneficiary; forced labour directed by the closest associates of the King himself."[6]

Morel had uncovered the economic logic of Leopold's reign. Leopold expected to make enormous profits in the Congo. But first the region had to be conquered and ruled, and this itself was immensely expensive, so expensive that Leopold had to borrow heavily to get his free state going. For a decade the region's ivory provided some of the money Leopold needed, but in the middle 1890s rubber supplanted ivory as the colony's most important product. World demand for rubber was soaring as technical innovations made the material more versatile and as such new products as the bicycle and automobile brought forth new needs for rubber tires.

The Congo's wild rubber was a very convenient resource for the cash-hungry king, as it occurred naturally and cost nothing to plant. The problem was that tapping the wild vines was difficult and painful: The vines were scattered through a trackless rain forest, and often the only practical way to turn the sap into rubber was for the harvester to spread it onto his body, wait until it dried, and pull it off, hair and all. The harvest was in fact so difficult that Leopold's administrators could not induce the Congolese to collect rubber voluntarily, in return for goods. So the free state turned to force, imposing a "tax" on the Congolese, to be paid in rubber.

The free state's soldiers used a myriad of methods to compel the population to harvest wild rubber. Sometimes they took the women and children of a village hostage, to be released only when the men delivered a set quota of rubber. At times local leaders were bribed to force their people to provide rubber. When all else failed, the soldiers burned recalcitrant villages to the ground and massacred their inhabitants as a lesson to neighboring villages on the price of disobedience.

Word of the free state's misdeeds eventually trickled out of the Congo. In 1899 the Presbyterian mission sent William Sheppard to investigate reports of conflict between the Kuba and a slave-trading, cannibalistic tribe called the Zappo Zaps. Sheppard headed back toward the capital of the Kuba and found to his horror that the region had been devastated. The free state's brutal rubber-gathering system had reached the Kuba, who had resisted being reduced to forced labor. Leopold's free state had hired the Zappo Zaps and dispatched them to pacify the Kuba, upon whom they brought down a reign of terror.

Sheppard eventually stumbled upon a group of Zappo Zaps whose leader recognized him. The local commander, Mlumba, knew Sheppard was a foreigner and assumed he was in league with the Belgians, and he boasted of destroying whole villages. Sheppard himself saw piles of bodies, portions of which had been carved into steaks for the consumption of the soldiers. Mlumba then, Sheppard wrote, "conducted us to a framework of sticks, under which was burning a slow fire, and there they were, the right hands, I counted them, 81 in all." Mlumba explained to Sheppard, "Here is our evidence. I always have to cut off the right hands of those we kill in order to show the State how many we have killed."[7] Leopold's logic was at work here too. The free state issued guns and ammunition to its mercenaries but found that they were more likely to be used for hunting than on state business. To prove that they were doing their duty, the soldiers had to demonstrate that the state's weapons and ammunition were being used for military purposes. The smoke-cured right hands of the soldiers' victims proved that the free state's money was not being squandered.

William Sheppard's eyewitness account of the atrocities in the Kasai region rocketed into the world's newspapers within weeks. Meanwhile Edmund Morel had followed up his discovery of Leopold's commercial fraud with a systematic effort to reveal Congolese reality to the world. He started a journal that published page after page of horrifying detail about the brutality of Leopold's administration. A few months after Sheppard's revelations an American businessman, Edgar Canisius, witnessed a punitive expedition by the free state's soldiers. In the course of six weeks the troops had, Canisius said, "killed over nine hundred natives, men, women, and children," all for the purpose of "adding . . . twenty tons of rubber to the monthly crop."[8] As reports like this proliferated, in 1903 the British House of Commons officially protested Leopold's reign. The British Foreign Office followed up by sending its consul in the Congo on a months-long investigative trip through the interior that confirmed the charges of Leopold's severest critics.

Morel's Congo Reform Association mobilized world opinion against Leopold and his looting of the Congo. The movement gained force quickly. It was supported by anti-imperialists, such as Mark Twain, whose 1905 *King Leopold's Soliloquy* is a bitter masterpiece of political satire. Even convinced imperialists joined the clamor against Leopold because his misdeeds discredited "responsible" colonial rule. In January 1905, indeed, one of America's leading imperialists, President Theodore Roosevelt, received William Sheppard in the White House and endorsed his efforts on behalf of the Congolese. For their more pragmatic part, the European powers were concerned that Leopold was not honoring his commitment to keep the Congo open to the trade and investment of others and was corruptly reserving profit opportunities to his henchmen.

Belgium's powerful Socialist Party and other Belgian reformers joined the attack, calling for the king's African empire to be turned over to the Belgian government, to be ruled in a more accountable way by a more appropriate colonial power. Only the most radical thought of the possibility of independence, for there were only two independent countries in all sub-Saharan Africa at the time. Leopold fought back, appointing a commission of inquiry. But Leopold's own commission found against him: "The exaction of a labor tax is so oppressive that the natives on whom it falls have little, if any[,] freedom. . . . The natives are practically prisoners within their own territory." The commission condemned the frequent "punitive expeditions . . . for the purpose of terrifying natives into paying a tax . . . the commissioners regard as inhuman."[9] King

Leopold was eventually forced to turn control of the colony over to the Belgian government, which eliminated the worst of the excesses.

William Sheppard's conflicts with the Congolese authorities were not over, however. In 1907 he wrote eloquently about how the rubber trade had destroyed the social structure of the half million Kuba:

> Only a few years ago, travelers through this country found them living in large homes, having from one to four rooms in each house, loving and living happily with their wives and children, one of the most prosperous and intelligent of all the African tribes, though living in one of the most remote spots on the planet. . . . But within these last three years how changed they are! Their farms are growing up weeds and jungle, their king is practically a slave, their houses are mostly only half-built single rooms and are much neglected. The streets of their towns are not clean and well-swept as they once were. Even their children cry for bread. Why this change? You have it in a few words. There are armed sentries of chartered trading companies who force the men and women to spend most of their days and nights in the forests making rubber, and the price they receive is so meager that they cannot live upon it.[10]

The outraged directors of the local chartered trading company, the Kasai Company, filed suit in Congolese court against Sheppard. Morel and the Presbyterians rallied a global network in support of Sheppard when he went on trial in Kinshasa. The U.S. government protested the trial, and the leader of Belgium's Socialist Party hurried to the Congo to serve as Sheppard's lawyer. The spectacle only highlighted the vicious nature of Leopold's rule and the profits made by his favored companies; eventually the judge dismissed the charges against Sheppard. After nearly twenty years in the Congo, Sheppard was ready to go home. He retired from missionary work and spent the twenty years until his death as a minister in Louisville, Kentucky. Leopold himself died in 1909, shortly after Sheppard's legal vindication, in as close to a state of disgrace as a reigning monarch could be.

Leopold's Congo Free State was the epitome of modern colonial evil. Sir Arthur Conan Doyle, author of the Sherlock Holmes mysteries, called Leopold's exploitation of the Congo "the greatest crime in all history, the greater for having been carried out under an odious pretence of philanthropy."[11] Hyperbolic as this may have been, it expressed a popular revulsion to the horrors of colonial misrule, a revulsion presented graphically by American jazz poet Vachel Lindsay in his epic poem *The Congo*:

Listen to the yell of Leopold's ghost
Burning in Hell for his hand-maimed host
Hear how the demons chuckle and yell
Cutting his hands off, down in Hell.

Leopold's twenty-five years of maladministration, plunder, and violence caused the unnatural deaths of millions of Congolese. But this
misrule caused far greater damage: the destruction of much of the
region's social structure. The colonial masters disrupted or devastated
local societies, exacerbated conflicts among the inhabitants of the area,
and gave the Congolese no opportunity to adopt and adapt what might
be useful from abroad. The colonial administration made it virtually
impossible for the residents of a region with extraordinary natural
resources to use them to develop their economy. Leopold never visited
the Congo; his interest was financial and political, not personal. But the
absentee landlord and his free state did the region enormous harm.
They are primarily responsible for the dismal economic performance of
the central African colony while they ruled it, and they bear major
responsibilities for its stagnation in subsequent decades.

Colonialism and underdevelopment

Mark Twain called Leopold and his kind "The Blessings-of-
Civilization Trust." Twain wrote of the trust: "There is more money in it,
more territory, more sovereignty, and other kinds of emolument, than
there is in any other game that is played."[12] Many trust members were,
like Leopold, single-minded in wringing value out of their possessions.
They extracted whatever resources they could in self-contained enclaves
of copper and gold mines or banana and sugar plantations. The enclave's
owners, customers, and sometimes even its workers had no long-term
interest in the region, and the impact on the local economy was minimal. Often, when the facilities needed workers, as in the Congo, the
colonial authorities imposed forced labor on local residents.

Such enclaves were little more than organized theft. Valuable
resources were taken away, with no wealth, technology, or training left
behind. The colonialists sometimes subjected indigenous inhabitants to
conditions close to slavery, disrupting their normal livelihoods and

destroying the local economy. Leopold in the Congo and the Portuguese in their colonies were the most prominent colonial exploiters. These regimes were so blatantly predatory that even at the time their exposure led to widespread outrage, as in the Congo.

Commercial concessions were only slightly less noxious than extractive enclaves. They were a throwback to the days of seventeenth- and eighteenth-century European mercantilism, when such charter monopolies as the Dutch East India Company and the Hudson's Bay Company were given control of whole colonies. In the modern cases, the colonial power assigned control of a promising region to a commercial concessionaire, whose goal was to maximize profits, not to develop the local economy. In the words of one of the managers of the British South Africa Company, which administered Northern Rhodesia (now Zambia), "The problem of Northern Rhodesia is not a colonization problem. It is . . . the problem of how best to develop a great estate on scientific lines so that it may be made to yield the maximum profit to its owner."[13] If commercial success and economic development went together, that was fine, but where they conflicted, the concessionaires' first responsibility was to their stockholders.

When small groups of Europeans colonized areas with large indigenous populations, there was the same potential for abuse as in the cases of unvarnished colonial pillage. This settler colonialism was fundamentally different from mass European migrations to such sparsely peopled areas as the Canadian prairies or Argentine pampas, where immigrants and their offspring were virtually the entire local population. A settler colony, in contrast, was ruled by an imported caste that dominated and controlled large indigenous populations. Some colonial authorities encouraged settler colonialism in order to develop sources of agricultural supply; some saw the settlers as a bulwark against native populations and other colonial powers. But economic development by way of settler colonialism was almost always a failure.

Settler colonialism typically involved giving land to Europeans to farm cash crops that the indigenous population did not grow. Settler experience often revealed the wisdom of the local inhabitants in not growing these crops, as the farms failed miserably. Settlers in fact sometimes purposely disrupted traditional economic activities in order to force the "natives" to work for them on the new farms. Many settlers were successful at commercial agriculture only because of subsidies from the authorities: credit and tax breaks; cheap infrastructure; privileged access to markets; expropriation of local property. In order to get six thousand

Europeans to settle in Kenya by 1913, the British had to give away land for next to nothing near a new railroad, expel thousands of Masai and Kikuyu from their homelands, assess hut and poll taxes in money to induce Africans to work for the settlers, and—it was alleged—coerce labor through friendly local leaders. And still Kenyan settler agriculture was largely a failure.[14]

There were some qualified successes, in which settlers managed to develop productive farms. In Algeria hundreds of thousands of Europeans settled along the Mediterranean coast after French rule had been consolidated in the middle 1800s. The region was similar to the south of France in climate and topography and suitable for crops well known to the French. Soon the settlers were exporting grain and wine, their competitive position bolstered by friendly colonial policy and cheap local labor. At the other end of the continent, parts of southern Africa, such as Rhodesia and the Cape Province, were also economic successes, in that the settler economies ended up being profitable and productive, largely of cash crops.

However, even the most vibrant settler societies were based on colonial policies that reserved economic benefits to the settlers—Algerian colons, white Rhodesians—and excluded local inhabitants. Settlers surrounded by populous indigenous societies depended on separate and unequal treatment of the locals. If equal rights had been extended to the rest of the population, the privileged position of the settlers would have been competed away by Arabs or Africans willing to work harder for less. What many settlers wanted was not the general development of indigenous agriculture but a captive, inexpensive labor force. Efforts to upgrade the conditions of the "natives" could fly in the face of settler needs for cheap labor. Most settlers thus opposed the assimilation of other colonial subjects into the social, economic, and political system.

Settlers opposed to bringing local populations into the colonial system sometimes came into conflict with the colonial powers themselves.[15] Originally the colonial governments welcomed a layer of Frenchmen or Britons to oversee their possessions. However, the locals could not profitably be subjugated by force forever, and the imperial powers eventually wanted to encourage involvement by the locals in colonial society—to co-opt them into the new order. Settlers opposed this co-optation because it implied a reduction in their special privileges. If Algerian Muslims or Kenyan or Rhodesian blacks were given full rights to land, public services, even the vote, there would soon be powerful pressures to eliminate the favors bestowed on the Europeans.

Settler opposition to local inclusion in the colonial system often blocked broad-based international economic integration and general economic development. The settlers restricted access to prosperity to themselves and their close allies; with most local inhabitants shut out, there was little prospect for broad-based growth. A more economically, socially, and politically inclusive Algeria or Rhodesia could have expanded economic opportunities for the home country, one reason, along with greater governability, why France and Britain eventually decided on the desirability of such inclusion. When settlers blocked democratization, they also blocked the social and economic development of the region, settling, as it were, for a larger slice of a smaller pie.

Even where foreign rule was not so pernicious as extractive and settler colonialism, it could still dampen local growth. Some imperial powers restricted trade in ways reminiscent of the European mercantilists, against whom New World independence movements and European liberals had fought. The mercantilists had forced colonies to buy and sell in mother country markets, overcharging the colonies for what they bought and underpaying them for what they sold. In addition to turning prices against the colonies, mercantilists sometimes discouraged or prohibited local manufacturing. Some modern imperial powers used mercantilist-style policies to force their trade and investment into colonial channels. This denied the colonies full access to the goods, capital, and technology of a vibrant world economy. Some great powers also forced independent developing countries to sign unequal treaties that provided industrial nations with preferential treatment.

Colonial neomercantilism and neocolonial trade treaties were impediments to development, but not substantial ones. The British and German empires were free trade, as was all of central Africa; formal tariffs were low where imposed; and informal trade diversion did not cost the colonies much. The unequal trade treaties also had limited effects: Countries that wanted to impose high tariffs, such as Brazil, Russia, and the United States, never agreed to them, and those that agreed had little interest in high tariffs. Indeed, when such countries as Siam and Japan were released from the unequal trade treaties, they barely changed their trade policies at all. So while the imperial powers did manipulate their trade with poor nations, this manipulation was not so sweeping as to retard economic growth in a major way.

In fact most imperial powers insisted that their colonial charges participate in the international economy. Their motivation was due not to colonial benevolence but rather to the fact that getting the resources of the colonies to market usually required active local involvement. In many societies, export goods were produced by local farmers. This was true of much of western Africa, Ceylon, and Southeast Asia, and colonial governments in these regions and elsewhere strove to draw their charges into world markets. They built railroads, roads, and ports; established judicial and monetary order; and encouraged traders to search the hinterlands for producers and consumers.

If anything, colonial rulers often did too little to allow colonial access to international markets. Sometimes this was because the imperial owner had acquired the territory for noneconomic reasons, such as to garrison troops or fuel ships. Sometimes it was because of the abysmal backwardness of the colonial power, as with the Portuguese and Spanish colonies. Sometimes it was because the colonial power relied on local rulers who themselves feared the effects of the international economy on their social control. In this regard, the inadequate provision of economic opportunities to colonial subjects—especially to nonwhite colonial subjects—was a major failing of most of the powers.

Sir W. Arthur Lewis analyzed the ultimate impact of even the most benevolent of colonialisms with his characteristic eloquence and restraint. Writing from personal experience—he was the first colonial subject, and the first person "of color," to win a Nobel Prize in Economics (he was from St. Lucia in the West Indies)—Lewis said in the 1970s:

> The backwardness of the less developed countries of 1870 could be changed only by people prepared to alter certain customs, laws, and institutions, and to shift the balance of political and economic power away from the old landowning and aristocratic classes. But the imperial powers for the most part allied themselves with the existing power blocs. They were especially hostile to educated young people, whom, by means of a colour bar, they usually kept out of positions where administrative experience might be gained, whether in the public service or in private business. Such people, they then said, could not be employed in superior positions because they lacked managerial experience, as well as the kind of cultural background in which managerial competence flourishes. One result of this was to divert into long and bitter anti-colonial struggles much brilliant talent which could have been used creatively in development sectors.[16]

These were sins of omission rather than commission. They involved inadequate attention to the prerequisites of economic development rather than active opposition to it. But such sins were real and important enough to be a serious cause of developmental failures in the years before 1914.

Colonialism hindered development to the extent that it impeded the colonies' economic integration with the rest of the world or impeded the ability of colonial subjects to participate in this process. This conclusion runs counter to the view that sees international trade and investment as the problem. Many anticolonial activists at the time made antitrade critiques of this sort, which remain popular in some circles today. They charged that the great powers threw the colonies into merciless global economic waters, subjecting poor regions to the constraints of world markets. This accusation is misguided, in at least two ways. First, the most noxious and objectionable colonial rulers used *restrictions* on trade, not free trade, to drain resources from their colonies. Second, engagement with world markets typically increased colonial economic growth dramatically. It is no coincidence that fast-growing Latin America traded more than three times as much as slow-growing Asia as a share of its economy, more than six times as much per person. When given the opportunity, the peoples of poor regions vigorously pursued the possibilities of enrichment held out by global capitalism. The colonial areas that grew fastest were those whose governments were most effective at smoothing pathways to and from global markets. Development problems were most severe when colonial regimes were unwilling or unable to allow the peoples of the colonies to take advantage of what the global economy had to offer.

Colonialism was only one among many factors that affected growth in the developing world, and it was not always a negative one. Effective colonial rule sped economic advance, just as venal colonial exploitation retarded it. Economically, most colonies were somewhere in between: provided with a modicum of administrative and other benefits; subjected to modest amounts of tribute and commercial discrimination. The relative unimportance of colonialism to developmental outcomes is clear in broader perspective: The variation in progress was just as great among noncolonies as it was in the colonial regions. While much of Latin America grew rapidly, for example, areas from Central America to northeastern Brazil stagnated dismally. Two of the world's most obvious developmental failures, China and the Ottoman Empire, were independent. Some colonial countries stagnated, as did some independent countries; other colonial countries grew rapidly, as did other independent countries. With the exception of cases of outright Leopoldian looting and privileged settler colonies, colonialism was not usually an insurmountable obstacle to economic development.

Misrule and underdevelopment

The economic policies of a nation's rulers were the main determinant of its economic development, whether the rulers were colonial or local. Economic growth required investment, easy contact with domestic and overseas customers, local skill acquisition, and access to foreign capital and technology. None of this could take place without support, or at least permission, from rulers.

The poor societies of the turn of the century were four-fifths agricultural, and their agriculture was extremely backward. By comparison, by 1700 Britain was less rural than this, and its farms were more productive.[17] To modernize, farmers needed to improve their lands, learn new methods, and plant new crops. Areas that grew rapidly—the rice lowlands of Thailand and Burma, the cocoa regions of West Africa, the coffee zones of Brazil and Colombia—teemed with independent farmers developing their lands. And their governments made it easy for their citizens to take advantage of economic opportunities.

One requirement of economic growth was economic infrastructure, services that facilitate economic activity. Farmers needed transportation to bring machinery in and crops out, information about techniques and markets, and credit. Rulers interested in economic growth made sure their people had reliable transport, communications, finance, and money.

Development also required subtler political and legal conditions, especially secure property rights. A commitment to protect private property was not necessarily a concession to privilege: in poor societies, the principal property owners were farmers. For them to take advantage of new economic opportunities, they had to set aside time, energy, and money in order to improve the soil. A farmer had to put his livelihood on the line in order to plant coffee trees, clear woodland, or irrigate. How could he undertake such risky investments if he could not be sure that their fruits would come back to him? If marauders could steal his animals and torch his fields? If local government officials could extort any wealth they saw being earned? If the national government taxed away all his profits?

Education to enhance worker skills and literacy also had a direct effect on productivity. Indeed, economic success tracked school enrollment almost perfectly. In the United States and Germany three-quarters or more of all primary school–age children were in school; in Japan, half; in Argentina and Chile, one-quarter. In addition to education, sanitation and public health were important, both for obvious social reasons and because they allowed people to be fruitful members of society.

Misrule was the principal barrier to economic growth. Misrule blocked farmers and miners from taking their goods to world markets. Misrule kept East Africans or Central Americans from improving their lands and towns. Misrule, whether by colonial authorities or by independent governments, effectively precluded development. And plenty of rulers, independent and colonial, were indifferent or hostile to the needs of economic development.

Sure signs of misrule were the absence of adequate transportation and communications, a paucity of banks, and popular mistrust of the national money. China's first railroad line was built twenty-five years after India's, by foreign merchants, and a year later the Chinese government tore it up and dumped it into the ocean.[18] As late as 1913 China had a smaller railroad system than tiny Japan and only one-fifth the rail mileage of India.

Another sign of misrule was the absence of a clear government commitment to a dependable economic environment, so that people could not take advantage of the opportunities the growing world economy had to offer. Traditional rulers were often loath to guarantee the rights of investors; after all, respecting private property rights meant restricting government prerogatives. It was not until the early years of the twentieth century that China took the elementary step of adopting a corporate code to allow companies to operate normally. Even then officials often ignored the rights of private citizens.

Misrule also involved a lack of government commitment to improve the quality of human life and labor. In India only one child in twenty was in school.[19] Some 92 percent of Egypt's adult population was illiterate in 1907, and there were no signs of government interest in reducing these numbers.[20] Many rulers—independent, neocolonial, and colonial—failed abjectly to provide basic education, sanitation, or public health.

Why did ruling classes condemn their societies to stagnation? In the colonies the answer might be that imperialist rulers were uninterested in local economic conditions. But many of the development failures were politically independent, and it is safe to presume that most rulers would prefer their societies' economies to grow than to decline—even if only to provide more tribute. It was not some simple lack of democracy; rulers almost everywhere were oligarchic, in rich and poor countries alike. Some sovereigns were simply less willing or able than others to enable broad-based economic growth.

Stagnation in Asia

The most striking failures to develop were China, the Ottoman Empire, and India. The world's three oldest civilizations had, of course, long histories of complex social organization. As in premodern Europe, the economies consisted almost entirely of local agriculture and handicrafts and had long been in rough balance—enough to feed and clothe the populace, not enough to provide a substantial surplus for investment and growth. Governments were expert at administering their far-flung societies, providing social stability and military security. The few advanced segments of the economy—long-distance and foreign trade and finance, incipient industry—were handled by distinct groups, sometimes of distinct ethnicity. These islands of economic activity were carefully monitored to avoid the emergence of alternative centers of power.

Ruling classes in the three countries feared that economic growth could provoke social changes that would make them ungovernable—at least ungovernable by their current governments. Ottoman, Chinese, and Indian rulers were primarily concerned with the stability of their social orders, and economic growth might well have destabilized them. Encouraging the emergence of a flourishing private sector meant committing governments to respect the rights of their subjects in unaccustomed ways. Creating the bases for modern economic growth meant joining the world economy, taxing the rich, educating the poor, upgrading rural transportation, developing local credit markets. Most of this implied social changes that were unwelcome to the countries' ruling classes. None of the three governments made real efforts to overcome the secular inertia until the late nineteenth century, by which time it was too late. Traditionalism impeded modernization.[21]

Defenders of the three governments have argued that geopolitical necessity forced them to subordinate development to foreign policy goals. The Ottoman and Chinese empires are said to have faced threats to their sovereignty that required them to defer economic development. For example, one reason given for the Chinese government's hostility to railways was that foreign militaries, merchants, or missionaries might use railroads to compromise the security of the country. Yet the choice itself was revealing. For one thing, it simply assumed that the Chinese themselves would not be able to adopt the new technologies, including military use of railroads, while the Japanese did just that. For another thing, denying the nation a revolution in transportation simply to refuse foreigners access to it implied that the threat to government influence outweighed the opportunity for economic growth. Imperial power and stability were more important than development. Eventually the imperial government reversed itself after it used railroads to move government troops around quickly during the Boxer Rebellion of 1899–1900, and it embarked on a program to try to build railroads, but this was forty years too late. The military necessity argument is precisely backward: The accelerating infringements on Chinese and Ottoman sovereignty over the course of the nineteenth and early twentieth centuries were a *result* of their economic inadequacies, not their cause.

In the case of India, its status as a militarily crucial jewel in the British crown is sometimes alleged to have retarded growth, because of colonial neglect of economic needs. It is true that military needs motivated the principal British expenditure in India, the building of an extensive railroad system. But far from retarding development, the railways were probably the single most important source of what economic successes India registered. This alone was insufficient, however. Both the British and their Indian allies were, like the rulers of China and the Ottoman Empire, primarily concerned with maintaining political control and regarded aggressive developmental policies with suspicion. [22]

By the last decades of the nineteenth century the disastrous development gap was clear, and reform movements grew in all three countries. There were many clearheaded and well-meaning agents of change, even inside government, but in most cases their efforts were hindered by continued imperial resistance.

Some of China's rulers, for example, embraced economic and political reform. But the government's reformist credentials were suspect, as the Chinese empress dowager showed when she backed the anti-Western Boxer Rebellion. Even the changes the Chinese government did implement were distorted by the influence of the traditional ruling classes.

One of the most pressing tasks was the development of modern industry, which was virtually nonexistent in China. Yet the few national and regional rulers who encouraged industry did so primarily as a way of extending their own influence. The provincial governor of Hubei and Hunan, for example, set up the Hanyang Ironworks under his personal auspices. He himself placed the mill's orders for equipment by way of the Chinese ambassador in London, apparently on the principle that he wanted the latest in British equipment. Given the governor's ignorance of metalworking, the blast furnaces were inappropriate for local ore, while the coal intended for the mill was unusable. To make matters worse, the mill was built in a location that was too small and too damp but that had the virtue of being within sight of the governor's palace. The mill cost a fortune and failed miserably. The economic historian Albert Feuerwerker studied a host of these last-ditch attempts by the imperial government to stimulate industry. In case after case the schemes enriched a few merchants and officials but did nothing to modernize the country's economy. "The overwhelming political weight of the scholar-gentry élite," he wrote, "was opposed or indifferent to industrialization."[23]

As entrenched interests sabotaged reform, opponents of the ruling classes picked up the banner of national renovation. Indian nationalists who wanted greater autonomy for the colony led the movement for economic development. Mid-ranking officers in the Ottoman Army spearheaded the drive for reform there. The Young Turks took power in 1908–1909, but their plans were overtaken by World War One. The war demonstrated just how calamitous delay had been, with massive Ottoman losses to foreigners and to indigenous nationalist movements. As the empire collapsed, another young officer, Mustafa Kemal (Atatürk), led the empire's remnants toward modernity as the new secular, republican Turkey. The relative successes of Atatürk's Turkey served only to highlight the retrograde nature of the regime it replaced.

New social and economic forces only came to the fore by revolution in China too. The imperial government's reform program was timid, and in 1911 a coalition of insurgent army officers and civilian opponents brought down the monarchy. Sun Yat-sen and his Nationalist Party led the rebel movement to declare a republic in 1912. But as in the Ottoman Empire, reform came too late to avoid a further deterioration of the country's condition. Warlords divided China into regional fiefdoms, leaving the nation nearly defenseless as a more powerful and industrialized Japan expanded its control of Chinese territory. No group or person could unify the country to fight against foreigners or to renew the national government. The result was nearly forty years of civil war and invasion, calamity after calamity demonstrating the extent to which the imperial system had left the country unprepared for the modern age. China's millennial civilization, like that of the Ottoman Empire and India, blocked rather than enabled the adoption and adaptation of modern economic activities.

Stagnation on the plantation

Entrenched interests could impede economic development even where the weight of history was not heavy. Rulers who needed plantation hands or mine workers to work for a pittance could lose the basis of their privilege if workers could move to more lucrative activities. Those who depended on captive workers had little interest in facilitating the transition of the masses to a new economic order. In contrast, elites that did not need masses of cheap labor could profit from a general increase in prosperity, by acting as bankers or merchants to thriving small farmers, taking up the lucrative export-import trade, or intermediating between foreigners and locals.

Whether ruling classes had interests compatible with development depended in part on the nature of the economy. Different crops or raw materials led to economic structures based on plantations, on huge mines, or on family farms, and these had lasting effects on social organization.[24] Some activities were particularly prone to create backward-looking oligarchs who retarded follow-on economic growth; other economic organizations encouraged the incorporation of the populace into economic and political life, stimulating further development.

The four principal export crops of the tropics contrasted strongly in their organization of production and in the societies they spawned. Coffee, cotton, sugar, and rice together accounted for more than half of the tropics' agricultural exports in 1913, and their impact on tropical societies could not have been more different. In common lore, sugar and cotton were "reactionary" crops, while coffee and rice were "progressive" crops; subsequent scholarship has largely confirmed this wisdom. The former were plantation products and created some of the world's most inequitable and torpid societies; the latter were small-farm products and provided opportunities for extensive economic growth.

Plantation owners usually farmed sugar and cotton with gang labor. Overseers drove rows of closely watched workers through the fields, with no need to reward individual initiative and motivation. For this and other reasons, there were substantial economies of scale in sugar and cotton: Large farms were more efficient than small ones, and small independent farmers could not compete with plantation owners.

Coffee and rice, on the other hand, were ideal smallholder crops. In the case of coffee, this was in part because picking coffee requires careful attention to detail; the berries (beans) mature at different rates and the picker must watch closely what he is picking.[25] Unlike in the case of sugar and cotton, large-scale gang labor was not practical. Economies of scale in coffee and rice were inconsequential, and small farmers dominated their production. And where the dominant crop was grown by independent smallholders, more broad-based and equitable patterns of political growth usually followed.

Latin America included both "reactionary" sugar and "progressive" coffee societies. Sugar, like cotton and tobacco, was originally grown on slave plantations. After abolition, technology and competition usually dictated that it continue to be grown on large plantations at very low wages. Where former slaves had a choice, they avoided plantations like the plague. The planters scrambled to increase the supply of labor and keep wages low. On the sugar islands of the Caribbean and in coastal Peru, planters brought in thousands of Indians and Chinese, often in indentured servitude. In northeastern Brazil, plantation owners did what they could to keep "their" laborers tied to the plantations: restrictions on mobility, debt peonage, coercion. The problem was exacerbated when Europeans began raising sugar beets and subsidizing beet sugar exports, driving sugar prices down.[26]

The bitter aftertaste of sugar dominance was shocking inequality. A wealthy elite lorded over an impoverished labor pool, with little incentive to encourage economic, social, or human development, all of which would simply have bid labor away from the sugar plantations. Comparable conditions prevailed in regions growing cotton on large estates with plenty of labor. Northeastern Brazil grew cotton as well as sugar, doubly damning its social structure. The economic and political orders reinforced the position of wealthy landowning and merchant classes with little reason to improve the quality of government, infrastructure, or schooling.

The results were often perverse. In Venezuela, for example, fine land in huge haciendas was surrounded by the poor dwellings of landless peasants. The large landowners—hacendados—used less than one-third of their land yet refused to rent the rest to the landless. If the hacendados had rented idle land out, farmworkers would not have been willing to work cheaply on the plantations. This would have deprived the haciendas of the labor needed to make the landed estates economically viable. So most of the fertile countryside lay idle. In the long run, this cannot have been in the landowners' best interests, for the perpetuation of landless misery severely restricted the home market, not to speak of the social unrest it fomented. But the landed oligarchs were more interested in their wealth and power in the here and now than in long-term development.[27]

These patterns repeated themselves in region after region and for product after product. Sugar had a retrograde social impact on the Dutch East Indies, the Philippines, Fiji, and Mauritius. Cotton in India and Egypt had effects comparable to those in northeastern Brazil, reinforcing the position of landed and commercial ruling classes. Some new crops, such as bananas in Central America and rubber in Malaya, created new plantation economies on largely vacant land, dominated in both cases by foreign corporations that employed landless workers, often imported from other poor regions expressly for the purpose.

In contrast, Latin America's coffee lands were among the great developmental successes of the decades before World War One. It is certainly not coincidental that coffee, like rice or wheat, was easy to grow at very competitive costs on small farms. It took a few years for new trees to mature, so that farmers needed either credit or savings, but unlike sugar or cotton plantations, small coffee farms could be extremely profitable. Over one-quarter of western Colombia's output in this period came from tiny farms of less than three hectares (7.4 acres). It was certainly possible for coffee to be cultivated on large plantations, and São Paulo's output was disproportionately from larger estates; but the region was also teeming with thriving small farms.[28] Indeed, one of the advantages of coffee was that small farmers could intercrop between the trees, providing both basic foodstuffs for their families and a valuable cash crop. And where farmers had an easy alternative of setting up their own lucrative smallholdings, even large landowners had to pay decent wages to farmworkers.

Whether the profile of coffee was of small family farms or larger estates with well-paid workers, coffee was associated with widespread prosperity. This was not simply because of high prices—cotton substantially outperformed coffee, rice, and cocoa between 1899 and 1913[29]—but because coffee by the very nature of its production was conducive to broad-based economic growth, and its benefits could not easily be contained within a small elite.

There were "progressive" crops other than coffee. Rice was the most important. Burma, Thailand, and Indochina, which accounted for three-quarters of the world's rice exports, experienced extremely rapid growth that was almost as inclusive as in the coffee regions.[30] So too was West African cocoa a smallholder crop. Moreover, where grains like wheat could be raised profitably on small farms, such as in Latin America's Southern Cone and parts of northern India, prospects for generalized prosperity were greater.

Brazil demonstrated the impact of different crops, for it contained both failed and successful regions. Its northeastern agriculture was based on large plantations growing cotton and sugar. Landowners relied on formerly slave and informally tied labor to keep its estates running. Plantation owners worked hard to keep farmworkers in their place, for without captive labor the plantations would collapse. At the other extreme, in the southeast around São Paulo, a vibrant agricultural economy based on coffee was developing. The constant demand was for more farmers, more labor, to open up new lands. Many farms were small, and many farmers worked for themselves; if they worked for others, they were paid decent wages and moved freely from employer to employer. Here the wealthy repositioned themselves in the export sector, finance, and commerce. This *Paulista* elite, no less self-interested than the northeasterners, encouraged the opening of new farmland and the development of ever more profitable farms. The northeast stagnated while the southeast boomed.

The country would have been best served if northeasterners had migrated south to the coffee farms, but this would have destroyed the economic base of the northeastern plantation owners. Instead northeastern rulers did what they could to keep their subjects down on the plantation: internal passports; a minimum of railroad building; discouragement of job advertisements and labor contractors. Desperate for labor, southeastern rulers brought in millions of laborers from southern Europe; the demand for labor was so great that state governments actively subsidized their passages.

The Brazilian experience recalls analogous regional differences in the United States. America's reactionary crops were the cotton, tobacco, and cane sugar of the South, while the progressive crops were the grain and cattle of the North and West. As in Brazil, the former plantation areas remained backward and stagnant for decades, while the small family farm and ranch regions grew dramatically. In fact the system of legal apartheid that reigned in the American South—with its social and political exclusion of the descendants of slaves, miserable educational system, hostility to labor recruiters, and underinvestment in transport and communications—was one among many such mechanisms to maintain an impoverished, captive labor force in a region whose oligarchs were dependent upon a ready supply of cheap unskilled labor.

The process was not simply economic, for there is no inherent reason why plantation agriculture cannot be efficient and dynamic; there were some rapidly growing sugar societies, such as Cuba. It was the broader impact of plantation agriculture that mattered, in its creation of a tiny elite that relied on a mass of low-wage laborers. In such a setting the scope for social mobility and political involvement was easy to limit, and the temptations for rulers to limit it were great. Where, on the other hand, many people had access to profitable small-farming opportunities, it was more difficult—and less necessary—for rulers to limit economic opportunities to the population.[31] Plantation societies and their similars tended to be or become highly unequal and polarized, subjugated by authoritarians. Their entrenched planter-based governments were rarely willing or able to encourage the socioeconomic development—of infrastructure, finance, and education—needed to allow the productive forces of the society as a whole to be brought to bear.

A similar process, by which the economy created concentrated interests that mishandled government and impeded economic growth, was associated with several raw materials. Some mining is similar to enclave agriculture, its economic impact restricted to the areas where the minerals are found. And much mining—copper, oil, silver—did in fact tend to create great divides between the mineral producers and the rest of society. How important this was depended on the social and political importance of the mines. A real difference between mining and farming was that because these societies were overwhelmingly agricultural, the export agriculture of the poor countries tended to involve very large portions of the population, while mining typically was carried out by small groups of isolated miners.

Mining typically had a powerful impact analogous to that of agriculture where it dominated the local economy, and that was only in a few regions, such as the gold-mining areas of South Africa. Where this was the case, as along the extraordinary mineral veins of the Transvaal, the results tended toward the same dual society characteristic of plantation regions. South Africa's social and political evolution was closely related to its domination by commercial farmers and mineowners, who relied on extensive supplies of cheap labor.

These experiences amount almost to a curse of natural resource wealth or at least certain kinds of resource wealth. Regions that were ideal for lucrative plantation crops or that had some kinds of valuable mineral deposits were likely to develop skewed social structures. They became dominated by entrenched elites with little interest in providing the infrastructure, education, or good government necessary for development to go beyond the initial natural resources boom. While there were exceptions, the striking fact is that the production of valuable crops and minerals in poor countries was commonly associated with poverty and inequality.

There was nothing deterministic about the impact of such natural resources. The purely economic characteristics of production were only the starting point for this downward slide. The most telling effects of these products were social and political, in creating powerful interests whose position relied on restricting access to social and political power. Early wealth might accumulate; but it would not diffuse, and without the broad mobilization of the population economic modernization did not take place. The process could be avoided, but the natural tendency of most such societies was for existing rulers to use the resource boom to consolidate their rule, but not to extend the benefits of development to the rest of the population.

Obstacles to development

There were as many reasons for stagnation, decline, and failure to develop in the poor regions of the world as there were unique societies in these regions. In some cases, colonial plunder was to blame. In others, the accumulated weight of centuries of traditional society stifled modern economic growth. In still others, plantation and mineral production threw up an entrenched elite, hostile or indifferent to the measures necessary for widespread development. Rational people pursuing their own interests obstructed development and destroyed the economic prospects of their countrymen.

Local rulers played at least an enabling role in virtually all the societies that failed to take advantage of the opportunities offered by the world economy before World War One. To be sure, avaricious foreigners—colonial predators, privileged settlers, monopolistic companies—were ever present. But some societies dealt with them more effectively than others, leaving open the question of why this was.

In the most egregious cases, social and political inequality gave traditional ruling classes little reason to encourage development and left the masses unable to overcome the obstacles created by their corrupt or incompetent masters. Where social organization gave the population access to new economic opportunities, and rulers supported—or at least did not discourage—these new opportunities, growth was rapid. But there were many societies in which these apparently minimal conditions did not hold.

Amid tantalizing vistas of great wealth pouring out of the pampas, poor regions speeding toward modernity, and three continents industrializing at breakneck speed, much of Africa, Asia, and Latin America remained desperately poor and economically inert. These regions represented some of the most difficult and enduring problems of the international order that was to collapse with the coming of World War One.

5

Problems of the Global Economy

The principal challenges to golden age global capitalism came from dissidents at the center of the system, not from the impoverished masses of Africa and Asia. British industrialists contested their country's commitment to free trade and global economic leadership. American farmers questioned the desirability of the gold standard. European labor unions and Socialist parties organized to remedy domestic ills long taken for granted. They all chipped away at the classical era's consensus on the primacy of international economic commitments over domestic concerns.

Free trade or fair trade?

In the 1880s dissenters from Britain's free trade orthodoxy originally demanded fair trade: retaliation against protective barriers overseas. Producers facing competition from recently industrialized nations led the charge. Textile and metalworking factory owners were incensed that Europeans and Americans sold freely in the British market, while their governments imposed heavy tariffs on British goods. The new competitors also took away British business in third markets—Latin America, Asia, eastern and southern Europe. Britain's premier industries came to rely more and more on sales within the empire, where business and cultural ties gave them an edge. By the early part of the century half the country's cotton textile exports, along with one-third of its exported galvanized iron, was going to India alone.[1] In one sense this was a success of empire in providing a captive market, but in another, it showed the distressing fact that previously dominant British industries could now compete with foreigners only with artificial imperial support.

The demand for fair trade transmogrified into a more general call for a revision of British trade policy. The charge was led by Joseph Chamberlain, a metal manufacturer who had served as mayor of Birmingham, head of the Board of Trade, and colonial secretary. Northern manufacturers agitated for protection under the aegis of the Tariff Reform League, formed in 1903. They often linked the demand for protection to proposals for imperial preferences, a system to provide Britain and its colonies and dominions with privileged access to each other's markets. This would have satisfied increasingly powerful protectionist interests in the rest of the empire—especially Canada, Australia, South Africa, and India—as well as provided an even more secure market for struggling British manufacturers.[2]

Supporters of tariff reform brought together protectionist sentiment, concern for empire building, and anxiety about the implications for British power of its lost industrial prowess. In the words of Chamberlain:

> Whereas at one time England was the greatest manufacturing country now its people are more and more employed in finance, in distribution, in domestic service and in other occupations of the same kind. That state of things . . . may mean more money but it means less men. It may mean more wealth but it means less welfare; and I think it is worthwhile to consider—whatever its immediate effects may be—whether this state of things may not be the destruction ultimately of all that is best in England, all that has made us what we are, all that has given us our power and prestige in the world.[3]

The general election of 1906 was largely a referendum on free trade. The financiers based in the City of London mobilized heavily to defend Britain's openness to trade, and they were backed by merchants and successful exporting industries. The protectionists lost resoundingly.[4] That year Joseph Chamberlain suffered a stroke that debilitated the principal spokesman of British protectionism. Both the man and the movement faded; Chamberlain died in 1914, and British demands for protection subsided until after World War One. The struggling industrialists had failed to revise British policy in their favor.

But it could no longer be taken for granted that Great Britain would forever accept the world's goods. Britain was losing its international economic position.

Britain's decline was only relative. Between 1870 and 1913 the size of the British economy well more than doubled; even if one takes into account population growth, British output rose by more than 50 percent per person in those years. Yet the gap between Britain and the rest of the world narrowed continually. British manufacturers were being beaten out of export markets, even out of the British market. The United States and Germany were the world's manufacturing dynamos; the United Kingdom maintained its leadership only in such services as banking, insurance, and shipping. It was no longer a given that the next power plant or railroad built in Africa or eastern Europe would be British; it was just as likely to be German, French, or American. Even in international investment, Continental financial centers—as well as New York—were challenging London's supremacy. It could hardly have been imagined that Britain's enormous industrial lead would last forever, but the speed of its erosion led many Britons to ask how this had happened, a question echoed by generations of economic historians.

One popular explanation is that British investors' enthusiasm for foreign ventures slowed down the British economy while speeding that of the recipients of British capital. After all, the country's investors sent half their savings abroad, and British borrowers sometimes complained that loans would be cheaper if they did not have to compete with the Canadian and Argentine provinces for the favor of London's bondholders. But profitable domestic investments had no trouble being funded. In addition, the money invested abroad earned handsome profits, which came home to increase national wealth and income.[5]

The British failed, it is sometimes alleged, to adopt new production and managerial techniques. Such countries as Germany and the United States had the advantage of lateness; they could set up new industries with recent advances already incorporated. The analogous disadvantage was of having industrialized fifty years before everyone else, so that introducing new technologies could mean scrapping existing, often still profitable equipment. In fact the increasing reliance on empire markets

for the country's traditional products postponed industrial modernization by providing an easy outlet for goods that did not require technological change. In the words of the economic historian Charles
Kindleberger, imperial exports "enabled the economy to evade the exigencies of dynamic change, away from cotton textiles, iron and steel
rails, galvanized iron sheets, and the like, to production . . . of the products of the new industries."[6]

British management practices too came from an earlier era before the
telecommunications and transportation revolutions of the late nineteenth century and before the rise of mass consumption of consumer
durables and of mass production. British firms tended to be smaller than
such German and American firms as Siemens and AEG or General
Electric and U.S. Steel. British companies were usually organized less
like modern corporations and more like family businesses, which many
of them still were. It is not clear, however, that this was such a bad idea.
It is possible that American firms were big because America was big,
that German firms were big because they were in monopolistic cartels,
and that the new managerial forms were not appropriate for British
industrial and labor relations.

Another candidate culprit for Britain's relatively slow growth was its
educational system. Critics blamed the nation's schools for inadequate
attention to technical training, excessive class-based rigidity, and insuf-
ficiently meritocratic principles of promotion and advancement. There
was certainly a hidebound strain in British society, whose potentially sti-
fling impact on economic advance was captured by the American novel-
ist Margaret Halsey: "In England, having had money . . . is just as
acceptable as having it. . . . But never having had money is unforgive-
able, and can only be properly atoned for by never trying to get any."[7]
While the country's social structure may not have sufficiently rewarded
entrepreneurship, and its educational achievements did not reflect the
industrial lead it had over other European countries, it is not clear that
these failings had substantial economic effects.

Whatever the sources of Britain's growth slowdown after 1870—and
probably there is something to each of the leading contenders—the
slowdown affected the country and the world. Many Britons came to
question previously unchallenged verities of their political economy,
such as free trade and global financial leadership. It is not surprising that
British manufacturers facing competitive pressure wanted supportive
government policy. Nor is it surprising, given the importance of empire
and dominion markets to the struggling industries, that this would take

the form of a call for protective barriers around the British Empire. In all this, the United Kingdom was much like other major industrial nations.

But the United Kingdom's central role in the world economy was predicated in large part on its being *unlike* other industrial nations, as it had been since the 1840s. Britain's commitment to free trade and financial openness was central to the structure and functioning of the world economy. It was one thing for such marginal countries as Russia and Brazil to impose protectionist barriers; even on the Continent, this was not of transcendent importance. But it was hard to contemplate a continuation of the economic Pax Britannica without Britain. A pillar of the classical world economic order had trembled.

Winners and losers from trade

Those outside Britain doing less well during the last years of the golden age also voiced concerns about the impact of economic integration. Even in the most rapidly growing countries during the decades before 1914, there were many who benefited little or not at all from their countries' economic growth.

The theoretical tools developed by the Swedish economists Eli Heckscher and Bertil Ohlin to understand international trade also help explain the winners and losers from integration. Heckscher-Ohlin theory predicts that countries rich in capital will export capital-intensive products (and capital), labor-rich countries will export labor-intensive products (and labor), while land-rich countries will export land-intensive products. Indeed, capital-rich Britain did export capital-intensive manufactures, while land-rich Argentina exported land-intensive farm products. The same went for imports: A country with very little capital (Argentina) imported capital and capital-intensive goods, while a country with very little land (Britain) imported land-intensive goods.

Twenty years after the Swedes first developed their approach to explain patterns of trade, two young Harvard classmates and neighbors extended it to demonstrate who is helped and hurt by trade. In a 1941 article, Austrian-born Wolfgang Stolper and American Paul Samuelson started with the observation that trade is particularly beneficial for producers of exports, while it can be especially harmful for producers that compete with imports. And Heckscher-Ohlin theory predicts that export producers are those that have what the country is rich in: capital in capital-rich countries, land in land-rich countries. As exports grow, demand for the resources used to make them rises: As a labor-rich country exports labor-intensive products, the demand for labor grows, so that wages also go up. Conversely, import-competing producers are those who have what is in short supply in the country: labor in labor-poor countries, land in land-poor countries. As imports grow and local producers are beaten out of the home market, their demand for the resources they use a lot of falls; as a labor-poor country imports labor-intensive products, the demand for labor declines, and so do wages.

Stolper and Samuelson showed that trade makes the national owners of a plentiful factor of production better off and the owners of a scarce factor worse off. Owners of abundant resources gain from trade, while those of scarce resources lose. An easy way to see the relationship is to consider a tangible resource like oil. In a country rich in oil, oil is cheap, and opening to trade is good for oilmen because it allows them to sell oil to foreigners. In a country poor in oil, where oil is expensive, opening to trade is bad for oilmen because it leads to oil imports that push the domestic price of oil down. Even if the resource in question is more general—land, labor, capital—the logic holds: Protection helps owners of a nationally scarce resource; trade helps owners of a nationally abundant resource.[8]

Even in an era of rapid growth, even in countries growing rapidly, even if free trade is the best possible policy for the economy as a whole, even orthodox economists accept that there are both winners and losers from freer trade. Winners and losers fought for policies to benefit themselves: Before 1914 owners of nationally abundant resources supported free trade, while owners of nationally scarce resources opposed it. A country such as Argentina, land-rich but capital-poor, exported land-intensive (farm) goods and imported capital-intensive goods. This was good for farmers, but not so good for capitalists, so farmers were pro-trade while urban capitalists were protectionist. A country such as Great Britain, capital-rich but land-poor, exported capital-intensive goods and imported land-intensive goods, so urban capitalists were protrade while farmers were protectionist.

The Stolper-Samuelson schema explains much of the politics of trade, and of economic integration more generally. Owners of nationally plentiful resources—capital, land, oil, labor—tended to favor international economic ties that made it possible to sell their resources or its products. A land-rich country had a comparative advantage in farm products and exported them, and this helped farmers; a land-poor country had a comparative *disadvantage* in farming and imported farm goods, hurting farmers.

In the late nineteenth and early twentieth centuries, indeed, farmers in land-rich countries were almost always free traders, whether they were plantation owners in Malaya, cattle ranchers in Australia, or wheat farmers in Canada. So too were capital-intensive manufacturers and investors in capital-rich countries mainly in favor of free trade and investment; witness the generally open policies of the wealthy countries of northwestern Europe. The Stolper-Samuelson argument held for *opponents* of global integration too; those whose resources were nationally rare were hostile to free trade and its complements. Labor in labor-poor Australia, Canada, and the United States was protectionist; industrial capitalists in such capital-poor countries as Russia and Brazil were protectionist; farmers in land-poor Europe were protectionist.

Protectionist interests were usually less influential than the internationalist groups that dominated the golden age: international bankers and investors, traders, competitive industrialists, export farmers and miners. But protectionists were always present, and they were powerful in some places, such as the United States and Russia, and times, during recessions. So long as the world economy grew and supporters of global integration could demonstrate to enough people the benefits of the free movement of goods, capital, and people, pressures for economic closure were staved off. It could not, however, be assumed that this would always be so.

Silver threats among the gold

If challenges in the British center of the system aimed at the classical world economy's free trade pillar, assaults at the periphery of the world economy gave its gold standard pillar the harshest tests. The challengers were rarely powerful enough or in important enough countries to unsettle the system as a whole, but they were substantial irritants. The fact that antipathy to the international gold standard was common even in good times also did not bode well for its ability to withstand economic difficulties.

Farmers and miners producing for world markets were the most vocal opponents of the gold standard. This was because a country that was on gold could not use currency devaluation to protect exporters from declines in the prices of their products. Many countries relied on one or a few crops or minerals, whose prices could fluctuate wildly from year to year. In a country on gold, these price movements immediately affected local producers because the national currency was in effect just a local version of gold, the global money: A price decline of 1 percent meant a 1 percent price decline whether it was expressed in gold pounds, gold dollars, gold pesos, or any other gold currency. All the twists and turns of world farm or mine prices were transmitted directly, by the gold standard, to farmers and miners. When world wheat, coffee, or copper prices dropped, prices of these commodities in Argentina, Colombia, or Chile dropped just as much—if the country was on gold.

Producers who faced competition from cheap *imports*, such as European farmers and American manufacturers, had an easy alternative: They could get tariffs to keep out foreign goods. But farmers and miners for export had no such choice. Their market was abroad, and tariffs to raise the price of coffee inside Brazil, the price of tin inside Malaya, or the price of cocoa inside the Ivory Coast would accomplish little. Producers needed to protect themselves from radical price declines on their export markets.

A devaluation helped exporters by increasing the amount of money they got for goods sold abroad. If wheat, coffee, or copper prices fell, a currency devaluation could offset the shock, keeping the domestic Argentine, Colombian, or Chilean price of those goods the same. For example, when world wheat prices dropped by about half during the late nineteenth century, the gold standard American price of wheat also fell by half, from a dollar to fifty cents a bushel. But in Argentina, which went off gold and devalued the peso, wheat prices paid to farmers were steady.

Chile accounted for nearly half of the world's copper production before World War One, and copper was typically half of total Chilean exports. But in one ten-year period the London price of a ton of copper fell continually from 70 to 40 pounds sterling. For American copper producers, Chile's principal competitors, this price decline was taken directly out of the prices they received. With the dollar on gold and fixed against sterling, this meant an analogous price drop, from about $340 to about $195 a ton. A similar collapse in Chile would have bankrupted copper miners, and much of the economy along with them. So the Chilean government devalued the peso against the gold currencies: In ten years the peso dropped from 0.18 to 0.10 pounds sterling, from 85 to 48 cents. This completely offset the world copper price collapse; in Chilean pesos, copper prices actually rose from 401 to 403 pesos a ton.[9]

A devaluation could not work miracles. When the currency depreciated, foreign goods became more expensive. Eventually these price increases were passed through to the domestic economy and contributed to inflation. As the Argentine peso fell, sooner or later other prices in Argentina went up, and the advantages of the devaluation were eroded. But in the meantime Argentina's wheat farmers had gained valuable time and money, while many American farmers had been driven off the land. Another group, debtors, actually liked the inflation that going or staying off gold brought. A homeowner, businessman, or farmer who owed money in the national currency could hope for inflation to reduce his real debt burden; a 50 percent rise in prices made fixed debts half as onerous.

Opponents of gold also disliked the government policies needed to keep a currency fixed to gold, which forced domestic prices, profits, and wages to adjust to changes in a country's international economic position. The government of a gold country could not respond to hard economic times with countervailing policy but had to reinforce the austerity imposed by foreign conditions. For the gold standard was expected to work best if governments allowed its recessionary effects to take their course, driving wages, prices, and profits down to allow a market-based recovery. A gold standard economy was supposed to change to fit the exchange rate, not the other way around.

For these reasons, most agricultural- and mineral-exporting countries stayed off the gold standard altogether or were on it only intermittently. The two alternatives to gold were paper currency and silver. Most Latin American and southern European countries issued paper money that was inconvertible, not exchangeable for gold. This was like today's paper money, in that it was issued by the government and its value was set on currency markets. The government acted to keep the peso or lira where it wanted. In the words of an American antigold senator from Nebraska, "We believe it possible so to regulate the issue of money as to make it of approximately the same value at all times." Another put it: "It is the cardinal faith of Populism . . . that money can be created by the Government in any desired quantity, out of any substance, with no basis but itself."[10]

The second alternative to gold was a silver-backed currency. Indeed, most of the world had used both gold and silver interchangeably for centuries before 1870. At that point a wave of silver discoveries drove the price of silver down by as much as half against gold, and governments generally chose one or the other. Almost all industrial nations followed Britain to gold. But China and India had had silver-based moneys for ages and stayed on that metal. So did such major silver producers as Mexico. For many other countries, staying on or going to silver was attractive. The price of silver generally declined against gold over the decades before World War One, so silver-backed currencies were weak. If silver prices dropped by 10 percent, so too did all currencies based on silver. This had the same effect as a depreciation, so that silver countries could give their exporters a competitive edge on world markets.

By the 1890s most industrial countries were on gold and most developing countries were on silver or paper money. The silver and paper countries realized palpable advantages. As gold prices rose against silver, the silver-based regions' exports became cheaper in the industrial world's gold currencies. Declines in the world prices of farm products and raw materials were compensated by analogous declines in the silver-backed and paper currencies, so that farmers and miners got paid just about the same in their own moneys. The competitive edge of silver did not matter much to most of the rich countries, for the developing regions mostly sold goods that industrial countries did not produce. If a decline in silver made Mexican copper or Chinese silk cheaper on European markets, this was all to the good.

However, those who produced the same things as the silver and paper regions faced a strong competitive threat from their depreciated currencies. Foremost among those affected was the United States, which specialized in many of the same raw materials and farm products as weak-currency Argentina, India, Brazil, China, and Russia: minerals, wheat, cotton, wool, tobacco. The result was that American farmers and miners lost business to the silver-based countries (and those on paper money). And because the United States was on gold, declines in the world price of wheat or wool simply cut into farm earnings. Struggling American farmers who flocked to the Populist campaign against gold and for silver thought, in the words of one, "that the yellow man using the white metal, holds at his mercy the white man using the yellow metal."[11] From the late 1880s onward the Populist firestorm reignited every time farm prices dropped, as farmers and miners tried desperately to get the dollar delinked from gold.

"You shall not," thundered 1896 Democratic-Populist presidential candidate William Jennings Bryan, "crucify mankind upon a cross of gold." America's farm and mining districts shared Bryan's defiance. In what was probably the first mass movement in American history, millions of people flocked to hear fiery orators denounce the Money Trust and its gold-backed stranglehold on the American economy. The Populists' platform insisted on immediate measures to jettison gold. The resulting depreciation would reverse the effects of the declining world prices of farm and mine goods, and whatever inflation might ensue would help lighten the load of heavily indebted farmers.

Bryan nearly won the presidency in 1896, at the height of farm distress; he ran again, and lost again, as the Democratic nominee in 1900 and 1908. This made the United States the only major exporter of farm goods and raw materials to stay on gold throughout the decades before World War One, if one leaves aside regions that were part of European empires, such as Australia and South Africa. Every other independent primary exporter—from Mexico to Russia and Japan, China to Argentina, even British India—spent much or all of this period on silver or paper money.

The United States was different because economically it was two immense regions with diametrically opposed views on gold. The farmlands and mining districts of the South, Midwest, Great Plains, and West were the world's greatest source of agricultural and mineral wealth. But the factory owners, merchants, and bankers of the Northeast and industrial Midwest made up the world's manufacturing powerhouse. The conflict of interest was direct. Every increase in farm prices made food more expensive to urban workers and raised industry's wage bill. Just so, every increase in industrial prices, including every tariff, took more away from farm families who relied on the cities for their clothing, farm implements, and other manufactured necessities.

Perhaps most important, the bankers and traders of New England and the Northeast staked their international reputation on the country's adherence to the gold standard. America's financial credibility depended on full participation in the club of rich nations, whose membership card was the gold standard. J. P. Morgan and his colleagues fought tenaciously to keep the dollar on gold. They did so in both the financial and political realms. In the former, Morgan arranged a series of international loans to allow the U.S. Treasury to defend the dollar when it came under attack on currency markets and to keep it tied to gold. In politics, starting with McKinley, anti-Populist candidates raised enormous sums from big northeastern businesses to help ensure their election. And America's gold bugs succeeded in fighting off the Populist hordes. The division of the country was close, though, with McKinley winning with just 51 percent of the popular vote. The geography of the divide was stark: A color-coded map of the 1896 election shows uninterrupted gold from the Northeast through the industrial Midwest, with a golden outpost in California and Oregon, but a solid silver South and Great Plains.

Commitment to the gold standard could not be taken for granted. A substantial decline in world prices would bring forth protests from the four corners of the earth and a stampede to leave the gold standard. Powerful groups around the world were willing to jettison their nations' ironclad commitments to gold when times were difficult.

The conflict over gold was typical of the frictions that affected the classical world economy before 1914. On the one hand, full participation in the global economy could be extraordinarily lucrative, to both countries and individuals. On the other hand, such participation typically required sacrifices. In the case of the gold standard, first-class financial citizenship was available only to those countries willing to subordinate the needs of their domestic economies to their commitments to gold. To be on gold and stay on gold meant giving up the ability to devalue to improve your competitive position. It meant agreeing not to stimulate your economy in hard times by lowering interest rates or printing money. It meant privileging the international standing of your currency over the state of the domestic economy.

These sacrifices were worth it to those whose livelihoods depended on the global economy, and the world's strongest supporters of the gold standard were international bankers, investors, and traders. This was especially the case because the sacrifices called for seldom affected these internationalist groups directly; financiers rarely had to face the threat of unemployment or drought. But people and groups whose interests were sacrificed saw little reason to suffer in order to sustain a global economic order that did not concern, and may even have harmed, them. The conflict between international and domestic concerns was present elsewhere: in trade policy; in immigration; in attitudes toward foreign lenders. So long as the world economy grew, the tension between national and global concerns could be managed. It would not always be thus.

Labor and the classical order

As the labor movement grew, it too came to represent a challenge to the established order. It was not that workers opposed global economic integration—in fact in many countries labor unions and Socialist parties strongly supported free trade—but that the demands of labor clashed with the classical liberal system's reliance on flexible wages and minimal government.

By the turn of the century industrial workers were the largest occupational group in most advanced societies. They had come to outnumber farmers by a lot in the United Kingdom, by a bit even in such still heavily agrarian countries as the United States and Germany. Workers had also developed labor organizations of great scope and sophistication. In the face of business and government hostility, labor unions had organized many of the skilled workers of western Europe, North America, and Australia. Unskilled laborers were less well organized, but as large-scale factory production expanded, they too were drawn toward the labor movement.

By 1914 British unions had four million members and German unions three million—well over one-fifth of the industrial labor force in each case. Working-class organization was even more successful in Scandinavia and moderately strong in North America; unions were present but less powerful in France and southern Europe. Despite variations, labor unions were a prominent part of the economic and political landscape in every industrial country—even in semi-industrial Argentina and Russia.

The working class supplemented its bargaining power in industry with a growing political presence, for many male workers gained the vote in the decades before 1914. The resultant rise of Socialist parties would have seemed unthinkable to both capitalists and workers a generation earlier. On the eve of World War One, labor-based parties with an avowedly anticapitalist message routinely got more than one-quarter of the vote in many industrial countries. In most of northern Europe, Socialist parties were getting one-third of the popular vote: 35 percent in Germany and 36 percent in Sweden. Representatives of the laboring classes were no longer relegated to the irrelevant margins of political life; the intellectual and ideological descendants of Marx and Engels had, 15 years after Engels's death, achieved an electoral prominence that the two founders of modern socialism would have found hard to believe.

Workers and their organizations sometimes engaged international economic policy issues, especially where labor was hostile to free immigration and free trade. This was the case in countries traditionally short of labor, such as North America and the other areas of recent European settlement, where restricting immigration was near the top of labor's wish list. The flow of people from low-wage Europe (and worse, even lower-wage Asia) would depress wages, and labor wanted it stopped. By the same token, the flow of cheap goods *made by* low-wage workers in Europe would depress wages in high-wage North America and Australia, and this drove labor movements in these countries toward protectionism. The anti-immigrant stance sat poorly with conventional socialist expressions of interest in cross-border solidarity; that may help explain why labor movements in these countries tended not to gravitate toward traditional European socialism.

However, in many countries the labor movement was firmly in the free trade, open borders camp. This was typically true in Europe, especially because the most important goal of European trade policies was to protect farmers, and agricultural protection made food more expensive for workers. Also, where migration was outmigration, as it was in Europe, the subsequent reduction of labor supply served to raise wages, not to lower them. In addition, many Europeans worked for industries that relied heavily on exports and could not afford retaliation from important markets. In some instances the divisions were more on the basis of industry than of class: Workers in Britain's export-driven coalfields supported free trade, while those in the hard-pressed textiles industry wanted the protection of imperial preferences as much as did their employers.

The international economic policy interests of labor—for or against trade protection, for or against controls on immigration—fitted easily into existing political economies. But the working classes were not often major players in debates explicitly concerned with the international economy because these issues were usually of secondary importance to labor. This relative absence of labor involvement in major foreign economic policy disputes was not, however, a true indication of the implications of the growth of the labor movement for the world economy.

Labor's general concerns were much more troublesome to the established order than were its specific policy positions on trade or immigration. As the working-class share of the population of industrial countries grew, its needs seemed increasingly inconsistent with important features of the classical open economies of the late nineteenth and early twentieth centuries. Most important, workers needed a cushion against unemployment. Farmers, the other big segment of the common folk, could fall back upon their land, crops, and villages when times were hard; they could grow enough to eat or rely on the assistance of relatives or neighbors if the problem was specific to their farm. Workers in big cities had, in the absence of their jobs, no property and no way to produce the necessities of life, and the anonymity of urban society reduced (although it did not eliminate) the availability of assistance from fellow workers. All they had was the minimal poor relief offered by private charities or the vestiges of medieval government aid to paupers, widows, and orphans.

Labor's central concern was protection against unemployment. As the working class grew, mutual aid societies developed their own unemployment insurance. Labor unions in the industrial city of Ghent, Belgium, early on provided union members with a basic income in case they lost their jobs. Only union members were eligible for the benefits, making labor organization that much easier. But these Ghent systems—unemployment insurance programs made up of union members in one city—could survive only if unemployment was scattered and limited. When serious economic downturns hit entire cities or regions, much of the area's working population could be left destitute, and the insurance pool would rapidly dry up. As local unemployment programs went bankrupt, municipalities and eventually national governments stepped in to take them over.

By 1913 many European towns and regions had unemployment compensation programs. But coverage was very spotty, and labor unions demanded more extensive, government-financed systems. Meanwhile some employers and other city dwellers came to the view that these schemes had their advantages. They stabilized local labor markets and dampened social unrest, and so long as government required nationwide participation and contributions their budgetary implications were limited.

There was also substantial business resistance to this "interference" with the workings of the labor market. In the absence of unemployment compensation, workers had little choice but to accept reduced wages in hard times, for the alternative was starvation. By putting a "floor" underneath workers' incomes, unemployment insurance—along with associated welfare and social programs—limited the ability of employers to cut wages. The growing organization of workers into unions had already restricted business control over wages; the new social programs restricted it further.

Because labor unions and social programs circumscribed the power of business to set wages, they excited the opposition of recalcitrant capitalists. The more control workers had over their lives, the less their wages and working conditions could be set at will by industry. Labor unions aimed to provide workers with guaranteed earnings, and this meant reducing the flexibility of wages and hours.

Working-class union and political action to temper the ability of markets to set wages freely had profound implications for global capitalism. It ran directly against the central importance of wage flexibility to the operation of most national economies and to their relationship with the international economy. In recession the very threat of unemployment was dire enough to force workers to accept large wage cuts, so recessions and even depressions typically led to reduced wages. Capitalists could cut wages and product prices, helping them restore sales and sustain profits. The consequence was that while business downturns caused pain and suffering, their impact on sales and profits was mitigated, and typically the downturn was quickly overcome. In fact the ease with which wages could be reduced gave employers little reason to lay off workers so that unemployment was often limited and of short duration. All this meant that there was little call for governments to intervene to soften the edges of the market economy's ups and downs.

Employers' freedom to force wages down was also essential to the functioning of the gold standard. Countries on gold were committed to keeping their economies in conformity with the gold value of the currency, making the national economy fit the currency. The most common way to trim an economy to sustain its gold parity (exchange rate) was to push wages down. If a country with a persistent trade deficit needed to restore balance, it would increase exports by cutting wages. If national producers faced import competition or were priced out of foreign markets, wages would be forced down until domestic products were again competitive.

Indeed, it was common under the gold standard for countries with rising prices simply to reverse the process and push prices back down. The American price level more than doubled after the country went off gold during the Civil War; to get back onto gold, the government tightened macroeconomic screws until prices had retreated by more than 50 percent. It is controversial today to impose austerity measures to reduce inflation—that is, to keep prices from rising. It would be unthinkable actually to force prices to decline by 20, 30, or 80 percent. The principal source of this unthinkability is the virtual impossibility of forcing workers to accept such drastic wage reductions. But such reductions were common under the gold standard; indeed, they were essential to the operation of this pillar of the classical world economy. To the extent that labor unions and such social programs as unemployment compensation reduced employers' ability to force wages down, they complicated the market processes that sustained the gold standard.

The burden of adjustment in the classical era was on labor. If business conditions worsened, wages were cut. Prices were usually cut also, so that a big drop in money wages might have only a modest impact on living standards. Profits usually suffered as well. But the essence of the adjustment required wage reductions. Under the gold standard, wages had to be cut in order to restore a country's competitiveness in export and import markets. The flexibility of wages, and of labor market conditions generally, was essential to the rules of the classical liberal game. But this wage flexibility became labor's principal target, as it tried to protect the working class from being the main victim of measures to ensure the smooth functioning of the world economy. And as the labor movement gained power and influence, it was able to protect workers from the dictates of domestic and international markets. However, this protection called into question the very workings of these markets or at least the ways that they worked in the era of gold standard globalization.

Tension between labor's efforts to shield itself from adverse market conditions and the business ethos of government nonintervention in markets was incipient in the years before 1914. In particular times and places it was an open and prominent issue. Most of the time the problem was barely a minor irritant. But the difficulties of satisfying the demands of both a growing labor movement and an integrated global economy proved critical and enduring.

The Gilded Age tarnished?

The world's economic and political leaders in the decades before World War One strongly supported global capitalism. Governments almost everywhere were committed to the free movement of goods, money, and people and to the rules of the gold standard. So too were they pledged to limit their involvement in national markets. The resulting economic order brought economic growth and social change to much of the world. It produced unimagined wealth for the developed nations, extended the benefits of industrial development down into the middle and working classes, and gave the hope of modernity to regions long mired in poverty.

But there were holes in the classical world economy. The world's most populous countries, China and India, benefited little from the heady growth of the late nineteenth and early twentieth centuries. Important parts of Africa, Latin America, and Asia were left behind. Even in regions that developed rapidly, the gains from growth were distributed very unevenly. Many people in even the most successful countries were left worse off. And economic growth and change in rapidly growing economies undermined social and political support for the classical prescriptions of global integration and minimalist government.

The economic achievements of the late nineteenth and early twentieth centuries were impressive, but this stage of development of global capitalism did not end well. The international economic order dissolved into the carnage of World War One and could not be reconstituted. The gold standard fell apart, never again to be fully restored. Global consensus on the movement of goods, capital, and people was rejected or seriously questioned as country after country closed its borders to trade, to immigration, to investment.

The classical era's seemingly rock-solid consensus on the primacy of international economic commitments eroded after 1914 and was washed away completely as the crash of 1929 swamped the world economy. Elite proponents of the old order abandoned their support for nineteenth-century internationalism. Fresh business and middle-class interests, for which the world economy was a distant concern where it was not a threat, entered the political scene. And the working classes brought novel pressures on governments to deal with domestic social problems.

It would be absurd to expect perfection from any economic order. Whatever flaws the classical world economy had, it was much better than what had come before. Moreover, whatever the justice of the complaints of contemporary critics, it was much, much better than its replacement, for the thirty years after 1914 saw the most devastating series of economic, political, and social collapses in historical memory. The one undeniable failing of the world economy in the decades before 1914 was that it was incapable of avoiding—indeed may have contributed to—what came after it.

PART II

THINGS FALL APART, 1914–1939

6

"All That Is Solid Melts into Air . . ."

Käthe Kollwitz was one of Germany's great expressionist artists. One of her sons, Peter, was killed on the battlefield in the first weeks of World War One. Kollwitz designed a memorial dedicated to him and the other war dead and had it erected in a German war cemetery in Flanders. The simple sculptures showed two figures, a grieving mother and father modeled on the artist and her husband, surrounded, as Kollwitz said, by the graves of "a flock of lost children." The memorial made a sensational impact on a generation still mourning millions of deaths. But for Kollwitz, despair for Europe's terrible condition deadened the cathartic effect of completing the memorial. As the memorial was put in place in 1932, Kollwitz wrote in her diary of "the unspeakably difficult general situation. The misery. The slide of humanity into the darkness of distress. The repulsive whipping up of political passions." Eventually Kollwitz and her husband saw their personal tragedy repeated, as their grandson, named Peter after his dead uncle, was killed on the eastern front during World War Two. Two weeks before the end of the second war, Kollwitz died; in her last letter, she wrote, "War accompanies me to the end."[1]

"All that is solid melts into air," wrote Karl Marx and Friedrich Engels in the *Communist Manifesto*. They were referring to how capitalist society was constantly remaking itself as its economic bases changed, so that "all fixed, fast frozen relations . . . are swept away." They could not have imagined the extraordinary speed with which previously existing global capitalist relations were swept away after 1914. Military conflicts of unprecedented ferocity tore Europe apart. The steepest economic decline in modern history led to trade and currency wars and financial hostilities. The generally free movement of goods, capital, and people among countries gave way to the aggressive closure of borders and markets. Within countries, sociopolitical calm shattered into bitter conflict.

Market internationalism before 1914 was not all good. Domestic and international stability often rested on political systems that excluded the middle and working classes and on governments that ignored the poor. Only toward the end of the golden age did the working classes gain significant political representation and governments begin to address the concerns of those outside the economic and political elite. Before 1914 the benefits of international economic growth were available only to some of the people some of the time.

But almost everything that came after 1914 was bad, or ended badly, for almost all the people almost all the time. Social conflicts became civil wars, and civil wars gave rise to brutal dictatorships; commercial conflicts became trade wars, and trade wars gave rise to shooting wars. The decades before 1914 should not be idealized, but the horror of the decades after it is hard to exaggerate. In an influential 1939 book the British historian E. H. Carr called the era the twenty years' crisis, which was wrong only by premature enumeration; the crisis lasted thirty years.[2] Those who characterized the interwar period as one of pan-European civil war were also optimistic, as it became a global war before it abated. Countries that had been allies became bitter enemies. Parties and classes that had worked together embarked on murderous crusades against one another. Nations and ethnic groups that had grown closer as the world economy tied them together found unimaginable ways to rid themselves of one another. Polarization at home fed antagonism abroad, and international conflict fed domestic extremism.

The virtuous circle of the late nineteenth and early twentieth centuries saw prosperity strengthen international economic cooperation and peace, both of which reinforced national accord. The consensus in favor of economic globalization and minimal government was held together by the apparent success of both trends. But after 1914 the world staggered around a vicious circle. Global economic collapse caused national crises, and national hardship drove domestic groups to extremes. The resulting economic nationalism, militarism, and war deepened international economic distress. The world spiraled downward, first slowly and then with terrible speed, as attempts to halt the descent failed.

Economic consequences of the Great War

War among the European great powers was no surprise, for geopolitical tensions had been high for several years before 1914. A century of debates has not succeeded in fully explaining the Great War, but there is little doubt that some of its sources were economic. Among the industrialized nations conflicts over their colonial and semicolonial interests grew, from Morocco to China and from the Persian Gulf to the Caribbean. Territorial discord, such as that over Alsace-Lorraine between France and Germany, was often heightened by the real or imagined economic value of the territories. Purely economic conflicts, such as trade disputes, often inflamed nationalistic sentiments, and vice versa. And the strivings for economic and political independence of peoples in central, eastern, and southern Europe threatened the Austro-Hungarian, Russian, and Ottoman empires and made these empires particularly sensitive to any disturbance in the military balance. Once the war began, in any event, the fighting turned out to be bloodier, less conclusive, and more protracted than anyone had anticipated. By the time the war ended late in 1918, its consequences were more important than its causes.

World War One and its immediate aftermath drew the belligerents out of the world economy and toward the war effort and pulled the United States into the resultant vacuum. The American economy had long been the world's largest, but before the war it was barely engaged with the rest of the world. World War One forced all Europe to depend on American capital, markets, and technology and to look to it for political leadership. The United States changed from a passive observer of the slow collapse of the classical order to an active leader of attempts to reconstitute it. "The change since 1914 in the international position of the United States" was, as the *New York Times'* financial editor wrote, "perhaps the most dramatic transformation of economic history."[3]

The first step in this transformation was the introversion of the

European belligerents. All had expected a short, sharp conflict, and as it became clear that hostilities would drag on, economies were reoriented toward the war. In early 1915 the British Navy blockaded Germany's North Sea ports, cutting off virtually all of the country's oceangoing trade, and the Central Powers ceased to play any appreciable role in the world economy. The Allies, on the other hand, remained major global economic actors. However, their prewar position was reversed. Before 1914 the United Kingdom, France, and Belgium were at the center of the classical order, supplying capital and manufactured products to the rest of the world. Now they had no capital or manufactured goods to spare and in fact needed to import both, and their demand for the rest of the world's raw materials soared with the need for food and inputs to make war matériel.

The United States was best positioned to meet the demand for food and armaments. In less than three years of official U.S. neutrality, from August 1914 to April 1917, American exports more than doubled. The country's trade surplus ran at five times prewar levels, accumulating to over $6.4 billion, almost entirely the result of trade with the Allies. American munitions sales abroad, just $40 million in 1914, were $1.3 billion in 1916. Agriculture boomed as Britain turned to North America to replace its traditional European food suppliers.

The Allies paid for their overseas purchases by selling what they could: goods, gold, and eventually foreign investments. This was especially the case for Britain, whose investors had large holdings of American stocks and bonds. As the British need for dollars grew desperate, the government bought two billion dollars of its citizens' American securities—at first on the market, then by requisition—sold them to American investors, and spent the proceeds on supplies. The British used as their purchasing agent and coordinator the firm of J. P. Morgan and Company, which had decades of experience selling American stocks and bonds to Europeans who wanted to invest in the United States. From 1914 to 1917 Morgan's purchases on behalf of its Allied clients averaged a billion dollars a year, one-quarter of all American exports. Morgan purchases exceeded the U.S. government's total annual prewar spending.

The British ran out of things to sell long before they satisfied their war needs. They would have liked to borrow the money, but at the start of the war the American government had decided that loans to the belligerents were inconsistent with neutrality. However, by summer 1915 the Allies' pressing needs along with the profitability of wartime sales led the administration of Woodrow Wilson to change policy. Treasury Secretary William McAdoo explained to Wilson, his father-in-law, that the Allied trade was important: "[T]o maintain our prosperity we must finance it. Otherwise it may stop and that would be disastrous."[4]

Morgan's reversed its traditional financial activities, now convincing Americans to invest in British and European loans. For a year and a half starting in October 1915, Morgan's and associated banks brought to Wall Street some $2.6 billion in bonds for the Allies. This was an enormous sum, double the entire outstanding debt of the U.S. government at the time.

As the belligerents deserted the developing world and even their own colonies in the battle for their homelands, the field was clear for American capital and manufactured exports. The most striking change was in South America, where European interests had been paramount for centuries. Even in the era of gunboat diplomacy, American influence had been limited to the Caribbean Basin. In less than a decade from the start of the war, the United States shot to financial, industrial, and commercial dominance in South America.

Britain's international economic leadership slipped away. The chairman of a British interministerial conference to consider how to reduce dependency on the United States reported glumly in late 1916 that "there was really nothing to deliberate about. . . . American supplies are so necessary to us that reprisals, while they would produce tremendous distress in America, would also practically stop the war." From his position in the Treasury, John Maynard Keynes reported to the British cabinet: "The sums which this country will require to borrow in the United States of America in the next six to nine months are so enormous, amounting to several times the national debt of that country, that it will be necessary to appeal to every class and section of the investing public. . . . It is hardly an exaggeration to say that in a few months' time the American executive and the American public will be in a position to dictate to this country on matters that affect us more dearly than them."[5]

The British had additional worries: that American investors would lose interest in lending to the Allies as the war dragged on, as J. P. Morgan warned its client governments in early 1917. However, American entry into the war in April made further private money unnecessary: The U.S. government made nearly ten billion dollars in government-to-government loans for the joint war effort. These loans eventually caused two controversies: first, accusations that they were meant to rescue the debts American bankers had arranged, symbolizing the willingness and ability of "Merchants of Death" to lead the nation to war for reasons of profit; second, charges and countercharges among Europeans and Americans over moral responsibility for the Great War, and American insistence that the debts be paid in full, in money, when many Europeans believed they had been paid in full, in blood.

The war devastated Europe but made the United States the world's principal industrial, financial, and trading power. American manufacturing production nearly tripled during the war years, from twenty-three billion dollars in 1914 to sixty billion dollars in 1919. In 1913 the European industrial nations combined—Germany, Britain, France, Belgium—produced substantially more than the United States; by the late 1920s the United States was outproducing these countries by nearly half.

From 1914 to 1919 America changed from being the world's biggest debtor to its biggest lender. The European powers were dependent on the United States for financial, commercial, and diplomatic leadership to rebuild from the most destructive war the world had ever known. While most of Europe recovered only haltingly, the United States went from strength to strength: The German and British economies did not get back to their prewar size until 1925, by which point the American economy was half again as big as it had been in 1914. Countries outside Europe, whose economic needs had long been satisfied by the Old World, now looked to the United States instead.

The United States led planning for the peace, including its economic aspects. Many in the United States, especially businessmen who had come to dominate world trade and finance overnight, welcomed the opportunity. As J. P. Morgan's most influential partner, Thomas Lamont, put it in 1915, "When that terrible blood-red fog of war burns away we shall see finance still standing firm. We shall see the spectacle of the business men of all nations paying to one another their just debts. . . . We shall see finance standing ready to develop new enterprises; to find money to till new fields; to help rebuild a broken and wreck-strewn world; to set the fires of industry blazing brightly again and lighting up the earth with the triumphs of peace."[6]

U.S. President Woodrow Wilson largely controlled the Paris Peace Conference's agenda. While the war raged, the Wilson administration listed its famous Fourteen Points, staking out a position known as internationalist in the American context for its emphasis on international diplomatic and economic cooperation. Wilson's third point called for the "removal, so far as possible, of all economic barriers and the establishment of an equality of trade conditions." This was not surprising from the leader of the free-trading Democratic Party, who had spearheaded a large reduction in American tariffs when he took office in 1913. It was associated with more general, and newfound, American sympathy for the free flow of goods and capital. This too was unsurprising given that the United States now dominated international trade and finance and given the prominence in the American delegation of such international-ist representatives of Wall Street as Morgan's Thomas Lamont, Norman Davis, Bernard Baruch, and a young John Foster Dulles.

The Wilsonian position was similar to the classically liberal British view, although its noneconomic components included a stronger insis-tence on self-determination for national groups (so long as they were not "colored"). This appeared to portend a considerable shift in America's role in the world political economy, from a peripheral, protectionist bor-rower with strong antigold leanings to a bulwark of the international economic order. As the United States took over Britain's economic posi-tion, it began to find more appealing the previously suspect British pro-clivities. Free trade, creditor cooperation, and the gold standard all looked much better from the commanding heights of the international economy than they had from its nether or even middling regions. Wilson argued to his countrymen, "We have got to finance the world in some important degree, and those who finance the world must understand it and rule it with their spirits and with their minds."[7]

The United States had an overwhelming influence on the Paris Peace Conference. The settlement followed Wilson's Fourteen Points and his blueprint for a League of Nations. American positions did not prevail everywhere: The United States acquiesced to the demands of its Allied associates on the payment of reparations by Germany. The French and Belgians, especially, insisted on a substantial indemnity to compensate them for the toll the fighting had taken on their territories. Most of the Americans, like many in Europe, thought these demands were exorbi-tant and perhaps uncollectible and would only inflame further conflict. But the French and Belgians insisted that the Germans pay for the loss of wealth and life. Despite these compromises, the overall shape of the postwar world was unmistakably American in design.

But the U.S. Senate repudiated Wilson's views, refused to ratify the Versailles Peace Treaty, and turned down American membership in the League of Nations that was meant to enforce the new world order. Domestic politics in the United States had not evolved as rapidly as its international economic standing. Many in the country believed that it was not in America's interests to be tied to European countries that seemed incapable of governing themselves, or their relations with others, without descending into murderous violence.

"In 1918," E. H. Carr wrote, "world leadership was offered, by almost universal consent, to the United States . . . [and] was declined."[8] Left to their own devices, the European powers did what they could to rebuild their own economies and the infrastructure of international trade, finance, and money. In this effort, they were hampered by the immensity of the problems they faced and by their deep disagreements.

Europe rebuilds

Central and eastern Europe were in the most severe disarray. The war and its aftermath swept away the four multinational empires that had made up the region. In the territory from Finland to Yugoslavia, Austria-Hungary's Hapsburg and Russia's Romanov dynasties shattered into pieces, and eastern Europe suddenly had a dozen new successor states and even a free city. The Ottoman Empire, which before the war had stretched from the Persian Gulf to Libya and from Albania to Yemen, was reduced to Istanbul, its Anatolian hinterland, and an adjacent sliver of Europe. Germany lost its colonies and much of its territory and population.

The successor states started from scratch, the spawn of defeated autocracies. They scrambled to turn former provinces into modern nation-states in the midst of famine and economic collapse. The new governments typically had few ways to pay their bills other than to print money. The result was a wave of inflation that destroyed the value of currencies, disrupted economies, and in extreme cases threatened the social fabric of nations.

The postwar inflations were not the gradual price increases of previous episodes; indeed, they prompted the invention of a new word, *hyperinflation*. By the time their governments stabilized prices, the moneys of Czechoslovakia, Finland, Yugoslavia, and Greece had lost 85 to 95 percent of their former values; those of Bulgaria, Romania, and Estonia between 96 and 99 percent. But these were not the most extreme cases. Hyperinflation in Austria and Hungary increased prices

14,000-fold and 23,000-fold respectively—not 14,000 and 23,000 percent, but to levels 14,000 and 23,000 times as high as at the outset. In Poland and Russia prices rose to 2.5 million and *4 billion* times their beginning levels. And, in the most famous case, when German hyperinflation ended in late 1923, prices were *1 million million* times—that is, 1 trillion times—their immediate postwar level. The German mark, previously valued at 4.2 to the dollar, ended up the experience at 4,200,000,000,000—4.2 trillion—to the dollar. In the final months of the German hyperinflation, the central bank had to print so much currency that it used more than 30 dedicated paper mills, 29 plate manufacturers, and 132 printing plants. On November 2, 1923, the government issued a banknote denominated at 100 trillion marks, worth $312.50. A bit over two weeks later, when the hyperinflation ended on November 20, the bill was worth $23.81.[9]

As inflation spiraled out of control, prices, wages, and currency values could not keep up. This gave rise to frantic attempts to compensate: Getting paid in the afternoon rather than in the morning meant a major pay cut, and holding on to paper money for more than a few hours could cost the holder most of its value. The chaotic instability of the relationship among prices, wages, and currency values led to bizarre misalignments with perverse effects.

In September 1922 Ernest Hemingway got what he called "a new aspect on exchange" when he and his wife took a day trip across the Rhine from the French city of Strasbourg to the German town of Kehl. With German hyperinflation in full swing, the mark's value against other currencies was dropping faster than German prices could rise. Prices on the German side were one-fifth to one-tenth of those in France. With the mark at about 800 to the dollar, Hemingway bought 670 marks:

> That 90 cents lasted Mrs. Hemingway and me for a day of heavy spending and at the end of the day we had 120 marks left!
>
> Our first purchase was from a fruit stand beside the main street of Kehl where an old woman was selling apples, peaches and plums. We picked out five very good-looking apples and gave the old woman a 50 mark note. She gave us back 38 marks in change. A very nice-looking, white-bearded old gentleman saw us buy the apples and raised his hat.
>
> "Pardon me, sir," he said, rather timidly, in German, "how much were the apples?"
>
> I counted the change and told him 12 marks.
>
> He smiled and shook his head. "I can't pay. It is too much."

He went up the street walking very much as white-bearded old gentlemen of the old regime walk in all countries, but he had looked very longingly at the apples. I wish I had offered him some. Twelve marks, on that day, amounted to a little under 2 cents. The old man, whose life's savings were probably, as most of the non-profiteer classes are, invested in German pre-war and war bonds, could not afford a 12 mark expenditure. He is a type of the people whose incomes do not increase with the falling purchasing value of the mark and the krone.[10]

The hyperinflation wiped out the life savings and purchasing power of millions of central and eastern Europeans.

A mix of austere fiscal policies and foreign support ended the inflations and hyperinflations. Governments reduced their need to print money by raising taxes and cutting spending. To regain public confidence, the monetary authorities usually had to prove that they had the backing of the major financial powers. This they did, typically, under the auspices of the League of Nations, in collaboration with the central banks of the leading western powers, and with the backing of private London and New York financiers.[11] Although difficult and socially costly, stabilization had largely been achieved within a few years.

The case of Germany was special in several ways. One was size. Hungary's debilitating hyperinflation did not affect the rest of the world as did the collapse of Germany, the biggest economy in Europe. Moreover, Germany was the principal defeated power (Austria-Hungary and the Ottoman Empire no longer existed, and Bulgaria was hardly a major player). Also, hyperinflation was closely related to reparations. The relationship was controversial: The Germans argued that attempts to squeeze money out of their struggling economy had caused the collapse; the French insisted that the Germans were printing money with abandon because they refused to make the serious efforts necessary to pay. Within Germany there were bitter debates over the appropriate attitude to take to the western powers, some counseling cooperation and others defiance. As the French insistently demanded payment, the German economy collapsed ever further.

Eventually it became clear that brinksmanship was harming all sides, and in late 1923 the German government undertook to get control of the economy. In 1924 the western powers and Germany negotiated the Dawes Plan, which committed two hundred million dollars to help stabilize the mark and regularized reparations payments by appointing an American supervisor. Because the U.S. government had withdrawn from active participation in European matters, the process was handled privately; half the loan was arranged by J. P. Morgan and Company, and the agent-general for reparations was an American Morgan associate.[12] By late 1924 Germany too had beaten back hyperinflation and begun to grow.

The macroeconomic collapses of the early 1920s left an enduring political legacy. The devastations of inflation further discredited traditional political leaders. In many countries politicians and big business seemed oblivious of the suffering hyperinflation and stabilization imposed on erstwhile middle-class allies. The wealthy could protect themselves as the national currency lost its value—by investing in real assets or taking their money abroad, for example—but the middle classes often had no recourse and lost all their savings in the space of months. The disorganization of the early 1920s seemed to demonstrate to the middle classes that prewar elites were unfit to rule. A Berlin small businessman recalled: "The inflation put a miserable end to all my efforts. I couldn't pay my people. My assets had melted away. Once again we experienced hunger and deprivation. . . . [T]he still somewhat prosperous middle class [*Mittelstand*] was destroyed, that middle class which was still an opponent of Marxism." On the basis of this experience, he remembered later, "I fled from a government that permitted such misery," joined the Nazi Party, and became a storm trooper.[13]

The economic failures of the early postwar years contributed to the rise of a New Right, and in the middle 1920s fascist-style movements gained favor, even power, throughout southern and eastern Europe. As Stefan Zweig, an Austrian Jew who left the Continent in 1934, reflected later, "Nothing ever embittered the German people so much—it is important to remember this—nothing made them so furious with hate and so ripe for Hitler as the inflation. For the war, murderous as it was, had yet yielded hours of jubilation, with ringing of bells and fanfares of victory . . . while the inflation served only to make it feel soiled, cheated, and humiliated; a whole generation never forgot or forgave the German Republic for those years and preferred to reinstate its butchers."[14]

The most dramatic collapse of prewar ruling classes was in Russia. Tsarist wartime failure led to a democratic revolution in March 1917, then in November to a seizure of power by the extreme antiwar, Bolshevik faction of the Russian socialist movement. The new government sued for peace and accepted harsh terms from Germany to achieve it, only to be torn by civil war until late 1920. By then, much to the surprise and chagrin of the West, the Bolsheviks were fully in control of the world's largest country.

Bolshevik leader V. I. Lenin was not alone in thinking that the Russian Revolution would be the beginning of a wave of radical revolts against European capitalism. In the year or so after the war ended, insurrections in Berlin and Bavaria, a Communist seizure of power in Hungary, and massive factory occupations in Italy all seemed part of a broader trend toward a workers' revolution. The mainstream of most Socialist parties faced real problems as it tried to resist the new Bolshevik-inspired factions. Most socialists had supported national war efforts, and this association with an unpopular war now tarnished their image. The socialists' electoral successes were also a mixed blessing, as they became implicated in ineffectual caretaker governments. Insurrectionary wings of every Socialist party ridiculed their attachment to national patriotism and the belief that the ballot box could change society. Eventually a new Communist International based in Moscow brought together the world's radical Socialist parties.

The early revolutionary optimism soon faded, leaving Lenin and his colleagues to run a shattered country that even in better days had not appeared to be promising soil for socialism. The new Soviet Union faced reconstruction from war, revolution, and civil war; it was hard to imagine building a new socialist society in a country which by 1920 had lost seven-eighths of its 1913 industrial capacity.[15] During the first postwar years the Soviets concentrated on bringing the economy back to life. The 1921 New Economic Policy permitted substantial private enterprise, especially in small business and farming, and encouraged the peasants to enrich themselves as best they could. By 1924, as elsewhere in the east, the economy had revived. The Soviet Union remained insular—in part by choice, in part because of the hostility of the capitalist nations that surrounded it—but gradually rebuilt economic ties with the rest of the world.

The western Allies faced fewer postwar difficulties than eastern and central Europe. Even in Belgium and northern France, where the destruction was most severe, normal economic activity quickly resumed. There was a rapid expansion of the western economies in 1919 and into 1920, followed by a sharp recession in 1920 and 1921, but by 1922 business conditions were returning to normality.

The Europeans attempted to reestablish normal international monetary conditions by restoring the gold standard, the centerpiece of the classical economic order. Two European monetary conferences, at Brussels in 1920 and Genoa in 1922, gave resounding support to this objective, but even countries that had not undergone massive inflation found its achievement difficult. In Great Britain prices had risen enough during and after the war that the attempt to go back to the 1913 exchange rate against gold required very restrictive monetary policies to cut wages, profits, and prices. Even then, when sterling returned to gold in 1925 at the prewar rate, much of British industry found itself priced out of world markets. Largely as a result, British unemployment stayed above 10 percent through the 1920s. The Scandinavian countries stabilized soon after Britain. Their close trade ties to the British market, and British-like overvaluations, also saddled them with double-digit unemployment for the entire decade: Norway's attempt to return to gold helped push its unemployment rate over 25 percent in 1927. Belgium and France went back onto gold soon after Britain, but unlike Britain, they did not attempt to restore their currencies' prewar values. This allowed them to go back to gold at relatively low cost and without imposing major competitive pressures on their industrial producers.

International trade also faced difficulties. Many governments that had imposed barriers to international trade and investment during the war found it difficult to remove trade protection after it. Even the British retained some of the trade barriers adopted in wartime. In the United States the trade liberalization enacted by Wilson and the Democrats in 1913 was reversed, and the Republican administration and Congress in 1921 and 1922 restored traditional protectionism. And most of the new nations in central and eastern Europe were more protectionist than the empires that had preceded them.

Despite difficulties and disappointments, by 1924 Europe had essentially recovered. European industrial production returned to its 1913 levels, although considerable differences existed within Europe. In the west industry produced 12 percent above 1913 levels, while central and eastern European industries lagged at over 20 percent below 1913 levels. The United States was far ahead, with manufacturing output nearly half again as large as in 1913.[16] In spite of the devastation of World War One, most countries' economies had returned to or near their prewar levels.

The twenties roar

An orgy of outward-looking international economic activity erupted. Between 1925 and 1929 the world's industrial production grew by more than one-fifth, even faster in Europe and North America. International investment reached levels reminiscent of its glory years in the early twentieth century, although now it came mostly from the United States rather than from Europe. Exports swelled to double pre–World War One levels; even when one accounts for inflation, world trade was 42 percent greater in 1929 than in 1913 and was a larger share of national economies.[17] The gold standard was back in place. The world economy appeared to be restored.

The economic expansion encouraged major social changes. In most of the industrial world the 1920s saw the rise of new mass production and mass consumption goods. Politically, virtually all democratic countries introduced female suffrage amid broader movements for the emancipation of women; the influence of labor movements and Socialist parties dramatically increased. Modernist and surrealist cultural movements revolutionized the arts, and jazz burst onto the international musical scene. The boom of the late 1920s was so pronounced, and its effects so broad and deep, that many countries gave it proper names: the Weimar Renaissance in Germany, the Baldwin Age in Britain, the Roaring Twenties and the Jazz Age in North America, the Dance of the Millions in Latin America.[18]

To some extent this growth involved catching up after wartime conditions. But it also had a powerful dynamic of its own, and its centerpiece was the United States. American capital and markets fueled economic growth from Europe to Asia and Latin America. American banks and corporations flooded the world with money and technology. Wall Street took over from London as the world's international financial center, while American corporations set up thousands of branch plants around the world. By 1929 the United States had accumulated over fifteen billion dollars in foreign investments, about half in loans and half in the direct investments of multinational corporations, and this did not include the many billions of dollars owed by foreigners to the U.S. government. The country had, in a little more than a decade, put together an international investment portfolio almost as large as that of the United Kingdom in 1913, which had been assembled over the course of more than a century. In the words of Secretary of State John Hay, "the financial center of the world, which required thousands of years to journey from the Euphrates to the Thames and Seine, seems passing to the Hudson between daybreak and dark."[19]

More than $1 billion a year in loans surged out of New York from 1919 to 1929. In peak years there were nearly one-third as many foreign bonds floated on Wall Street as bonds of American corporations.[20] From 1924 to 1928 Americans lent an average of $500 million a year to Europe, another $300 million a year to Latin America, another $200 million to Canada, another $100 million to Asia. Americans seemed to have an inexhaustible interest in financing ventures in lands few had heard of a decade before; 36 American investment banks fought over the privilege of floating the bonds of the city of Budapest, 14 competed over Belgrade, and a village in Bavaria looking for $125,000 found itself convinced to borrow $3 million.[21]

The United States accounted for more than half the new loans, but it was not alone in this recovery of international finance. Especially after returning to gold, the London markets reopened, as did lending from Paris, Amsterdam, and other smaller European creditor capitals. Britain took up about a quarter of the new loans of the 1920s, other European countries another quarter.[22] After ten years of domestic preoccupations and restrictions on international business, neither borrowers nor lenders seemed able to get enough of the revival of world capital markets.

American industrialists also searched the world for profitable investment opportunities—not loans but "direct" investments in branch plants and other subsidiaries. American firms invested more than five billion dollars over the 1920s, by the end of which American corporations were well established in every major economy, and many minor ones as well. Even American commercial banks, which before the Federal Reserve Act of 1913 had largely been prohibited from operating overseas, got into the act and by the late 1920s had nearly two hundred branches abroad.

The boom of the 1920s was even more pronounced outside Europe. In Latin America, American loans and American direct investment were associated with the region's most rapid growth in memory. Latin America grew more than half again faster than western Europe and North America in the 1920s.[23] In the process, its industrial structure matured substantially; by 1929, for example, Brazil produced three-quarters of the steel it needed.[24] Around the region, economies modernized, enlarged working and middle classes became politically prominent, and democratic regimes stabilized.

America in isolation

These years of recovery and boom were reminiscent of the golden age before World War One, but with the United States replacing the United Kingdom at its center. In the earlier era London financed economic activity all over the world, largely by loans but also by private corporate investment. Debtor countries earned the money they needed to pay interest and principal by exporting to Europe, especially to the large and open British market. And the system was held together by a commitment to a common monetary standard, gold. By 1925 a comparable system was in place, as capital flowed from the United States to the rest of the world, the rest of the world sold heavily into the American market, and almost all major currencies were back on gold.

However, the second incarnation of this order brings to mind Marx's observation that while history may repeat itself, it is "the first time as tragedy, the second as farce." For while the economic cornerstones of the two eras were similar—the world's access to the capital and markets of the United Kingdom and the United States respectively—the behavior of the center countries diverged fundamentally.

The classical gold standard before 1914 was centered on London and held together by the United Kingdom.[25] Great Britain's overwhelming commercial and financial influence, combined with its business and political elite's unshakable commitment to the world economy, allowed the British government to act as decisively as necessary to stabilize international monetary and financial relations.

While the United Kingdom was, in John Maynard Keynes's words, "the conductor of the international orchestra," it could not have sustained the gold standard without the other players.[26] The stability of the classical gold standard relied on strong support from France and Germany and smaller European nations. For example, when the 1890 collapse of Barings, a major British bank, threatened to destabilize the London markets, the central banks of France and Russia lent to the Bank of England; the mere knowledge that these large sums were available helped calm investors. In 1898 the British and French helped stabilize German financial markets; a few years later the Austrians in their turn helped calm the Berlin market. At least seven more times between 1900 and 1914 the French stepped in to assist the British in a display of what the Bank of France called "the solidarity of financial centers."[27]

Neither British leadership nor European cooperation was altruistic. The leaders of British business depended for their incomes upon the smooth functioning of the world economy. The British economy, and its principal firms and investors, relied on foreign investments, foreign trade, and international finance. Moreover, France, Germany, Belgium, the Netherlands, Austria, and Russia were tightly integrated into the London-centered monetary and financial order; instability at the center would be transmitted outward, challenging the bases of support of the political and economic leaders of other countries in the system. The wealth and power of the captains of European finance and industry depended on the London-based system of international trade and payments. It was in every powerful group's interests to maintain this balance.[28]

But if before 1914 enlightened self-interest provided the gold standard with both a reliable conductor and a harmonious orchestra, neither could be taken for granted after 1920. The orchestra's disarray was most obvious: Whatever common economic concerns the continental Europeans might have, they were no match for the economic continuation of the trench warfare of World War One. The armistice had only ushered in another stage in Franco-German conflict, as the French, Belgians, and Germans fought pitched battles over reparations. The French had no intention of bailing out a country that most Frenchmen believed had not yet paid for its military aggression, and no German politician could be seen as pandering to the international bankers and their accessories in what most Germans believed was a criminally unfair peace treaty. Almost every country in Europe took one side or the other. Even technical monetary and financial issues were drawn into the bitter diplomatic conflict.

The absence of a reliable conductor of Keynes's golden orchestra constituted the most serious gap in the interwar political economy. The similarity between the international economic role of pre-1914 Britain and post-1920 America was as striking as the difference between their international political roles. The United Kingdom and the United States were the principal industrial, financial, trading, and investing nations of the respective eras. As the years after World War Two were to demonstrate, there was only a short step from American economic hegemony to American political leadership in international economic matters. Yet from 1920 until the eve of World War Two the United States refused to get involved.

American capital and markets dominated the world economy in the 1920s as much as their British counterparts had before 1913, but the U.S. government was almost wholly absent whereas that of Britain had been ever present. Even if it had wanted to be engaged—and it did not—the U.S. administration was prohibited by Congress from official involvement in international discussions of economic (and most other) issues. The Federal Reserve Bank of New York, which was close to the international bankers on Wall Street, made a concerted effort to participate in global economic affairs, but it did so surreptitiously. Indeed, the American representatives to international monetary meetings were usually private bankers from J. P. Morgan and Company. American trade policy was resolutely protectionist, even though it was well understood that this kept the country's overseas debtors from earning dollars needed to service their loans. Even the country's commitment to gold was suspect, for a new wave of antigold populism swept the American farm belt as agricultural prices dropped by one-third.

American isolationism was government policy from March 1920, when the U.S. Senate turned down Woodrow Wilson's peace plans and U.S. membership in the League of Nations. It was confirmed and deepened in November, when national elections gave the Republicans control of the presidency and the Congress. Although some Republicans supported the League, the Republican administrations and Congresses that governed the country until 1933 were led by men who viewed American involvement in the affairs of Europe with suspicion or disdain. This view extended to virtually all aspects of international economic diplomacy and colored every global economic issue until the early 1930s.

American policy was at the core of reparations, the central postwar financial issue. The attempts of Germany's moderate Weimar governments to maintain their international commitments were unpopular with a bitter German public, and many Europeans began to regard the harsh payments schedule as counterproductive. But the European Allies still owed the United States government ten billion dollars, and the French and Belgians saw reparations as a necessary evil so long as the U.S. government continued to insist on being repaid. There was an easy way out of the logjam: forgive the war debts. "Those debts," as J. P.

Morgan put it, "should be cancelled."[29] In return the Allies could reduce their reparations demands. This would have attenuated economic pressure on Germany, which fed into political tension, which exacerbated nationalist and revanchist sentiment, which impeded joint international economic action.

But a succession of American Congresses and presidents categorically refused renegotiation of war debts. While many in Europe regarded the war debts as having been paid in full with the blood of millions of young men, most Americans regarded the debts as debts, pure and simple. In the words of Calvin Coolidge, "They hired the money." So long as the Americans insisted on being paid, the French and Belgians insisted on reparations.

If the United States would not lessen the burden of war debts and reparations, it might at least have made it easier for the Europeans to earn the money needed to meet their obligations. The American market, the world's largest, was in fact opened substantially by new trade legislation in 1913. But when the high-tariff Republicans returned to office, they raised trade barriers back to and above their earlier levels. The congressional response to economic difficulties in Europe was in fact further protection—in 1921, in 1922, and in 1930, with the extreme Smoot-Hawley Tariff. American investors resisted American protection, as trade barriers made it hard for the countries that owed them money to earn dollars. "Having become a creditor nation," pleaded New York banker Otto Kahn to his countrymen, "we have got now to fit ourselves into the role of a creditor nation. We shall have to make up our minds to be more hospitable to imports."[30] The pleas of the free traders went unheeded, for the interests of America's lenders and America's protected industries were diametrically opposed. One wanted foreigners to have easy access to the American market so that they could service their debts; the others wanted the American market as closed as possible to foreign competition.

The irony of America's inconsistent international position—financial leadership and political indifference or hostility—was not lost on the American public. Franklin D. Roosevelt made much of the contradictions of Republican international economic policy in the 1932 presidential race, comparing it with the fantasy world of *Alice in Wonderland*:

A puzzled, somewhat skeptical Alice asked the Republican leadership some simple questions:

"Will not the printing and selling of more stocks and bonds, the building of new plants and the increase of efficiency produce more goods than we can buy?"

"No," shouted Humpty Dumpty. "The more we produce the more we can buy."

"What if we produce a surplus?"

"Oh, we can sell it to foreign consumers."

"How can the foreigners pay for it?"

"Why, we will lend them the money."

"I see," said little Alice, "they will buy our surplus with our money. Of course these foreigners will pay us back by selling us their goods?"

"Oh, not at all," said Humpty Dumpty. "We set up a high wall called the tariff."

"And," said Alice at last, "how will the foreigners pay off these loans?"

"That is easy," said Humpty Dumpty. "did you ever hear of a moratorium?"

And so, at last, my friends, we have reached the heart of the magic formula of 1928.[31]

Even technical consultations between American policy makers and foreigners were impeded by the isolationist Congress and executive. A conference of central bankers to discuss the European situation, proposed in 1921 by the Federal Reserve and the Bank of England, was vetoed. Even when much of the initiative came from the United States, as with the Dawes and Young plans of 1924 and 1930, official American participation was impossible; J. P. Morgan and other New York financiers were the American counterparts to the finance ministries and central banks of Europe. The contrast with British leadership of the pre-1914 Pax Britannica was striking.

Other functions that the governments of the pre-1914 economic leaders had carried out were "privatized" because of America's official isolationism. For example, during the golden age of international lending before World War One, committees of creditors—private bondholders and governments together—had typically overseen the finances of indebted countries in economic trouble. With the United States unwilling to participate, the role of creditor oversight fell to private citizens, most prominent among them Edwin Kemmerer, the "international money doctor." Kemmerer, a Princeton economist whose first job had been as a financial adviser to America's Philippine colony, advised many poor governments on how best to structure their economies so as to attract American capital. His private involvement spanned a twenty-year period, over which he worked for Mexico, Guatemala, Colombia, Ecuador, Peru, Bolivia, Chile, Germany, Poland, Turkey, China, and South Africa. His recommendations—invariably for balanced budgets and the gold standard—carried great weight with American lenders, so governments tried to follow them. As Kemmerer wrote, "a country that appoints American financial advisers and follows their advice in reorganizing its finances, along what American investors consider to be the most successful modern lines, increases its chances of appealing to the American investor and of obtaining from him capital on favorable terms."[32]

Many Americans supported American involvement. What was known as internationalism was especially strong in regions, and sections of the population, with important foreign economic interests. First and foremost were the banks and corporations whose overseas investments and sales had grown rapidly after 1914. Many farmers who produced for export sympathized with government support for the reconstruction of overseas markets and were historical free traders. Variants of Wilsonian internationalism continued to be the official Democratic Party position, and there was a strong internationalist faction among Republicans, especially big-business Republicans from New York and other financial centers.

But economic and political isolationists dominated the American political system. Some isolationists were right-wing chauvinists; others were left-wing anti-imperialists. Some objected to overseas involvement on moral grounds, others out of pragmatism. The traditional American clash of cultures between an Anglophilic elite and patriotic masses played a part. But from an economic standpoint, the overriding source of America's schizophrenic international position was the uneven nature of the country's overseas involvement. The classical British economy had been heavily directed outward, toward foreign markets, foreign suppliers, and foreign investment. In the United States, however, international economic exposure varied tremendously. Wall Street was deeply engaged, as were many farmers and some of the country's leading industries. But the bulk of American industry continued to look inward and remained insular and protectionist. For the internationally oriented industries—machinery, motor vehicles, rubber, petroleum—overseas investments were ten to twenty times as important as they were for the rest of the manufacturing sector.[33] A powerful and dynamic segment of the American economy was heavily involved in the world economy—indeed was leading the world economy—but the bulk of the country's economic leaders remained hostile or indifferent to conditions abroad. America had no British-style consensus for international involvement or leadership.

A world restored?

The American absence was a major weakness of the postwar world economy. But astute observers noted other, less obvious causes for concern. Keynes identified how the interwar international and domestic political economies had changed from the Victorian ideals to which most governments aspired.

Keynes was himself a creature of the late Victorian age.[34] His father was a star pupil of Alfred Marshall, the preeminent British economist of the late nineteenth and early twentieth centuries. John Neville Keynes followed in Marshall's footsteps as a Cambridge don, although to Marshall's disappointment he did not become a professional economist; eventually he became the principal administrative officer of Cambridge University. Keynes's mother was a social reformer who served as the first woman mayor of Cambridge. Their son was true to both the academic and political strains in his family.

John Maynard Keynes was born in Cambridge in 1883. After a brilliant career at Eton, he returned to Cambridge as an undergraduate in 1902. He distinguished himself in mathematics, and his work in economics (only then beginning to be treated as a separate subject) attracted the attention of Marshall, who knew him through his father. But although Keynes much admired "my old master who made me into an economist,"[35] the young man's first love was philosophy, and members of his circle spent much of their time in heated debates over philosophical issues. As Keynes's authoritative biographer, Robert Skidelsky, has noted, in Keynes's cohort "Radicalism at Cambridge" revolved around "Sodomy and Atheism," and Keynes threw himself enthusiastically into both.[36] After several years of scholarship and homosexual affairs, Keynes graduated and, after considering an academic career, joined the civil service in the India Office.

Keynes had an abiding interest in politics but little respect for politicians. From an early age he thought the Victorian infatuation with monarchy laughable. As a teenager Keynes wrote sardonically, upon getting a view of Queen Victoria herself, that "doubtless owing to the coldness of the day, her nose was unfortunately red"; upon seeing Kaiser Wilhelm, he remarked that "his moustache was quite up to my expectations."[37] Keynes's attitude toward elected politicians was also dismissive, especially when (as was common) he thought them intellectually inadequate. He preferred to affect policy from the outside, as a provider and supporter of good ideas—and a critic of bad ones.

Keynes's first stint in government lasted only two years. He was very successful at the India Office, but in 1908 Marshall retired and nominated Keynes for a position in economics at Cambridge. Keynes accepted and spent the rest of his life as a Cambridge economist. Out of his India experience, however, he developed his first book, *Indian Currency and Finance*. Published in 1913, while Keynes sat on a royal commission on the subject, the book was very well received and helped establish him as a leading economic expert. His principal point was that India's modification of the gold standard—what he called a gold exchange standard—was actually an improvement, allowing for "scientific management" of monetary conditions. The Indian system was less rigid than the textbook gold standard and gave the government a desirable flexibility to respond to local conditions. The book's economic ideas were traditional but demonstrated that Keynes was looking for ways out of the monetary straitjacket of gold standard orthodoxy.

On trade policy, Keynes's views were strictly liberal and "Liberal," in the party politics of the day. He stated the case for free trade, and against the protectionist movement for tariff reform, in an argument to the Cambridge Union in 1910: "The Tariff Reform case rests on the principle of making things relatively scarce. To those who are concerned with making these things, this is no doubt advantageous. But it causes an amount of distress more than equivalent elsewhere. The community as a whole cannot hope to gain by making artificially scarce what the country wants."[38]

Keynes was also a central figure in Britain's most important cultural coterie. The Bloomsbury Group had coalesced around writers, philosophers, artists, and others, many of them friends of Keynes from Cambridge days. Among its members were Leonard and Virginia Woolf, Clive and Vanessa Bell, Lytton Strachey, and E. M. Forster. The Cambridge economist helped bankroll the group's collective activities, and he leased the houses in which many of them lived and gathered for meals and discussions. Keynes's involvement with Bloomsbury was in keeping with his modernist rejection of Victorian morals and beliefs; the homosexuality of his Cambridge set was connected to an intense focus on beauty and friendship in contradistinction to traditional emphases on duty and religion. And while Keynes's professional activities were far closer to the mainstream than those of his fellow Bloomsberries, to use their own name for themselves, he fitted in well as a cultured sophisticate and a powerful, philosophically insightful intellect.

World War One drew Keynes back toward government, where he soon became the Treasury's principal financial expert. Although he came to oppose the war and applied for conscientious objector status (gratuitously, as he must have known, given his government service), Keynes took enthusiastically to the task of finding a way of financing the war effort without bankrupting the government. As the war dragged on, he became more disheartened. "I work," he told a friend, "for a government I despise for ends I think criminal."[39] His work for the government caused friction with other Bloomsberries, who could not fathom how he separated his antiwar views from his exertions on behalf of war finance. But Keynes found the financial problems intellectually engaging and believed that despite his misgivings—his conscientious objection was more over mandatory conscription than the war itself—Britain deserved victory.

Keynes was the chief Treasury representative on the British delegation to the Paris Peace Conference that designed the postwar settlement. Once more Keynes was sickened by political realities, especially by the European Allies' insistence on exorbitant reparations. President Wilson had told the British, "[H]ow can your experts or ours be expected to work out a *new* plan to furnish working capital to Germany when we deliberately start out by taking away all Germany's *present* capital?" Keynes disliked the preacherly Wilson, but he admitted the "substantial truth in the President's standpoint."[40]

Keynes regarded the conditions imposed on Germany as "wickedness and folly." In May 1919, as the proceedings wound down, he wrote a friend:

> Certainly if I were in the Germans' place I'd die rather than sign such a Peace. . . . But if they do sign, that will really be the worst thing that could happen, as they can't possibly keep some of the terms, and general disorder and unrest will result everywhere. Meanwhile there is no food or employment anywhere, and the French and Italians are pouring munitions into Central Europe to arm everyone against everyone else. I sit in my room hour after hour receiving deputations from the new nations, who all ask not for food or raw materials, but primarily for instruments of murder against their neighbors. And with such a Peace as the basis I see no

hope anywhere. Anarchy and Revolution [*sic*] is the best thing that can happen, and the sooner the better.[41]

At the beginning of June 1919 Keynes left the British delegation and government in disgust; three weeks later the former belligerents signed the Treaty of Versailles. Keynes returned to England and in less than five months drafted a searing indictment of the settlement. *The Economic Consequences of the Peace* was part chronicle, part explanation, part polemic, but most of all, it was a damning denunciation of politicians whom Keynes portrayed as shortsighted, grasping, and dishonest. The demands on Germany were immoral and impossible; insistence on the terms of the treaty would only bring disaster. Should they stand, "vengeance, I dare predict, will not limp. Nothing can then delay for long that final civil war between the forces of reaction and the despairing convulsions of revolution, before which the horrors of the late German war will fade into nothing, and which will destroy, whoever is victor, the civilization and the progress of our generation."[42]

The book was an international phenomenon. Keynes's economic analysis was acclaimed, his political acumen celebrated, his style admired. Within six months the book's English edition had sold a hundred thousand copies, and within a year it was out in twelve languages— remarkable for a work that included complex analysis of an intricate international agreement. Keynes was now a global political figure and the world's best-known economist. And he had shown how this particular attempt to restore the pre-1914 world order had failed.

Keynes's emergence as a powerful critic of the great powers redeemed him with his Bloomsbury friends, but he soon taxed their understanding by marrying Lydia Lopokova, a renowned ballerina from St. Petersburg. Keynes's new lifestyle astonished most of his friends and angered some of them. But he remained happily married to Lopokova until his death.

Over the course of the 1920s Keynes developed his analysis of the changing postwar political economy. His previous economic views had been as traditional as his lifestyle was unorthodox; as his lifestyle became more traditional, his economics became more heterodox. Keynes played a central role in Britain's principal economic policy debate of the 1920s, over whether and how the country should return to the gold standard. The government had taken the pound sterling off gold when the war started, and prices had risen 150 percent. There had been substantial price declines after the war, and many in the financial and investing communities wanted a return to gold as soon as possible, at the pre–World War One exchange rate ("parity") of $4.86 per pound sterling. This would have required further deflation, but supporters argued that it would be relatively simple to force wages and prices down, as had so often been done under the classical gold standard.

But Keynes, like some other economists, noted that wages and prices had become less flexible. The economy was simply not adjusting as it had before 1914. It had become exceedingly dangerous "to apply the principles of an economics, which was worked out on the hypothesis of *laissez-faire* and free competition, to a society which is rapidly abandoning these hypotheses."[43] The principal problem was the rigidity of prices and especially wages, which no longer declined as needed to keep business conditions and employment stable. Keynes told a group of London bankers, "The business of forcing down certain levels of wages . . . into equilibrium is almost hopeless, or it will take a long time."[44]

The modern world had evolved toward a more organized capitalism, one with substantial wage and price rigidities. The industrial countries' political economies were not what they had been in the golden age. The simpler industrial economies that prevailed before World War One had been heavily populated by independent farmers, small businesses, and individual workers. Small firms and disorganized workers had approximated the textbook examples of market economies: They reacted to conditions as price takers, receiving whatever prices or wages the market dictated. But the industrial economies had changed. Large corporations had accumulated enough market power to exercise some control over their prices. Labor unions had become more common, so that workers too could affect wages. Even where unions were weak or absent, the increasing complexity of industrial production put a premium on a reliable, skilled workforce that could not simply be fired and rehired at will. There were important industries in which firms and unions were more like price makers, determining—within constraints, of course—prices and wages.

The greater organization of many product and labor markets meant that prices and wages might not decline as needed to sustain or restore balance in the economy—or to allow the pound sterling to be linked to gold at its 1914 exchange rate. Large corporations could decide that profits would be maximized by selling fewer cars at a higher price, rather than let prices be driven down. Workers organized into unions could resist wage cutting. Firms in many industries were reluctant to fire high-quality well-trained workers that they might not be able to rehire later. Prices and wages did react to supply and demand, but in many portions of the industrial economies the reaction could be slow and partial.[45]

In December 1923, as the debate on gold raged, Keynes published *A Tract on Monetary Reform*. He argued that governments should act to stabilize wages and prices, rather than passively wait for them to adjust. In one of his most famous passages, he ridiculed the orthodox argument that short-run adjustment problems should be ignored in order to allow the market mechanism and the gold standard to restore normal conditions in the long run: "[T]his *long run* is a misleading guide to current affairs. *In the long run* we are all dead. Economists set themselves too easy, too useless a task if in tempestuous seasons they can only tell us that when the storm is long past the ocean is flat again."[46]

Keynes powerfully opposed the attempt to put sterling back on gold at its 1914 exchange rate. After the Conservatives took over in late 1924, it fell to their chancellor of the exchequer, Winston Churchill, to decide. In the public press, before parliamentary committees, and in private letters, Keynes argued that the policies necessary to return the pound to its prewar parity "would probably prove socially and politically impossible."[47] He railed against those who argued for pushing down the wages of such workers as coal miners in order to speed adjustment: "Like other victims of economic transition in past times, the miners are to be offered a choice between starvation and submission, the fruits of their submission to accrue to the benefit of other classes. But in view of the disappearance of an effective mobility of labor and of a competitive wage level between different industries, I am not sure that they are not worse placed in some ways than their grandfathers were. . . . *They* (and others to follow) are the 'moderate sacrifice' still necessary to ensure the stability of the gold standard."[48]

He lost the battle but won the war. Churchill decided for gold, and in April 1925 the pound was restored to its prewar parity. The result was stagnation and high unemployment in the United Kingdom until the Great Depression made matters even worse. In the meantime Keynes echoed his earlier public denunciation of bad public policy with a pamphlet entitled *The Economic Consequences of Mr. Churchill*, in which he explained the dire implications of the measures adopted.

Keynes eventually attacked the gold standard itself, the very core of the classical worldview. He labeled the gold standard a "barbarous relic" and called for an active monetary policy to keep employment and the economy stable. Keynes refined his argument through the rest of the 1920s, culminating with the 1930 publication of *A Treatise on Money*. He was alarmed, he told a director of the Bank of England, "at seeing you and others in authority attacking the problems of the changed postwar world with . . . unmodified pre-war views and ideas. To close the mind to the idea of revolutionary improvements in the control of money and credit is to sow the seeds of the downfall of individualistic capitalism. Do not be the Louis XVI of the monetary revolution."[49]

But gold had a magnetic pull on national political economies. Gold represented the stability and prosperity of the pre-1914 world economy. All that going off gold would do, went the standard line, would be to allow governments to debase currencies with no real impact on the economy. Pragmatic concerns also motivated the supporters of gold. Financial institutions, and the "creditor classes" in general, held assets denominated in gold-backed currencies. A devaluation meant a corresponding decline in the value of stocks or bonds issued in that currency. To reduce the gold value of, say, the pound sterling was to reduce the value of investments in sterling stocks, bonds, and other financial instruments. Hard-money supporters of the gold standard regarded a government commitment to gold as tantamount to a government promise to secure the value of their property. Gold protected investors, and gold guarded against inflation; devaluation was expropriation. Keynes's arguments had little power in the battle with such entrenched interests. It took a decade, and a depression, to give widespread credence to Keynes's objections to orthodoxy.

Into the void

America's isolationism left the world economy without the political engagement of its leading member. Great power rivalry blocked cooperation on the international monetary, financial, and commercial front. The evolution of modern industry reduced the efficacy of prevailing economic policies. The very centerpiece of the attempt to restore global economic integration, the gold standard, was flawed.

But American money kept flowing to Europe, Asia, and Latin America, in spite of America's official absence. So long as the rest of the world could tap American capital and American markets, the world economy kept growing. The institutional and other infrastructure that had helped stabilize the world economy before 1914 was gone, but the world made do without it. An apparently endless stream of dollars seemed a reasonable substitute. There was, in any event, little alternative.

7

The World of Tomorrow

Flushing, Queens, was a marshy wasteland used for garbage dumps, when it was used at all. But on April 30, 1939, after years of planning and construction, Franklin D. Roosevelt opened the New York World's Fair there. The fair's "World of Tomorrow" was a spectacular exhibition of scientific and industrial advancement. "We seem to be moving steadily," one observer wrote, "toward a splendid future. Here are many of the creative things that humanity has done. Here are evidences of what humanity wants to be and do."[1]

Sixty nations had pavilions at the New York fair, but the corporate exhibits made the biggest splash. The fair displayed technological wonders, products, and processes that boggled the minds of the more than fifty million people who visited it in the summers of 1939 and 1940. At the center were the fair's two symbols, the gleaming white Trylon and the Perisphere. The former was a needle seven hundred feet tall; the latter was a globe from the inside of which visitors could see a display of an imagined democratic and properous future.

No imagination was needed to see the remarkable things on exhibit in Flushing. At the entrance to the RCA building was a specially manufactured version of one of RCA's new home televisions. Because many viewers thought the new machine involved trickery, RCA made the display out of Du Pont's brand-new transparent Lucite so that all its internal workings were visible. The "Phantom Teleceiver" was only one of a host of television-related exhibits. One showed how a living room could be remodeled to include televisions along with the then common radios and record players, as well as such other new devices as a household sound movie projector and a fax machine. The *New York Sun's* correspondent reported on the experience: "Television—radio with pictures. Here are the machines. Beautiful cabinets, too, and there's the screen up in back there, just like a motion picture show. The camera's ready in New York and the sending antennas are all set. Turn the switch and here we are in Flushing and seeing a bus on Fifth Avenue! A miracle of the future already operating in the present."[2]

New uses of electricity were on display. Albert Einstein ceremonially flipped the switch for the fairground's night lighting, the first use of fluorescent streetlights. Westinghouse demonstrated the Nimatron, an "electrical brain" (early computer), an electric eye, a sterilizing ultraviolet lamp, and a robot named Elektro and his dog, Sparko. The pavilion highlighted a "Battle of the Centuries" between two methods of dishwashing, Mrs. Drudge by hand and Mrs. Modern by electric dishwasher. Not surprisingly—it was the Westinghouse exhibit, after all—the dishwasher always won. General Electric featured an earsplitting demonstration of artificially produced lightning and thunder.

The General Motors pavilion included the fair's most popular attraction, the Futurama, which took visitors on a tour of the United States of 1960. The exhibit, called "Highways and Horizons," emphasized how a national highway system (still only a dream) would transform the country. The *Sun* reporter told of the visit as one walked toward the Futurama:

> You step onto a moving floor . . . and you take a seat. . . . The chairs slide onward and presently the first vista of the futurama unfolds itself as it might be seen from a low-flying plane, speeding up a beautiful valley. Miniature towns and cities lie there, set forth in marvelous detail. . . . And everywhere there is the constant never-ending flow of automobile traffic. There are 50,000 small-scale cars in view at various times and 10,000 of them are in actual operation. They speed at fifty miles an hour and more on special lanes for fast traffic. They stop under control towers and wing over bridges of several decks. . . . Streamlined trains, daring in design, slide into tunnels under high mountains and emerge to climb through the snowy peaks. Great transport planes lie in the airports while automobiles speed between railroads and airfields.[3]

General Motors' new world, with cloverleafs that allowed traffic to flow with no stop signs and no traffic lights, had the *New Yorker*'s E. B. White dreaming of "the life which rests on wheels alone . . . going a hundred miles an hour around impossible turns ever onward toward the certified cities of the flawless future."[4] As they left the General Motors pavilion, visitors were given buttons that read "I have seen the future."

The exposition could not escape the military and economic realities of 1939. Germany did not send an exhibition, and the Soviet pavilion did not reopen for the 1940 season. The pavilions of Czechoslovakia, Lithuania, and Poland remained open even after their homelands had been overrun by invading armies. Meanwhile admissions and sales were affected by the still-depressed economic conditions, and the fair went bankrupt and was put under new management in its second year. It closed after its scheduled two-summer run a financial failure.

But the New York World's Fair of 1939–1940 succeeded grandly in showcasing the new technologies of the era. The future would feature innovative new products and processes, developed and manufactured by enormous corporate entities. An array of new goods—the automobile, the radio, the motion picture, the airplane, the refrigerator—transformed everyday life, as they did modern economies.

In every leading economy except Germany's, labor productivity grew more rapidly from 1913 to 1950 than it had in the forty years before World War One. Despite world wars and economic crises, the productivity of the industrial countries of western Europe, North America, and Oceania more than doubled.[5] Important new products and industries were developed, and the organization and management of the modern corporation were revolutionized.

The new industries

New products and industrial processes were the most important sources of rapid productivity growth from 1914 to 1939. World War One had accelerated the development of the chemicals industries, and shortly afterward plastics and synthetic fibers (especially rayon) came to market. The use of electricity in production supplanted other forms of energy, as electric power grids were rationalized and improved. New steel alloys and new ways of refining petroleum were developed, facts of special importance to the making and operation of automobiles and airplanes. These innovations spurred productivity growth, and since most of them required large-scale operations, they also spurred the expansion of big plants and firms.

For most people, the most visible evidence of technical change was the rise of new household machines. Some had existed before 1914, but only as novelties; many were commonplace by 1939, so that some historians speak of a consumer durables revolution in the interwar years. American production and application outpaced those of the rest of the world. Before World War One about one-tenth of the finished goods American consumers bought were consumer durables; by 1929 the proportion was one-quarter. Almost all the increase was in motor vehicles and such home appliances as radios and refrigerators.[6] Other developed countries were not that far behind the United States in the availability of consumer durables, although lower incomes, political instability, and war restricted demand and supply.

The invention of the vacuum tube a year or two before World War One made the home radio feasible; regular broadcasts in the United States, Holland, and Britain demonstrated its commercial viability between 1920 and 1922. By 1939 there were twenty-eight million home radios in the United States, fourteen million in Germany, nine million in Britain, five million in France. The home refrigerator was introduced in the United States in 1916 for nine hundred dollars, an amount that was more than double the cost of a Model T Ford and one that would have taken the average industrial worker nearly eighteen months to earn. But by the late 1920s the average price had fallen to below three hundred dollars, substantially less than the new Model A Ford; the average worker could now pay for a refrigerator with three months' wages. By this time nearly a million units a year were being sold; on the eve of World War Two annual sales reached almost three million, and half of American homes had refrigerators. Electric stoves, heaters, and water heaters proliferated over the 1920s, both in the United States and in Europe. So too did such smaller electrical appliances as vacuum cleaners and irons become common possessions of American and western European families.[7] This is not to speak of such minor conveniences—albeit ones whose absence is hard to imagine—as the zipper, masking and adhesive tapes, and, in 1924, sliced bread.

The airplane was at the other end of the spectrum of new products in affordability. Before World War One it was a curiosity with little use for serious transportation; the first enclosed passenger cabin was demonstrated only a couple of years before the war. The war led to many improvements in design, and in the 1930s air travel came into its own. It was still prohibitively expensive for most people, and the workhorse DC-3 (which carried twenty-one passengers) was introduced only in 1936, but by 1939 air transportation had been established, including over the transoceanic routes of Pan American Airways.

The impact of the radio, the refrigerator, the airplane, and even the zipper on life in the 1920s and 1930s paled in comparison with that of the automobile. The motor vehicle transformed societies, provided unprecedented individual mobility, and freed people from the constraints of preexisting transportation just as fundamentally as the railroad had freed them from the tyranny of water transport.

Automobile production became the centerpiece of modern economies. The motor vehicle industry was soon the largest in every major developed country, and many other industries were devoted to satisfying the demands for inputs for the production of automobiles. By 1929, when the United States produced 5.4 million motor vehicles, the industry was accounting for about one-fifth of the total national consumption of tin, nickel, and steel—more than half of all strip steel. It also used about one-third of the nation's output of aluminum and three-quarters or more of its plate glass and rubber.[8] An industry that had barely existed fifteen years earlier—in 1913 America produced fewer than a half million vehicles—now dominated the economy.

The meteoric rise of the auto industry was especially pronounced in the United States. High incomes and great distances made the motorcar particularly attractive to American households; by 1921 the United States had over ten million cars on the road, more than ten motor vehicles for every one in Europe. Smaller home markets and a later start in mass production slowed the European industry down, for it meant that cars were much more expensive in Europe than in the United States. In 1922 a well-paid American worker could buy a Model T with about ten weeks' wages, while an analogous French worker would take more than a year to earn enough to buy an equivalent car, the Citroën 5 CV.

Europeans soon joined the automotive age. In 1930, after ten years of vertiginous sales, the ratio of American to European registered motor vehicles had already dropped from 10:1 to 5:1. By the middle 1930s the British motor industry was the principal user of such industrial inputs as steel and tin. While the auto industry was not as central to western Europe as it was to the United States, it was still the most important industry in all the major economies.

The automobile came to define modern industry. In 1939 there were twenty-nine million motor vehicles on American roads, another eight million in Europe, and several million more in other parts of the world. Another seven or eight million cars were being produced every year, and trends everywhere were upward.

The new corporations

The automobile industry highlighted the managerial and organizational innovations that created the modern corporation. Many of the productivity advances between 1914 and 1939 would have been impossible without the new kinds of companies that developed along with new technologies and products.

Large companies were nothing new; the trust movement of the decades before 1914 had created some highly oligopolistic industries. A few of these large firms, like the railroads, presaged the new forms of organization, as they managed complex and interrelated economic interests. But many early trusts and holding companies were simply attempts to restrict competition, just like large businesses going back to the merchant princes of the British East India Company.

The new corporations of the interwar years, however, grouped independent operations into one integrated multiplant corporation in order to address complicated problems of coordination. They brought together in one enterprise disparate activities—research, design, production, distribution, advertising—that had previously been carried out separately. They could see a product through from raw materials to final purchase, and beyond to consumer finance and service.

Technological advances that increased the scale of production caused some of the corporate evolution. In fifteen years, between 1914 and 1929, the average American blast furnace, steelwork, and dyestuff factory tripled or quadrupled its production. In 1909 the average American bicycle factory had 46 workers and produced about seven bicycles a day. By 1929 the average such factory had 209 workers and turned out forty-five bicycles every day.

The new economies of scale were obvious in automobiles. The most important were realized when Henry Ford introduced a moving assembly line in 1913, ten years after his Ford Motor Company had been formed and five years after the launch of the Model T. It was patterned on the disassembling lines of Chicago meatpackers, along which animal carcasses swung as they were taken from boxcars on the hoof and back to boxcars in cans, boxes, and crates. The assembly line reduced craft labor to simple repetition, fine-tuned the speed of assembly, and turned auto manufacture into mass production.

The assembly line installed in Ford's Highland Park plant in 1913 reduced the time necessary to make a Model T chassis from over twelve man-hours to ninety minutes.[9] The average auto plant before the assembly line in 1909 had fewer than two hundred workers and made fewer than 10 cars a week; by 1929 the typical auto factory had nearly a thousand workers and made more than 400 cars a week. This meant that while there were actually more automobile factories in the United States in 1909 than in 1929, auto production was 126,000 in the first year and 5.4 million in the latter and that the average American autoworker produced ten times as many cars in 1929 as in 1909.[10]

Factories this large and productive did not necessarily require large corporate owners. There were huge textile mills all over the industrial world, but they were typically specialized, even one-plant companies. Most industries had a series of separate steps in bringing goods from raw materials to market, with each step accomplished by an independent company. Plantations grew cotton; railroads brought it to port; shippers hauled it to users; textile mills turned it into cloth; wholesalers sold it to clothing factories or retailers. Even where the corporate units were large—and railroad, shipping, and textile companies could be very large—they had one or a few related activities. They dealt with customers and suppliers at arm's length, en masse. Textile mills and clothing manufacturers bought cotton or cloth from a wide variety of sources and sold their wares on the open market.

Automakers found that this sort of organization did not work for them. Automobiles used hundreds, even thousands of different components and parts. Many of the parts used to make Chevrolets or Model As were specific to these makes and models, so that there was no readily available market for them. This left the automakers at the mercy of their suppliers and their suppliers in turn at the mercy of the automakers. The reliability of each party was crucial to the other, and there was no room for failure. The unique nature of many parts and components also made it difficult to agree on a fair price for a good that had only one supplier and only one purchaser. The result was that the car companies' relations with suppliers (and with distributors) were precarious. A delay by one parts manufacturer could endanger an entire line of cars, just as a delay in one line of cars could endanger the livelihood of a parts manufacturer.

Henry Ford saw early on that he needed a reliable source of components to operate his assembly lines effectively. During World War One he began building an enormous integrated complex on the River Rouge near Detroit. The plant ultimately had a workforce of 120,000 and redefined modern manufacturing. As two automotive historians put it, "The Rouge, which covered 2,000 acres and boasted the longest assembly line in the world, was the hub of Henry Ford's industrial empire, as well as a monument to the man himself. Iron and coal arrived on his private boats, fresh from excavation in his own mines. Rubber was imported from a Ford-owned plantation in Brazil. Wood came from trees harvested on Ford land. The Ford Motor Company had become the largest privately owned company in the world."[11] The vast and interconnected scale of production that Ford developed was so extraordinary that in many parts of the world modern mass production came to be known as Fordism.

General Motors, a holding company from its 1908 start, was the greatest managerial innovator in the industry. Over the course of the 1920s Alfred P. Sloan and his team created a sophisticated management system. They divided the company into units whose products were clearly differentiated—Chevrolet, Cadillac, Oldsmobile, eventually GM's producers of tractors, refrigerators, and airplanes—and that ran separately but had a common management.

GM strove to take over more and more links in the chain of production and sale of its cars. As with Ford, the strategy grew out of difficulties in securing and maintaining reliable sources of supply for crucial parts. Early on GM's most important independent supplier was Fisher Body, which made the chassis for all its cars. But after a decade of difficult contractual and other problems, GM took over Fisher Body in 1919. GM management resolved never to allow its massive operations to be held hostage by one unreliable supplier or distributor.

By the middle 1920s General Motors was owning outright, or had nearly exclusive relations with, many of its most important suppliers, such as AC Spark Plugs, Delco, and Fisher Body. GM had a vast network of dealers, over which it exercised tight control. The General Motors Acceptance Corporation was a huge financial subsidiary that lent money to its customers so they could buy their cars "on time." The corporation also used its powerful position in industrial research, production, and marketing to introduce new lines of consumer products, notably the Frigidaire home refrigerator.

Managers applied the new methods to research and development and to marketing. Automakers, who needed to marshal and protect new technical advances, gathered industrial research under their own roofs rather than buy it from independent laboratories that might reveal proprietary information to competitors. The same was true about marketing these image-sensitive products. General Motors and other automakers brought design, engineering, advertising, and marketing into the corporate network.

The corporation of a new type self-consciously kept its technological, managerial, and marketing expertise *inside* the company. While an important part of the automotive story was that in the United States in 1929 more than five million cars were produced in only 244 auto assembly plants, a bigger part of the story was that three enormous firms— General Motors, Ford, and Chrysler—accounted for more than four-fifths of all these cars.

The new corporations were multiplant. The auto firms had highly diversified factories making everything from spark plugs to window glass for their automobiles, in addition to the assembly plants. The new motor vehicle companies were also managerial: They coordinated and administered the elaborate process of automobile production and distribution. The modern corporation separated management from ownership, for running a complex enterprise was a professional undertaking that required specialized expertise. Family-owned companies in these industries declined in favor of companies owned by anonymous shareholders and run by professional managers.

Auto corporations were also vertically integrated, bringing together successive stages in production and distribution. Most earlier firms had controlled one limited industrial process, and the auto companies had typically started in this way, buying parts and putting them together into cars. But over time they integrated backward in the production process to control the supply of less finished inputs and forward to control the distribution and sale of their products. This vertical integration meant that an automaker might have divisions to mine iron ore and coal, smelt steel, build chassis and parts, design and assemble automobiles, send them out around the country (on company-owned railroads), advertise and sell them through corporate networks, and finance their purchases through a financial arm. The automobile corporations were leaders in mass production, mass distribution, and vertical integration. They brought into the firm a range of activities that had previously been carried out on open markets: research, design, production, distribution, and marketing. They were also overseen by corporate headquarters that specialized in being corporate headquarters, not in the production of automobiles itself.

The automakers were only the most visible of the new corporations. The United States was increasingly dominated by large, diversified, vertically integrated corporations. The new companies clustered in businesses that depended on mass production, mass consumption, technological innovation, and often customer recognition. There were branded consumer nondurables such as processed foods, cigarettes, and toiletries: Armour, Borden, Pillsbury, Campbell, Swift, American Tobacco, and Procter & Gamble. Another type was in consumer durables, automobiles of course but also other similar goods and appliances: Firestone, Remington, Eastman Kodak, Singer, General Electric, and Westinghouse. A related kind of firm produced machinery for industrial and agricultural (as opposed to household) users: Allis-Chalmers, American Can, Deere, International Harvester, the steel and metalworking firms. Finally there were chemical and petroleum firms: Du Pont, Allied Chemical, Union Carbide, all the big oil companies.[12]

These behemoths of industry shaped production and consumption in ways never before imagined. Corporate design, advertising, and marketing seemed to mold customer demand to meet supply rather than the other way around. And of course corporate dominance of markets raised the specter of anticompetitive behavior. This was true both because the new corporations did so much internally rather than in the marketplace and because of the obvious possibilities of collusion among the few huge companies that dominated increasing numbers of industries. Indeed, while General Motors was a leader in automobiles, it too was arguably integrated into a bigger complex. Du Pont was the principal shareholder in GM, and Pierre du Pont was the chairman of GM's board. In turn, GM was Du Pont's largest customer, because of its massive use of Du Pont's quick-drying paints to cover GM cars. More and more of what had previously been governed by the market seemed to be carried out in exclusive relationships within or between enormous corporations.

The new corporations also brought research and development into the firms themselves. Before the turn of the century most innovations had been developed by individual scientists and engineers or by groups in independent laboratories. As the need for new research and development soared, so did the desire to keep discoveries proprietary, and more and more industrial research was integrated into the new corporations, to be done in internally controlled labs. The era of the inventor, epitomized by Thomas A. Edison, faded and was replaced by corporate research and development. Corporations concerned about controlling their own technological horizons expanded in-house scientific laboratories spectacularly. In 1921 about twenty-eight hundred scientists worked in such corporate labs. By 1946 there were forty-six thousand scientists in industrial research facilities, and these in-house laboratories had 93 percent of all the scientists employed in industry. Scientific personnel as a share of total industrial employment went up sevenfold in these twenty-five years. The image of the inventor in a small stand-alone laboratory faded, to be replaced by American Telephone and Telegraph's Bell Telephone Laboratories or by similar operations run by Du Pont, General Electric, and the like.[13]

Research and development were integrated primarily in those industries where the modern corporations prevailed, for the reasons to bring science into the firm were similar to the reasons to bring in other component parts of the industrial process. In 1940 more than four-fifths of research staffs in industry were in the sectors that were also strongholds of the new corporate form: food processing, chemicals, petroleum, rubber, machinery, transport equipment, and instruments.[14] The new corporations changed fundamentally not only the ways in which goods were made, advertised, and distributed but also the ways in which products and production processes were invented, developed, and designed.

The United States led the way in the new corporate forms, but other industrial countries were close behind. The paths to the new corporation differed.[15] The long European tradition of organized cartels meant that it was common for some of these cartels to form themselves into horizontally integrated firms. For example, the six largest German chemical firms operated as a loose federation from 1916 to 1925, at which time they decided to merge to become IG Farben.[16] British companies tended to be slower to adopt the new forms perhaps because long-standing relationships between customers and suppliers in the oldest industrial nation were enough. France was slower still, probably because of the backwardness of the country's consumer markets and financial system. But while there were laggards, by the eve of World War Two all the major industrial economies were dominated by very large, diversified, integrated corporations.

The new multinational enterprises

The new corporations also spread past the water's edge. During the 1920s modern multinational corporations made their first significant appearance. Again the United States took the lead, and again the automobile was the quintessential corporation of this type. American firms set up or bought thousands of subsidiaries in Europe, Canada, and Latin America.

Investors had long gone abroad in search of profits, but the forms taken by this search were changing. During the classical era, capital flowed out of western Europe in enormous quantities. Most of this was in the form of loans, in which the foreign firm or government simply got money to use for whatever it chose. Control of the investment, in other words, stayed in the hands of the borrower. Some European overseas investment was in fact direct, with managerial control vested in the European investor. But almost no foreign direct investment before World War One was in manufacturing. Typically, it was in raw materials and agriculture—copper mines, sugar or banana plantations, oilfields— or in utilities and railroads. This was also the case for Americans, almost all of whose overseas direct investment before 1914 was in Latin America, almost all of it in primary production.

American vertically integrated corporations expanded their horizons abroad, introducing the manufacturing multinational corporation (MNC). They brought new products, marketing, managerial, and production techniques with them, and soon American car, appliance, and other brands were household names in Europe and Canada. Ford, Westinghouse, and the others used their experience building networks of factories, suppliers, and distributors around the United States to set up similar networks in Europe. The process was accelerated to some extent by European trade barriers, which made it hard for American firms to export to European markets and gave them reasons to jump tariff walls to set up local factories. However, the real impetus for corporate expansion was the same one that had prevailed inside the United States: the great advantages of an integrated corporation to make and sell the mass-produced mass consumption goods.

By 1929 American foreign direct investment was $7.9 billion, equal to more than 5 percent of total American corporate and farm wealth (up from 2 percent in 1900). Of this, nearly half remained in Latin America, heavily oriented toward primary production and utilities. Most of the rest was in Europe and Canada, and in both cases the bulk of the American investment was in manufacturing.[17] American corporations had about four hundred subsidiaries in Britain and about two hundred each in France and Germany.

American corporations went almost entirely into the new fields dominated by American products, production processes, and corporate forms. Four such industries—motor vehicles, machinery, chemicals, and rubber products—accounted for well over half the manufacturing multinationals, even though they were barely one-fifth of domestic manufacturing investment. By the 1930s the local affiliates of Ford and General Motors were leaders of the auto industry in the United Kingdom and Germany. In the UK, Ford and GM's Vauxhall produced a substantial proportion of the nation's motor vehicles; in Germany, Ford and GM's Adam Opel had half the total auto market.[18] International Harvester, Eastman Kodak, Singer, Otis Elevator, General Electric, Gillette all brought their production and their products to Europe and had enormous success.

Down on the farm

The final decline of backward agriculture in the developed world was another source of rapid productivity increases. This was a socially wrenching process, but it undoubtedly increased economic efficiency. In the average industrial country before World War One about a third of the working population was farmers; by the end of World War Two this proportion was below one-sixth and falling fast. The trend was evident even in two extreme cases, agrarian France and industrial Britain. In the former, farmers in 1913 were 41 percent of the workforce, which declined to 28 percent in 1950; analogous figures for the United Kingdom are 12 and 5 percent. Shifting labor out of backward farming and into advanced industries and services increased overall productivity—even if it destroyed rural communities and lifestyles.

The rise of the new machines, including farm machinery and the automobile, was intricately linked to the modernization of agriculture. The mechanization of American agriculture dramatically increased the ability of a few workers—perhaps a family and a few seasonal hands—to cultivate very large farms. Between World War One and the late 1940s output per farmer skyrocketed in the United States. Around 1915 it took one man-hour to produce 1 bushel of wheat, 1.3 bushels of corn, or 3 bushels of cotton. Thirty years later a man-hour produced three times as much wheat or corn and twice as much cotton. The yield per acre did not change much over this time, but machinery reduced drastically the need for farm labor.[19]

European agriculture, already crippled by World War One, was further hit by imports from the more efficient farms of the New World, Australia, and the developing countries. Before the war Europe produced 56 percent of the world's wheat, but by the late 1920s it was producing only 39 percent. Even in absolute terms, European grain farming fell short: Overall wheat output dropped by over one-fifth in fifteen years, from the eve of World War One to the late 1920s. Most extensive European farming, such as in grains, endured only because of government subsidies and trade protection.

The full mechanization of American farming and the advent of the automobile age brought traditional rural life in the United States to an end. The desolate symbol of the country's agrarian troubles, the exodus of hundreds of thousands of farmers from the dust bowl of Oklahoma and Arkansas to California, was only the most graphic expression of how the conclusive industrialization of America was emptying the country's farmlands.

While the European experience was less dramatic, there too millions of farmers left the countryside for the cities. Traditional European rural life did not survive the combined onslaught of imported food, mechanization, and the automobile. Some traditional farming hung on into the 1950s, especially in more backward areas or where aided by government support, but Europe was no longer agricultural. Brutal as this process was, it shifted European and North American labor from where it was redundant to where it was needed.

New societies

Technological and organizational changes also affected social structures and politics in the industrial countries. Most obvious was the rise of labor and of the Socialist and Communist parties with which it affiliated.

As industry shifted toward very large companies and very large factories, labor's strength grew. Larger plants and firms were generally easier
to unionize, both because the concentration of people made union
organizing more effective and because large corporations could not call
upon the personalistic ties with employees that smaller firms often cultivated. In addition, large corporations in new industries tended to be
less hostile to unionization than smaller-scale and older industries. An
enterprise like General Motors had several features that made it less set
in its antiunion ways than, say, a textile company. First, such firms were
dependent on complex integrated operations and needed a stable and
reliable labor force; that was why they usually paid high wages.
Unionization might help guarantee the stability of the workforce, and
sometimes the unions self-consciously promised to do so. Second, labor
costs were a much smaller share of production costs for the new industries than for older, labor-intensive ones; much of the cost of production
was in machinery, research and development, and marketing. Third, the
interwar turn toward trade protection meant that wage increases would
not lead to competitive threats from imports. Fourth, because the firms
tended to dominate their markets with products to which consumers were
loyal, they could often pass increased labor costs on to consumers with little loss of sales. Americans were not going to switch from GM cars to
Fords if prices went up a percent or two—and especially not if both GM
and Ford were unionized, so that wages went up together.

The growth of unions complemented the growing dominance of western Europe and North America by large corporations. Firms got bigger
and bigger and controlled their markets more and more; it was only natural that their workers would try to follow suit to gain control over their
working conditions. Few capitalists welcomed unions, but the new corporations were less virulently antiunion than the older, smaller, more
labor-intensive firms.

World War One and the Great Depression of the 1930s gave an enormous push to growth of labor movements. The war led everywhere to an
increase in labor influence. For one thing, the departure of millions of
young men to the front made labor scarce, so that those who remained
had greater leverage. For another, almost every socialist movement supported its country's war effort and during or after the war was rewarded
with enlargement of the scope of permissible labor activity and with supportive government programs. In addition, the shock of the Russian
Revolution of 1917, and of the insurrectionary movements in central
Europe right after World War One ended, led many European rulers to

view concessions to moderate working-class movements and parties as a price worth paying to reduce the appeal of homegrown bolshevism.

The Depression of the 1930s also pushed labor forward. The crisis increased the appeal of unions that could protect workers in their places of employment and of labor-based parties that could protect workers in the political arena. After the 1933 Nazi disaster the Communist movement dropped its hostility to the less revolutionary Socialist parties in favor of an alliance with other progressive organizations. This made Left and Center-Left governments a possibility in many remaining European democracies. The failures of the traditional parties, the threat of fascism, and the prospect of broad labor-oriented governments came together to draw masses of workers and others to the Left.

Labor influence increased most strikingly in the European political arena. Almost everywhere labor-based parties were the largest or second-largest vote getters, typically receiving over one-third of all votes cast. Britain was on the low end, with the Labour Party getting 30 percent of the vote in 1922; Germany was on the high end, as the two Socialist parties combined nearly had a majority in 1919. Over the 1920s Socialist votes usually held fast. Some Socialist supporters went over to the new Communist parties, especially in France and Germany. In most cases, the socialist movements were able to sustain strong parties and substantial political influence, participating at least as coalition partners in many western European governments at some point in the 1920s.

The Great Depression brought Left governments, or coalition governments dominated by the Left, to power in most of the European democracies, for at least a trial run. Labour in Britain, the French Popular Front, and a wave of socialist-led governments in Scandinavia remade the political map of Europe as previous political pariahs were called upon to try to deal with the desperate conditions. Some experiments failed, as did Labour in Britain and, more bloodily, the Spanish Popular Front; others began a long-lived social democratic evolution, as in a Scandinavia solidly socialist by the middle 1930s.[20] One might also consider Franklin Roosevelt's New Deal and the remaking of the Democratic Party an analogous movement toward a Center-Left presence in the United States. Whatever the national particulars, there was a clear left wing to all democratic political systems, toward which the bulk of the working class, and often many others, gravitated and which often rode the electoral path to power.

There was a roughly equal and definitely opposite political reaction on the Right. New types of movements of the extreme Right arose under various names, all ultimately related to the fascism introduced by Benito Mussolini in Italy and refined by the Nazis in Germany. By the middle 1930s the new fascist Right was powerful, or in power, in most of Europe. Economic trends were an important backdrop to the rise of the Ultraright. For what was new about the New Right was not its extreme antisocialism and nationalism, or even its anti-Semitism, but its melding of these hallmarks of reaction with a passionate mass base that could be mobilized on the streets and at the ballot box.

The Ultraright capitalized upon the social dislocations and political discontent brought about by structural changes in the industrial economies. As enormous corporations came to dominate industrial economies and farming was modernized, what Marxists called the petite bourgeoisie or middle strata were squeezed. Small businesses faced fierce competition from large corporations, while small farmers confronted both cheap imports and the growth of large-scale machinery-intensive farming in Europe itself.

Almost every European ultraright wing or ultranationalist movement found its principal base of mass support among small business people or small farmers, or both. These were the groups most fundamentally displaced by interwar developments, and they had little voice in established political institutions, which had evolved toward the class-based labor-capital divide Marx had anticipated and encouraged. The main opponents of large corporations were the socialists and Communists, but small business or farm owners were rarely sympathetic to the labor-based demands of these movements. Nor did traditional liberal and conservative parties, with their strong orientation toward stable businesses, the landed gentry, and professionals, have room for déclassé shopkeepers and destitute farmers.

In some instances the Left or traditional Center and Right did get middle-class and farm support; but this was a relative rarity, and where it occurred, the Ultraright typically found little favor. Unfortunately for Europe and the world, it was more common for beleaguered shopkeepers and farmers to turn away from traditional parties and toward protest movements that attacked both big business and labor. Fascism and its variants were perfect vehicles for their demands, given the peculiar fascist mixture of anticorporate, antilabor, and antiforeign rhetoric. In some nations, where there were many Jewish-owned businesses or small-town Jewish merchants, the anti-Semitic views of much of the European Ultraright resonated with businessmen and farmers who saw Jewish competitors, creditors, or middlemen as part of the problem.

Anxious Main Street tradesmen and small-town farmers targeted big corporations as the interwar economy spiraled downward. The troubled lower middle classes also scorned the Left parties whose responses to the crisis were driven primarily by the concerns of labor. This discontent found a ready home in the reactionary movements that swept southern, eastern, and central Europe from the early 1920s onward. These movements promised a fascist middle way between corporate capitalism and proletarian socialism.

Advances and retreats

A belief that technological development translates automatically into economic growth is strained by the interwar years. These decades witnessed some of the most important technical developments in history, both in the laboratory and in the factory. Many of the products and processes we associate with modern economies were introduced or implemented in the 1920s and 1930s. These years also saw the full development of the modern corporation and of its international counterpart the modern multinational corporation.

This economic evolution fed two powerful political processes. On the one hand, the triumph of big business in modern industry brought forth a powerful labor movement. By the 1930s it was common for European governments to include parties whose principal base of support was in the working class. Many such governments were in fact led by Socialist parties, and some even included Communists as alliance partners.

On the other hand, the continued modernization of Europe crushed more of the continent's middle sectors, especially small businesses and farmers. These marginalized groups provided the mass base for the fascist movements that came to rule Europe as the interwar period ended.

8

The Established Order Collapses

In January 1936 Britain's Left Book Club commissioned George Orwell to investigate social conditions in the country's depressed economy. The result, *The Road to Wigan Pier*, shocked the nation with its descriptions of destitution and despair. Orwell summarized the bewilderment and pervasive misery that had descended upon the unemployed, depicting the "decent young miners and cotton-workers gazing at their destiny with the same sort of dumb amazement as an animal in a trap. They simply could not understand what was happening to them. They had been brought up to work, and behold! it seemed as if they were never going to have the chance of working again."[1]

The economic collapse of 1929–1934 was unprecedented in its depth and breadth. There had been cyclical crises before, but never like this. The economies of the industrialized world disintegrated for five years and more, as output dropped by one-fifth and unemployment went above one-quarter of the labor force almost everywhere. Financial and currency crises ricocheted around the world in the space of weeks, binding economies together as they plummeted downward. No major nation was spared.

Carl Sandburg had called Chicago "City of the Big Shoulders" and described it "Laughing the stormy, husky, brawling laughter of Youth, half-naked, sweating, proud to be Hog Butcher, Tool Maker, Stacker of Wheat, Player with Railroads and Freight Handler to the Nation." But now Chicago was not laughing or proud; in the winter of 1930–1931 a reporter wrote of this capital of American industry, "You can ride across the lovely Michigan Avenue bridge at midnight with the lights all about making a dream city of incomparable beauty, while twenty feet below you, on the lower level of the same bridge, are 2,000 homeless, decrepit, shivering and starving men, wrapping themselves in old newspapers to keep from freezing, and lying down in the manure dust to sleep."[2] The halting recovery of the 1920s had come to an end.

The end of the boom

The end started innocently enough, with a gradual decline in growth outside North America. In 1928 farm conditions in the major producers took a turn for the worse, while much of Europe and Asia began to fall into recession. The United States continued to boom. With foreign investments less attractive, American capital headed home, and the stock market surged remarkably: The Dow Jones Industrial Average rose nearly without interruption from 191 early in 1928 to 381 in September 1929.

A doubling of stock prices in little over a year far surpassed any return available abroad, and the supply of American money to the world dried up. In the first half of 1928 new American lending to foreigners averaged $140 million a month. This declined by half to $70 million between mid-1928 and mid-1929 as money flooded into the stock market, and by the last half of 1929 foreign loans were down by another half, to $35 million a month. If one takes into account money coming back to the United States as debts were repaid, an even starker picture emerges: A net outflow of $900 million in 1927–1928 turned into a net outflow of just $86 million a year between 1929 and 1931.[3]

When the American money that had fueled world economic growth headed homeward, it turned a mild recession elsewhere into a full-fledged crisis.[4] As money flowed into the United States and the dollar, investors unloaded other currencies. European governments facing a sell-off on the foreign exchanges responded as usual, raising interest rates and imposing austerity. Higher interest rates were supposed to attract capital back to the economy and its currency, while austerity would restrain wages and profits in order to make the country's goods more competitive on world markets.

Even the American authorities faced serious challenges. The Federal Reserve wanted to curb what it regarded as excessive speculative behavior on Wall Street, by raising interest rates to draw money away from stocks and make it harder to borrow. But an increase in American interest rates would suck capital out of Europe and Latin America, making business conditions more difficult there. If the Fed kept interest rates steady, the stock market bubble would continue; if it raised interest rates, it would worsen Europe's economic problems. In the event, the Fed thought that its principal commitment was domestic, and in August it raised interest rates a percentage point to persuade investors to avoid further stock market speculation. In fact the stock market did begin to decline, in late summer and early fall of 1929.

In late October 1929 the frenzy came to an end. In three weeks the market lost all the ground it had gained in the previous year and a half. In three months American industrial production fell by 10 percent and imports by 20 percent. Prices of commodities dropped astonishingly steeply. In the summer of 1929, when economic contraction was already in the air, rubber was going for 21 cents a pound; by early 1932 its price was 3 cents a pound and still falling. Other raw materials prices came down almost as dramatically; copper, for example, went from 16 to 5 cents a pound. Farm products were just as hard hit: From summer 1929 to their trough in late 1932 or early 1933, silk dropped from $5.20 to $1.25 a pound; cotton, from 18 to 6 cents a pound; coffee from 23 to 8 cents a pound. It was not just poor countries' products that suffered, as a bushel of corn fell from 92 to 19 cents, and wheat, the world's most important crop, dropped from $1.50 a bushel in summer 1929 to 49 cents a bushel at the end of 1932.[5]

Manufactured goods prices declined, but not so fast. By one measure, while American farm prices fell by 52 percent between 1928 and 1933, prices of metal products and building materials dropped by 18 percent, while consumer durables prices fell 8 percent.[6]

Commodity-producing nations were especially hard hit by the combined effect of price declines, the slump in American and European demand for their exports, and the cutoff of American lending. Within a few months of the American stock market crash, Argentina, Australia, Brazil, and Canada responded to the collapse of their export prices by formally or informally taking their currencies off gold. Their defection from gold standard rules was worrisome, but they were after all relatively minor economies facing a very serious commodity price collapse.

Industrial country governments, however, had another idea of what to do about the price declines: nothing. Received wisdom and prewar experience said that the recession would correct itself. Once wages got low enough, capitalists would start hiring back workers; once prices fell far enough, consumers would start buying. As prices and wages dropped, demand would rise, until balance was restored.

The Fed turned to the usual monetary tools to impose a sharp and quick bout of austerity. This policy of liquidationism aimed to force down prices and wages so that excess stocks of labor, food, and goods would be liquidated. The advice of Treasury Secretary Andrew Mellon to President Hoover was typical: "Liquidate labor, liquidate stocks, liquidate the farmers, liquidate real estate . . . purge the rottenness out of the system."[7] So the Fed kept interest rates relatively high—2.5 percent at a time when prices were falling at about 15 percent a year—and attempted to oversee an orderly working out of what it believed was a typical cyclical decline. Prices and wages would fall, and eventually the economy would rebound.

But the results were troubling, not only in the United States but in virtually all the developed world. American industrial production dropped 26 percent from its August 1929 peak to October 1930, prices by 14 percent, personal income 16 percent.[8] The average household had lost the income gains of the previous five years and more, and there was no sign of an end to the decline. Unemployment too was on the rise: From 3 percent in 1929, the jobless rate went to 9 percent in 1930 and to 16 percent in 1931. In Germany the collapse was even faster, from 8 percent unemployment in 1928 to 22 percent in 1930 and 34 percent in 1931.[9] The already weak British economy turned down further, bringing with it the Scandinavian and Baltic countries in its commercial orbit. Japan was dragged down by the lending cutoff and a 43 percent decline in the price of silk, its principal export, over the course of a year. Only France seemed immune to what was now clearly a worldwide crisis, and by the end of 1930 the French expansion too seemed precarious at best.

Governments redoubled efforts to shore up confidence in their financial prudence and commitments to gold. The leaders of the principal central banks consulted almost continually to try to craft a way out. There even seemed to be progress on the issue of reparations, as a European conference chaired by American businessman Owen Young agreed to regularize German payments. The Young Plan also established a Bank for International Settlements to help smooth the process and provide a venue for international monetary and financial cooperation.[10] And in February 1930 an international conference to reduce trade barriers was convened.

But these international initiatives were ineffectual, especially without real American involvement. Most governments had to rely on their own efforts to try to pull themselves out of the decline. Great Britain seemed uniquely suited to search for imaginative alternatives. In July 1929 a minority Labour government headed by Ramsay MacDonald took power, ruling with the support of the Liberals and the backing of some of the country's leading economic thinkers, including Keynes. Yet the government was immobilized by the conflicting pull of its constituents. On the one hand, it held firm to the country's commitment to free trade, balanced budgets, and the gold standard; on the other, it was desperate to respond to the demands of collapsing industries and unemployed workers. In the end it temporized feebly for two years.

Germany, probably hardest hit by the crisis, was torn apart even more completely. Two years of traditional austerity succeeded only in driving unemployment to astronomical levels. The Center-Left coalition government collapsed early in 1930, to be replaced by the government by decree of Heinrich Brüning, a prominent Catholic politician. Brüning seemed to have no new ideas and called a new election in September 1930. The principal result was a great increase in political support for the two parties least committed to orthodoxy, the Communists and the Nazis. The former took 13 percent of the vote, up from 10 percent two years earlier; the latter increased their popular votes from under 3 percent to 18 percent. The country divided into warring factions, with its international economic relations one of the principal battlefields. Still, the government did almost nothing to counteract the slump. This inaction was immensely costly; even modest measures to stimulate the economy would, subsequent analysis has shown, have been enough to stop the Nazis' electoral advances.[11]

The U.S. government too turned inward toward traditional American responses to economic downturns. The first such response was trade protection. From the middle of 1929 through early 1930 Congress worked on the Smoot-Hawley Tariff Act, which promised to raise substantially American trade barriers. Despite pleas from foreign trade partners and from a petition of 1,028 American economists, Congress passed the bill, and President Herbert Hoover signed it in June 1930. Within a few months other countries also began raising their own trade barriers, whether for their own reasons or in retaliation.[12]

But economies did not recover, and unemployment kept increasing. In 1933, the fifth year of the downturn, American unemployment was 25 percent, and it stood at comparably high levels elsewhere. This was long past the time when "natural" economic forces should have kicked in to set economies right. Deflation and liquidation, far from rekindling economic growth by lowering prices and wages enough to encourage new investment and consumption, seemed to be deepening the decline.

And the economic decline was astoundingly deep. Industrial production dropped precipitously, typically by between 20 and 50 percent over a two- or three-year period. In the 1920–1921 recession the American economy had contracted by 4 percent; between 1929 and 1933 it shrank by 30 percent. The American economic collapse was one of the worst in the world, but other countries were not far behind. The 1928–1935 peak-to-trough decline in GDP—that is, the fall from the high point in 1928 or 1929 to the nation's low point, typically in 1932 or 1933—was of 25 to 30 percent in the United States, Canada, Germany, and several Latin American countries and of 15 to 25 percent in France, Austria, and much of central and eastern Europe.[13]

The downturn fed on itself, in large part through what economist Irving Fisher called debt deflation. During the 1920s there had been a big increase in lending, and even many consumers had come to rely on installment credit to purchase the new consumer durables. Debtors could not service their debts when incomes collapsed while debt obligations stayed constant. Deflation forced debtors to reduce consumption and investment, leading to further price declines. By the beginning of 1934 in the average American city over a third of home mortgage holders were behind in their payments; in Cleveland the proportion was nearly two-thirds.[14]

Distress was especially pronounced among people or countries that specialized in raw materials and farm goods, whose prices had fallen two or three times more than those of other goods. By 1933 nearly half of all American farmers were behind in their mortgage payments, and over that year some two hundred thousand farms were foreclosed. The foreclosure rate was ten to twenty times normal; in some states one-quarter to one-third of all farms were foreclosed between 1928 and 1934.[15] The United States, like almost every country, experienced massive agricultural bankruptcies and rural unrest.

And still political and business leaders followed the prescriptions of previously prevailing wisdom. The generally accepted view of business cycles was that an upswing led to speculative excesses, which had to be cleared away by an inevitable downturn. The liquidation of past errors was a good thing, and attempts to mitigate its effects were counterproductive. The liquidationists insisted that the boom of the 1920s had to be unwound in order to set the economy back on a healthy path. That meant liquidating bad investments, bad loans, and useless products. This was difficult but necessary, for as Lionel Robbins put it in 1935, "Nobody likes liquidation as such. . . . [But] when the extent of malinvestment and over-indebtedness has passed a certain limit, measures which postpone liquidation only make matters worse."[16] The intellectual pedigree of this view was impeccable, and it had seemed to work well in previous crises. Traditionalists argued that government inaction—even action to accelerate the "purgative" effects of the downturn—would eventually speed recovery. Don't just do something, they said to governments, stand there.

Herbert Hoover, after the fact, blamed the paralysis of his administration in part on the prevalence of these views: "The 'leave-it-alone liquidationists' headed by Secretary of the Treasury Mellon . . . felt that government must keep its hands off and let the slump liquidate itself. . . . He held that even panic was not altogether a bad thing. He said: 'It will purge the rottenness out of the system. High costs of living and high living will come down. People will work harder, live a more moral life. Values will be adjusted, and enterprising people will pick up the wrecks from less competent people.' "[17] Support for liquidationism was not based only on moral and intellectual appeal; businessmen had self-serving reasons to justify layoffs and wage cutting. Orthodoxy was especially strong among businesses that relied on large amounts of labor, for which reducing wages was crucial. Firms in more capital-intensive lines, such as the auto, machinery, and petroleum industries, were less sensitive to labor costs, and they were more likely to argue that wage cutting was self-defeating because it reduced consumers' purchasing power.[18] But many businessmen naturally endorsed the idea that lower wages were needed.

The reward for enduring all these rigors was supposed to be that eventually the wave of deflation and bankruptcies would create the conditions for its reversal and recovery. Yet traditional inaction, which had previously righted troubled economies, did not work. Prices and wages continued to fall, failures proliferated, unemployment rose further and further, and there was no sign of a turnaround. The generally self-equilibrating mechanism of pre-1929 business cycles was broken.

Why weren't the old solutions working? As Keynes had anticipated, reduced flexibility of prices and wages meant that the postwar economy was not responding as before to a slump. Oligopolistic firms that cut back on sales while keeping prices high produced less than they otherwise would; unions that held out for higher wages at the expense of lower employment restricted the supply of available jobs. Firms and unions with market power could produce less and sell at a higher price, leaving machinery and workers idle. In sectors that approximated pre-1914 conditions, such as agriculture, prices fell precipitously, while farmers produced as much as or more than before. But the orthodox purgative mechanism that depressions were supposed to activate was not operating in many parts of the economy and was not rekindling overall economic growth.

As the new wage and price rigidities imposed themselves, recovery lagged and dragged. Unemployment remained high in almost every country, even as real wages—the purchasing power of wages relative to prices—stayed steady or even rose, especially in sectors dominated by large enterprises or unionized labor, or both. In the United States, for example, the average hourly wage of manufacturing workers went from fifty-seven cents in 1929 to fifty-four cents in 1934, a fall of 5 percent, while consumer prices dropped over 20 percent. Even with 22 percent of the labor force unemployed and millions of Americans looking desperately for work, the real wages of those with jobs were much higher in 1934 than in 1929. As late as 1939, with American unemployment still 17 percent, real wages were 15 percent higher than in 1934—and fully 40 percent higher than in 1929. Real wages tended to increase or stay constant in oligopolistic industries—utilities, finance, manufacturing—but declined by 15 to 25 percent in such competitive sectors as farming, domestic service, and construction. While as much as a quarter of the labor force was out of work and clamoring for jobs, wages in many industries were high and rising.[19]

There was nothing reprehensible in capitalists and workers banding together to protect themselves by keeping prices, profits, and wages as high as they could. The fact that this interfered with the orthodox adjustment mechanism is not necessarily a strike against it. After all, adjustment drove economy-wide wages down very far very fast, and while recovery might be quick, the pain and suffering of the crisis were very severe. The ability of many firms and unions to resist price and wage cuts kept factories more idle and unemployment higher than otherwise, but it also provided better wages and earnings to the labor and capital that were employed in these privileged sectors. How one weighed this trade-off depended on which side of the scale one occupied; the gains of employed workers resulted, to some extent, in the continuing unemployment of others.

Deflation was not the solution and might be part of the problem. Indeed, eventually many governments harnessed corporate and union efforts to sustain prices and wages to a more general attempt to reverse the deflationary circle. Fascist regimes encouraged corporations to cartelize to keep prices from collapsing. Social democratic governments brought labor and capital together to hammer out agreements to prop up wages and prices. America's New Dealers railed against "cutthroat competition" and used new laws and regulatory agencies to facilitate corporate and labor organization that they hoped would reverse the deflation. In many cases, governments themselves organized markets against deflation such as by launching agricultural programs to keep farm prices high. All these measures were undoubtedly motivated by a mix of concern over deflation and the more prosaic desire of producers to keep the prices and wages they charged as high as possible.

The deflationary damage was done by the time governments got involved. For nearly five years after the Depression began, many prices, especially of primary products, collapsed. But deflation did not perform as anticipated and, as before 1914, set the stage for recovery. Wage and price rigidities meant that contrary to the prescriptions of orthodoxy, contraction did not give way to recovery.

Gold and the crisis

Deflation and prolonged depression triggered financial and currency panics that moved around the world, at times like a gradually spreading stain, at times with lightning speed. Shocks were carried from country to country by skittish investors shifting money from one market to another. Proliferating bankruptcies raised the specter of bank failures, and when depositors pulled their money out, they turned fear into reality. Beginning in May 1931, panics swept from Austria through Poland, Hungary, Czechoslovakia, and Romania and eventually to Germany, then to Switzerland, France, the United Kingdom, Turkey, Egypt, Mexico, and the United States. In six months, eighteen national banking systems had faced the financial abyss.[20] In the five years before the summer of 1929, there were only four appreciable national banking crises; in the five years after, there were thirty-three.

"These heroes of finance," Henrik Ibsen had written, "are like beads on a string—when one slips off, all the rest follow."[21] The effects of financial failure were profound; by the end of 1933 half the American financial institutions in business in 1929 were gone.[22] The impact was not felt only by bankers; alarmed lenders stopped supplying funds to almost all borrowers. Farm bankruptcies could, by scaring bankers and investors, dry up money available to industry.

Financial difficulties brought national banking systems and the international financial system to a standstill. As heavily indebted people and countries cut back on their purchases and investments, this reinforced the vicious debt-deflation cycle, further depressing local and world prices.[23]

Governments searching for alternatives to deflationary paralysis and financial ruin ran into an apparently immovable international object, gold. Attempts to halt deflation and raise prices were blocked by government commitments to the gold values of their currencies. As two economic historians put it, the gold standard's "rhetoric was deflation, and its mentality was one of inaction."[24] Countries on gold had to let prices take their course, for national prices were simply a local expression of world prices. Attempts to print money would lead investors to sell off the (debased) national currency for gold. The gold standard ruled out monetary stimulation, and there were no other options. Almost nobody supported deficit spending—Roosevelt's campaign against Hoover in 1932 attacked the president's inability to balance the budget—and trade protection, another common remedy, had been tried everywhere and found wanting. Gold ruled.

Gold retarded a government response to the crisis, and it also sped the international transmission of financial shocks. The slightest hint that interest rates in, say, Belgium, might go down led investors to pull money out of Belgium and put it somewhere safer. As capital fled Belgium, the fears became self-fulfilling: Money became scarcer, debtors defaulted, and banks failed. Governments were besieged by speculative flows of "hot money" seeking short-term security and returns. As Herbert Hoover put it, gold and financial movements were "a loose cannon on the deck of the world in a tempest-tossed era."[25]

Far from absorbing shocks, the gold standard heightened their effects. When investors took money out of a country, they had to sell the national currency. To get money out of Belgium, for example, speculators had to convert Belgian francs into more reliable sterling or dollars or into gold. As they sold francs to the Belgian government for gold or dollars, eventually the authorities would run out of either or both and would have to go off gold. The government needed to raise Belgian interest rates in these circumstances to entice investors to continue to hold assets in the franc—Belgian government bonds, for example—and to stave off a run on the currency. In this way, the gold standard *required* that national governments passively accept international financial exigencies, even if this meant sacrificing local conditions to maintain the exchange rate.

Countries with weak banking systems were particularly likely to collapse under the strain of financial and currency attacks. Where banks were tied to industry, as in much of central Europe, financial distress was quickly transmitted to the rest of the economy. Banks that relied on money from abroad—half of Germany's bank deposits belonged to foreigners in 1930—were especially exposed, for foreigners could pull their money out with ease. But vulnerability to international financial whims was universal and contributed to the speed with which the Depression became, and remained, global.[26]

Financial and currency pressures began a string of national crises that brought the international monetary and financial system to a halt. In May 1931 the Creditanstalt, Austria's largest bank and a longtime Rothschild affiliate, failed. The government stepped in immediately and tried to mobilize support from other European capitals, but to no avail. Even in these dire straits, the political flaws in the interwar order intervened. Before the French would assist in stanching the effects of the failure of the Creditanstalt, leading French politicians insisted that Austria renounce a planned customs union with Germany; the Belgians and Italians supported the French.[27]

The problem soon became familiar. Depositors would not keep money in banks in danger of closing, so a run on the banks developed at the first sign of difficulties. As a nation's banks threatened to collapse, people scrambled to get their money out of the country; nobody wanted to leave funds in a financial system in the process of disintegration. No amount of austerity and no interest rate increases would attract money back to the currency of a country in the throes of a bank panic, and rumors that the currency would be taken off gold and devalued accelerated the rush to cash in stocks, bonds, and money for gold or a reliable currency. The vicious circle fed on itself, as expectations of a devaluation could cause a bank panic, while bank panics triggered devaluations. The interrelated banking and currency crises so crippled credit markets that lending virtually ceased, and even businesses that might have wanted to expand had no way to borrow the money to do so.

Within a week of the Creditanstalt failure in May 1931, bank runs spread from Austria to neighboring Hungary. Within a month they reached Germany. Investors got money out of the banks, out of questionable national currencies, into gold or dollars, as soon as possible, and so these interconnected economies pulled one another down. President Hoover attempted to help hold off disaster by proposing on June 20, 1931, to allow war debtors to suspend payments on their obligations to the U.S. government for a year. Still, savers all over central Europe were gripped by the fear that bank failures would strike the continent's leading economy and force Germany off gold. They were right. Again, attempts to gather support from the French and British were complicated by political hostilities. Before the French would help the Germans deal with the financial crisis, they insisted on further reparations payments and disarmament. But these political maneuverings took far more time than the Germans had.

In July 1931 the German government closed its banks and suspended the convertibility of the currency into gold and foreign exchange. The exchange rate was kept officially steady, but it was now virtually impossible to exchange the German currency for gold, dollars, sterling, or anything other than German goods.[28] The German decision excited more fears, which soon turned to the financial cornerstone of Europe, the United Kingdom.

Over the late summer, as the pound sterling was sold off by worried investors, the British government struggled to support the pound without austerity. In late August the Labour government collapsed and was replaced by a National Government, also headed by Ramsay MacDonald but now with substantial Conservative support. Almost immediately the new government took sterling off gold, devaluing it for the first time in peacetime since the gold parity was established by Sir Isaac Newton in 1717.

The pound fell by nearly one-third against the dollar in a couple of months, from its historical $4.86 to $3.25. As sterling dropped, a host of other countries followed Britain off gold: the Scandinavian and Baltic states with close ties to the British market, then Japan, then much of Latin America. Most of these countries also imposed substantial barriers to trade. Britain abandoned nearly a century of free trade; in February 1932 the National Government imposed tariff protection, then negotiated special preferences for the empire and a few favored trading partners. After decades resisting protectionism, the United Kingdom established an imperial bloc that shared preferential trade relations and a sterling bloc that shared depreciated currencies. Trade with the rest of the world fell precipitously, but exports to the sterling area—the empire, the Nordic and Baltic countries, Argentina, and a few others—rose from 50 to 60 percent of Britain's total exports.[29] Other imperial powers tightened economic ties with their colonies, and in 1931 Japan expanded its colonial area by occupying and annexing Manchuria in northern China.

By the end of 1932 effectively only two groups of countries were left on gold: the United States, and a French-centered gold bloc that included Belgium, Luxembourg, the Netherlands, Italy, and Switzerland. The remaining gold countries faced strong competitive pressures in both their own and third markets, as the depreciations made British, Japanese, and other goods much cheaper. And the tariff barriers imposed in the European empires, Japan's expanding imperial sphere, the United States, and Latin America reduced trading possibilities still further.

Government use of currencies as competitive weapons threw additional uncertainties into the international financial and monetary order. The "butter war" between New Zealand and Denmark was symptomatic. The two countries were Great Britain's principal suppliers of butter, which was in turn the principal export of each nation. Early in 1930 the government of New Zealand devalued its currency by about 5 percent against the pound sterling, which gave its exporters a cost advantage over Danish producers. The Danes hoped that by following the British devaluation of September 1931, they would redress the balance, but the New Zealanders also followed the British pound downward. In September 1932 the Danes devalued their currency 5 percent more against the pound. Four months later the government of New Zealand retaliated with a further 15 percent devaluation, and a month after that the Danish government responded with yet another 17 percent devaluation. By the end of 1933 the two currencies were back to roughly where they had started against each other, but four years of competitive devaluations had heightened political tensions and protectionist pressures in both nations.[30]

Still the economic situation deteriorated. At the end of 1932 world trade was at barely one-third its 1929 levels. International financial markets were almost completely inactive. The world's leading trading

nations had turned toward protectionism. In the United States industrial production stood at half its 1929 levels, and unemployment was 24
percent; it was 44 percent in Germany.[31] Latin America was hit by the
double whammy of falling prices and falling demand; between the two
the region had to reduce its imports by more than half over the first
three years of the Depression. Almost every country in the region was
now in default, with the notable exception of an Argentina desperate to
stay in the good graces of its British trading and financial partners.[32]

Yet many voices called for a reaffirmed commitment to gold. In the
United States itself, a month before leaving office, President Hoover
spoke contemptuously of those who would "inflate our currency, conse-
quently abandon the gold standard, and with our depreciated currency
attempt to enter a world economic war, with the certainty that it leads
to complete destruction, both at home and abroad."[33] France and its
gold bloc neighbors did not give up their attachment to gold until 1936,
more than seven years after the slump had begun.

But policy makers in the remaining gold countries were racked by the
contradiction between the desire to get the economy going and the need
to defend the currency. The American authorities were besieged after
the British devalued against gold in October 1931. Investors cashed in
their dollars for safer gold, while American bank depositors pulled
money out of the banks in anticipation of a financial crisis. The Fed
responded in classic gold standard fashion, raising interest rates from 1.5
to 3.5 percent in a week to keep money in the country and in the banks.
The logic was clear but perverse. Without the commitment to gold, the
Fed could have lowered interest rates, stimulating the economy by making borrowing, spending, and investment easier. Instead, shackled to gold
standard requirements, the world's most important central bank imposed
ever more austere and restrictive monetary policies.[34]

The American elections in November 1932 brought Franklin D.
Roosevelt to the presidency, and the Democratic sweep of Congress
seemed to give him a free hand. This encouraged the internationalists
who had been pushed aside by American isolationism in 1920; after all,
the president-elect himself had been the defeated Wilsonian vice presidential candidate in 1920.

But the Democratic landslide provoked currency panic. The
Democrats relied for support on farmers who had been clamoring for a
devaluation since before the Depression began. By 1933 American farm
prices were barely half their already depressed 1928 level, while other
prices had gone down by much less: 8 percent for consumer durables,

18 percent for metal products.[35] As the four months from election to inauguration dragged on, Roosevelt was careful not to say what he would do about the dollar's gold value, but members of his future cabinet were not so coy. Henry Wallace, a prominent farm leader already announced as the new secretary of agriculture, said six weeks before the new administration took office, "The smart thing would be to go off the gold standard a little further than England has."[36]

As soon as it came into session, Congress took up measures to force the dollar off gold. It seemed clear that one way or another, the dollar would be devalued. A run on America's banks ensued, starting in February and spreading throughout the country until the eve of Roosevelt's inauguration on March 4, 1933. As in Austria, Germany, and Britain, the expectation of a devaluation led people to cash in dollars and buy gold. Once he took office, Roosevelt closed the nation's banks and announced emergency measures to stabilize the financial system. For a few weeks the dollar held steady as it seemed the administration might recommit to gold. But in mid-April Roosevelt confirmed the speculators' expectations and took the dollar off gold.

For three months the Roosevelt administration pushed the dollar down, so that it dropped against sterling from $3.42 back roughly to the $4.86 price it had held before the pound's devaluation. The dollar floated, generally downward, for another six months until in February 1934 Roosevelt refixed the dollar at $35 an ounce, more than two-thirds below the long-standing $20.67 per ounce gold parity. As if to reinforce his sense of priorities, over the summer of 1933 Roosevelt effectively shut down a World Economic Conference in London that had been trying to work out some form of international monetary cooperation. In a strongly worded message on July 3, the president insisted that "the sound internal economic situation of a nation is a greater factor in its well-being than the price of its currency." He lashed out at "the old fetishes of so-called international bankers," which were, he said, "being replaced by efforts to plan national currencies with the objective of giving those currencies a continuing purchasing power."[37] It was hard to imagine a more trenchant rejection of the traditional rules of the classical international economy. The day the dollar was taken off gold, Budget Director Lewis Douglas said glumly, "This is the end of Western civilization."[38]

In retrospect, most analysts have accepted the synthesis of Barry Eichengreen, who adopted Keynes's epithet for gold as the title of his account of the interwar economy, *Golden Fetters*:

The gold standard is the key to understanding the Depression. The gold standard of the 1920s set the stage for the Depression of the 1930s by heightening the fragility of the international financial system. The gold standard was the mechanism transmitting the destabilizing impulse from the United States to the rest of the world. The gold standard magnified that initial destabilizing shock. It was the principal obstacle to offsetting action. It was the binding constraint preventing policymakers from averting the failure of banks and containing the spread of financial panic. For all these reasons, the international gold standard was a central factor in the worldwide Depression. Recovery proved possible, for these same reasons, only after abandoning the gold standard.[39]

From the darkness

By 1933 the world economy was dead in the water. Trade, investment, and lending were at small fractions of previous levels. Economic activity in every country was down by unprecedented amounts; all the hard-won gains of the 1920s were gone. Economic warfare waged across Europe and the Atlantic: War debts were repudiated, trade wars declared, competitive devaluations and exchange controls celebrated, reparations denied. All this fed into an atmosphere of desperation, political polarization, and mutual recrimination.

At the economic nadir of the Depression, governments became willing to jettison failed policies and try new ones. John Maynard Keynes, sensing the opportunity to influence policy makers and public opinion, swung into action. He derided the "imbecility" of the orthodox and their commitment to liquidationism: "It would, they feel, be a victory for the mammon of unrighteousness if so much prosperity was not subsequently balanced by universal bankruptcy. We need, they say, what they politely call a 'prolonged liquidation' to put us right. The liquidation, they tell us, is not yet complete. But in time it will be. And when sufficient time has elapsed for the completion of the liquidation, all will be well with us again."[40] Keynes would have none of this: "The voices which . . . tell us that the path of escape is to be found in strict economy and in refraining, wherever possible, from utilizing the world's potential production are the voices of fools and madmen."[41]

Keynes watched with approval as the United Kingdom went off gold, a move he called a "most blessed event."[42] He even abandoned his long-standing support for free trade in the face of the economic disaster. "We do not wish," he told an Irish audience, "to be at the mercy of world forces working out, or trying to work out, some uniform equilibrium according to the ideal principles of *laissez-faire* capitalism." Keynes remained an internationalist in all things cultural and intellectual, but the dire straits in which the peoples of all nations found themselves called for attention to national conditions first and foremost. "Ideas, knowledge, art, hospitality, travel—these are the things which should of their nature be international. But let goods be homespun whenever it is reasonably and conveniently possible; and, above all, let finance be primarily national."[43]

Keynes had lost the battles of the 1920s—over Versailles, monetary policy, and the British return to gold—but the spectacular failure of the world economy seemed to prove him right. Gold was definitively out of favor. Farmers had long railed against it. Now workers, who were paying a stiff price in unemployment for the pervasive deflation, joined in. British labor leader Ernest Bevin argued that "only the rentier classes stood to gain" from maintenance of the gold value of the pound sterling and that "the deterioration of the conditions of millions of workers was too high a price to pay for the maintenance of . . . international banking in London."[44] Industrialists likewise favored the freedom to devalue and help them compete with foreigners.

Many economists, like Keynes, challenged the gold standard. In the United States one of the more curious was a Cornell agricultural economist named George Warren. Warren had spent a lifetime studying prices in the United States, especially farm prices. He had put together price data from newspapers, catalogs, contracts, and hundreds of other sources, in an obsessive effort to figure out how and why they moved. After decades of study Warren came to believe that when the price of gold in dollars went down, farm prices went down, while when the price of gold in dollars went up, farm prices went up. The weaker the dollar was against gold, the higher were American farm prices. Warren had many ideas about why farm prices moved this way, most of them wrong. But he was convinced that reducing the gold value of the dollar would raise farm prices. The way to do this was to go off gold and devalue.

Most serious American economists scoffed at Warren. His ideas had little grounding in established theory, and the evidence was circumstantial at best. But when Franklin Roosevelt came to office in 1933, he was desperate to do something about what he called the threat of "an agrarian revolution in this country."[45] His decision to take the dollar off gold and devalue it was influenced by the man derided as Rubber Dollar Warren.

Rubber Dollar Warren, it turned out, was right (even if for the wrong reasons). As the dollar declined, prices of agricultural products and other primary commodities soared. In March 1934, before the devaluation began, American farmers were getting thirty-five cents a bushel for their wheat. By July they were getting eighty-seven cents, an increase of nearly 150 percent in a few months. The Moody's index of staple commodity prices, which measured a range of farm and raw materials prices, rose by about 70 percent over the three months from April to July 1933. And the price increases were effective in turning the tide of the crisis: They gave relief to farmers and other debtors, reversed the downward spiral of deflation and financial distress, and restored confidence. As the first three months of devaluation progressed, the Dow Jones Industrial Average rose by over 70 percent, reflecting the changed climate of opinion.[46]

The U.S. government, freed from the constraints of the gold standard, was able to expand the money supply, raise prices, and put the economy back on track. In the first year after the dollar was devalued, the Federal Reserve expanded the monetary base by 12 percent, and it kept up this rate of growth until 1937, by which time the money supply was nearly 50 percent higher than in March 1933. With more money in circulation, prices rose continually, and the reversal of deflation was instrumental in bringing the economy out of the Depression. Deficit spending played little or no role, as the Roosevelt administration did not really begin to experiment with fiscal policy until 1938 and 1939, when the worst of the Depression was over. The virtual entirety of the recovery in the United States was due to the relaxation of monetary policy, made possible by the devaluation. By one estimate, if policy had not been changed, the American economy would have remained stagnant and as late as 1942 would have been half the size it actually was.[47]

The American experience was typical: The commitment to gold deepened and lengthened stagnation, and going off gold allowed recovery to begin. The contrast can be seen by comparing countries that went off gold early in the Depression with those that held on until later. In 1930 and 1931 wholesale prices in all the countries on gold declined by about 13 percent a year. The deflation essentially stopped there for the United Kingdom and the countries that accompanied it off gold in late 1931, for once they were off gold they were free to stimulate their economies. Meanwhile deflation continued to plague the nations that kept their currencies on gold. The impact was not just on prices; between 1932 and 1935 industrial production in countries off gold grew by 6 percent a year, while it declined by 1 percent a year in the gold standard countries.[48]

As new policies were adopted, a gradual recovery began in 1934 and continued until 1937. As economies revived, the western nations tried to reconstruct their international trade, financial, and investment relations. The Roosevelt administration led the British and French in September 1936 to a tripartite monetary agreement, which committed the three governments to mutually support one another's currencies. The agreement was an attempt to build a modified international monetary system without gold standard fetters. It was soon joined by Belgium, Luxembourg, the Netherlands, and Switzerland. And almost immediately after America's Reciprocal Trade Agreements Act of 1934 allowed the executive to agree to reduce tariffs in return for reductions proffered by other countries, American trade barriers began going down.

Western governments also adopted domestic programs to cushion the blow of unemployment, facilitate union organization, and incorporate labor movements into politics. The American New Deal and the French Popular Front government were merely the most prominent examples of such trends. A similar and even more pronounced evolution took place in Scandinavia, where Socialist governments led the way toward trade liberalization. Out of the economic carnage of the Depression emerged the beginnings of the modern welfare state, understood as the general acceptance of government provision of social insurance, basic social policies, and macroeconomic management to attempt to avoid economic volatility. In the west, new people, parties, and classes tried an array of new policies that insisted on, rather than reject, the possibility of satisfying *both* domestic and international economic commitments and that insisted on, rather than reject, *both* a market economy and active government involvement in the economy.

Governments in central, eastern, and southern Europe and in Japan turned inward when the crisis hit. In this they were like the rest of the world. But unlike western Europe and North America, these regions were soon ruled by new fascist or protofascist governments that continued to reject the international economy. These governments brought the concept of autarky—forcible separation from the rest of the world—to economic organization, where it remained a good description of fascist attitudes toward the world economy.

Along with economic autarky, the fascist path involved severe controls on labor. Existing labor movements were wiped out, along with the Socialist and Communist parties with which they were affiliated. They were replaced with government-controlled "labor fronts" that told workers what their interests were, then met them. It was not so much that labor's interests were ignored—the Nazis engineered the most rapid and lasting reduction in unemployment in the industrial world—as that there was no possibility for these interests to be expressed independently. Fascist governments could also push businesses around if they got in the way of important policy goals, but large corporations were better able to resist or blunt government pressures than were disorganized workers. The fascist and neofascist political economies of central, eastern, and southern Europe and of militarist Japan contrasted with those of the west, then, on both major dimensions. The west looked to rebuild international economic integration, while the fascists looked to protect themselves from it; the west brought organized labor into the heart of government, while the fascists destroyed their labor movements.

The semi-industrial Soviet Union and Latin America found different alternatives to both pre–World War One orthodoxy and western social democracy. The Soviets constructed a Communist autarky, even as they engineered the most rapid industrialization drive in history. In Latin America and other developing regions, the prior vocation of producing food and raw materials for export could not survive in a world in which primary product demand and prices were chronically depressed. Forced back on its own devices in the 1930s, the developing world refocused its energies on national development. Urban society and modern industry grew rapidly in semi-industrial areas of Latin America and the Middle East.

Despite the divisions and differences, a common thread tied together all the industrial and semi-industrial countries' responses to the Depression. All of them—except for the Soviet Union, which pursued organized socialism—in one way or another implemented some sort of organized capitalism. Governments supported cartels to stabilize prices, permitted or encouraged the coordination of wages, and manipulated macroeconomic policy to affect national economic conditions. The chaos of the first few years after 1929 left its mark everywhere. And everywhere this mark pointed away from laissez-faire and toward vigorous government involvement in the economy. The experimentation was tentative in some countries, revolutionary in others, but everywhere the way had been cleared for new approaches to the problems of modern economies.

Out with the old . . .

The Depression's ferocity was at root the result of the clash between the interests and ideas that had reigned before 1914 and the new economic and social developments that had altered the world since then. In the face of the original downturn, governments followed policies inherited from classical global capitalism, whose supporters were many and powerful among ruling circles. These presupposed an earlier economy of small firms, disunited workers, and textbook conditions of perfect competition—as well as a political system that could resist pressures to alleviate the suffering of workers and the poor. But industrial economies were now dominated by huge corporations, mass production, and complex consumer products; labor unions were much stronger than before World War One; and political systems were far more democratic. Classical policies to confront the catastrophe ranged from useless to counterproductive, yet governments, driven by faith in gold standard solutions, soldiered on as conditions worsened.

The new, organized capitalism of big businesses and powerful labor movements, along with financial fragility and wage and price rigidity, made the classical adjustment mechanism obsolete. Competitive orthodoxies were inadequate for the problems of the organized democratic industrial capitalism that had evolved out of the global capitalism of the golden age. At the same time, European conflicts unresolved at Versailles and American reluctance to get involved in the affairs of the Old World blocked the collaboration among financial centers that had helped them over the difficulties that arose before 1914. The Depression's harshness reflected a fundamental inconsistency between the traditional principles of the pre-1914 classical world economy and the new organization of domestic and international societies.

The old guard of international bankers, imperial investors, powerful industries, and landed aristocracies tried traditional measures to deal with the crisis. They hewed to the international gold standard and international financial commitments and maintained a concomitant hostility to interventionist government policy. They proved completely unable to address national economic crises and domestic social emergencies. The traditionalists' insistence on bankrupt policies only inflamed their opponents in the labor movement, in the business community, among small businesses and farmers and intellectuals. Ultimately, the failure of the classical nostrums brought forth new ideas and new groups, and soon power changed hands everywhere.

The continuing crisis eventually drove classes and countries toward new ways of counteracting the Depression. Some looked to the political extremes for answers, seeking in communism or fascism the solution to the apparently intractable problems of orthodox capitalism. Others, even among the political and business classes that had long run society, were equally eager for new approaches, in this case to save capitalism rather than to replace it. New forms of economic and political organization called for new ways of dealing with them, and countries crawled their way out of the Depression toward these new ways.

The classical world economy had failed. The halting recovery, the preliminary steps at reconstituting international economic order, the islands of growth in the midst of stagnation, and the newly available products and techniques could not disguise this basic fact. The old order did not deliver economic growth, or stability, or protection from chaos. It had not brought peace and cooperation and may indeed have inflamed conflicts among nations. Critics of global capitalism—whether fascist or Communist—seemed vindicated by its inability to overcome the troubles of the period from 1914 to 1939. The fact that rapid economic growth was restored only with the rush to rearm was cold comfort indeed.

9

The Turn to Autarky

In March 1933 Adolf Hitler shocked the world by appointing Hjalmar Schacht to take charge of the German economy. Schacht was Germany's best-known economic policy maker and a pillar of international gold standard orthodoxy. There was, the *Economist* wrote, "no leading banker in the world who more fervently preached balanced budgets, adherence to the gold standard, the removal of restrictions on the free movement of capital and the rest of the elements of the orthodox faith."[1] Middle-class Germans idolized the man who had ended inflation. Germany's captains of industry trusted him as a prominent financier. Foreign statesmen and investors admired Schacht as a reasonable inter-locutor during the difficult negotiations over war debts and reparations.

But Schacht abandoned orthodoxy after 1929 and proposed new methods to deal with the crisis. His new methods involved separation from world markets, forceful state intervention in the economy, and massive public works. His plans required a strong government to imple-ment them, and he turned to the Nazis to engineer this turn away from global capitalism. Germany's paragon of classical economic internation-alism led the country to a rejection of every classical principle.

Schacht had company, for the Depression convinced almost everyone of the bankruptcy of traditional economics and politics. The world economy's ancien régime—global markets for capital and goods, the gold standard, minimal government involvement in the economy—seemed to have worked reasonably well before 1914. But during the 1930s international markets collapsed, governments were forced to intervene to save national economies, and people everywhere looked to replace failed traditionalism.

Like Schacht, much of the world found its way to the alternative of autarky, economic self-sufficiency. Countries across southern, central, and eastern Europe—from Portugal to Latvia and from Germany to Greece—adopted some variant of autarkic fascism. The countries of Latin America converged on autarkic developmentalism. The political economies of other independent developing countries looked strikingly like those of Latin America, as did the more advanced colonies.

One after another semi-industrial country embraced the new economic nationalism. Romania and Mexico, Argentina and Japan, Italy and Russia all rejected the gold standard, imposed prohibitive trade protection, tightly controlled foreign investment, denounced foreign bankers and the debts they were owed, and force-marched modern industrial growth. An entire stratum of the global social structure—the middle class of nations, neither rich nor grindingly poor—moved along a path that was at great and sometimes violent variance with that of western Europe and North America.

Semi-industrial self-sufficiency

One needs to know only one thing to determine whether a country moved toward autarky and authoritarianism or remained economically open and democratic: whether it was an international debtor. Every autarkic regime—fascist states in Europe, the Soviet Union, developmentalist governments in Latin America and Asia—ruled a net debtor nation. Every debtor country went the way of fascist or nationalist autarky; every creditor country remained democratic and committed to international economic integration. (Czechoslovakia and Finland were in rough international financial balance.)

The debtor nations were different because they were semi-industrial. They were poor enough to rely on exports of primary products (raw materials and agricultural goods). But they were rich enough to have thriving urban industries that produced for the domestic market. They were poor enough to need foreign loans but rich enough to be credit-worthy. Their powerful export sectors coexisted with growing domestic industrial sectors. The coexistence of internationalist and nationalistic sectors of the economy gave rise to conflict once the world economy crashed.

Until the Depression the debtor countries' governments played by international financial rules, for only those that conformed to creditors' expectations were able to borrow. They relied on foreign trade, loans, and investment. They struggled to tie their currencies to gold and their markets to the rest of the world.

The ruling classes of the debtor countries depended upon the international economy. Bankers and traders, large landowners, export manufacturers, miners and lumber barons and oilmen all had global ties. Their leading firms borrowed abroad or were owned by foreigners; when their governments had deficits, they financed them in London or New York or Paris. So long as the world economy performed well, these countries did well, sometimes spectacularly well.

But the debtors' economic growth created new social groups that were less enthusiastic about the global economy. Industrialists producing for the domestic market wanted protection from foreign companies; urban workers resented making sacrifices to support a gold standard from which they got little benefit.

Interwar realities further undermined the debtor nations' conservative internationalists, challenging both their conservatism and their internationalism. First came the new mass politics, as economic growth, World War One, and the worldwide rise of the socialist and Communist movements all helped labor and the Left gain in size and power. The "middle sectors"—small businessmen, artisans, small farmers—too were increasingly active politically. The millions of workers, farmers, and others battering at the gates of autocratic regimes could not be ignored. By the early 1920s mass movements of the Left and Right were threatening the political hegemony of the traditional ruling classes.

The second source of the conservatives' weakness was the collapse of their economic basis with the Great Depression. Ragnar Nurkse, an Estonian economist at the League of Nations, reported, "During the international financial crisis . . . it was a popular joke in some countries to compare foreign credit to an umbrella which a man is allowed to borrow as long as the weather is fair, but which he has to return the moment it starts raining."[2] As world markets broke down, those in the semi-industrial nations who depended on contacts in London, Paris, and New York found their foreign partners weak, bankrupt, or gone.

The obligations inherited from the open economy aggravated the suffering as the crisis persisted. Foreign bankers and their domestic allies had saddled countries with massive debts, whose payment meant disaster. Global investors and traders imposed the tyranny of gold, which had led to ruin. Local agents of world markets had delivered the nation into debt slavery.

New groups created or mobilized since the turn of the century poured into the vacuum left by the debilitated conservatives. The open economy was challenged by those who wanted protection from, not access to, foreigners. Old alliances collapsed, and new ones were formed.

As the debtor countries turned toward autarky during the 1930s, they rejected their foreign debts, reliance on world markets, and comparative advantage. Their previous areas of specialization were taxed to stimulate sectors of the economy that had been hamstrung by foreign competition, especially national industry. They gave up on foreign capital and markets and turned inward to the domestic market and domestic finance. Their governments took on the thoroughgoing transformation of the national economy.

The semi-industrial countries had depended on classical rules. They had given pride of place to international economic opportunities, export agriculture, raw materials, and export industries over domestic manufacturing and domestic food production. With world markets and their local representatives in disarray, the autarkies turned away from international competition and toward the use of national resources to meet national demands. This led to a cascade of measures to reinforce economic nationalism from Japan to Portugal and from Brazil to Germany.

Schacht and the Nazis rebuild Germany

Hjalmar Schacht was a stereotypical German of the old school, with a stiff high collar, a prim Prussian wife, and an obsessive concern for propriety and prestige. Like John Maynard Keynes, he was a product of the classical economic order, bred to support the orthodoxies of the past: the gold standard, balanced budgets, and free trade. Schacht's turn to Hitler symbolized the marriage of convenience between rabble-rousing fascists and conservative German businessmen. The Nazis needed Schacht to bolster their ties to Germany's business leaders; Schacht and his business supporters needed the Nazis to address the country's economic problems.

The architect and engineer of Nazi economic nationalism was the son of progressive internationalist parents, a Danish aristocrat and a German from the Schleswig-Holstein region that was constantly changing hands between Denmark and various German jurisdictions (Schacht's hometown of Tinglev is currently in Denmark).[3] His parents emigrated to New York in the early 1870s; his father became an American citizen and was an active supporter of progressive American causes. They moved back to Germany just before their second child was born, apparently because conditions in their homeland had improved. The couple named the boy Hjalmar Horace Greeley Schacht, after the New York presidential candidate and newspaper publisher who had published Karl Marx's dispatches from Europe.

After a mediocre university career, Hjalmar did his graduate work in political economy. He was uninterested in scholarship and was baffled by the abstract philosophical questions asked him during his oral doctoral examination.[4] Schacht wanted the degree only to go into business, and in 1903 he went to work for the Dresdner Bank, one of Germany's largest. Schacht married his longtime sweetheart, Luise, whose reactionary Prussian background—her father was an imperial police inspector—complemented Schacht's nonconformist origins. Schacht served briefly in government financial administration during World War One, only to become entangled by accusations that he had used his position to benefit the Dresdner Bank. After the war Schacht became one of two principals in another leading financial institution, the Danatbank.

Schacht distinguished himself from his colleagues primarily by his political ambitions. He himself dated his fascination with politics to when he was eleven years old and saw Kaiser Wilhelm II in Hamburg. The young Schacht was awed by the pomp and circumstance of the imperial visit. "Power is an empty word," he later wrote, "until one has seen a display of power. . . . I suddenly grasped the meaning of the word 'Politics.' "[5]

His first major foray into the political arena came the day the defeated Germans signed the armistice that ended World War One. Schacht and other liberals believed that only an alliance between the moderate business classes and moderate socialists could save Germany, and the German Democratic Party was formed as, in Schacht's words, "a middle-class Left which will throw in its lot with the organized workers in the coming Coalition Government."[6]

Schacht's Democratic Party occupied a crucial position in the democratic Weimar Republic, as the most progressive bourgeois party and one of the socialists' principal parliamentary allies. Schacht and the Center-Left Democrats stood for a classical liberal economy, tempered by extensive social programs—market capitalism with a human face, so to speak. The Democrats included some major business figures, drawn primarily from the internationalist wing of German capitalism. They were hostile to the radical Left for its socialism and to the radical Right for its extreme nationalism and economic interventionism.

Schacht's activism in the Democratic Party propelled him into domestic and international renown. By November 1923 the German inflation had reached its high point. Communist revolutionaries threatened to take power in several German states and cities; Adolf Hitler's Nazis attempted a coup in Munich. The Center-Left government needed somebody to stave off economic collapse, but the German central bank was headed by an unreliable conservative who had done nothing to stop the inflation. Schacht had impeccable financial and political credentials, as a banker and a member of a liberal democratic party.

On November 13, 1923, at the age of forty-six, Hjalmar Schacht became Germany's commissioner for the national currency. Two days later the printing presses were stopped, and Schacht announced a new rentenmark, backed by real property and exchangeable for old marks at the rate of one trillion to one. On November 20 the old central bank head died. The government appointed Schacht president of the Reichsbank—as the candidate of the Left, over the objections of the conservative parties and of almost the entire Reichsbank board of directors.

With Schacht as currency commissioner, the mark's value held steady for the first time in years. He obtained foreign support for the mark stabilization, while the government raised taxes and cut spending to help avoid a return to deficit spending. By spring 1924 the terrible German inflation was over, and on the streets of Germany Schacht was credited with this achievement.

Schacht knew that the German economy could not fully revive until the reparations issue was untangled, so he helped negotiate the August 1924 Dawes Plan to regularize German's international financial position and allow the country access to foreign capital. For the next six years Schacht was Germany's principal representative in international eco-

nomic affairs, traveling throughout Europe and North America to negotiate war debts, reparations, trade, and currency matters. His pro-
nouncements were at the center of international politics and economics.
And while he was strongly nationalistic, he was also one of the world's
most effective spokesmen for gold standard orthodoxy.

But Schacht was above all a pragmatist, and the Depression shook his
faith in the practicability of traditional solutions. He broke definitively
with the past in 1930, as he struggled to renegotiate Germany's obligations. Schacht felt betrayed by the German government, whose desperate financial straits were driving it toward policies he regarded as fiscally
irresponsible, and by his foreign friends, who were pressing the German
nation for concessions Schacht believed were unacceptable. After fighting on two fronts, against profligacy at home and exploitation abroad, in
March 1930 Schacht resigned his position as president (for life) of the
Reichsbank.

In late 1930 Schacht contacted the Nazis through Hermann Göring.
In January 1931 he met with Adolf Hitler and began pressing others in
ruling circles on behalf of the view that Hitler should be brought into
government, marshaled and tamed on behalf of a conservative program
to meet the emergency. In spring 1931 he told an American journalist,
"No, the Nazis cannot rule, but I can rule through them."[7] Over the
course of 1931 and 1932, Schacht became convinced that, in his words,
"this party would take the leadership in the coming government."

In October 1931 Schacht appeared at a public meeting of the German
Far Right, dominated by Hitler, and gave a bitter speech attacking the
government. His wife, Luise, who had been an early Hitler supporter,
was ecstatic. As the Nazis rolled up electoral successes, Schacht wrote
to Hitler, "[Y]ou can always count on me as your reliable assistant."[8]
Even after the Nazi vote declined in the November 1932 elections,
Schacht's endorsement was splashed all over the front pages of the
German press: "There is only one man who can now become
Chancellor, and that is Adolf Hitler."[9]

Soon Hitler was chancellor, appointed by conservatives who saw him
as a last resort. As more elections loomed, Schacht served as a crucial
intermediary between sympathetic businessmen and the Nazis. In late
February 1933 Hitler and Göring met with a score of prominent financiers and industrialists to secure their political and financial backing.
Göring played for support with the promise that if the Nazis won this
election, it would "be the last one for the next ten years, probably even
for the next one hundred years."[10] After the Nazi leaders left the room,

Schacht turned to his colleagues: "All right, gentlemen. Now to the cash register!"[11] He collected three million marks for the Nazis and their allies, who won the March 5 election, the last one in prewar Germany. Two weeks later Hitler appointed Schacht president of the Reichsbank.

Hjalmar Schacht was never a member of the Nazi Party and did not share many of its principles. But like many others in the conservative wing of the business community, he saw the Nazis as capable of exercising power to reassert German nationalism. Nazi economic ideas ranged from unformed to bizarre, and Schacht was confident that he could fill the policy vacuum. No other political force could hold Germany together against the threat of communism and chaos, and Hitler seemed willing to give Schacht free rein.

Despite his classical and orthodox origins, Schacht shared some important ideas with Hitler. He had come to regard the Left with suspicion, even hatred. He saw the western powers as exploitative. He believed that the government needed to use centralized power to restart the economy without rekindling inflation. Schacht was also an easy anti-Semite in the way of many traditional Germans of his generation: "Jews must reconcile themselves to the fact that their influence among us is over, once and for all. We want to keep our people and our culture pure and our own."[12] At the same time, he abhorred the vulgarity of the Nazis and their violent anti-Semitism. He argued against restrictions on Jewish businesses and helped design an emigration scheme that saved the lives of many German Jews.

Despite their differences, in 1933 both Hitler and Schacht agreed that the overwhelming need of the moment was to stimulate the economy and reduce unemployment. Schacht wrote, alluding to the fact that he did not share all of the Nazis' views: "Since I was now given the opportunity of ending unemployment for six and a half million persons, all other considerations must give way. . . . It was not from personal ambition, or agreement with the National-Socialist Party, or greed of gain that I took up my former post, but simply and solely out of burning anxiety for the welfare of the great masses of our people."[13]

Hitler himself had a clear view of how Schacht could suit the Nazis' needs. "He is," Hitler later told some colleagues, "a man of quite astonishing ability and is unsurpassed in the art of getting the better of the other party. But it was just his consummate skill in swindling other people which made him indispensable at the time."[14] The new Reichsbank president was respected by those from whom the Nazis needed support or at least forbearance, and he was willing to take bold economic measures to confront Germany's economic crisis. In return for his success, Hitler awarded Schacht the post of minister of the economy in July 1934 and a year later made him the plenipotentiary general for the war economy. Schacht had complete control over German economic policy.

Hitler gave Schacht absolute power over a German economy in shambles, with more than a third of the workforce unemployed. The Nazis' political priority was to destroy the Left and labor, but their economic priority was to end the grinding unemployment that had made the Left powerful and attractive in the first place. Hitler made this goal clear to Schacht, who designed the so-called Schacht Plan to rebuild the economy, avoid inflation, restore order in the country's foreign trade, and permit rearmament.

Schacht effectively ended unemployment within three years. The Nazi government created a half million jobs for young adults, sending them out to do community chores or farmwork. Another half million of the unemployed were sent to build roads, repair bridges, and help with public works. The government cut wages to encourage owners to hire new workers and gave employers subsidies to increase their workforces. General government spending increased from a 1929 level of 16 percent of GNP to 23 percent in 1934. Much of this spending was concentrated where it would reduce unemployment: construction, transportation, work creation, rearmament. In two years, from 1932 to 1934, these four categories went from just 15 percent to more than half of government spending. Even if rearmament is excluded, employment-creating programs went from under two billion marks in 1932 to eight billion in 1934, from 10 to 35 percent of total public spending. The Nazis also helped their political support bases: They gave tax and loan relief and price supports to farmers and government contracts to small businesses. This all involved substantial budget deficits, averaging nearly 5 percent of GNP over the first four years of Nazi rule—deficit spending substantially higher than that pursued elsewhere. By 1936 the economy was essentially at full employment, and in 1937 and 1938 labor shortages began to surface.[15]

Such programs would normally have raised fears of inflation, but as Schacht wrote with understatement, "National Socialism introduced in Germany a state-regulated economy which made it possible to prevent price and wage increases."[16] Wage increases were out of the question, for the Nazis destroyed the labor movement and instituted a reign of terror in the workplace. Hitler assured Schacht that Nazi deficit financing would not lead to price increases, as his regime would alter conventional economic relationships: "[T]he first cause of the stability of our currency is the concentration camp."[17] In Hitler's words, "Inflation is lack of discipline. . . . I'll see to it that prices remain stable. That's what my storm troopers are for. Woe to those who raise prices. We don't need legislation to deal with them. We'll do that with the party alone. You'll see: once our storm troopers visit a shop to set things right—nothing similar will happen a second time."[18]

Schacht also used the regime's political power to implement a form of autarky that became known as Schachtian economics. The government enforced tight control on the use of foreign currencies and on Germans' taking their money abroad. All payments on the country's foreign debts—not to speak of reparations—were suspended. Schacht put in place a system of multiple exchange rates, offering better currency prices to favored industries and foreign allies. The capital and exchange controls kept as much money at home as possible, allowing the Nazi government to channel financing to public works, industrial development, and rearmament.

The Thousand-Year Reich also built a trade network in eastern and central Europe in order to prepare its sphere of influence. Schacht designed elaborate preferential trade schemes, forcing unfavorable terms on countries in the Nazis' economic and political orbit. In the late 1920s Germany accounted for about 15 percent of the total trade of Hungary, Romania, Bulgaria, Yugoslavia, Greece, and Turkey; by the late 1930s this was up to nearly 40 percent on average, more for some countries. The share of Germany's total trade accounted for by these six countries tripled in this period, as the formerly informal German economic area became a formal economic and diplomatic reality.[19]

Schacht led German economic policy from the depths of depression to recovery and autarkic reconstruction, but his success created the conditions for his own irrelevance. The Nazis had needed him to provide credibility with foreigners, domestic capitalists, and the German middle classes. His job was now essentially done, and after 1936 he found himself in increasing conflict with the Nazi government.

For one thing, the Hitler regime had so centralized political power and financial resources that private capitalists were less important than they had been when the Nazis took power. By 1938 the Nazis had more than five hundred important state-owned firms, half of all investment was being carried out by the state, and government spending was 34 percent of GNP, up from 15 percent in the late 1920s.[20] For another thing, while Schacht and like-minded businessmen had supported autarky as a way to focus on national economic growth, they were not in favor of long-term separation from the world economy. But it eventually became clear that the Nazis had no intention of rebuilding economic ties to the West. Finally, Hitler's increasingly bellicose intentions worried Schacht and other business leaders; it was one thing to rebuild Germany's international position, quite another to provoke a Continental war.

The Nazis reduced Schacht's influence as they consolidated power. All through 1936 the architect of the recovery was increasingly ignored. Hermann Göring increased his control over economic policy, standing for the subordination of economic policy to the government's political and military goals. "I do not," said Göring, "acknowledge the sanctity of any economic law."[21] To Schacht this was heresy, as was the Nazi leader's refusal to safeguard the role of private business. Göring tackled Schacht head-on: "Against this conception of liberalism and economics we set our conception of national socialism and that is: In the center of economy stand the people and the nation, not the individual and his profit; work and economy are exclusively only there for the whole people."[22] After trying to counter the trend, in summer 1937 Schacht stopped going to his office in the ministry; in November, Schacht's resignation from the cabinet was announced.

"Der Führer," quipped *Time* magazine, "has fired the Schacht heard round the world."[23] A bit more than a year later Schacht was relieved of the Reichsbank presidency too. From 1938 on Schacht was on bad terms with the Nazi government. For his part, the former financial dictator participated in a series of plots against Hitler. After the failure of the most important such coup attempt, in July 1944, Schacht was arrested. He remained incarcerated for four more years, first in Nazi prisons, then in the Dachau concentration camp, finally in a succession of Allied and German prisons.

Schacht was one of the twenty-four original Nuremberg defendants and one of three to be acquitted. He was then indicted by the postwar German authorities but was eventually released. He served as a financial consultant for another decade or so and died at the age of ninety-three in Munich in 1970. His life had spanned nearly a century and several eras, from a child admirer of Kaiser Wilhelm, through financial leadership during the pre-1914 golden age, to attempts to restore normality in the 1920s, through the rise and fall of the Thousand-Year Reich, to beneficiary of the postwar German Miracle. Yet Hjalmar Horace Greeley Schacht's finest hour was also his most morally questionable: He crafted an extraordinarily effective response to the Depression, which strengthened the most murderous government of modern times and laid the foundation for the most devastating war in world history.

Autarkic economic policies

Like Germany, the other autarkies promoted national production for national use, especially industrial growth. Everywhere the turn inward was justified as necessary to modernize the economy; continued reliance on world markets would only reinforce backwardness. Germany was an industrial power, and Italy was relatively developed; but their analogous goal was to strengthen industry to avoid dependence on hostile foreigners and eventually to provide the wherewithal for reassertion of their military capabilities. Some governments also supported agriculture—not the export-oriented farmers of the previous open economies but those who could assure food self-sufficiency.

The autarkies pursued industrial modernization by the time-tested means of making industrial investment exceptionally profitable, raising the prices industry received and lowering the costs it paid. In this they followed a long tradition. The mercantilist empires of the seventeenth and eighteenth centuries had forced colonies to sell their raw materials cheap and buy their manufactured goods dear, channeling profits to metropolitan traders and manufacturers. Such later developers as the United States had repeated this pattern: High tariffs on manufactured goods forced farmers and miners to pay inflated prices to industry while delivering their food and raw materials at prices set on world markets. Both mercantilism and neomercantilist protectionism turned the terms of trade in favor of industry, raised the price of goods industry sold and lowered the price of goods industry bought.

The autarkies turned the internal terms of trade in favor of industrial investment, against agriculture and against consumption. Government directed resources out of the export-oriented primary producing sectors of the past and into the inward-oriented industrial sector of the future and out of the pockets of workers and farmers and into industrial investment. Expensive manufactured consumer goods and low wages translated into lower living standards for workers. This was true despite populist rhetoric and high-visibility government programs. The Nazis trumpeted the dignity of farming and labor, but real wages in 1938 were still below their 1933 (and 1929) levels, and artificially low farm prices contributed to a flood of farmers off the land and into the cities.[24] Real wages in Italy at the end of the 1930s had regressed to pre–World War One levels, 20 percent lower than they had been in 1921, before Mussolini took power.[25] In the Soviet "dictatorship of the proletariat," the industrial transformation of the economy was accompanied by severe hardships for much of the working class.[26]

Subsidizing industry at the expense of traditional economic activities required a complex range of follow-on policies. Higher prices for industry required strict controls on foreign trade to keep out cheaper competitors. Governments imposed high tariffs, quotas and other restrictions, or outright prohibitions on foreign goods. Many took over all foreign trade themselves. Germany and its central and eastern European trading partners developed barterlike clearing arrangements, so that German aspirin sent to Hungary was balanced by Hungarian wheat sent to Germany.[27] This steep protection, whatever its form, led to import substitution, the replacement of previously imported goods with local products. Efforts to restrict trade succeeded: Germany's foreign trade in 1938 was barely one-third of what it had been in 1928, and the decline among other autarkies was only slightly less dramatic.

Foreign investors could have leaped trade barriers to take advantage of the government subsidies and incentives to domestic industrial investment, but this would have displaced local businesses. So governments reserved national industry to nationals, by controlling foreign investment. Existing multinationals were subjected to stringent regulations, forcibly sold off to local investors, or simply taken over by the government. New investment was strictly limited, often to keep out firms that would compete with local companies and let in only those whose production would complement that of national firms. Foreign companies were prohibited from sending profits home, forced to hire more local citizens, and assessed higher taxes.

Governments defaulted on their foreign debts and scaled them back to fractions of the original amounts, in order to save precious capital and foreign currency for industry. Governments imposed stringent controls on capital movements as well as currency trading, in order to force domestic investors to keep their money at home to provide capital to industry. Governments doled out foreign currency to benefit favored sectors and forced overseas earnings to be surrendered to the government.

The rate the government charged those permitted to buy foreign currencies might vary by the priority of its use. A government trying to encourage local steel production, for example, could allow the import of iron ore or coking coal at a very favorable exchange rate and charge importers a very unfavorable rate for finished steel imported. This encouraged the import of inputs and discouraged the import of the final product. Local citizens who took vacations abroad might be charged a particularly expensive exchange rate to reduce foreign travel and stimulate domestic tourism. Firms that wanted to import spare parts could be given a favorable exchange rate if the parts were not locally available, but an unfavorable rate if locally made versions of the parts could be substituted for imports.

The autarkies' currency manipulations usually meant leaving the gold standard, which was in any case the principal prop of the hated international financial aristocracy. Governments often kept the currency "overvalued," artificially strong in terms of others, again in service of national industry. An artificially strong ("appreciated") currency made foreign goods cheaper and domestic goods more expensive, which would have hurt national industry in the previous open economies. But now, with economies effectively closed to competitors, overvalued currencies made it cheap for manufacturers to import raw materials, iron and steel, spare parts, and other inputs they needed.

In addition to protection from foreigners, industry got positive support. Governments gave preferential loans, subsidies, and tax treatments and used government spending directly and indirectly to spur demand for manufactured goods. Most of the autarkies dramatically expanded the public sector to include many new productive activities—in the Soviet Union, to include almost everything. These closed economies could not rely on imports of basic industrial goods, and such projects were usually too big or unprofitable for local capitalists, so governments set up a rash of state-owned basic industrial corporations. The enlarged state sectors came to produce steel and chemicals, provide electric power and transportation, mine coal and oil, all for the sake of industrial development.

Industry grew at a pace that ranged from the respectable to the remarkable. From its Depression low point, industrial output in western Europe and North America had barely regained 1929 levels by the late 1930s, but it doubled and more in Germany and Poland, in Japan, in Brazil, Colombia, and Mexico and more than quadrupled in the Soviet Union. [28]

The autarkies pursued national industrialization by concerted, sometimes extreme means. They took money for industry out of traditional farming and mining, which were anyway associated with the spent ruling classes of the past. They took more money for industry out of mass consumption, which would anyway have been wasted on the ungrateful and antinational proletariat (said the fascists), the ungrateful and antinational petty bourgeoisie (said the Communists), the ungrateful and antinational oligarchies (said the developmentalists). The mix of policies varied, but the core was similar everywhere: Throw all available resources into industry. This was done with antilabor vengeance by the fascists, with anticapitalist fervor by the Communists, and with patriotic ardor by the nationalist developmentalists.

Europe swings to the Right

Germany was only the most important of the dictatorships of the Right that rolled like waves from southern Europe through the rest of the continent. The first set came as part of a conservative reaction to the social unrest of the years after World War One. Between 1920 and 1924 the tottering democracies of Italy, Spain, Hungary, and Albania succumbed to new dictatorships; in 1926 Portugal, Poland, and Lithuania fell. The second set came with the Depression: Yugoslavia in 1929, Romania in 1930, Austria in 1932, Germany in 1933, Latvia, Estonia, and Bulgaria in 1934, Greece in 1936. While Spain redemocratized in 1930, ultimately the fascists under Francisco Franco emerged victorious from a bloody civil war.

"Dictatorships today," said Portuguese dictator António Salazar, "no longer seem to be parentheses between regimes."[29] By 1936 every country in southern, central, and eastern Europe—with the lonely exception of Czechoslovakia—was a reactionary despotism. Not all fitted the textbook description of fascism: totalitarianism with a mass populist following and a disdain for the conventional Right. But this phalanx of fascist and authoritarian tyrants represented a clear alternative to liberal capitalism, economic internationalism, and democracy.[30] Only western Europe was untouched, although several western European countries had notable homegrown fascist movements and by 1941 Nazi occupations had felled most remaining European democracies, leaving only Switzerland, Sweden, Finland, Britain, and Ireland.

The fascist and neofascist regimes counted on enthusiastic support from the New Right, drawn from the urban lower-middle classes and small farmers, and more measured collaboration from traditional conservatives in big business and big agriculture. Semi-industrial Europe's traditional and New Right made common cause against labor and the Left, and agreed to close the economy to foreign competition. In some cases, such as Germany and Italy, the fascists seized and consolidated power with the support of the conservatives. In others, traditional conservatives—such as Admiral Miklós Horthy in Hungary or the kings of Romania, Bulgaria, Greece, and Yugoslavia—ruled with the support of local fascists. Either way, the relationship was symbiotic: Traditional conservatives needed the fascists' mass base; the fascists needed the conservatives' credibility with big business.

The two most important fascist regimes, Germany and Italy, were larger and more developed than other fascist lands, but in both countries fascists preached hatred of left-wing labor, foreign bankers, and domestic business with strong foreign ties. Germany's export industry and finance had been one of the bases of the Weimar Republic, in alliance with the Socialists and with the support of Anglo-American loans and diplomacy. (At least some of the anti-Semitic bent of the fascists was related to the fact that in Germany and much of eastern Europe, many of the internationally oriented businesses were owned by Jews.) In Italy the alliance that brought modern industry and labor together from the turn of the century until the early 1920s (known as the Giolittian system) had also relied on integrating the country into the world economy. The failure of the old order brought democratization and international economic integration in Germany and Italy to an end just as certainly as did the fall of Brazilian coffee or Romanian oil.

Fascism's typical mass base was among farmers, small businessmen, handicraft workers, and white-collar functionaries; these groups were two-thirds of the Nazi Party in 1935 while they were just a quarter of the German population.[31] They yearned for an earlier era in which they had had a privileged position and saw modern industry and labor as the cause of their social dislocation. But fascists understood that they could not rule without big business and large landowners and sought their support or at least cooperation. The wealthy appreciated the antisocialism of the fascists, even if they disdained their lower-class origins and

populist hysteria; fascism promised to halt the increase in labor costs
that had disrupted big industry and big agriculture.[32]

Fascist supporters among capitalists, landowners, farmers, small businessmen, and functionaries were tied together by hatred of the powerful socialist movements that had emerged from World War One. They
saw as their principal enemies labor and social democracy and those segments of the business, professional, and political classes that had tolerated and worked together with them. But the reasons for this animosity
to labor and its allies differed, and the peculiar mix of déclassé middle
sectors and capitalist upper classes had strange effects. In both Italy and
Germany much of fascism's mass appeal was due to its anticapitalist
rhetoric, but Hitler and Mussolini quickly made their peace with big
business and large landowners—on terms largely dictated by the dictators, to be sure—and relied increasingly on their collaboration. After all,
the fascists' grandiose plans required the economic wherewithal that
only the investing classes could provide.

As Hjalmar Schacht's experience demonstrated, the fascists were hard
put to satisfy these two broad constituencies—antilabor capitalists and
landowners, on the one hand, and discontented lower middle classes, on
the other. Fascists celebrated agrarian traditionalism but accelerated
industrialization. Their rhetoric trumpeted individualism and independence, but their policies championed monopolies and cartels. Fascist ral-
lies gloried in the splendor of supposed imperial pasts while demonizing
the imperialist powers. Fascism concurrently embraced both reaction
and radical change, preached a return to the moral certainties of a
preindustrial idyll, but promised rapid advance to modern industrialism.
The contradictions of fascist rhetoric reflected the contradictory nature
of its support base, which eventually led to disagreements over which of
the conflicting goals was to take priority.

But first the fascists had to consolidate their hold on power. Most of
them took over amid economic distress and social unrest and spent their
initial years on emergency footing, dealing with both. Social unrest was,
in the first instance, easy: It was repressed, often brutally, as labor
unions and Left parties were outlawed and their leaders jailed, exiled, or
murdered. But repression was not enough and could not work forever;
the fascists had to a large extent come to power because they promised
to solve dire economic problems.

So the first economic order of business was to engineer recovery, and
this the fascists did. The new dictatorships used reflation, deficit

finance, new taxes, and spending simultaneously to reward their mass followers in city and countryside and jump-start stagnant economies. As in Germany, fascists virtually everywhere started with a rapid demonstration that they could bring the country out of crisis, along with quick payoffs to their core supporters. In Italy, as in other countries where dictators took power in the 1920s, the economic problems were less immediate and severe. Mussolini assured Italian industrialists and landowners that the fascist regime would follow policies they trusted, and until the Depression the Italian macroeconomy was run on standard conservative lines. At the same time, Italy's fascists undertook major programs to secure their political bases of support among the lower middle classes. They filled in marshes, distributed land to farmers, raised the salaries of public employees, and redoubled public construction projects.

Fascist success in pulling economies out of the depths of the Depression had several sources. As in the Third Reich, they used violence to achieve economic goals. Keynes himself wrote in the Preface to the 1936 German edition of his *General Theory* that the book's argument was "much more easily adapted to the conditions of a totalitarian state" than to a democracy. The fascists also stimulated economic recovery by signaling to the business community that its troubles were over: no more strike waves; no more Bolshevik threat; no more political instability. All this gave capitalists strong reasons to catch up on a backlog of profitable investments. They brought money out of mattresses and foreign bank accounts and sank it into a now-hospitable business climate. Finally, fascists were less constrained from experimentation than were the western democracies: They were implacable opponents of the foreign and domestic standard-bearers of gold standard orthodoxy, and the pursuit of new paths was a point of pride rather than a difficult break from tradition. This allowed them to try out program after program until they figured out what worked.

Having addressed the immediate crisis, fascist rulers turned to their longer-term goals: unquestioned political control, accelerated industrial development, autarky, military expansion. Independent political organizations were liquidated and replaced with easily controlled channels by which citizens might try to express their opinions: Nazi labor fronts, fascist "corporations" (industry guilds) that included both management and labor, all under the supervision of the fascist state.

Economic policy shifted from crisis management to remaking society, often in ways that troubled the business allies of the fascists. As the 1930s wore on and the fascists implemented their programs—which included priority to state industry and the subjugation of private business to military adventurism—much of the traditional business community found itself farther and farther from power. Schacht's estrangement from the Nazis was typical of tensions between the fascists and big business as war clouds gathered. In Italy, as in Germany, Mussolini exerted ever-tighter control on foreign trade and channeled it toward allies and the new Italian miniempire, an effort that took on greater urgency in 1935, when the League of Nations slapped sanctions on Italy for its aggression against Ethiopia. The turn to greater autarky and away from markets in western Europe and North America troubled industrialists in many fascist countries. With recovery in place, they were interested in reestablishing economic ties with the industrial countries rather than in suppressing them.

But as fascist economics took hold, the ability of the business community to resist them declined. By the late 1930s Mussolini's regime, like that of Hitler, was running major parts of Italian finance and industry. Under the auspices of several enormous state-owned holding companies, the Fascist government controlled nearly half of the country's share capital, almost all bank lending, and most of the country's steel, machinery, shipping, electrical, and telephone sectors.[33] The "little dictatorships" of southern, eastern, and central Europe followed suit: State-sponsored firms accounted for two-thirds of Bulgaria's industrial output in 1937, the public sector for two-thirds of total investment in Poland throughout the late 1930s.[34]

While relations between business and the fascist state were uneasy over some issues—extreme autarky, government controls on the economy, the diversion of resources to the military—in other dimensions fascist policies were in line with business preferences. The fascists suppressed wages and ignored or actively discouraged mass consumption. All available wealth was thrown into investment for industrialization, modernization, and militarization. They gave primacy to heavy industries, not to consumer goods production.

The German experience was especially striking, for the stagnation of mass living standards came in the context of a booming economy. Despite full employment and complete recovery, real wages in 1938 were still well below 1932 levels and had stagnated for four years; wages fell from 64 percent of national income in 1932 to 57 percent in 1938. Consumption dropped even more precipitously in the same years, from 83 to 59 percent of national income. In 1937 the average German working-class family was eating substantially less meat, milk, eggs, vegetables, and sugar than in

1927; only the consumption of rye bread, cheese, and potatoes had increased.[35] German workers had little to celebrate, but for business this was a decidedly favorable component of Nazi economics.

The fascist dictatorships varied widely. German income per person was three to five times that of the rest of fascist Europe; Germany was less than one-third rural while most of eastern and central Europe was 75 to 90 percent rural.[36] Even in agriculture, Germany was a relatively advanced farming nation while eastern Europe was extraordinarily backward; farmers in Germany in the 1930s used between fifty and five hundred times as much fertilizer per acre as did farmers in eastern Europe, where agricultural productivity often was lower than it had been at the turn of the twentieth century. Two-thirds of Bulgaria's plows were still wooden in 1936.[37] This helps explain why the fascist and proto-fascist movements of eastern Europe tended toward peasant radicalism, for their farm populations were truly miserable and their agriculture desperately needed modernization. The prospects for rapid industrial development in Albania or Lithuania were hardly comparable to those in Italy, Poland, or Hungary; the possibilities of anything approaching autarky were laughable in Estonia or Latvia with their tiny populations, while they were considerable in Germany and Italy, and even such middle-size countries as Spain and Poland could contemplate substantial industrial self-sufficiency.

Halfway across the world the Japanese government took on many fascist features. Like Germany and other semi-industrial countries, Japan had established a fragile democracy and a generally open economy in the 1920s. Neither survived the Depression. Japan's analogue to Hjalmar Schacht was Korekiyo Takahashi, a respected banker and politician who had been president of the Bank of Japan, prime minister, and finance minister in several democratic governments. As in Germany, a crisis government backed by businessmen and the military brought Takahashi in as finance minister to try to control a failing economy. Takahashi, despite his orthodox background, experimented with reflationary measures similar to those used by other autarkies. He took the yen off gold and engineered a massive depreciation in 1931. This led to an export boom that flooded world markets with Japanese textiles, toys, shoes, and other cheap goods. As this petered out in the face of foreign protectionism and the limited growth of world markets, Takahashi turned to deficit spending to keep the economy going. Over the course of the 1930s the economy grew an impressive 72 percent.

Meanwhile the Japanese military and its allies, including powerful business groups, clamored for imperial expansion abroad and discipline at home. They eclipsed the remaining moderates in government, seized Manchuria in 1931, formally allied with Germany, and went to war with China in 1937. In 1936, when Takahashi, like Schacht, warned of the economic implications of military adventurism, the Japanese militarists had him assassinated. From then on, the militarists' hold on economic policy and political power was unchallenged. They purged the political system of the last vestiges of democracy and pushed economic policy toward rapid industrialization and the consolidation of the influence of large-scale industry and finance. An integral part of these plans was the construction of a semiautarkic East Asian Co-Prosperity Sphere, which was to serve to speed Japan's industrial development. The path would, as elsewhere, lead to war.[38]

At its height the fascist economic order—the fascist states, those they had occupied, and their colonies—included virtually all of Europe and the Middle East and much of Asia and Africa. Perhaps half the world's population lived in, or under the rule of, fascist political economies. Neither communism nor liberal democracy had had anything like the reproductive and expansionary success of fascism. While the defeat of Germany, Italy, and Japan in World War Two made fascism an anachronism, surviving only in a few risible backwaters—Spain, Portugal, Greece—in the late 1930s fascism was a serious contender for international economic supremacy.

Socialism in one country

The other self-conscious candidate to supplant western liberal capitalism was the central planning of the Union of Soviet Socialist Republics. The Soviets built their form of socialism during the Depression, amid massive social and economic upheaval. The Bolshevik Revolution had lopped off the investing classes of Russian society, leaving a country made up of industrial workers and managers, government functionaries, small businessmen, and peasants—especially peasants. Communist support was in the cities: The industrial proletariat was strongly favored by Soviet policy, as were industrial managers, many of whom were Communists promoted from the shop floor to supplant the technicians of prerevolutionary Russia. In public administration too the

Bolsheviks gradually replaced unreliable bureaucrats with loyal party members. However, neither peasants nor small businessmen had much use for Communist theory or practice—not a minor problem in a country where these two groups together were 90 percent of the population.

During the 1920s the Soviet regime promoted a private-public hybrid economy that accepted the private farm and small business sectors. Modern industry, finance, and utilities were run by the government, which also controlled foreign trade and investment. But agriculture remained almost entirely private—and after all, four-fifths of the population was in farming—as did most domestic trade and small-scale industry. The public sector accounted for a tiny proportion of the labor force. This hybrid produced relatively rapid growth rates and had brought most branches of the economy back to prerevolutionary levels by 1926 or 1927. Even foreign trade revived, although at much lower levels than before 1914. The Soviet Union was no market economy, but there was little planning; the state-owned firms ran themselves, as islands of modernity in a sea of rural backwardness.

This was not a stable balance of economic or political forces. The model socialist society the Bolsheviks had in mind could not be confined to isolated urban pockets of support for, or at least absence of active hostility toward, Soviet rule. The Communist mission required the construction of a modern industrial society; it was hard to imagine a proletarian dictatorship without a proletariat. And the wealthy entrepreneurs in the vibrant private sector were a latent threat to the regime. The Bolsheviks regarded much of the peasantry too as inherent opponents of the urban-based Communist regime, whose goals after all did include the liquidation of private property. Moreover, Soviet agriculture was disdained—not entirely inaccurately—as hopelessly backward, useful only as a potential source of food, materials, and labor for industry.

Joseph Stalin and his supporters began pushing the country toward rapid industrialization after 1928, when they consolidated their control of the Communist Party and the government. The first five-year plan, of 1928–1933, called for a substantial expansion of state control of the economy and for enormous new investments in industry. The Soviet industrialization drive had many domestic sources, especially the Communists' concern at ruling a preindustrial society with only the support of a tiny urban industrial sector, but international conditions were also an important impetus for the turn inward. First and foremost, Stalin and the Soviets were convinced that they would eventually be attacked by some or all of the capitalist powers. They did not have much time to build an industrial sector large enough to provision an army capable of beating back such a military challenge. The hostile diplomatic environment helped justify Stalin's insistence on a forced march to industrialization. The hostile international economic environment had the same effect. Some of Stalin's opponents had argued that more gradual, less violent means could be used to industrialize, but these plans involved grain exports to pay for imported machinery for industrial development. The collapse of world commodity markets made these proposals unworkable. So in the Soviet Union, as in so many other countries, the Depression reinforced an economic turn inward.

As in the other autarkies, the resources for rapid industrial development were largely taken out of agriculture and out of consumption. In the case of the Soviet Union, the state turned the terms of trade against agriculture even as it launched a sweeping assault on private farming. If the peasants would not voluntarily assist in the industrialization drive, their resources would be corralled and commandeered. The regime forced peasants into collective farms under quasi-governmental control. In 1928, 97 percent of the country's farmland was in private production; by 1933, 83 percent was in the collectives.[39] Not surprisingly, farm production stagnated under this punishment, dropping by more than a quarter between 1928 and 1932 and barely returning to 1928 levels by 1939.[40] Rather than surrender their animals to the collectives, farmers slaughtered and ate or sold what they could; from 1928 to 1933 the country's stock of pigs and cattle went down by half, of sheep and goats by two-thirds.[41]

The government required collective farmers to sell their crops to the government at artificially low prices, providing cheap food and raw materials for industry. In addition, it forced grain out of the collective farms to sell abroad; in 1931, as famine threatened, one-sixth of the country's wheat and grain harvest was exported to buy machinery and equipment for the new factories, railroads, and utilities.[42] The government's success at hobbling the peasantry made farming so unattractive that tens of millions of rural inhabitants fled the countryside to provide a cheap labor source for industry.

The government also squeezed consumers to industrialize the country, raising prices and reducing the availability of consumer goods as it threw resources into heavy industry. Overall, consumption's share of the economy declined by one-third between 1928 and 1937, from 82 to 55 percent of national income. About half of this was poured into investment; the other half went to current (noninvestment) government spending, divided equally between military and nonmilitary purposes. The tax on consumption was especially visible in the government's bias toward heavy industry and against consumer goods (light) manufacturing. Between 1928 and 1938 woolen and cotton fabric output increased at barely the rate of population growth, while steel output quadrupled and truck and tractor production went from 2,500 to 250,000 a year.

The Soviets needed some way to manage this increasingly complex and increasingly government-run economy. Over the course of the first and second five-year plans, between 1928 and 1937, they improvised their way toward an organizational structure for Soviet planning that endured for decades. [43] At the top was the State Planning Committee, Gosplan, under which were a series of industrial ministries with responsibility for particular sectors (iron and steel, chemicals). Every five years the government determined a general orientation for the economy. Gosplan used this to formulate goals for a five-year plan, in consultation with managers and administrators who knew conditions in the industries and regions. Gosplan then ordered enterprise managers to fulfill annual production requirements in line with this plan.

Planners set prices, like production targets, centrally. The central planners sometimes took into account the desire to balance supply and demand, but they had many other concerns as well, such as favoring the cities over the countryside and heavy industry over light industry. This led to some strange results: In 1932 rye flour was 12.6 kopecks a kilo, while rye bread was 10.5 kopecks a kilo, implying that the flour might actually lose value by being made into bread.[44] This was due not to the quality of Soviet bread but rather to pricing policies motivated by political rather than market considerations—in this case, the desire to keep food prices for urban workers low. Enterprise managers used prices almost entirely for accounting purposes. While firms' managers and workers could be rewarded for good performance, the usual capitalist market indicators—prices, profits, losses—were irrelevant. Factories did pay for their deliveries from other factories—shoe manufacturers paid for leather; tractor manufacturers paid for steel—but the money left over after paying costs was turned over to the government, while firms that lost money got the difference from the government. It could not be otherwise with prices set for noneconomic reasons. How could a bakery be expected to make money if it was not allowed to charge enough for bread to cover the cost of flour?

The economy was managed by a system of material balances. Each ministry was expected to produce and deliver a given number of tractors or shirts, and in turn each ministry assigned analogous goals to the enterprises it controlled. Central planners had to make sure that factories were supplied with what they needed: tractor factories with steel, garment factories with cloth. Gosplan had to make sure that the country was going to produce enough steel to cover the needs of tractor manufacturers and other users, enough cloth for garment manufacturers and other users, and so on. The central planners were charged with making sure that it all turned out to be roughly in balance.

Planners defined their goals in terms of the material output of factories, power plants, and farms. This raised problems of quality—a million pairs of poorly made shoes was still a million pairs—which Gosplan and the ministries had to monitor. The Communist Party, with members in every enterprise, served as something of a parallel system to ensure everything from labor discipline to managerial commitment.

Soviet autarkic planning was a stunning success in many ways. The best statistics available indicate that from 1928 to 1937 industrial production went up fivefold. Steel output rose from 3 to 13 million tons, coal from 36 to 128 million tons. Lenin had preached, pragmatically, "Communism is Soviet power plus the electrification of the whole country," and electricity production shot up from 5 billion killowatt-hours in 1927 to 36 billion in 1937. Millions of people moved off the farm and into industry and related activities. From 1926 to 1939 the number of farmers dropped from sixty-one to forty-eight million, while the number of workers in industry, construction, and transport went from six to twenty-four million. Agricultural workers fell from four-fifths to half the labor force, while industrial and related workers went from 8 to 26 percent.[45]

The country industrialized in a decade, and per capita GDP rose by 57 percent between 1928 and 1937.[46] This achievement was especially remarkable with the rest of the world mired in unemployment and stagnation, and even the most successful industrial countries, Norway and Sweden, grew only half as rapidly as the USSR. Although consumption was severely limited, Soviet living standards also appear to have risen, by 27 percent according to one estimate. The government's principal bases of support—urban workers, bureaucrats, Communist Party members—received most of the benefits of rapid development, while farm incomes grew little or not at all.[47] The broader price was enormous. Government coercion, indifference, and disorganization left parts of the countryside stripped of grain, and millions of peasants died of famine in the terrible years of 1932 and 1933. Moreover, the use of terror against those believed to stand in the way of industrialization poisoned Soviet politics and society for generations.

But by the late 1930s the Soviet Union had leaped to the first rank of industrial nations. Soviet steel production in 1940 put it behind only the United States and Germany. This was true only of basic industrial goods, not of living standards, but as World War Two began, this was certainly relevant. And Soviet industrialization was accomplished with an almost complete separation from the rest of the world economy and with a new system of central state ownership and control. Soviet industrial success provided a striking alternative both to the reformed liberal capitalism of the West and to the garrison capitalism of the fascist powers. To the developed world, Soviet socialism held out the promise of a full-employment system in which human design, rather than profits, determined the shape of the economy. To the developing world, Soviet socialism seemed to produce rates of growth and development that no capitalist economy had ever equaled. The full importance of these trends was not evident in 1939, for the USSR remained on the fringes of the world economy. But for millions of people around the world, Soviet socialism offered a serious alternative to capitalism's fascist, social democratic, and underdeveloped variants.

Development turns inward

The 1930s were also a turning point for the developing world, especially for those poor regions that had already achieved a level of industrial maturity. This included most of Latin America; such other independent developing countries as Turkey, Egypt, and Siam; and some of the more developed colonies, such as British India and French Algeria. China shared much with these regions, although it was racked by civil war and Japanese invasion.

These areas had developed substantial urban industrial economies during the decades of openness before 1929. In some cases, such as India and China, urban industry was tiny relative to the rest of the economy—although large in and of themselves, given India and China's sheer size—while in others, such as Argentina, Chile, and Turkey, industrial development was quite advanced. All had been drawn into the world economy as export-oriented producers of primary products, but the wealth accumulated on this basis had created urban centers whose fortunes increasingly diverged from those of farmers and miners. Most obviously, the exporters were free traders—they wanted access to world markets and to be able to buy manufactured goods as cheaply as possible—while the new industrialists demanded protection from foreign competitors.

The collapse of world trade fatally weakened export interests, and urban groups came to dominate economic policy. In fact, for the developing world, Depression-era conditions prevailed until the middle 1950s. The Depression was succeeded by World War Two, which only further closed the world economy; after the war, reconstruction and the Cold War once more preoccupied the developed nations until the end of the Korean War in 1953. So from about 1929 to about 1953, Africa, Asia, and Latin America were cast adrift economically from the industrialized world. In the course of those twenty-five years, the more advanced developing nations broke from their open economy pasts in favor of a new model based on domestic industries producing for protected domestic markets.

This transition from primary exports to domestic industrialization repeated that of many countries that came before. For example, the early political economy of the United States was dominated by southern cotton and tobacco interests hostile to the protectionism of northern industry. Conflict grew over the early nineteenth century, deepened by differences over slavery, until the Civil War decided matters in favor of the North and set the country on a resolutely protectionist path. In Latin America and other advanced developing nations, the Depression and subsequent years played a role analogous to that of the Civil War in the United States: It brought down internationalist economic interests and brought nationalists to the fore.

The Depression in the developing world called an entire socioeconomic order into question. A way of life based on exporting to Europe and North America was particularly vulnerable to the downturn, for primary prices went down much faster and farther than did industrial prices. From the late 1920s to the late 1930s, prices of the principal developing country mineral exports fell 60 percent; prices of sugar, coffee, and cotton declined by two-thirds or more; the price of rubber went down 80 percent. This was on top of an already weak performance in the latter part of the 1920s. Overall, an index of principal agricultural products declined 30 percent between 1925 and 1928, then fell another 66 percent to 1932, so that in this last year the index was more than 75 percent below its 1925 level.[48] Other prices fell too, but not as much as primary products. This meant that the developing regions were earning much less on their exports and paying only slightly less for their imports.

The terms of trade of the poor regions dropped precipitously. This standard measure of the relationship between export and import prices for Latin America, for example, fell by 44 percent between 1928 and 1932. This meant that the prices of Latin American exports fell 44 percent farther than the prices of its imports so that with the same volume of exports the region could buy only 56 percent as many imports as in 1928. But this was not all, for the Depression reduced not only the price but the actual volume of developing country exports as demand in rich regions plummeted. Even as Latin America's terms of trade dropped 44 percent from 1928 to 1932, the volume of its exports fell by another 22 percent. Between the fall in relative prices and the fall in volume demanded, in 1932 Latin America could only afford to import 43 percent of what it had had in 1928.[49] In some countries the shock was even greater. Chile relied on copper and nitrates for almost all its exports, and these were especially hard hit by the Depression. By 1932 Chile's imports had dropped by 87 percent in three years.[50] The impact on agrarian countries was roughly equivalent to what would be the impact on a farm family if, between falling prices and falling demand, its crops brought in less than half the customary income: a corresponding collapse in the ability to buy from the rest of the world (the rest of the economy, in the case of the family).

The international financial collapse intensified the shock. When the New York and London markets dried up, the borrowing nations lost their principal cushion against adversity. In addition, while prices that debtors earned on their goods plunged, the debt burden was fixed in dollars or sterling. So the debtors were expected to make fixed interest payments out of drastically reduced export earnings. Peru was a typical example. In 1929 the country's exports were $134 million, and debt service—interest and principal on the foreign debt—was $13 million, 10 percent of this. By 1932 exports had collapsed to $38 million but debt service owed was $14 million, more than one-third of export earnings.[51] The same grinding reality held for commitment to the gold standard; the costs of sustaining it during the present emergency were astronomical, as gold and hard currencies had gotten ever more difficult to earn.

This enormous shock provoked a uniform response by the poor countries. Where they had a choice—that is, where they were not colonies or otherwise occupied by a financial power—they took their currencies off gold, depreciated, and introduced inconvertible paper money. Also, rather than use scarce gold and hard currency to service debts owed to financial markets that seemed unlikely to revive, almost all independent developing countries defaulted and imposed controls on the movement of currencies and capital. Even in the colonial countries the Depression undermined the position of foreigners in the economy. Three-quarters of the foreign-owned sugar factories in Java went out of business. European expatriate bureaucrats and employees all over Southeast Asia were dismissed; they were simply too expensive. Millions of Indian and Chinese migrant workers left or were sent home.[52]

This chain of events—export collapse, currency depreciation, debt default—threw the developing regions back on their own economic devices. Like farm families whose money earnings were cut in half, the developing nations bought less from others and produced more on their own. The effect was more or less automatic: Goods produced at home were cheaper; goods from the industrial countries were more expensive. The developing regions experienced a natural process of import substitution as domestic production replaced goods previously imported. Entrepreneurs quickly seized the opportunities, including to develop local uses for previously exported farm and mine goods in manufacturing.

World economic events were reinforced by national policies, as governments scrambled to reorient economies away from exporting and toward domestic production for domestic use. The large currency depreciations made imports more expensive, while emergency trade barriers raised import prices yet further. Turkey and Egypt, Thailand and Chile, even the colonial authorities in India erected barriers to imports, provided cheap loans for domestic producers, and built up roads and other infrastructure to encourage national industrial development. Government corporations took over railroads, electricity, oil wells, steel, banking, and foreign trade.

Everywhere in the developing world, local production for local consumption—mainly local manufacturing—soared. Egypt had previously exported raw cotton and imported cloth, but the collapse of the world price of cotton while world textiles prices remained high made this unattractive and even impossible. Enterprising Egyptians began using local raw cotton to make clothing and textiles, and soon a substantial industry was in place, bolstered by new trade barriers. Over the course of the 1930s Egyptian employment in clothing, footwear, and textiles manufacturing doubled while Egyptian production of mechanically woven cloth increased 700 percent.[53] By 1939, three-quarters of the local textile market was supplied by local products, up from barely one-eighth ten years earlier. Meanwhile local production came to fill between 90 and 100 percent of the local demand for alcohol, cigarettes, sugar, boots and shoes, cement, soap, and furniture.[54]

China in the 1930s was preoccupied with overcoming the political and military fragmentation of the country. Even so, the Nationalist government of Chiang Kai-shek's Kuomintang attempted to spur industrial development. After 1929 the government increased trade protection very substantially, especially for the products of such domestic industries as clothing and textiles. In five years average tariffs went from 3 to 27 percent of imports; by 1933 tariffs on some cotton goods were over 100 percent.[55] The central government also used public banks and government spending to stimulate modern investment, as did some of the provincial governments. But these measures were too late to have much effect on China's impoverished and underdeveloped economy, in which all modern industry was only 3 percent of GDP. The government's attentions were in any case absorbed by Japanese encroachments on Chinese territory and, after 1937, by a full-scale Japanese invasion. Despite these dire conditions, the Chinese government did continue to pursue industrial modernization and set up or took over nearly a hundred basic industrial facilities.[56]

Even countries long dedicated to farming and mining, and heavily oriented toward foreign markets, turned their economic structures around. Brazil's export agriculture in the 1920s had grown nearly three times as fast as industry. But in the 1930s, with the collapse of coffee prices, the depreciation of the Brazilian currency, and new tariff protection, industry grew ten times faster than export agriculture, doubling from 1929 to 1938.[57] Turkish tariffs more than tripled, and the country's manufacturing went from 9 to 17 percent of GNP in just ten years after 1929.[58] While all through the 1930s Chile's mining output remained below pre-Depression levels, industrial production grew 48 percent from 1932 to 1937, and output of cotton fabrics quintupled.[59] By 1935, 97 percent of Chilean consumption of nondurable consumer goods was domestically produced, as was 60 percent of metal products, machinery, and transport equipment.[60] Even Colombia, a quintessential agrarian exporter dedicated single-mindedly to coffee, was powerfully affected. Between 1928 and 1939 Colombian primary production rose by one-third, but manufacturing increased two and a half times. By 1945 Colombian production of cotton textiles was nine times what it had been in the 1920s, of cement thirty times.[61]

The poor regions simply could not afford to import and had to produce more at home. The economic imperatives behind this import substitution were so powerful that the process went on even in many colonies. India's British rulers found it impossible to maintain the colony's financial obligations without increasing revenues; that meant raising tariffs, even over the strenuous protests of the Lancashire cotton goods manufacturers. More generally, the collapse of export earnings meant that keeping the colony on a sound financial footing required import substitution. And Indian industry boomed, nearly doubling in size from 1928 to 1938. By the late 1930s India was producing 95 percent of the cement it used (up from 51 percent in 1919), 71 percent of its own tinplate (up from 25 percent), and 70 percent of its steel (up from 14 percent).[62]

Some of the very poorest colonies had limited possibilities for import substitution, and in some instances the colonial powers resisted it. Such areas as sub-Saharan Africa and Indochina did not experience so marked a Depression-era process of local industrial development. The British, who acceded to Indian demands for industrial promotion, were better able and more willing to resist such demands in regions where industrialists and their supporters were weak. Chancellor of the Exchequer Neville Chamberlain reported to his colleagues in 1934: "While it is improbable that West Africa would set up factories to compete with those at home, there [is] a real and serious danger of such factories being established in Malaya and possibly other parts of the Colonial Empire, and we might well be faced with very serious developments of a problem of industrial competition of which we [have] already had some experience in the case of India."[63] But overall, the 1930s were a time of inward-looking industrial transformation in most of the developing world.

The inward turn had important political ramifications. In the independent developing countries, the previously powerful primary exporting groups were weakened. As rubber collapsed in Malaya and copper collapsed in Chile, the political dominance of the rubber and copper barons faded. In almost all the major countries of Latin America the 1930s saw the eclipse of the agroexporting oligarchy of Latin American nationalist disrepute. In its place came new urban groups whose interests were domestic, not international: manufacturers, the middle classes, the labor movement. Turkey's nationalist leaders tightened their control. The Siamese monarch was displaced by a nationalist military coup and made an essential figurehead. Everywhere the new watchwords were *developmentalism* and *nationalism*, concerted government policies to speed industrial development and a redoubled emphasis on producing for the *national* market, with profits going to *national* firms.

Developmentalism was often associated with populist politics and policies, reflecting the mobilization of urban middle and working classes. The populists aimed to weaken the traditional elite's hold on social and political power. They introduced new social policies—unemployment insurance, public housing, public pensions—as well as encouraged the organization of workers and other urban dwellers.

The new regimes gave different weights to nationalism, developmentalism, and populism. Mexico marched forward on all three fronts. President Lázaro Cárdenas took office in 1934 and built a new political and economic order out of the results of a bloody revolution between 1910 and 1920 and a decade of postrevolutionary reconstruction. Cárdenas promised organization and good wages to the urban working classes, employment to the middle classes, and land to small farmers and, in part to defuse American concern, invoked Roosevelt's New Deal as a model. Cárdenas nationalized the country's foreign-owned oil wells in 1938; he also set up a government-run power system and made the public sector the centerpiece of industrial policy.

The Mexican example was striking for its revolutionary and nationalistic fervor, but comparable movements came to the fore elsewhere. The Brazilian "Revolution of 1930" eventually brought Getúlio Vargas to office as a nationalistic dictator with semifascist leanings. Chile's leftist parties came to power democratically as a Popular Front, and despite the ideological differences, both Brazilian and Chilean systems ended up heavily oriented toward nationalist industrialization. Thailand was not as developed, but there too the military leaders of the 1932 revolution poured resources into state-led industrial development, aimed in part at displacing European and Chinese businessmen.[64] Argentina took a more circuitous course to a similar destination. During the Depression the agroexporters remained powerful, in part by working out privileged access to the British Empire's markets. But an urban nationalist backlash brought a new military regime to power in 1943, and the government was eventually dominated by a middle-ranking officer named Juan Domingo Perón. Peronism was a unique Argentine blend of nationalism, developmentalism, and populism, drawing the urban masses into the battle against the traditional agrarian elite, including with such symbolic acts as burning down the elite's flagship Jockey Club.

Similar trends took hold in the more advanced colonies, foremost among them India. New groups of Indian businessmen, strengthened by industrialization in the 1930s, became convinced that economic development demanded greater autonomy from the empire. As the economy grew and diversified, more of the population gravitated toward the burgeoning Congress movement, which eventually won power electorally in 1937.[65] The Indian nationalists demanded that they be permitted to do what the independent developing countries were doing: raise tariffs, default on the foreign debt, devalue the rupee. The British met many of these demands, but they could not overcome the fundamental conflict between the interests championed by Indian nationalists and the countervailing interests of British exporters, bondholders, and taxpayers. The government of India's ability to address domestic concerns was hampered by its commitments to its British overseers.[66] This helped set India—and some of the other more advanced colonies—on a course that eventually led to independence.

Where colonial political economies were weaker or colonial rulers more hostile, the result was even more polarized and conflictual. In such areas the Depression led to the same dire problems for primary producers, but there was little scope for industrial diversification in a way that was consistent with colonial rule. In the words of one West African leader, "It is not enough to live in the old agricultural economy. We must manufacture and buy our own goods. We must industrialize our country."[67] But colonial rulers were rarely willing to speed industrial development in regions they regarded as ill suited to modern manufacturing. The result was often the eruption of rebellions with a radical and nationalist tinge eventually led by Communists in Vietnam and Indonesia and by leftist nationalists in French and British West Africa. Some colonialists believed resistance to local development was shortsighted. For example, the governor-general of Indochina wrote in 1937: "It is impossible to conceive that Indochina should remain forever in a state of economic vassalage, under the pretext that it must not compete with French products either in France or at home."[68] But such views did not prevail against the powerful interests in a continuation of the status quo.

The Depression's impact on the developing countries was more mixed than in the industrial world, where hardly a positive trend could be discerned. To be sure, the disintegration of the world economy hit the developing world hard, especially the collapse of primary prices and the disappearance of international loans. Yet as Latin America, the Middle East, Africa, and Asia were forced back on their own devices in the 1930s, they found some aspects of the experience encouraging. Urban society and modern industry grew rapidly. With them came new groups and classes—businessmen, professionals, workers—that would lead these regions toward more democracy and, in the case of the colonies, independence.

The autarkic alternative

The interwar implosion of the international economy drove most of the world's nations inward. The Soviet regime raced to modern industrial growth with brutal single-mindedness and central planning, trampling its rural population in the process. Governments in central, eastern, and southern Europe invoked a new fascist ideal as they stamped out labor, the Left, and eventually all opposition in the march toward militaristic self-reliance. The upper tier of developing countries in Latin America, the Middle East, and Asia rejected Europe and North America to build national economies on nationalist principles; the colonies prepared themselves to do the same.

The global economy in the 1930s offered little more than the promise that international integration might eventually make people and societies better off in a world restored, a world yet to come. Promises were no substitute for results, though, and the classical model of economic openness was short on results. Fascism, communism, and nationalist developmentalism delivered. They provided jobs, industrial development, modernization, and, less tangibly, national pride and cohesion. Fascism and communism did so at the expense of liberty and on the backs of their chosen enemies of the state; developmentalism was rarely more humane. An alternative was slow to develop.

10

Building a Social Democracy

In 1933 John Maynard Keynes wrote: "The decadent international but individualistic capitalism in the hands of which we found ourselves after the war is not a success. It is not intelligent. It is not beautiful. It is not just. It is not virtuous. And it doesn't deliver the goods."[1] Yet the industrial democracies, unable to develop an alternative, floundered through the first years of the Depression. A few did better than others, but none did well, certainly not so well as Germany and other fascist regimes. Governments in most of western Europe and North America tried deflation, then a series of stopgap macroeconomic measures, then trade protection but did not make much of a dent on unemployment or stagnation. Many in the industrialized democracies were drawn to the German or Soviet model to replace the market system and to autarkic economic nationalism to replace reliance on the world economy.

The democracies began to find an alternative in the middle 1930s. Parties of the Left came to power, with working-class and agrarian bases of support. They enacted more interventionist economic policies, expanded social programs, and increased government spending. And the new governments rebuilt cooperative economic ties among the democratic states.

The new alternative was social democracy. The modern social democratic welfare state would not truly be constructed until after World War Two, but by the late 1930s its foundations were in place in western Europe and North America.

Swedish and American roads to social democracy

Social democracy was a new social and political order, even if most of its features had precedents. Governments backed by coalitions of workers and farmers took responsibility for macroeconomic management, social insurance and social security, and labor rights. Two countries' experiences are particularly instructive: Sweden and the United States.

In the 1920s the Swedish Social Democratic Party polled over 35 percent of the vote and participated in government several times. In the 1932 elections the Social Democrats took 42 percent of the popular vote (Far Left parties took another 8 percent) and came close to a majority in the lower house of Parliament. They formed a government with the Agrarian Party, improved their position in the 1936 elections, and ruled Sweden for forty years thereafter.[2]

The first pillar of social democracy in Sweden was countercyclical demand management, government commitment to alleviate the business cycle. This was hardly controversial at the depth of the Depression, when everyone was looking to end the crisis. Social Democratic governments went further, attempting to reduce the amplitude and frequency of cyclical downturns in general, to maintain full employment. They used monetary policy to keep prices from falling or rising too much and fiscal policy (government spending and taxation) to sustain economic activity.

The Swedish government pioneered active monetary management. After the Conservative government took the currency off gold in 1931, it asked three eminent economists how it should manage the country's money. The economists recommended an active monetary policy to keep consumer prices steady where they were at the time of the September 1931 devaluation. The central bank accordingly promised "to prevent the price level in Sweden from following the downward international price trend."[3] The Socialist-led coalition that took power in

1933 reaffirmed this course. The Swedish government's explicit public commitment to price stability attracted international attention, especially as the Swedish economy quickly recovered.

Sweden's government took longer to use its second major macroeconomic tool, fiscal policy. Even many who advocated looser monetary policy believed that deficit spending was folly. The country's leading economist, Gustav Cassel, argued that if the government borrowed heavily for job-creating public works, the effect would be that "the private sector's supply of capital will dry up or at least be curtailed to the highest conceivable degree."[4] Cassel's colleague Eli Heckscher believed that private enterprises used money better than governments and that deficit spending was bad medicine, "the kind of medical treatment which used to be applied by market horse-traders with old nags for sale. They gave them a half a stoup of aquavit to make them pirouette as they had done in the springtime of their youth, only to revert, of course, to their former sloth once the intoxication wore off."[5]

Sweden's labor-based government, with unemployment at 25 percent, needed to do more than lower interest rates and wait for recovery. Some government advisers, like Heckscher's student Bertil Ohlin, recognized "the inadequacy of price stabilization" and argued that monetary policy was not enough. The unions demanded government efforts to put the jobless to work. So between 1933 and 1935 the Social Democrats implemented emergency and public works that employed an average of sixty thousand workers and gave another thirty-five thousand cash assistance. The deficits needed to run the "Crisis Policy" were small, 2 or 3 percent of GDP, and the policy was phased out after 1935. By then Sweden was recovering from the Depression, primarily because of the devaluation and the gradual improvement in international conditions. Nonetheless, the deficit-financed job programs set a precedent of concerted government spending to reduce unemployment.[6]

After countercyclical macroeconomic policy, the second pillar of Swedish social democracy was social insurance. The country had instituted some social policies in the first decades of the century, but they were very limited. Social Democratic leader Gustav Möller recalled the fate of his mother, the widow of a blacksmith who died of tuberculosis at forty-one. "There was," Möller said, "no public pension for my grandmother that could lighten mother's burden; there was no aid for widows with children and miserably low incomes; society did nothing to eliminate housing that helped cause people to become deathly ill and depart from life at a relatively early age; there were no legally regulated working hours; there was no paid vacation, still less the possibility of house-wives' vacations." Möller became the minister of social affairs in the 1930s and pressed for sweeping social reforms "to prevent the occur-rence of fate's like my mother's."[7]

During the 1930s Sweden implemented most of the programs associ-ated with the modern welfare state.[8] The government adopted unem-ployment insurance in 1934 and mandated universal participation in a national health insurance program a few years later. It instituted mater-nity, infant, and child care; subsidized school lunches; increased old-age pensions; and made housing grants and subsidies to poor families. By the late 1930s the Swedish government was providing its people some-thing approaching cradle-to-grave social assistance, even if benefit lev-els were relatively low. The Social Democrats had kept their promise to mitigate the social effects of a market economy.

Swedish farm policy also had a social dimension, for there was sub-stantial rural poverty. But the motivations for agricultural assistance were more political than social. The Swedish Social Democratic success relied on an alliance with the Agrarian Party—the "cow trade" or "cowli-tion" (kohandel), as the Swedes called it. Before this, the free trade labor movement and the protectionist farmers were at loggerheads—workers wanted access to cheap imported food, and farmers wanted access to low-wage labor—but during the Depression they made a deal, giving the Agrarians tariffs and price supports for dairy products, meat, bacon, eggs, and other locally produced food goods, in return for sup-porting the Social Democrats' prolabor policies. As the 1936 Social Democratic election platform put it, with some resignation, "the Swedish working class will pay the price necessary to guarantee workers in agriculture and small farmers a tolerable living standard."[9] The farmer-labor alliance, unusual before the 1930s, became a hallmark of the social democratic welfare state.

The social democratic solution included the incorporation of labor into the political system. In Sweden this meant organized consultation between business and labor leaders to manage industrial relations. During the early 1930s many Swedish businesses remained hostile to the Social Democrats, but the 1936 elections made it clear that the Left was going to dominate politics for the foreseeable future. The Social Democrats' finance minister Ernst Wigforss told business leaders that capitalists "should not base their actions on the assumption that the present political tendencies of the state will abate, that a political change will occur in the near future. . . . On the other hand, this also means that the representatives of political power admit the necessity of maintaining favorable conditions for private enterprise."[10]

At the end of 1938 representatives of the government, business, labor unions, and others signed the sweeping Saltsjobaden accord. Business and labor agreed to manage labor relations at a centralized, nationwide level. More broadly, in the words of political scientist Peter Gourevitch, "the terms of the agreement were business acceptance of Social Democratic government, high labor costs (high wages and the benefits of the welfare state), full-employment fiscal policy, and government activism for social services, in return for labor peace in labor markets (i.e. no strikes), continued private control over property and capital markets, and openness in relation to the world economy."[11] The Social Democrats were now allied with one traditional antagonist, farmers, and at peace with another, big business. Social democracy had arrived.

Across the Atlantic a different political configuration led to similar outcomes. The Hoover administration's policies were belated and ineffectual, when not actually harmful. The Democrats did not seem to offer anything more novel, and in fact Franklin D. Roosevelt ran for president in 1932 on a platform that accused Hoover of insufficient commitment to orthodox economic policies. He complained, for example, that the Republicans were not balancing the federal budget: "Let us have the courage to stop borrowing to meet continuing deficits. . . . Revenues must cover expenditures by one means or another. Any government, like any family, can for a year, spend a little more than it earns. But you and I know that a continuation of that habit means the poorhouse."[12]

Once he was in office, Roosevelt reversed himself and abandoned traditional austerity. He took the dollar off gold and devalued, which helped recovery. Within a hundred days the Roosevelt administration adopted emergency programs to regulate industrial prices, support agriculture, and build and manage large public works. These early measures smacked to many of fascism, with their attempt to encourage businesses to cartelize and set prices and the administration's hostility to international economic cooperation. The more controversial of them were in any case ruled unconstitutional by the Supreme Court, and by 1935 the Roosevelt administration had settled on a different course, sometimes called the second New Deal. This included job-creating government programs, social insurance, and labor rights. An array of "alphabet soup" federal agencies and programs—the Works Progress Administration (WPA), Civilian Conservation Corps (CCC), Agricultural Adjustment

Administration (AAA), and dozens of others—created social democracy American-style.

The New Deal government focused on reducing unemployment and providing social insurance. In March 1935 Congress approved its largest peacetime allocation ever, almost five billion dollars, for unemployment relief. Much of this went to the WPA, which eventually put nearly nine million people to work to build 650,000 miles of roads, 800 airports, and hundreds of thousands of public buildings, parks, bridges, and other projects. Other billions of dollars went to cash relief to the indigent who could not work.

A few months later Congress passed the Social Security Act, the country's first national social insurance system. Roosevelt recommended it "to provide at once security against several of the great disturbing factors of life—especially those which relate to unemployment and old age." The act provided for a public pension system with benefits for widows and other survivors, disability insurance, and relief for the aged, children, and the blind. It also established the nation's first unemployment insurance scheme, to be run by the states.[13]

Farm policy, as in Sweden, reflected the new farmer-labor coalition. Before the 1930s American labor had typically been hostile to agrarian demands for farm supports that would raise food prices, just as American farmers had opposed industrial demands for trade protection that would make manufactured goods more expensive. The New Deal forged a new Democratic alliance of urban labor and southern farmers, with some support from midwestern farm state Republicans. Roosevelt poured billions of dollars into farm debt relief, cash payments, and price supports. These programs, it is estimated, saved nearly two hundred thousand American farm families from foreclosure and assisted millions more in less dramatic ways.[14]

New Deal programs were motivated by pressing political imperatives, not by a conscious desire to engage in deficit spending. Indeed, Roosevelt constantly promised to balance the budget and vetoed some congressional spending bills because he thought they were profligate. Even at the peak of their activity, in the midst of the worst economic crisis in the nation's history, New Deal governments ran deficits of only 3 or 4 percent of GDP. But the government was spending at an unprecedented rate, as nondefense federal spending increased from 3 to 10 percent of GDP between 1927 and 1936. Given the commitment of the Roosevelt administration to balance the budget, most of this increase was financed by higher taxes. The administration became more tolerant of deficits after the 1937–1938 recession, which was probably worsened by budget-balancing efforts, but by then it was hard to distinguish deficit spending for countercyclical purposes from preparations for rearmament.

As in Sweden, the reorientation of economic policy was accompanied by a transformation of labor's role in politics. The Roosevelt administration's biggest innovation in labor markets was the 1935 National Labor Relations Act, which set up a procedure for the recognition of unions and required employers to bargain with them. When the crafts-dominated American Federation of Labor seemed slow to take up the new opportunities, the upstart Committee for Industrial Organization worked to organize the nation's labor force. Organizing drives, punctuated by highly visible demonstrations, sit-down strikes, and public protests, swept through the country's steel, auto, tire, and rubber industries. In 1930 the country had barely three million union members, representing less than 11 percent of the nonagricultural labor force; by 1941 there were nine million union members, and they were 23 percent of the labor force.[15] The labor movement had become an integral part of the New Deal Democratic coalition, and the business community was resigned to its influence.

The federal government dramatically increased its role during the New Deal. This was the American analogue to European measures to remake national labor and social policies. The Roosevelt administration centralized government spending: In the late 1920s state and local government spending was nearly three times federal nondefense spending, but by 1936 federal nonmilitary expenditures were substantially greater than state and local combined.[16] The federal government expanded its regulation of everything from banking and monetary policy to electric utilities and social insurance. The New Deal remade a highly decentralized political economy, with low levels of social insurance and limited labor rights, into a new federal government committed to demand management, national social programs and public works, and a place for labor in collective bargaining and in politics.

Most industrial nations moved in similar directions. In Denmark and Norway, powerful Socialist parties led worker-farmer alliances to power.[17] In Belgium and Switzerland, multiparty coalitions enacted substantial social reforms and organized national consultations between business and labor.[18] In Canada and New Zealand, conservative governments reacted to the Depression with reform measures; when the Left (Liberals in Canada, Labour in New Zealand) came to power in 1935, it extended these reforms.

In France, a Popular Front took power in dramatic circumstances. Initially, unstable centrist and Center-Left governments confronted the crisis weakly, although they introduced minor reforms, such as a family allowance and subsidized housing. In February 1934, right-wing rioting racked Paris. The Communists, sobered by the fascist threat and by Hitler's recent rise to power in neighboring Germany, dropped their previous hostility to the Socialists and proposed a common platform. The resulting Popular Front was, as its leader Léon Blum said, "a reflex of instinctive defense . . . against the prolongation of the economic crisis which was crushing the working classes, the farmers, the middle class of the country."[19]

The Popular Front swept the 1936 elections, and in June 1936 Blum took office as France's first Socialist (and first Jewish) premier, in the midst of a massive strike wave. A day after taking office, Blum brought together business and labor representatives to hammer out the Matignon agreement, committing management to recognize labor rights and raise wages substantially. Within two months the Popular Front government enacted 133 laws. The Left government reformed the central bank, put in place massive public works and new agricultural supports, and mandated unemployment insurance, a new collective bargaining system, a forty-hour workweek, and two weeks' paid vacation. Although the Popular Front ruled for less than two years, it had a lasting effect both on legislation and on the political position of labor.[20]

Great Britain lagged behind. Despite the fact that the Labour Party was in office when the Depression hit, despite the power of British organized labor, despite a long tradition of social reform, despite the influence of John Maynard Keynes, successive British governments did little to follow the examples of western Europe and the other Anglo-American nations. The same was largely true of Australia and the Netherlands. In these three countries, demands for social democratic measures may have been tempered by the fact that they already had relatively extensive social insurance systems.

By the late 1930s the alternative to fascism and communism was in place. Every advanced industrial country except Germany and Italy remained democratic, and almost every industrial democracy traced the basic outlines of the social democratic welfare state. Governments were committed to stabilize the business cycle, provide social insurance, and reserve a central place for organized labor in politics and society.

Keynes and social democracy

The reasons for the development of the new social democracy are not obvious. A common view is that Keynesian economic ideas triumphed. This was certainly Keynes's own view, not so much of his own success as of the general way in which economic policies evolved. He wrote in 1936: "The ideas of economists and political philosophers . . . are more powerful than is commonly understood. Indeed the world is ruled by little else. Practical men, who believe themselves to be quite exempt from any intellectual influence, are usually the slaves of some defunct economist."[21]

Keynes's ideas were certainly influential. Keynes was well known for his polemics on Versailles and the gold standard and for his analysis of how government mishandling of monetary policy had contributed to the ills of the era. These views were not unique to Keynes, though. With his 1930 book *A Treatise on Money*, he began developing more innovative interpretations of contemporary economic problems. He expounded this view in more and more detail—in print, in his well-attended Cambridge University lectures, and in presentations to other economists around the world. By 1932 the basic lines of the Keynesian approach to the Depression were clear. It took Keynes three more years to build a theoretical edifice with which he was satisfied, which he published in 1936 as *The General Theory of Employment, Interest, and Money*.

Keynes's principal contribution to the economic debates of the time, and to economic theory, had to do with fiscal policy. Most economists already regarded budget deficits in times of crisis as unavoidable; after all, they were almost automatic, as economic decline reduced tax revenue much more quickly than spending. Keynes went further, to argue that deficit spending was essential to reactivate stagnant economies. The economy was caught in a trap, from which only government spending could free it.

Keynes put investment at the center of his argument. In most classical approaches, investors simply responded to profit opportunities: If wages got low enough, new investment would be forthcoming, and the economy would revive. But Keynes understood that investment depended also on *expectations* of the behavior of others. No capitalist would expand his factory if there was no prospect of demand for his products—no matter how low wages or interest rates were. If all capitalists invested on the basis of how they expected other capitalists (and consumers) to behave, the economy could be "stuck" in a self-reinforcing trap, a bad equilibrium. Expectations of stagnation would depress investment, which would ensure continued stagnation.

The market economy would *not* right itself. The problem was what today might be called a coordination failure: If every capitalist invested, hired more workers, and produced more goods, demand would rise, and there would be a market for the goods; but since no one capitalist could be sure that this would happen, all preferred to hold on to their money and keep things as they were. In Keynes's words, "An individual may be forced by his private circumstances to curtail his normal expenditure, and no one can blame him. But let no one suppose that he is performing a public duty in behaving in such a way. The modern capitalist is a fair-weather sailor. As soon as a storm rises, he abandons the duties of navigation and even sinks the boats which might carry him to safety by his haste to push his neighbor off and himself in."[22]

The usual monetary stimulus could not overcome this depressed equilibrium because it relied on lower interest rates to spur investment. If capitalists did not anticipate a recovery, however, no rate of interest was low enough to induce them to invest; why produce goods that would not be sold? Investors preferred to keep their money in cash rather than lose it, so even zero interest rates could not stimulate investment. "I am not confident," Keynes wrote at the depth of the Depression, "that on this occasion the cheap-money phase will be sufficient by itself to bring about an adequate recovery of new investment. It may still be the case that the lender, with his confidence shattered by his experiences, will continue to ask for new enterprise rates of interest which the borrower cannot expect to earn."

Keynes had an alternative:

. . . direct state intervention to promote and subsidize new investment. Formerly there was no expenditure out of the proceeds of borrowing that it was thought proper for the State to incur except for war. In the past, therefore, we have not infrequently had to wait for a war to terminate a major depression. I hope that in the future we shall not adhere to this purist financial attitude, and that we shall be ready to spend on the enterprises of peace what the financial maxims of the past would only allow us to spend on the devastations of war. At any rate, I predict with an assured confidence that the only way out is for us to discover some object which is admitted even by the deadheads to be a legitimate excuse for largely increasing the expenditure of someone on something![23]

Government could break out of this vicious circle by borrowing and spending heavily. This would stimulate demand and change expectations; capitalists would see the new conditions and would increase investment, increase employment, and increase output. Countercyclical fiscal policy—deficit spending—could alter expectations and get the economy going.

To some, Keynes's ideas were almost Marxist in their reliance on government. At times, in fact, Keynes characterized his ideas provocatively. "The State," he wrote in the *General Theory*, "will have to exercise a guiding influence on the propensity to consume partly through its scheme of taxation, partly by fixing the rate of interest, and partly, perhaps, in other ways. . . . I conceive, therefore, that a somewhat comprehensive socialisation of investment will prove the only means of securing an approximation to full employment."[24]

In fact, as Keynes himself noted, his message was profoundly anti-Marxist, because it allowed the government to overcome the weaknesses of the capitalist economy. Keynes accused the classical economists, who argued that government could not improve conditions, of being the true allies of Marxism: "The Marxists have become the ultra-orthodox economists. They take the Ricardian [classical] argument to show that nothing can be gained from interference. Hence, since things are bad and mending is impossible, the only solution is to abolish [capitalism] and have quite a new system. Communism is the logical outcome of the classical theory."[25] Keynes, on the other hand, wanted more energetic attempts to save the market economy, without which, he said, "the existing order of society will become so discredited that wild and foolish and destructive changes will become inevitable."[26]

Keynes inspired a reformist zeal, as reflected in the memories of a Cambridge student who called the development of the ideas in the *General Theory* "joyful revelation in dark times. We thought that Keynes had . . . found the 'flaw in the capitalist system' and had proclaimed its remedy. . . . The mystery of contemporary iniquity had been unveiled by a masterpiece of sustained intellectual effort. . . . Thus the *General Theory* was to us less a work of economics theory than a Manifesto for Reason and Cheerfulness. . . . It gave a rational basis and moral appeal for a faith in the possible health and sanity of contemporary mankind such as the youths of my generation found nowhere else."[27]

Keynes had a powerful effect on modern economics, even though many historians of economic thought would argue that what he said was not actually new.[28] This was true about specific policies, such as deficit spending, and about the theoretical justification for these policies. But Keynes's 1936 book fundamentally rethought modern economies and government policy. And in fact Keynes and his followers did remake economics, if not always in ways he might have endorsed. Keynes invented modern macroeconomics, the analysis of such general economic variables as unemployment and output, and in his wake came generations of new economic thinking.

Nonetheless, he had very limited influence on government policy, and his ideas did not affect the evolution of the social democracies in the 1930s. For example, Keynes's principal weapon of macroeconomic policy was fiscal, deficit spending. Yet very few democratic governments in the 1930s made conscious, concerted, or sustained use of fiscal policy as a tool against the Depression. Governments that ran budget deficits saw them as necessary evils and always promised to reduce them as soon as possible. Expansionary monetary policies were much preferred and seemed to work reasonably well. And Keynes had nothing to say about social insurance, labor unions, farm subsidies, or the other policies that were central to the emerging social democratic welfare states.

Keynes did participate in important discussions of policy. He visited the United States in May 1934, talked to scores of New Dealers, and met with Franklin Roosevelt for an hour. Their meeting had no discernible impact on Roosevelt, who said that Keynes seemed "a mathematician rather than a political economist."[29] But Keynes was enthusiastic about American policy, calling himself "more of an admiring observer than . . . an instructor."[30] He supported the administration in public lectures and meetings with business leaders, academics, and others, which helped counter some of the anti-Roosevelt sentiments of business and economic traditionalists. His principal suggestion, in an open letter to Roosevelt published by Walter Lippmann in the *New York Times*, was that emergency federal spending be increased from three hundred million to four hundred million dollars a month, hardly a revolutionary contribution.

Despite his importance to the development of economic theory, Keynes was just one of many voices arguing for countercyclical macroeconomic policy. The Stockholm school of young economists is credited by many—especially in Sweden—with inventing Keynesianism before Keynes. In the United States in the early 1930s Utah's Marriner Eccles was one of a group of iconoclastic businessmen who argued for government to assume major fiscal tasks in a way that later became known as Keynesian. Eccles, a provincial banker with a high school education, was blunt: "A bank cannot finance the building of more factories and more rental properties and more homes when half of our productive property is idle for lack of consumption and a large percentage of our business properties are vacant, for want of paying tenants. The government, however, can spend money, because the government, unlike the bankers, has the power of taxation and the power to create money and does not have to depend on the profit motive. The only escape from a depression must be by increased spending. We must depend upon the government to save what we have of a price, profit, and credit system."[31] The Roosevelt administration spotted Eccles early on, and the president appointed him head of the Federal Reserve in 1934, a post he held until 1948.[32]

Keynes believed that policy makers were subconsciously applying the ideas of defunct (or, in his case, living) economists, but the experience of his own ideas was much the opposite. Political leaders all over the industrial world were clawing their way toward a new political economy that could pull away from the maelstrom of the Depression. That political economy included loose money, public works, and intensive employment programs. Keynes the public figure applauded developments that had taken place independently of Keynes the economist. Eventually economists would find Keynes's writings valuable in constructing a theoretical edifice appropriate to understanding the new social democracies. For the origins of these social democracies themselves, we have to look elsewhere from the world of ideas.

Labor, capital, and social democracy

Social democracy was not an application of Keynesian thinking, but its developers shared with Keynes the idea that governments needed to act forcefully to save modern capitalism. Like him, the pioneering Scandinavian Social Democrats had long since decided that their duty was to make capitalism work better. The trinity, according to the Danish party newspaper in 1926, was "seriousness, a sense of responsibility, and a sense of the public interest."[33] The New Dealers too saw the goal as stabilizing democratic capitalism; as Roosevelt said in 1938, "the very soundness of our democratic institutions depends on the determination of our government to give employment to idle men."

Every element of the social democratic model could be justified on these system-sustaining grounds. Macroeconomic management overcame the failure of capitalists to act in their own best interests; if fear drove investment and consumption down, to the detriment of all, governments could push it back up, to the benefit of all. Social insurance helped cushion the blows of unpredictable business cycles, and not only for workers.[34] Unemployment compensation stabilized the economy, as a downturn automatically increased government spending to pay jobless benefits, thus counteracting the downturn. The same was true of poor relief. The Depression provided the impetus for the general establishment of such social insurance systems.

Social security for the aged, national pensions, and health insurance all helped society as well as their direct beneficiaries. They freed people from the severest worries of providing for adversity, so that they could focus on education, production, and civic life. And as decades of European experience had demonstrated, these socially beneficial measures could not effectively be supplied by private enterprise or citizens' self-help. Central state provision of social insurance was an economic and social necessity.

Modern societies may simply have required social democratic welfare states to survive. It is otherwise hard to explain why every industrial society developed social insurance schemes whose similiarities far outweigh their differences. Yet this development was not smooth or even, and it often came after substantial political battles. Social democracy may have provided for the common weal, but the opposition it provoked makes it hard to believe that it would have been adopted without strong and determined supporters.

The working class was the principal protagonist of social democratic evolution. Workers were most directly affected by the economic uncertainties that social insurance hoped to redress. They did not have wealth or land to protect themselves against unemployment, sickness, or disability, nor did they earn enough to save for retirement—should they be lucky enough to survive until retirement age. From the onset of the Industrial Revolution, workers organized self-help societies and trade unions. But labor attempts at social insurance were rarely fully successful. Local unemployment insurance schemes, probably the most important such projects, were bankrupted by business downturns that brought the whole region down because there were simply too many unemployed to support. Indeed, many countries' social insurance systems started with bailouts of bankrupt local unemployment funds, which were converted either to government programs or to subsidized voluntary ones.[35]

The working class and its parties demanded social insurance. They also insisted that government counter economic crises with reflation, job creation, and other macroeconomic measures—or at least that it not exacerbate crises with deflation and austerity. Labor's push for these social policies was reinforced by the crisis of the 1930s. The plight of workers was too dire to be ignored, and in fact problems that had previously seemed unique to workers now affected broader segments of society. While the received wisdoms of previous ruling classes seemed to have failed, labor and Socialist parties offered a clear democratic alternative. Sweden's Social Democratic prime minister explained that the Depression galvanized society:

> The economic crisis has been a powerful preacher against an arrangement where suddenly the rug is pulled out from under masses of people who have struggled honestly to secure their houses and families and where the entire society and all social classes are threatened with ruin. It doesn't pacify people to know that similar catastrophes have happened before; it's not enough for them to know that there is social assistance to save them from starvation; they will not be quieted by the idea that society supposedly lacks the capacity to protect them against economic accidents. That the enormous resources of modern society should be employed to secure people's livelihoods is a fundamental demand.[36]

Countries with powerful labor movements and powerful Socialist parties turned most quickly to social democracy. By the time of the Depression, Scandinavian Socialists had larger shares of the vote than anywhere else and were the largest parties in their respective countries. Their labor movements encompassed large proportions of the labor force—well over one-third of wage earners in Denmark and Sweden even at the depth of the Depression. Belgium was close behind. The economic, social, and labor policies of social democracy were adopted quickly and thoroughly in these countries.

A powerful working class helped explain the adoption of social democratic policies in several countries, but it cannot explain the entire phenomenon. Labor was powerful in Great Britain and Australia, yet social democracy lagged there. The United States had a tiny labor movement and no socialism to speak of, but the New Deal was a radical example of the turn to social democracy. In fact in many countries, including the United States, the growth of the modern labor movement was as much a *result* as a cause of the new reforms. American unions had no more members in 1935 than in 1925. The passage of the National Labor Relations Act in 1935 allowed American labor unions to grow as fast as they did, more than tripling their size over the next ten years.[37] So while powerful labor movements helped speed the rise of social democracy, they were not the whole story.

A united working class helped promote social democracy, but a divided capitalist class—the support or forbearance of important businessmen over the opposition of others—was also crucial. A singular feature of the 1930s was the prominence of corporate backers of the macroeconomic, social, and labor reforms associated with social democracy. Some of them may have been social reformers by nature, conviction, or religion. But many in the business community had pragmatic reasons to welcome, even advocate the new policies. There was another great mass of businesses that found little reason to oppose social democratic measures. The American experience is striking, as American employers had long been among the most hostile to labor and social reform.

The new focus on macroeconomic management appealed to many businessmen. They welcomed measures to restore normal business conditions. Looser monetary policy lessened the burden of corporate debt, while increased government spending meant more orders for business—directly in some cases, indirectly in others. Lower interest rates and budget deficits worried some, especially in the financial community, but they were a distinct minority so long as economies remained depressed. Policies to stimulate economies met little resistance, and some enthusiastic support, from most corporate circles.

Social insurance measures were also less controversial than they had been. As governments adopted social insurance schemes, many firms found their impact trifling. Capitalists quickly realized that so long as all companies were required to contribute to unemployment and pension programs, social insurance did not affect competitive conditions. In fact companies that had themselves provided in-house unemployment and pension schemes were happy to relinquish this responsibility. "Industry," wrote the editor of *Iron Age*, the organ of the American metal industry, "is in sympathy with the broad objectives leading to social security" and has "no objection to having these burdens transferred to Uncle Sam's shoulders."[38]

Some in the business community even thought such programs good for their businesses. Modern corporations for which reliable and motivated employees were crucial had long used higher wages and better working conditions to attract a high-quality workforce. Over the course of the 1920s and 1930s many of them found that reducing workers' uncertainties also helped stabilize and improve the labor force. They attempted to maintain good relations with their workers, even during the Depression—as with International Harvester, which purposely declined to cut wages after 1929. Many American companies, prominently Eastman Kodak and General Electric, started internal unemployment, pension, and health insurance programs to enhance the attractions of their jobs and attract the best workers.

These welfare capitalists, as historians call them, may have provided such benefits to workers out of an enlightened social consciousness, but this was a self-interested enlightenment. Support for social insurance was strongest in industries where the quality of labor was particularly important, and where wages were a relatively small component of total costs. It was easier for a capital-intensive company like General Electric or International Harvester, which relied on dependable and committed labor forces, to support measures that increased wage costs than it was for companies in an industry such as footwear or garments, where labor turnover in the best of times was very high and where wages were the largest cost firms faced. Even if modern capital-intensive industries were more favorable to social insurance, they did not relish being the only businesses bearing added costs. They might be willing to provide these programs privately, but they preferred universal provision in order to, as a group of firms put it, "equalize cost burdens among competitors."[39]

Business leaders from these kinds of industries were prominent in the New Deal's development of social security programs. Executives from Eastman Kodak, General Electric, Goodyear Tire and Rubber, and Standard Oil of New Jersey (another high technology and capital-intensive firm) helped design New Deal social insurance legislation. Others had decided that these social democratic reforms were no danger and could even help organize and stabilize the economic environment.

Similar considerations were at work in the business attitude to labor relations. In labor relations business views were typically tolerant at best, for even progressive employers were wary of ceding workplace control to organized labor. It was more a matter of which firms had the least to lose, rather than anything to gain, from recognizing labor unions.

Again, capital-intensive firms for which labor costs were less relevant and companies for which the quality and stability of the workforce was especially important were in the forefront of recognizing labor unions and working with rather than against them. Retail merchants such as Filene's were also supportive. Like many of the other corporate liberals, retailers depended on loyal and high-quality employees and could pass on additional costs to consumers—if all of them did so. Retailers generally supported labor legislation that, in the words of the San Francisco retailers' grouping, "takes the question of wages very largely out of competition and saves them from the necessity of holding wages down to the level of their hardest and shrewdest competitor."[40] In fact the only major American business group to back the 1935 Social Security Act was the National Retail Dry Goods Association, whose members included Macy's and Sears, Roebuck.

Even in Sweden, where labor unions and the Social Democrats were extremely strong, the cooperation of segments of the corporate world was central to the development of social democracy. Sweden's famous national wage-setting arrangements grew out of an alliance between workers and employers in the metalworking industries. In 1933 and 1934 a long construction strike and rapidly rising wages in the building trades threatened to price Swedish machinery out of world markets. Unions and management in the export-oriented metal industries wanted to hold down wages in construction, so as to protect the competitiveness of Swedish metalworking exports. The employers' federation and the labor federation came together to impose national wage restraint. Social democratic accountability for the national economy implied that unions would have to be "responsible," and centralization of wage bargaining was an effective way for Social Democratic, labor, and business leaders to ensure the compatibility of wage increases with national economic goals. The result was a system that worked very much to satisfy some of Sweden's important export industries.[41]

Many American industries, however, opposed the New Deal furiously. The Liberty League, led by Du Pont and the Morgan partners, brought together business enemies of social democratic policies. Labor-intensive companies rejected a benevolent view of New Deal reforms; they could not count on recouping the burden of expensive social and labor legislation because labor was too large a share of their costs. Further problems confronted industries that competed internationally because not all countries adopted the social insurance and labor reforms of the era. Even many corporate liberals worried about this, and General Electric proposed tax breaks for firms facing competitors from laggard countries. Indeed U.S. Steel stalled its negotiations with the CIO's Steel Workers' Organizing Committee until an international cartel agreement was reached that sheltered the American market; two days later, freed from concern about foreign competition, the company agreed to recognize the union.[42]

Despite continued opposition to social democracy from many business quarters, during the 1930s many capitalists came to support, or at least drop their opposition to, social reform. It might even be argued that social democracy reflected a coalition between farmers and organized labor, on the one hand, and the more modern portions of the business community, on the other. Capitalists in more technologically advanced industries, with more capital-intensive production, organized in new corporate forms for which workforce quality and stability were key, had reasons to support (or at least refrain from opposing) social insurance, labor rights, and other social democratic measures.

The sources of social democratic evolution were several. It was certainly motivated in part by broad sociopolitical concerns, by the belief that, in Keynes's words, "decadent international but individualistic capitalism . . . doesn't deliver the goods." Without general sentiment for change, democratic regimes could certainly not have adopted the sweeping measures that they did. The labor movement was the proximate spark for many of the reforms that were eventually implemented. And the active support or passive acceptance of portions of the business community was important for the adoption of social democratic social and labor policies. Broad social needs, labor demands, and capitalist acceptance all contributed to rebuild the industrial order.

Social democracy and international cooperation

As the industrial world turned toward social democracy, it also attempted to rebuild more open and cooperative international economic relations. This was the case for several reasons. First, labor and socialist movements in many advanced countries had long been free traders, in part to ensure cheap food and other consumption products to urban workers. Second, most of the business supporters of social democracy were in technologically advanced, internationally competitive industries, for which protectionism was anathema. Third, as the decade wore on, it became obvious that the western democracies would need to work together against the fascist autarkies.

The small social democracies of western Europe led attempts to reconstruct international trade and finance; they had long free trade histories and could not seriously consider an autarkic alternative. At the depth of the Depression in 1932, Scandinavia and the Low Countries agreed to reduce tariffs among themselves by half over five years. This Oslo Group of small, open western European economies was the nucleus of attempts to rebuild the trading system. Support for these attempts soon came from an unexpected quarter, the New Deal administration of Franklin Roosevelt.

The United States was the Western world's most protectionist country. But the Democrats dissented from the high-tariff policies of the long-dominant Republicans and even succeeded in lowering trade barriers during the brief Democratic ascendancy from 1913 to 1920. The South was the principal support base for free trade, for exports of cotton and tobacco were crucial to the region. In addition, the party garnered backing from corporate free traders dismayed by Republican tariff raising, especially after the Smoot-Hawley Act of 1930.

The administration was initially racked by infighting over trade policy. But soon Secretary of State Cordell Hull, who had fervently supported free trade for years as a senator from tobacco-exporting Tennessee, gained the upper hand. In summer 1934 Congress passed Hull's Reciprocal Trade Agreements Act, which permitted the president to negotiate tariff reductions of up to 50 percent with other countries, without congressional approval. Within five years, the United States had signed twenty trade agreements covering 60 percent of the nation's imports. The Oslo Group in western Europe and the United States in the Western Hemisphere were pulling for a rebuilt trading order.

France and Britain went along reluctantly. Initially they instituted restrictive empire preferences. France reduced its trade barriers only after the Popular Front had taken office. Eventually the British also started to back down from their preferential imperial trading system; Canada and other important members had already started to defect, and the United States complained incessantly about the empire's discriminatory practices. The French and British agreed to support a study by former Belgian Prime Minister Paul van Zeeland that in early 1938 recommended concerted efforts at trade liberalization. By the eve of World War Two the industrial democracies were committed on paper to reducing trade barriers, and some of them had in fact begun to move in that direction. The war intervened before further progress could be made.[43]

International monetary relations took a similar course. As the French Popular Front government prepared to take the franc off gold in 1936, it consulted with the British and Americans to avoid a new round of competitive depreciations. The eventual devaluation of the franc, at the end of September 1936, was announced as part of a three-country understanding. "A streak of sunlight," enthused the *New York Times*, "had broken through the dark clouds of nationalism. International cooperation was still possible."[44] Within a few months the three signatories to the Tripartite Monetary Agreement, joined by Belgium, the Netherlands, and Switzerland, had extended the arrangement to provide for the stabilization of their currencies' values. While the Tripartite Agreement was hardly earth-shattering, it was, as a prominent New York banker put it, "a challenge to the application of economic nationalism in monetary affairs."[45] This was not a return to the old gold standard, but something new, based on governments' commitments to help defend one another's currencies with only a limited link to gold. It hinted, as Leon Fraser of the First National Bank of New York put it, at "a union of what was best in the old gold standard, corrected on the basis of experience to date, and of what seems practicable in some of the doctrines of 'managed currencies.' "[46] Exactly what this union would be would have to wait until after World War Two, when these monetary designs would be elaborated and expanded. But the seeds of a new international monetary order had been planted.

From the ashes

The Depression destroyed the established order. The pre-1930 system was based on internationalist gold standard orthodoxy, limited government role in the economy, and the political predominance of business. The calamity of the 1930s swept away the classical order's commitment to the international economy and to the market. Germany, Italy, and their fascist brethren rejected global integration and the market in favor of autarky, state intervention, and antilabor repression. In the industrial west, a coalition of labor, farmers, and progressive capitalists replaced laissez-faire with a new social democracy that managed the macroeconomy and provided a range of social services and social insurance.

Hjalmar Horace Greeley Schacht and John Maynard Keynes represented these polar responses to the Depression. The two men had rejected gold standard orthodoxy in favor of vigorous government action. Both Schachtian and Keynesian economics stood for government intervention, fiscal activism, restrictions on international investment, and controls on trade. Schacht gravitated toward fascist autarky, Keynes toward social democratic interventionism.

In 1934, at the depth of the Depression, the pragmatic Schacht was running the world's second-largest economy, while the scholarly Keynes was writing a work of abstract economic theory. This flowed from their intellectual and personal makeup: The German was a conformist Prussophile who worshiped power and the powerful, the Englishman a heterodox homosexual who believed in the power of ideas and disdained politicians. But the differences also reflected global political and economic realities: Schachtian economics was admired and emulated in dozens of autarkic regimes in Europe and Latin America, while Keynesian economics only gradually gained intellectual and political favor.

The tables were turned ten years later, in 1944. While the Englishman toasted the west's acceptance of his design for the postwar world economy, Gestapo agents were on their way to arrest the German. While Schacht pleaded for his life at Nuremberg, Keynes presided over the negotiation of a new economic order to be built on the ruins of the war the Germans had lost.

PART III

Together Again, 1939–1973

11

Reconstruction East and West

The Western Allies began to plan the peacetime economic order as soon as war broke out. In fact American postwar planning began long before the United States entered the conflict. Less than two weeks after hostilities erupted in Europe in late summer 1939, the State Department and the New York–based Council on Foreign Relations set up study groups to report on how the United States might pursue its world vision. Once the United States entered the war, official planning began in earnest, and hundreds of government, business, and academic experts worked to design the peace.

Previous international economic systems had evolved by the interplay of markets and politics. But during World War Two, Western leaders were consumed by the fear that the peace settlement would recapitulate the disasters that followed World War One. They left nothing to chance. International negotiations determined the shape of the world's economic system, and governments wrote the rules of the global economic game.

The United States leads the way

The most important task for those who wanted to lead the postwar world toward greater economic integration was to ensure that the United States was engaged. Conditions in the Allied leader were favorable, unlike in the interwar period, when the American internationalism associated with Woodrow Wilson had been unpopular or ignored. Businessmen and policy makers who had never abandoned economic internationalism could now put their goals back on the agenda. Leon Fraser, president of New York's First National Bank, insisted as early as 1940 that there was no reason to delay tackling three principal evils: "economic nationalism, trade barriers, and war." He said: "These three dis-Graces go hand in hand, and always have. To give profound consideration to our public policies concerning them, even while a battle is raging, is really not so incongruous, so impotent, or so inappropriate as it first appears, any more than one should desist from inquiring into the fundamental causes of a plague while people are dying of it." It was especially important that the United States lead in the right direction: "As America goes, so goes the world, for our influence is so great, our strength so dominant, that our policy, once clearly adopted and followed, is likely—nay, is certain—to be the guidepost for the remainder of the globe."[1]

An official American view coalesced over the course of the war, despite differences within the Roosevelt administration, Congress, and the population. Leading government and business circles came to focus on three components of the postwar order: freer trade, international monetary stability, and the recovery of international investment.

The emerging American vision began with freer trade. Secretary of State Hull, who dominated the administration's trade policy, held the traditional free trade views of a Democrat from the export-oriented South. He pushed the president to negotiate tariff reductions under the terms of Hull's pet Reciprocal Trade Agreements Act of 1934. His motives were not just to find markets for American goods, for he had a Wilsonian belief that, as he put it, "unhampered trade dovetailed with peace; high tariffs, trade barriers, and unfair economic competition, with war." Skeptics could scoff, Hull said, but "it is a fact that war did not break out between the United States and any country with which we had been able to negotiate a trade agreement. It is also a fact that, with very few exceptions, the countries with which we signed trade agreements joined together in resisting the Axis. The political line-up followed the economic line-up."[2] As one of Hull's supporters put it, "If soldiers are not to cross international borders, goods must do so."[3]

The free traders were bucking a century of American protectionism, and in many corporate quarters support for trade barriers persisted. But enthusiasm for trade liberalization had grown, and by the end of the war it was a popular, if not universally held, view that freer trade was in America's interest. There were practical reasons for this conversion. Many American industries had used their technological edge to become exporters and foreign investors. This expanded support for freer trade from its traditional farm export base. And as the war dragged on, it became obvious that Americans would not face much foreign competition after the fighting ended. Many protectionist industrialists changed their views once they saw that they had much to gain from trade liberalization and much to lose from continued British and European trade barriers.

In addition, Britain's imperial preferences had shocked Americans who relied on access to the markets of the British Empire. Hull pointed to American egg exports to Canada as an example. Under pressure from farmers, Congress had raised the duty on eggs from eight to ten cents a dozen with the Smoot-Hawley Tariff. This reduced the already small number of Canadian eggs bought in the United States by 40 percent, from 160,000 to under 100,000. The British imperial trade area (which included Canada) countered by increasing the duty on eggs to the same ten cents a dozen (from the previously low three cents). This drove America's very considerable egg exports to Canada down by 98 percent, from 11 million to under 200,000. American protectionism had backfired.[4]

American free traders saw the British Empire's preferential system as, in Hull's words, "the greatest injury, in a commercial way, that has been inflicted on this country since I have been in public life."[5] The United States was in a strong position to insist on its goals: Britain needed the Americans to fend off the Nazis. Even businessmen and politicians sympathetic to the British cause were enthusiastic about using the wartime emergency as a fulcrum to pry open empire markets.

In March 1941 Congress agreed to a lend-lease agreement with Britain, over the objections of the still-powerful isolationists. This arrangement allowed the United States to "lend" military and related equipment to the Allies, on the fiction that it would be returned once used. Republican leader Robert Taft complained that "lending military equipment is like lending chewing gum, you don't get it back," but the subterfuge helped sidestep isolationist objections to outright grants. The plan promised to avoid the war debts that had bedeviled the settlement of World War One; new Allied debts to the United States would be forgiven more or less automatically. American war matériel could begin flowing to the British, even though the United States was not yet a belligerent, and the British would not have to pay for this aid.

But lend-lease came with strings, including a British commitment to freer trade. In August 1941 President Roosevelt and Prime Minister Winston Churchill announced an Atlantic Charter stating joint war aims, which included "to further the enjoyment by all states . . . of access, on equal terms, to the trade and to the raw materials of the world." Shortly after the United States entered the war, the two countries signed a comprehensive lend-lease agreement that committed them both—meaning Great Britain—to "the elimination of all forms of discriminatory treatment in international commerce, and to the reduction of tariff and other trade barriers." The implications were clear to all. Undersecretary of State Sumner Welles was exultant. "The age of imperialism is ended," he said, using the then-popular definition of imperialism as any arrangement that reserved the benefits of empire to countries other than the United States. The British had bent to the American view that "every nation has a right to expect that its legitimate trade will not be diverted and throttled by towering tariffs, preferences, discriminations or narrow bilateral practices."[6] Within a year American and British planners began to design an International Trade Organization to manage the reduction of trade barriers.

Anglo-American discussions of international money and finance went on parallel to negotiations on trade. Starting in 1940, John Maynard Keynes and Harry Dexter White, representing the British and American treasuries, respectively, drafted proposals for postwar international monetary relations and global investment. These plans were less controversial than trade. Trade policy pitted powerful firms whose profits depended on protection against other powerful firms whose profits depended on the removal of trade barriers. But just about everyone stood to gain from the restoration of a functioning international monetary system.

Most wanted to continue the international monetary cooperation established in the late 1930s, under the Tripartite Monetary Agreement among the Western Allies. Debate focused on the gold standard, with many international bankers convinced that a renewed gold standard would best meet their needs. The *New York Times*, reflecting Wall Street views, opined that "the gold standard was, without any international agreements, the most satisfactory international standard that has ever been devised." The newspaper insisted: "It is often said that the gold standard 'failed.' The truth is that governments sabotaged it deliberately, because it interfered with nationalistic 'planning' that governments preferred to stability of exchange rates. . . . It is not necessary to invent elaborate technical devices to secure monetary stability. The nineteenth century developed them through the gold standard."[7]

But many industrialists and organized labor were wary of attempts to return to gold on a pre-1914 basis. They did not like the inflexibility of gold, under which the government could not use monetary policy to stimulate the economy and could not devalue to improve industry's competitive position. Politically sensitive bankers, aware that a simple return to gold was unlikely, were willing to settle for a modified dollar standard. The chairman of Chase believed that it was feasible that "the dollar would constitute a sure anchorage for the currencies of other nations and would become a generally acceptable international medium of exchange."[8] Not coincidentally, a dollar standard would give American international banks, like Chase, a privileged position in international financial markets.

By early 1944 Keynes and White had hammered out a compromise between the international stability of a gold-dollar standard and the national flexibility of managed currencies. Countries would join an International Monetary Fund (IMF), contribute gold and their own currency to the common fund, and link their currencies to gold at a fixed rate. The fund could lend them money in hard times, and currency values could be changed if economic conditions warranted. The Keynes-White plan balanced the objectives of the American and British governments: currency stability with flexibility, gold backing without rigidity.

Keynes and White anticipated that governments would restrict short-term capital flows to stabilize their currencies because they believed that the detrimental effects of speculative investments outweighed the benefits of free capital movements. This, along with the reliance on currency management, inflamed hard-line supporters of gold, such as the New York banker who railed about the absurdity of treating all currencies as equal: "They put in lei, lits, lats, and rubles, and they take out dollars. We are entitled to use the lei, the lits, the lats, and the rubles."[9] But such objections were on the margins of public debate. As Keynes put it, "the plan accords every member government the explicit right to control all capital movements. What used to be heresy is now endorsed as orthodoxy."[10]

Despite their antipathy to short-term ("speculative") investments, Keynes and White wanted to ensure that long-term ("productive") investment would flow to regions that needed it. The war-torn countries of Europe and Asia, especially, needed massive loans to rebuild their infrastructure. Two things had impeded this sort of investment in the past. First, international finance often got embroiled in diplomatic disputes. A series of studies in the 1930s had concluded that otherwise desirable international capital movements needed to be separated from interstate politics. Herbert Feis, a prominent State Department adviser, wrote that if the future was to be happier than the past, "capital which moves abroad will not carry with it the power of an organized national state, nor will it be forced to serve the political purposes of the state."[11] And Eugene Staley's widely read *War and the Private Investor* was emphatic: "The factor of national allegiance must be detached from migratory capital." In the future, Staley wrote, "the functions of investment promotion and protection should be lodged in various agencies representing the world community and having a world-wide jurisdiction."[12] The scholars were starry-eyed, but they captured a widespread belief that international investment should be uncoupled from diplomatic intrigue.

The second impediment to international investment was that lenders had become reluctant to fund large projects, such as railroads and ports. These projects were crucial to the viability of other private investments, but the time horizon required was so long that risk-averse investors avoided them. Private investment in Europe, for example, required massive investments in the continent's roads, railroads, and ports, but these were themselves unlikely to be funded by wary private investors.

Keynes and White proposed to solve the problem with an International Bank for Reconstruction and Development (World Bank), backed by the governments of the major financial powers. The bank could borrow on private markets at low interest rates (because of its backers' guarantee) and relend to projects that would facilitate other private investment. The scheme, in one form or another, went back to the early 1930s, and even financial conservatives supported it. The agency would supplement, not replace, private lending, funding undertakings whose completion would enhance the profitability of private investment.

At the beginning of July 1944 nearly a thousand delegates from more than forty countries gathered at the Mount Washington Hotel in the New Hampshire resort of Bretton Woods. Over the next three weeks, under the leadership of Keynes and White, the delegates finalized plans for the IMF and the World Bank—and for the postwar monetary and financial order. The resulting Bretton Woods system was unique. There had never been an international agency like the IMF, to which member governments agreed to subject their decisions on important economic policies. Nor had a multilateral organization such as the World Bank existed, with billions of dollars to lend to governments around the world. The organized capitalism of the new social democracy, which had swept the domestic political economies of the Western capitalist nations, was applied at the international level.[13]

Before the war in the Pacific ended, the U.S. Congress approved the Bretton Woods Agreements Act, over opposition from isolationists and a few international bankers. In March 1946, with Europe and Asia in shambles, the inaugural meetings of the International Monetary Fund and the World Bank were held in Savannah, Georgia.

Keynes was disappointed by the final evolution of the Bretton Woods institutions, for he believed that politicians were perverting good ideas—in particular, his good ideas. Keynes the British nationalist was dismayed by the naked exercise of power by Americans who, he complained, wanted to "pick out the eyes of the British Empire."[14] He had criticized the Allies in 1919 for imposing a postwar settlement that was unjust to the vanquished; now he thought that the United States was imposing an unjust settlement on one of the victors, the United Kingdom. This should have come as no surprise: The Americans and the British wanted institutions that served their interests, but the British expected to be borrowers while the American expected to be lenders. Conflicts of interest were inevitable, and power relations ensured that American interests prevailed. Like many Britons, though, Keynes had not understood how completely political realities had changed, and he was bitter at his homeland's loss of influence.

He also believed that a cooperative international agreement was being undone as Americans reworked the Bretton Woods institutions to guarantee American predominance. Keynes's distaste for American manipulation of the Bretton Woods settlement was heightened by his personal ambivalence about most things American. He was, after all, an English gentleman—now Baron Keynes of Tilton—from a cultural and intellectual world alien to the sensibilities of even those Americans whom he liked. A ditty that circulated during the negotiations summarized the opinions he transmitted:

> In Washington Lord Halifax
> Once whispered to Lord Keynes,
> "It's true *they* have all the money-bags
> But we have all the brains."[15]

In addition, Keynes the economist abhorred the politicization of his carefully designed mechanisms to deal with economic problems. At the inaugural meeting in Savannah, he delivered an allegorical warning about the dangers of capture of the institutions by politicians. Drawing on the ballet *The Sleeping Beauty*, which he had just seen, he referred to the fairy godmothers of the Bretton Woods institutions, who had endowed them with Universalism, Courage, and Wisdom. He hoped, Keynes said, that no "malicious fairy, no Carabosse" would turn the two institutions into political instruments. The likely target of this veiled attack was the American treasury secretary, Fred Vinson, who grumbled, "I don't mind being called malicious, but I do mind being called a fairy."[16] Keynes celebrated as much of his vision was brought to fruition, but he fumed at how the realities of power politics, and especially the realities of American power, undermined his idealistic hopes for the Bretton Woods organizations. He returned to England after this bittersweet experience, already in very poor health after years of overwork. A few weeks later, on the morning of Easter Sunday, he died suddenly in his bed at home.

But Keynes and White had written the ground rules for the new economic order. The two principal Bretton Woods institutions defined the capitalist world economy in the twenty-five years after World War Two. Their organizational specifics did not matter much, for they evolved in ways not anticipated by their founders. The point was broader, as one of the American negotiators later observed: "The major significance of Bretton Woods was the death blow it represented in victory over the economic isolationism of the prewar period and the serious threat that with military victory this country would again revert to economic nationalism. Thus, the question of how effective the Bank and Fund may have been in the light of postwar events (many of them not foreseeable except by hindsight) is not nearly so important as having established the principle of U.S. cooperation in the solution of the international economic problems of the future."[17]

The immediate task

The Bretton Woods plans proved irrelevant to the immediate task of rebuilding the economies of the former warring nations. The world's most terrible war had been more destructive of economies and societies than anyone had anticipated. Postwar GDP per person in the Continental Allies—the Soviet Union, France, Belgium, Netherlands, and others—was less than four-fifths of what it had been in 1939; in most, 1946 levels were lower than those of the early 1920s. Conditions in the vanquished nations were far worse. Industrial production in 1946 Germany was one-third that of 1936, and overall output per person in the defeated nations of the Axis was less than half what it had been before the war. In Italy and Japan, 1946 levels were roughly equivalent to those of 1910, in Germany to 1890, in Austria to 1870. The war on the Continent had thrown back the winners' economies twenty-five years, while those of the losers had lost forty, fifty, even seventy-five years.[18] German living standards before the war were comparable to those of Great Britain and about four-fifths of the United States; by 1946 they had sunk to barely one-third of British and one-quarter of American levels, roughly comparable to Spain or Peru.

Western Europe's changed international economic position seemed likely to hamper recovery. To rebuild, the Continent needed to import food, raw materials, and capital equipment. But the Europeans had exhausted much of their ability to earn money to pay for imports. They had sold off most of their foreign investments to pay for the war, losing the earnings from these investments. The Cold War cut off Western Europe's access to the markets of Eastern and Central Europe. The Europeans' empires were crumbling, restricting their privileged access to the markets and raw materials of former colonies. Even Europe's ability to carry its goods to and from markets was hobbled: The combined merchant fleets of the European continent, three times as large as that of the United States in 1939, were reduced to less than half of it in 1947.[19] Western Europe's capacity to import was barely one-third that of 1938.[20]

Meanwhile the United States and the rest of the Western Hemisphere basked in prosperity. The American economy grew by 50 percent (in real terms, adjusting for inflation) during the war, from 1939 to 1946; Canada and Latin America grew even faster. The relative weights of the

American and European economies changed fundamentally. In 1939 the U.S. economy was just half the size of the economies of the eventual belligerents in Europe, Japan, and the Soviet Union; by 1946 the American economy was larger than all the others combined. The combined steel production of Germany, Britain, and the USSR in 1939 had been more than 15 percent greater than that of the United States; in 1946 it was less than half as great.[21]

Europe and Japan were crushed or exhausted; the United States was wealthy and powerful, and its involvement would determine the speed of recovery. The memory of American withdrawal after World War One weighed heavily on European leaders. Their concerns grew as the Republicans swept the House and Senate in 1946, for the isolationist wing of this party remained strong. This time around, Americans who wanted the United States to take a leading role won out. Had American policy makers learned their lesson? Almost certainly not. With few exceptions, the isolationist leaders of the 1920s remained isolationists in the 1940s. But now they were outnumbered.

America turned outward after 1945 because of changed conditions, not changed minds. The United States was now unchallenged in world trade, finance, and investment. The dollar no longer shared monetary leadership with the pound sterling and the French franc; most British and French overseas investments had been liquidated. Europe seemed to have an insatiable hunger for the products of America's manufacturing powerhouse, rather than compete with American industry. Exports at war's end were twice as important to American industry as they had been in the 1930s, while import competition was much weaker. This economic change was reflected in the altered views of some members of Congress, now more interested in finding markets for American goods than concerned about foreign competitors.[22]

The fact that American power had grown and European flagged made it clear that the United States would have its way with the rest of the world. At Versailles and after, Woodrow Wilson and his colleagues had faced European intransigence on issue after issue and had been forced to conciliate on such important matters as German reparations. Now America's Western Allies were at the mercy of the United States. Britain and France expressed their concerns forcefully, and sometimes American policy makers listened; but there was no pretense of an equal partnership. It was easier to "sell" American international involvement at home when this involvement was on American terms.

The newfound power and influence of the Soviet Union also changed American views. Soviet society had suffered terribly from the war, but its military successes left it dominant east of the Rhine, and by the end of the war the Soviet industrial plant was going strong. The Soviets and their Communist supporters in Europe also emerged from the war with a vastly improved reputation. The Communists had an unquestioned record of suffering at the hands of the fascists. While many Socialists, Christian Democrats, and others had behaved nobly, there were enough exceptions to cast shadows on non-Communist movements and parties.

Some believed that American predominance, Western European decline, and Soviet power and influence presaged a continued wartime alliance, led by an American-Soviet condominium, to defang the defeated nations and reconstruct Europe. There were supporters of this view in the American administration, including Secretary of the Treasury Henry Morgenthau and former Vice President Henry Wallace. Morgenthau's Treasury even drew up a plan to deindustrialize Germany, restricting it to agriculture and light industry in order to purge the Nazi regions of its military-industrial complex.

But hostility between the United States and the Soviet Union grew as the war ended. Ideological differences between the two social orders may have been too great, or political competition in European countries between Communist and non-Communist parties too fierce. Conflict may have been an inevitable consequence of the tension that ensued as each superpower faced the unwelcome ascendance of the other. Perhaps the hostility could have been avoided, but it was not. By 1947 Europe was dividing into pro-American and pro-Soviet blocs, and each bloc leader took on the task of holding its clients together economically and politically. The United States and the Soviet Union took responsibility for rebuilding Western and Eastern Europe respectively.

America's role in capitalism's reconstruction combined global economic and anti-Soviet goals. Some American corporate and government leaders were enthusiastic about the second chance at economic internationalism and used the Soviet threat largely to justify the attempt to build an American-centered global economic order. Others tolerated the economic components of American hegemony, but only in service of the struggle against the Soviet Union and communism. The result has been called the centrist consensus, but it was more a compromise than a consensus.

Dean Acheson, present at the creation

Dean Acheson was one of the principal architects of this compromise over American postwar policy. Acheson was in many ways a quintessential New England WASP, the son of an Episcopal bishop of Connecticut who went to Groton, Yale, and Harvard Law School. But he was also atypical: His parents were Canadian, they were hardly wealthy, and he was a lifelong Democrat. Acheson was deeply affected by his clerkship for Supreme Court Justice Louis Brandeis, a judicial progressive wary of monopoly and sympathetic to social reform. Acheson's Washington law firm was a pillar of the establishment, and Acheson was prominent in the Washington elite; but he also served as legal counsel to the International Ladies' Garment Workers Union.

Acheson represented the new breed of American interwar businessmen, politicians, and journalists who combined a commitment to Wilsonian internationalism, the modern business community, and social reform. These strands came together in the 1930s in the New Deal, while analogous combinations came together in Western Europe as the new social democracy grew there. There was no contradiction in Acheson's mind between economic globalism and domestic reform.

Acheson became undersecretary of the treasury in 1933 and was immediately caught between his Wall Street and reformist tendencies. Roosevelt's decision to take the dollar off gold was resisted by the Treasury, which was close to traditional business sentiment and financial orthodoxy. When Acheson strenuously opposed the new currency management, the president forced him out of office after six months. As the Depression dragged on, Acheson became a supporter of the New Deal, defending labor organizers in court and working enthusiastically (against many of his Wall Street friends) for Roosevelt's reelection. Acheson was powerfully interested in international affairs and powerfully opposed to isolationism; he ran against and beat Senator Robert Taft, the country's leading isolationist, for a seat on Yale's governing council.[23]

Late in 1939 Acheson presented his worldview in a forceful and widely remarked speech at Yale. Although he was still a private citizen, his sentiments represented the opinion of those who wanted to pull the United States toward international economic leadership. "The economic and political system of the Nineteenth Century," said Acheson, "has been for many years in the obvious process of decline. The system is deeply impaired." Its foundations were gone: "We can see that the credits which were once extended by the financial center of London no longer provide the means for the production of wealth in other countries. We can see that the free trade areas, which once furnished both a market of vast importance and a commodities exchange, no longer exist. We can see that British naval power no longer can guarantee security of life and investment in distant parts of the earth."

Acheson argued that a better future required American leadership:

> . . . making available capital in those parts of Europe which need productive equipment upon condition that Europe does its part to remove obstructions to trade within itself and provide, so far as it can, scope for commerce. We can join in offering a broader market for goods made under decent standards and, in this way, a means of purchasing essential raw materials. We can join in providing a stable international monetary system under which credits can be made and repaid and goods purchased and sold. We can join in removing exclusive or preferential trade arrangements with other areas created by military or financial conquest, agreement, or political connection.[24]

He worked for all these things over the next dozen years, financing Europe in return for a commitment to European economic cooperation, reducing American trade barriers, creating a stable monetary order, and breaking down foreign protectionism. In January 1941 he was invited back into the administration, as assistant secretary of state for economic affairs. He had already shown more flexibility than in the debate over gold, suggesting in a prominent letter to the *New York Times* the legal expedients that would allow for lend-lease aid to Britain. Once in the administration, Acheson negotiated the terms of the formal Lend-Lease Agreement with Keynes. He headed the State Department's team at Bretton Woods and helped draft the monetary agreements. A year later Acheson led the administration's drive to secure congressional support for the Bretton Woods Agreements. He told Congress that the new system was crucial to American exports and that American exports were crucial to American prosperity: "We cannot go through another ten years like the ten years at the end of the Twenties and the beginning of the Thirties, without having the most far-reaching consequences upon our economic and social system. . . . The important thing is markets. . . . You must look to foreign markets."[25]

With the Bretton Woods institutions in place, American policy turned to immediate problems of reconstruction. Acheson was again at the center of the storm, as undersecretary of state in the new administration of Harry Truman. The economic internationalists wanted to restore London as a financial center, as a first step to revitalize world markets. The United States and Canada extended a five-billion-dollar loan to Britain (three-quarters from the United States, one-quarter from Canada), in return for British agreement to remove many restrictions on trade and investment. Most important, the United States insisted that Great Britain remove currency controls so that private investors and traders could freely exchange sterling for dollars. This return to convertibility, the ability to convert European currencies to "hard" currencies, was central to the restoration of normal business. Without it, currencies other than the dollar were not truly backed by gold, and countries with inconvertible currencies could not fully engage in international trade, payments, and investment.

The American leaders saw the loan to Britain as crucial to European reconstruction. Now they had to convince skeptical Americans, including U.S. senators and congressmen, of the wisdom of sending billions more dollars across the Atlantic for an economic goal that seemed to be of interest only to a few banks and industries. The purely economic arguments for the loan failed, and the Truman administration decided to market it as the cement for a Western alliance against the Soviet Union, even though at this stage in early 1946 the direction of American-Soviet relations was still unclear. Acheson's collaborator Joseph Jones told one senator, "If these areas are allowed to spiral downwards into economic anarchy, then at best they will drop out of the United States orbit and try an independent nationalist policy; at worst they will swing into the Russian orbit."[26]

Acheson was anathema to the conservative isolationists who had opposed internationalism after World War One and who challenged its revival now. But he persuaded them that economic engagement would serve their anti-Soviet goals. He argued that the loan made geopolitical as well as economic sense, and the battle was all but won when Arthur Vandenberg, ranking Republican on the Senate Foreign Relations Committee, warned: "If we do not lead some other and powerful nation will capitalize on our failure and we shall pay the price of our default." By the same token, the Republican leader in the House saw it as determining "whether there shall be a coalition between the British sphere and the American sphere or whether there shall be a coalition between the British sphere and the Soviet sphere." This was almost certainly overblown. Acheson's biographer concluded that "Acheson regarded it as unfortunate that the loan had to be justified with veiled illusions to the Soviet threat, but he accepted it as a price that had to be paid to secure the support needed."[27]

The British loan made it through Congress, but the economic policies the loan was meant to support collapsed. When sterling returned to convertibility in July 1947, every investor who could changed pounds into dollars. Within weeks the billions were dissipated, and the government had to slap on currency controls. European reconstruction would require more massive initiatives than previously anticipated.

In February 1947 the administration went back to the House and Senate, now controlled by the Republicans, to plead for assistance for countries such as Greece and Turkey. Again the economic arguments were ineffectual. But by now the Soviet threat was more credible, as relations with the Soviet Union deteriorated rapidly, and Undersecretary Acheson and Secretary of State George Marshall knew that the Republicans were more concerned about the spread of communism than about free trade. In private, Vandenberg warned Truman that there was just one way to get popular support for the economic aid: "Mr. President, the only way you are ever going to get this is to make a speech and scare the hell out of the country."[28] Truman made such a speech in March 1947, announcing the Truman Doctrine.

Three months after the Truman Doctrine committed the United States to a global effort against the Soviets and their allies, Secretary of State Marshall launched the Economic Recovery Plan, the Marshall Plan. This sent about $13.5 billion to Europe to rebuild the economies of the Western Allies; a parallel program sent another half billion dollars to Japan. Acheson replaced Marshall as secretary of state in early 1949, just in time to oversee the creation of the North Atlantic Treaty Organization, an American military bloc to accompany its sphere of economic influence. The following year Acheson facilitated a French-German plan to unify their coal and steel industries, the first step on the road to a Common Market. The foundations of the postwar world were in place.

Dean Acheson had been, as his memoir's title put it, "present at the creation" of a new world economy. In his ill-fated six months at the Treasury in 1933, he had fought for gold standard orthodoxy against new, more flexible policies. He returned to policy making in 1941 to help slip a few destroyers past a wary Congress to the beleaguered

British. Lend-lease, Bretton Woods, and the British loan clarified how America intended to reorganize the world economy. The Marshall Plan cemented the new community of interest, and a link to Cold War diplomacy secured American domestic support. Out of the ruins of the ancien régime, Acheson and his colleagues achieved his 1939 goals: American aid to Europe, European economic cooperation, a new global monetary and investment system, and trade liberalization.

The United States and European reconstruction

American government loans and aid were the country's first contribution to Western European and Japanese postwar growth. The United States sent over ten billion dollars in emergency assistance to Europe and Asia immediately after the war, in large part to provide food and other necessities to populations that were sometimes near starvation. The Marshall Plan and a parallel Japanese program were oriented toward economic reconstruction. The cost, about fourteen billion dollars, was more than 5 percent of America's 1948 GDP; an analogous share of America's GDP in the year 2000 would have been more than a half trillion dollars. In its first year of operation, Marshall Plan assistance was between 3 and 6 percent of most Western European recipients' national incomes, on average about one-quarter of their total investment; for some small countries, Marshall Plan aid was more than one-tenth of national income.[29]

American markets were another resource the Western Europeans and Japanese tapped to fuel reconstruction. The Europeans were desperate for American food, raw materials, and capital equipment. American aid and loans were not enough, and at some point the Europeans would have to pay for imports with goods they sold. For the first time in memory, the American market was relatively open to Europeans. European exports increased again when the Korean War began in 1950, as the need for war-related matériel pumped up American demand.

Europe and Japan embarked on an American-based export boom that continued through the 1950s. Western Europe's exports in 1946 were barely equal to those of the autarkic conditions of 1938, at eight billion dollars. By 1948 they had doubled, and by 1951 they had risen to twenty-seven billion. In 1948 West German exports were just a billion dollars, which paid for only half the country's imports; by 1951 exports were four billion dollars, more than the nation's import needs. West German industrial production, led by exports, nearly tripled over the three-year course of the Marshall Plan.[30] Although German performance was most striking, all of Western Europe grew extraordinarily quickly. Steel production in Germany, France, Italy, and Benelux combined jumped from twelve million tons in 1946 to forty-one million tons in 1952. By 1953 output per person in every Western European country, and in Japan, was above 1938 levels and rising fast. The three biggest economies, Britain, France, and Germany, had by 1951—six years after the war ended—surpassed their record of recovery during the entire period from the end of World War One through the Depression of the 1930s.[31]

The political environment the United States established had at least as big an impact as direct American aid and trade. American support for the new economic institutions, American leadership of the Western bloc, and American engagement in world affairs during the Cold War all combined to reassure investors in Europe and Japan that conditions would be stable and predictable. This contrasted with the 1920s, when international and domestic conflict unsettled political economies and dampened investment. The price was acceptance of American dominion within its bloc, but European and Japanese leaders were weak enough, and their views close enough to those of the United States, that this was a price worth paying.

The United States bankrolled the two functioning Bretton Woods institutions, the IMF and the World Bank, and provided them with their Washington headquarters. By joint agreement, the bank's president was an American, the fund's a European; but American predominance was taken for granted in both organizations as it was in NATO and other Western partnerships. Neither the fund nor the bank did much through the 1940s and early 1950s. The bank's reconstruction tasks had been rendered irrelevant by America's postwar aid; its development mission was caught in lengthy discussions of how best to carry it out. In monetary relations, European countries tightly controlled their currencies, strictly limiting the degree to which private citizens could convert national money into gold or dollars. Only the U.S. dollar and a few other currencies were freely convertible. But the dollar had been fixed at thirty-five dollars per ounce of gold since 1934, and this commitment, as well as America's support for the Bretton Woods order, provided a reliable monetary anchor for international trade, finance, and investment.

The gold-dollar standard provided international monetary stability, while the United States did not try to force a reconstituted gold standard rigidity on national policies. This was brought home in September 1949, when the United Kingdom devalued the pound sterling by 30 percent, to $2.80. The IMF was simply informed of the move, which was followed by similar devaluations against the dollar in Europe and other regions accounting for two-thirds of world trade. In a gold standard world this might have been seen as the opening shot in a currency war; in the Bretton Woods environment it was regarded as a necessary adjustment to increase the ability of struggling economies to export.[32] The new monetary order and the United States further demonstrated their flexibility with the development of a multilateral clearing system, the European Payments Union. This effectively encouraged Western Europeans to trade more with one another, even if it came to some extent at the expense of the United States. The message was clear: The desire for international currency stability would be tempered by the need for national macroeconomic health.

International trade was liberalized as international monetary relations stabilized. However, the process did not start propitiously. Across Washington from where the IMF and the World Bank were growing up, the International Trade Organization (ITO) was being strangled in its cradle. American protectionists found it too free trade, free traders too protectionist, and the Truman administration never bothered to submit the enabling treaty to a Congress that was sure to defeat it.

Trade liberalization went forward over the ITO's dead body. In 1947, in Geneva, two dozen Western countries signed what was supposed to be an interim General Agreement on Tariffs and Trade (GATT). The agreement reduced many trade barriers and provided a forum within which the industrialized nations could consult and negotiate over trade policy. The Western industrial nations had embraced the goal of freer international trade.

Political support for the new order had to be secured. The economic component of stabilization was important, as a stable international economic order would reinvigorate business communities demoralized by depression, class conflict, interstate and civil war. But there were many domestic political issues to be addressed. Capitalists in Europe and Japan were at best unpopular, at worst tainted by collaboration with fascism. The war had left the Right discredited and even illegitimate, and there was little Center to counter the Left. As Dean Acheson recalled, "only in Britain and Russia did people have any confidence in government, or social or economic organization, or currencies. Elsewhere governments had been repudiated, or abolished by the conquerers: social classes were in bitter enmity, with resistance groups hunting out and executing, often after drumhead trials, collaborators with the late enemy."[33]

In most of Europe the Left dominated postwar politics. The Socialists built on their already powerful position, while the Communists turned popular desires for socioeconomic change and popular respect for Soviet (and, in many places, Communist resistance) wartime achievements into support at the ballot box and in labor unions. The first elections after the war typically gave the Socialists and Communists combined the largest share of votes in Parliament, often a clear majority. Communist parties joined ruling coalitions in France, Italy, and Belgium. This could not survive the Cold War, and the Communists were thrown out of these governments in 1947. At the same time some of those tarnished by association with the fascists, who had been purged in the early postwar months, were allowed back into business and government. Nonetheless, labor movements and Socialist parties were central to the new politics of Western Europe.[34]

Postwar politics was much broader—and more left-leaning—than had been accepted before the war. The Center before 1939 typically described an alliance between agrarians and traditional (business-based) liberals. In the conditions of the late 1940s the centrist spectrum spread from the Christian Democrats through the Socialists. And despite some American aversion to supporting such socialists as British Labour, the new governments counted on strong support from the United States as they charted a course toward full membership in the Western economic order.

The Soviet Union builds a bloc

The starting and ending points of reconstruction in the East were different from those in Western Europe. To begin with, the devastation was unimaginably greater in Central and Eastern Europe, where the most destructive battles of the war were fought. More Russians died in the three-year siege of the city of Leningrad than Americans and Britons combined during the entire war; two million German and Russian soldiers died in the battle for Stalingrad, which was left a pile of rubble. During the most critical portion of the war, from the invasion of Russia in June 1941 until the Allied landings in France in June 1944, 93 percent of the German Army's casualties were suffered on the eastern front.[35]

By the end of the war the Soviet Union had lost some twenty million people, more than half of them civilians. Tens of millions of Soviet citizens were homeless, and in the western part of the country, which had been occupied by the Germans, some four-fifths of prewar industry had been put out of commission. The government had moved many factories to the Urals and beyond, allowing heavy industrial production to continue and even grow a little during the war. But consumer goods and food output were barely half the already low prewar levels, and the cost of rebuilding the country's ruined cities, farms, and factories would be immense.[36]

Most Eastern European countries also suffered severe war damage as Soviet, partisan, and Axis armies fought over them. The Soviet-occupied sector of Germany was as much in ruins as the American, British, and French sectors. Only Bulgaria, Albania, and the Czech lands had been spared substantial losses. In the region as a whole, agricultural production had dropped to one-quarter below its prewar levels, industrial production to half or less.[37]

For the losers—the eastern part of Germany and its former allies Bulgaria, Hungary, and Romania—the destruction of war was compounded by reparations. The Allies had agreed on cash and equipment transfers to the victors. The United States and its allies soon suspended these transfers in the western parts of Germany, especially once the Cold War led the West to regard a strong and prosperous Germany as more useful than a poor and weak one. The Soviets continued to exact reparations, Cold War or no. They dismantled nineteen hundred German plants and shipped them to the Soviet Union. The Soviet government also took over, but left in place, over two hundred large East German factories, accounting for about one-third of the zone's industrial production, and kept possession for almost ten years. Between reparations payments and the costs of occupation (which the Germans, by Allied agreement, were supposed to bear), East Germany paid perhaps one-eighth of its national income to the USSR for a decade after the end of the war.[38] Romania and Hungary too were assessed substantial reparations obligations in cash and kind, mostly to the USSR; Bulgaria had to pay more modest amounts to Greece and Yugoslavia.[39]

Conditions in the East were even more unsettled than they had been after World War One. Hungary experienced the worst inflation in world history. When the war ended, the U.S. dollar traded at 1,320 pengös, already a severe collapse from the 5.4 pengös to the dollar of 1938 or the 44 pengös to the dollar of 1944. By the end of 1945 Hungarian prices had risen four hundred-fold, and the pengö had dropped to 290,000 to the dollar. As 1946 began, prices began to rise so fast the money supply could not keep up, and the currency became next to worthless. By summer 1946 prices were tripling every day and more. In the mad rush, wages lagged far behind and fell as low as one-eighth of 1938 levels in terms of purchasing power. By the end of July one U.S. dollar was worth five nonillion pengös (a nonillion is ten followed by thirty zeros). The government printing presses could not keep pace with the wild inflation, and at this point all of Hungary's banknotes in circulation combined were worth about one one-thousandth of an American cent.[40] While the Hungarian hyperinflation was extreme, many Eastern European countries experienced traumatic collapses of their economies.

In addition to general dislocation and confusion, by the end of the war the economic organization of Eastern Europe was profoundly different from that of the West, even before it felt the full impact of the Soviet Union. Most of the region had gone down the path of autarky and government control of the economy before 1939, and wartime conditions—whether under German occupation or as part of the Nazi-led alliance—had led to a further centralization of state ownership and control of the economy. The already large public sectors were swelled by war-related demands and by the expropriation of the properties of Jews and other "undesirables." With liberation, the new authorities took over properties belonging to Germans, war criminals, and collaborators, further expanding the state sector. The region's already weak business classes were further weakened as the war ended since many fell into the categories to be expropriated.

Postwar confiscations also changed the agrarian structure. Millions of ethnic German farmers were expelled, and their farmlands were taken, along with the large estates and other properties seized from collaborators and war criminals. This land was distributed to the region's poor or landless peasants, and these rough-and-ready measures were often supplemented with more systematic land reforms. By 1946, with few Communist policies in place, Eastern and Central European economies were already dominated by state-run industry and utilities and aggressively reformed agriculture. The business communities and middle classes were small and weak, while the Communists had been bolstered by their wartime records and alliance with the Soviet Union.

In these conditions, the public Soviet line toward the region seemed plausible. Communist leaders said that these countries would follow a new "people's democracy," neither Soviet-style socialism nor Western capitalism. An alliance of the working class, the peasantry, and the fragile "national bourgeoisies" would—under Communist leadership, to be sure—reconstruct mixed economies. This "third way" in the Soviet zone of influence paralleled social democracy in the American zone and reinforced the hopes of some for a postwar accommodation between East and West.

Whatever the true prospects for a non-Soviet road to socialism, domestic and international conditions did not allow such a road to be taken. Relations between the Communists and their alliance partners in Eastern and Central Europe deteriorated along with relations between the Soviet Union and its wartime allies in Western Europe. By 1948 the "people's democracies" were heading toward Soviet-style centralization. Governments nationalized most remaining large private enterprises, set up central planning systems that put a premium on heavy industrial development, and restricted international trade.[41]

In January 1949, a few months after the Marshall Plan came into effect, the Soviet Union and its allies in Eastern Europe created the Council for Mutual Economic Assistance (CMEA, or Comecon). The CMEA may have been meant as a counterweight to the Western alliance, but it played little economic role; autarkic economic policy limited the possibility of any mutual economic assistance. The Soviets reduced or eliminated remaining reparations payments and established some preferential trading arrangements, although many in the region believed that these arrangements were especially preferential to the Soviet Union. Most of the region's trade was on a strictly bilateral country-to-country basis and limited in volume and effect. The USSR encouraged its allies to pursue the Soviet-style path of autonomous industry-led economic development. The curious breach between Stalin and Tito that led Yugoslavia, previously the most Stalinist of regimes, to break away from the Soviet sphere, was only a slight diversion from the consolidation of central planning from the Elbe to the Pacific.

The new members of the Soviet bloc and the Soviet Union itself rebuilt from war damage very quickly. By 1950 Soviet industrial production was nearly double that of 1945 and well above prewar levels.

Despite serious farm problems, living standards seem to have recovered the ground lost to war and reconstruction. The same was true in Eastern Europe, where every country's industrial production had surpassed prewar levels by 1949.[42] Even in Hungary the currency was stable, inflation was under control, and income per person was 15 percent higher than it had been in 1938. Hungarian agriculture lagged below prewar levels, but given the chaos of the immediate postwar period, the restoration of economic stability and growth was a remarkable achievement.

Economic trends in the Soviet Union and its allies were especially important because the Communist world was expanding outside Europe. By the time Comecon was created, Communist-led governments controlled most of China and northern Vietnam, as well as all of northern Korea. Early indications from all three countries were that the new governments intended to pursue some variant of the central planning pioneered by the Soviet Union.

Central planning was no longer a Russian oddity but a worldwide alternative to market capitalism. For the first time the issue was brought to the Third World by the Chinese Revolution, Vietnamese success in halting French recolonization, and the political influence of Communist parties in other colonies. Now hundreds of millions of inhabitants of the colonies, and of such newly independent nations as India, could examine the differences between centrally planned socialism and market capitalism to see which better suited their conditions. Up to then the principal division of the world had been between rich industrial countries and poor agrarian countries. Now there was a second dimension and two possible paths toward advanced industrial status: capitalist and Communist.

The Communist part of the world was a new economic pole. For the first time there was an existing option for people, parties, and countries dissatisfied with the inequality and unpredictability of capitalism. Fascism had had a certain appeal for populists in the industrialized world and nationalists in the developing and colonial countries, but World War Two ended that hope. Social democracy held out the prospect of incremental reform, but its promise was too modest for those looking for a radical solution to the grinding poverty of the poor regions and even for many people in the industrial nations.

Soviet-style socialism seemed to deliver rapid growth, egalitarianism, and social improvements. The result made many leftists uneasy, as witness the common appellation of "really existing socialism" that most of the Western Left used, simultaneously admitting that communism's centrally planned economies were the only socialism extant and distinguishing them from a more desirable but nonexistent form of socialism. Nonetheless, the rise and consolidation of a socialist world of Communist-led countries gave hope to millions that there was indeed a way to avoid the impersonality of capitalism's market forces and their tendency to work against the interests of the poor and powerless.

Two syntheses

In the golden age of global capitalism, ruling classes pushed and pulled their societies toward domestic and international markets. They were little concerned for, and often actively hostile to, policies to ameliorate the poverty of the world's majority. Proponents of this orthodoxy argued that global economic openness was inconsistent with policies to mitigate domestic poverty. The fascist movements of the interwar period accepted this argument and acted on the principle that neither economic integration nor social reform was desirable. They rejected both the international economy and social reform in pursuit of nationalist autarky.

Out of the liberal thesis and its fascist antithesis came a postwar synthesis, predicated on the conclusion that both liberalism and fascism had been wrong. There were two strikingly different versions of this synthesis, West and East. Both rejected fascism's abandonment of social reform and embraced social change. But their attitudes to the classical liberal view of global capitalism were diametrically opposed. The West wagered that liberalism had been wrong about the incompatibility of global capitalism and the market with social reform. The West aimed to prove that economically integrated market economies could adopt equitable social policies, that economic openness could go along with the new social democratic welfare states.

The East's Communists made an equal but opposite wager: that liberalism had been right about the incompatibility of integration and reform, that social change meant rejecting global and national markets. Central planning aimed to prove that the demands of poor people and poor countries for equity and development could be met only by separating from world markets and by eliminating markets more generally.

For the next twenty-five years the principal global geopolitical goal of the American and Soviet leaders of the capitalist and Communist worlds, respectively, was to prove the other side wrong. One side was intent on proving that global capitalism could be good for growth and equity; the other, on proving that development and equity could best be achieved by rejecting global capitalism.

12

The Bretton Woods System in Action

In August 1945 Charles de Gaulle visited Washington and compared notes with Jean Monnet, who was procuring supplies for de Gaulle's new government. "America's dazzling prosperity," Monnet recalled, "astonished him." General de Gaulle had visions of French grandeur, but Monnet told him they were misplaced: "You speak of greatness," he said, "but today the French are small." The way forward was to "modernize themselves—because at the moment they are not modern. They need more production and more productivity. Materially, the country needs to be transformed."[1] The same could have been said about all of Western Europe. It was a half century behind the United States; even after reconstruction, per capita GDP in Western Europe in 1950 was equivalent to that of the United States in 1905.

Less than twenty-five years later the gap had effectively closed. Between 1870 and 1929 Western European output per person doubled, and that was seen as a remarkable achievement. In the Bretton Woods period Western Europe's per capita output doubled in sixteen years, from 1948 to 1964, and then kept growing.[2]

A few years earlier the world had focused on the contrasts between Nazi Germany and New Deal America, fascist Italy and social democratic Sweden, militaristic Japan and struggling Britain. Now these countries had a common economic, political, and social order and similar standards of living. Between 1945 and 1973 the "First World" of rich democratic welfare states coalesced. In 1961 these countries formalized their club as the Organization for Economic Cooperation and Development (OECD).[3]

The industrial West rebuilt its political economies on the basis of compromise among nations, classes, parties, and groups. Governments balanced international integration and national autonomy, global competition and national constituencies, free markets and social democracy. The middle ground reigned at home and abroad. The United States removed most of its trade barriers but accepted European and Japanese protection. The Europeans negotiated an economic and political union that respected national differences. Governments pulled down barriers to cross-border trade and investment but protected weaker firms. Labor and capital cooperated to keep profits and wages high, trading labor rights for labor peace. Socialists and conservatives, Christian Democrats and secular liberals worked together to build modern welfare states.

Postwar growth accelerates

The postwar compromises grew out of the agreements signed at Bretton Woods in 1944. The Bretton Woods system maintained the spirit, if not always the letter, of the Bretton Woods Agreements: international integration tempered by government concern for national constituencies; markets tempered by social reforms; American leadership tempered by Western cooperation.

The Bretton Woods system delivered the goods: economic growth, low unemployment, and stable prices. Japan was the most dramatic success story: Its output grew eightfold in just twenty-five years. The Asian nation's postwar miracle began with a quick recovery during the American occupation and accelerated after 1950 as orders poured in to supply American troops during the Korean War. The Japanese learned new methods, created new industries, searched out markets abroad, and quickly became a major force in international trade.

Japanese industrialists moved quickly to adopt technologies developed in the previous thirty years. They drew on a backlog of new products as well as a highly trained and very cheap labor force. Japanese companies in the 1950s and 1960s spent one-quarter to one-half of all their research and development budgets to buy foreign technology. Sony, for example, started life in 1946 as a repair shop and first made an electric rice cooker that did not work. Over the next few years it made cheap copies of the tape recorders American occupiers had brought to Japan. In 1953 it licensed from Western Electric the right to produce the new transistors that Bell Labs had recently invented. Sony turned out its first transistor radio—the world's second—in 1955 and brought a miniaturized "pocket radio" to market two years later. Meanwhile companies like Honda in motorcycles and Toyota in automobiles were carefully imitating American production techniques to supply the Japanese market.

The Japanese government supported manufacturers with tax breaks, subsidies, cheap loans, and other assistance. The domestic market grew spectacularly after decades of crisis and war. In the early 1950s virtually no Japanese households owned televisions, washing machines, or refrigerators; ten years later half of them owned all three, and by 1970, 90 percent of the country's families had the three appliances. This helped fuel a revolution in basic industry: Steel production went from less than ten million tons in the early 1950s to almost a hundred million tons fifteen years later.

The government also encouraged firms to produce for export, especially with a very weak yen that made the country's goods highly competitive and that made it extremely profitable for Japanese companies to sell overseas. By the late 1950s Sony was marketing its radios in the U.S. market, Toyota its cars, and Honda its motorcycles. Honda set up a factory in Los Angeles in 1959 and one in Europe in 1962. Japanese companies had become well known to Western consumers, and in 1961 Sony became the first Japanese company to sell stock in the United States. By the 1960s Japan's manufacturers were a major force in world trade.

Japan achieved remarkable economic success in the first twenty-five postwar years. In 1950 Japan was roughly as developed as the United States had been in 1850, measured by GDP per person. By 1973 its GDP per person was equivalent to American levels of 1963 and as high as that of Western Europe. Japan started out the postwar period economically a century behind the United States; in 1973 it was ten years behind. The world's second-largest market economy had made up nearly a hundred years in less than twenty-five.[4]

Postwar economic growth was extraordinary everywhere, not just in

Japan. The advanced capitalist nations as a whole grew three times as fast as in the interwar years and twice as fast as before World War One. In 1948 the industrial nations combined (Western Europe, North America, Australia, New Zealand, and Japan) produced $3.7 trillion, expressed in 2000 dollars. By 1973, the combined output of these twenty-one countries was $12.1 trillion, well more than three times as much.[5]

American growth was not slow: Output per person there grew 75 percent, and Americans were prosperous. But Europe and Japan grew much more rapidly. The farther behind countries started, the more quickly they caught up. Had this pace continued, by the year 2000 the United States would have been one of the poorer countries in the OECD.[6]

A 1950 observer would have been hard put to anticipate this convergence among the countries that eventually formed the rich world club of the OECD. At that point Western Europe's GDP per person was 10 percent below that of Argentina; France's was over 15 percent lower, Germany's over one-third lower, Italy's 45 percent lower, Spain's less than half. Germany and Italy were poorer than Chile; Japan was poorer than Peru. Between 1948 and 1973 continental Western Europe and Japan vaulted over a host of other countries to join the United States, United Kingdom, and other Anglo-American nations at the top of the world's social ladder. By 1973 Spain had gone from being half as rich as Argentina to being richer than Argentina; Western Europe on average was now 50 percent richer than Argentina. Germany and Italy were two or three times as rich as Chile, Japan three times as rich as Peru.

After the former belligerents had rebuilt their industrial facilities by the early 1950s, they turned to adopt new technologies. Few of the interwar advances in products and production of the 1920s and 1930s had been put into place outside North America. The automobile, the most conspicuous symbol of American affluence, was the most important such product. In the United States in 1950 there were more than 40 million automobiles on the roads. This was about 7 cars for every car in Europe; there were more motor vehicles in the state of California than on the entire European continent. By 1973 Europe had been motorized. In less than twenty-five years the number of passenger cars in Germany went from a half million to 17 million, in France from 1.5 million to 14.5 million, and so on. The region in 1973 had ten times more cars than in 1950, nearly 60 million passenger cars. Scandinavia's 17 million people now had more cars than all 300 million people in Western Europe had had just two decades earlier. There were now 102 million cars on American roads, so the American-European ratio was now just 1.7 to 1.

The Europeans quickly caught up with other new consumer durables—refrigerators, washing machines, eventually televisions. The new synthetic fibers and petrochemicals, which had taken America by storm before World War Two, reached Europe and Japan in the 1950s. The moving assembly line came to Europe as a relative novelty in the 1940s. As the Europeans and Japanese introduced new products and technologies, the lag was overcome. Production of new chemicals, automobiles, television sets, and synthetics such as nylon grew at two or three times the American rate in the 1950s and 1960s.

Western Europe and Japan caught up between 1948 and 1973 in part because millions of their people left farming. European and Japanese agriculture had long been inefficient, with millions of poor peasants stuck on marginal land. Only the collapse of international trade in the interwar period, reinforced by trade barriers, had maintained these oversize farm sectors. In countries with modern agriculture, by 1950 farmers were typically around 10 percent of the labor force (13 percent in the Netherlands, 11 percent in the United States, 6 percent in the UK). But more than half of the workers in Japan, nearly half in Italy and Spain, one-quarter in most of the rest of Western Europe were still in agriculture. Europe and Japan had far more farmers than their relatively poor land could support, meaning they had generally miserable living standards. Over the next twenty years, farm populations in Western Europe and Japan shrank to well below 10 percent of the total workforce on average—in the case of Italy, down from 45 percent in 1950 to 17 percent in 1973. Labor moved out of unproductive agriculture into more productive manufacturing and services.[7]

Postwar international trade and investment also catalyzed Western European and Japanese growth. From 1913 to 1950 world trade and investment stagnated, and governments reinforced this trend by building barriers to foreign goods and companies. European and Japanese manufacturers and farmers, insulated from world markets, carried on without having to introduce new industrial processes or products. Economic isolation was a major cause of the backwardness of European and Japanese industry and agriculture in 1950. Just as world economic collapse dragged Europe and Japan down between the wars, so the revival of world trade and investment after World War Two spurred them on. These economies suddenly had access to a dynamic world trading system. Foreign corporations, especially American multinationals with the latest products and processes, were eager to invest in Europe and Japan.

America's international position had changed fundamentally. Before World War Two the United States had been inhospitable to foreign goods and generally uninterested in foreign markets. Now it sucked in imports from the rest of the world and exported enthusiastically. American trade in the 1950s was two or three times as great as interwar levels, even controlling for inflation. Companies in Europe and Japan could sell what they produced in the American market and buy the most modern capital equipment and supplies from the United States. The ready availability of the enormous American market changed the attitudes and behavior of European and Japanese producers.

The industrial world now also had access to American capital, primarily in the form of foreign direct investment. American firms' investments in Europe and Japan went from two billion dollars in 1950 to forty-one billion in 1973.[8] The American multinationals that established affiliates abroad brought with them the latest technologies, marketing, and management techniques.

American markets and capital helped reorient the world's industrial economies. America's conversion from insulation to integration sparked a revival in world trade and investment, which drove a burst of growth in Western Europe and Japan, which in turn contributed to the dynamism of the world economy, itself reinforcing the trend toward global economic integration. All good things went together in a virtuous circle of commercial integration, multinational corporate expansion, economic growth, and prosperity. The hopes of the designers of the Bretton Woods system were fulfilled.

Jean Monnet and a United States of Europe

A French brandy salesman named Jean Monnet was central to one remarkable Bretton Woods–era development, Western Europe's creation of a common market.[9] Monnet, the eldest son of the chairman of a producers' cooperative, was from the town of Cognac. As a young man Monnet traveled the world to market the family wares, from the Yukon to rural Egypt. He spent a long time in North America, giving him an understanding of American business practices, business partners in the United States, and good English.

Monnet had an exporter's belief in economic internationalism. He was a globe-trotter long before people realized that the globe could be trotted. A convoluted episode from his personal life is illustrative. In 1929 Monnet fell in love with a married woman, the Istanbul-born daughter of an Italian publisher of a French-language newspaper. In 1935, in an era of difficult divorces, they arranged to converge on Moscow, he from financial consulting in Shanghai, she from her temporary home in Switzerland. There Silvia took out Soviet citizenship and took advantage of the liberal Soviet divorce code to divorce her husband and marry Monnet. They moved to Shanghai, then set up housekeeping in New York, in part because they needed to stay away from Europe to avoid a custody dispute over Silvia's daughter by her first husband. Over the next decade they moved back and forth among New York, Washington, London, Algiers, and (once the daughter was grown) Paris.

Monnet never ran for or held elected office, but he was an exceptionally effective administrator and negotiator. During World War One he was the French representative on a joint Allied supply commission. After the war he served five years as deputy secretary-general of the League of Nations with principal responsibility for economic affairs. In this capacity Monnet oversaw efforts to stabilize and reconstruct the economies of central and eastern Europe and experienced the League's inability to secure American involvement.

In 1923 Monnet returned to private business as the European partner of Blair and Company, a Wall Street investment bank. For Blair, Monnet led private-public stabilization programs in Poland and Romania. He left Blair in the early years of the Depression, but his consulting firm remained a fixture on Wall Street and in international finance, negotiating loans and other business in China, Europe, and North America.

Monnet had close contacts with America's most important international financial, political, and legal figures. He consulted frequently with official and financial America, advising the Roosevelt administration on lend-lease and American bankers on international affairs. He became good friends with some of the country's interwar and postwar leaders, including senior Morgan partners Thomas Lamont and Dwight Morrow, Averell Harriman, John McCloy, and Dean Acheson. Monnet had especially close ties to John Foster Dulles, then a Wall Street lawyer; they worked together on the Polish loan program, and Dulles bankrolled Monnet's New York financial consulting firm.

Many American international bankers believed that the interwar period had demonstrated that the political and economic fragmentation of Europe was untenable. As Dulles put it in 1941, "the reestablishment of some twenty-five wholly independent sovereign states in Europe would be political folly." The United States should "seek the political reorganization of Continental Europe as a federated commonwealth."[10] America's internationalist political and business leaders believed that a United States of Europe was essential to the prosperity and stability of the continent—and to America's interests there.

It was natural that the principal protagonist of a common market in Western Europe was immersed in American business and political circles. This was not for the reasons some Gaullists focused on, that Monnet was a tool of American imperialism. Monnet believed that the new industrial capitalism would look American and that Europe's economic and political fragmentation crippled its ability to take advantage of the new mass production and mass consumption. American-style industrialism required a market the size of the American market, corporations as big as American corporations, financial markets as deep as Wall Street. European businesses could not compete with American businesses without a home base like that of the United States, and if they could not compete, they could not tap the potential of the Continent. That was the challenge Monnet aimed to take up with European integration.

During World War Two, Monnet worked tirelessly in Washington and New York to channel supplies to the French and British. He served de Gaulle and the Free French in North Africa and in France upon liberation. As director of the new Planning Commissariat he formulated the Monnet Plan for reconstruction, and his superministry was the principal French conduit for Marshall Plan aid.

In 1948 and 1949 the hardening of the Cold War and the establishment of a unified Federal Republic of Germany made clear to Monnet that relations between France and Germany were at a turning point. Some in France wanted to turn toward their empire, perhaps in alliance with the United Kingdom. But Monnet believed that the future lay in an economically integrated Europe with American support, with or without Britain.

Coal and steel had been the source of conflict between France and Germany for a century. The two countries had vied for control of the coal of the Ruhr, the iron ore of Lorraine, and the steel mills of the Saar since the modern German state was formed. They could continue to compete over these resources, an outcome the United States opposed vehemently, or they could cooperate. In May 1950, Monnet came up with a plan to put French and German (and other consenting European) coal and steel production under a joint authority, with common regulation and a common market. French Foreign Minister Robert Schuman (himself from Lorraine) obtained the consent of the Germans and the approval of Dean Acheson in advance of a meeting of foreign ministers from the United States, Britain, and France, and despite British resistance, the Schuman Plan was sprung on the world.

The new European Coal and Steel Community (ECSC), which was joined by France, Germany, Italy, Belgium, the Netherlands, and Luxembourg, was the nucleus of broader economic cooperation on the Continent. The United States had long favored this sort of arrangement, as had the smaller countries; Franco-German rivalry and British opposition had been the principal stumbling blocks. Monnet's Schuman Plan dissolved the Gordian knot by pooling the complementary resources of France and Germany under an independent agency.

Jean Monnet was the first president of the ECSC when it opened in 1952. The community integrated the six nations' iron, coal, and steel sectors and quickly created a common market. Monnet's ECSC High Authority got a hundred-million-dollar loan from the United States and soon began to borrow privately. Within a few years the ECSC was the largest foreign borrower on Wall Street.

The unification of Europe's coal and steel production was only a start. In 1955, Monnet moved on from the High Authority. He brought together some of the most influential business and political figures in Europe as a private Action Committee for the United States of Europe, to spur governments toward economic integration. The Action Committee pointed the way to a joint effort in atomic energy, the European Atomic Energy Community (Euratom), and, most important, to the Common Market, or European Economic Community (EEC). Both of these opened for business at the beginning of 1958.

A dozen years after Europe had torn itself apart, the principal belligerents were building a confederation. By the 1960s the six core Western European nations were creating a unified market. In 1971, after years of wavering (and French resistance), the United Kingdom joined the original six, along with Ireland and Denmark. At this point the European Community (EC) was as large an economic unit as the

United States, with a quarter more people. Monnet dissolved his Action Committee in 1975, for its work was over. The United States of Europe was no longer a pipedream but a reality. The next year a unanimous declaration of the heads of state of the nine EC member states made Monnet an honorary citizen of Europe.

European unification embraced the Bretton Woods compromises. On the one hand, it was the most ambitious trade liberalization in history, eliminating tariffs among six (then nine) rich societies. The result was an integrated Continental market that free traders only dreamed about in the nineteenth century. On the other hand, the purpose of the exercise was to improve the ability of European business to compete internationally. And the new Common Market did not shy away from keeping out foreign products in sensitive industries; the common tariff on passenger cars was a steep 17.6 percent. Indeed, in agriculture, the Common Market developed a complicated scheme of subsidies, cash payments, support prices, and barriers to trade, the Common Agricultural Policy. Similarly, a foundation stone of the European communities was that integration should reinforce, not threaten, the region's reformist bent. Competition would not be permitted to undercut national social and labor standards by social dumping, as it was called. High standards would reinforce productivity growth, which would permit funding of the region's generous welfare states. European economic integration fused classical liberalism and social democracy, with great success.

Bretton Woods in trade

During its 1948–1973 heyday the Bretton Woods system involved relatively free trade, stable currency values, and high levels of international investment. None of these components evolved as the founders had foreseen. The role of the United States was more central than expected, and the compromises were more extensive than, and different from, planned.

The liberalization of world trade was the first and probably most important achievement of the Bretton Woods system. This took place without the organization planned to handle it, for the treaty creating the International Trade Organization (ITO) was never ratified by the United States. The institution that took its place, the General Agreement on

Tariffs and Trade (GATT), itself came to be a pillar of the Bretton Woods institutional order.

In April 1947 representatives of twenty-three countries met in Geneva to bargain over their tariffs. After six months of negotiations, these original GATT members signed over a hundred agreements, affecting more than forty-five thousand tariffs that covered about half of world trade. The bargainers cut tariffs by greater than one-third on average and agreed not to discriminate among countries. This was enshrined in the principle of unconditional most-favored-nation treatment, a concept that went back to nineteenth-century British trade relations. The principle required governments to offer the same trade concessions to all. Any reduction in trade barriers between two GATT signatories was automatically offered to all GATT members; countries could not discriminate against the products of one nation in favor of the products of another. The result was a global liberalization of trade.

The GATT, unlike the other two Bretton Woods institutions, was not an independent organization but rather a forum within which countries met. The first few GATT meetings, called rounds, were organized on a country-to-country (bilateral) basis. Assume, for example, that country A was a major exporter of steel to country B, and country B was a major exporter of shoes to country A. Country A would ask country B for a reduction in the tariff on steel exported from A to B, in return for a similar reduction in the tariff on shoes exported from B to A. If the two countries agreed, they would announce the new lower tariffs on steel and shoes and would apply them to all GATT members (under the most-favored-nation principle). This reduced trade taxes on thousands of individual products, then extended the reductions to all GATT members. The procedure allowed a gradual and general reduction in trade barriers.

Two more GATT rounds between 1949 and 1951 reduced trade barriers further. By 1952 tariffs on imports into most European and North American countries were about half their prewar levels. The commitment to trade liberalization was clear, although average tariffs in the United States, the UK, France, and Germany remained between 16 and 19 percent.[11] After a few years GATT negotiations resumed, with three more rounds between 1956 and 1967. The Kennedy Round of tariff reductions that ended in 1967 reduced average tariffs on nonagricultural goods to below 9 percent, probably their lowest since the middle of the nineteenth century. The industrialized countries had removed most barriers to nonagricultural trade among themselves.[12]

World trade exploded after 1950. Exports grew more than twice as rapidly as the economy, 8.6 percent a year.[13] This was an unprecedented increase in world trade. During the glory years of classical liberalism before 1914, world trade volume doubled every twenty to twenty-five years. Over the first twenty-five postwar years, the volume of world trade doubled every ten years.[14]

Country after country experienced remarkable export booms. Measured in the prices of the day (current dollars) in 1950, Western European exports were $19 billion; by 1973 they were $244 billion; German exports alone went from $2 billion to $68 billion. In 2000 dollars, controlling for inflation, Western European exports went from $150 to $960 billion, and German exports from $17 to $255 billion. In the same period, American exports went from $13 billion to $71 billion in current dollars, $56 billion to $230 billion in 2000 dollars. Japanese exports, as the sole developed Asian nation catapulted into world markets, went from just $825 million in 1950 to $37 billion in 1973 in current dollars, from $4.6 to $125 billion in 2000 dollars.[15]

By 1973 international trade was two or three times as important to every OECD economy as it had been in 1950, more important than during the decades before World War One. Western Europe, for example, exported 16 percent of all it produced in 1913. In 1950 this was down to 9 percent, but by 1973 it had shot up to 21 percent. To put it differently, in 1913 Western Europe exported about $800 per person (in 2000 dollars). By 1950 this had fallen to $650 per person, but in 1973 the region exported over $3,300 for every man, woman, and child. For the most trade-oriented societies, figures were even more striking. In 1973, Belgium and the Netherlands exported about half of what they produced, over $7,500 for each of the twenty-three million inhabitants of the two countries (again, in 2000 dollars).[16]

Like the Bretton Woods system in general, trade liberalization depended on compromise. Attempts to liberalize agricultural trade would have been a source of conflict, for all the developed capitalist countries had farm support programs and politically powerful farmers. So GATT negotiations left farm products alone, as it did with trade in services, which would have been just as controversial.

The developing countries would not have gone along with rapid reduction of trade barriers. Latin America's industrialization drives, like those of Europe and North America in the nineteenth century, relied on trade barriers to stimulate national industry. The new free nations of Asia, Africa, and the Caribbean relied on trade protection to build national markets and reserve them for locally produced goods. Developing countries from Argentina to India and from Iran to Zambia rejected free trade in favor of protectionist industrial development. And so the GATT largely exempted developing countries from its rules.

Too stringent an application of the principle of universalism—that trade reductions negotiated with one country had to be granted to all—would have kept countries that wanted to form customs unions from doing so. But even foreigners whose products were discriminated against preferred a regional common market to smaller, divided national markets. So when the issue arose—as in the 1950s, when six Western European countries began working toward a common market—the GATT made an exception for members of customs unions, which were allowed to favor one another's products. All these exceptions removed contentious issues from discussion, allowing more tractable bargains to be struck.

The Bretton Woods monetary order

Bretton Woods was a success in monetary relations too, even though the system only casually resembled the plans of its founders. What had been designed as a multilateral system presided over by the IMF turned into a dollar-based system with little IMF role. Initially, the currencies of Europe and Japan were too weak to return to full convertibility into gold or dollars, so until 1958 the world economy ran on dollars. In the last week of 1958 most European currencies were made convertible, freed for trading on open markets. From then until 1971 the international monetary system was based on a U.S. dollar worth one thirty-fifth of an ounce of gold and on other currencies linked to the U.S. dollar at fixed exchange rates.

The essence of the Bretton Woods system was as Keynes and White had intended, a middle ground between gold standard rigidity and interwar insecurity. Unlike on the gold standard, governments other than the United States could change their currencies' values as needed, although frequent changes were frowned upon. Virtually every developed country devalued against the dollar in 1949. Canada let its dollar float against the U.S. dollar for all of the 1950s and early 1960s; France devalued the franc several times; the pound was devalued in 1967; Germany and the

Netherlands revalued (increased the value of) their currencies a couple of times. But exchange rates were stable enough to encourage international trade and investment, disturbed only when governments found themselves facing serious economic strains.[17]

The Bretton Woods monetary order permitted, even required, governments to restrict the short-term movement of capital across borders. This gets to the very essence of the Bretton Woods monetary compromise. The system let countries run monetary policies in line with their own conditions, even if they differed (within limits) from the policies of others. Governments could meet the demands of their constituents, say, for lower inflation or to stimulate the economy. Of course countries and their peoples differed in what they wanted. France and Italy were particularly worried about unemployment and cared more about this than they did about a little inflation. Germany was growing very fast with little or no unemployment, and its people had terrible memories of hyperinflation, so German governments faced few demands for stimulative policy and a general antipathy to inflation.

Different countries had different monetary policies, especially different interest rates. All through the 1960s Italian and French governments kept interest rates 1 or 2 percent lower than in Germany, which may have helped keep unemployment low but led to inflation 1 or 2 percent higher in France and Italy than in Germany. An investor could earn much more in real terms (after inflation) from a German bond than from an identical Italian or French bond. The real long-term interest rate in Germany in the 1960s was 4.4 percent, compared to 2.2 percent in Italy and 1.8 percent in France (and 1.7 percent in Japan).[18] This is a big difference, one investors would surely notice.

If interest rates differ between two countries with fixed currency values, investors will take their money from the low interest rate to the high interest rate country. In the 1960s they would have pulled money out of France and Italy and put it in Germany, and they would have kept doing so until interest rates in France and Italy went up to German levels. It was this problem that led Keynes and the other architects of Bretton Woods to want controls on short-term international investments. They did not want to restrict the ability of companies to invest in other markets—what they often called productive investment—or of governments to borrow abroad. However, they did want to make it difficult or impossible for investors to speculate on interest rate differences among countries with flows of what was branded "hot money."

For national governments to pursue their own monetary policies, with fixed exchange rates, they had to make it hard to send short-term investments from one country to another. So the Bretton Woods system presupposed capital controls, taxes or prohibitions on moving money across borders for "speculative" purposes. The Europeans had a solid array of such measures, relaxed but not removed after the 1950s. The United States imposed controls on American investments abroad in order to keep American interest rates low. Otherwise, with nominal long-term interest rates at 5 percent in the United States and 6.7 percent in Germany (2.5 and 4.4 percent in real terms), money would have rushed out of the United States and to Germany, almost as quickly as out of France and Italy.

The Bretton Woods monetary compromise kept currency values stable and currency markets open to encourage trade and long-term investment, but it imposed barriers to financial flows to permit governments to follow their chosen policies. The monetary stability of the 1950s and 1960s contributed to the growth of international trade and investment, while national governments were able to pursue macroeconomic policies in line with national conditions.

International investment under Bretton Woods

Long-term international investment, like money and trade, took directions not foreseen by the founders of the system. The International Bank for Reconstruction and Development (World Bank) had been expected to lend heavily to Europe and Japan for the reconstruction of basic infrastructure—roads, ports, railroads—and to do the same for the developing and colonial world. This would help allow private investment flow around the world. The World Bank's reconstruction mission was displaced by the Marshall Plan and the unexpected rapidity of the postwar recovery. After fifteen years of relative inactivity, it did begin to lend to developing countries, a billion dollars a year by the middle 1960s. But the international investment the World Bank helped stimulate turned out not to be the private lending of earlier eras.

For centuries foreign loans were the principal form international investment took. European investors lent billions to the New World, the colonies, Russia, Japan, and other Europeans before World War One; America became the world's chief lender in the interwar years. After

1929 private international lending practically disappeared. The defaults and other conflagrations of the 1930s scared bankers and bond markets off, domestic profit opportunities were more than attractive enough, and Bretton Woods capital controls discouraged foreign loans.

International investment did grow, but in the form of multinational corporations. Such foreign direct investment (FDI), to establish branch plants and affiliates abroad, was not new. In the 1920s and 1930s many American corporations had exploited their competitive position by setting up (or buying) facilities in other countries. But multinational corporate investment had always been a far smaller portion of world investment than international lending. However, by 1950 American multinational corporate investment was twice as large as portfolio investment in foreign loans and stocks; by 1970 it was four times as important. International lending did not recover—not among developed countries, not to developing countries. Before World War Two the typical international investor was a bondholder or banker who lent money to foreign governments and corporations. In the Bretton Woods era the typical international investor was a corporation that built factories in foreign nations.

The kinds of direct investments being made were also relatively new. Before World War Two the typical foreign direct investment was in agriculture or mining in a developing country or colony; in 1938 two-thirds of all international direct investment were in poor regions. American corporations had more than three times as much invested in Latin America than in Europe, mostly in mines, farms, oil wells, and utilities. By the 1960s the typical foreign direct investment was a factory in a developed country. Now American companies had three times as much invested in Europe and Japan than in Latin America, primarily in factories.[19]

By 1973 multinational corporations had invested two hundred billion dollars around the world, three-quarters of it in the advanced industrial countries. Half this FDI came from the United States, and nearly a fifth of all American corporate profits were made on foreign investments. European and Japanese corporations were catching up too.

In every industrial country the largest corporations were heavily multinational—whether because they owned a lot abroad or because they were owned by foreign companies. In 1973 five of the top ten American corporations (all oil companies) made 80 percent or more of their profits abroad; Ford, Chrysler, ITT, and IBM made half. America's multinational corporate affiliates produced nearly three times as much abroad as the country exported—$292 billion in overseas production and $110 billion in exports in 1973. In fact sales by foreign branches of American firms back to their owners in the United States accounted for one-third of all of America's imports. The largest American firms relied heavily on their overseas investments, which were a more important element in its international economic position than its trade. The same was true for most other developed countries; foreign direct investment was the leading edge of international economic integration.[20]

This was also true of the countries in which multinational corporations invested. In Europe multinational corporations—especially American multinationals—were everywhere, with one-quarter or more of manufacturing sales in most countries. Over half of Canadian industry was controlled by foreign firms. Manufacturing in developing countries was even more dominated by multinationals, as foreign companies accounted for one-third to half of industrial output in most of Latin America. Multinational corporations typically clustered in the more technologically advanced or visible industries: chemicals, electrical machinery, pharmaceuticals. In these lines of business, foreign companies could be 80 or 90 percent of the industry, pushing local firms out of the market or buying them up.[21] Even in the United States foreign corporations were becoming a substantial presence; in the early 1970s over a million people in the United States worked for foreign corporations. This was less than 2 percent of the labor force, but the number was growing rapidly and was substantially higher in some industries.[22]

Automobiles and computers, two industries central to the postwar period, were among the most "multinationalized." The automobile sector was the predominant force in every nation's industrial economy: one-sixth to one-quarter of manufacturing employment, 5 to 8 percent of total employment. The indirect effects of the auto industry meant that for every ten workers in automobile manufacturing in the United States, for example, there were another fifteen who owed their jobs to the car sector—four in metalworking, two in machinery, two more in textiles, rubber, and glass, and so on. Vehicles and parts were one-tenth of the major industrial economies' exports and were central to the growth of foreign direct investment.

By the late 1960s American manufacturers had a major share of dozens of other automobile industries. They accounted for over one-quarter of the European car sector. Ford and GM were the second and third "European" car manufacturers (after Fiat), and Chrysler was seventh. The American firms had more than half the British market and 40 percent of Germany's. Ford's British and German affiliates accounted for one-quarter of Ford's global sales and employment; GM's (called Vauxhall and Opel, respectively) for one-eighth.[23]

The computer industry was small, especially relative to auto, but by the early 1960s it was clear that it would be key to a host of new technologies. And although many early innovations were European, by the late 1960s the industry was controlled by American multinationals. American companies made over 80 percent of Europe's computers, and another 10 percent were made on licenses from American firms. IBM alone had 82 percent of the German market, 63 percent of the French. The American firms dwarfed European competitors—IBM employed four times as many people in data processing than the eight largest European companies combined—and bought up or drove out of business all but a few of their European rivals. The global computer industry was dominated by American multinational corporations.[24]

International investment boomed after World War Two for the same reasons trade grew so rapidly: economic growth, monetary stability, reductions in barriers, general government support. This investment took the form of FDI for somewhat more complex reasons. One reason was the rise of mass production and mass consumption in many industries, which gave very large firms important advantages. The centrality of the automobile—and other consumer durables such as the record player, washing machine, and refrigerator—to the economies of North America, Europe, and Japan gave an advantage to firms that had innovated their development, production, and marketing. The same was true of consumer products for which brand name recognition was crucial—toothpaste, soap, records, pharmaceuticals—so that established companies, again, had an advantage. Many of these were American, although by the 1960s European and Japanese multinational companies were also powerful.

A second reason for the proliferation of multinational corporations after World War Two was the persistence of trade barriers. Many American industrial firms had strong export sales to foreign markets. But as firms abroad adopted new products and processes, local competition increased, and sometimes governments raised trade barriers to keep American and other foreign goods out. American companies had to choose between forgoing the protected market and setting up a factory in it and producing locally for local consumption. If the market was important enough, and the American firm's advantage large enough, this made economic sense. So a great deal of foreign direct investment was tariff-jumping, allowing American (and eventually European and Japanese) producers to supply the French, Brazilian, German, Japanese, or Indonesian markets even behind high trade barriers.

These tariff-jumping multinationals were especially prevalent in Europe. The Common Market nations of Germany, France, Italy, Belgium, the Netherlands, and Luxembourg eliminated barriers to trade among themselves and adopted a common tariff against the products of others. The result was the world's second-largest market. The EEC's population was as big as that of the United States, its economy was about two-thirds the size of America's, and trade among its members was the most rapidly growing component of world trade. For some EEC countries, sales to other EEC consumers were especially important as a replacement for their vanishing colonial markets. The French economy, for example, was completely reoriented. In 1952 France's principal market was in its colonies and former colonies. They took 42 percent of French exports, more than two and a half times as much as French sales to the other five countries that would form the Common Market (less than 16 percent). By 1973 its five EC cofounders took half of French exports, while the former colonies were down below 10 percent.[25] A European market was emerging out of a patchwork of national markets.

No major international company could ignore the Common Market, but EEC tariffs were a substantial impediment. By 1968 in the automobile industry, for example, there were no tariffs on cars sold among members of the EEC, but the Common Market's common external tariff of 17.6 percent on passenger cars brought in from outside was a nearly prohibitive tax on imports. Any car company that wanted to sell in Europe had to produce in Europe. The common tariff would have tacked 17.6 percent on to the price of Ford exports from Detroit to France or Italy, but exports from Ford Werke in Germany to France or Italy were tariff-free. The same was true of GM's sales from its German affiliate, Opel, and Chrysler's sales from its French affiliate.[26]

By the 1960s Ford, Fiat, Colgate, Bayer, Coca-Cola, and Philips were household words—and big employers—in most of the world's major economies. To some, multinational corporations were an unwelcome economic, political, and cultural intrusion; to others, they presented opportunities for technological and financial enrichment. Whatever the interests involved, international investment—like international trade and monetary integration—succeeded in tying the industrialized world together more tightly than it had been since 1914.

Bretton Woods and the welfare state

Bretton Woods allowed the sweeping liberalization of international trade and investment to coexist with a sweeping extension of the public sector.[27] From 1950 to 1973 the average industrial country's public sector rose from 27 to 43 percent of GDP. Social transfers, the core of the social security and insurance systems, went from an average of 7 to 15 percent of GDP.[28] By the late 1950s Sweden had universal pensions, health insurance, industrial accident and disability insurance, child and family allowances, poor relief, subsidized low-income housing, and compulsory schooling until age sixteen.[29] While the extent and coverage of the Swedish system were broader than most, the rest of the industrial capitalist world was in line with the Swedish pattern. Everywhere except Japan, the government protected citizens against the vagaries of unemployment, sickness, disability, old age, and poverty.

The rapid growth made possible by postwar integration allowed governments to extend existing programs and create new ones with little controversy. This was reinforced by the fact that wealthier societies tend to be more generous with their social policies, and the rise of so many OECD members into the ranks of the wealthy led to increased social spending.

Postwar social spending may itself have been a political prerequisite of economic integration. Economic openness had long been controversial. Some economic interests—especially big businesses and investors—expected to gain from integration, but others were less enthusiastic. There were intransigent opponents of liberalization, who knew that they could not compete in world markets, but their numbers were typically small. More important were the companies, workers, and farmers that were wary of, but not inalterably opposed to, the uncertainty economic openness would bring. Integration into world markets expanded opportunities but also meant that the country would be buffeted by conditions beyond its control.

Winston Churchill's closest adviser expressed the fear of this middle group when he warned of the potential effects of allowing the pound to become internationally convertible too soon: "If a 6 percent Bank Rate, 1 million unemployed and a two-shilling loaf [of bread] are not enough, there will have to be an 8 percent Bank Rate, 2 million unemployed, and a three-shilling loaf. If the workers, finding their food dearer, are inclined to demand higher wages, this will have to be stopped by increasing unemployment until their bargaining power is destroyed. This is what comfortable phrases like 'letting the exchange rate take the strain' mean."[30] Economic openness was associated in the minds of many with arguments that global economic imperatives required recession, bankruptcies, wage cutting, and layoffs.

A social safety net promised to reduce the uncertainties of global markets; it could cushion the austere downside of economic integration, while allowing capitalists, farmers, and workers in potential exporting sectors, and consumers of cheaper imports, to benefit from international trade. The welfare state thus helped neutralize an important source of potential opposition to liberalization.

It is no coincidence that the small European countries led in implementing the social democratic welfare state. The small size of the "Nordics" (Norway, Sweden, Denmark, and Finland), "Alpines" (Switzerland and Austria), and "Benelux" (Belgium, the Netherlands, and Luxembourg) meant that their economies were heavily oriented toward exports, imports, and cross-border investment. Even at the depth of the Depression of the 1930s these countries maintained generally open trade policies. (Agriculture was an exception, but all nine were largely industrial societies by the 1930s.) A correlate of this interwar openness, however, was a broad network of social policies. By a variety of different routes, these societies arrived at a similar synthesis of economic openness and comprehensive social insurance.

Where protectionism was not a viable option, capitalists, farmers, and workers agreed on government programs to protect the victims of world market forces. One Swedish conservative leader suggested thinking of "society as an organization for equalizing risks and for providing minimum standards of security not just for the badly-off, but also for the industrious."[31] The result was generous social programs, a prominent political role for socialists, extensive labor-capital cooperation to restrain wages and maintain full employment, and aggressive employment and worker-training schemes, along with a firm commitment to market capitalism and to free trade and investment.[32]

Even most of Europe's Christian Democratic parties joined this conversion to moderate anticapitalism. The German Christian Democrats' programs insisted that "the capitalist economic system has not done justice to the vital interests of the German people" and that "the new structure of the German economy must start from the realization that the period of uncurtailed rule by private capitalism is over." France's

Catholic party spoke of a "revolution" to create a new order "liberated from the power of those who possess wealth."[33] And this was from the Continent's principal conservative parties!

The new consensus reflected the domestic social democratic compromises of the 1930s and their international variants at Bretton Woods. It brought socialist, not Communist, labor together with the business and middle classes to support a reformed market economy. This rankled some traditional conservatives, including many in the United States who had trouble considering a British socialist (Labour) government as a bulwark of Western capitalism. But in order to secure the backing of the socialists and their working-class base for the Bretton Woods order, European governments had to accommodate union organization, social welfare policies, and wage increases.

In the United Kingdom the postwar order was mapped out during World War Two. A government commission headed by Sir William Beveridge called, in great detail, for a comprehensive system of social insurance. The result was electric; as one Labour Party leader put it, "in one of the darkest hours of the war, at the end of 1942, the Beveridge Report fell like manna from heaven."[34] The report became a best seller, and successive British governments implemented its recommendations for a national health service, universalistic benefits, and other elements of the modern welfare state. As the war wound down on the Continent, every new government implemented sweeping social reforms. The unified western sectors of Germany also moved in this direction, as German conservatives put what they called a social market system in place. It combined social insurance, a substantial public sector, and workers' councils that gave labor a voice in management decisions.[35] And the United States and Canada had built a broad consensus in favor of social reform and economic integration over the course of the 1930s and 1940s.

The social democratic welfare state was an integral part of the Bretton Woods system. It facilitated political agreement, especially between labor and capital, on the desirability of international economic integration. And while business prospered, the working classes also did very well. One-third to two-thirds of the labor force was in unions, and parties of the Left were in power more often than not. Government policies softened the swings of the business cycle; expansions were more than twice as long, recessions barely half as long, as during the gold standard. Unemployment averaged just 3 percent in the main OECD countries, compared to 5 percent during the gold standard and 8 percent in the interwar years.[36]

Societies became more equal and poverty declined. In the United States, which had one of the less aggressive welfare states but some of the best statistics, the proportion of the population below the official poverty line went from more than one-third in 1950 to barely 10 percent in 1973.[37] And all this went hand in hand with a high level of international trade and investment. The combination of the welfare state and the Bretton Woods order seemed to show that classical liberals, fascists, and Communists alike were all wrong: Modern industrial societies could be committed simultaneously to generous social policies, market capitalism, and global economic integration.

The success of Bretton Woods

The Bretton Woods system governed the international economic relations of the advanced capitalist countries from World War Two until the early 1970s. The industrialized nations turned away from economic nationalism and conflict. But they did not return to the laissez-faire of the years before World War One, with its presumption that the requirements of international success trumped the problems of unemployed workers and struggling farmers.

During the 1950s and 1960s the industrialized West navigated a middle road. The new order combined internationalism with national autonomy, the market with the social, prosperity with social stability and political democracy. It allowed both international economic openness and controls on short-term investment, protection for agriculture, and such preferential trading arrangements as the European Common Market. It mixed probusiness policies with substantial government involvement in the economy, an extensive social safety net, and politically powerful labor movements. The result was a blend of active markets and aggressive governments, big business and organized labor, conservatives and socialists. This order oversaw the most rapid rates of economic growth and most enduring economic stability in modern history.

13

Decolonization and Development

"Long years ago we made a tryst with destiny," Jawaharlal Nehru reminded his countrymen on the eve of India's independence, referring to their decades-long struggle for self-determination. "And now," Nehru told the Constituent Assembly on August 14, 1947, "the time comes when we shall redeem our pledge, not wholly or in full measure, but very substantially." When the new government assumed power from the British, it confronted the bloodshed of partition, economic stagnation, and generalized poverty. Yet Nehru and his colleagues saw this new start as a singular opportunity: "A moment comes, which comes but rarely in history, when we step out from the old to the new, when an age ends, and when the soul of a nation, long suppressed, finds utterance. . . . We have to build the noble mansion of free India where all her children may dwell."

How would the new Indian government, and others like it, redeem its pledge? How could it overcome decades, even centuries of stagnation? There were no ready-made blueprints to copy, no simple principles to follow. As the colonies achieved their freedom and the Latin American countries emerged from the enforced isolation of the Depression and World War Two, they struggled toward a new strategy for national development.

The formula adopted was economic nationalism. While the developed capitalist countries abandoned the inward orientation of the 1930s, the developing world embraced it enthusiastically. The developing countries closed themselves to foreign trade and pursued rapid industrialization. The newly independent colonies followed suit, keeping out foreign goods and often foreign capital to build up independent national economies. Within a decade of the war's end a Third World of non-aligned countries was navigating a nationalist course between the global integration of the capitalist First World and the central planning of the Communist Second World.

Import-substituting industrialization

Latin American countries (and the handful of other independent nations in the developing world) were isolated from the world economy from 1930 until the early 1950s by trends in the world economy itself. The collapse of the international economy left the region to its own devices. Countries organized around producing coffee, cattle, or copper for export now had virtually no market for their principal goods. Consumers accustomed to manufactured products from North America and Europe found these goods prohibitively expensive or simply unavailable. New industries grew to satisfy local demand, and the export farming and mining sectors shrank.

Urban classes and masses expanded to fill the economic, social, and political vacuum left by the disintegration of the traditional open economies. Latin America was transformed from a bastion of open-economy traditionalism to a stronghold of economic nationalism, developmentalism, and populism. An implicit alliance for national industrial development, including urban businessmen, middle-class professionals and government employees, and industrial labor, came to dominate the region. The alliance was explicit in the analysis of much of the Left, which saw it as an anti-imperialist coalition between national labor and national capital. A self-consciously nationalistic business community, often fluent with quasi-Marxist rhetoric about the dangers of foreign capitalism, led the way. Luiz Carlos Bresser-Pereira, a leading Brazilian businessman and intellectual, wrote about how the 1930s "crisis of imperialism, based on the international division of labor, constituted an opportunity for Brazil's development." He characterized the opportunity, as seen and seized by his colleagues in industry after World War Two: "Nationalism, which was the basic ideology, and industrialism and developmental interventionism . . . were above all else in service to the emerging industrial bourgeoisie. What we are calling the Brazilian national revolution had as its central objective the transformation of Brazil into a truly independent nation. Industrialization, to be carried out by the industrial entrepreneurs with the aid of the state, was by far the best method to reach this goal."[1]

By the late 1940s the principal Latin American countries were industrial and urban, with one-fifth of output and employment in manufacturing, a level similar to the United States in 1890. One-quarter of the population lived in cities of more than twenty thousand, more than in continental Europe in 1900. Literacy was over 80 percent in the Southern Cone of Argentina, Chile, and Uruguay. Much of the region was democratic, with powerful labor movements and middle classes. The stereotype of Latin America twenty years earlier had been a mass of peasants overlorded by a quasi-aristocratic landowner; now it was a teeming industrial metropolis ringed by shantytowns. This had come with a closing to the world economy, in part by necessity but also, increasingly, by choice. In 1950 the region exported just 6 percent of its output, the larger countries less: 2 percent in Argentina, 4 percent in Brazil. The Mexican metamorphosis was striking: In 1929 exports were 15 percent of Mexican output, but in 1950 they were just 3.5 percent.[2] Amid depression and war most world trade was declining, but the decline was much greater in Latin America. And unlike those elsewhere, Latin Americans seemed to agree that this was a good thing.

Supporters of autarky in Latin America came to the fore in the 1930s and 1940s and emerged from World War Two even more powerful. The earlier turn inward was driven by external conditions, but the postwar restoration of world trade did not lead Latin Americans to reverse course. Too much had changed. Industrialists who had not confronted imports for over twenty years did not relish new foreign competition. Politically, Latin American sympathizers of autarky were in command (as opposed to Western Europe and Japan, where they had been defeated). Nationalist manufacturers, small businessmen, professionals, labor unions, and intellectuals shared the goal of industrialization, and foreign competition threatened this goal. Champions of open trade, the export farmers and miners, were out of favor or (in the case of mining) had been nationalized.[3]

Latin America repeated a trajectory followed by other nations that shifted from being free trade primary exporters to protectionist industrializers. The colossus to the north was the most prominent example: The United States started as an exporter of raw materials and importer of manufactures, and its cotton- and tobacco-exporting South battled its protectionist manufacturing North for decades. Eventually urban industry prevailed, and American economic policy turned against farmers and miners to support protected industries. The result was rapid industrialization, the consolidation of the national market, and maybe even a spur to nationalist solidarity. The American precedent—and that of Canada, Germany, Japan, and others—was a model for many of America's southern neighbors.

In the 1950s Latin America moved from an emergency response to the collapse of world markets to a conscious effort to restrict foreign trade. This policy, known as import-substituting industrialization (ISI), aimed to substitute domestic industrial production for goods that had previously been imported. The principal method was to make domestic manufacturing more profitable.

The first component of ISI was high barriers to trade. By the early 1960s tariffs on manufactured imports averaged 74 percent for Mexico, 84 percent for Argentina, and 184 percent for Brazil.[4] These barriers made many manufactured imports prohibitively expensive; in some cases, imports were simply forbidden. Not all industrial products were kept out, for the manufacturing industries needed machinery, spare parts, and other inputs. But virtually anything that was made in a Latin American nation was sheltered from foreign competition, its price often two or three times that of similar products on world markets.

Governments also provided subsidies and incentives to industry. They gave industrial investors tax breaks and cheap credit from government banks and gave local industrialists preferential access to imported capital goods, parts, and raw materials. Governments manipulated the currency to provide cheap dollars to manufacturers so they could buy foreign equipment and inputs. Sometimes there were different exchange rates for different products, so that dollars were expensive to buy imports that competed with local producers, but cheap for local producers who wanted to buy machinery abroad.

Latin American governments took over much of the industrial plant. They ran the railroads, shipping lines, telephone networks, electric power systems, and other parts of the infrastructure; in this they were like much of Western Europe. But Latin America's governments also owned many of the region's steel mills, chemical factories, oil wells and refineries, mines and smelters. The public sector accounted for one-quarter to one-half of all investment in the region's economies, mostly in industry and related sectors. Supporters of this public-sector expansion believed that private investment could or would not finance basic industries; steel and chemicals factories were beyond the means of Argentine or Mexican capitalists and were too important to leave to the vagaries of private investment. In addition, public ownership allowed the government to sell such basic inputs as steel, electric power, chemicals, and transport to private industry at artificially low prices that, once more, encouraged industrialization.

These policies spurred impressive industrial development. From 1945 to 1973 Mexico's industrial production quadrupled and Brazil's increased eightfold. The number of motor vehicles on the two countries' roads went from under half a million to six million; by 1973 their automobile industries, nonexistent twenty years earlier, were turning out over a million vehicles a year. The vast majority of the manufactured goods the region consumed were now produced at home rather than imported. For example, by the early 1960s Brazil's industries were supplying 99 percent of the country's consumer goods, 91 percent of its intermediate inputs (such as steel and chemicals), and 87 percent of its capital goods (machinery and equipment).[5] At that point the Brazilian economy, which was roughly the size of the Dutch economy, was close to self-sufficient in manufactured goods.

Industrialization was largely financed at the expense of the primary exporting sectors. Farmers and miners paid much more for the manufactured goods they consumed but sold their own products at world market prices, and their taxes subsidized favored industries. This was no accident; the farmers and miners had lost the battles of the 1930s and 1940s. The industrial cities turned the terms of trade against those who had for long decades monopolized the political, social, and economic order in favor of traditional exports. After all, that is what the industrial North had done in the United States from the Civil War until the 1930s, and it succeeded exceedingly well.

Twenty-five years of purposive import-substituting industrialization, on top of twenty years of import substitution forced on Latin America by world conditions, gave the region a formidable industrial economy by 1973. At that point the continent's principal countries—Brazil, Mexico, Argentina, Colombia, Venezuela, Chile—were roughly as industrial and as urban as Western Europe and North America. Between 61 and 81 percent of their people lived in cities, depending on the country (the figures for the principal OECD countries ranged from 73 to 89 percent). Between 29 and 42 percent of their output came from industry (the range in major rich nations was from 29 to 48 percent).[6] Sophisticated industrial sectors dominated these economies.

Latin America certainly was different from the developed world in 1973. Most obviously, it had only one-third the average income. It also had many more people in agriculture: one-fifth to one-half, a level higher than that of Europe forty years earlier. Poverty was rampant and showed no sign of improving. While industry was large, it was not particularly efficient, with prices above world market levels. This was made possible by high protective barriers, and the Latin American economies were among the most closed markets in the world. They had in fact become more closed over time; even the Soviet Union traded more with the rest of the world in 1973 than in the 1950s, but not Latin America. Despite these unusual features of ISI, there was little questioning in the region of import substitution as a method of development. It had after all achieved its goal. Latin America had industrialized.

The rush to independence

The years from 1914 to 1945 affected the rest of the developing world as they did Latin America. Most of Africa, the Near East, and Asia remained colonial. Even in the colonies, though, isolation from the world economy stimulated urbanization and industrialization, strengthened local business and middle-class interests, and weakened the export economy. It undermined the supporters of colonial rule and reinforced the influence of those wary of or hostile to colonialism.

Nonetheless, at the time of World War Two the European empires were at their height; outside Latin America, only a handful of poor countries were even nominally free. While the French and British promised their more rebellious charges additional rights, and the United States promised the Philippines independence, the results remained to be seen. The developing world outside Latin America circa 1945 was a colonial world and appeared likely to remain so.

Yet colonialism collapsed with remarkable speed; by 1965 it had disappeared, with some trivial exceptions and the anomalous Portuguese fascist empire, which resisted the inevitable for another ten years. A few years after the end of World War Two almost all of colonial Asia was independent. The Japanese had left Korea and Taiwan, the French Indochina, and the Dutch the East Indies; French and British mandates in the Near East (Syria, Lebanon, Israel, Jordan) all were free. Most important, the jewel in the crown of the United Kingdom, a British India that had stretched from Iran to Laos, was now—after a paroxysm of bloody internecine warfare—four free nations: India, Pakistan, Burma, and Sri Lanka. Most of North Africa gained its freedom over the course of the 1950s; starting in 1957, sub-Saharan Africa was quickly liberated (again, with the exception of the Portuguese colonies), as was the remaining Asian possession, Malaysia. By the middle 1960s America's control over Puerto Rico made it arguably the world's principal colonial power (again, excepting the Portuguese), an ironic outcome, given the long-standing anticolonialism of the U.S. government.[7] The fact that twenty years after World War Two the largest colony of a major nation was not India or Algeria, the Congo or Indonesia, but a tiny island in the Caribbean showed how much had changed.

Colonial rule collapsed so rapidly for several reasons. The first was the economic and political evolution of the colonial societies. After 1914 those who wanted to modify or reject the classical colonial economy grew continually in wealth, power, and influence. The same economic and political processes that changed the course of Latin American development were going on in Africa and Asia: the rise of urban and industrial centers; dissatisfaction with primary production for export; the desire for diversification and industrialization.

Colonialism was also undermined by global problems that isolated the colonies from the world economy, impeded the export economy, stimulated urbanization and industrialization, and built up local business and middle-class interests. The interwar years' economic difficulties weakened supporters of colonial rule and strengthened those wary of or hostile to colonialism. Sometimes conflict between the colonial powers and the new social groups erupted into open military rebellion against colonial rule, as in Indonesia and Indochina. Elsewhere, the threat of anticolonial uprisings was a powerful brake on great power ambitions.

So the colonialists attempted to meet local demands. India, which already had the right to decide its own tariffs, was given extensive self-government in 1937. Other possessions were granted similar increases in local power. However, for many colonial leaders this only highlighted the irrelevance of colonial rule. Either imperial control was a veneer or it was real. If the former, then there was no reason to keep it; if the latter, all the more reason to leave. This view was especially strong when settler populations, ranging in size from substantial in Algeria to modest in Rhodesia to tiny in Kenya, delayed or halted reforms. If a few thousand European settlers in Kenya could keep the British Empire from granting elementary rights to Africans, why should an African regard the empire as anything but a tool of oppression?

There were also forces for change in the colonial powers themselves.[8] Before World War Two colonialism had been justified on diplomatic and economic grounds. Now geopolitical justifications were not credible; the strategic positions of Britain, France, the Netherlands, and Belgium consisted of huddling under the American nuclear umbrella, for which colonies were neither necessary nor encouraged by the holder of the umbrella. Economically the importance of the colonies diminished continually after the war. Europeans traded and invested more and more with their neighbors and with the United States. In addition, the colonies were largely irrelevant to the new industries that had gained in importance: automobiles, consumer durables, aircraft, computers. As European foreign investments shifted away from raw materials and plantations and toward manufacturing, economic support for colonial rule eroded further. Manufacturing multinationals had little need for colonialism and often profited handsomely from the high tariffs newly independent nations imposed. Even where colonial trade and investment remained desirable, the United States put constant pressure on the Europeans to open their colonial markets, but what economic good was a colony if one had to share it?

The final, perhaps decisive reason for the rapid march of independence was American insistence. The United States had opposed colonialism for decades. Ideology and morality may have played a role in this position, but self-interest was paramount. The United States came very late to the race for colonies and ended up with few of its own; colonial economic exclusivity hit American goods and capital hard. The Cold War added further motives for American anticolonialism. The Soviet Union had good anticolonial credentials and used the European empires as evidence of how Western capitalism subordinated the developing world. After 1949, Communist China's voice was added to this, with great credibility, for China had been one of the most tortured victims of Western imperialism. With so much of the world under European colonial control, it was hard for the United States to make a case for the evils of Soviet domination. The longer the Europeans ruled, the more they pushed Africans and Asians toward the Communists in the search for allies.

American anticolonialism brought Europe's colonialists up especially short during the Suez crisis. In October–November 1956 troops from Israel, France, and the United Kingdom attacked Egypt, ostensibly to secure the Suez Canal but really to try to topple the regime of radical nationalist Gamel Abdel Nasser. American Secretary of State John Foster Dulles was furious, and not for any love of Nasser. The invasion provided powerful ammunition for Soviet and Chinese attempts to convince the developing world that capitalism was brutal and unfair. Even more galling, it came in the midst of Soviet suppression of an anti-Communist revolt in Hungary and shifted world attention away from a demonstration of Soviet brutality to yet another instance of Western aggression. A month that should, in Dulles's view, have been a propaganda triumph for the West became a disaster. To make matters worse, the Anglo-French-Israeli invasion drove Egypt's regime even closer to the Soviet Union.

The British and French quickly found out how the economic weight of the United States restricted their options. The crisis led to a sell-off of sterling, and the United States abruptly cut the British off from financial support. The British government, which five years earlier had regarded Egypt as an effective protectorate, had no choice but to back down in humiliation.[9] Anticolonial activists were reinvigorated by this demonstration of colonial impotence, even as the resolve of Europe's colonialists weakened. A year later Ghana became the first sub-Saharan colony to gain its independence from Britain, followed in 1958 by French Guinea. As the collapse of colonialism worsened France's impasse over Algeria, the French political system imploded; Charles de Gaulle, summoned to restore the nation, supervised French withdrawal from the land it had long argued was as French as Marseilles. Within four years of Suez, all of French Africa was independent, with British Africa close behind.

ISI in theory and practice

Latin America was a guide to much of the developing world after 1945. After all, before 1945 Latin America was close to the total of independent developing countries. There were a few free states in the Near

East (Turkey, Iran, Iraq), but their sovereignty was recent or questionable; Liberia, Ethiopia, Afghanistan, and Siam were too poor to matter; and China was unique. The principal model for a poor former colony was Latin America, which had been independent for over a century. Latin America's industrial development indicated to others that such a path was open to them. (Several other independent nations, such as Turkey, were in fact pursuing ISI themselves.) Enthusiasm grew for Latin American–style national industrialization, as for the view that independence was a prerequisite to its adoption.

In addition to a practical model, Latin America provided intellectual arguments for ISI. Latin American theorists argued, against the classical liberalism of mainstream economists, that it was good for economic development to protect and subsidize industry. The Latin American view brewed in the cauldron of the Santiago, Chile, office of the United Nations Economic Commission for Latin America. ECLA (in Spanish, CEPAL) was headed by an Argentine economist and former central banker, Raúl Prebisch, and attracted leading scholars. The ECLA view, formed by the early 1950s, had great intellectual resonance elsewhere in the developing world.

ECLA extended existing arguments for the infant industry protection and subsidization of industry. Like nineteenth-century German and American protectionists, it pointed out that industries with substantial scale economies are by definition uncompetitive when they are small and that countries could not simply start from nothing with large industries. A common metaphor was that wings cannot have evolved on birds one feather at a time; countries could not develop modern industry by starting with tiny shops if they were open to foreign competition. The new infant industries had to be nurtured until they reached the scale necessary to be able to compete internationally.

ECLA (and the *Cepalistas*, as they were known) further argued that industrialization had positive effects on society that were not reducible to industrial output. There were, they said, externalities or spillovers, benefits that other members of society realized simply from the expansion of industry. The benefits included social cohesion as cities and factories developed, a more highly skilled labor force, higher levels of political knowledge and involvement, and other such advantages. The spillovers could also be economic, as industries encouraged the formation of backward and forward linkages. A firm making shoes developed links "backward," to the producers of leather, rubber, and other inputs, and "forward," to the wholesalers and retailers of the finished products.

The shoe industry did more than make shoes; its demand for inputs and supply of output broadened and deepened the local economy. Industrialization had general positive social and economic effects.

The most novel argument of the *Cepalistas* was first put forth by Prebisch in the late 1930s. He claimed that the prices of raw materials and agricultural products tended to decline over time, while the prices of manufactured products tended to rise. He argued:

> Manufacturing industries, and therefore industrial nations, can effica- ciously control production, thereby maintaining the value of their prod- ucts at desired levels. This is not the case with agricultural and livestock countries, for as is well known, their production is inelastic on account of the nature [of production], as well as the lack of organization amongst agricultural producers.
>
> In the last depression these differences manifested themselves in a sharp fall in agricultural prices and in a much smaller decline in the prices of manufactured articles. The agrarian countries lost part of their purchas- ing power, with the resultant effect on the balance of payments and on the volume of their imports.[10]

The problem, Prebisch said, was that markets for manufactured goods were controlled by a few oligopolistic firms that made sure that prices rose whenever possible and did not fall even in adverse market condi- tions.[11] On the other hand, markets for primary products were very com- petitive—there were millions of wheat or coffee farmers—and prices moved up and down very easily. In times of crisis, manufactured prices did not decline as rapidly as primary prices, while in good times they rose more quickly. The result was that the terms of trade of countries that specialized in primary products deteriorated: They got less for what they sold and paid more for what they bought. Producing more of the same would only make matters worse by driving primary prices down further. The way to break out of the vicious circle was to change the composition of countries' products, to get out of primary products and into industry.

Other economists contested ECLA's arguments. Opponents of infant industry protection said that infant industries never grew up, just con- tinued to get protection and that the spillovers were much smaller than the costs of creating inefficient industries. They alleged that the ECLA policies would create bloated industries producing expensive, techno- logically backward, low-quality, goods. Skeptics challenged Prebisch's charge that the terms of trade of the developing world deteriorated.

Even if it were true, the solution was not protection and subsidization; after all, primary exports brought prosperity and industry to Canada, Australia, even the United States.

The ECLA view found overwhelming support in the colonial and postcolonial world, whatever its intellectual merits. The new governments' principal supporters were in the urban capitalist, middle, and working classes and had little sympathy for the primary-exporting model. Europeans or their allies often dominated production of agricultural goods and minerals for export; where primary producers were indigenous they were usually politically fragmented and weak. Industrialists, professionals, government employees, and factory workers were well organized, often had close ties to the military, and controlled the cities.[12] The battle over development strategy was over before it began; import-substituting industrialization was the universal postcolonial solvent.

Nehru leads India to industrialization

After Jawaharlal Nehru reminded Indians of their "tryst with destiny" in his August 1947 speech as the country's first prime minister, he looked toward the future. "That future," he said, "is not one of ease or resting but of incessant striving so that we may fulfil the pledges we have so often taken and the one we shall take today. The service of India means the service of the millions who suffer. It means the ending of poverty and ignorance and disease and inequality of opportunity. . . . [A]s long as there are tears and suffering, so long our work will not be over."

Nehru led independent India for fifteen years, attempting to make good on his pledges. When he took office in August 1947, he had more than thirty years of political experience behind him. This included governing many of India's provinces and negotiating with the British over the terms of the empire's disengagement. But his most important formative experiences were as a leader of the world's principal anticolonial movement.

Nehru was the eldest son of a prominent lawyer and member of India's aristocratic Brahmin class. He was born in 1889 and had a series of Western tutors before going to Harrow, an exclusive English boarding school. From Harrow Nehru went to Cambridge, where he received a degree in the natural sciences. He then went back to London to qualify for the bar and become a lawyer like his father. In 1912, after this thoroughly English education, Nehru returned to India, "perhaps," as he later put it, "more an Englishman than an Indian . . . as much prejudiced in favor of England and the English as it was possible for an Indian to be."[13] Nehru's father was already a moderate leader of the Indian National Congress Party, and despite his Anglophilia, the son was also a nationalist. The younger Nehru first met Gandhi in 1916 at a Congress Party convention, and by the early 1920s he and his father had moved to a more radical proindependence position.

The Nehrus and other members of India's upper and middle classes turned to support full independence for several reasons. World War One and the interwar years impressed on Indians that colonial rule was unnecessary. The country did fine when separated from the empire by war, reconstruction, and depression. Increasing British grants of autonomy proved that Indians were perfectly capable of ruling themselves and that locally designed policies were more likely to suit local needs. The empire offered its infrastructure and defense, but at an increasingly burdensome price—especially in the light of the brutality of some British actions, most prominently the massacre of hundreds of peaceful demonstrators at Amritsar in 1919.

India's large and growing modern ruling elite was hamstrung by its British overlords. Nehru and the Congress movement saw little reason to continue the relationship. Nehru's was no jingoistic reaction, nor was it a Gandhi-like harkening to Indian traditionalism. Nehru's vision for his native land was refracted through essentially European lenses; as he put it, "I came to her via the West, and looked at her as a friendly Westerner might have done. I was eager and anxious to change her outlook and appearance and give her the garb of modernity."[14] The former Cambridge science major and London barrister wanted to bring modern science and technology to the country, not return it to its traditions.

The British resisted independence. In 1921 the colonial authorities jailed the younger Nehru for the first of many spells (he spent over one-third of the time between 1921 and 1945 in prison). Upon his release he became the general secretary of the Congress Party, developing his political skills and knowledge of the country. In 1926 and 1927 Nehru and his wife and daughter went to Europe and the USSR. There Nehru was exposed to the international anticolonial movement and to Soviet socialism. The prospects both for anticolonial unity and for noncapitalist development impressed him deeply. Upon his return, Nehru served again as the Congress's general secretary and then, in 1929, became president of the party. It was soon clear that Nehru (whose father died in 1931) was second only to Gandhi in the nationalist leadership.

In the ten years' run-up to independence, Nehru (called Pandit, or "teacher") blended socialism and nationalism with a focus on achieving the possible. British attempts to conciliate led to provincial autonomy and to the election of Congress governments in most provinces in the late 1930s. As war threatened in Europe, the Indians had to take a position. Nehru, who spent time in Europe again in 1936, as his wife was dying in a Swiss sanitorium, was very sympathetic to the anti-Nazi cause. But he and the Congress insisted that Indian support for the war effort be contingent on a commitment to independence that the British would not provide. Nehru spent most of the war in prison, but even before his release he began negotiating with the British. He worked closely with Lord Mountbatten to ensure as smooth a transition to independence as the inherent difficulty of the process allowed, especially given the mounting hostilities between Hindus and Muslims that eventually led to the partition of the nation into two countries, India and Pakistan.

In power, Pandit Nehru continued to emphasize economic nationalism and industrial development. Unlike Latin America, India emulated aspects of Soviet planning, using a series of five-year plans to guide the country's industrialization. The government emphasized investment in the infrastructure and basic industry, to further the development of a modern manufacturing sector. Nehru was direct about priorities: "If we are going to industrialize this country we are not going to industrialize it by having a multitude of industries supplying consumer goods. These are useful, no doubt, but if we industrialize we have to have certain basic, key[,] and mother industries in the country: the machine-making industry, the steel industry, and so on, out of which other industries grow."[15] During the country's three five-year Nehru plans, which took India from 1951 to 1966, government made half of all industrial investment, and half of that went to the iron and steel industry.[16] In the 1950s and 1960s, while production in the textile sector rose by one-third, in the machinery industry it increased more than fifteenfold, and it more than quadrupled in basic metals.[17]

Nehru espoused a socialist vision, as did most Indian political leaders, but he was a pragmatist. The government was firm in its commitment to private businessmen, whom Nehru often defended: "It has been often said that capital is shy . . . but it is shy because the capitalists who are private entrepreneurs are not quite sure how long they will exist in the country. I therefore suggest that we should give them a fair chance and ask them to make a fair profit. . . . It is essential for us to give an opportunity to the private entrepreneurs and give them a surety to go on working for the sake of production."[18]

India's economic policies were similar to conventional Latin American–style import-substituting industrialization. The government implemented trade protection, subsidized credits, tax incentives, and other measures in ways familiar to Latin Americans. The five-year plans had rhetorical flourishes unlike those of the more conservative Latins, but in practice the Indian government exercised little Soviet-style planning. India's government did pay more attention to rural conditions than did the Latin Americans. Of course the country was much more rural than Latin America, and India's lively parliamentary democracy meant that politicians could not ignore farmers. While extensive land reform and agricultural improvements did not redress the overall bias in favor of the cities and industry, the farm sector was less punished in India than in many other developing nations.

India's policies achieved results similar to those of other ISI economies. Indian agricultural production in the first twenty-five years of independence barely kept pace with population growth, but manufacturing grew three times as fast. By the early 1970s India was producing over five million tons of steel (up from under a million at independence), sixteen million tons of cement (up from under three million tons), and a million tons of fertilizer (up from less than ten thousand tons). The country made its own railroad cars and automobiles and had a thriving machinery industry.[19] Nearly 90 percent of the textile machinery the country used was manufactured domestically, along with 98 percent of its aluminum and 99 percent of its iron and steel (all these had been primarily imported at independence). Industry was only 16 percent of the economy's output, but the sheer size of the subcontinent meant that India had one of the developing world's largest manufacturing sectors.[20]

Industrialization was accompanied by the fastest economic growth in Indian history. The most careful estimates available indicate that in 1950 Indian output per person was less than 10 percent higher than it had been a century earlier. This masked ups and downs—up until World War One, down thereafter—but overall the late colonial Indian economy was stagnant. Between 1950 and 1975, however, it grew by nearly 50 percent, even taking rapid population growth into account. Although this rate of growth was slower than that realized in many other developing countries, it was respectable by Indian standards.

Indian economic achievements fulfilled only one part of Nehru's ambitions for the country. He believed that India could help change the very nature of the international economy. There was after all no voice for the recently independent nations of Africa and Asia. To remedy this shortcoming, in 1949 Nehru called an Asian-African conference in New Delhi, and in 1954 he joined the leaders of Pakistan, Sri Lanka, Burma, and Indonesia in Colombo, Sri Lanka, to plan for a broader meeting. In April 1955 twenty-nine African and Asian nations convened in Bandung, Indonesia. The meeting was attended by a veritable who's who of the world's anticolonial eminences: U Nu (Burma), Norodom Sihanouk (Cambodia), Zhou Enlai (China), Gamel Abdel Nasser (Egypt), Nehru (India), Sukarno (Indonesia), Muhammad Ali Bogra (Pakistan), Carlos Romulo (the Philippines), Prince Faisal (Saudi Arabia), and Pham Van Dong (North Vietnam).

The Bandung Conference signaled the arrival of a new presence on the world stage. Nehru called it "part of a great movement of human history," marking "the political emergence in world affairs of over half the world's population."[21] Dozens of developing countries demonstrated their intention to steer a middle course between the United States and the USSR. The final Bandung Declaration included five principles proposed by Nehru to avoid conflict and oppose imperial intervention. Nehru's success in guiding Indian society toward independence and neutrality was replicated at the international level. The Third World was a political force, and Nehru was one of its leaders.

When Pandit Nehru died in 1964, his vision was secure. India was industrial, its strong public sector working alongside a powerful private business community. The nation's democracy was stable. Despite a disastrous war with China in 1962 and border conflicts with Pakistan, India was a major player in world politics, both on its own and at the head of the Third World's nonaligned movement. Africa and Asia no longer relied upon Europe for their administration, investment, and industry. The two continents were independent, growing rapidly, and increasingly self-confident. Nehru's successes were widely enough recognized in his homeland that within two years of his death, his daughter, Indira Gandhi, was prime minister.

The Third World embraces ISI

As in India, the nationalist reorientation of postcolonial economies led to rapid industrialization. New governments following ISI shifted resources and people from farming and mining to manufacturing, from the countryside to the cities. African and Asian industries developed impressively, albeit not as broadly and deeply as in Latin America. Nations with prior histories of manufacturing, such as Turkey and India, now had major industrial plants. Countries with rudimentary industrial facilities, such as Iraq and Korea, now boasted extensive manufacturing sectors. Areas that had never had any modern industry, such as Kenya and Thailand, now had rapidly growing industries. By 1973 the Industrial Revolution seemed to have taken hold in Africa and Asia, as it had several decades earlier in Latin America.

Economic growth was rapid in the postcolonial Third World. Most of Asia and Africa grew at 2 or 3 percent a year per person, after decades, perhaps centuries, during which growth had rarely, if ever, been above 1 percent a year. In some countries, such as Egypt, the Ivory Coast, Nigeria, Indonesia, and Thailand, output per person doubled or nearly so in twenty-five years. And this does not include South Korea and Taiwan, which achieved probably the fastest economic growth in history, GDP per person tripling or quadrupling in twenty years.[22]

The economic structure of the new nations was transformed. In a generation, agrarian societies shifted toward industry and the cities. By 1970 industry was accounting for one-quarter or more of the production of Sri Lanka, Indonesia, Thailand, Malaysia, and the Philippines—all preindustrial societies before 1950.[23] Middle Eastern countries that started with tiny manufacturing sectors experienced a major acceleration of industrial growth, and by the early 1970s many of the nonoil economies of the region were producing more in industry than in agriculture. In Turkey and Egypt, employment and output in manufacturing grew very rapidly, and despite their strong farm economies, industrial output passed agriculture sometime in the 1970s.[24] Sub-Saharan African countries with virtually no manufacturing underwent serious import-substituting industrialization. The share of Nigerian GDP that came from manufacturing went from under 3 percent at independence to 10 percent in the 1970s, as industry grew nearly 11 percent a year.[25]

ISI in these countries was similar to that in Latin America, only more so. Countries with little manufacturing needed even greater protection and subsidies to incubate new industries. Nations whose capitalists were weak needed even more strenuous involvement by the government. Some of the more extreme applications of ISI were in some of the least developed countries in Asia and Africa. Critics considered these to be parodies of an already bad idea, but in Nigeria and India, Kenya and Malaysia, the political influence of those with powerful financial, ideological, or political interests in industrialization produced an extreme focus on manufacturing.

Trade protection in these countries was extremely high, even though their industries were embryonic. Protective barriers in Egypt and India roughly doubled industrial prices. Trade declined precipitously; exports went below 2 percent of Indian output. The foreign trade of Turkey, despite centuries of commercial ties to Europe and a favorable location, dropped from 25 to 30 percent of the economy in the 1920s to below 9 percent in the 1970s.[26]

Government was much bigger in these least developed countries than in Latin America. In fact, ISI was commonly promoted as part of a local form of socialism. Supporters of Indian socialism, Arab socialism, Burmese socialism, and African socialism all presented them as a combination of central planning and social democracy, bundled together with rapid industrialization and nation building. Governments employed vast portions of the population, or owned much of the economy, or both. Nasser's Arab socialist government nationalized all of Egypt's banks and insurance companies and much of its manufacturing. The Egyptian public sector owned 90 percent of factories with more than ten workers and accounted for one-third of the labor force and nearly half of output. The government of Ghana employed fully three-quarters of all those in the formal (modern) sector of the economy; although those with such formal-sector jobs were only one-tenth of the total, this meant that the urban employed were overwhelmingly government employees.[27]

This extreme turn to ISI in countries with little industry to start with had several roots. Ideologically, industrialization was closely associated with sovereignty, just as the export economy was connected to colonial rule. Powerful urban interests stood behind this ideological justification, and the rural opposition had been decimated by the departure of the colonialists or was inherently weak and disorganized. The contest between the army, government employees, local capitalists and professionals, and labor unions, on the one hand, and the rural poor, on the other, was no contest indeed. There were few political obstacles to turning everything to industrialization.

Many of the Asian and African excesses were due to the relatively lower level of development of these societies, which made it easier for a tiny elite to distort policy in its favor. Latin American societies were more developed, their economies more mature, their political systems more responsive. After all, while Europe was twice as rich as Latin America in 1950, Latin America was in turn more than three times as rich as Africa and Asia. The gap between Latin America and the rest of the developing world was much larger than the gap between Latin America and the rich countries. The large countries of Latin America were following industrial policies like those of late-nineteenth-century America or Germany, at a level of development roughly equivalent to that of late-nineteenth-century America or Germany. Such policies were unlikely to be suited to countries as poor as Bangladesh or Tanzania, whose level of development was below that of eighteenth-century Europe.

Most of Asia and Africa followed Latin American–style ISI, even to extremes, but a handful of countries in East Asia tried something different. South Korea, Taiwan, Singapore, and the British colony of Hong Kong pushed their manufacturers to export to developed country markets. Hong Kong was close to a free trade city, but the other three had tried ISI in the 1950s and early 1960s. However, in the middle 1960s they turned toward what has been called export-oriented industrialization (EOI), encouraging industrialists to produce for export. These governments too intervened heavily in the economy—— but in this instance to encourage exports. They gave subsidies and incentives to export industries, such as cheap credit to firms that exported and tax write-offs for export profits. The public sector often owned as much of the economy as in Latin America, including all of South Korea's banks and much of its basic industry. While the rest of the Third World turned industry inward, the export-oriented countries pushed it outward. This meant relying on often volatile international markets, but it had the advantage of forcing national manufacturers to produce goods that met rigorous technological, quality, and price standards.

The East Asians turned to EOI in part because they had few natural resources to export to pay for necessary imports, and the only way to earn foreign currency was to export manufactures. The South Korean and Taiwanese governments also had geopolitics on their side; their importance to the United States gave them guaranteed access to American markets. Whatever the source of the policy, it was remarkably successful. South Korean and Taiwanese exports grew at 20 and 16 percent a year between 1950 and 1973, their output per person at 6 and 5 percent a year respectively. In 1950 the two East Asian countries were poorer than the Philippines, Morocco, or Ghana; by 1973 they were two or three times richer. EOI seemed, if anything, more successful than ISI, although it was still only a curiosity confined to the East Asian fringe.

The modern spread of industry

Between 1939 and 1973 developing countries opted for inward-oriented nationalist import-substituting industrialization. Latin America and the few other independent nations started down this path in the 1930s. They were followed by three waves of liberated colonies: Asia in the 1940s, the Middle East and North Africa in the 1940s and 1950s, sub-Saharan Africa in the late 1950s and 1960s. All of them kept out foreign industrial products, boosted local production for local consumption, and promoted cities and industries at the expense of the countryside and farmers. Even the handful of export-oriented countries in East Asia achieved industrial development, relying on exports rather than import substitution.

Almost all these developing nations did well. Despite the undeniable excesses of ISI in many Asian and African countries and even in Latin America, the 1960s were relatively good times. Economies grew; - industrialization sped ahead; living standards improved. Import substitution appeared a successful economic concomitant to national political independence.

14

Socialism in Many Countries

Nikita Khrushchev's visits to the United States in 1959 and 1960 made headlines around the world. When the Soviet leader angrily banged his shoe on the desk in front of him while speaking at the United Nations in 1960, Westerners ridiculed the unsophisticated peasant now leading the world's largest country. But when he boasted that the economy of the Union of Soviet Socialist Republics would be larger than that of the United States by 1980, nobody laughed. The Soviets had beaten the Americans into space with *Sputnik* in 1957, and a year later they launched the first manned space vehicle. Crude or not, Soviet socialism seemed a serious rival to capitalism.

In 1939 socialism existed only in one country, the Soviet Union.[1] Granted, the USSR was the world's largest nation, a major industrial power and a force in world politics, but it was still a semi-industrial country with few economic ties to the rest of the world. It had turned away from the world economy and the market less than ten years earlier, and Soviet central planning was an anomaly restricted to one country with 8 percent of the world's population. No other government was remotely interested in socialist central planning, and even in the Soviet Union its future was unclear.

By the time Khrushchev visited the United States, Soviet-style socialism was firmly in place in more than a dozen countries with over a third of the world's people. A considerable minority of developing country governments espoused centrally planned socialism as an ultimate goal. The world's most populous country, China, was socialist; the second most populous country, India, was politically allied with the Soviet Union. Communist movements were powerful all over the developing world and in some Western European countries. A Communist optimist had grounds to believe that it was only a matter of time before most of the developing world and even large parts of the developed world would adopt some version of Soviet socialism.

Meanwhile the socialist countries were revising, reforming, and modernizing the Soviet model. Even the Soviet government saw flaws in the system as created in the 1930s and planned to perfect it. The future of Soviet-style socialism, and by inference of Western capitalism, depended on these efforts to improve central planning.

The socialist world expands

Within five years of the end of World War Two, socialism stretched from the center of Europe to the Pacific. The Cold War led to a rapid imposition of the Soviet model in Central and Eastern Europe. Between 1949 and 1953 the socialist nations of Central and Eastern Europe— East Germany, Czechoslovakia, Poland, Hungary, Albania, Romania, Bulgaria—copied the USSR's centrally planned economy (Yugoslavia was the only exception). By 1952 the state sector was controlling between 97 and 100 percent of manufacturing everywhere but East Germany, and even there the figure was 77 percent. Agriculture was socialized more gradually, but by 1953 state and collective farms had over half the farmland in Bulgaria and Czechoslovakia and nearly that in Hungary.

There were variations, even with Yugoslavia's independent search for worker-managed socialism left aside. Some countries allowed substantial scope for private business, especially in farming and such small-scale services as restaurants, repair shops, and retail trade. Given the special status of East Germany, a fairly large private sector was still in place there in 1953. Planning varied from country to country, for these nations were at very different levels of development; output per person in industrial East Germany and Czechoslovakia was three times what it was in Romania, Bulgaria, and Albania. But by 1953 all these countries had rejected markets in favor of central planning.[2] These commonalities were formalized with the 1949 creation of the Council for Mutual Economic Assistance (CMEA, or Comecon), meant to be a socialist counterpart to the Bretton Woods order. But economic ties among the new governments were limited inasmuch as they were pursuing an autarky in which trade, even among socialist nations, had little place.

Three new socialist governments were in power in Asia, in China, North Korea, and North Vietnam. The Chinese Revolution alone more than tripled the population living under communism. These three nations were much less developed than the other socialist countries, and much more rural. The Asian path to socialism they took was more agrarian and began more modestly. They carried out extensive land reforms, expropriating most of the land held by wealthy landlords and distributing it to poor and landless peasants. The Asian Communist regimes also embarked on ambitious state-led industrialization programs, with Soviet advice and money, along centrally planned lines.

Communist governments in Europe and Asia were constructing replicas, with varying degrees of slavishness, of Stalin's Soviet Union. They adopted basic features of Soviet-style central planning: government ownership of industry, infrastructure, trade, and much of agriculture; an emphasis on industry over agriculture; tight controls on markets; high or prohibitive barriers to foreign trade and investment. The amount of private farming, degree of centralization, and extent to which prices were permitted to move freely varied. Nonetheless, the general outlines of the centrally planned economies were similar from Prague and Sofia through Kiev and Moscow, to Beijing and Hanoi.

The socialist world divides

After Stalin died in March 1953, the socialist world's orderly forward march broke apart, and national paths separated. Most of Central and Eastern Europe and the Soviet Union softened the Stalinist model, providing more benefits to consumers, less favor to heavy industry, and more marketlike incentives to managers and workers. China moved in the opposite direction, radicalizing its version of central planning and collective agriculture. These different trends in economic policy were matched by a growing schism between the two Communist giants.

Stalin's death revealed political, social, and economic strains in the socialist camp. Conflict erupted within the Soviet Communist Party, out of which Khrushchev emerged in control. He caught the world's attention with an electrifying 1956 speech to the party charging Stalin with a perversion of the ideals of socialism. The leadership agreed on economic reforms, although it was not clear what those reforms might be. The upheavals in the USSR were mirrored in Central and Eastern Europe, where Stalinist leaders were typically replaced by reform-minded "national Communists" who wanted to modify socialism. Economic and social (and sometimes political) reforms swept the USSR and Central and Eastern Europe.

The most immediate source of tension was popular dissatisfaction. Riots broke out among workers in Berlin in June 1953. Discontent spread throughout Eastern Europe and could not simply be ascribed to antiproletarian counterrevolutionaries, for workers were among the most aggressive in their grievances. The 1953 Berlin riots paled by comparison with the upheavals in Hungary and Poland in 1956. In both cases, while there were certainly anti-Soviet and antisocialist components to the uprisings, substantial portions of the working class and of the local Communist parties actively or passively supported change. The USSR and its local allies quickly suppressed the revolts, but the regimes that came to power after the 1956 events were led by moderate Communist reformers with reasonable national credentials, a history of opposition to the hard line, and a modest claim on popular support (Gomulka in Poland, Kádar in Hungary).

The poor quality of life of the average citizen was the principal source of popular discontent. The Soviet government privileged heavy industries over light (consumer goods) industries and industry over agriculture, arguing that sacrifices to speed basic industrialization now would permit a stronger overall industrial base later. Whatever merit this position had in 1930s Soviet conditions, it was incongruous in the 1950s, especially in Central European countries that already had significant manufacturing sectors. The bias toward basic industry meant that there were serious shortages of consumer goods, including housing, and the neglect of agriculture meant that the supply and quality of food were poor. Soviet consumers in 1938 may have been willing to endure spartan conditions to prepare for the Great Patriotic War against Nazi invaders, but Hungarians, Poles, and even Soviets in the 1950s were not so motivated. The problem was exacerbated by widespread knowledge of Western prosperity. The Central European countries were near or next to flourishing capitalist societies, and television and radio reinforced the impression that the East was falling behind. Even Soviet citizens were coming to understand how large was the gap in living standards.

"If we were to promise people nothing better than only revolution," Khrushchev is said to have explained, "they would scratch their heads and say: 'Is it not better to have good goulash?' " What came as a result to be known as goulash communism was adopted by the Soviets and their Central and Eastern European allies. Governments shifted resources into consumer goods industries, housing construction, and other services and raised wages.[3] They deemphasized heavy industry and increased the supply of shoes, clothing, phonographs, and other consumer goods. They promised to build millions of new apartments, and the Soviet authorities vowed in 1957 that within a decade no Soviet family would have to share an apartment with another family.[4] The new emphasis on improving the quality of life of the populace had dramatic and quick results: From 1953 to 1957 real wages in Eastern Europe rose by between 30 and 60 percent.[5] Discontent tailed off.

Government neglect of farming had led the supply of food to stagnate. Farm prices were set so low that farmers had little incentive to produce, and the government had spent almost nothing on agricultural improvements. Soviet farms in 1953 produced less grain and potatoes than in 1940, and had fewer cattle, pigs, and sheep. With growing populations, this could not but be reflected on city dwellers' tables. Government policies that made farming unprofitable had also left the rural areas themselves impoverished. Practically the only way farmers could make decent livings was to sell what they grew on their tiny personal plots.[6]

Khrushchev was from the country's Ukrainian breadbasket and fancied himself an agricultural expert. From the start of his rule he poured money into agriculture. This doubled the number of tractors and combines on the farms in ten years and increased the use of fertilizers and irrigation. He also spent vast sums to open up tens of millions of hectares of unused land to grain farming, mostly in southern Siberia and Kazakhstan.

The Soviets reorganized agriculture as well. The government raised agricultural prices, and collective farm earnings went up by more than one-third in a few years. It merged collective farms to make them more efficient; by 1960 the average collective farm had four hundred households on three thousand hectares of sown land, with thirteen hundred head of cattle and nine hundred pigs in common. More machinery, larger farms, and higher farm prices all substantially improved rural living standards and the supply of agricultural products; between 1953 and 1965, after years of stagnation, food production rose by nearly three-quarters.[7] Eastern European governments also improved farm conditions. After 1956 Poland and Hungary disbanded many collective farms. By 1960 some 90 percent of Polish farming was private, and there was no pressure from the government to change this. Hungary rebuilt collectives on terms more attractive to farmers. Elsewhere, although farmers were cajoled or compelled to join collective or state farms, farm prices were relatively favorable, and privately tended household plots were permitted and even encouraged. In Eastern Europe, rural conditions and farm output improved, as meat consumption doubled or nearly so in the decade to 1965.[8]

These changes in Eastern Europe and the Soviet Union largely accomplished their purposes. Economic growth remained strong and improved conditions in the cities and countryside. People were able to buy consumer goods beyond bare necessities—cameras, washing machines, phonographs, even cars—to live in decent housing, and to take advantage of a wide array of social and educational services. By the late 1960s Eastern European and Soviet levels of ownership of telephones, radios, and television sets were approaching those of Western Europe. While the Communist Party and the central planners remained in control, economic and political constraints were not so heavy-handed as they had been before 1953.

The conditions of the 1960s reflected informal political and economic compromises. Socialist governments were supported by the party members and industrial managers who ran these societies. Higher wages and favored access to services privileged the urban working class. Farmers, professionals, and others were allowed to make decent livings so long as they accepted the leading role of the Communist Party and, in Eastern Europe, the alliance with the USSR. The primacy of the one-party state was the price of improved living standards and reduced interference in private life.

The changes of the 1950s improved living standards, but governments in the Soviet Union and Eastern Europe knew there were still problems with their economies. The Soviets seemed to realize that the forced march methods of the 1930s, successful as they may have been in those circumstances, were poorly suited to the problems of the more advanced industrial economy that had emerged by the 1950s. Even Stalin, shortly before his death, recognized that mechanisms to industrialize rapidly were not necessarily the same as those needed to manage the growth and development of a mature economy. Rapid industrialization had relied on extreme centralization, coupled with disciplinary threats to managers. Such quasi-military arrangements might work for quasimilitary means, but they had real shortcomings in more normal times.

The two most pressing structural economic problems were overcentralization and a lack of incentives. Ministries were centrally organized by industry, with iron and steel, for example, completely separate from chemicals; ministry planners safeguarded their own empires and were loath to cooperate with other ministries. So instead of a steel factory's getting supplies, say, from a neighboring factory that had a stock of them, it would have to requisition the supplies from the central ministry officials in Moscow. Factory managers commonly employed "finders," who roamed the countryside looking for things their factory needed but could not get centrally, to exchange for goods the factory had in excess. Khrushchev attempted to deal with this by establishing more than a hundred local planning authorities and devolving authority down to the local level. The Brezhnev-Kosygin regime that replaced Khrushchev in 1964 rolled back decentralization but continued to give local managers more authority over their enterprises.

Another problem was that of incentives. The Soviets had never relied entirely on exhortation and ideological ardor to motivate workers and managers, but they had not used economic rewards very extensively. They feared that rewarding results would lead to substantial inequalities among people and regions, which the regime regarded as undesirable. It was also not clear how to measure success in a centrally planned system. Prices were set centrally, so the profitability of a firm depended mostly on pricing decisions that were not controlled by the firm's manager or workers. If planners, realizing that monetary outcomes were meaningless, tied rewards to quantitative measures, factories would turn out large quantities of goods with little regard to quality. It was not the manager's fault if central planners set prices so that the enterprise spent more than it earned or if planners told him to make products consumers did not want; nor was success on these fronts the result of managerial excellence.

Most Soviet analysts believed that while crude forms of central planning may have been appropriate for economic growth of the 1930s and 1940s, they were no longer. In the earlier period the principal goal was "extensive" growth that brought underutilized resources into the economy. The government moved workers off the land and into industry, pulled unused land into production, and poured money into basic industry. Because the economy was rudimentary, the planners could easily measure and assess the goods produced—grain, steel, petroleum. With basic industrialization complete, the Soviet economy had to undertake "intensive" economic growth, making more effective use of the productive capacity already in place. But without stronger incentives, managers and workers were unlikely to take risks to increase productivity. Why should managers take time and energy to develop innovative productive techniques when they would not be rewarded for such achievements?

Even in the 1930s the Soviets attempted to get prices closer to realistic levels and to use rough measures of profitability to figure out which enterprises were performing well. In the 1960s reformers started using marketlike forms to reward enterprises, managers, and workers. Some of the first salvos were fired in 1956 by a Soviet economist, Evsei Liberman, who argued for the use of profits and prices to reward firms' managers and workers. In 1962 the Communist Party newspaper *Pravda* allowed Liberman to set forth his promarket ideas, and the ensuing public debate indicated that the Soviet authorities were considering major reforms. The new Brezhnev-Kosygin leadership applied moderate incentive-based measures in 1965. Decisions previously made at the center were passed down to the enterprise. Firms were allowed to keep some of their profits and distribute them to managers and workers, in bonuses or in kind (housing, vacations, social services).

The Soviets also began to rethink their international economic ties, accepting that the USSR "has been wasting time and effort reinventing processes and commodities that had previously been developed in other advanced countries."[9] They increased foreign trade dramatically, both with other socialist countries and with the capitalist world; by 1973 trade was three times as important to the Soviet economy as it had been in 1950. Foreign investment was much more welcome than before, and in August 1966 the government signed a $1.5 billion contract with Fiat to build a state-of-the-art automobile factory in a new city to be called Togliattigrad, after a postwar Italian Communist leader.[10]

Eastern European countries experimented with more radical variants of market-oriented forms. The Czech regime went farthest between 1966 and 1968, only to find the Czech road to socialism (or away from Soviet-style socialism) blocked by a Soviet invasion. However, Hungary's regime implemented radical reforms at much the same time and apparently satisfied the Soviets that this implied no threat to bloc security. By the early 1970s most Hungarian prices were being determined by supply and demand, and profits were being retained by firms and their employees. Other Central and Eastern European countries also decentralized planning and increased the role of prices and profits.[11]

Political obstacles often impeded the Soviet and Eastern European reforms. Entrenched interests fought changes that threatened them. Enterprise managers who suffered from the increased competition the reforms brought attempted to get them reversed or revised. Industrial managers were important supporters of the Communist regimes, so their concerns constrained what governments could do. In the USSR, where managers had built powerful social and political positions over decades, many of the Brezhnev-Kosygin reforms were stymied almost as soon as they were announced. Nonetheless, economic management in Eastern Europe and the Soviet Union in 1973 was very substantially different from the pre-1953 Soviet model. And the economies of the region did very well up to 1973. Economic competition between the industrial capitalist West and the industrial socialist East was very much alive.

The Chinese road

Most of the people living under socialism, however, were driven in a very different direction as the People's Republic of China moved toward extreme methods of Communist-style modernization. While the rest of the socialist camp reformed, moderated, and revised Stalinist principles, the Chinese (and their Albanian allies) expanded them in search of rapid industrialization and agrarian transformation. They created enormous farm communes to accelerate progress from capitalism to communism, politicized all aspects of economic policy, and curtailed ties with the rest of the world. From the middle 1950s until the middle 1970s, China went down the path of ever-greater urban and rural radicalism.

The Chinese Communists who took power in 1949 faced conflicting demands, which were reflected in factional conflicts within the party. One difficult dimension was the country's long-standing urban-rural divide. The Communists had support in the countryside and understood the need to keep their peasant base in a country that was almost entirely rural. The Communist Party also had support from the urban working class and shared with the rest of the Third World the desire to industrialize rapidly. But proindustrial policies typically implied antiagricultural measures, so that urban and rural interests were likely to clash.

On another dimension, the world's most populous country had long been beset by disorder bordering on anarchy, and a prime goal was simply to hold the nation together. But the Communists also wanted thoroughgoing economic and social change, and such change risked massive conflict; they might have to choose between order and change. Yet another tension was between the Communists' nation building, on the one hand, and China's participation in the worldwide Communist movement, on the other—between nationalism and internationalism.

The first few years after the revolution were dedicated to reconstruction and reform. The new government redistributed land, nationalized large private enterprises, and expanded the public sector. The first five-year plan, from 1952 to 1957, set the country on a Soviet-style path. Planners gave heavy industry half of total investment, despite the fact that it was a minuscule share of the economy. Soviet technical and financial aid built several hundred major manufacturing plants, and with concerted government attention and Soviet help, industry grew very quickly. In five years overall industrial production doubled; cement and electric power output tripled; steel production quadrupled.[12]

Originally farmers were left on their own. Almost no public money was put into agriculture, but at least there were no attempts to drain massive resources from the villages to the cities. The rural population was so enormous that modest agricultural taxes yielded enough money for industry, and Soviet aid also helped fund the new industrial capacity. The Communists could not risk the antagonism of more than four-fifths of the country; they were a much more rural party than the Soviets had been (two-thirds rural as opposed to two-thirds urban). The Communists made only modest efforts to encourage farmers to join cooperatives. At the end of 1954 less than 2 percent of the country's peasants were in cooperatives, and almost none in collective farms. An optimistic Central Committee resolution anticipated that 20 percent of the country's farmers might join cooperatives (not collective farms) by 1957; Mao Zedong took the radical view that the whole peasantry could conceivably be in cooperatives by 1960.[13]

This gradualism was soon abandoned. Relations between the Chinese and the Soviets became increasingly strained after 1956, and in any event, the Soviet money was borrowed, not given, and would eventually come to an end. More important, it became clear that the farms were providing only a modest surplus to invest in industry and the cities. Some Communist leaders were willing to accept this, opting for a lengthy transition to socialism and industrial development. Mao Zedong and his supporters thought that this implied abandoning their goals. But how could they get the resources for rapid economic change? The peasantry could not be squeezed as in the USSR; they were too close to subsistence, too numerous, and too politically important.

Mao and his supporters tried to increase farm production with major changes in agricultural organization. In October 1955 the party suddenly began a big push for collectivization, and in a remarkable turnaround, by the end of 1956 nearly 90 percent of Chinese peasants were in collective farms. Soviet collectivization had taken nearly ten years to reach this level, required enormous brutality, and led to massive problems. Chinese collectivization appeared smooth and relatively problem-free. Each new collective farm was generally organized to coincide with one traditional village, with about a hundred households. Moreover, collectivization was not accompanied by Soviet-style requisitioning of grain at absurdly low prices.

Problems quickly arose. Apparently Mao had hoped that a reorganized peasantry would increase farm output so much that there would be plenty to allow farm incomes to rise *and* to fund industrial investment, new infrastructure, and better living standards. But this was not the case, and once more the government faced the prospect of extracting more from the farmers. Mao chose to deal with the problem differently. In the winter of 1957–1958 the government organized the collective construction of irrigation and other waterworks. These drew together hundreds of millions of people from many different collectives and appeared a great success; the Chinese boasted of building the equivalent of three hundred Panama Canals in the course of a year.[14] Mao and his supporters saw a way out of their quandary: Larger collectives could bring together the peasants in even more effective campaigns. They pushed to amalgamate ten, twenty, or thirty collective farms into single units that would share labor, machinery, leadership, and just about everything else.

In a matter of months toward the end of 1958 the Chinese took what they called a Great Leap Forward that reorganized 99 percent of the country's peasants into enormous communes with as many as thirty thousand members. The communes were much more "communistic" than the collectives, sharing everything from child care to food in communal messes. As the Central Committee put it enthusiastically, "The people have taken to organizing themselves along military lines, working with militancy, and leading a collective life, and this has raised the political consciousness of the 500 million peasants still further. Community dining rooms, kindergartens, nurseries, sewing groups, barber shops, public baths, happy homes for the aged, agricultural middle schools, 'red and expert' schools, are leading the peasants toward a happier collective life and further fostering ideas of collectivism among the peasant masses." This was, the party said, "the fundamental policy to guide the peasants to accelerate socialist construction, complete the building of socialism ahead of time, and carry out the gradual transition to communism."[15] The party encouraged the new communes to build small-scale industry, and soon a million tiny blast furnaces were producing iron and steel around the countryside.

The Great Leap Forward nearly took the country over a cliff. The huge communes were much too large for meaningful farming. Peasants who could get food and other services for free had little reason to work and much incentive to eat, so consumption went up while production went down. The 1958 harvest had been very good—perhaps one reason for the optimism of the Great Leap—so euphoria lasted for a while as stocks were depleted. But the 1959 and 1960 harvests dropped, by about one-quarter, and food supplies dwindled. By 1960 the countryside was in serious trouble. Food production was down precipitously, and the country's transport and distribution systems were in disarray. In the end the Communists, who prided themselves on eradicating hunger and want, presided over one of history's most massive famines. Between fifteen and thirty million people starved, and a panicked government sent thirty million city dwellers to the countryside because it had no way to feed them.[16]

The government returned to more modest forms of agricultural organization. The average commune was divided into three and reduced largely to an administrative unit. The government entrusted control of the land and farming to production teams of twenty to forty households, often coinciding with traditional extended families (clans). The private family plots were reinstated, along with greater leeway for private part-time businesses (handicrafts, trade, repair shops) to help farmers make ends meet. Some areas even reintroduced individual peasant farming.[17] The government focused on ensuring the food supply, concentrating machinery, irrigation, and fertilizer in the most productive regions. The movement back toward markets and the emphasis on higher-yield areas increased inequality between richer and poorer farmers. The Communist leadership was dismayed by this, but radical leveling had been disastrous.

The battles were not over, however. In 1966 Mao Zedong and his supporters attempted to reverse the reformist course of economic policy. The Great Proletarian Cultural Revolution, as it came to be called, pushed economic management back in a more revolutionary direction. The radicals objected to the use of nonideological technicians and experts, to large wage differentials between skilled and unskilled workers, to inequality in the countryside. They charged that the more moderate course of the early 1960s was taking China down the "capitalist road" of the revisionist Soviets, from whom the Chinese had split. The Cultural Revolution tore the country apart in factional conflict, including armed battles between supporters and opponents of one or another political tendency. The conflict disrupted the economy, and uncertainty about economic policy dampened growth. By the early 1970s, although the Cultural Revolution was still officially in progress, the government had settled into a more moderate course similar to that of the early 1960s.

Wild swings in economic policy took their toll. From the revolution until the end of the first five-year plan, GDP per person grew a remarkable 57 percent. The Great Leap drove output down by one-quarter in five disastrous years. During the retrenchment from 1962 to 1966, growth bounded ahead by another 43 percent, only to be driven down 12 percent by the first three years of the Cultural Revolution. Once the Cultural Revolution cooled off, from 1968 to 1973, the economy grew again by one-third. Despite the ups and downs, overall Chinese economic growth averaged 2.9 percent a year per person, which compared favorably with other developing nations and particularly with India. But this comparison masked lost opportunities, for India was a slow grower among less developed countries. If China had sustained its 1950–1958 growth rate, by 1973 the country would have been almost three times richer than India, more than twice as rich as it actually was, within reach of South Korean and Taiwanese levels of income per person.[18] China's factional conflicts and the twists and turns of its economic policies put out of reach the extraordinary developmental success that much of East Asia was experiencing.

The ups and downs were the result of fundamental tensions in Chinese society. Attempts to spur economic growth increased inequalities among regions, groups, and classes, which clashed with the Communists' goals and with the interests of some of their important supporters. But attempts at radical social change depressed the economy, and China was much too close to subsistence to risk this. The moderates argued for the "economistic" needs of a desperately poor country, the radicals for the "utopian" goals of their revolutionary tradition. Modest doses of both might have been manageable; instead China was driven from one position to another.

Nonetheless, in the early 1970s the Chinese government had some important achievements. Economic growth had not been anything like that of its East Asian capitalist neighbors, but it also had not been as slow as that of capitalist India. Social conditions had improved substantially, in health care, education, and nutrition. China was hardly a shining beacon of unmitigated socialist success, but its experience was positive enough that the socialist path remained attractive to others in Africa, Asia, and Latin America.

Socialism in the Third World

China's example inspired many in Africa and Asia, as did the Vietnamese and Korean experiences. North Vietnam was admired for its tenacity in what was widely seen as a continuing anticolonial liberation war. The willingness of a small, backward country to confront the American superpower raised the stock of socialism in the developing world, for many in the Third World resented America's perceived neglect of or hostility to the cause of economic development. North Korea had a similar appeal and seemed to have achieved some success in autarkic industrialization. By the early 1970s many African and Asian countries had allied themselves either with the Soviet Union or with China and espoused general approval—albeit only partial imitation—of the socialist path. The liberation movements in Portugal's African colonies, in Rhodesia, and in South Africa also identified with the USSR or China. Some of this was undoubtedly due to an opportunistic alliance with their enemies' enemies, for the white minority African regimes were seen as having the active or passive support of the West. But there was also a certain faith that the socialist road was appropriate to conditions of underdevelopment.

The socialist experience that most captured the imagination of the developing world, however, took place in the most unlikely of spots. The Cuban Revolution gave socialism a toehold off the shore of the world's capitalist powerhouse, in a former playground of America's upper classes, far from the Eurasian center of Communist power. Cuba's audacity in confronting the United States, its revolutionary fervor, and its achievements impressed millions in Latin America, in Africa and Asia, and even in the industrialized world.

Cuba had been a U.S. dependency, formally or informally, since American troops defeated the Spanish in 1898. By the 1950s the island was well off by Latin American standards, not as rich as Argentina, not as poor as Mexico or Brazil, about equal to Chile. Yet to many Cuba seemed a grotesque parody of development. The corruption of the country's political leaders was matched by the decadence of Havana's hotels, casinos, and brothels. Apart from tourism, the island depended on a sugar sector much of which was owned by Americans and relied on privileged access to the American market. Dependence on the United States may have enriched many Cubans, but it did not alleviate the grinding poverty of many others, such as the landless farmworkers or the inhabitants of sprawling slums surrounding the cities. Showy wealth in the midst of poverty, dependence, and nationalism created deep-seated Cuban resentment toward the island's ruling class and its American protectors.

Fidel Castro and his thousand or so fighters entered Havana on January 1, 1959, without opposition, for the brutality of dictator Fulgencio Batista had, after twenty-five years of misrule, run its course. Cuban supporters of Castro—at first almost everyone—shared a desire for some simple things: national independence, economic growth, diversification away from sugar, and a reduction in inequality. The revolutionary regime's attempts to achieve these goals quickly led it to ever more extreme measures and eventually to a full-fledged embrace of communism. Radicalism may have been inevitable: When the government tried to reduce foreign dependence and inequality, it ran up against powerful American interests, and the only alternative source of support seemed to be the USSR. American antagonism was especially worrisome in the light of the recent experience of Guatemala, where in 1954 the United States had engineered the overthrow of a democratically elected government that had adopted some mildly nationalistic measures.

By 1961 the Cuban government had carried out a major land reform, nationalized most of the private sector, begun to adopt central planning, essentially made the Communist Party official, and allied itself with the Soviet Union. Over the next decade, economic policy swung back and forth between Soviet- and Chinese-style positions. The problem was like that in China. The Cuban government wanted to reduce the role of sugar and exports and to industrialize, and it wanted rapid growth and greater equality. However, attempts to twist the economy away from tropical agriculture and toward modern industry slowed growth, especially since the expropriation of foreign firms left Cuba without access to Western technology and capital. By the same token, measures to reduce inequalities among groups and regions dampened growth, both because they left many producers with little incentive to work and because they drove hundreds of thousands of skilled Cubans to emigrate. The reality appeared to be that industrialization, economic independence, and greater equality meant economic stagnation, while rapid economic growth meant accepting a sugar-based agrarian economy and only a gradual reduction in inequality.

By 1970, after ten years of twists and turns in policy, the Cuban government had settled into a local variant of Soviet central planning that attempted to balance these goals. Radical economic transformation was scaled back, and diversification of the economy, assisted by substantial Soviet financial and technical aid, proceeded only gradually. Some regional, group, and class inequalities were accepted, although the revolutionary regime provided high levels of social services to all. While the ten years of experimentation had taken a toll on economic growth and the government's popularity, the first socialist country in the Americas was flourishing.[19]

The fact that socialism in Cuba, Vietnam, Korea, and China appeared capable of addressing some serious problems impressed many millions. Socialism certainly had costs in political and economic liberty, but there were virtually no democracies in the non-Communist developing world either. China, Cuba, and other poor socialist countries had not magically eliminated the trade-offs facing underdeveloped countries. Governments still had to make hard choices—between city and countryside, industry and agriculture, social services and productive investment, growth and equity. Nonetheless, within a decade or two of their respective revolutions, these countries had eradicated the appalling disparities between wealth and income of an India or a Brazil, and (with the exception of the Great Leap fiasco) hunger and malnutrition had disappeared. Health care, education, and other social services were much better than in comparable capitalist developing countries. On balance, the socialist nations had chosen equity and economic diversification at the expense of special-ization and rapid growth, and the results impressed many dissatisfied with the glaring inequities of capitalist development.

A socialist future?

For twenty-five years after 1948, the centrally planned economies did very well. The Soviet Union and Eastern Europe grew faster than Western Europe; China grew faster than India. In Bulgaria and Romania output per person more than tripled between 1950 and 1973; in all Europe only Spain, Portugal, and Greece grew faster. Countries that had been overwhelmingly rural and agricultural became urban and industrial. The backward societies of Eastern Europe changed espe-cially dramatically. Farmers were 82 percent of the Bulgarian popula-tion in 1948, more than ten for every industrial worker; twenty-five years later there were more workers than farmers, and industry accounted for more than three times as great a share of the economy. Romania had had virtually no industry before World War Two, but by the early 1970s it had produced seven million tons of steel a year and exported enough of it to worry Western European and American steelmakers.[20]

Rapid growth and social change were accompanied by greatly improved social services such as health care and education. Illiteracy was essentially eliminated, even in China. Medical care was free and plentiful, and many socialist countries had more doctors and hospital beds per person than did industrialized capitalist nations. Infant mortal-ity plummeted, often below that of much wealthier countries; by 1970 it was lower in Czechoslovakia than in Austria, lower in Bulgaria than in Greece, lower in East than in West Germany. Life expectancy rose, and incomes became more equal.

In the early 1970s Communists ruled unchallenged over both the world's largest country and its most populous. Despite the bitter division between the USSR and China, the prospects for socialism seemed good. The Soviet camp's reformed central planning seemed to provide steady improvements in living standards. China was stable and growing. Several dozen poor nations and liberation movements counted them-selves as members of the socialist camp.

Socialist central planning, which first appeared to be a temporary strategy for the Soviet Union to prepare to fight off foreign invaders, had established itself as an alternative economic order. It rejected international integration, and the market more generally, and appeared to be a viable option for countries attempting to develop quickly and equitably and even for developed countries that wanted to avoid the evils of capitalist uncertainty and inequality. Capitalism appeared to require a sacrifice of social conditions to accelerate industrialization, but the centrally planned economies seemed to have achieved both growth and social equity. Karl Marx certainly did not envision a socialist camp made up mostly of poor countries, and Vladimir Lenin would have been disappointed that the only developed areas under Communist rule had been annexed by military means. Yet communism ruled one-third of the planet and had millions of adherents.

15

The End of Bretton Woods

On Friday, August 13, 1971, President Richard Nixon and his economic team slipped out of Washington to the presidential retreat at Camp David. Presidential speechwriter William Safire shared a car to the heliport with Herbert Stein, a member of the Council of Economic Advisers. When Safire asked what the meeting was about, Stein said cryptically, "This could be the most important weekend in the history of economics since March 4, 1933." Safire, who had little background in economic issues, thought hard about the reference and came up with his best guess, "We closing the banks?," referring to Franklin Roosevelt's bank holiday during the darkest days of the Great Depression. Stein laughed and elaborated: "Hardly. But I would not be surprised if the President were to close the gold window." This didn't help Safire, but the speechwriter realized it had to be serious on the helicopter ride to Camp David. A Treasury official who had joined them, told of the prospect, "leaned forward, put his face in his hands, and whispered, 'My God!'"[1]

The topic at Camp David was whether to make the most momentous economic decision of the postwar period, to "close the gold window" and take the U.S. dollar off gold. On the world's currency markets, investors were attacking the dollar, selling it off because they expected President Nixon to devalue the U.S. currency. Once Nixon and his advisers gathered, Secretary of the Treasury John Connally presented the issue: "What's our immediate problem? We are meeting here because we are in trouble overseas. The British came in today to ask us to cover $3 billion, all their dollar reserves." Under the Bretton Woods monetary order, other governments could redeem dollars for gold. Since they expected that the dollar would be devalued—its gold value would be reduced—it made financial sense to unload as many dollars as possible. "Anybody can topple us—anytime they want," said Connally; "we have left ourselves completely exposed."

The United States could counter the sell-off, but to defend the dollar, it would have to raise interest rates, cut spending, restrain wages and profits, and drive the economy into recession. No government would relish this prospect, and Richard Nixon's political memory made him particularly unwilling to tighten economic policy. Nixon regarded his close loss to John F. Kennedy in the 1960 presidential election as the result of the Fed's willingness to raise unemployment to defend the dollar. He remembered the impact of recessionary policy well: "All the speeches, television broadcasts, and precinct work in the world could not counteract that one hard fact."[2] About his earlier experiences, Nixon said sardonically, "We cooled off the economy and cooled off 15 senators and 60 congressmen at the same time."[3] As a presidential election year approached, the administration opposed raising American interest rates to make the dollar more attractive to investors.

The country's trade position also increased pressure to devalue. Prices in the United States were rising faster than prices abroad, so foreigners bought less from the United States while Americans bought more from abroad. Imports grew twice as fast as exports, and in 1968 the country imported more automobiles than it exported, a striking blow to what had been the nation's flagship export product. The AFL-CIO, long a supporter of freer trade, turned toward protectionism. Two protectionist trade bills came closer to passage than any such legislation since the Smoot-Hawley Tariff of 1930. By 1971 the United States was importing more than it exported, its first trade deficit in living memory. The strong dollar meant expensive American products, and expensive American products meant competitive pressures on American manufacturers.

Thirty years of American commitment to the Bretton Woods monetary order stood against these domestic considerations. If the United States did not defend the dollar, it would need to break the link to gold and devalue it. This would bring down the Bretton Woods system that was the centerpiece of the international economy.

Those at the Camp David table understood the trade-offs between international economic interests and domestic politics. Peter Peterson recommended the president focus on how a devalued dollar would protect American companies from imports: "Let's get competitive. Businessmen will like that." Paul Volcker, then undersecretary of the treasury, noted that gold had never been politically popular in the United States and referred to William Jennings Bryan's 1896 antigold rhetoric: "There is a certain public sentiment about 'a cross of gold.' " Nixon was wary of this last argument; he made a face and pointed out that "Bryan ran four times and lost."

Arthur Burns, chairman of the Federal Reserve Board, was the closest to Wall Street of any of those present. Burns was reluctant to go off gold and made the financial markets' arguments in favor of maintaining the monetary system that had served them so well. Safire reported the exchange:

> Burns: "But all the other countries know we have never acted against them. The good will—"
> Connally: "We'll go broke getting their good will. . . . Why do we have to be reasonable?"
> Burns: "They can retaliate."
> Connally: "Let 'em. What can they do?"
> Burns: "They're powerful. They're proud, just as we are. . . ."
> Connally: "We don't have a chance unless we do it. Our assets are going out by the bushel basket. You're in the hands of the money changers. You can see the result of this action will put us in a more competitive position."
> Burns: "May I speak up for the 'money changers'? The central bankers are important to you."[4]

Burns's invocation of the country's international economic obligations did not convince Nixon. The central banker's case was probably weakened by the fact that the administration had been at odds with the Fed for much of the previous year. Burns insisted on greater austerity and more inflation control, while the president resisted measures to slow down the economy. As the administration ignored Burns's insistence on the need for action, pundits joked, "Nixon fiddles while Burns roams."[5]

Domestic political imperatives overpowered international commitments, and on August 15, 1971, Richard Nixon took the dollar off gold. Over the next few months the dollar dropped by about 10 percent. Nixon reinforced the impact of the devaluation by imposing a 10 percent import tax to protect American producers, and he also introduced wage and price controls. Although the major financial powers attempted to patch together a reformed Bretton Woods system, in 1973 the Nixon administration again devalued the dollar by 10 percent. Trade moved back into surplus, the economy picked up speed, and unemployment declined.

But Bretton Woods was dead. The IMF staff circulated an obituary notice in the fund's Washington headquarters: "R.I.P. We regretfully announce the not unexpected passing away after a long illness of Bretton Woods, at 9 P.M. last Sunday. Bretton was born in New Hampshire in 1944 and died a few days after his 27th birthday. . . . The fatal stroke occurred this month when parasites called speculators inflated his most important member and caused a rupture of his vital element, dollar-gold convertibility."[6] After nearly thirty years the balancing act between national economic concerns and international economic integration had failed.

The compromises unravel

The early 1970s were the high-water mark of the postwar world economy. Almost all the industrialized nations, centrally planned economies rich and poor, developing countries, and former colonies grew rapidly and continually. Prosperity reigned in the advanced capitalist world, which defied the conclusions drawn by many in the interwar years, jointly satisfying international and domestic concerns, markets and social reform, capitalists and labor.

The Bretton Woods system combined freedom to address national concerns with international economic integration. Its compromises spurred international trade, investment, and finance, and this very success eventually undermined the agreements. Growing economic ties among countries led to concern that the world economy restricted national policies and to equal and opposite concern that attachment to national goals hamstrung the full development of global markets.

The biggest challenge came on the monetary front, to the gold-dollar standard that was the centerpiece of the postwar order. The challenge struck the very core of the system, forcing the American government to choose between its international obligations and its domestic goals.[7] Under Bretton Woods, the dollar was fixed to gold at thirty-five dollars per ounce, while other currencies were fixed to the dollar. Governments were expected to refrain from changing their exchange rates, even when they might have liked to do so—for example, to devalue and make domestically produced goods more competitive with foreign goods. The rules of the game were not very binding for twenty or more years after World War Two. Governments other than the United States could change exchange rates without disrupting the system, and most industrialized countries devalued or revalued at some point; Canada even floated the Canadian dollar against the U.S. dollar. Even if they did not devalue, governments could change interest rates to affect local conditions. If France was in recession, the central bank could lower French interest rates to stimulate the economy.

Two trends, both of them results of the success of the Bretton Woods order, undermined the system. The first was the restoration of international finance. This was important because the dormancy of international financial flows had been one reason governments remained able to manage their own monetary policies. If world financial markets had been active in the 1950s and 1960s, lower interest rates in France than in Germany would have led investors to take their money from Paris to Frankfurt, counteracting the policy. But short-term money flows were practically nonexistent, in part because of the trauma of the 1930s, in part because of booming opportunities at home, in part because of capital controls. This insulated monetary conditions in one country from those in others and gave governments some policy independence. World financial markets revived over the course of the 1960s. By the early 1970s the global financial system was holding about $165 billion, and international lending was running at about $35 billion a year. Now short-term investors—speculators, to use a loaded term—could move money in response to differences in national monetary conditions and could threaten the independence of national macroeconomic policy.

The first change contributed to the second, pressure on the American dollar. This too was a measure of systemic success, as it was largely due to the growing economic importance of Western Europe and Japan. When the United States dominated the world economy, nobody questioned the reliability of the U.S. dollar. But as the American share of the world economy shrank, the divergence of American monetary conditions from those of its partners became untenable. Investors around the world began to doubt the U.S. government's commitment to its exchange rate. The Bretton Woods system could survive a devaluation now and again, but that did not apply to the dollar. The gold standard was based on gold; the Bretton Woods system was based on a gold-backed dollar, and the U.S. government was finding it hard to maintain the value of the dollar. Shoring up the dollar required the United States to bend to its international commitments, and Americans were unaccustomed to subordinating national concerns to international markets.

Trouble first came in 1959 and 1960, when an American payments deficit led to a loss of confidence in the dollar. The Federal Reserve raised interest rates in order to increase foreign demand for dollars, which drove the U.S. economy into a recession (whose political effects Richard Nixon remembered thirteen years later). For the first time since the 1930s American monetary policy subordinated national goals to international ones—in this case, enduring a recession in order to defend the dollar. As the 1960s continued, the problem was made more pressing by the two wars the country was fighting: the Vietnam War and the large increase in social spending known as the War on Poverty. Neither was universally popular, and the administrations of Lyndon Johnson and Richard Nixon resorted to deficit spending. This drove inflation in the United States appreciably higher than in most of its partners.

The result was a "real appreciation" of the dollar, an artificial strengthening of the American currency. The dollar's exchange rate—its price in terms of other moneys—was being held constant, while American prices rose. This meant that foreigners could buy less with their dollars. Bretton Woods rules required people around the world to accept dollars as if they were worth one thirty-fifth of an ounce of gold, or four deutsche marks, or five francs, but in fact they were worth less than this, by some calculations 10 or 15 percent less. This was good for Americans in many ways. They could buy more foreign goods with the strong dollar, make foreign investments more cheaply, and travel more cheaply to foreign lands. In 1971 Americans bought twice as much in manufactured imports and invested twice as much abroad as they had in 1967, while the number of Americans traveling abroad more than doubled. The government could meet its foreign policy commitments in artificially strong dollars. And the Bretton Woods system gave foreigners little choice but to take these dollars.

The real appreciation of the dollar had advantages to Americans, but it threatened Bretton Woods. The monetary system depended on a dollar that was "as good as gold," but the inflationary erosion of the dollar's real value made foreigners reluctant to hold the currency as it lost purchasing power. Instead foreigners used unreliable dollars to buy reliable gold. From 1961 until 1968 investors and governments abroad cashed in seven billion dollars, taking up more than 40 percent of America's gold reserve. The French were particularly critical of America's privileged position; Charles de Gaulle complained bitterly of the country's use of "dollars which it alone can issue, instead of paying entirely with gold, which has a real value, which must be earned to be possessed, and which cannot be transferred to others without risks and sacrifices."[8] The French in fact bought up three billion of the seven billion dollars drained from American gold reserves.

The major financial powers worked together to try to protect the dollar, selling gold and buying up dollars to raise the currency's price. The United States imposed capital controls, taxes on American foreign investments, to stem the outflow of dollars. But there were too many people wanting to get rid of too many dollars; at the low point, on one day in mid-March 1968, four hundred million dollars were presented for redemption. This made it too expensive to defend the gold-dollar price, and the major powers allowed a private market to develop alongside the official market in which the dollar traded only at the official thirty-five-dollar-per-ounce price. But the problem would remain so long as people did not regard the dollar as reliable. French President Georges Pompidou complained: "We cannot keep forever as our basic monetary yardstick a national currency that constantly loses value. . . . The rest of the world cannot be expected to regulate its life by a clock which is always slow."[9]

So long as people around the world lost confidence in the dollar and sold dollars for gold, stopgap measures would not suffice. There was not enough gold in the world, let alone in American reserves, to buy up all the world's dollars. Eventually the United States would run out of gold, and the promise that the dollar was as good as gold would not be honored. The only lasting solution was to impose austerity on the U.S. economy to restore the purchasing power of the dollar. This would bring American prices down and raise the dollar's true worth toward its official value. Or the American authorities could raise American interest rates high enough to attract foreigners back to dollars; if the Federal Reserve raised interest rates two or three percentage points, investors might buy more American bonds, increasing the demand for dollars and shoring up their price. Neither measure was acceptable to the Nixon administration in the run-up to the 1972 presidential election.

The Bretton Woods monetary order collapsed for political, not technical, reasons. The original gold-dollar system was politically attractive because it stabilized currencies to promote trade and investment, without tying national governments' hands to any great degree. Yet as the world economy became more integrated, the system became more like the gold standard. Governments had to mold domestic policies to fit the exchange rate, to sacrifice national goals in order to sustain a currency's international value. There was no secret about how to do this: If domestic prices rose to make a currency "overvalued," they needed to be brought back down by raising interest rates, cutting government spending, reducing consumption.

The relative importance of currency stability and policy independence to a government determined whether it was worth making these sacrifices. Banks, corporations, and investors that would lose from a change in the currency's value supported austerity. On the other hand, workers and corporations whose jobs and profits would be cut to fit the currency opposed propping up an exchange rate that had little impact on them. In very open economies, in which much of the population was involved in world trade and investment, there was often support for austerity to sustain the currency; but the United States was relatively closed—even after the expansion of the postwar period, trade was less than 10 percent of the economy—and voters would never put international monetary order above domestic prosperity. The U.S. government was simply unwilling to trim its economy to fit its currency commitments under the Bretton Woods system and chose instead to bring the system to an end.

Challenges to trade and investment

The same political factors that challenged the monetary system also threatened international trade and investment. Just as the success of Bretton Woods sped its own demise, so too did the extraordinary growth of trade and direct investment spark debates that called their future into question.

Postwar trade liberalization had a particularly great impact on Western Europe and Japan, which emerged from thirty years of protectionism ready to take advantage of world and American markets. They embarked on successful export drives: By 1973 trade was more than twice as important to Western Europe than it had been in 1950, four times as important to Japan. Much of the prosperity of these years depended on tapping the technological, scale, and other possibilities of a growing world market.

The rise of Japan as an export power was especially striking. In 1950 the country exported less than one-twelfth as much as the United States. By 1973 Japanese exports were more than half those of the United States, and growing quickly. While in the 1950s Japanese exports were mostly such labor-intensive goods as clothing and toys, by the late 1960s Japan was a force in the world market for sophisticated manufactured products. The country's steelmaking capacity went from 1 million tons in 1950 to 117 million in 1974, at which point the country's largest steel company was almost one-half again bigger than U.S. Steel. Japanese output per worker in the automotive industry in the 1950s was one-tenth that of the United States (and one-third that of Europe). By 1973 the productivity of Japanese and American autoworkers was roughly equal, and double that of the Europeans. Japanese steel, machinery, and automobile producers were major players in foreign markets, especially in North America.[10]

But one country's exports are another country's imports. And while trade in, say, coffee, between Colombia and Germany is uncontroversial—Colombian coffee growers are not competing with Germans—trade in automobiles or television sets creates a backlash. German, Italian, Japanese, and others' cheap exports of textiles, steel, clothing, and machinery to other countries were a boon to consumers but a bane to the producers of goods that competed with them. One of the principal battlefields, as with the gold-dollar standard, was inside the United States. As more European and Japanese steel, textiles, footwear, and clothing came into the United States, American producers fought for protection.

GATT members had agreed not to raise nonagricultural tariffs, so those who wanted shelter from foreign competition found other means. One was to accuse the foreign seller of dumping, selling the product below its cost of production in order to corner a market. Dumping was against GATT rules, and countries could impose special taxes on goods that were found to be dumped. But dumping is often in the eyes of the beholder—one firm's dumping is another's attempt to compete—and antidumping complaints were often simply protectionist demands.

Another innovative way to keep imports out was to convince producers to restrict their own sales, as the United States did in 1968 by getting Japanese and European steelmakers to limit exports to the American market. But why would foreign producers go along with these

Voluntary Export Restraints (VERs)? Sometimes affected industries used the stick, threatening antidumping or other punishments. They could also hold out a carrot of higher profits for the foreigners themselves, sharing the benefits of protection with the overseas producers. Export restraints limited supply, so they kept the American price of the good high; this was, after all, the reason American manufacturers wanted to keep imports out. The higher American price allowed foreigners as well as Americans to sell their goods for higher prices in the American market. In the end, even foreign producers could charge more money per unit on lower volume. In essence, the VERs created a cartel between American and foreign producers to keep American prices higher than world market prices.

These new nontariff barriers (NTBs)—antidumping suits, VERs, and other devices—did not reverse the effects of the earlier liberalization, but they did hint that the balance of political forces was shifting in favor of the new protectionism. This was especially true in the United States. There had been broad consensus in favor of freer trade, especially between big business and the labor movement. Many big corporations and many big unions were in major exporting industries—autos, steel, rubber, machinery. But as these sectors faced more competition on world and domestic markets, their labor and capital switched to protectionism. The liberalism of the postwar trading order had originated with American pressure, and an American turn toward protection seemed likely to reverse the course of global trade integration.

There was a similar backlash against foreign direct investment. For many years after World War Two, multinational corporations (MNCs) were generally in favor. They brought in capital, along with modern products, technologies, and management techniques. They were typically in advanced industries; indeed, Latin Americans often distinguished between "bad" British pre-1930 investments—mines, plantations, railroads, government loans—and "good" American investments in modern manufacturing. Unlike old-style international lending, foreign direct investment (FDI) did not create obligations for national policy makers; there was no government guarantee that the foreign company would make money. The MNC might get all the profits, but it took all the risks, and it brought in technology, capital, and jobs. By the early 1970s there was two hundred billion dollars in FDI outstanding, with tens of billions of dollars in new investments made every year.

But as foreign corporations grew, so did reservations about their impact. Local competitors complained about the foreign giants that dominated local markets. Some were concerned that foreign managers would be less sensitive to national social, cultural, and political norms. The result was a greater wariness of foreign direct investment. A leading French journalist, Jean-Jacques Servan-Schreiber, wrote the most prominent example in 1967, a tract that quickly became the fastest-selling book in modern French history. *The American Challenge* pointed out that the principal beneficiaries of European integration were American corporations. The Common Market, Servan-Schreiber said, "is basically American in organization." This was because "American firms, with their own headquarters, already form the framework of a real 'Europeanization.' " Unlike European companies, American MNCs had a truly European vision: "This is true federalism—the only kind that exists in Europe on an industrial level. . . . Europe has almost nothing to compare with the dynamic American corporations being set up on her soil." And this would be fatal to European society, for "the confrontation of civilizations will henceforth take place in the battlefield of technology, science, and management." Servan-Schreiber meant his book more as a clarion call to European modernization than an attack on the United States, but he did identify a choice that many Europeans found increasingly clear, and increasingly troubling, between "building an independent Europe or letting it become an annex of the United States."[11]

In developing countries, large foreign corporations could have a powerful and unwelcome impact on local politics. The outrageous activities of the U.S.-based International Telephone and Telegraph Company (ITT) in Chile demonstrated the threat. ITT first tried to keep Socialist Salvador Allende from being elected president in 1970 and, when this was unsuccessful, participated in a series of plots to try to overthrow him. The sorry story ended with a coup that destroyed one of Latin America's sturdiest democracies and brought a murderous dictatorship to power. The notion that American companies could be complicit in such matters, long derided by Westerners as feverish imaginings, was soon proved accurate by a congressional investigation, and this fed sentiment against MNCs.[12]

Many countries began restricting multinational corporations in the 1960s. Canada monitored and controlled new investments, while France used administrative means to limit the impact of foreign companies. The French also attempted to convince their European partners to adopt regional controls, with limited success. Japan had long had strict limits on foreign direct investment. But the most sweeping efforts were in the developing world. From Mexico to Nigeria, from Peru to India, foreign corporations were excluded from many industries, and foreign ownership was strictly limited, often to a minority share. Many developing countries allowed FDI only if the foreign company did not compete with local firms, shared ownership with local investors, brought in important new technologies, and agreed to reinvest most of its profits. Governments subjected foreign companies to closer scrutiny and greater controls.

Conflict over domestic economic issues also began to rise in the industrialized world. In France in May 1968 student protests led to a general strike that lasted weeks; in Italy workers struck continually during the "Hot Autumn" of 1969. In almost every country in Western Europe, at some point between 1968 and 1973, there was a period of strikes at five to twenty times normal levels. In many instances, the strikes took place or soon moved outside the normal trade union channels, challenging the traditional (typically Communist or socialist) leadership of the labor movement.

One reason for the increase in labor-capital conflict was that for twenty years wages had lagged behind growth in productivity and in economic activity.[13] At the beginning of the postwar period, workers were willing to forgo wage increases to help economies recover; but recovery was long since over, and a new working-class generation wanted a larger share of the postwar expansion. This was compounded by a European recession in the middle 1960s, which led businesses to try to hold down wages. By the late 1960s there was a decade of accumulated grievances ready to burst into protest.

More immediately, inflation was heating up in Europe as it had in the United States, and workers were trying to make up lost ground. Unions and management in Europe had typically collaborated to sustain wage increases and job creation, but the rapid rise in prices undermined many of the agreements. Workers demanded protection against inflation, but unions were often bound by commitments to management, so the protests regularly were against both management and union leaders who insisted on holding to previous contracts.

Heightened labor-capital conflict and the growing backlash against trade and foreign direct investment indicated that the political and economic bases of the international order had changed since the 1940s. Then almost everyone in the developed world had agreed on the need to overcome bitter domestic class conflict, to raise a pathologically low level of international trade and investment, and to organize the international monetary system to this effect. By the 1960s all this had been achieved with great success. At this point one body of opinion looked with enthusiasm toward a deepening of international economic integration, while others thought that economic integration had gone quite far enough. The breakdown of the Bretton Woods monetary system itself, along with the broader politics of international economic relations in the late 1960s and early 1970s, demonstrated that opinion was increasingly divided on how far global economic integration should go. A simple progression toward greater openness could not be assumed, and might meet with great resistance.

Crises of import substitution

While the developed capitalist world reconsidered its march toward the international economy, the developing world was questioning the wisdom of protectionist industrial development. Import-substituting industrialization (ISI) had many successes, but many undesirable effects.[14]

ISI caused chronic problems with the balance of trade and payments. Import substitution was supposed to reduce reliance on world trade, but every nation needed to import something not available locally—raw materials, machinery, spare parts. The more a country industrialized, the more it needed these imports—what economist Carlos Díaz Alejandro called "the import intensity of import substitution."[15] But countries needed to export to earn money to buy imports, and ISI was strongly biased against exports. Trade protection and overvalued exchange rates raised domestic prices and made exports less competitive, and export taxes discouraged foreign sales. The industrializing countries were unable to export enough to buy the imports they needed.

Some imports could be paid for with foreign aid and loans from such international institutions as the World Bank. But these funds were limited. Private foreign investment brought in some foreign currency, but not enough. After 1967 a few better-off developing countries were able to borrow from northern lenders to pay for imports—three or four billion dollars a year by the early 1970s. But these loans had to be repaid, so they only postponed the reckoning; anyway, they were not enough money, and they were available to only a few nations. Developing countries needed to export more to pay for needed imports, and the political economy of ISI made this exceedingly difficult.

The typical ISI economy went through periodic balance of payments crises. The faster the economy grew, the more it needed imports; but exports could not keep up with imports, and so the country ran out of foreign currency. The government restricted imports to essentials and raised interest rates to bring money into the country and keep it at home. It devalued the currency to raise the price of imports and make exports more attractive, also reducing the country's purchasing power. The result was usually a deep recession. Companies under pressure cut wages and laid off workers. The collapse of the local economy curtailed imports, while a weaker exchange rate, high unemployment, and lower wages made it easier to export. Soon exports were again greater than imports, growth restarted, and the cycle began again. But successive rounds of these crises eventually endangered the social, economic, and political order.

ISI countries also tended to run substantial budget deficits and inflation, which made these crises worse. Governments subsidized industrial investment, gave tax breaks to industrial investors, and targeted spending at politically important groups. But spending chronically outpaced government revenue, and these budget deficits were usually covered by printing money. The resulting inflation made domestic goods more expensive, reducing exports still further; it decreased tax income as taxpayers delayed tax payments to make them in less valuable money; and it drove economic activity into gray and black markets. By the 1960s many ISI economies had been caught in a vicious cycle of balance of payments deficits, budget deficits, inflation, and recession.

Brazil's import substitution realized substantial achievements and created substantial problems. The second-largest economy in the developing world after India, Brazil was a major industrial nation by 1960. It produced almost all the final goods it consumed, built world-scale steel and automobile industries, and constructed a brand-new capital city, Brasília, in five years. But industrialization required imports of equipment, machinery, chemicals, and spare parts, as well as the petroleum required for the nation's millions of new cars. Brazil's exports could not keep up. Over half of its exports was still coffee, and most of the rest were such traditional products as cotton, sugar, tobacco, and iron ore. Efforts to encourage exports of the new manufactured products failed; in 1960 Brazil exported less than half of 1 percent of its manufacturing output.

The result was a series of balance of payments crises. In 1963 exports were still well below their levels a decade earlier. More important, exports fell behind imports despite the government's efforts to keep imports to a minimum. Meanwhile budget deficits grew, and inflation ratcheted up from around 20 percent in the 1950s to 96 percent in 1964. Businessmen protested high interest rates, workers struck against wage reductions, and the country's conservative military faced the specter of social unrest and even revolution. In April 1964 a coup replaced the elected government with a military dictatorship that ruled for more than twenty years. Austerity measures and a deep recession brought the deficits and inflation under control, but basic problems remained.

The Brazilian pattern was repeated all over the developing world: payments crises, inflation, social unrest, then military coup, repression, and austerity. In Chile the final paroxysm came during the presidency of Socialist Salvador Allende, with the 1973 military coup that overthrew him; in Argentina, with the return to office of Juan Perón and his wife and the 1976 military coup that overthrew her; in Turkey, with military interventions in 1960 and again in 1971; in the Philippines, with the imposition of martial law and the assumption of dictatorial powers by Ferdinand Marcos in 1972; in Indonesia, with the bloody military takeover of 1965. Even the two leading democratic ISI countries tottered, as Mexico's government massacred hundreds of student demonstrators in 1968 and India's Prime Minister Indira Gandhi declared an extralegal state of national emergency in 1975. The tensions of import substitution created a volatile mixture of economic problems and nationalist, populist, and developmentalist pressures, culminating in political unrest and often authoritarianism.

ISI also seemed to have nasty effects on poverty and income distribution. The industrial bias against agriculture worsened rural poverty in societies that were heavily rural. Masses of farmers migrated to the cities to look for jobs in the new industries. But import-substituting growth was very capital-intensive: The government subsidized investment, so industrialists used lots of capital and not much labor. Most of the farmers who flooded into the cities found that they could not get the jobs industrialization had promised. ISI countries ended up with "dual" economies: on the one hand, modern, capital-intensive industries with skilled, well-organized workers earning relatively high wages; on the other, a mass of struggling farmers and urban poor frozen out of the modern economy, consigned to subsistence wages, and excluded from the social protections modern-sector workers received.

Brazil's farm sector lagged behind the rest of the economy, especially in the backward northern parts of the nation, which in 1970 had 40 percent of the country's people but barely 20 percent of its income. In the poorest northeastern states, income per person was one-sixth that of industrial São Paulo State; the average urban worker made three times as much as the average rural worker. [16] Brazilian economist Edmar Bacha described his country as "Belindia," one small part Belgium, the huge remainder India.[17] Migrants fled India for Belgium, north for south. Yet employment in the modern sector was hard to find. The priority industries created few jobs; in the early 1960s the rapidly growing sectors of electrical equipment, transport equipment, and chemicals accounted for one-third of manufacturing output but barely one-tenth of manufacturing employment. Most migrants were relegated to the informal sector, working as day laborers and domestic servants and at other jobs that usually paid below the country's legal minimum wage. The country's cities were ringed by crime-ridden shantytowns with minimal services, burgeoning populations, and little access to the benefits of Brazil's industrial growth.

Brazil's income per person grew by one-third between 1960 and 1970; but the conditions of the bottom four-fifths of the population barely improved, and those of the poorest third probably worsened. Brazil became the world's most unequal society: The richest 5 percent of the country earned as much as the poorest 80 percent, twice as much as the poorest 60 percent. A country that prided itself on its modern industry, cosmopolitan metropolises, and modernistic capital city had a child mortality rate three times that of Cuba, six times that of the United States, well above that of such poor countries as Paraguay and Jamaica. More than one-third of Brazil's primary-age children and more than half its secondary-age children were not in school. [18]

Brazil could at least point to rapid growth, but other societies were doing much less well. Between 1950 and 1973 Chile grew at just 1 percent a year on a per person basis, Argentina at 2 percent, India at 1.6 percent. These were not bad numbers by the countries' historical standards, but they were far below the world average. Moreover, in the fast-growth conditions of the 1950s and 1960s, not taking advantage of opportunities had dire consequences. If Argentina had (like Brazil) grown 4 percent a year rather than 2 percent, by 1973 it would have been as rich as France; if Chile had (like South Korea) grown 5 percent rather than 1 percent, it would have been as rich as Germany. India in 1950 was only slightly poorer than South Korea and Taiwan; by 1973 Korea was three times richer, Taiwan four times richer.

The inward-oriented industrializing nations could not take part in the trade boom of the Bretton Woods period. Between 1950 and 1973 Latin America's exports fell from 8 percent to 3 percent of the world's total. Argentina's extraordinary natural resources made it a major world exporter, and in 1950 it exported roughly as much as Italy. But by 1973 Argentine exports were down to one-seventh Italy's, and were equal to those of Finland, which had one-fifth the people and one-quarter the economy. India in 1973 exported less than either South Korea or Taiwan, even though its population was seventeen times that of Korea and forty times that of Taiwan, and its economy five times the size of Korea's and ten times the size of Taiwan's.[19]

The East Asian export-oriented model seemed to avoid some of ISI's problems. In 1973 Korea exported 41 percent of the manufactured goods it produced, Taiwan 50 percent, as opposed to 3 or 4 percent for Latin America.[20] South Korea and Taiwan were so successful at production for export that they did not run into the serious balance of payments problems common elsewhere. They specialized in labor-intensive manufactures for export, and their firms needed all the cheap labor they could get, so plenty of jobs were created. The need to keep goods competitive on world markets made it essential to keep inflation under control. These benefits had costs. The East Asian exporters did not develop dualistic economies with high modern-sector and low informal-sector wages, but they were forced to keep *all* wages low, often with labor repression, to make their exports cheap. Their exchange rates were undervalued to maintain competitiveness, depressing the purchasing power of the local working and middle classes. Conservative macroeconomic policies led to low inflation but also meant that governments provided little in the way of social insurance. Still, the export successes added to the pressures to reevaluate import substitution.

The beneficiaries of ISI, however, blocked attempts to reform it. Industries had come to rely on protection from imports and were not enthusiastic about foreign competition. Firms that received government subsidies and tax breaks threatened to go out of business if they were revoked. Those whose wages or consumption had been propped up by government programs tried to keep these programs from being cut. There was some tinkering around the edges of ISI. One reform was the "rationalization of protection," the reduction of some trade barriers. And many governments began to use export subsidies and tax incentives to encourage industries to export. However, decades of import substitution had created entrenched interests that made a revision of the policy difficult.

One response to what came increasingly to be seen as a stagnant, stultifying system was an upsurge in revolutionary sentiment. In Latin America, especially, the existing order was criticized for its inequality and social failings, for its tendency to rely on foreign corporations, for its privileging of wealthy local businesses. The Cuban alternative looked attractive to a generation of students and to many in the working classes. Latin America lacked a strong socialist or Communist tradition, but labor and student unrest, radical organizations, and even urban guerrilla warfare increased. The problems of ISI seemed to feed a broader discontent with the capitalist world economy.

There were also official dimensions of this discontent. Third World governments, frustrated by problems at home, looked to the possibility of organizing themselves globally. The nonaligned movement launched at Bandung in 1955 grew into a United Nations lobby, the Group of 77 developing countries. The G-77 attempted to counter the economic influence of the developed world, pressing for changes in the rules of the international economic game to make it easier for poor countries to play. The less-developed countries (LDCs) pushed for higher prices for exports, more aid and loans, and greater access to OECD markets. This led to some concessions, but not enough to make a difference. The dilemmas of import-substituting industrialization persisted.

Socialism stagnates

The socialist world also faced increasing difficulties. In the Soviet Union and even in much of Central and Eastern Europe, economic reforms slowed or stopped. The problem was, once more, political. Decentralization would inevitably reduce the influence of the central authorities, while market-oriented changes would draw resources away from enterprises and regions that were poorly managed or simply had less economic potential. While these reforms would improve the overall functioning of these economies, they would also increase inequality between groups and regions. The Communists, however, were ideologically committed to equity and relied for a measure of mass support (or at least forbearance) on the poorer segments of society. Perhaps more important, the reforms threatened the position of the managerial and technical elite that was tightly intertwined with the Communist leadership.

Reform threatened the social and political balance of the socialist societies. The Communists' political base was primarily among those who benefited from central planning, and dismantling central planning directly threatened them. The situation was similar to that of ISI countries in the developing world. Economic policy in the centrally planned societies had entrenched firms and industries that relied on government support and protection—just as ISI industries relied on ISI—and that resisted attempts to reduce the support and protection they received. By the early 1970s the flurry of reformist activity of the 1960s had ceased. The Soviets reversed or ignored the "Kosygin reforms" of 1965. The Czechs were forced back to standard Soviet principles after the 1968 Soviet invasion. Even the Hungarians, who had gone farthest in a reform direction, backpedaled in the early 1970s. A process of ossification set in. The existing economic order was running out of steam, but there were too many political obstacles to substantial economic policy changes.

Economic growth in the centrally planned economies slowed continually over the late 1960s and early 1970s. What growth there was did not raise living standards enough to keep populations satisfied. The Soviets were ever more hated in Central and Eastern Europe, and the Communists were increasingly out of favor even with the Soviet population. In December 1970 in Poland this sentiment erupted into strikes and demonstrations in the country's Baltic shipyards, some of its most important industrial facilities. The regime responded with violent repression, and many demonstrators were killed. This abject failure led to the replacement of the Polish leader Wladyslaw Gomulka in favor of the more moderate Edward Gierek who tried to raise living standards quickly (in part by borrowing from Western banks). Even Gierek and other leaders of a second wave of attempted reforms could not break the logjam of entrenched interests.

Meanwhile another serious economic obstacle was becoming clear. By the 1960s the advanced capitalist world was adopting a host of new electronic technologies. The transistor and the laser transformed everything from consumer products to industrial processes and telecommunications. Computers became a mainstay of business and government, and other advances accumulated rapidly.

But the socialist countries were falling behind technologically, apparently as the result of systemic flaws in the centrally planned order. The reforms of the 1960s, although incomplete, enabled Comecon members to produce reasonably good buses, machine tools, cameras, and automobiles. But these were products of an earlier era, not of the new electronic age. Scientific education and research in the Soviet Union and Eastern Europe were excellent, but they were almost never applied to industrial innovation and production. It took all the resources the Soviet Union could muster to keep up with the United States in military technology, and then it was only marginally successful. In civilian industry the Soviets and their allies were a generation or two behind.[21]

Central planning in fact gave managers few reasons to develop and adopt new technologies. The system rewarded reliability and stability over risk taking, for planners needed to be sure that every link in the chain of production was secure. A manager who stuck with tried-and-true methods and fulfilled his quota was safe; one who experimented with a new process or product and failed was in trouble. This much would be roughly true in a market economy, but if the innovative gamble paid off under capitalism, the manager would be handsomely rewarded. In the command economies, however, there were few positive incentives for innovation. Inventors had few rights; the government strictly restricted profits from individual achievement, and nobody could get rich by coming up with new things to make or new ways to make them. The system's focus on tangible targets also made many innovations hard to measure or confirm; improvement in a product's quality might be a matter of opinion. The central planners' emphasis on quantitative goals, and the limits on individual rewards, worked against innovation; the risks of a new method were great, the potential rewards limited.

The technological divide between the Comecon countries and the West grew continually after 1960. Soviet successes in space and military applications obscured this in the public mind, but those in the know, including Comecon governments themselves, recognized that the general technological level of the centrally planned economies was falling ever farther behind. Socialist governments increased spending on science and technology, introduced more bonuses for inventions, and tried other measures but could not overcome the bias against risky innovation in the command economies.

The Soviets and their allies tried to bridge the technological gap by importing from the West. Some of the technology imports were turnkey factories that Western companies sold and set up as fully functioning modern production facilities. Comecon nations also bought large amounts of advanced machinery and equipment, although they were hamstrung to some extent by a Western embargo on anything that could be used for military purposes. For a system that prided itself on its scientific basis, it was a startling admission of inferiority to rely on imports from the West as its principal method of technical advancement. Soviet and Eastern European trade with the West skyrocketed, increasing tenfold between 1950 and 1973, tripling as a share of the socialist economies. Trade with the West plugged other holes in the centrally planned economies. The seemingly intractable retardation of Soviet agriculture led to demands for Western grain to feed the Soviet people. The government invited in foreign firms to exploit natural resources and borrowed heavily abroad. The USSR looked like a developing country, exporting raw materials and taking out loans in order to import machinery and food.

Trade with the West was not the answer to the problems of socialism. For one thing, the Soviets and their allies had very little that they could export. The socialist nations had an antiexport bias even more pronounced than that of the ISI economies. They were not oriented toward production for world markets: Input costs were so high as to make prices prohibitive, firms were not rewarded for earning foreign currency, and many manufactured goods were so shoddy as to be unmarketable. At some point natural resource exports—petroleum, gold, timber—would not be enough to pay for necessary imports. That point had not come by the early 1970s, but the warning signs were there. The reform programs had stalled, and the central planners struggled with poor living standards, technological backwardness, and declining growth rates. The glory days of socialism, like those of Bretton Woods and of ISI, were over.

End of an era

The postwar era ended in the early 1970s. The developed capitalist world had come out of World War Two with a compromise that blended international economic integration with national policy independence, the market with the welfare state. The Bretton Woods compromises succeeded on all dimensions: They provided rapid growth, extensive social policies, and a level of international economic integration unseen since the 1920s.

By the early 1970s the compromise between the international and the national was fraying. Trade competition, capital flows, and currency movements impeded domestic economic performance, and a backlash set in. Even, perhaps especially, the United States was increasingly reluctant to privilege international economic commitments over domestic goals. The gold-dollar standard collapsed, and trade protection rose.

In the Third World the impressive march of industrial development flagged. Lagging exports and persistent balance of payments problems slowed industrialization. To many the march now seemed too forced and had left too many poor people behind. The socialist world's increased output and industrial development were not reflected in living standards, and this led to popular dissatisfaction. Governments of both developing and socialist economies tried to enact reforms, but entrenched interests stymied them.

The postwar order had achieved the goals of its architects. The advanced capitalist countries got economic integration, coupled with the welfare state and national macroeconomic management. The developing countries got intensified industrialization, coupled with protection from foreign economic influence. The socialist countries got rapid industrial and economic growth, coupled with an equitable distribution of income. But in all three groups of countries the joint achievement of these goals had become more difficult over time. Economic integration challenged national demand management; ISI led to periodic crises and greater inequality; socialist central planning slowed economic growth. The way forward was not clear.

PART IV

GLOBALIZATION, 1973–2000

16

Crisis and Change

After 1973 the accumulated tensions of the postwar era came to a head. Growth in the advanced capitalist countries slowed to half its postwar rate for over a decade. Unemployment doubled and tripled, as more people pounded pavements in Western Europe and North America than at any time since the 1930s. Inflation went to three or four times the postwar average, and the price of oil, the industrial world's lifeblood, rose from three to thirty dollars a barrel. Global financial markets grew to unimaginable size. Hundreds of billions of dollars flowing around the world bounced currencies up or down 10 percent in a few days. Developing and socialist countries borrowed a trillion dollars, then collapsed in a wave of defaults that rivaled those of the 1930s and domestic economic crises often worse than those of the 1930s.

Nationalists and internationalists, free marketeers and interventionists, leftists and rightists fought over the course of national and international political economies. Political positions polarized: Businessmen bitterly opposed labor unions and the welfare state; labor vigorously embraced antibusiness stances. The centrist consensus of the 1950s and 1960s disintegrated. Dictatorships democratized, democracies collapsed; socialists took power in traditionally conservative countries, conservatives displaced socialists in others. The balance of power shifted away from those committed to the global economy toward those who wanted to limit or roll back international economic integration. The 1970s and early 1980s looked ominously like the 1930s, an antechamber to autarky and even military hostility, as relations between the United States and the Soviet Union deteriorated.

Oil and other shocks

Governments tried to invigorate their economies once the Bretton Woods monetary straitjacket was removed. As international finance revived, the gold-dollar standard had made it hard for governments to lower interest rates or increase spending without having to worry about the impact on currency values. The collapse of Bretton Woods removed the exchange rate constraint, and governments were free to stimulate their economies. The world economy surged between 1970 and 1973, as industrial production in the major economies rose 15 to 25 percent. The money supply grew by 40 percent between 1970 and 1973 in the United States, by 70 percent in Britain in 1972 and 1973. This led to inflation, and prices crept up all over the world.

Boom times in the industrial economies increased demand for the agricultural goods and raw materials that the Third World exported, and their prices soared. Between 1971 and 1973 the prices of copper, rubber, cacao, and coffee, for example, doubled or more. This was passed on to consumers, and food prices in the United States rose by 20 percent in 1973 alone. The price hikes accelerated, and in 1974 the American price of bread, potatoes, and coffee went up by one-quarter, and of rice by two-thirds, while sugar prices doubled.

Then there was oil. The world price of oil had lagged behind inflation for decades, and in 1960 the major developing country oil producers— Iran, Iraq, Kuwait, Saudi Arabia, and Venezuela—had formed the Organization of Petroleum Exporting Countries (OPEC). Its principal goal was to raise the royalty and tax rates private oil companies paid their hosts, which required coordination among producing governments (and the avoidance of undercutting). OPEC accomplished a bit, recruited a few more member countries, and benefited from the commodity boom of the early 1970s. In fall 1973, in the midst of war between Israel and its Arab neighbors, OPEC broke off talks with the oil companies, and its

Arab members doubled the price of oil to more than five dollars a barrel. Two months later OPEC doubled it again to nearly twelve dollars a barrel. Some in the West believed that such market manipulation could not be sustained, but soon it was clear that a small group of developing countries had dramatically changed the terms on which they sold their goods.

OPEC could quadruple the price of one of the world's most important commodities for several reasons. There were few readily available substitutes for oil, so price increases did not reduce consumption very much. Also, just a few of OPEC's core members controlled a very large share of the world's oil. The Persian Gulf "oiligarchies"—Saudi Arabia, Kuwait, Qatar, and the United Arab Emirates—had nearly half the world's oil reserves, a quarter of its output, and tiny populations. With fewer people than the Netherlands, they earned more from oil than Japan did from all its exports—by 1980 enough to pay each of their inhabitants an annual income two to three times greater than what the average American earned. They did not need to sell oil quickly and could hold it off the market to keep prices high. An additional source of power was the solidarity of OPEC's Muslim members in and around the Middle East who shared cultural and political ties. Further, some American policy makers saw higher oil prices as a way of channeling aid to allies in Saudi Arabia and Iran that was easier than going through Congress.

The oil producers were powerful, and consumers were helpless. Oil supplied half to three-quarters of the energy of the industrial world, and most industrial countries relied heavily on imports from OPEC. Alternative energy sources could be developed, but this would take years and hundreds of billions of dollars. OPEC had an extraordinary influence over world oil prices. Other Third World commodity producers—of copper, coffee, iron ore, bauxite, and bananas—tried to emulate OPEC, but the oil sector was unique.

The oil price increases had an immediate and electrifying impact. Prices soared within days. The German government gave emergency oil supplies to manufacturers who were running out of fuel and whose products would be ruined if their factories shut down. Japanese taxicab drivers demonstrated, and housewives hoarded toilet paper and laundry detergent. French government inspectors made spot inspections and fined managers of buildings that were heated to over twenty degrees Celsius (sixty-eight degrees Fahrenheit). American motorists faced gas station lines an hour or two long, and signs reading SORRY, NO GAS TODAY sprouted on the country's highways. The U.S. government created a new Department of Energy, and the American president called the oil crisis "the moral equivalent of war."[1]

The rapid growth of the early 1970s, the commodity boom, and the oil shocks all increased inflation. In 1974 consumer prices around the industrial world shot up: by 12 percent in the United States, 14 percent in France, 16 percent in Britain, 23 percent in Japan. Some of this was due to OPEC, but the best estimates are that the oil shocks themselves accounted for only one-quarter of the inflationary surge of the period.[2] The oil price hike was a one-time shock with contradictory consequences for other prices. On the one hand, petroleum was widely used throughout the economy, so there were upward pressures on other prices. On the other hand, with oil more expensive, consumers had less to spend on other things, demand for them fell, and other prices might actually have dropped. The result depended largely on government policy, especially monetary policy. If Bretton Woods had still been in place, the need to sustain fixed exchange rates would have forced most governments to restrain or reduce other prices—probably by raising interest rates, adding further to the recessionary impact of OPEC. With most currencies floating, however, governments were free to "accommodate" the price hikes by increasing the money supply to allow the oil shock to translate into price rises without forcing austerity. This led to a jump in inflation, which averaged nearly 10 percent for the OECD through the rest of the 1970s—three or four times higher in most countries than the average since World War Two. The monetary stability that had prevailed for nearly thirty years came to an end.

Despite these policies to stimulate economies, the world plunged into the steepest recession since the 1930s. In 1974 and 1975 industrial output dropped by 10 percent in the industrial world, and unemployment rose almost everywhere to levels thought of as unacceptable. By the end of 1974 the American stock market was at barely half its 1972 level. The world financial system was hit by the two biggest bank failures since the Depression, of the Franklin National Bank in the United States and the Bankhaus Herstatt in West Germany. New York City was unable to pay its debts and bills and was put in financial receivership by its creditors and the state government. Some of this was due to the OPEC shock, which was the equivalent of a tax on oil consumers, equal to about 2 percent of the GDP of the industrial countries.[3] But the effect was magnified by the great uncertainty that ensued.

Rising prices and sinking economies caused something close to panic. Businessmen and workers in the industrialized world were accustomed to growth, full employment, and stable prices; a generation of Europeans, North Americans, and Japanese had known only prosperity. As the recession continued, governments everywhere faced insistent demands that something be done. Labor unions mobilized to protect themselves against the erosion of their wages. Britain's coal miners slowed work and then struck in early 1974, eventually forcing the country onto a three-day workweek; over the next five years nearly twelve million workdays a year were lost to strikes in the United Kingdom, more than triple the rate of the 1950s and 1960s. Italy's labor unions forced adoption of an "escalator"(*scala mobile*) that tied wages to inflation. Labor unions also pressed for greater worker influence on the economy. The German Social Democratic government gave workers direct influence on managerial decisions ("codetermination"), while the new British Labour government enacted a string of prolabor regulations. In Spain and Portugal, democratization substantially increased Left and labor influence; for most of 1975 Portugal was ruled by a Communist-influenced government that was probably the most left-wing regime in modern Western European history.

In Sweden in 1975 the Social Democrats proposed the novel Meidner Plan (named after its architect, a leading economist). This would have allocated some of each company's profits to a union-controlled fund as shares in the company, giving labor unions partial ownership of more or less the entire private sector. Within a couple of decades, under the plan, most firms in Sweden would be owned by unions. The plan was not anticapitalist in theory—the firms would run on normal business principles, and high profit rates were one goal of the proposal—but it would have implied a radical shift in economic and political power, and it polarized labor-capital relations.[4]

This social strife changed the political landscape of the industrial world. In February 1974, in the midst of the coal miners' strike, the British Conservatives were voted out of power, an electoral verdict repeated in another general election in October. The Dutch socialists won power for the first time in fifteen years. Italy's Communists committed themselves to a "historic compromise" with capitalism, then put on a stunning electoral performance in 1976 and became informal members of the ruling coalition. On the other hand, in September 1976 the Swedish Social Democrats were turned out of office, ending over forty years of socialist rule. Two months later Gerald Ford became the first incumbent American president to lose an election since Herbert Hoover.

Despite the galloping inflation, governments avoided serious austerity measures that would worsen already tense class and social relations. Even though it was clear that loose monetary policies were not easing recessionary conditions, only continuing to fuel inflation, governments dreaded the consequences of a serious attack on inflation: recession, business distress, unemployment, and political conflict. Stagnant business conditions and continuing inflation saddled the Western world with stagflation, an ugly word for an unpleasant reality.

A second round of OPEC oil shocks in 1979 and 1980 reinforced the belief that the world economy was out of control or at least beyond the control of the advanced capitalist countries. A fundamentalist Islamic revolution overthrew the shah of Iran, one of America's closest allies; then war broke out between Iran and Iraq. OPEC decreed a near tripling of oil prices to thirty-three dollars a barrel, while prices went over forty dollars a barrel on the open market. OPEC did not fully sustain these high prices; new sources of supply had been developed, conservation and alternative energy sources restrained consumption, and members of OPEC cheated on agreements to control supply. Nonetheless, oil prices remained around thirty dollars a barrel, and another round of price shocks hit the world.

Governments created millions of jobs in the public sector and pumped billions of dollars into struggling economies. Between 1971 and 1983 the average industrial country's government increased spending from 33 to 42 percent of the economy, much more in some—from 45 to 66 percent of GDP in Sweden, from 49 to 66 percent in the Netherlands.[5] The industrial countries hired a million new public employees every year, and by 1983 governments were accounting for one-fifth of all jobs on average and as much as one-third in some countries. Few governments could afford to raise taxes to cover the expense, so budget deficits crept up to cover as much as one-fifth of total public spending in some countries, approaching 10 percent of their economies.

Governments borrowed in part because interest rates were falling behind inflation, so that borrowers effectively got free money from investors. In 1974, for example, while consumer prices rose 12 percent, the U.S. Treasury paid under 8 percent to borrow (with six-month securities). This was true for every year but one between 1973 and 1981, and similar relationships held for most industrialized countries. It was relatively painless to finance social programs with borrowed funds so long as money was available at interest rates below inflation ("negative real interest rates"). However, inflation and deficit financing were not permanent solutions to the economic difficulties.

Conservative governments in France and Sweden defended their economic programs from bitter labor opposition and eroding business support. The government of Italy, despite two IMF programs, a succession of leadership shake-ups, and Communist participation in government, failed to bring the budget and inflation under control. Britain's governing Labour Party split into warring leftist and centrist camps, with the Left program calling for radical changes in economic policy; in the Conservative Party, a previously marginalized right wing gained control under Margaret Thatcher. In March 1979, after a dismal winter of public-sector strikes, the Labour government fell to the first parliamentary vote of no confidence in over fifty years; two months later Thatcher became prime minister after a landslide victory. In the United States, President Jimmy Carter lost public confidence as unemployment stayed high and inflation approached 15 percent.

Carter referred to the prevailing attitude as "malaise," which description brought him popular disapproval but seems appropriate. Unlike the situation in the 1930s, there was no street warfare between Left and Right, no clear labor-capital class conflict. Instead the advanced capitalist nations seemed to degenerate into political free-for-alls, as remnants of previous coalitions grabbed for what they could. The constituent parts of the postwar centrist consensus—Europe's social democrats and Christian Democrats, America's New Deal coalition—could not reconstitute themselves. Old recipes for economic growth and political stability did not work, and although new nostrums proliferated, there was little support for any of them. The postwar order was in its death throes.

The 1970s were even more trying times for developing countries already struggling with the accumulated problems of ISI. The rapidly industrializing LDCs continued to have trouble paying for imports to fuel industry. Stagnation in the West reduced the demand for their products, while inflation raised the price of the manufactured goods they needed to import. To make matters worse, most developing nations were oil importers and faced much more expensive oil import bills. The first oil shock added about thirty billion dollars to the import bill of non-OPEC developing countries; the second oil shock, almost fifty billion. The desire for industrialization was unabated, but its cost was rising.

Foreign borrowing allowed the more advanced developing countries, now known as newly industrializing countries (NICs), to continue to invest in industry. The developing world had long gotten dribs and drabs of funds from the public development banks, such as the World Bank and the Inter-American Development Bank; now, for the first time since the 1920s, they could get money from private international bankers. The NICs took tens of billions a year from banks and bondholders on the off-shore markets. Latin America borrowed $50 billion in 1981 alone, at which point the region owed $300 billion to foreigners. The Third World as a whole owed $750 billion abroad, three-quarters to private financiers.[6]

Developing country debt created a strange triangle. The oil price explosion gave OPEC members far more money than they could spend, and they deposited much of it—about $150 billion between 1974 and 1980—into the world's financial markets. International bankers were eager to lend OPEC's "petrodollars," and among the principal users of these funds were the nonoil developing countries— the NOPECs, as they were called—which needed to pay for more expensive oil. Oil-importing developing nations borrowed $200 billion between 1974 and 1980 in part to pay for oil from OPEC, which deposited its earnings in the international banks, which then lent them back to the developing countries to pay for oil. This was only one aspect of Third World borrowing, but it highlights how the trends of the 1970s were not sustainable.

Borrowing did not go only to pay for oil. Many oil exporters, especially those with substantial populations such as Mexico and Indonesia, also parlayed their newfound wealth into collateral against which they could borrow heavily. The principal goal of the new loans in almost all countries, indeed, was to sustain industrial development. Tens of billions of dollars in borrowed money went to build steel mills in Brazil, shipyards in South Korea, and petrochemical plants in Mexico. Most loans went to a dozen better-off developing countries, from Brazil and Mexico to South Korea and Turkey; private bankers had no interest in the poorer nations of South Asia and Africa. From 1973 to 1981 the major borrowers broadened and deepened their manufacturing sectors. Much new investment was financed with debt that had to be paid back in foreign currency, so the NIC governments needed to increase manufactured exports. This was easy for the export-oriented NICs in East Asia, but it led traditionally closed economies, such as Brazil, to begin to encourage exports. From 1967 to 1981 the dozen big borrowers increased manufactured exports from $15 billion to $190 billion. This was a success for the countries and for their creditors, but it flooded the advanced industrialized countries with cheap manufactured imports and increased import competition for the industrial world's struggling steel, auto, textiles, and shoe industries. The export achievements of the borrowers increased trade conflict in the OECD.

The world descended into ever-greater polarization. East-West geopolitical competition heated up. Soviet troops installed a Communist government in Afghanistan, Vietnamese troops occupied Cambodia, and a virulently anti-Western Islamic revolution surged to power in Iran. Pro-Soviet regimes consolidated their power in the former Portuguese colonies in Africa, in Angola with the help of thousands of Cuban troops. A leftist government took office in formerly white-ruled Rhodesia, now Zimbabwe. In America's Caribbean backyard, revolutionaries overthrew pro-American dictators in Nicaragua and Grenada and threatened others in Guatemala and El Salvador. Polarization went both ways: China, now firmly in the American camp, turned toward Western-oriented reforms. The USSR was also threatened by the eruption of new strikes in Poland, which eventually led to the recognition of Solidarity, the first independent labor union in a Communist country.

International financial markets were just as unsettled. The Carter administration tried to stimulate the economy but succeeded only in undermining confidence in the U.S. dollar, which dropped by one-third against the yen and the deutsche mark. During the four years of the Carter administration, American banks and corporations nearly tripled their foreign investments, to $530 billion, in part because of misgivings about the country's economic future. Investors searched frantically for safe harbors, driving gold above three hundred dollars an ounce in summer 1979 and above eight hundred dollars an ounce in the winter—twenty times its Bretton Woods price of a few years earlier. The members of the European Union, in what appeared a desperate attempt to protect themselves from the crisis, launched a European Monetary System (EMS) to manage their currencies jointly and avoid the panic afflicting the dollar.

The world faced difficult times from 1973 until the early 1980s. Growth slowed, prices rose, recessions hit, and unemployment grew. Governments accustomed to the growth and prosperity of the previous thirty years seemed unable to deal with the downturn and its resulting conflicts. So they threw money at the problems. Governments in the advanced capitalist world threw money that they printed or borrowed into social spending, unemployment benefits, subsidies to businesses, and public job creation. Governments in the better-off developing countries threw money that they borrowed abroad into redoubled industrialization drives. Both strategies helped avoid further strife. Neither strategy was sustainable.

The Volcker counter-shock

On August 6, 1979, the United States turned from crisis and polarization toward transformation and resolution. On that day President Jimmy Carter installed Paul Volcker at the head of the Federal Reserve. Volcker had served in the Nixon administration, then as president of the Federal Reserve Bank of New York. He was closely associated with Wall Street and enjoyed the confidence of the international financial community. He was pragmatic and sensitive to political and business pressures, but he strongly believed in the free movement of goods and capital and strongly opposed inflation and budget deficits.

Paul Volcker could not get Cuban troops out of Angola or restore labor peace to Britain. But he calmed financial markets by changing the tenor of economic policy in the United States. Within weeks of taking over at the Fed, Volcker committed the American central bank to do whatever was necessary to bring inflation down. The Federal Reserve pushed short-term interest rates up from about 10 percent to 15 percent and eventually above 20 percent. He kept American interest rates at these extraordinarily high levels for almost three years, until late 1982. This drove the economy into two successive recessions, reduced manufacturing output and median family income by 10 percent, and raised unemployment to nearly 11 percent. But the Volcker shock got inflation below 4 percent, and it stayed roughly this low or lower for the next twenty years. In the words of one economist, this was "perhaps the most important monetary policy action since the catastrophic failure of the Federal Reserve to resist the monetary collapse of the 1930s."[7]

Volcker's massive shock to the economy pushed real (after-inflation) short-term interest rates up from near or below zero to 10 percent. This killed inflation and more broadly shifted the balance of power toward investors. Inflation and negative real interest rates had been a major burden on the financial community. Higher real interest rates increased the return on capital; financial investors who could barely keep up with inflation in the 1970s could now earn the highest profit rates in memory. Policy after 1979 strongly favored the financial community and investors. Although others in the working and middle classes were also weary of inflation and welcomed its defeat, the price was high. The end of the inflationary spiral forced companies to take a hard line on wages. Before, when prices and wages rose constantly, firms could pass them on to consumers in higher prices, confident that this would be part of a broader trend and would not lose them business. Now the knowledge that inflation had stopped meant that firms could not raise prices at will and had to control wages. In addition, the increase in the cost of borrowing forced companies to economize on other costs, such as labor. American real wages dropped by more than 10 percent between 1978 and 1982 and continued to decline even as the economy began growing again. The real wages of American workers did not begin rising for ten years, in 1993, by which time they had fallen 15 percent below 1978 levels.[8]

High interest rates quickly spread to the rest of the advanced capitalist countries. Other governments could not ignore them, for American interest rates could draw capital from all over the world. Investors would not buy German bonds at 7 percent when U.S. government bonds were earning 15 percent. Governments had a choice, though. They could keep interest rates low, allow money to flow out, and avoid the recession. This would force the national currency to decline in value as investors sold it off and also implied that inflation would continue. Such a course, however, would put governments at odds with bankers and investors, who abhorred both devaluation and inflation.

The high-interest-rate, low-inflation policy was often linked to a rightward political turn. The new Conservative government of Margaret Thatcher in Britain, which took office a few months before Volcker, embraced the new policies. A year and a half after Carter had appointed Volcker, in the midst of a recession caused by the Fed, Ronald Reagan swept into offfice with a conservative agenda similar to Thatcher's. In 1982 Germany's Christian Democrats took power, defeating the Social Democrats for the first time in nearly fifteen years.

The new macroeconomic realities imposed themselves even where there was no clear ideological shift. France and Spain voted in their first Socialist governments in nearly fifty years, and Italy got its first Socialist prime minister, but the Left and Center-Left governments faced stark choices. Their social goals were increasingly at odds with global austerity and with their membership in the European Monetary System, which tied currencies to the deutsche mark. As the Germans and their fellow EMS members (Benelux and Denmark) followed the Americans and raised interest rates, France and Italy had to decide whether to stay with their EU partners or go it alone. Businesses and others interested in European and international markets fought for the governments to follow the German example, while the Communists and left-wing socialists, including much of the labor movement, opposed this turn. After two years of conflict, in 1983 the French Socialist government opted for the EMS and austerity, and the Italians followed in 1985. Country after country fell into line with the United States, putting in place what German Chancellor Helmut Schmidt bitterly called "the highest real interest rates since the birth of Christ."[9] Growth slowed, and unemployment rose everywhere.

The debtor nations of the developing world continued to need to borrow billions. But the Volcker interest rate hikes pushed the base lending rate to which Third World commercial debts were pegged from 10 to 20 percent in two years. Real interest rates on LDC debt barely kept up with inflation between 1974 and 1980, but they shot up to 6 percent in 1981, then to 8 percent in 1982 and stayed there. Because existing debt was indexed to American interest rates, each one percentage point increase in American rates cost the Third World's debtors another four or five billion dollars a year in additional interest payments. Two other shocks compounded the impact of American policy on the Third World: The 1979–1980 oil price increase raised import costs for all the oil-poor LDCs, while the recession in the West reduced demand for developing country exports. These three factors—interest rate increases, oil price hikes, and recession in the OECD—increased the need for foreign money even as it became less available. The debtors hung on by using new loans for the oil bill and for interest payments on previously borrowed money. In the last half of 1981 Latin America borrowed a billion dollars a week, mostly to pay off existing debt.

In summer 1982 the carousel stopped. Mexico announced that it had run out of money, and within weeks private lending to the developing world dried up. The flow of funds shifted abruptly from southward to northward. In 1981 twenty billion more dollars had flowed into Latin America than flowed out; in 1983, as lending ended and governments scrambled to pay their debts, a net twenty billion dollars flowed out of Latin America. The most recent round of developing country borrowing came to a sudden, shuddering halt.

This ushered in a debt crisis of 1930s proportions.[10] Like its predecessors in the 1930s and throughout the nineteenth century, the 1980s debt crisis had a self-reinforcing nature. As in a bank panic, when lenders worried that poor country governments might not repay them, they stopped lending. This left developing country governments without a financial cushion, and in desperation they stopped payments to their creditors, thus scaring international bankers even further. The more countries ran out of money, the less bankers lent, and the less bankers lent, the more countries ran out of money. In the space of weeks some of the most rapidly growing economies in the world were suddenly cut off from the bank lending they had relied on for ten or fifteen years.

One after another the major debtor governments struggled to generate the foreign currency and government revenue needed to pay their creditors, until eventually their economies collapsed. By 1983 thirty-four developing and socialist countries were formally renegotiating their debts, and a dozen more were in serious trouble. Latin America was spending nearly half its export earnings to pay interest and principal on its foreign debt, leaving little to buy the imports it needed. The creditors organized themselves to protect their interests, creating a standard format for debt negotiations. A debtor would go to the International Monetary Fund to plan a program of macroeconomic stabilization and economic adjustment. The IMF and the debtor would agree on targets for inflation, government spending, budget deficits, and the like. If the IMF was satisfied that the government was going to change policies, the fund would lend a small amount of money, in installments, which could be halted if the government failed to meet its commitments. Private international bankers regarded an IMF agreement as a seal of approval and required debtors to go to the fund before they would renegotiate debts.

Most debtor economies remained depressed for years. The 1980s were a lost decade for Latin America: Income per person declined by 10 percent, real wages fell by at least 30 percent, and investment fell even further, while inflation rose above 1,000 percent in many countries.[11]

This lost decade witnessed two surprising developments. The first was a wave of democratization. In 1980 there were two elected civilian governments in South America; by 1990 there were no dictatorships left. The crisis led to more democratic rule in dozens more countries outside Latin America, from South Korea to Thailand, from the Philippines to Zambia. To some extent this reflected a tendency to throw out whatever government was in office during the crisis. Democratization may also have resulted from business, middle-class, and popular revulsion at how insulated authoritarian regimes had misused borrowed funds and a hope that representative government would avoid the more egregious of these mistakes.

The second outcome of the crisis was that the heavily indebted countries jettisoned import-substituting industrialization. Foreign loans had helped keep ISI in place, paying for the imported capital equipment and raw materials, subsidies, and public investments that governments needed to sustain inward-oriented industrial development. When the loans dried up, governments could not run budget deficits, so they had to stop providing costly subsidies to industrialists. Countries could not borrow to cover trade deficits and had to generate more foreign currency to service their debts, so they had no choice but to increase exports. Over five to ten years after 1982 one developing country after another liberalized trade, deregulated banks, sold off government enterprises, raised taxes and cut spending, and integrated its economy into world markets.

After the turn to anti-inflationary austerity in the OECD and the turn away from import substitution in the developing world came the greatest change of all, the collapse of communism. Conditions in China, Eastern and Central Europe, and the Soviet Union were dismal, but they had been that for quite a while. The economic problems of the late 1970s and early 1980s, however, led to a socioeconomic earthquake, in whose aftermath these countries turned away from central planning and toward international markets.

The earliest changes came in China and Vietnam, which inhabited an entirely different economic reality from the rest of the socialist bloc. Vietnam and China were among the world's poorest countries, with tiny industrial sectors lost in a sea of peasants whose living standards had barely changed in a century. By the late 1970s both countries were facing serious economic problems, and in 1979 they turned more or less simultaneously toward market reforms. The first step in both cases was a radical reform of farming, effectively turning it back to individual households.

The two countries were four-fifths rural, so simple agricultural reforms brought capitalism and markets to the vast majority of the population in one fell swoop. Within five years China's billion farmers were fully engaged in capitalist agriculture, and the real income of the average Chinese farm family had doubled. The rural reforms became the launching pad for further private and semiprivate enterprise. Farm villages, private individuals, rural and urban collectives, and other groups outside the control of the central state set up nonagricultural enterprises that, like the farms themselves, ran on market principles. Within ten years of the original agricultural measures, a million and a half of these town and village-run enterprises had fifty million employees. Between private agriculture, collective and local enterprises, and the growing number of foreign firms, almost the entire economy was outside the state sector. Even in industry, the last redoubt of government enterprises, the central state accounted for barely half of output.[12] The Chinese government did not tackle the remnants of the centrally planned system head-on but instead overwhelmed them with a proliferation of market-based successes. State-owned enterprises reformed gradually, as even the most retrograde of managers in the state sector eventually woke up to the opportunities presented by China's market economy.

The Chinese government pushed its economy vigorously toward global markets. It opened special export-oriented economic zones in coastal regions, eased the way for foreign investment, and borrowed heavily abroad. Within a decade, from 1978 to 1988, China's exports went from less than ten billion dollars to nearly fifty billion dollars, its foreign debt from under a billion to forty-two billion dollars. The new, effectively capitalist China became a major player in the world economy. The domestic results were nothing short of remarkable. In twenty years, from 1958 to 1978, Chinese output per person had grown by about a third. In the subsequent ten years, as the country turned to domestic and foreign markets, its output per person doubled. There were problems: The gap widened between rich and poor regions and people; foreign influences were not welcomed by all; a new post-Communist oligarchy arose. But it was hard to criticize a five- or sixfold increase in the rate of growth of a country whose biggest problem had long been economic stagnation.

While China boomed, the Soviet Union stagnated. Soviet output per person grew 75 percent between 1958 and 1978, twice as quickly as China's; but in the subsequent ten years, while China doubled its economic size, the Soviet economy grew by only 7 percent. Moscow could not ignore this, both for obvious economic reasons and because China was a major military adversary. The economic success of the rival to the east and its ever-closer ties to the Western capitalist world forced the Soviets to rethink their policy.

The USSR began to change after Brezhnev's death in 1982. After two interim rulers died, in 1985 Mikhail Gorbachev took power. Almost immediately, he announced the urgent need for political opening (glasnost) and economic restructuring (perestroika). Gorbachev bulled his way through entrenched interests built up over decades and put in place ever more radical economic reform measures, insisting that his goal was to modernize socialism rather than return to capitalism. He also tried to relax tensions with the West. The Soviets made it clear that they would no longer intervene in the domestic affairs of their Eastern European allies. The ruling Communists in Poland, then Hungary, followed by the rest of Comecon eased themselves out of power, by remarkably nonviolent means in all cases but Romania. In 1989 the Berlin Wall was breached, then opened, and in 1990 the two Germanys were reunified.

As Gorbachev struggled to manage what was now frankly a transition to a Western-style economy and democracy, in 1991 the USSR collapsed. Communist rule, authoritarian politics, central planning, and the Cold War all had ended, far more quickly and peacefully than anyone imagined possible. It remained to disassemble an economic and political system and build a new capitalist order, in the midst of social and economic turmoil. But the turn had been accomplished, in the Communist world as previously in the advanced capitalist and developing worlds.

The crisis of the 1970s drove political economies everywhere toward international and domestic markets; the greater the transformation, the later it started. Between 1979 and 1985 the advanced industrial countries turned from the conflict and confusion of the 1970s to financial orthodoxy and economic integration. Starting around 1985, the developing countries left fifty years of import substitution behind and moved aggressively to export, open their markets, privatize, and deregulate. The socialist economies (other than China and Vietnam) came last, after 1990, but they gave up central planning and moved toward capitalism at speeds varying from rapid to breakneck.

Globalism

Those who stood for the integration of national and global markets, and for the market more generally, had triumphed. But bringing inflation down and pushing the rate of return on investments up were a turning point, not an end point. In the OECD, victory over inflation was barely achieved when deficit spending surged so rapidly as to dwarf that of the 1970s. The Reagan administration in the United States led the way, with the greatest peacetime accumulation of government debt in history. The administration slashed taxes, bringing the top marginal rate down from 70 to 50 percent immediately, then to 38 percent a few years later. Reagan also accelerated Carter's expansion of military spending. Drastic tax cuts, increased military spending, and higher interest rates made deficits inevitable. The federal budget was in surplus from 1978 to 1981 (as adjusted for the impact of the business cycle and inflation) but then collapsed into deficits that averaged nearly two hundred billion dollars a year, over 3 percent of GDP, for Reagan's two presidential terms and his successor George H. W. Bush's single term.

Presidents Reagan and Bush drove federal government debt from under one trillion to over four trillion dollars in twelve years. They more than doubled the federal debt per person, a ratio that had declined throughout the postwar period. They also doubled federal debt as a share of GDP, from a postwar low of 33 percent in 1981 to 66 percent in 1993.[13] Most of this was due to the tax cuts, which even after subsequent reversals left the federal government with about a hundred billion dollars less every year than it otherwise would have brought in. The experience was extraordinary, as much for its economic significance as for the incongruity of conservative administrations' simultaneously preaching the virtues of small government and running breathtakingly large deficits.

The Reagan and Bush–era deficits had some clearly political roots. Tax reductions were immensely popular with the wealthy and with upper-middle-class voters for whose loyalties the Democrats and Republicans were battling. Increased military spending was also popular, both with more security-conscious members of the body politic and in parts of the country and the economy that depended heavily on defense spending. Some members of the administration believed that the tax cuts would pay for themselves in higher growth, but they did not. Some Reagan conservatives considered "their" deficits a means to limit government programs of which they disapproved: If future governments were saddled with big debts, they would not be able to expand spending.

Paul Volcker watched the process with dismay. He reflected later:

> The more starry-eyed Reaganauts argued that reducing taxes would provide a kind of magic elixir for the economy that would make the deficits go away, or at least not matter. . . . But some of their arguments made me wonder why we bothered to collect taxes at all. The more realistic advis-

ers (everything is relative) apparently thought the risk of a ballooning deficit was a reasonable price to pay for passing their radical program; any damage could be repaired later, helped by a novel theory that the way to keep spending down was not by insisting taxes be adequate to pay for it but by scaring the Congress and the American people with deficits.[14]

David Stockman, who directed Reagan's Office of Management and Budget and saw with increasing alarm the decay of attention to either, remarked bitterly a few years later that out of the experience "what we got was $1.5 trillion worth of cumulative deficits, radical deterioration of our internal and external financial health, and a political system that became so impaired, damaged, fatigued, and bloodied by coping with it year after year that it now functions like the parliament of a banana republic."[15]

The Reagan deficits were part of an international expansion of government budget deficits. By the late 1980s growth in North America, Europe, and Japan was back on track, inflation was low and declining, but budget deficits were very high. They were typically 3 or 4 percent of GDP in the largest countries, 5 percent in Canada, the Netherlands, and Spain, 9 percent in Ireland, 11 percent in Greece and Italy. Governments were particularly attracted to deficit spending for two reasons. The first was a basic fact of macroeconomic policy: that fiscal and monetary policies can substitute for one another. A government can try to stimulate the economy either by looser money or by running deficits (or both). By the middle 1980s OECD governments had stopped trying to affect their economies with inflationary monetary policy. However, they could still use fiscal policy: taxing, borrowing, and spending. The decline of active monetary policy was accompanied by a rise in the use of active fiscal policy. This was especially clear in the countries of the European Union that tied their currencies to the deutsche mark and handed over their monetary policies to the German central bank. The Irish, Dutch, and Italian governments could not change their own interest rates, but they could borrow billions to keep their economies going. The American experience was similar: Monetary policy focused on keeping inflation low, but fiscal policy was still available to a government that wanted to pump up political support.

Another source of the deficits of the 1980s and 1990s was that the growth of world financial markets made deficit financing much easier. In 1973 the total pool of capital available on international (offshore) financial markets was $160 billion, and some $35 billion was lent out every year. At the time these seemed impressive numbers, for there had been next to no international lending for nearly half a century; but by the early 1980s international capital markets were about ten times larger, at $1.5 trillion, and international lending was about $300 billion a year. The global financial system continued to grow, and by the early 1990s it held over $5 trillion and was lending out over $1 trillion a year.

OECD governments could finance deficit spending very easily from this enormous pool of capital. Previously, in financially closed economies, deficits had to be borrowed at home, and what was lent to governments was not available to be lent to the private sector. Government borrowing raised interest rates, increased the cost of capital to businesses, and "crowded out" private investment, as the expression went. A government such as that of Ireland, whose borrowing needs were often over 15 percent of its GDP, could not possibly borrow only at home. Now governments could draw on a large pool of foreign capital, so deficit spending did not come at the expense of domestic private lending or investment. With money readily available, there was no need for higher interest rates. The country could eat its cake and have it too, by borrowing from abroad to cover deficits. By the middle 1980s a hundred billion dollars a year were flowing into the United States from abroad, largely in loans to the U.S. government. Sometime in 1988 the United States became a net debtor to the rest of the world for the first time since World War One. The American economy depended on deficit spending, which in turn relied on foreign money.

Eventually the debt would have to be repaid. For a politician, however, eventually is a long time, certainly farther in the future than the next election. Nonetheless, as deficits rose, so did concern—especially in the financial community—that government borrowing was becoming a habit. Financial investors began to complain that continued deficits were unsustainable and to warn that governments needed to "put their houses in order." Governments that had spent great political capital regaining the confidence of investors by fighting inflation now faced new complaints about deficits.

The United States' reliance on foreign funds also had some negative domestic effects. Money that came into the country from overseas increased demand for the U.S. currency; foreigners lent to the U.S. government by buying Treasury securities, which meant buying dollars. This drove the value of the dollar up by more than 50 percent in just five years. The strong dollar of 1981–1986 allowed Americans to buy foreign goods cheaply. But it devastated American manufacturers and farmers, who faced competition from dramatically cheaper foreign goods. In 1980 American industries exported 26 percent of what they produced, while 20 percent of the manufactured goods Americans consumed was imported, a manufactured trade surplus equal to 6 percent of GDP. Five years later, American manufactured exports were down to 18 percent of production, and imports were 32 percent of consumption, a deficit of 14 percent of GDP. In five years the share of imports in American consumption of a wide range of goods—shoes, machine tools, clothing, computers, home appliances, home furniture—doubled. As overall employment rose 10 percent, the number of manufacturing jobs fell 5 percent. Formal requests for trade protection doubled, as American industrialists and farmers complained that they could not compete so long as the dollar was so high.[16] Foreign governments expressed concern that the dollar's rise destabilized financial markets. The effects of the strong dollar helped convince the U.S. government of the need to cooperate with other financial powers to bring the dollar down and of the desirability of coming to grips with the American budget deficits.

The developed countries began reducing deficits in the early 1990s, raising taxes and cutting spending. In many cases the fiscal retrenchment appeared as, and sometimes was, an attack on the social democratic welfare state. Governments cut some social programs, but the ultimate result was to stabilize, not reduce, the size of government. By the late 1990s the typical industrial country's government was still spending over 40 percent of GDP; but budget deficits were down to a fraction of their earlier levels, and many countries, including the United States, were running substantial budget surpluses.

There were three distinct macroeconomic phases during the thirty years after the end of Bretton Woods. The 1970s were a decade of high and rising inflation. In the 1980s the developed countries defeated inflation but built up enormous budget deficits. During the 1990s governments reduced or closed these deficits. By the end of the century most developed countries had low inflation, small, if any, budget deficits, and a substantial public sector and an extensive net of social insurance programs.

Regionalism and globalism

As they revised their macroeconomic policies, the developed countries also redoubled their integration into the world economy. They started with a renewal of regional integration. The European Union (EU) added new members south and north during the 1980s and 1990s: Greece, Spain, Portugal, Austria, Sweden, and Finland. It also deepened its economic integration. In the early 1980s, with the continent mired in Europessimism and Eurosclerosis, the members of the EU began planning a radical merger of their markets. Governments and big business agreed that a fully unified European market was needed to help rejuvenate the European economy. This consensus cut across ideologies and was spearheaded by the Center-Right government of Germany, the Socialist government of France, and the Conservative government of Britain. Economic sectors that had new technologies, streamlined organization, and the world economy in their sights hoped for a relaunched regional integration.

EU members approved the Single European Act in 1986 and put it in place gradually between then and 1992. Plans for a single market moved more rapidly than anticipated. With powerful economic interests behind the process, all sorts of barriers dropped. The union eliminated or harmonized the regulation of investment, migration, product and production standards, professional licensing, and many other economic activities. By 1993 the EU was in some ways a more integrated unit than the American states or Canadian provinces, for EU member states had given up many of the powers that North American federal units retain.

The economic and political momentum created by the formation of a single market pulled EU members toward an even more ambitious proposal, the unification of their currencies. In 1991 EU members adopted a new Treaty of European Union, generally known as the Maastricht Treaty after the small city in the Netherlands where it was signed. The treaty called for more cooperation on several dimensions, including broad foreign policy, and it increased the political weight of the European Parliament, an elected body that is the legislature of the European Union. The centerpiece of the Maastricht Treaty, however, was monetary union. In 1999 the new common European Central Bank introduced a common currency, the euro. Three countries remained outside the euro zone: the United Kingdom, Sweden, and Denmark.

Nonetheless, the European Union now had all the economic hallmarks of a country: a single market, a single currency and central bank, a common trade policy, and common economic regulations on such matters as antitrust and the environment. For all economic intents, Western Europe was one economic unit—indeed, by most measures, the largest economic unit in the world, bigger than the United States and more than twice the size of Japan. In addition, there were more than a dozen countries around its borders at various stages of accession to the union, from Estonia to Malta, the Czech Republic to Turkey.

North American businesses also saw regional integration as a way to improve *their* competitive positions. First, the United States created a Caribbean Basin Initiative that gave countries in and around the Caribbean privileged access to the American market. The next step was northward. The United States and Canada had long-standing investment and trade ties, and in 1987 they signed a free trade agreement. This started them on the road to a European-style single market, albeit without the concomitant political and foreign policy implications.

Five years later Mexico joined in, and in 1994 the North American Free Trade Agreement went into effect. Over the next ten years NAFTA removed virtually all barriers to the movement of goods, capital, and services among the three countries. The result was the gradual creation of a single North American market, although immigration was excluded from this liberalization. NAFTA pioneered in bringing developed and developing countries into a free trade area. Many countries in Latin America wanted to affiliate with NAFTA. and some even adopted the U.S. dollar to replace their own currency. There were serious prospects for extending NAFTA to countries in and around the Caribbean Basin and other parts of Latin America.

At the same time, the world's third-largest trading bloc was formed in South America. Between 1985 and 1990 Brazil and Argentina negotiated a trade area that eventually included Uruguay and Paraguay as full members and Chile and Bolivia as associates. The Southern Common Market—Mercosur in Spanish—was in place by 1994. Among the four members and two associates, it drew together 250 million people with a combined output of nearly two trillion dollars—fourth only to the EU, NAFTA, and Japan as a global trading power. As with the EU and NAFTA, governments and businesses in Brazil and Argentina were eager to combine their markets to provide a larger home base from which to compete on world markets. By combining forces, the Mercosur members also hoped to attract more foreign investment, as global companies were more interested in a larger combined market than in any one of the four members alone. As in the developed world, Mercosur marked the definitive victory of those economic interests that saw their future in exporting, borrowing abroad, or partnering with foreign companies.

With regional integration the antechamber to broader liberalization, in 1994 the long-stalled trade negotiations of the Uruguay Round were concluded. The new agreements extended trade liberalization to new issues and drew in new and future members from the developing and formerly Communist nations. The Uruguay Round also created a new institution, the World Trade Organization, to replace the GATT. The WTO, unlike the GATT, is a permanent organization with powers of its own, largely to mediate trade disputes. Its founding consolidated the open trading system.

Global finance and national financial crises

As trade was liberalized, governments of developed countries also removed the last barriers to the free flow of money and capital, and many developing countries reduced controls on cross-border investment. By the late 1990s international financial activities were so intertwined with domestic financial markets that for all intents and purposes there was one global financial system that included all the developed countries and many developing and formerly Communist countries. Pensioners and small investors routinely included foreign stock and bond funds in their portfolios, even when the foreign securities were Chilean, Czech, or Korean. Most countries also liberalized domestic banking, leading to a wave of mergers of the world's leading financial institutions.

The economic internationalists predominated at a truly international level, as most developing and former Communist countries now fully participated in the world economy. Developing and transitional nations integrated into international markets and reduced government involvement in their domestic markets. Despite the difficulties of macroeconomic stabilization, adjustment, economic reforms, trade liberalization, and privatization, most governments stayed the course. Governments all over Central and Eastern Europe, Latin America, Africa, and Asia reduced trade barriers, welcomed foreign investment, implemented austerity measures to bring inflation and budget deficits down, and sold off government enterprises.

By the middle 1990s a host of middle-income nations—countries like Mexico and Brazil, Hungary and Lithuania, Korea and Thailand—had converged toward the international economy and the market. Almost all were also under democratic civilian rule. The return of developing and transitional countries as international borrowers symbolized their success. The heavily indebted countries had worked for a decade to overcome the crisis that began in 1982, and now they regained access to foreign loans.

The freewheeling finance of the 1990s was worlds apart from that of the 1970s, when a few better-off LDCs and centrally planned economies negotiated big loans from a few dozen huge international banks. Now governments and corporations in developing and transition economies dipped directly into a swirling international financial system. Mutual funds, investment trusts, and banks in the rich countries brought small investors, retirees, union pension funds—anyone with even modest savings—into direct contact with stocks and bonds from Bangkok to Budapest to Buenos Aires, from Seoul to St. Petersburg to São Paulo. A phalanx of countries in Latin America and East Asia, having graduated from being poor to less developed, then to Third World and newly industrialized, were now simply emerging markets, emerging just as a new product might. The same was true of the former centrally planned economies, which went from central planning to transitional and then, again, to emerging.

International investors now included dozens of countries in Latin America, East Asia, and Central and Eastern Europe in their portfolios as a matter of course. These countries had attained something approaching full membership in the global economic order. Mutual and pension funds might now consider Mexico, Hungary, and Korea for investment portfolios as routinely as, say, Siemens and Unilever. Free trade and the WTO, financial integration, and the emergence of the emerging markets reflected the consolidation of a new economic reality, the general acceptance of world markets for goods and capital—*globalization,* in a buzzword.

But freewheeling trade, money, and finance sometimes careened into economic crises of frightening speed and size. Countries and companies tightly tied into world markets were more susceptible to international financial forces; governments and firms were held to more rigorous global standards than they were used to. With hundreds of billions of dollars sloshing around the globe, from country to country, in minutes, investors' views of country and corporate creditworthiness were essential. Governments and managers had to worry much more than before about how their actions would be interpreted by domestic and foreign investors, who could be skittish and fickle.

International competition weakened some major banking systems. The savings and loan crisis in the United States was an early example. Small financial institutions made very risky loans as they struggled to compete with larger international counterparts, while regulators and politicians delayed clamping down on the politically influential bankers. Eventually the savings and loan industry disintegrated, requiring an infusion of at least two hundred billion dollars in taxpayers' money. Scandinavia, Japan, and other nations were hit by similar collapses of previously sheltered financial systems.

The developing country debt crisis of the early 1980s turned out to be only a hint of how quickly and completely modern financial markets could turn from euphoria to collapse. The new round of crises focused on exchange rates, and began with a currency market attack on European monetary unification. Since about 1985 most of the members of the European Union had held their currencies fixed against the deutsche mark. New EU members Spain and Portugal, prospective members Sweden, Norway, and Finland, and reluctant Europeans like the United Kingdom all had joined the German-led currency bloc, which after the 1991 Maastricht Treaty moved toward a single currency. But even as more European nations signed up for the Economic and Monetary Union (EMU) and a common currency, the apparently stable monetary arrangement collapsed.

When Germany unified, the country's monetary authorities were concerned that massive government spending on its east would lead to inflation, so it raised interest rates quickly and steeply. This forced other European countries whose currencies were tied to the deutsche mark to raise their interest rates as well, a move that shoved them into a recession made in Germany. German policy confronted European governments with a stark choice between continued membership in the deutsche mark bloc, on the one hand, and avoiding a recession, on the other. The rest of Europe was already mired in recession and double-digit unemployment, and there was little political support for more austerity. To make matters worse, in June 1992 Danish voters turned down a referendum to ratify the Maastricht Treaty on EMU, and public opinion polls indicated that French voters might do the same in September. If the Maastricht Treaty was dead, governments had less reason to keep their currencies fixed against the deutsche mark.

In the summer of 1992 currency traders began anticipating that Britain and Italy would not maintain their currencies' pegs to the deutsche mark. Investors sold off their holdings of these currencies, which only intensified speculation that the pound and the lira would be devalued. The British and Italian governments bumped interest rates up; but eventually the cost seemed extreme, and both devalued their currencies. Foreign exchange traders attacked other currencies in the months that followed. Governments tried to hold on to the link to the deutsche mark—at one point the Swedish central bank pushed interest rates to 500 percent—but the cost was too high.[17] Eventually Ireland, Spain, Portugal, Sweden, Norway, and Finland all devalued their currencies, and it appeared that progress toward monetary union had been reversed.

The European crisis was short-lived, and the region's economies rebounded after they had delinked from German monetary policy. The damage to monetary unification was repaired quickly and effectively enough to move forward with plans for the euro. But the enormous resources of international financial markets had been brought to bear to attack currencies deemed unreliable and to force governments to devalue and change other policies.

Within a year this point was brought home to Mexico.[18] With NAFTA in effect, the Mexican government wanted to hold the peso steady against the U.S. dollar. Also, in the run-up to a hotly contested presidential election the government wanted to keep the peso strong and Mexican incomes high. The economy grew quickly and drew in over thirty billion dollars in foreign investment in 1993. But in January 1994 a rebellion broke out in southern Mexico, and in March one of the ruling party's leading presidential candidates was assassinated. As the election year of 1994 wore on, the government struggled to maintain its commitment to the peso, both to uphold its reputation and because the strong peso increased the purchasing power of Mexican consumers.

But currency traders did not believe that the government could hold to its promises. Investors got more and more skittish, and the narrowness of the ruling Partido Revolucionario Institucional's victory in the August 1994 presidential election was not reassuring. The PRI's secretary-general was assassinated in September, further scaring investors. As the new government took office in December, currency traders sensed they could take a "one-way bet" against the peso: If it was devalued, they won, and if it wasn't, they didn't lose. As the speculators sold off the currency, the government spent billions, but a few days before Christmas 1994 it floated the peso, which promptly sank. Yet another government had been forced to devalue its currency.

Mexico, unlike Europe, was hit by a banking crisis as a result of the currency collapse. When the peso was strong, many banks and companies borrowed heavily in dollars. The devaluation of the peso triggered mass bankruptcies as the real cost of dollar debts soared. The peso dropped in the space of a month from about thirty cents to about fifteen cents, so the real burden of a $1 million foreign debt on a Mexican company doubled from about 3.3 million to 6.6 million pesos. Many indebted firms collapsed, followed by their domestic bankers, and within weeks the country was in the throes of a financial panic. The country plunged into a deep crisis, as output dropped 6 percent, and inflation soared above 50 percent. Greater catastrophe was averted only when creditor governments, led by the United States, along with the IMF and other international financial institutions came through with tens of billions of dollars in distress lending to pull Mexico through the trough of the crisis. Still the fallout of the Mexican crisis, picturesquely called the tequila effect, was felt all over Latin America, which plunged into recession.

The next round of currency and financial crises was the most dramatic. Most of the countries of East Asia, especially Korea, Thailand, Malaysia, and Indonesia, were models of financial orthodoxy and conservative social policies: minimal inflation, small budget deficits, low levels of social spending, and few labor rights. And in 1997 the East Asian economies were booming. Their apparently endless potential drew in foreign money: Thailand's foreign debt tripled from thirty to ninety billion dollars in three years to 1996, while Indonesia's doubled from twenty-five to fifty billion dollars. During the early 1990s about fifty billion dollars a year flowed into East Asia from global financial markets, with tens of billions more in direct investment from multinational corporations. The prosperity brought with it higher prices that made exporting less profitable, so that much of the new investment was—as usual in periods of financial euphoria—concentrated in real estate, commerce, and finance itself. By 1996 and early 1997 exports were lagging, inflation was rising, and banks were taking on more and more debt. Soon investors began to anticipate devaluations and started selling off East Asian currencies.

Despite assurances from governments, the IMF, and other international financial leaders, investors continued to get out of Asia. In a now-familiar spiral, the flow became a flood, then a deluge, then a panic. The sell-off spread from Thailand and the Philippines to Indonesia and Malaysia, then to Taiwan and Korea. The size and efficiency of international financial markets seemed to facilitate the attacks, by making it remarkably easy for investors to speculate against government attempts to defend their currencies. Joseph Stiglitz, then chief economist at the World Bank, gave an example of the process:

> Assume a speculator goes to a Thai bank, borrows 24 billion baht, which, at the original exchange rate, can be converted into $1 billion. A week later the exchange rate falls; instead of there being 24 baht to the dollar, there are now 40 baht to the dollar. He takes $600 million, converting it back to baht, getting 24 billion baht to repay the loan. The remaining $400 million is his profit—a tidy return for one week's work, and the investment of little of his own money. . . . As perceptions that a devaluation is imminent grow, the chance to make money becomes irresistible and speculators from around the world pile in to take advantage of the situation.[19]

Within weeks of the initial attack the currencies of Korea, the Philippines, and Malaysia had dropped by 40 percent, that of Thailand by 50 percent, and of Indonesia by 80 percent. Money ran out of these economies as fast as it had run in: The $50 billion annual inflow of the early 1990s turned into an outflow of over $230 billion between 1997 and 1999. Stock prices collapsed by 80 and 90 percent, even more in the formerly booming real estate market; by the end of 1997 shares in the Thai property sector were down 98 percent from their 1993 high.[20] After years of extraordinary growth—10 percent a year was common—the economies of Indonesia, Thailand, and Malaysia contracted by 15, 10, and 8 percent respectively in a matter of months. It would be years before they would recover their precrisis levels. The backwash eventually helped drive Russia and Brazil into similar crises.

The world's financial leaders saw the Latin American, East Asian, Russian, Turkish, and other crises of the 1990s as threats to the international economic order. International financial organizations and creditor governments mobilized over $50 billion for Mexico in 1995, almost $120 billion for the three principal Asian crisis nations (Indonesia, Korea, and

Thailand) in 1997 and 1998, and another $70 billion for Russia and Brazil in 1998 and 1999. Critics charged that taxpayers were being forced to bail out foolish investors and bad governments, but financial leaders insisted on the need for a quick response to avoid financial contagion.

Problems and all, the end of the century was reminiscent of its beginning, dominated by globe-straddling markets. The world economy had, after a tortuous journey of nearly one hundred years, been reintegrated. Trade was nearly twice as important to national economies as it had been at the turn of the twentieth century. Foreign investment was immeasurably greater, and global financial markets swamped national markets. Goods and money moved around the world faster than ever before and in much greater quantities. The global capitalism of the start of the century had returned.

17

Globalizers Victorious

In summer and early fall of 1997 Malaysia faced the gravest economic crisis in its history. Prime Minister Mahathir bin Mohamad blamed international financiers. On July 24 Mahathir charged bitterly, "Anyone with a few billion dollars can destroy all the progress we have made." The problem was an undue attachment to globalization, which allowed currency markets to drive down the value of the Malaysian ringgit. "We are told," he said, "we must open up, that trade and commerce must be totally free. Free for whom? For rogue speculators. For anarchists wanting to destroy weak countries in their crusade for open societies, to force us to submit to the dictatorship of international manipulators."[1]

Trouble had started when the currency of Thailand came under speculative pressures in early summer. On July 2, after months of desperate measures, the Thai authorities devalued the currency. Within a few days the Philippines, Malaysia, Singapore, and Indonesia faced attacks on their currencies; eventually Vietnam, Hong Kong, Taiwan, and Korea joined the list of victims. By September 1997, when the World Bank and IMF held their annual meeting in Hong Kong, all of East and Southeast Asia was engulfed in a financial and economic crisis that threatened decades of economic progress.

Mahathir took his case directly to the IMF and World Bank meeting.

"Society must be protected from unscrupulous profiteers," he told the delegates and financiers. "I am saying that currency trading is unnecessary, unproductive, and immoral. It should be stopped. It should be made illegal." The country he had led since 1981 had made substantial economic progress in those years. The economy had tripled in size; output per person had doubled. These achievements were under attack by "the great fund managers who have now come to be the people to decide who should prosper and who shouldn't."[2]

The root of the problem, Mahathir said, was the subjection of developing countries to the whims of global markets. "All along," he complained, "we had tried to comply with the wishes of the rich and the mighty. . . . We did all that we were told to do. But when the big funds use their massive weight in order to move the shares up and down at will and make huge profits by their manipulations then it is too much to expect us to welcome them, especially when their profits result in massive losses for ourselves." Financial openness had gone too far and had served only one purpose: "[T]he currency traders have become rich, very very rich through making other people poor."[3]

Prime Minister Mahathir attached names to the faceless international markets trying to destroy the economy he ruled. He aimed his charges of immorality at George Soros, one of the world's most prominent financiers. "The poor people in these countries will suffer," Mahathir said, "and these are the people who have to be protected from George Soros, who has so much money and power but is totally thoughtless."[4] For months Mahathir had lashed out at Soros and other "ultra-rich people," whose "wealth must come from impoverishing others, from taking what others have in order to enrich themselves."[5]

The target of the Malaysian prime minister's assault answered the charges the next day. "Dr. Mahathir's suggestion yesterday to ban currency trading," said currency trader Soros, "is so inappropriate that it does not deserve serious consideration. Interfering with the convertibility of capital at a moment like this is a recipe for disaster. Dr. Mahathir is a menace to his own country."[6]

Soros spoke out for global capitalism. "There can be no doubt," he said, "that global integration has brought tremendous benefits. Not only the benefits of the international division of labor which are so clearly proven by the theory of comparative advantage, but also dynamic benefits such as the economies of scale and the rapid spread of innovations from one country to another. . . . Equally important are the non-economic benefits, the freedom of choice associated with the international movement of goods, capital, and people, and the freedom of thought associated with the international movement of ideas."[7]

But Soros was only an investment fund manager, while Mahathir was a national leader and a guiding light of the Third World's nonaligned movement. Over the following year Mahathir steered a nationalist course. In September 1998 he sacked his finance minister, deputy prime minister, and designated successor, Anwar Ibrahim, over Anwar's support for financial integration. Mahathir imposed capital and currency controls on the Malaysian economy and stepped up his attacks on international financiers. He charged the unfortunate Anwar with a bizarre array of corrupt practices and homosexual behavior, and Anwar was convicted a few months later.

In another era the vitriolic Mahathir-Soros exchanges and the Malaysian prime minister's nationalistic rhetoric might have presaged long-lasting measures to turn the economy away from global markets. Yet within a couple of years the episode had largely been forgotten. After a severe recession the Malaysian economy began growing again. Despite the capital and currency controls, Malaysia continued to rely heavily on the international economy. Mahathir was indeed careful to avoid a blanket condemnation of global capitalism. "We want to embrace borderlessness," he said, and "We have always welcomed foreign investments, including speculation." It was just that "we still need to protect ourselves from self-serving rogues and international brigandage."[8] Despite the vehemence of Mahathir's economic nationalism, he never really questioned the goal of economic openness. Despite the great shock that international markets administered to the East Asian economies and the wave of crises the shock caused, the advance of global economic integration was barely slowed. How and why had international markets overcome their association with "self-serving rogues" and devastating crises to gain acceptance by almost every government on earth?

New technologies, new ideas

Dizzying technical change in the late twentieth century strengthened supporters of global economic integration. Innovations in transportation and telecommunications shrank the costs of international exchange. Supertankers and containers cheapened oceangoing shipping; goods that had been prohibitively expensive to ship across the Pacific or Atlantic were now common cargo. The price of shipping a ton of cargo dropped by three-quarters over the course of the century, and better refrigeration and air transport allowed producers to ship raspberries and roses across oceans economically. The introduction in 1970 of jumbo jets carrying more than four hundred people and the subsequent deregulation of airline routes transformed flying from a luxury to an ordinary expense for many in the industrialized world; the real cost of air passage dropped 90 percent from 1930 to 2000. Satellites and fiber-optic cables reduced the cost of long-distance communication to a fraction of former rates. In the 1920s the average American worker would have had to work three weeks to pay for a five-minute telephone call from New York to London; in 1970 the same call would have cost eight hours' wages, by 2000, about fifteen minutes. The Internet gave hundreds of millions of computer users instantaneous access to information from around the world. Cellular telephones and other wireless devices allowed constant contact among business partners, families, and friends.

The most striking technological advances of the last quarter of the twentieth century were in microelectronics. In the 1950s producers and consumers marveled at the transistor, a component smaller than a postage stamp that replaced vacuum tubes as the backbone of electrical appliances. Transistorized radios, televisions, and production equipment put previously unimaginable power into tiny packages. All this was as nothing compared with the microchip invented in the late 1960s, a silicon wafer on which transistors and other components could be printed as integrated circuits. By the middle 1970s chips a few millimeters square could be inscribed with two thousand transistors, making possible handheld calculating machines with more power than had been packed into the room-size vacuum tube computers of the 1940s. By the end of the century microchips were holding over a billion transistors each; a thousand-dollar personal computer was more potent than anything available to the largest corporations and governments in the 1970s—at about one ten-thousandth of the price.[9] Miniaturization allowed for cellular telephones, handheld computing and communications devices, and other powerful tiny machines.

The new computing and telecommunications encouraged international economic integration. They reduced the costs of trading and investing and of monitoring overseas interests. In addition, some of the most important component parts of the new high-tech sectors were intangible—software and programming, for example—and it would be technically difficult to impede cross-border trade in them. Finally, the vast research and development and related requirements of the high technology industries meant that profitability required extremely large-scale production or distribution, typically only available by taking advantage of global markets.

The new inventions had their most powerful globalizing impact on finance. Massive computing power and inexpensive telecommunications made it easier and faster to move money around the world and harder for governments to control these flows. Modern telecommunications sped access to the offshore markets, allowing an astronomical growth of international financial transactions. By the end of the century *daily* foreign exchange transactions were $1.5 trillion. Many transactions were purely speculative, drawing the fire of such politicians as Prime Minister Mahathir and leading such critics as British writer Susan Strange to write of casino capitalism.[10] The huge increase in overall transactions was part of a more general expansion of international finance. International bankers and investors widely applied the new technologies, which helped knit together global financial markets. Financial transactions across borders and oceans became as easy as domestic business.

On one level, these developments did not fundamentally change international trade and investment from conditions of the beginning of the twentieth century. The telegraph allowed nearly instantaneous communication from market to market; ground and water transportation was roughly as fast in 1900 as in 2000. However, the cost of transportation and telecommunications had dropped remarkably. The Internet grew astronomically; by 2001 more information could be transmitted in a second over a single cable than in 1997 had been sent over the entire Internet in a month.[11] These technological changes made international economic involvement very attractive and militated against a return to protectionism.

Technological change alone could not secure national commitments to world markets; continued growth in the world economy was important to global integration. The great technological advances of the interwar years did not stave off descent into autarky in the 1930s; the appeal of the automobile, phonograph, and radio could not prevent the collapse of world trade and investment. Over the first, worst years of the Great Depression, from 1928 to 1933, when world trade shrank by more than half, economic openness was unattractive or downright dangerous.

Even countries that tried to keep up their foreign economic ties were bucking powerful economic tides.

But even during the troubled 1970s and 1980s, international finance and trade grew faster than national economies. Economies stagnated in the 1970s, but world trade tripled between 1973 and 1979; even with inflation taken into account, this was a very substantial increase. The growth in international finance and investment was even more striking. In the 1930s cross-border lending and investment essentially stopped, but from the early 1970s to the early 1980s new foreign investment by multinational corporations soared from about $15 billion to nearly $100 billion a year, while international lending went from about $25 billion to about $300 billion a year. International financial markets grew from $160 billion in 1973 to $3 trillion in 1985. The availability of unimaginable sums of money, with hundreds of billions of dollars lent out every year, held most countries' interest in the benefits of economic openness.

Latin America had powerfully different experiences with international finance in the 1930s and the 1970s. In the 1930s there was effectively no new foreign investment in the region, whether by multinational corporations or by international lenders. By contrast, during the crisis years between the early 1970s and the early 1980s new foreign lending to Latin America accelerated from half a billion to fifteen billion dollars a year; the region's debt to private lenders went from under thirty billion dollars in 1973 to over three hundred billion dollars in 1983. New investment in Latin America by multinational corporations grew as well, from a billion to five billion dollars a year. The conditions of the 1930s made it futile to maintain international economic ties, since there was next to nothing to tie to. But the enticements offered by the world economy in the 1970s were more seductive than they had been for the previous fifty years. This drew governments toward international economic integration, even in developing and centrally planned economies where commitment to economic openness was weak at best.

New technologies and flourishing international trade and finance were not sufficient, on their own, to confront entrenched ideologies, political positions, and interests. Since 1945, after all, the reigning consensus, certainly in the import-substituting LDCs and the semiautarkic centrally planned economies (CPEs) and even in the social democracies of the industrialized West, had been guarded in its enthusiasm for markets. Supporters of redoubled economic integration faced the longstanding objections of those for whom restrictions on markets were desirable ways to achieve social and political goals.

In the 1980s, however, a new ideological wave swept the world. Politicians, analysts, and interest groups attacked government involvement in the economy after generations of general acceptance. Their preferred macroeconomic policies were often joined together under the rubric of "monetarism." They also pushed to privatize or deregulate companies owned or controlled by the government. The backlash against state involvement in the economy was associated with the conservative governments of Ronald Reagan and Margaret Thatcher and with belief in what Reagan called "the magic of the marketplace."

The new view had clear prescriptions. It called for strong measures to beat inflation. This hostility was associated with the increasing academic prominence of monetarists, who held that inflation was entirely the result of the government's printing more money than necessary. Monetarism harkened back to pre-Keynesian arguments that government manipulation of the money supply could have at best a short-term impact on the economy but in the long run would only lead to higher prices. The scholarly argument was more subtle, and the differences with Keynesians less evident, for both approaches allowed governments to use monetary policy to reduce the impact of such adverse events as recessions and depressions. But where Keynesians welcomed government management of the macroeconomy, monetarists like Nobel laureate Milton Friedman distrusted it. Friedman and other monetarists wanted governments to increase the money supply only to keep up with the growth of the economy, rather than use it to try to alleviate temporary economic problems. They rejected the loose monetary policies of the 1970s, when governments allowed inflation to grow for fear that the alternative, high unemployment, would be worse. Monetarists argued that inflation itself was corrosive and called for a new government commitment to bring inflation down.

Anti-inflationary verve was linked to a belief that economic problems should be dealt with by getting the government out of the economy, rather than by imposing more government macroeconomic management. The previous consensus embraced public programs and government regulation, but the new view advocated lower taxes, less spending, and fewer regulations. In the United States supporters of supply-side economics argued that tax reductions would increase growth so much that they would actually raise government revenue, for a smaller share of a larger pie is better than a larger share of a smaller pie.

The new view urged governments to privatize or deregulate large portions of the economy. Governments in the industrialized world sold off hundreds of businesses they had long owned—a trillion dollars' worth of privatization during the 1990s. Western Europe's governments sold four hundred billion dollars in telephone companies, steel mills, electrical utilities, banks, and other companies to new private owners. At the same time, governments drastically revised their control of private firms. The movement for deregulation began in the United States in the middle 1970s. Over the next ten years the Carter and Reagan administrations cut by two-thirds the share of the economy covered by tight regulatory controls: air, rail, and road transport; telecommunications; petroleum and natural gas; finance. Other industrial countries followed, deregulating everything from telephone companies and airlines to stockbrokers.

By the end of the 1990s the industrial economies were freer of government control than they had been since the 1930s. This triggered an extraordinary consolidation of large private firms. In 2000, $3.5 trillion in mergers were announced around the world, about half in the United States and most of the rest in Western Europe. This was about five times the 1990 level, which had been thought of as high at the time.[12] Mergers, formerly almost always contained within national boundaries, were increasingly international; in 2000 about one-quarter of all merger activity was across borders. The $203 billion acquisition by Vodaphone (UK) of Mannesmann (Germany) in 2000 involved as much money as *all* the international mergers and acquisitions carried out in 1991, 1992, and 1993 *combined*.[13]

Deregulation and privatization were both cause and consequence of technical change and global economic integration. The most commonly deregulated or privatized industries—finance, telecommunications, transportation—had experienced major technological advances or big increases in the importance of global markets, or both. New technologies made older, regulated or government-owned sectors obsolete, and the global market opened rich vistas for previously insular national firms. In banking, for example, increased global financial activity in the 1960s and 1970s, coupled with rapid technical change, led governments to deregulate and privatize national financial systems in the 1980s and 1990s. Reinvigorated financial markets in turn redoubled the pace of international integration and technological innovation.

The new point of view, variously called free market, neoliberal, or orthodox, embraced anti-inflationary austerity, tax and spending cuts, privatization, and deregulation. The "Washington Consensus," as it was tagged by economist John Williamson, was soon the organizing principle for most discussions of economic policy.[14] The Washington

Consensus resonated with increasing force in the developing world as it struggled through the debt and growth crises of the 1980s and in the Communist world as it moved away from central planning in the 1990s. By the end of the century there was more agreement on economic doctrine than at any time since 1914. Communist, radical, developmentalist, and populist alternatives to orthodoxy were weak or nonexistent; it was difficult to find supporters of planning, import substitution, or widespread state ownership anywhere in the world. There was disagreement "inside the tent" among market-oriented thinkers, but few questioned the general superiority of markets as mechanisms of economic allocation.

Globalizing interests

The global sweep of market-oriented orthodoxy may have appeared an ideological hurricane, but the turn toward markets had tangible sources in politics and economics. The change in ideas was more *result* than cause; conceptual change followed material change. The victory of monetarism over Keynesianism is one example of how ideology could mask pragmatic motivations. When Federal Reserve Chairman Paul Volcker announced in October 1979 that the American central bank would target the money supply rather than interest rates, this was widely trumpeted by supporters as a triumph of monetarist theory. Monetarists thought of the rate of growth of the money supply as "their" key policy target. However, Volcker's reasons were far more down-to-earth. Changing Fed operating techniques to "focus on the money supply" was, he explained, "a way of telling the public that we meant business," in order to "have a chance of affecting ordinary people's behavior." Nobody at the central bank had any academic illusions about what the change in procedure meant in practice. "The basic message we tried to convey was simplicity itself," said Volcker. "We meant to slay the inflationary dragon"even if it meant extremely high interest rates and a slowed economy.[15] But the ostensible turn toward monetarist theory provided an intellectual patina for what was in fact a simple, if dramatic, change in monetary policy. Popular discussions of the new austerity measures were peppered with references to "monetarism," taken to mean stringent inflation fighting, but this bore little or no resemblance to the theory as elaborated by academic economists. This is not to say that economic ideas had no effect, only that it is hard to trace the policy revisions of the 1980s and 1990s to any significant shift in economic theory.

Economic policy changed because politics changed. Two developments were especially important. First, there was an increase in the size and cohesion of firms and industries that wanted international economic integration and that wanted governments to change their involvement in national economies. Second, there was growing popular concern about high unemployment, slow growth, and inflation, which left voters and others open to new policies.

By the early 1980s much of the public had lost patience with rising prices. The populations of Western Europe and North America had not experienced inflation during the first twenty-five postwar years, and when it began to creep upward in the early 1970s, many were caught off guard. As the price level doubled by the early 1980s, savings and earnings eroded, and concern mounted. Inflation hawks, especially in the banking and investing communities, had always seen inflation as a major economic threat. Now inflation was eating at middle-class living standards, and pivotal segments of the electorate—white-collar workers, small businessmen, retirees—wanted it to be brought under control. Many Britons and Americans gave the benefit of the doubt to the Thatcher and Reagan adminstrations' hard-line anti-inflation policies. In the heyday of Bretton Woods almost nobody would have considered bringing inflation down by 10 percent at the cost of raising unemployment by 10 percent, but in country after country over the 1980s recessionary policies that would have seemed unthinkable ten or fifteen years earlier were put in place. Voters appeared to agree that it was worthwhile, for they reelected the inflation fighters. Even though the battle against inflation was packaged with fiscal austerity and a redoubled commitment to global trade and investment, there was surprising mass political support for it.

Powerful economic interests in competitive and technologically advanced industries also fought for liberalization and economic integration. Technical advances increased the importance of the global economy for many of the world's leading firms. New products and new production techniques became the core of a high technology sector that took center stage in all industrial countries. In 1979, eighteen of the twenty-five largest American corporations were in oil and manufacturing; just three were in high technology and telecommunications. By

1999 thirteen of the top twenty-five were in high technology and telecommunications, with just two in petroleum and manufacturing. Also, the new high-tech corporations dwarfed earlier companies: The single largest firm in 1999, Microsoft, was worth as much *in real terms* (that is, after correcting for inflation) as the top twenty-five *combined* had been twenty years earlier. Company number twenty-five, Yahoo!, after only six years in business, was worth more in inflation-adjusted dollars than the country's three largest oil companies combined (Exxon, Amoco, and Mobil) had been in 1979. [16] Companies of previously unimaginable size whose business was unthinkable without microelectronics—Microsoft, Intel, America Online—now dominated the American economy and that of all industrial countries.

Most of these high-tech companies were viable only with global markets. Cellular telephones were typical. In 2000 about 400 million handsets were sold, and market leader Nokia sold about one-third of them. The five million people in Nokia's Finnish home base accounted for only a sliver of the 128 million Nokia telephones sold, and even the European market was not remotely sufficient. Only a truly global market could support the vast research, development, and marketing expenses necessary for Nokia to remain an industry leader. [17]

The ease with which money could move from place to place gave internationalist economic interests an added reason to want further international economic integration. The explosion in capital mobility made it easier for dynamic companies to borrow, easier for investors to shift funds across borders from less to more productive uses, easier for the successful companies to buy up or supplant laggards. They also put pressure on governments to adopt policies friendly to international investors.

Walter Wriston of Citibank, perhaps the most powerful international banker of the 1980s, saw the new capital mobility and telecommunications as part of the evolution of an "information standard" that allowed markets to monitor governments. "The gold standard," he said, "replaced by the gold exchange standard, which was replaced by the Bretton Woods arrangements, has now been replaced by the information standard. Money only goes where it's wanted, and only stays where it's well treated, and once you tie the world together with telecommunications and information, the ball game is over. The information standard is more draconian than any gold standard. They think the gold standard was tough. All you had to do on the gold standard was renounce it; we proved that. You cannot renounce the information standard, and it is

exerting a discipline on the countries of the world." The result has been
to give international investors enormous influence over governments
and their policies: "There's not enough money in the world to support a
currency with dumb fiscal and monetary management. There are
60,000-odd terminals out there in the trading rooms of the world, and
those guys are about as sentimental as a block of ice. Politically, the new
world is an integrated market in which nobody can get away with what
they used to. You can't control what your people hear, you can't control
the value of your currency, you can't control your capital flows."[18]

The globalized economy allowed newly industrializing nations to take
advantage of their cheap labor to produce steel, clothing, simple
machinery, and other basic industrial goods for world markets.
International corporations could combine high technology management
and research and development in the north with low-cost manufacturing in the south.

However, the new global industries threatened old industries in the
north with unwanted competition. Europe was mired in economic stagnation, with high inflation in many countries and high unemployment
everywhere. In the United States the skyrocketing value of the dollar
after 1980 drew in cheap imports that put American producers on the
defensive. Japanese sales to the United States mounted from under six
billion dollars in 1970 to over thirty billion in 1980 to eighty billion dollars in 1986. The competition struck some of the country's strongest traditional industries and biggest exporters; in just ten years after 1975
automobile imports went from twelve billion to sixty-five billion dollars.

Europe's and North America's old-line industries responded to the rising tide of imports with a protectionist backlash. Steel, auto, textile, and
other manufacturers clamored for help, and many got it. European and
North American governments forced Japanese producers to limit their
sales, raising the cost of the average car by hundreds of dollars in order
to provide breathing space for hard-pressed European and American
car manufacturers. Imports of semiconductors from Japan, and of steel
from a host of industrialized and newly industrializing countries, were
severely restricted. A succession of new blocks to imports—nontariff
barriers (NTBs)—evaded earlier commitments and kept foreign goods
out of the European and American markets. Europe turned inward, and
the Reagan administration, despite its free market rhetoric, adopted the
most sweeping protectionist measures since the 1930s.

Yet the new protectionism called forward a powerful countervailing
trend. Manufacturers in industrial countries pushing for trade protec-

tion faced opposing demands from investors with stakes abroad and from internationalized corporations eager for access to Brazilian auto parts, Indian computer programmers, and Korean electronic components. Many firms in Europe and North America had come to see unconnected national markets as insufficient; they needed a larger and more diverse customer and supplier base. Big European companies required a larger base of operations than France or Denmark could provide. Europe's high technology and other industries needed access to the cheap labor of the south, the highly skilled workers of the north, and the financial markets of London. Globally oriented American banks and companies, although they had a larger natural home, also chafed at the constraints one country imposed. While old-line industries clamored for and got shelter from competition, multinational enterprises and international banks in North America and Western Europe groped toward new ways to build and maintain powerful competitive positions. This involved both defeating the protectionists and finding a way forward toward greater integration.

During the 1970s and early 1980s in Europe and North America political conflict raged. In the United States economic nationalists and internationalists jostled for dominance over economic policy. Much of American labor and many American manufacturers had switched in the early 1970s from supporting free trade to demanding protection from foreign competitors. When Richard Nixon took the dollar off gold and slapped a 10 percent surcharge on imports, it seemed the country might head toward a Depression-style turn inward. But the big American companies that depended on exporting their products, importing foreign inputs, and making international loans and investments fought back. International banks, oil companies, and high technology firms grouped themselves into lobbying groups like the Emergency Committee for American Trade to fight growing protectionist sentiment. Their executives joined with like-minded politicians, intellectuals, and others from Europe and Japan in the Trilateral Commission, a transnational talking shop to try to safeguard international economic cooperation.

Powerful supporters and influential opponents of further global integration clashed. Financial communities fought for a hard line against inflation and against labor movements horrified by tight money that drove unemployment up to levels not seen since the 1930s. The wealthy pushed for tax cuts, while the poor fought to protect their programs from being targeted for spending reductions. Business communities supported privatization and deregulation, while trade unions tried to block what they saw as thinly veiled attempts to cut wages and employment. Some regarded the waves of corporate consolidations as an indication of the revival of a vibrant private sector, while others saw a return to the days of the robber barons.

In case after case, and country after country, globalizers defeated their opponents. They rolled back supporters of economic nationalism, labor and the Left, and commitments to extensive social policies. In part this was due to attrition; the difficult economic climate picked off the more vulnerable firms and industries. Over time there were simply fewer opponents of the new global capitalism. At the same time, the growth of trade and investment strengthened internationalist firms and industries.

Technical progress, macroeconomic trends, the explosion of international finance, and the changing composition of business reinforced those who wanted further economic integration. While hard times excited protectionist sentiment and led many to want governments to give priority to domestic problems, in the end the difficult decade from the early 1970s to the early 1980s led to redoubled economic globalization. The world moved quickly toward ever more impressive levels of cross-border trade, investment, and finance.

George Soros makes markets

When Malaysian Prime Minister Mahathir bin Mohamad fulminated against George Soros as the source of his country's difficulties, the connection seemed natural even to those who supported Soros. For George Soros epitomized global markets. He did so in the economic sphere, as his financial activities seemed capable of bringing down currencies and governments. He did so in the political arena, as he plowed billions of dollars into trying to influence governments around the world. He also brought his financial and political clout to bear on the very organization of the world economy.

All this was a long way to come for the son of a Budapest attorney, born Dzjchdzhe Shorash in 1930.[19] Like most prosperous Hungarian Jews, the assimilated and cosmopolitan family was forced into hiding by fascism and the Holocaust. In the war's aftermath the teenager moved to London. Supporting himself as a waiter, a housepainter, and an apple picker, Soros studied philosophy with no great success. After a stint selling handbags, he disappeared into the middle ranks of British investment banking. After a few years he moved to New York.

On Wall Street, Soros played his several languages, European contacts, and business sense into a career in the then tiny foreign investment community. He went to work for the international banking firm of Arnhold and S. Bleichröder. This association was doubly appropriate. For one thing, the company, which had been the Berlin agent of the Rothschilds since the 1830s, had taken corporate refuge from nazism in 1937, so Soros found himself in an environment heavy with fellow Central European émigrés. For another, the firm's pedigree foreshadowed Soros's own path. The Bleichröder patriarch, Gerson, had been an extraordinarily powerful financial adviser and confidant of German Chancellor Otto von Bismarck's in the late nineteenth century. The elder Bleichröder was the first Jew to become a hereditary Prussian nobleman, was generally believed to be the richest man in Germany, and had privileged access to Europe's most powerful statesmen. [20]

Soros was to follow in Bleichröder's footsteps, but he began prosaically, by profiting from the gradual revival of global finance. Arnhold and S. Bleichröder reacted to the 1963 imposition of American capital controls by taking much of its international business offshore. In 1967 Soros set up his first investment company; two years later he established an innovative investment vehicle based in the Caribbean offshore financial haven of Curaçao, free from government controls and from capital gains taxes. This Double Eagle Fund was an early hedge fund, a barely regulated private investment company open only to wealthy individuals willing to take greater risks than traditional financiers. The fund was tremendously successful—a thousand dollars invested at its inception would have grown to four million dollars by the year 2000, an average annual return of over 30 percent—and Soros struck out on his own in 1973. In the early 1980s he was called "the world's greatest money manager" by the international bankers' trade journal, *Institutional Investor*.

Soros's reputation soared in 1992, when he bet billions of dollars against the British government and won. The British had announced that they would keep the pound sterling fixed against the deutsche mark, as part of the growing movement for European monetary union. However, the attempt was politically unpopular in Britain, and Soros thought it could not last. He was right, and the British government gave up and devalued the pound in September 1992. Soros's speculation against sterling earned him a billion dollars, and related speculative investments against other European currencies earned him another billion.

To many, it appeared that a wealthy investor had single-handedly forced a major government to reverse economic course. The perception of a unique Soros touch was exaggerated, for speculation against the pound was widespread. Nonetheless, Soros's experience brought home the fact that governments were under massive pressure to satisfy international investors, even if the domestic political costs were high. And while Soros went on to lose money on similar bets over the course of the 1990s—most prominently in Russia, where he may have dropped two billion dollars—he also successfully bet against governments.

His investment activities made him particularly controversial in countries, such as Malaysia, hit by currency crises. When Prime Minister Mahathir accused Soros of bringing the country's economy down, he was expressing a broadly held view that global capital markets had gone too far in constraining government policies. The spirited row between the two focused at times on serious issues, such as whether primary responsibility for the troubles of a country like Malaysia was to be sought in bad policies or amoral speculators. But there was also a strain of conspiratorial nationalism in the assault, as when Mahathir invoked Soros's Jewishness as part of his accusations: "In reality it is a Jew who triggered the currency plunge, and coincidentally Soros is a Jew. It is also a coincidence that Malaysians are mostly Moslem. Indeed, the Jews are not happy to see Moslems progress. If it were Palestine, the Jews would rob Palestinians. Thus this is what they are doing to our country." Mahathir was not alone in seeing the revival of a Jewish international finance antipathetic to the national dignity of other nations; Ukrainian nationalists also attacked Soros as "a member of a group that has demonstrated itself to be hostile to the success of the Ukrainian state, and that in fact has an overriding interest in a Ukrainian economic collapse."[21] Tension between global finance—of whatever religion—and nationalism had once more come to the fore.

Soros's extracurricular activities went beyond those of a simple banker. In 1979 he began to spend his money to help undermine Communist governments in Eastern Europe. He started small, buying a few hundred photocopiers for Hungarian institutions to circumvent prohibitions on forbidden literature. During the 1980s he spent hundreds of millions of dollars to support dissidents in Central and Eastern Europe and the Soviet Union; in 1990 he founded a new Central European University, based in Prague and Budapest. Soros's financial and philanthropic activities put him in a unique position to encourage the development of capitalism and democracy in the former Communist countries. His Open

Society Institute continued this work through the 1990s, to the tune of hundreds of millions of dollars a year. Soros also bankrolled such varied programs as campaigns to legalize marijuana in the United States, for better treatment of Roma (Gypsies) in Eastern Europe, and for the promotion of democracy in Haiti and Mongolia.

A leading financier might be expected to promote market societies, but Soros's philanthropy also put a premium on political democracy and human rights. The commitment was genuine: The first president of the Open Society Institute was Aryeh Neier, former head of the American Civil Liberties Union and Human Rights Watch and a well-known American supporter of human rights. This emphasis on social justice certainly reflected Soros's personal quirks, but it also represented concern that global capitalism could not be sustained if masses of people were excluded from the mainstream of economic and political life. "The global capitalist system," Soros said, "has produced a very uneven playing field. The gap between rich and poor is getting wider. This is dangerous, because a system that does not offer some hope and benefit to the losers is liable to be disrupted by acts of desperation."[22] Soros was a strong supporter of open societies on both principled and pragmatic grounds, believing that the new international economic order necessitated a commitment to social justice.

Soros argued fervently that global capitalism would be safe only if attention were paid to national and social concerns. The international economy, he believed, required a better social and political infrastructure and new international institutions. He also insisted on more effective regulation of global investments and their effects. "There is," he said, "a serious mismatch between the political and economic conditions that prevail in the world today. We have a global economy but the political arrangements are still firmly grounded in the sovereignty of the state. This would not be a cause for concern if free markets could be counted on to take care of all needs; but that is manifestly not the case." Soros proposed a raft of international institutions to try to deal with these new global problems, including a reinvigorated United Nations that would take on features of a world government. Closer to his own interests, he said, "Now that we have global financial markets we also need a global central bank and some other international financial institutions whose explicit mission is to keep financial markets on an even keel."[23]

Despite the dissonance of an international financial speculator calling for more regulation and a wealthy investor expressing concern for social justice, there was an underlying unity to Soros's position. Markets, especially those as precarious as financial markets, often need governments to stabilize them; the collapse of the interwar years had definitively established this in national financial markets. Yet there is no world government coterminous with world markets, and this led to Soros's fears. Soros, and many of his partners in international finance, support efforts by governments to stabilize and regulate the markets in which they operate. They believe in international markets, to be sure, but they also want to avoid the political and social conflicts that have beset international finance in the past. Soros became a voice for purposive government action to make the world safe for global markets, just as he had been a powerful proponent of reducing government intervention in Eastern and Central Europe in order to make them hospitable to market society.

At the end of the twentieth century Soros represented both the achievements and the anxieties of international finance. The global financial system held trillions of dollars and moved hundreds of billions of dollars around the world with extraordinary speed and efficiency. Neither governments nor their peoples could ignore the opinions and actions of international investors, and global capital markets conditioned economics and politics around the world. Although there was an undercurrent of social discontent, of nationalism, and of concern about financial instability, these were the troubles of a newly triumphant global capitalism, which had vanquished central planning, economic insularity, and resurgent protectionism and could move on to the task of completing the integration of the world economy.

Trade unblocked

Soros could take satisfaction from the turn toward economic openness in Eastern and Central Europe, in China, and in the developing world. When China turned away from central planning and India dropped import substitution, one-third of the world's people were pulled out of decades of economic isolation into the mainstream of the global economy. Similar developments in the former Soviet bloc and Latin America affected another billion people. From a world historical and human standpoint, these were the cardinal developments of the last quarter of the twentieth century.

From an economic point of view, however, North America and Western Europe defined the world's course. These two regions, with one-tenth of the world's population, accounted for half the world economy and two-thirds of world trade. When, between 1985 and 2000, they accelerated the integration of their trade, investment, financial, and monetary affairs, the impact overwhelmed the rest of the world economy.

The path forward was indirect and controversial. After weathering the crises of the 1970s and early 1980s, supporters of economic integration in North America and Western Europe focused on new *regional* trade agreements. Western Europeans turned the European Union into a true single market within which goods, services, capital, and people moved freely, then moved on to create a single European currency, the euro. The United States, Canada, and Mexico created the North American Free Trade Agreement, another huge area moving toward free trade among its members. By the end of the century Western Europe was a single economic entity in virtually all dimensions, and North America was close to one. Other regional trade agreements proliferated elsewhere in the developed and developing worlds.

Two large trading areas emerged. The European Union headed one that included Central and Eastern Europe, the former Soviet Union, and former European colonies in Africa and Asia. The United States led the other, which comprised the Western Hemisphere. Some feared that the new regionalism would lead, as the old regionalism had in the 1930s, to a general closure of international trade. Others saw the trade blocs as precursors to broader liberalization. In the phrase of economist Robert Lawrence, the question was whether the regional trade agreements would be "building blocs" or "stumbling blocks" on the road to an integrated world economy.[24] The EU's various efforts led to talk about the threat of a new Fortress Europe. Similar concerns were expressed by many in Asia over the new integration efforts that led to NAFTA and Mercosur.

The new regionalism turned out to be very different from that of the imperial systems of the 1930s. The principal proponents of the trade agreements were internationalists, not traditional protectionists trying to carve out sheltered regional markets. Businesses were happy to have privileged access to the larger home markets the new blocs represented. But the real attraction of the blocs, to their main supporters, was the opportunity to strengthen business in global competition. The larger blocs made exports cheaper to produce, allowed firms to grow, made it easier to attract foreign investment, and encouraged the consolidation of banks and corporations. Larger regional markets meant more economies of scale, bigger companies, a better position in the increasingly heated international competition for customers and capital. The dynamics of NAFTA and the EU could perhaps best be seen by looking at their domestic opponents, who concentrated in traditional declining industries desperate for defense from imports from lower-cost producers in Mexico and Southern Europe, respectively. The defeat of the opponents of NAFTA and European integration was a victory for those who supported broad international economic integration.

Regional integration in the 1990s became an important component part of the overall process of economic globalization. The single European market, with a single European currency and common economic regulation, had most of the economic effects its business supporters had anticipated. Five trillion dollars in mergers and acquisitions created a host of European business behemoths. The market position of leading European banks and corporations improved so dramatically that they went on buying sprees outside Europe as well, investing more than 150 billion dollars a year in the United States alone in the late 1990s. Redoubled integration put much more pressure on less efficient firms and sectors, many of which went out of business or were bought by regional leaders. But overall European integration strengthened Europe's big businesses in world and European markets.

NAFTA too had powerful effects. Between 1993 and 2000 American trade with its NAFTA partners grew nearly twice as fast as trade with the rest of the world, from under $300 billion to over $650 billion. Investment also soared, as Canadian and American firms could now produce in Mexico, where wages were lower, without worrying about getting products back to market. The Mexican economy, the smallest and least developed of the three, was the most affected. By 2000 the country had weathered a currency and banking crisis, a restructuring of its financial system, and a reorientation of its trade and was tightly tied into the North American economy. North America was well on the way to forming an integrated economic entity.

Even Mercosur, more recent and less ambitious, had striking effects on its members. By the end of the century it was a recognizable economic bloc; domestic and foreign firms alike were making production and investment plans on a Mercosur-wide rather than a national basis. Over the course of the decade trade among Mercosur members increased fivefold, from one-twelfth to one-quarter of their total trade.

In the late 1990s the bloc was the single most important site for foreign investment in the developing world, attracting every year about twenty billion dollars in multinational corporate investment and many more billions in foreign loans.

The advances in regional economic integration were part of the broader success of the supporters of economic internationalism. After fifteen years of bitter battles from the early 1970s through the middle 1980s, initiative shifted to interests, politicians, and ideologies associated with economic integration. During the 1990s the issue was decided in favor of supporters of global integration. There was hardly universal agreement on free trade, but official policy came to accept it as a matter of course.

The forces for global capitalism at the end of the twentieth century proved extremely powerful, as they had been at the end of the nineteenth. Earlier economic globalists weathered the Great Depression of 1873–1896, with its mass populist movements and recurrent debt crises. The recent course of globalization survived global recession, persistently high unemployment in Europe, social disintegration in the former Communist countries, and contagious crises in Asia and Latin America. Technological advances, the power of internationalist economic interests, and trends in global politics reinforced the globalizing trend.

The advanced industrial world created continental markets in Europe and North America. The developing world dismantled import substitution and developmentalism. The former Communist world turned toward the market at home and abroad. The interests, and the ideas, favorable to economic globalization dominated world economics and politics. The globe was once again capitalist, and capitalism was once again global.

18

Countries Catch Up

In 1961 Seoul, the capital city of South Korea, was a pitiful sight. Its inhabitants, an American visitor wrote, "live in miserable jerry-built shacks, and few of them have been able to find jobs. Beggars, some apparently only two or three years old, are commonplace, along with venders who squat for hours on the sidewalks, offering passersby cigarettes, chewing gum, combs, cheap jewelry, toys, whistles, abaci, and live dogs. The dogs bark constantly; they sound hungry, too."[1] In the years after the end of the Korean War, South Korea was an impoverished, unstable dictatorship. One authoritarian regime was forced out of power in 1960, but less than a year later another military coup brought yet another general to power. The new dictatorship of Chung Hee Park governed a destitute nation.

The misery of Seoul contrasted with the glistening progress that had been made by the country's former colonial master across the Sea of Japan. John Lie was born in 1959 in South Korea and moved to Japan soon afterward, but his family went back frequently to visit relatives. He could make comparisons easily:

> Seoul in the early 1960s was my childhood conception of backwardness. While I marveled at traffic jams in Tokyo, I was horrified by the oxcarts

tottering along on Seoul's dusty roads. Tokyo seemed indisputably modern, with its international-style high-rises, electronic toys, flush toilets, air conditioners, and refrigerators. Seoul, in contrast, appeared unmodern with its Japanese colonial-period architecture, wooden toys, non-flush toilets without toilet paper, and, at best, electric fans and ice blocks. Tokyo was dynamic—new buildings popping up everywhere, store shelves overflowing with new products; Seoul was stationary, trapped in tradition. In Tokyo I gorged on caramels and chocolates sold in tidy stores; in Seoul, I gagged on grilled grasshoppers peddled on the street. Going to restaurants in South Korea, I was incredulous that rice . . . couldn't be served on certain days because of government restrictions.[2]

Indeed, South Korea was one of the world's poorest countries in the early 1960s. Most of the newly independent nations of sub-Saharan Africa were better off, and Latin America was more than three times as rich. Per capita income in South Korea was, by some measures, lower than in the North. Prospects for improvement seemed dim. The country relied heavily on aid from its American patrons, and the United States had grown exasperated by the succession of lethargic and corrupt governments.

Twenty-five years later the country had been transformed. After John Lie returned to Korea as a young man in the late 1980s, he wrote: "I encountered upper-middle-class housewives sporting *haute couture* and affluent youths leading lives of invidious distinction and dissolution. Clean and well-lit coffee shops had replaced the dark and dingy cafes; McDonald's and Pizza Hut, the noodle shops and cheap eateries. . . . What makes these changes and contrasts all the more striking is that they occurred during a mere generation."[3]

When South Korea hosted the 1988 Olympics, the world got to see the progress the country had made. A new democratic system was being consolidated, and a popularly elected president shared power with a legislature controlled by the opposition. Beyond the political changes and the gleaming athletic facilities, the country's overall economic advancement was on display. The change was remarkable. British Marxist Perry Anderson wrote in wonderment: "Seoul is now the third largest city in the world, as a municipal unit—bigger than Tokyo or Beijing. Size is no guarantee of modernity, as the desperate inequality and violence of the two greatest of all urban concentrations, São Paulo and Bombay, testify. But that is still the Third World. Seoul is not part of it. What a Londoner notices first is the ways in which the city is more advanced than his own." The Korean experience, Anderson wrote, was unprecedented:

"No other society in the world has industrialized in depth as fast. A historical process that took at least three generations in Japan has here been accomplished in one. The tempo of the change has no precedent. In the past twenty years, the exodus from agriculture has been three times greater than in Italy, four times greater than in Japan, five times greater than in France and seven times greater than in Germany. The proportion of the population living in cities of over one million is now the highest on earth."[4]

By 1996, thirty years after the beginning of Korea's transformation, the OECD had recognized the Korean reality and made the country a member of this international club of rich nations. South Korea had "graduated" from the developing to the developed world. It had gone from a level of development lower than that of the Philippines and Thailand, of Ghana and the Congo to one higher than that of Greece or Portugal, comparable to that of Spain, New Zealand, or Ireland. In the early 1960s there was one motor vehicle for every 830 Koreans, and one telephone for every 250. Thirty years later there was one car for every 5 Koreans, and one telephone for every 2. In the early 1960s the average Korean girl got less than three years of schooling; in the mid-1990s, more than nine years.[5]

Observers were wrong only in thinking that the Korean case was unique. Taiwan, Singapore, and Hong Kong grew roughly as fast, or even faster. And a second generation of East Asian tigers was close behind: Thailand, Malaysia, even China. In all these cases, the extraordinary pace of economic catch-up was directly related to ties with the international economy. The integration of the world economy in the last part of the twentieth century created great opportunities for specialization and growth. Governments and companies in poor countries could take advantage of the rich world's demands for cheap products and lucrative investment opportunities. They could orient their production to hundreds of millions of prosperous consumers and attract the capital of the world's wealthiest banks, corporations, and investors. Many did just this, leading to a burst of growth in parts of the developing world.

The global capitalism of the end of the twentieth century, like that of the fifty years before World War One, offered powerful incentives to people, groups, companies, and countries. The opportunity to sell to and borrow from the whole world, rather than one nation, allowed firms to specialize in their most profitable activities. Under import substitution, Mexico had failed to create a viable car industry, but now it took by storm the global market for auto parts. Farmers in Argentina and New

Zealand made fortunes selling winter fruits and vegetables to Northern Hemisphere consumers, an opportunity possible only with a global market for raspberries. Companies in Thailand and Turkey, previously constrained by the difficulty of borrowing at home, now had access to cheap and plentiful foreign finance. These countries and their citizens took advantage of global markets to specialize and speed their growth.

Global markets imposed constraints along with the opportunities. Owners of enormous pools of capital could scour the globe for the most attractive investment sites. Whether they were seeking inexpensive labor, ample natural resources, skilled technicians, favorable regulations, or big markets, investors had access to virtually every nation. If investors disliked a government's policies or a company's balance sheet, money would flow out as it had flowed in—only faster. If consumers lost interest in a gadget or a style or cut back on spending in a recession, the producing factories, countries, and regions could be shuttered. Global markets expanded both the possibilities available to their participants and the disciplines imposed upon them.

Global production and national specialization

Production became global in the last quarter of the twentieth century, as corporations outsourced the components needed to make a product to factories in many nations. At the end of the century world trade was two or three times as important to the economies of developed countries as it had been in the 1960s, and this made it easy for firms to relay goods and services from place to place. Companies could locate research and development, marketing, manufacture, and assembly thousands of miles away from one another, for economic, political, or regulatory reasons, then ship the ultimate product to consumers everywhere. Economist Robert Feenstra spoke of "integration of trade and disintegration of production," the one allowing for the other.[6]

By the 1990s it was remarkably easy to disperse production around the globe. Public attention had focused on multinational corporations in the early 1970s, when they invested $10 billion a year internationally, $2 billion in the developing world. By 2000 foreign direct investment by multinational corporations (MNCs) was running at about $1 trillion a year, of which about $250 billion was going to the developing countries,

more than a hundredfold increase. Other forms of international investment grew even more rapidly. By the latter part of the 1990s private
international lending and other investment (in addition to that of
MNCs) was also about $1 trillion a year. This volume of international
investment meant that any reasonable proposal to set up a mine, mill, or
mall would attract interested investors.

The products that entered world trade were increasingly international
in both origin and market. The quintessentially American Barbie doll,
for example, was by the middle 1990s a quintessentially global product.[7]
Its manufacture started with molds that Mattel in the United States
made available to factories in Southeast Asia. Taiwan and Japan supplied
plastic and hair. Chinese firms provided cotton cloth for dresses. The
dolls were assembled in Indonesia, Malaysia, and China, then shipped
to Hong Kong and from there to Mattel's customers in the United States
and elsewhere. Almost every major corporation was global: Three-fifths
of IBM's sales were outside the United States; four-fifths of
Volkswagen's were outside Germany.

Whether globalized production was organized inside or outside the
networks of multinational corporations, factors of production flowed
away from less profitable and toward more profitable places and uses.
Trillions of dollars in the world's offshore financial markets looked continually for lucrative opportunities, wherever they might be found.
Thousands of companies from dozens of countries scrambled for low-
cost loans to expand their operations. The result was new industries in
Indonesia, new start-ups in Silicon Valley, new buildings in Brazil, new
highways in Hungary. International finance, investment, and technology
sped the globalization of production, as resources in search of profits
moved from place to place in ever-greater quantity and at ever-greater
speed.

This continual reallocation of production led to heightened specialization among countries and regions. Goods previously made in one country could now be divided into a dozen parts, with each part
manufactured in a different nation. Firms could disaggregate production into minute components and fine-tune their investments to take
advantage of the benefits of many disparate locations. Global production allowed companies to reduce their costs and gave developing countries opportunities to occupy profitable economic niches.

Globalizing forces pushed and pulled different parts of the world into
an ever-finer division of labor. Areas with high levels of education specialized in headquarters operations, research and development, and

related activities. Those with many well-trained workers focused on production that required high skill levels. Countries with masses of unskilled workers built on their comparative advantage in cheap labor, just as those with abundant natural resources exploited these resources. Global capitalism drew hundreds of millions of people in East Asia, Latin America, and elsewhere into production for world markets.

Greater specialization could be both blessing and curse. Its attractions were tempered by the fact that it made some lines of business of long standing obsolete, increasing the competition that companies and countries faced from others. Europe and North America could not compete with China and Mexico in producing things that used lots of unskilled labor, and the north's traditional manufacturing industries shrank as those of the south expanded. In the developed countries, manufacturing employment went from 27 percent of the labor force in the early 1970s to under 18 percent in the late 1990s. While in 1970 there were two American service workers for every manufacturing worker, by 2000 the proportion was five to one.

As regions with abundant unskilled and semiskilled labor were drawn into the world economy, they began taking over the manufacture of goods that required intensive use of this type of labor. Steel was typical. In 1975 there were almost no steel mills in the developing world, and those there were had to be heavily subsidized and protected by governments. Raw steel production in the developing world was barely one-fifth that of Western Europe and North America; all the developing countries put together produced less than half as much steel as the United States. Twenty-five years later the world's most competitive steelmakers were largely in Latin America and Asia. Developing country steelmakers in 2000 produced much more raw steel than Western Europe and North America combined. Indeed, the six big emerging market steel producers—China, South Korea, Brazil, India, Mexico, and Taiwan—together made nearly three times as much steel as did the United States.[5] Over the last twenty-five years of the twentieth century there was a massive reallocation of industrial production from the rich countries to the developing world.

The growth of industry in the developing nations of the south paralleled the experience of an earlier era. In the late nineteenth and early twentieth centuries globalization led to impressive economic growth in many areas of the New World, Africa, and Asia. The rapidly growing regions flooded the developed world with cheap farm products and raw materials. This was a boon to European manufacturers that used the imports and to consumers but it wreaked havoc with traditional agriculture in Europe. In the late twentieth century the newly industrializing countries flooded the developed world with cheap manufactured goods. This helped the European and North American industries that used the cheap manufactured imports and consumers, but it wreaked havoc with traditional industry in Western Europe and North America. Both processes were the inevitable effects of specialization in an integrated international economy: Swedish and Italian farmers in 1900 could not match the low costs of farmers on the Great Plains and the pampas, just as British and American unskilled laborers in 2000 could not match the low costs of those of China and Mexico. European agriculture declined in the earlier era just as Western European and North American industry declined in the later period. And just as primary production in the New World and other regions boomed before 1914, basic manufacturing in East Asia, Latin America, and elsewhere grew rapidly after 1973.

Export-led growth on the edge of Europe and Asia

An astounding example of economic catch-up involved Western Europe's four poorest countries. In the 1950s and early 1960s brutal military dictators ruled the backward nations of Spain and Portugal; the fragile democracy of equally backward Greece collapsed in 1967. Ireland, although democratic, was almost as poor. In these four peripheral countries of Western Europe, income per person in the 1950s was less than half that of France or Germany, well below that of Chile and Argentina. Their economic and social conditions were extremely low by European standards, and they had some of the worst poverty in the allegedly industrial world.

All four countries began to modernize their economies around 1960. Ireland went first, turning away from import substitution and toward production for export in 1958. The government vigorously pursued foreign, mainly American corporations that could take advantage of a well-educated, English-speaking, cheap workforce in Europe. When Ireland entered the European Union in 1973, foreign investment and economic growth increased. The island nation eventually shifted from low-wage manufactures to higher skills and high technology. Soon Ireland made one of every three computers bought in Europe. In 2000 the "Celtic

Tiger," with fewer than four million people, passed the United States as the world's leading exporter of software, and its per capita income passed that of its old colonial master, Great Britain.[9] Dublin was one of Europe's most prosperous cities.

Spain, Portugal, and Greece shifted gears with more difficulty than Ireland, for they had fascist economic legacies to overcome. But once their dictatorships were gone, they turned toward European integration: Greece joined the EU in 1981, Spain and Portugal in 1986. This accelerated their economic opening. While in 1980 the two Iberian countries traded much less with the EU than with the rest of the world, by 1990 their EU trade had nearly quintupled and was more than twice as important to them as their other commerce. In fact Ireland, Spain, and Portugal were among the more enthusiastic participants in the creation of the Economic and Monetary Union (Greece joined later, in time for the final launch of the euro in 2002). All four countries attracted many multinational corporations and banks and eventually played host to some ten thousand affiliates and subsidiaries of foreign corporations. Indeed, in the fifteen years after 1985, foreign direct investment in the four nations went from $25 billion to $210 billion; about one-tenth of all their investment came from foreigners.

By the end of the century Spain, Portugal, and Greece were unmistakably developed and European, with income per person approaching that of Italy and of Sweden and double that of Chile. The countries' social progress was even more impressive. In 1970 Portugal's infant mortality rate was sixty-one per thousand, roughly equal to that of Mexico or Malaysia; by 2000 it was under six per thousand, better than that of the United States. In the late 1960s there was just one telephone and one television set for every twenty Portuguese, while by 2000 there was one phone and TV for every two residents and one car for every three— numbers similar to those of the rest of Western Europe. While the Portuguese race from backwardness to modernity was particularly swift, those of the other nations on Western Europe's perimeter were nearly as impressive.

This pace of growth was possible only with access to the markets and capital of Europe and the world. National firms were freed from the constraints of small home markets, now able to sell to hundreds of millions of Europeans, if not to the entire world. Access to foreign capital made it possible to finance investments that local capitalists could not or would not. Industries specialized and productivity advanced, leading to some of the most rapid growth on record. While outlying Western European nations are hardly comparable to developing countries, many elements of their catch-up was to be repeated in newly industrializing countries: production for export; attraction of foreign investment; heavy investment in upgrading the local labor force and building infrastructure.

East Asia's poor countries were the most impressive followers of the European periphery onto the path of convergence. Four of them in particular—South Korea, Taiwan, Hong Kong, and Singapore—were so successful as to "graduate" from the developing world. By 2000 Hong Kong and Singapore had per person outputs above most of Western Europe, while Taiwan came close and South Korea trailed by only a bit. All four had some unusual characteristics: The first two were island city-states (and Hong Kong was not even a state), while Taiwan and South Korea were parts of divided nations and military protectorates of the United States. Nonetheless, they were similar enough to other developing countries that their experiences could not be written off as anomalies.

South Korea and Taiwan started from almost nothing in the middle 1950s, after their devastating civil wars. For a decade or so they adopted typical import-substituting policies, but without the long-standing independent experience of Latin America, the East Asian nations' new industrial sectors were weaker and less committed to protectionism. In the late 1960s both countries began to encourage their capitalists to produce industrial goods for foreign, especially American, consumers. They used many techniques to push exports: cheap loans and tax breaks to exporters; a very weak currency to make Korean and Taiwanese products artificially cheap. Both governments continued to protect their own industries but emphasized export production. Unlike most of Latin America and Africa, the two East Asian economies—as well as, even more, Hong Kong and Singapore—had few exportable natural resources and had little choice but to take advantage of low wages to produce simple manufactures to sell abroad. The new development strategy of export-oriented industrialization (EOI) promoted and subsidized manufacturing for foreign markets.

By the late 1970s South Korea and Taiwan were flooding world markets with toys, clothing, furniture, and other simple manufactures. Korean exports went from $385 million in 1970 to $15 billion in 1979, 90 percent of them manufactured goods. International banks and corporations found the East Asian exporters increasingly attractive. They were stable dictatorships backed by the United States, and their strong export performances promised a steady stream of dollars to pay back foreign lenders. The two countries borrowed heavily, using the money to build up their industrial base. Korea's government pursued heavy industrial development by sponsoring modern steel mills, chemical factories, and a new auto industry. By the early 1980s the country had the world's largest private shipyard and largest machinery factory. Unlike most developing countries, Korea's policy makers and businessmen decided to try to set up a car-making industry without multinationals. In the 1970s the government helped local auto firms borrow abroad and buy foreign technology and expertise. Soon cars made by Hyundai, Daewoo, and Kia were sold all over the world.

When the debt crisis hit in 1982, South Korea and Taiwan were far less seriously affected than Latin America. Their businesses were used to selling abroad and could increase exports rapidly to service their debts. After a couple of difficult years the "Asian Tigers" resumed their rapid growth, shifting from simpler to more complex manufactured goods—from toys to computers, from clothing and footwear to bicycles and cars. This progression echoed the course of Japanese industrial development, with a twenty-year lag; just as Japan had gone from simple low-wage manufactures in the 1950s to more complex machinery and consumer appliances in the 1970s, so the two former Japanese colonies did much the same between the 1970s and the 1990s.

Soon South Korea and Taiwan were selling sophisticated mid-market industrial products. Korean cars were a particular success: By 2000 the country produced nearly three million vehicles a year, about half for export. South Korea was also a world leader in ships, television sets, and consumer electronic equipment; Taiwan was the world's third-largest producer of computer products, after the United States and Japan. By the turn of the century both countries had living standards roughly on par with Spain and Portugal. During the 1990s they democratized as well, seeming to contradict the criticism that the East Asian model required dictatorial regimes that could repress the working class to keep labor cheap.

The East Asians appeared to point the way forward to the rest of the developing and transitional countries, at a time when traditional import substitution had run out of steam and central planning had collapsed. The path of export-oriented industrialization meant opening to the world economy, drawing in foreign investment and loans, and producing for foreign markets. It meant wholehearted integration into the global division of labor. This ran counter to decades of development theory and practice, but within a few years the new strategy had been adopted by almost every country in the Third World.

East Asian and Latin American followers

The near neighbors of the four East Asian Tigers quickly turned toward export promotion. Thailand, Malaysia, the Philippines, and Indonesia, four heavily agrarian countries, had failed to industrialize with import substitution. While their governments continued to back national businesses, even continuing to protect them from foreign competition, these governments abandoned ISI in favor of export-led industrialization. In a matter of years all four became major industrial exporters.

The newer Asian exporters benefited from the successes of the four front-runners. As South Korea, Taiwan, Hong Kong, and Singapore developed, their living standards and wages rose so quickly that they became unattractive to the most labor-intensive manufacturing. Industries priced out of Singapore and Taiwan found cheap labor in Thailand, Malaysia, and Indonesia, whose governments seemed skilled at both managing the economy and controlling (and repressing) political unrest. Foreign capital flooded into the three Southeast Asian economies and eventually into the politically less stable Philippines, and soon manufactured exports flooded out. Like the initial four East Asians, these four Southeast Asian countries were close American allies and feared Communist insurgencies. These strategic realities undoubtedly made it more attractive for them to integrate into the American-led world economy.

No such geopolitical rationale explains the two most remarkable Asian transformations, Communist China and Vietnam. China in the late 1970s and Vietnam in the mid-1980s turned aggressively toward the international economy. Vietnam's shift was striking, given its decades of war with the West, but its penury led it to turn to market reforms and globalization. From near-total economic isolation in the early 1980s, by 2000 Vietnam was exporting a billion dollars' worth of shrimp, a billion of rice, and five billion of manufactured goods. After decades of war and stagnation the Vietnamese economy tripled in size in fifteen years.

China's shift was far the more important because it involved the world's most populous nation. The Chinese government returned farmland to private farmers, removed the central government from most economic activities, set up special zones for export production, and welcomed foreign corporations. The country's output quadrupled in twenty years, and living standards tripled. In 1992 China surpassed Japan as the world's second-largest economy.

The Chinese growth explosion was closely linked to its embrace of the world economy. Chinese exports went from $20 billion to $200 billion in twenty years, manufactured exports from under $10 to over $170 billion. By the late 1990s foreign corporations were investing $35 billion a year in the Asian giant. China, whose role in the world economy had been small before World War One and trivial during fifty years of civil war and central planning, was on the verge of becoming one of the world's largest exporters.

The comparison between China and India was striking. In the late 1970s the two countries' output per person was roughly the same, but in 2000 China's was double that of India. In part as a result of this unfavorable comparison, India's commitment to a closed economy eventually yielded to the Asian rush. The government started to liberalize both the domestic economy and foreign trade and investment in 1990. The software industry's impressive success took advantage of some unusual components of India's comparative advantage. The country's excellent universities, insufficient jobs for college graduates, and English language made it an ideal site to recruit software engineers. Many went to North America to work, but more stayed in India to write code for companies at home and around the world. By the end of the century the nation's software exports were one of its leading economic activities, bringing in over six billion dollars a year, double Indian clothing sales abroad.

Asia was first off the blocks in the renewed race for global capital and markets, but Latin America was not far behind. The Latin American turn toward globalization was pioneered by Chile in the 1970s, under the military dictatorship of Augusto Pinochet. The country had been one of the Western world's most protected markets, with tariffs of 250 percent and more. The Chilean generals associated import substitution with the populist developmentalism that helped the Left win elections, and within a few years of the 1973 coup the dictatorship had virtually eliminated trade protection and thrown open Chile's financial markets. The economy came crashing down during the debt crisis, but after 1985 the military regime returned to its path of economic integration. Chile had a ten-year head start on the rest of Latin America with privatization, trade openness, and financial integration, and it adopted relatively extreme variants of the new orthodoxy, such as eliminating public pensions in favor of a private social security system. The democratic election of a civilian government in 1989 overcame the wariness with which many Latin Americans regarded the Chilean example. When the Center-Left coalition chose to continue Chile's market-oriented policies, it reduced the policies' taint by association with the bloody Pinochet regime.

Chile's turn toward exports paid off in the 1990s, as the economy doubled in size; in 2000 it was the richest country in Latin America. This growth was driven by Chile's ties to the rest of the world economy: By the end of the century its trade was thirty billion dollars a year and foreign investment another five billion dollars, many times previous levels. The new globalist Chile took advantage of long-distance transport and communications to specialize in some unusual product niches. The country's long, rugged coastline proved perfect for raising salmon, and starting from nothing in 1986, Chile quickly became the world's second-largest exporter of the fish, supplying more than half the salmon eaten by discerning Japanese consumers. Chile's Southern Hemisphere location and temperate climate were ideal for raising summer fruits during the North American and European winter, and over the course of twenty years the country tripled the land sown to fruits and tripled yields on this land. Consumers in rich countries came to regard as natural the December arrival of Chilean grapes and peaches. By 2000 Chile was earning nearly four billion dollars a year selling newly developed products. Chile provided a textbook lesson in how economic integration spurred specialization: Export possibilities drove farmers to expand fruit production and entrepreneurs to start up the salmon-raising industry.

Within ten years the rest of Latin America followed Chile's example and moved into world markets. Mexico, the region's second economy after Brazil, liberalized its trade and investment policies after 1985. During the 1990s domestic policy change and the formation of NAFTA transformed Mexico from a self-contained, import-substituting country to a free-wheeling, free-trading integral part of the North American economy. In just ten years the country's total trade nearly quadrupled; manufactured sales abroad shot from about $10 billion to $120 billion, while foreign investors poured $20 billion a year into NAFTA's low-wage member. While the metamorphosis was particularly striking in the case of Mexico, virtually all Latin America followed suit.

The Marxist sociologist takes power

Fernando Henrique Cardoso became Brazil's finance minister in 1993, after decades of theorizing, writing, and debating about development. He was steeped in politics almost from his birth in 1931—his grandfather and father were prominent Brazilian generals, and his ancestors include many national political leaders—but at an early age Cardoso chose the life of the scholar and embraced Marxism and socialism instead of his family's traditional Brazilian nationalism.[10]

Cardoso turned toward academia after college in the 1950s and studied sociology in Brazil and in France. His Ph.D. thesis examined Brazilian race relations, and his next major project investigated the political attitudes of Brazilian capitalists. He was a founding member of Brazil's most famous Marxist study group. After Brazil's 1964 military coup, the thirty-three-year-old Cardoso fled the country for Chile, where he wrote a series of influential studies of Latin American development. After a stint at the University of Paris, he returned to Brazil in 1968 to teach at the University of São Paulo, only to be forced from his post by the military dictatorship. With support from the Ford Foundation, Cardoso and several other similarly unemployed scholars set up a respected center for social scientific research in São Paulo. By the early 1970s Cardoso had a worldwide reputation as a scholar of development—and as an intellectual almost uninvolved in practical politics. In fact Fernando Henrique Cardoso espoused a radical Marxism that virtually dismissed, and certainly did not engage with, the Latin American political mainstream.

Cardoso's Marxism was revolutionary—"the important question," he wrote, "is how to construct paths toward socialism"[11]—but unlike many others on the Left, he believed that the Third World could develop. Cardoso was associated with one position in a controversy that raged during the 1960s and 1970s among Marxists and neo-Marxists. On one side were hard-line dependency theorists, who insisted that the backwardness of the Third World was due to an economic order controlled by North American and Western European imperialism. Colonialism had retarded development in Africa, Asia, and Latin America, they argued, and the imperialism of the multinational corporation similarly retarded growth. The only alternative was thoroughgoing socialist revolution, although some conceded that extreme nationalism and closure to the world economy might help.

While Cardoso agreed that developing countries' options were limited, he argued that they had more room to maneuver than the hardliners believed. Dependency did not, he maintained, rule out development. To those who saw socialism as the only alternative to underdevelopment, Cardoso insisted that a modernizing government could be supported by the middle classes, progressive capitalists, and labor. On the basis of his study of Brazilian society and of Brazilian businessmen, he believed that governments could create local capitalist economies that were not simple appendages of the American Empire. In all this Cardoso was heavily influenced by the experience of the Brazilian dictatorship. After 1967 the country's economy tripled in size in less than fifteen years. Cardoso did not doubt that the country was developing, even if it was flawed by the antidemocratic nature of the Brazilian state and business community.

Where some saw contact with the world economy as an obstacle for developing countries to overcome, Cardoso argued that it was an essential feature of their growth. He dismissed the view of Communists and others on the Left that local capitalists would be nationalistic members of an anti-imperialist alliance. He insisted that "the dominant classes, given the increasing internationalization of production, are forced to make deals with foreign interests and to reorganize the internal system of economic exploitation in order to cope with new realities."[12] In much of Latin America, he wrote, "the state embodies an alliance between the interests of the internationalized sector of the bourgeoisie and those of the public and entrepreneurial bureaucracies. The local bourgeoisie links itself to these sectors."[13] This alliance might have authoritarian and other retrograde tendencies, but it also could push poor countries toward rapid economic development.

Events soon gave Cardoso the opportunity to test his theory that the right government with the right policies could cure some of the ills of underdevelopment. By the early 1980s economic mismanagement had driven Brazil into chronic hyperinflation and crisis, even the country's business elite seemed eager for change, and the once-proud military dictatorship was in disorderly retreat. In 1978, taking advantage of the political opening, Cardoso ran for senator from São Paulo State as a candidate of the legal opposition. He came in second, and when the winner became state governor in 1982, by Brazilian law Cardoso entered the Senate. He lost a hard-fought campaign for mayor of the city of São Paulo in 1985, but he remained a prominent senator and was a leader of the Constituent Assembly that wrote the country's new democratic constitution. Cardoso now tried to harness his radical beliefs to practical political reform. He insisted: "I am favorable to abolishing the system of exploiters and exploited! But this is a statement of faith, which has perhaps a biographical or moral importance. What is important is to develop a political attitude, not a moralistic attitude. What is important is to know which forces are moving in a given direction, to introduce the act of faith into the reality of the current situation."[14]

Cardoso's estimate of the "reality of the current situation" led him to call for Brazil to jettison protectionism and statism. He told the Senate in January 1988: "Choosing development implies a process which, for lack of a better name, I will call 'modernization,' but which in truth is the 'globalization' of the economy. . . . Brazil cannot isolate itself, anachronistically, with an outdated policy of autarchy which runs the risk of turning it into a huge Cambodia."[15]

Meanwhile the Brazilian political system was collapsing. The first civilian government did not resolve the country's economic problems, and in 1990 the country elected a little-known provincial politician, Fernando Collor de Mello, to the presidency. Two years after taking office, Collor de Mello was impeached for corruption, dishonesty, and general incompetence, and a caretaker coalition took over. A few years earlier Cardoso had helped create a new Social Democratic Party, and the Social Democrats participated in the postimpeachment government. Cardoso became foreign minister in 1992, then finance minister in 1993. He entered government at a critical juncture: Inflation was over 2,000 percent, manufacturing production had dropped nearly 20 percent in three years, and Brazil's trade was stagnant. A succession of government plans to rein in the crisis had failed, and the country's characteristic optimism was in short supply.

As finance minister Cardoso in 1994 introduced yet another plan, this one called the Real Plan, named for the new currency pegged at one real to the dollar. The plan succeeded where others had failed largely because Cardoso was willing to impose austerity where others had not. Inflation came down quickly, and the economy remained strong. In the early euphoria of the Real Plan, Cardoso was elected president of Brazil.

He pushed on with his economic reforms, reduced trade barriers, deepened the country's commitment to the Mercosur customs union with Argentina, Paraguay, and Uruguay, and sold off a hundred billion dollars' worth of public enterprises, including flagship electric power, telecommunications, steel, and railroad companies. Within four years inflation was down below 10 percent, Brazil's trade had doubled, and the economy was growing. It had become a magnet for foreign lenders and investors, drawing in tens of billions of dollars every year.

Cardoso's former friends on the Left severely criticized his embrace of international trade and investment and his enthusiasm for dismantling much of the public sector. The president dismissed the criticisms as "pure posturing, on a purely ethical plane. . . . They do not see reality, they do not see the real social patterns, they do not see that which is changing. They do not see even the facts. This prevents political action."[16] He insisted on the need to adapt to changing realities, even while holding to his principles. "We must continue to be, in this sense, socialists," he said in 1997, "concerned about the social. But this cannot be done in the old fashioned way, as if it were possible, by an act of political will, to push a button and make things happen."[17]

Cardoso was a master of practical politics. He became the first elected president in forty years to serve out a full term, and in 1998 he won an unprecedented second term in office. The 1998–1999 currency crisis cast a shadow on the government's economic management, but the Marxist sociology professor had succeeded where so many others had failed. Cardoso's government had tamed inflation and a runaway public sector, cut trade barriers, and turned the country's economy toward world markets. The president was unmoving in his belief that his political actions were consistent with his theoretical commitments. He argued that he was "making it possible for the most advanced sectors of capitalism to prevail. It is certainly not a regime at the service of monopoly capitalism nor of bureaucratic capitalism, but of that capitalism which is competitive under the new conditions of production. It is, in this sense, socially progressive."[18]

After the "lost decade" of the 1980s, with debt crisis and depression, hyperinflation and political disarray, Cardoso's Brazil was mightily transformed in under ten years. The Cardoso government dismantled its dominant role in production and eliminated most of its controls on foreign trade. Brazil's businesses entered world markets with an enthusiasm not seen since the coffee boom of the 1920s, while foreign investment flooded into the subcontinent with equal enthusiasm. Brazil vaulted from economic near isolation to vigorous engagement, leading the world's third-largest trade bloc. It was too early to tell if the Marxist professor's hypothesis—that good government and globalization could lead to economic development—was confirmed. But Brazil was an undisputed part of the evolving international division of labor.

Eastern Europe joins the West

After the Berlin Wall fell, it was common to wonder whether the formerly Communist nations of Central and Eastern Europe could ever be on track to catch up economically with the West. The answer to the question is ambiguous, for several reasons. For one thing, the statistics are hard to evaluate, both from the era of central planning and from the period of very rapid flux since then, and by the end of the century results were still unclear. For another, it is hard to compare living standards in a centrally planned economy with those in a market economy; how can we weigh the cradle-to-grave security of communism against the consumer and job freedom of capitalism? Finally, the experiences of the transition economies varied widely: Between 1990 and 2000 Central Europe and the Baltic states did vastly better than most of the constituent parts of the former Soviet Union.

The 1990s were extremely difficult for all of Central and Eastern Europe, especially for the former Soviet Union. Optimists point to a tier of high achievers in Central Europe: Poland, Hungary, the Czech Republic, Slovakia, and Slovenia, along with the Baltic nation of Estonia. Even among these showcases of capitalism, Poland was the only unambiguous case of improvement; its economy grew by one-third between 1990 and 2000. In the rest of the region, output per person in 2000 was barely at its 1989 levels. Conventional measures of economic growth did not provide clear evidence that these transitional nations were converging on Western living standards.

The Central Europeans (and perhaps the Balts) nonetheless began to catch up with Western Europe in several ways. One way was political, with the consolidation of democracy and of European-style social welfare states. Another was institutional, as the legal and political groundwork was laid for capitalism. Financial systems, commercial networks, and regulatory administrations all developed to promote the new economies. Finally, and perhaps most important, these countries entered the economic orbit of the European Union. They reoriented their economies away from the Soviet Union and its allies and threw themselves enthusiastically into the Western European single market. After negotiating the terms of their eventual entry into the European Union, the more advanced Central European nations implemented European policies and prepared for full membership in the EU. They searched out ways to take advantage of their geographical and economic characteristics to attract foreign investment and to sell their products in Western markets.

Some Central European countries had a head start. Hungary, Poland, and Slovenia had reformed substantially during the era of central planning and were already familiar with a competitive business environment—albeit not quite as competitive as that of true capitalism. The former Czechoslovakia had long-standing industrial experience, for the Czech lands had been one of Europe's leading manufacturing regions for a century, and some of its products had remained well regarded even during the Communist era. Estonia, with a linguistic and cultural affinity for its Finnish brethren fifty miles away, had been something of a gateway to the West even under the Soviets.

Still, skeptics doubted the ability of people in Central Europe to adapt to a capitalist social order with which only the elderly had any personal experience. They speculated that the region's social and cultural realities would slow the move to the market. But in fact this first tier of Central European countries jumped quickly into a market economy and global markets. This occurred even though democratic elections often brought former Communists back into power, as happened in Poland and Hungary. The Left remade itself as the social democratic guarantor of capitalism with a human face and carried through with privatization and other elements of the move to the market. Political stability, reform progress, skilled and cheap labor, and active business communities made them attractive to multinational corporate investment. This was true both for companies that wanted access to the growing Central and Eastern European consumer markets and for those that wanted to use the transition countries as platforms to produce cheap exports for sale in the West. Over the 1990s Hungary with ten million people drew in twenty billion dollars in foreign direct investment, more than Russia with its two hundred million people. Poland attracted thirty billion dollars from foreign corporations, the Czech Republic fifteen billion.

Corporations flocked to the region. Western European firms moved quickly to rebuild commercial ties that had been cut for decades and to carve out production sites and markets in the EU's rediscovered hinterland. American and Asian firms seeking a low-cost springboard to the EU market also took up the opportunity. Daewoo spent $1.5 billion to build two Polish auto plants; Sony set up state-of-the-art factories to make consumer electronics in Hungary; Goodyear took over a Polish tiremaker; Volkswagen bought up the Czech Republic's respected Skoda automaker. Sweden's Electrolux, the world's leading producer of kitchen appliances, turned a musty Hungarian state refrigerator producer into one of the region's industrial showcases.

Western European companies were especially eager to buy up existing factories or set up new ones in Central Europe to improve their global competitive position. The former Communist region's skilled workers and low wages made it a natural place to produce parts and components for the integrated European industrial economy. In 1991, for example, Thomson—a French conglomerate whose consumer electronics division sells under such names as GE, RCA, and Telefunken— snatched up a failing Polish television factory that made barely a hundred thousand picture tubes a year. Soon Thomson Polkolor's now sparklingly efficient plant produced nearly five million tubes, two-thirds of them for foreign sale. Overall, Poland exported a half billion dollars in TV sets and much more in components, and fully half of Poland's total exports came from the local affiliates of multinational corporations.

By the end of the century Central Europe was crucial to the European economy as the principal local supplier of low-cost, high-skilled labor. The region's companies supplied axles to Volvo, furniture to IKEA, and electronic equipment to Philips. Central European products were indispensable to cost-conscious EU manufacturers facing competition from North America and East Asia. Just as Mexico and the Caribbean Basin were drawn into an integrated North American production complex, so did the Central and Eastern Europeans establish a vital position in the European industrial economy. In 1990, when the Berlin Wall came down, few would have anticipated that by 2000 the Central European nations would be integral to the European Union's economy.

A new international division of labor

Phalanx after phalanx of developing and transitional countries marched into the new international division of labor, sorting themselves according to the economic characteristics most likely to succeed. The first four East Asian Tigers—South Korea, Taiwan, Hong Kong, and Singapore—used low wages to stake early claims as producers of such labor-intensive manufactures as clothing, shoes, and furniture. As industrial success caused wages to rise and price them out of these markets, they moved on to take advantage of their still-moderate labor costs, relatively skilled workers, and now substantial industrial experience to progress into such mid-range manufactures as consumer electronics and computers.

A new wave of East Asian nations—Thailand, Indonesia, and especially China—quickly filled the market position vacated by the earlier industrializers. East Asian nations in 2000 ranged across the regional division of labor from poorest to richest, from most labor-intensive to highest technology, from lowest- to highest-skilled workers—in other words, from China, through Taiwan and Korea, to Japan. Japan was the financial and technological leader. South Korea and Taiwan had skilled workers, technicians, and managers and concentrated on manufacturing such sophisticated products as computers, automobiles, and electronic equipment. The newer industrializers, especially China, dominated the market for labor-intensive goods.

Developing countries everywhere looked for ways to succeed as investment sites or export platforms. Location was one such attraction. Mexico's proximity to the American market enabled it to assemble goods for reexport, a process that the rest of the Caribbean Basin tried to emulate. Central Europe played on its ability to serve as an adjunct to the single European market. Chile and New Zealand turned another locational feature, their site in the Southern Hemisphere, into an off-season fresh food production advantage.

Natural or human resources also provided the springboard to success. China had low wages, as did some other poor countries of Asia. Brazil and Indonesia had minerals; Thailand and Vietnam had tropical agriculture and aquaculture. India's wealth of well-trained, English-speaking engineers provided the foundation for one of the world's leading software industries.

Countries drawn into the cutthroat rivalry of world markets were driven to hone their competitive skills and to focus on what they did best. As they did so, their economies became more efficient and grew rapidly. These were the success stories, the supporting arguments for global capitalism. Their achievements were real, in economic growth, in living standards, even—in most cases—in broader social development. Some took issue with the cost of the transition, or with the increased vulnerability to international economic volatility, or with the greater penetration by foreign influences. But the enthusiastic globalizers of East Asia and Latin America shared in the rapid economic growth of the late twentieth century.

19

Countries Fall Behind

When the people of Zambia celebrated the creation of their new nation in 1965, they had reason for optimism. The country was one of the better-off former colonies in Africa—not rich but prosperous and promising. Zambia and South Korea were at roughly equivalent levels of development; but Zambia was rich in copper, and its government was honest and trusted, while South Korea had no resources to speak of, and its leaders were despised and ridiculed. The British colony of Northern Rhodesia had been a major world copper producer for over twenty years. The newly elected president, Kenneth Kaunda, was popular at home and respected abroad for his intelligence and seriousness of purpose.

Thiry years later the average Zambian had barely half the income he'd had at independence, and Kaunda had been voted out of office in disgrace. After just thirty years South Korea was now *eighteen times* richer than Zambia; the average Korean produced as much in three weeks as the average Zambian did in a year. South Korea was on the verge of joining the developed world, but the economy of Zambia and countries like it had failed so miserably that new categories were being invented: the Fourth World, the least developed countries, failed states.

Zambia was not alone. Amid encomiums to the peace and prosperity that global capitalism was to bring, the last decades of the century could be cruel to the poor. The world's poorest countries, especially in sub-Saharan Africa, experienced little or no improvement in living standards, and often substantial declines. Many formerly centrally planned countries ended up poorer than before the transition to capitalism. Even among the better-off developing nations, debt and currency crises interrupted economic advance, and the success stories of the 1980s turned out to be less impressive after all. Overall, by 2000 poverty was afflicting some one-third of the developing world's 5 billion people. This reflected some improvement since 1985, for the *share* of the world's population living in poverty had declined, but the *number* of poor people had risen by 100 million, to 1.6 billion.[1]

The benefits of global economic integration did not seem to have reached the billions of people who were falling farther behind the rich. Even more alarming, hundreds of millions had suffered a real decline in living standards: Not only did they not keep pace with residents of the faster-growing countries, but they were also actually becoming worse off. From 1973 to the end of the century output per person doubled in the advanced capitalist countries and tripled in the rapidly growing nations of Asia. In what economist Angus Maddison called the 168 "faltering economies" of Africa, stagnant Asia, Latin America, Eastern Europe, and the former Soviet Union, output dropped 10 percent.[2] These countries had more than one-third of the world's population, and none had done better than cling to a low rung on the developmental ladder.

The abject growth failures at the end of the twentieth century were hardly relevant to the world economic order. The poorest countries represented only a tiny share of world trade, investment, and production. Even if one uses the most generous of estimates and inflates them to reflect actual purchasing power, Africa from Algeria to Zimbabwe produced barely 3 percent of the world's output. Africa's most populous nation, Nigeria, with 110 million people, had an economy smaller than Switzerland, with 7 million people. The continent, with a population of 800 million, roughly equal to that of all the industrial countries of Western Europe, North America, and Japan combined, had a smaller economy than Italy or California. Even the direst economic events in so small a portion of the global economy had little direct economic impact on the rest of the world.

Nonetheless, there were two reasons for concern about the grim conditions of one-quarter of humanity. The first was moral: One could hardly speak seriously about global economic progress when there were more malnourished children in Africa and South Asia in 2000 than there had been in 1975. The second was pragmatic: The widening gap between rich and poor posed potential threats even to the rich. Political resentments among people who blamed their social ills on global capitalism could turn into hostility to the West. More pathetically, societies in the throes of developmental disaster could collapse into chaos and disorder, with frightening consequences for the health and safety of their neighbors and others. The glaring gap between wealth and poverty called out for attention—although rarely with much response.

Reform and transition disappointed

By the turn of the new century the path to growth seemed to run inevitably through globalization, yet this path was littered with disappointments. Scores of countries in the developing and Communist worlds had turned away from protectionism and planning and toward the market, yet few of them had realized substantial improvements in living standards. The reasons for these frustrating performances ranged from bad policies and poor implementation to bad luck and political troubles. The disappointments revealed that there was no simple solution to the problems of development and that the obstacles to success could be daunting.

Some of the disappointments were due to foot-dragging in adopting new policies. Many countries came late, reluctantly, and partially to accept that import substitution and related strategies were not working. Egypt, for example, started dismantling its "Arab socialism" before 1980, but economic change was intermittent at best. Most Egyptian efforts to liberalize were incomplete, and many were reversed before they were fully implemented. Politics ruled: Reform of trade and industry meant attacking special interests in the bureaucracy and the business community, while budgetary reform meant cutting social services, a course that fueled the radical Islamist opposition movements. Twenty years of halfhearted economic reform brought the country's seventy million people little more than economic stagnation.

Halfway around the world, similar disappointments ensued after the mass protests of the Philippines' People Power movement chased

Ferdinand Marcos from office in 1986. The country entered a new era committed to reform, and democratic governments promised to dismantle the "crony capitalism" of the Marcos regime. Here too changes were politically difficult and were put into effect slowly and poorly. The results were as mediocre as in Egypt: By 2000, per capita income was barely equal to what it had been in the fading years of the Marcos dictatorship. The island nation's relative performance was particularly dismal: In 1980 the Philippines and Thailand had roughly similar standards of living, but by 2000 Thailand had an income per person triple that of the Philippines.

The former Soviet bloc presents striking cases of partial reform and economic disenchantment. No one expected that it would be easy to overcome decades of central planning and economic isolation. The technical and organizational problems of establishing a market economy were compounded by political and social obstacles. Entrenched interests characterized the transition economies. Bureaucrats, factory managers, and other insiders knew how to work the system to their benefit and used that knowledge as the system unraveled. They blocked unfavorable economic change, staked out monopoly positions for themselves and their firms, and acquired control of the most valuable assets of companies that were supposed to be privatized.

While members of the former ruling groups blocked or subverted economic change, the general public was itself wary of marketization. Residents of the Soviet bloc had come to depend on communism's social stability, full employment, readily available and inexpensive social services, and education. With capitalism came risk, the threat of poverty, and even hunger. People would not throw themselves into the market without a safety net, and governments faced insistent demands for social services even as they ran out of money. These factors slowed economic reform throughout the former Soviet Union and the more backward Balkan nations—Albania, Bulgaria, Romania, and the former Yugoslavia.

Few anticipated the economic collapse that attended the transition from socialism to capitalism. In 2000 real income per person in the former Soviet Union was barely half what it had been a decade earlier. The economy had dropped to barely one-third its 1989 size in the southern tier of the former USSR, an area with eighty million people stretching from Moldova and Ukraine, through Armenia, Azerbaijan, and Georgia, to Central Asia. In these countries, the standard of living was comparable to that prevailing before World War Two; the transitional collapse had set them back more than fifty years. In Russia and Belarus, Lithuania and Latvia, and parts of Central Asia, output per person hovered around half its prereform levels, roughly equal to the living standards of 1960.

In most of the former Soviet Union during the 1990s, the proportion of the population in poverty went from 2 percent to over 50 percent. This was particularly shocking against the historical backdrop of a socialist system that had, whatever its failings, provided an effective social safety net to protect citizens from abject impoverishment. It was especially galling to the average citizen, for the galloping immiseration took place even as high-fashion boutiques, exclusive nightclubs, and luxury car dealerships sprang up all over Moscow, St. Petersburg, and Kiev to service a new generation of privatization millionaires, robber barons of the new capitalism.

Social and health conditions deteriorated alarmingly, especially in the former Soviet Union. It may have been inevitable that as the country's socialist system collapsed and the market took over, the gap between rich and poor would grow. But the speed at which inequality grew and the size of the gap between rich and poor were a shock: In the space of ten years Russia went from having a distribution of income roughly as egalitarian as Scandinavia to being as socially polarized as such sub-Saharan African nations as Zambia. By 1998 the richest 10 percent of Russians was earning twice as large a share of the country's income as they had ten years before, while the poorest half earned only half as much. [3] The economic upheavals decimated the country's health, in part because health care spending dropped by two-thirds. Male life expectancy declined precipitously in the early 1990s, bottoming out at fifty-seven years, comparable to that of Pakistan. The overall adult male death rate was more than one-quarter higher in 1999 than it had been in 1990, a phenomenon virtually unprecedented in modern countries, except in times of war.

Given this collapse in living standards, a decade after the former Soviet Union and its former allies started down the path to capitalism, public opinion was unenthusiastic about the choice. Country after country in the former Soviet Union and Eastern Europe voted in governments led by the former Communist Party. Many of the Communists had remade themselves as Western European–style Social Democrats, but still the sight of Lithuania and Poland, Ukraine and Hungary freely electing Communist governments just a few years after the Berlin Wall came down was striking. Support for erstwhile Communists there, as elsewhere in the former Soviet bloc, largely reflected the belief that the transition to capitalism had been too harsh, and its social costs too high, and that the Communists would restore balance between markets and social policies.

Estonia and Uzbekistan were the only two countries of the former Soviet Union whose economies were roughly back to their 1989 size by 2000. They represented extremes: Estonia was the most European of former Soviet states, Uzbekistan one of the most Muslim; Estonia was the most thoroughly reformed and democratic, Uzbekistan one of the more authoritarian and economically unchanged. The reasons for their relative success—if an arduous ten-year battle to stand still can be considered success—were diametrically opposed: Estonia succeeded because it reformed most completely, Uzbekistan because it changed almost not at all. Nonetheless, they were the exceptions. The rest of the former Soviet Union stumbled along a path of incomplete economic and political change and fell farther and farther behind the West.

Conditions elsewhere in the former Soviet bloc were not so dire, but hardly cheerful. Central and Eastern European countries adopted market economies vigorously. They fell less and recovered more quickly, so that by 2000 living standards had climbed back to, or above, prereform levels. The more backward, less reformed economies of the Balkans were on average about one-fifth poorer than they had been at the end of the Communist era. As in the former USSR, extremes of wealth and poverty proliferated. Many found it hard to accept that it would take decades to approach the living standards prevailing a few hundred miles away, across the Danube. Millions of Eastern Europeans fled westward, joining Turks and North Africans on the lower rungs of the employment ladder in cities from Madrid to Berlin.

Desperate people around the region also flocked to absurdly improbable get-rich-quick investment funds. Romania alone had six hundred such Ponzi schemes; the largest, Caritas, promised to double investors' money in three weeks. It drew in one-fifth of the country's population before it collapsed with more than a billion dollars in unrecoverable debts. In Albania, the poorest country in the region, the pyramids sucked in half the population and grew to equal the size of the nation's economy. When they, inevitably, collapsed, the ensuing financial panic, political crisis, and rioting in the streets forced the Albanian government, many of whose members and supporters had promoted the schemes, to make good on some of the investments, at a cost equal to three-quarters of its annual budget. The ease with which classic Ponzi schemes drew in Russians, Czechs, and Bulgarians reflected a combination of disappointment with the realities of market societies and delusion about what a market economy could provide.

Parallel disappointments afflicted Latin America, where globalization bore fewer tangible fruits than its supporters had hoped. Most of the region followed Western advice with more fealty than adepts of the Washington Consensus dared hope, but many regional economies were stagnant or worse. After fifteen years of stabilization, adjustment, and economic reform, only one Latin American country, Chile, had an output per person unambiguously higher in 2000 than it had been in 1980. A few others might have grown slightly, but the rest were no better off or were substantially worse off. This was distressing, for such countries as Mexico and Argentina had been models of privatization, trade liberalization, and macroeconomic integrity. After the terrible "lost decade" of the 1980s, they had implemented wrenching reforms that promised renewed growth. But reality disappointed; what growth there was in the 1990s was eroded by recurring crises and recessions.

Some Latin American problems were due to incomplete or insufficient adoption of new policies. For example, some countries flung their doors open to foreign finance without modernizing their domestic financial structures and regulations. At times the resulting inflows of capital overwhelmed national banking systems and contributed to devastating banking crises. In other instances, governments were caught between the desire to keep currencies strong to control inflation and the conflicting desire to keep currencies weak to stimulate exports. This led to currency crises—Mexico in 1994, Brazil in 1998–1999, Argentina in 2001–2002—that stopped growth. The region's transformation did lead to manufacturing industries with better quality, higher technology, and more consumer choice. Moreover, the experience of Chile, where the fruits of reform were not fully realized for fifteen years, held out hope for the rest of the region. Still, disappointment pervaded Latin America as the new century began.

The experience of the 1990s demonstrated the pain and difficulty of undoing decades of economic policies. Economic, political, and social relations had developed under the old orders of import substitution and central planning, and it was complicated to unravel these policies. Even where, as in much of Latin America and Central Europe, there was support for reform and the policy changes were reasonably well implemented, growth was slow or negative. Much of the former Soviet Union and the Balkans, where there was less enthusiasm for reform efforts and less willingness to make sacrifices on their behalf, risked long-term stagnation. At the turn of the twenty-first century the promise of globalization remained only that, a promise, for many of the developing and transitional economies that had embraced it.

Developmental disasters

While the economic experiences of Latin America and the former Soviet bloc were disappointing, those of some other parts of the developing world were truly disastrous. The real economic catastrophes were mostly in sub-Saharan Africa and the Middle East, with a peppering of other cases in Asia and the Caribbean Basin. Portions of the developing world spun downward into abject poverty and despair.

No place matched the appalling decline in Africa. Not every country on the continent was a disaster. The southern African nations of South Africa, Swaziland, Botswana, Namibia; the Mediterranean countries of North Africa; and Gabon and Congo, two tiny oil producers, were on average three or four times better off than the rest of the region. But the remaining forty-three African nations and their half billion people were collectively the poorest in the world, and getting poorer; between 1980 and 2000 their average income dropped by one-quarter. The enthusiasm and optimism of newly independent Africa in the 1960s collapsed into unprecedented failure, as most of these countries ended the century poorer than they had been at independence.

These impoverished—indeed impoverishing—African nations took many paths to economic retrogression. Some could point to factors beyond their control. World oil price increases created serious problems for countries dependent upon imported oil; the same was true of declines in prices of the region's principal export commodities, such as cocoa and copper. Some scholars argue that climate and disease make the tropics particularly inhospitable to modern economic activity; infectious diseases such as malaria are difficult to control, and extreme heat or rainfall makes for adverse labor conditions. Others emphasize the difficulties of poor natural transportation compounded by bizarre boundaries the colonial powers imposed. Indeed, most African nations are tropical, landlocked, or both.[4] Yet daunting as development may be in the objective conditions facing the very poor countries, national experiences have been remarkably diverse. Compare, for example, similar countries one of which has succeeded while the other has failed: Botswana-Zambia, Gabon-Zaire, Thailand-Burma. Many countries have adjusted to the shock of rising import prices or falling export prices. The greater accomplishments of some countries than others in their neighborhood, and with similar products, argue for causes other than a blanket geographical condemnation to destitution.

Postcolonial regional, political, ethnic, and other conflicts took their toll. Angola descended into civil war immediately after independence from Portugal in 1975, as regional, ideological, and ethnic factions battled for control. Despite extraordinary natural resources—oil, diamonds, coffee—twenty-five years of warfare condemned Angola to finish the century two-thirds poorer than at the time of independence. At the other corner of the continent, Ethiopia's people barely had time to celebrate the overthrow of Haile Selassie in 1974 when the country plunged into fifteen years of conflict, first within the new military regime and then between the government and rebel groups. The 1991 victory of the rebels led to a few years' peace, but eventually war with Eritrea broke out. Countries like Angola and Ethiopia and dozens of others among the poorest of the poor spent so much time, energy, and money on military and civil conflict that it is not surprising that little remained for economic development.

Then there was the new category of "failed states," countries that ceased to exist as organized entities. The appellation was controversial, but countries like Afghanistan, Somalia, Liberia, Yemen, and Sierra Leone fell for extended periods into something approaching anarchy, with no established government and an atmosphere of terror and lawlessness, a breakdown of the existing social order with no replacement in sight. Slow economic growth was trivial compared with the murder of hundreds of thousands of civilians by marauding bands or with the genocide that tore Rwanda apart.

Nonetheless, these tragedies are not principally to blame for the economic disasters of the least developed countries. Economic failures were more commonly *causes* of civil war and government breakdown than their result; the rulers' inability to provide the basic needs of their people led to the collapse of their rule. The fact that such countries as Ghana, Haiti, Sudan, Liberia, Afghanistan, and El Salvador were poorer in 1980 than twenty years earlier was a major source of the conflicts that consumed them and dozens of other nations after 1980. What produced the developmental disasters of the late twentieth century? External events and uncontrollable internal strife were debilitating, but failures of government, not force of circumstance, produced the collapses.

The Zambian road

Kenneth Kaunda led the Zambian people to independence and ruled for nearly thirty years after liberation. Despite his political effectiveness during the struggle for liberation and an apparently sincere dedication to his people's well-being, he presided over a catastrophic economic failure.

The sorry saga began stirringly. Kaunda was the eighth child of a Church of Scotland minister from what is now Malawi. When he was born in 1924, his parents were missionaries in the northern stretches of the British colony of Northern Rhodesia (the future Zambia). The 1920s saw two important developments: First, the British South Africa Company's charter in Southern Rhodesia (the future Zimbabwe) expired, and white settlers took control of the self-governing colony; second, copper was discovered in Northern Rhodesia. By the early 1940s Northern Rhodesia had a booming copper sector and Southern Rhodesia's white-run agriculture was thriving. Kenneth Kaunda graduated from the only secondary school in the colony open to Africans and began work as a schoolteacher. Early on he became active in African self-help groups and independence organizations.

During the 1950s anticolonial African activists squared off against both white settlers and the British government. The British wanted to merge Northern and Southern Rhodesia, along with Nyasaland (now Malawi), into a settler-dominated federation. Kaunda and other Africans opposed federation vigorously, largely under the leadership of the African National Congress (ANC). After federation in 1953 Kaunda became the ANC's secretary-general. For five more years he was one of the organization's top leaders, promoting everything from boycotts of segregated shops to civil disobedience. As editor of the ANC's magazine Kaunda was arrested and served a two-month term of hard labor. Eventually he found himself at odds with more moderate groups in the ANC and led a breakaway Zambia African National Congress (ZANC). Arrested again by the British in 1959, Kaunda emerged from prison to lead a new United National Independence Party (UNIP). In 1964, as the federation splintered into its component parts—Nyasaland into Malawi, Northern Rhodesia into Zambia, Southern Rhodesia into white-ruled Rhodesia—Kaunda won handily a free election for Zambia's presidency.

Zambia appeared an ideal candidate for success, for it had extraordinary mineral wealth and a skilled and committed leadership. The copper belt stretched for over a hundred miles along the Congolese border and hosted a chain of thriving mining towns and cities. The new nation was, it was commonly said, "born with a copper spoon in its mouth."

But the steady stream of earnings from the country's copper mines had perverse effects on long-term development. The government, anticipating that copper money would keep flowing into the country, faced little pressure to develop the rest of the economy. Easy copper revenues encouraged Zambians to spend much of their time trying to get a share of the copper wealth. Mine workers expected high wages, city dwellers wanted high-paying government jobs and cheap food, and Zambians in general took for granted government-funded social programs and political patronage. Like the offspring of wealthy parents absorbed with spending their inheritance rather than figuring out how to earn money on their own, Zambians spent easy copper money rather than plan an economic future that did not rely on mineral wealth.[5]

During the first ten or so years of the country's independent existence, the new government implemented Zambian control of Zambian society with increasing confidence. Kaunda evinced a balanced approach to economic development, telling an English audience a year after independence: "The major aim of our economic development plan is to make the economy less dependent on minerals whilst ensuring that economic advance is spread as widely as possible. But this cannot be done by holding back mineral developments because we need the mineral output to earn foreign exchange. And pushing mineral production needs balancing; otherwise we would add to the already excessive income differentials."[6] The Kaunda government encouraged copper development, even while trying to control aspects of the foreign-owned mining operations that rankled nationalist sentiments.[7] The mining companies were ordered to promote more Zambians to managerial positions and pay more taxes to the government. The new policies gave jobs to Zambians, while expanded government spending increased the educational, health, and social services available to the rapidly growing population.

But Zambia, like most developing countries in the late 1960s, turned away from foreign ownership of raw materials production. Like most

African leaders, Kaunda saw tightened government control over the economy as necessary for the country's social progress. He promoted what he called Humanism as Zambia's guiding philosophy, with socialism the "instrument for building a Humanist society."[8] In order to move the country, in his words, "from Capitalism to Humanism through Socialism,"[9] in 1968 Kaunda launched a new economic orientation in a speech at Mulungushi, near the capital of Lusaka. Under the new Mulungushi program the state took over the copper mines, and within a few years Kaunda had nationalized companies in other key sectors of the economy: manufacturing, trade, transportation, construction, and others.

The founder of Zambian Humanism did not believe in state central planning, however. Kaunda foresaw, he said, that "the public sector will co-exist peacefully and indeed co-operate with the private sector, but more and more, as the economy expands, the public sector will engage in and establish industries which are nationally important especially in those areas where the private sector may for one reason or another be unwilling or unable to engage."[10] The principal purpose of the Mulungushi reforms was nationalistic, not socialistic. Given the huge size of the foreign businesses and the small size of the Zambian private sector, it was necessary, Kaunda said, "to give Zambian enterprise certain areas in which to operate without competition from expatriate business." The goal was "to remove foreign domination of our economic life by acquiring control of most major means of production and services while, at the same time, establishing a firm foundation for the development of genuine Zambian business."[11] As elsewhere in the developing world, the government promoted import-substituting industrialization, protecting local manufacturing with high trade barriers.

The nationalized copper mines brought the Zambian government a massive stream of income. Copper accounted for over 90 percent of exports, half of government revenue, over one-third of the economy's total output. The government spent copper wealth liberally to expand educational opportunities, train indigenous civil servants, improve health care, and build up public services. Mineral profits also made it possible to pay high wages to the country's powerful copper miners, who had been at the forefront of the independence movement that Kaunda had led. Copper money permitted the government to mandate high wages for other urban workers and to subsidize the prices of basic foodstuffs. Since copper supplied virtually all of the country's export earnings, the government did not have to worry about the uncompetitive nature of the new Zambian industries.

Copper money allowed the Kaunda government to solidify a political support base of businessmen, mine workers, government employees, and city dwellers generally. In 1972 Kaunda decreed that henceforth the country would be a single-party state with his United National Independence Party (UNIP) in command. The party dispensed patronage in return for political support. Party members and supporters were given priority for jobs in the huge public sector, for cheap loans, and for public services; those without paid-up memberships were denied access to transportation, markets, and health care. Agricultural credit was used to build support for UNIP; as one local party leader put it, the goal was "to make our best party men into farmers; we cannot stand anyone who is not UNIP."[12] The party leadership isolated and expelled opposing factions and consolidated control over the political system, the bureaucracy, and the media.[13] "By 1975," scholar Michael Bratton wrote, "UNIP had been transformed from a party of participation to a party of control."[14]

Kaunda's success began to fade even as he consolidated his single-party state. Copper prices rose after independence, and by 1974 they were double what they had been in 1964. After 1975, however, they weakened substantially, declining in some years, in others barely keeping up with inflation. Stagnant copper prices meant stagnant government revenues, but the government's supporters expected a growing stream of benefits. Soon the Kaunda administration's network of supporters began to disintegrate as the government lost the financial resources to hold it together. With copper prices weak, the state mining companies tried to restrain wages, but the mine workers' union was powerful enough to block this. As copper revenues fell, the government needed manufacturers to produce more for export, but they were so uncompetitive that they had little hope of selling abroad. The neglect of agriculture had depressed farm production, so that one-quarter of the country's food had to be bought abroad even as foreign currency to pay for food imports dried up. The bloated public sector, which accounted for three-quarters of formal employment, had to be cut back, but government employees were heavily unionized and politically central to the ruling party's hold on power.

The choices of the early days came back to haunt Kaunda. The government had used copper money to buy political support or acquiescence from protected industries, miners, beneficiaries of government services, consumers of subsidized food, and government workers. But as copper earnings declined, the Kaunda administration needed to reduce what it gave miners, government workers, and other recipients of government largess. The Zambian government was a political hostage of the political supporters it had come to rely on—and whom it could no longer satisfy.[15]

As the Kaunda government ran out of money, it was forced away from its developmentalist and social welfare commitments. In October 1985, with the economy collapsing and the government under pressure from the IMF and World Bank, Kaunda turned toward economic reform. The government freed many prices, removed controls on the currency, restrained the wages of public employees, laid off some government workers, and reduced subsidies that kept the price of food—especially the national staple, cornmeal—artificially low.

The measures led to unrest, riots in the copper belt, and a series of strikes that came close to shutting the country down. In May 1987, faced with a continued erosion of popular support and mounting discontent within his own party Kaunda repudiated the reforms and reversed course. But the government did not have the resources necessary to satisfy its opponents or even to sustain its supporters. Strikes and civil unrest recurred as wages fell behind prices. Frederick Chiluba, the head of the country's labor union federation, attacked the government at every opportunity, insisting on an end to one-party rule. In June 1990, new food riots broke out as cornmeal prices rose again. Meanwhile the already unsettled political life of the country was made even more volatile as the country fell victim to the AIDS epidemic that was sweeping Africa. By 1991 one-third of all pregnant city women tested were HIV-positive, as were an estimated one-fifth of all adult Zambians. Not only had Kaunda's government overseen the collapse of the country's economy, but it was also presiding over the horrible deaths of large portions of the nation's population.

Kaunda agreed to multiparty elections. In October 1991 the Movement for Multiparty Democracy led by trade union leader Chiluba outpolled Kaunda's party three to one. In the copper belt, Chiluba got 90 percent of the vote, but the defeat was overwhelming everywhere; of Zambia's nine provinces, Kaunda took only one. After nearly forty years as Zambia's national leader, first in the struggle for independence and then as its only president, Kenneth Kaunda left office. Zambia was far poorer than it had been at independence, with no easy way out of its predicament.

African catastrophe

Zambia was hardly alone in its economic collapse or in the political sources of its tribulations. Protracted and systematic misrule led many countries to fall behind the rest of the world. Only powerful social and political pressures could lead governments to persist in such destructive policies. Governments actively discouraged producers in Africa from doing what they did well, for political reasons. In an attempt to move away from the agrarian past and present, rulers discriminated against agriculture and favored manufacturing. Governments taxed industrious farmers on fertile land, driving many of them out of farming, but richly subsidized investors who set up factories whose output was unmarketable.

Tanzania provided sad examples of the punishments inflicted on agriculture and the failures of hothouse industrialization. The prominent African liberation leader Julius Nyerere ruled the country directly or indirectly from independence in 1961 until 1990. Nyerere, intent on transforming the country's traditional economic base, tried a number of innovative rural initiatives. But these measures could not overcome the extraordinary antiagricultural bias of the government's development policies, which severely depressed the return to farming. This was an unnecessary disaster for a country that was more than 90 percent rural, with substantial potential for such export crops as coffee, cashews, and tea.

Meanwhile taxpayers and foreign donors poured money into manufacturing ventures that were worse than worthless. The Morogoro shoe factory was financed with forty million dollars in World Bank funds and opened in 1980 to great fanfare. It was to be one of the world's largest shoe factories, with a capacity of four million pairs a year, of which three million were expected to be exported. Exports would allow the government-owned mill to pay back the World Bank and generate profits. But neither the government nor the World Bank took into account the extremely high price of electric power in Tanzania, the poor quality of local hides, its high tariffs on imported materials, and the scarcity of labor capable of working modern assembly lines. Nor was the factory, with steel pillars, aluminum walls, and no ventilation, designed for Tanzania's tropical climate. The venture was a disaster. It never turned out more than 4 percent of its capacity, at its best a few hundred pairs of shoes a day. The factory never exported a pair of shoes. The shoes the company made were actually worth less than the overpriced inputs used to produce them, and by the middle 1980s the firm was losing a half million dollars a year, not counting the cost of servicing the World Bank debt. A visitor to the plant in the early 1990s was told that the absent manager was suffering from severe depression, caused in part by the stress of a constant stream of people interested in visiting the spectacular failure.[16] The company was sold to private investors in the early 1990s, but they could not overcome the folly of building a shoe industry on such flimsy foundations, and the factory soon closed.

Worthless industrial projects sprouted all over Africa, unable to operate even with billions of government dollars. Morogoro shoe was small change compared with some of the other white elephants. Nigeria's Ajaokuta steelworks was intended to be one of the continent's flagship steel mills with a workforce of ten thousand. The undertaking devoured more than four billion dollars over twenty years without ever producing steel; half the money was estimated to have ended up in the pockets of successive generations of Nigerian public and private figures. By the end of the century goats and cattle were wandering through the nearly deserted steel mill, even as the government promised to pour another half billion dollars into the project in yet one more effort to bring it to completion.[17] All this for the purported benefit of the 10 or 15 percent of the population that lived in the cities, while agriculture sank farther and farther into penury.

These apparently perverse government policies had a logic that grew out of resource endowments, social and political institutions, and economic conditions. The colonial political economies had relied on exporting primary products to the mother country: copper from Congo to Belgium, coffee from Kenya to Britain, cacao from Côte d'Ivoire to France, petroleum from Angola to Portugal. The opponents of colonialism naturally were hostile to these export ties and to those who benefited from them. The governments of most newly independent countries sought to downgrade these traditional economic activities in favor of new ones, especially manufacturing.

The desire to industrialize Tanzania or Ghana was understandable, but government attempts to do so bled farmers dry. Farm prices were kept low to supply cheap food to city dwellers, while prices of urban products and services were very high, both of which squeezed the profits out of farming. After all, the cities were the repositories of modernity, as well as the main political bases of the postcolonial governments, including their armies and bureaucracies. In this calculation, the new African rulers were similar to proponents of import substitution in Latin America, forced industrialization in the Soviet Union, or industrial protection in late-nineteenth-century America: Policy would channel resources into the urban economy in order to industrialize the country. But Africa was far less developed than any of these societies had been when they embarked on their developmental journeys; many African countries had 90 percent or more of the population living in the countryside and only the most rudimentary of industrial and urban sectors. It was one thing to push farm prices down artificially in Mexico or Turkey where half the country was farmers and half city dwellers; but when nine-tenths of the country were farmers, the effect was quite different. The average African economy in 1960 was comparable to that of Latin America or Russia a century earlier, in 1860. When the Soviet and Latin American industrialization drives began in the 1930s, they had developed far beyond the economies of postcolonial Africa.

In the African context, soaking the countryside to modernize the cities had almost entirely negative effects. It impoverished farmers but had almost no impact on industrial development; there was simply too little to build upon. The Nigerian electric power grid was so inadequate that the country's small manufacturers spent on average three times as much buying their own power generators as they did on all their other capital equipment and machinery combined. Instead of improving economic infrastructure, government services, or social services, the money taken from farmers went to bloat public-sector salaries, or to line the pockets of the rich and powerful, or to reward regime supporters. As governments imposed rules that turned profitable economic activities into losing or illegal ventures, public employment became the default option for city dwellers; nearly three-quarters of Ghana's formal labor force was employed by the government.[18]

African economies grew for a few years after 1960, but from about 1975 onward problems multiplied. Agriculture and mining, the region's former mainstays, were bled dry. Manufacturing was so weak and inefficient as to provide few jobs and fewer opportunities for economic growth. Governments spent more and more money, including aid money, to keep dictatorial regimes in power or simply to enrich the dictators themselves. From the middle 1970s until the end of the century sub-Saharan Africa was the only region of the world to experience negative growth in virtually every dimension.

The continent's impressive natural resource base seemed to be no help. To some it even seemed a major contributor to the African disaster. Governments of countries with rich resource endowments had little incentive to undertake or encourage the difficult efforts needed to make agriculture or industry productive and competitive, for they could simply sell diamonds or oil and live off the profits. A steady flow of earnings from copper mines or sugar plantations enriched rulers, rewarded supporters, and bought off potential opponents. Easy money from primary products reduced the pressure to find new, more dynamic development policies. While the governments of South Korea and Taiwan, with virtually no natural resources, had no choice but to encourage enterprise and education, the rulers of Zaire and Angola had easily exploitable minerals to sell abroad and little incentive to undertake the difficult measures to foster long-term economic growth and development. There seemed to be a "curse of resource riches" that dragged countries down.

Horror stories proliferated, not only about projects but about whole countries gone awry. One of the region's largest and most richly endowed nations, Zaire (now Democratic Republic of the Congo), was ruled virtually from independence by Joseph Mobutu, whose extraordinary venality spawned a new term, *kleptocracy*. By the early 1980s he had accumulated a fortune estimated at four billion dollars—ten years' worth of the country's exports—and mansions all over the world. By the time Mobutu was overthrown in 1997, the fifty million people of this Western Europe–size country were among the poorest on earth—possibly poorer than they had been a hundred years earlier.

The Congo's experience was more the norm than the exception. Country after country in sub-Saharan Africa collapsed economically under the weight of terrible policies and terrible politicians. Geography, resource endowments, and history may have presented governments with obstacles, but none of the disaster was predetermined. Virtually all of it resulted from powerful political pressures—from business interests, the military, government employees, ruling parties—that pulled governments away from promoting economic and social development and toward ensuring their own hold on power. Governments everywhere, of course, are concerned about their survival. But during the disastrous decades of postcolonial sub-Saharan Africa, rulers' desire for political survival seemed the principal obstacle to the survival and prosperity of Africans.

Plague, destitution, and desperation

Development failures in Africa, the Middle East, and elsewhere and the paucity of Western charity consigned hundreds of millions of people to appalling suffering. The consequences of economic collapse were felt most immediately and most keenly by the weakest—the young, the old, the infirm. In many African countries, one child in five died before his fifth birthday.[19] At the turn of the twenty-first century, between one-third and one-half of the children of South Asia and sub-Saharan Africa were malnourished, about 150 million children in all. Half of the two regions' women and one-third of the men were illiterate, and there were many countries in which female illiteracy was around 90 percent. Over half the people of the two regions subsisted on less than an internationally comparable poverty line, and around the world, there were 1.6 billion people living below this line.

The most striking result of the socioeconomic breakdown of sub-Saharan Africa was an AIDS epidemic comparable to medieval plagues. Assisted by the parlous state of nutrition and health care and by government neglect, the disease spread with extraordinary speed during the 1990s. By the end of the century nearly thirty million Africans had been infected with HIV; in southern Africa, as many of one-quarter of all adults. In some southern African cities, nearly half of pregnant women tested were HIV-positive, and almost half of them would pass the virus on to their children. Twelve million Africans died of AIDS during the 1990s, and as the new century began, more than two million people a year, including half a million children, were dying of the disease. Africans accounted for some four-fifths of all the world's AIDS deaths, and the epidemic had created more than twelve million AIDS orphans in the region. Nearly a million were in Zambia alone, where one in six children had lost a parent to AIDS.

Sub-Saharan Africa, although the world's most strikingly miserable region, was not alone. In dozens of countries elsewhere in the developing world, people's livelihoods deteriorated considerably over the last two decades of the century. Most had already been poor and ended the century even poorer. Economic collapse led to crumbling nutrition, health care, and education, as well as bitter political conflicts, including civil wars and genocides.

The development failures entailed massive human suffering, a monumental humanitarian crisis. A billion people in the developing world did not have access to clean water, and over eight hundred million were malnourished. A billion people lived in housing that did not meet the minimal standards of the United Nations. Nearly a billion had no access to any form of modern health service. This was the human impact of the gap between the very poor and the rest of the world's population. By 2000 the richest 1 percent of the world's population earned substantially more than the poorest half; indeed, the combined wealth of the world's two hundred richest individuals—more than a trillion dollars—was greater than the combined annual income of the poorest half of the world's population.

The amounts of money necessary to end this deprivation were, by industrial country standards, trivial. Experts estimated that eighty billion dollars a year would provide every inhabitant of the developing world with basic food needs, health care, education, water, and sewers. This was a trivial amount, three cents of every ten dollars of the rich world's income, less than a hundred dollars a year for the average inhabitant of the developed world, less than 8 percent of the combined wealth of the world's two hundred richest individuals. The price of ensuring that everyone in the world had basic nutrition and health was less than the amount Americans and Europeans spent on pet food in an average year.

Yet even that much aid to the poorest of the poor was not forthcoming. Foreign aid to poor countries declined almost continually. This was true of aid measured as a share of the industrial world's economies. In 1970 most developed countries agreed to try to give 0.7 percent of their GDP in aid. By 1990 it had reached a level of about 0.35 percent, but by 2000 it had fallen back again to only 0.2 percent of the GDP of the developed nations. Aid even declined in actual dollar amounts too. In real terms, controlling for inflation, the fifty-three billion dollars in development aid given in 2000 was nearly one-third less than what had been given in 1990. Aid given to the very poorest countries declined even more rapidly than overall aid.

The moral implications of grinding poverty in the poorest countries, growing wealth in the rich countries, and tiny levels of aid are not unambiguous. In many instances, humanitarian aid did not reach its intended beneficiaries, ending up instead in the pockets of the Third World rich, confirming the common charge that government was taxing poor people in rich countries to benefit rich people in poor countries. There was also evidence that giving humanitarian aid to incompetent, venal, or corrupt governments could *reduce* the governments' efforts to improve; after all, they could now rely on foreign donors to remedy their worst failings. Many governments played on geopolitical realities to extract aid that went only to enrich them and their supporters. Zaire's Mobutu, for example, was expert in playing the capitalist West off against the Communist East. Americans and Soviets alike subjugated economic and moral concerns in Africa to Cold War geopolitics—even if that meant countenancing or bankrolling policies that deepened the misery of the masses.

Only sustained economic development could ultimately solve these problems. This was largely the responsibility of the people of the poor countries themselves. Even so, it was hard to justify the paltry levels of Western foreign aid and easy to find good purposes to which more aid could be put. But as Africa spiraled downward, the advanced industrial countries did little. The end of the Cold War pushed Africa even lower on the West's agenda since the region had lost its principal leverage over Western governments, its role in U.S.-Soviet competition. The pitiful levels of northern aid in the prosperous 1990s highlighted the general unwillingness of the rich world to provide even humanitarian support to the poor countries of the world.

Those incapable of appreciating moral arguments for increased levels of assistance to the world's poor might have been moved by more pragmatic considerations. The countries with the most dismal socioeconomic indicators—those ranked lowest on the United Nations' Human Development Index—included those with the most brutal and prolonged political and civil conflicts: Rwanda and Burundi, Sierra Leone and Ethiopia. Apart from the moral imperatives, the cost of cleaning up after these conflicts almost certainly exceeded what the cost of assistance to avoid them might have been.

While Africa's wars and genocides did not pose a threat to the security of the industrialized world, other poor, troubled regions did. The world's poorest economic performers included countries that were the homes, or home bases, of violent extremists with strong anti-Western views. During the 1990s an "arc of anarchy" spread across parts of the Islamic world, from former Soviet Central Asia, through Afghanistan and Pakistan, to Yemen, Sudan, and Somalia. Virtually all these countries were at or near the bottom of any list of human and social development, and economic failure led to a broader breakdown of societies and states. Social unrest rose, and governments were even less able to provide for the basic needs of the population. In some instances, such as Somalia and Afghanistan, there was no functioning government apparatus. Even where governments held on to power, as in Egypt and Pakistan, their failure to protect the poor from economic stagnation left a vacuum into which fundamentalist extremists could step with needed social services. To the list of the Muslim world's developmental disasters one could add Iran, Iraq, and Syria, although their economic failures were related to their positions as international political pariahs. In these countries, people who felt threatened or left behind by globalization joined a strong drumbeat of protest against the West.

At the end of the twentieth century four hundred million people in the region stretching from Egypt to Pakistan and from Central Asia to Somalia were living in conditions of economic stagnation and social deprivation. These conditions bred powerful anti-Western sentiments and fed into violent movements, whose most common theme was a rejection of Western economic and cultural integration. The waves of terrorist attacks by Islamic extremists that swept across the West highlighted the fact that large parts of the Muslim world had been in social and economic decline for decades and that the West could ignore this trend only at its peril.

Successful economic development was desirable not only on moral and humanitarian grounds but as a means to help resolve some of the world's most difficult political and military problems. However, social and political realities were powerful obstacles to developmental success in many parts of the world, and even governments attempting to rectify their situation found the international diplomatic and economic environment highly constraining, even hostile. While much of the world's population leaped toward modern economic growth, led by China and India, other hundreds of millions of people fell farther behind as the century came to an end.

20

Global Capitalism Troubled

Delegates to the Third Ministerial Conference of the World Trade Organization (WTO) converged on Seattle, Washington, on November 29, 1999. Diplomatically sensitive and technically complex issues filled the agenda: opening a new round of trade talks; reducing barriers to trade in farm goods and services; revising the WTO's definition of dumping; adding labor and environmental standards to trade agreements. Prepared for difficult and acrimonious negotiations among trade delegations, the representatives of the United States, Europe, Japan, and the developing countries drifted into Seattle.

The WTO delegates were totally unprepared for what met them as they arrived in Seattle that rainy Monday. Tens of thousands of antiglobalization activists were already in the coastal city. On the eve of the opening ceremonies, thousands of protesters encircled the site of a delegates' reception, then moved on to a mass meeting nearby. At the harbor, protesters organized a Seattle Tea Party reminiscent of the Boston Tea Party of 1773. Under the slogan "No Globalization without Representation," they dumped offending goods into the water: Chinese steel, symbolizing unfair trade practices; beef treated with hormones and shrimp caught in nets that endangered sea turtles, representing environmentally suspect goods whose trade the WTO would not allow nations to restrict.[1]

The next morning the protests shifted into high gear. Demonstrators blocked intersections leading to the downtown area where opening ceremonies were planned. As police tried to disperse the protesters, trade unionists began meeting at Memorial Stadium about a mile away. "The WTO," James Hoffa, president of the teamsters' union, told twenty thousand trade unionists, "is a mistake. . . . Worker rights [*sic*] has to become a part of the agenda for every one of these meetings."[2] American labor leaders accused the WTO of ignoring labor rights by not allowing restrictions on the trade of goods made in sweatshops or with child labor. "The rules of this new global economy," charged the head of the country's garment and textile workers' union, "have been rigged against workers, and we're not going to play by them anymore." John Sweeney, president of the AFL-CIO, America's labor federation, concluded: "Until the WTO addresses these issues, we should not and must not permit our country to participate in a new round of trade negotiations."[3] Hoffa told the crowd: "We are walking into the pages of history. We will have a place at the table of the WTO, or we will shut it down."[4] The trade unionists hit the streets and headed for the downtown site of the ministerial meeting's opening ceremonies.

Tens of thousands of other demonstrators also headed toward the city center. While the demonstrations swelled, small groups of anarchists bent on violent protest raced through the streets. The police attempted in vain to control the crowds, and within a couple of hours tear gas pervaded the meeting areas.

By the middle of the afternoon the center of Seattle was a chaotic mass of demonstrators, police, tear gas, delegates, and vandals. Concerned about security, the Secret Service would not let the leaders of the American delegation leave their hotels. Only a handful of official delegates made it to the Paramount Theater for the opening ceremonies, which the organizers reluctantly canceled. The city's mayor declared a 7:00 P.M. to 7:30 A.M. curfew in the area surrounding the meeting sites and called out the National Guard, while police used tear gas, concussion grenades, pepper spray, and rubber bullets to clear out demonstrators.

Wednesday morning, December 1, the WTO ministerial meeting finally got under way. The meeting was a failure on its own terms; the delegations could not agree on any important issue. But around the world headlines focused on the protests rather than on the trade talks that the demonstrations had delayed. As he headed toward the meeting, U.S. President Bill Clinton called the peaceful protests "healthy," citing them in support of his argument for a more socially conscious approach to the link among trade, labor rights, and the environment. "Trade is now no longer the province of CEOs, organized interest groups that deal with the economy and political leaders," said Clinton. "This whole process is being democratized, and we're going to have to build a new consensus that goes down deeper into every society about what kind of trade policy we want."[5]

The Battle of Seattle represented a general challenge to the world economic order. International institutions that had long labored in obscurity were now a lightning rod for those wary of global integration. One of the coalitions leading the protest explicitly stated why the WTO deserved such an assault: "The central idea of the WTO is that *free trade*—actually the values and interests of global corporations—should supersede all other values. Any obstacles to global trade are viewed with suspicion. In practice, these 'obstacles' are the laws of nation-states that protect the environment, small businesses, human rights, consumers, labor as well as national sovereignty and democracy. The WTO views these as possible impediments to 'free trade,' and they become subject to challenge within closed WTO tribunals. . . . Offending countries *must* conform with WTO rules, or face harsh sanctions."[6]

Very public challenges to global capitalism emerged in the last years of the century. In protests from Seattle to Prague, Washington, and Genoa, millions of activists targeted the WTO, the World Bank, the IMF, the Group of Seven industrial countries, and other international economic organizations at the types of meetings that had previously attracted no attention. As the WTO's ministerial meeting and the Seattle protests wound down, antiglobalization author and activist Naomi Klein wrote that they reflected a "face-off . . . between two radically different visions of globalization. One has had a monopoly for the last 10 years. The other just had its coming-out party."[7]

Financial fragility and the unholy trinity

Antiglobalization protests challenged the economic order from the outside, but the most serious threats to the system came from within.

The most "globalized" component of the international economy, finance, seemed to be its weakest link, as the global financial system was hit by wave after wave of currency and banking crises. Beginning in Europe in 1992, shocks shot from continent to continent: Mexico, East Asia, Russia, Brazil, Turkey, Argentina and beyond. Each round involved hundreds of billions of dollars, drew in international institutions, private investors, and national governments, and threatened the very stability of the international economy. Countries as different as Britain, Thailand, Brazil, and Turkey tried desperately to protect their currencies as investors drained billions of dollars out of them, until eventually each government had to give up and let its exchange rate collapse—often with disastrous effects for the local economy. How had one of global capitalism's greatest promises, access to open international capital markets, turned into its greatest threat?

The answer to this question goes back to an unlikely place, Canada in the 1950s. At that point Canada faced problems that anticipated those eventually confronted by the rest of the world. The Canadian economy was very tightly tied to that of the United States. Money flowed freely across the Canadian-U.S. border, and trade with the United States was crucially important to Canada. This presented Canada with a trade-off akin to that faced later by "globalized" economies. Canadians wanted a stable and predictable Canadian-U.S. dollar exchange rate, to facilitate trade, travel, and investment. But they also wanted their government to control Candian monetary policy so that it could lower unemployment or reduce inflation as necessary. The two goals were incompatible. With one Canadian dollar freely exchangeable for one U.S. dollar, and money free to move from Canada to the United States, whatever interest rates were in the United States they had to be in Canada. If money markets paid less in Canada, people would take money out of Canada and into the United States until interest rates rose. Canada was so integrated into the U.S. economy that if its exchange rate was fixed, it could no more have an independent monetary policy than Illinois could. So Canadians had to choose which they valued more: a stable exchange rate or an independent monetary policy. In the 1950s they chose the latter; in 1962 they went back to the former.

The Canadian controversies over how to deal with its early "globalization" experience engaged the interest of a young Canadian economist at the IMF, Robert Mundell. In the early 1960s Mundell systematized the Canadian problem as the dilemma of a financially open country. He pointed out that a country financially linked to others had to choose between having its own national monetary policy, on the one hand, or having a stable currency, on the other; it could not have both. If Canada tied its dollar to the U.S. dollar, it had to have American monetary policy; if it wanted its own monetary policy, it had to allow its currency's value to fluctuate.

Mundell's impossibility theorem, sometimes called the unholy trinity, showed that countries could have only two of three generally desirable things: capital mobility, a stable exchange rate, and monetary independence. If capital was free to move into and out of a country, fixing its currency to that of another country was like adopting the other country's money, and that meant accepting the other country's monetary policy as well. Mundell's analysis was particularly relevant to Canada in the 1950s and 1960s because money flowed easily across the Canadian-American border. Given Canadian financial integration, the country had to choose between the remaining two: either a stable exchange rate or monetary independence.

The Canadian conundrum was a curiosity in the 1950s and 1960s. Everywhere except across the U.S.-Canadian border, financial flows were tightly regulated by capital and currency controls. Countries could have both currency stability and their own policy autonomy with little difficulty.

By the 1990s the Mundell dilemma had ceased to be a theoretical curiosity and had become the central reality of international money and finance. Mundell's analysis was vital to understanding global capitalism—and to his recognition with the Nobel Memorial Prize in Economics in 1999. Most countries were now integrated into international financial markets, so the Canadian trade-off was nearly universal: Either give up control over national monetary policy, or give up a stable currency. The problem was anything but theoretical to those caught on the horns of the dilemma. For Argentines in 1999, for example, the choice was stark: Stay the course and keep the one peso–one dollar link at the cost of widespread and rising bankruptcies and unemployment, or devalue to salvage the national economy at the cost of a massive financial and currency crisis. The issue was neither arcane nor academic to people desperate for both stable currencies *and* locally appropriate policies, forced to choose between them.

The revival of world financial markets after the 1960s created the conditions that led to endemic currency and banking crises in the 1980s and 1990s. Governments of globalized economies needed their currencies to be stable, but they also needed to respond to national conditions that called for currencies to be devalued. The problem was reminiscent of gold standard conflicts between international commitments to gold and domestic economic concerns.

The developing country debt crisis of the 1980s was barely resolved when a massive currency crisis hit the members of the European Union in the run-up to monetary union. In 1992 EU members tied to the German deutsche mark were forced to accept sky-high interest rates, recession, and more unemployment. Governments wanted to hold their currencies fixed against the deutsche mark, but they also needed to avoid sending millions more people onto the unemployment rolls. The conflict between the two goals became too powerful to ignore, and eventually most European governments devalued their currencies. In 1994 the Mexican government was similarly torn. The strong peso was a symbol of the government's resolve to control the macroeconomy, but a strong peso priced Mexican products out of the North American market and drove Mexican interest rates ever higher to keep money at home. Neither development was consistent with government goals of orienting the Mexican economy toward its NAFTA partners and stimulating investment with low interest rates. Defending the currency meant abandoning other important objectives, and a combination of economic and political pressures would not let the government ignore these inconsistent aims.

Countries from East Asia to Brazil, Russia, Turkey, and Argentina faced all the contradictory pulls of the new environment's Mundellian trade-offs. They desperately needed capital mobility to attract investment into their economies, but they suffered severely from giving up their monetary independence. The more they incorporated their economies into the global financial system, the more their national economic policies were constrained. Emerging market governments were under pressure to do inconsistent things: Sustain financial integration; maintain an independent monetary policy; keep the currency stable; keep the exchange rate weak to stimulate exports; keep the exchange rate strong to moderate the foreign debt burden. When something went wrong with this balancing act, it went wrong in a big way.

Most currency crises also caused bank panics. Local banks borrowed heavily in foreign currency, which they then lent to domestic firms at profitable rates. This was fine while it lasted. But it meant that if the national currency declined in value, the foreign debt burden rose: If the peso was worth five cents, a one-million-dollar foreign debt was twenty million pesos, but if the peso was devalued to four cents, the debt rose from twenty to twenty-five million pesos. When a currency crisis hit, it could bankrupt large portions of the private sector, drive domestic banks to bankruptcy, and cause a national financial panic.

These crises threatened the stability of international finance itself. The world's biggest banks and investors lent enormous amounts to a few countries, and major losses might have triggered a wave of bank runs. In the early 1980s crisis, the five biggest Latin American debtors owed more to U.S. banks than the capital of the entire American banking system. For five years the creditor banks, their governments, and the International Monetary Fund managed the crisis to contain fallout for the global financial system. The banks took some losses, creditor governments provided subsidies and other assistance to calm financial waters, and debtor nations eventually paid off their debts. The impact on the countries that had fallen into debt crisis was severe; but the crisis was contained, and international financial markets continued to grow. In subsequent crises, similar coalitions of international banks, creditor country governments, the IMF, and other international financial institutions threw hundreds of billions of dollars at problems in attempts to avoid international financial panic.

International financial markets coexisted with national currencies. Governments wanted to stabilize exchange rates, while global investors trolled for currencies to attack. Powerful groups pushed for financial integration and currency stability, while other powerful groups advocated monetary and financial independence. Debtors demanded a strong currency, while exporters insisted on a weak one. Most of the time these global and national pressures balanced, but when they entered into open conflict, something had to give—usually some unfortunate country's currency. Recurring crises threatened the international economy, just as they had before 1914 and in the 1930s.

The strains on the international financial system suggested more basic problems. There was, some said, a crisis of economic governance caused by the mismatch of *international* financial markets and *national* regulation and control. Some argued that global capitalism required global economic management, a new financial architecture with the International Monetary Fund as a global monetary and financial authority. The IMF could function as a world central bank to counteract international currency and financial panics. But only a few bankers and academics actually supported giving so much power to the IMF. In the absence of global regulators that encompassed global financial and money markets, crisis management rested with national governments that were beset by enduring conflicts of interest and opinion.

Globalized finance highlighted the dilemmas of international economic integration. World financial markets allowed governments, firms, banks, and people around the world to borrow far more than they could have otherwise. But just as they directed untold billions toward favored countries and companies, global markets directed billions more away from those that fell out of favor. The speed and size of international financial markets made these flows extraordinarily volatile. International financial integration could make good times even better and bad times even worse. This did not threaten just the countries that financiers deserted, because one nation's collapse could be transmitted to others, to an entire region, or to the whole world. Financial instability had, after all, lengthened and deepened the Great Depression of the 1930s, and the world might not be better prepared to handle a truly major crisis in the twenty-first century than it had been in 1929. The currency and banking crises of the 1990s demonstrated that the largest and most efficient international financial system in history had a downside: Its very size and speed gave it the potential to destabilize the entire world economy.

"The three scariest words"

Another threat to global capitalism came from its very essence, competition. As country after country joined the global economy, competitive pressures threatened many powerful interests. The threat was symbolized by the reentry of the world's largest country into the world economy.

"The China price," reported *Business Week*, had become "the three scariest words in U.S. industry."[8] Factory wages in the United States were more than thirty times Chinese levels—over eight hundred dollars for a forty-hour week versus about twenty-five dollars for the same forty hours—and while American workers were more productive, there were many companies and industries that simply could not make up for such massive wage differentials. This led to concerns that a global economy would create a "race to the bottom," forcing conditions down to the lowest common denominator prevailing in poor nations. Would wages in North America and Western Europe be pushed to Chinese or Brazilian levels? Would similar pressures erode social welfare policies and regulations to protect the environment and labor?

Neoclassical trade theory in fact predicts that international economic integration will depress wages in the industrial countries. Trade encourages factor price equalization, as it reduces differences among countries in the price of productive factors (land, labor, skilled labor, and capital). Unskilled wages are very low in poor countries that have a lot of unskilled labor. As nations with many unskilled workers export goods that use a great deal of unskilled labor, this raises the domestic demand for labor and increases national wages. But in rich countries a similar process works *against* unskilled workers. The rich countries export goods that use a lot of capital and very little unskilled labor so that the demand for unskilled labor decreases, and wages fall. According to trade theory, trade reduces the wage differences between rich and poor countries because wages in poor countries rise and wages in rich countries decline. Integrating the economies of poor and rich countries means that workers in rich countries are now in direct competition with workers in poor countries.

Labor economist Richard Freeman summarized the pressure succinctly. "Are your wages," he asked in a prominent article, "set in Beijing?"[9] The answer to Freeman's question has been hotly contested. The real wages of unskilled American workers stagnated or declined for most of the latter part of the twentieth century. Some analysts blame this on technological change, in particular the growing importance of microelectronics and computers, which works against those workers without computer skills. But increased competition from low-skilled, low-wage labor in other countries caused at least some of the dismal performance of American unskilled workers. The impact on Europe was different: Europe's much higher minimum wages and greater controls on firms laying off workers made the competitive effect felt through lower job creation rather than wages. Competitive pressure from low-wage imports may explain why the real wages of American unskilled workers declined after 1973 and why European unemployment hovered around 10 percent from 1980 until the end of the century. The logic is compelling: Unskilled North Americans and Europeans are harmed by competition from unskilled Moroccans or Mexicans.

Just as integration allowed firms to choose low-wage countries, it also allowed them to choose countries with more business-friendly regulations and lower taxes. This could create a similarly slippery slope in social policy and regulation, draining business away from North America and Western Europe with their high taxes, generous social policies, and stringent controls on environmental pollution, health and safety, and labor rights. In the European Union, northern Europeans worried about social dumping, businesses and jobs fleeing regulatory controls in Scandinavia and other social democracies for the looser strictures of Spain or Greece, fears that only expanded as Eastern and Central Europe joined the European Union. The opening of the developing world to international trade and investment raised the specter of social dumping on a global scale.

Throughout the 1990s labor unions, students, and other activists mobilized against the threat that economic integration would erode wages and social policies and formed the new antiglobalization movement that erupted in the 1999 Battle of Seattle. The labor movement interest was straightforward, to avoid cutthroat competition with low-wage workers and low-standards countries. As the American AFL-CIO said simply, "The global economy and the race to the bottom have lowered the standard of living for working families, while making the world's rich even richer."[10] First and foremost was the ability of capitalists to flee rich countries in search of more friendly regions: "Today, multinational corporations can move capital thousands of miles with the click of a mouse and send jobs halfway around the world in the time it takes numbers to travel along fiber-optic cable. These companies— many of them American—search the globe for the lowest possible labor costs and weakest environmental safeguards."[11] Labor union demands for stricter controls on "sweatshop labor" in the developing countries reflected both working-class solidarity and a more prosaic desire to reduce competitive pressure.

Human rights activists and environmentalists also eyed economic integration with apprehension. Just as corporations could seek lower wages, they could also look for pollution-friendly regimes, dictatorships that violated human rights, and other miscreants. These critics believed that global economic integration meant "free trade for corporations, but severe controls upon nations and citizens that try to protect the safety of their food, their jobs, small businesses or Nature" or that globalization was "homogenizing global cultures and values."[12]

In the words of a European campaign to "clean up" the world garment industry, "incentives for foreign investors include not only low wages, but also the suspension of certain workplace and environmental regulations. If a government does attempt to strictly enforce these regulations, you can bet that many investors will quickly pack their bags for another country that is even less strict and is more accommodating."[13] A coalition of militant American antiglobalization groups labeled globalization "a conspiracy against the environment . . . a conspiracy in favor of freeing corporations from democratic laws that regulate their excesses."[14]

A cultural component to the complaints about globalization focused on a decline in diversity, a consequence of the world economy's leveling and Americanizing tendencies.

> With economic globalization [wrote one umbrella organization] diversity is fast disappearing. The goal of the global economy is that all countries should be homogenized. . . . [E]conomic globalization and institutions like the World Bank and the WTO promote a specific kind of homogenizing development that frees the largest corporations in the world to invest and operate in every market, everywhere. For these agencies and corporations, diversity is not a primary value: efficiency is. Diversity is an enemy because it requires differentiated sales appeal. What corporations love is creating the same values, the same tastes, using the same advertising, selling the same products, and driving out small local competitors. Mass marketers prefer homogenized consumers.[15]

The new antiglobalization movement was amorphous, and its targets varied. Some efforts focused on individual corporations or industries, using shareholder activism or consumer boycotts to convince companies to agree to codes of labor or environmental conduct. Others emphasized the need to affect the policies of governments in the industrial world— for example, to impose sanctions on governments in the developing world that did not respect human or labor rights. These efforts often conflicted with the international institutions that had arisen during the Bretton Woods era to manage world trade, finance, and investment. The most common new initiatives, such as attempts to restrict national imports from countries alleged to violate human and labor rights or environmental principles, were efforts to use trade barriers in ways that ran counter to existing international trade rules.

Labor, environmental, and human rights activists found themselves drawn into confrontation with the GATT and its successor, the WTO. The GATT ruled against American attempts to ban imports of tuna caught with nets that might trap dolphins. The WTO prohibited European restrictions on the import of hormone-fed beef. And the international trading system's rules did not allow restrictions on the trade of goods made in sweatshops or with child labor. The American textile and garment workers' union argued: "[C]orporations can't treat the globe like their own private sweatshop. Strong worker rights and environmental protections must be included in every international trade agreement." But, it protested, "The current rules of the global economy were written by corporations and the politicians who support business interests."[16] The December 1999 Seattle demonstrations were but the first of a series of large antiglobalization mobilizations. Previously the GATT and WTO, Group of Seven, and other international economic institutions had been virtually unknown. Now millions of people were taking to the streets to protest features of world trade law or to reform the bureaucratic nature of trade tribunals that only a handful of people had even heard of a decade earlier.

Complaints from the developing world were often equal but opposite to those coming from the industrial countries. While northern activists were particularly interested in raising labor, health, and environmental standards in poor countries, governments and businessmen in industrializing nations frequently opposed these standards and regarded them as thinly veiled trade protection. Complaints about standards, they argued, were simply the latest way to keep Asian or Latin American products out of lucrative northern markets. Many activists in the developing world also believed that the use of trade or other economic measures to force changes in Brazilian or Indian policies was an exercise in neocolonialism. Even those in Africa, Asia, and Latin America sympathetic to criticisms of global capitalism were troubled by the ease with which antiglobalization movements in Europe and North America fed into what they regarded as thinly veiled protectionism or neoimperialism.

Some developing country spokespeople and activists regarded North American and European activists as tools of their governments. They pointed out that the Clinton administration had itself pushed labor and environmental standards onto the trade agenda and found it suspicious that at Seattle President Clinton and the demonstrators agreed on forcing developing countries to adopt labor, social, and environmental policies designed in the United States. In the aftermath of the 1999 Seattle meetings, respected Indian spokesman and journalist Chakravarthi

Raghavan wrote that there was "little doubt that the Clinton White House had planned a controlled 'street protest' by organized labor and some of the 'environment' groups, in order to 'persuade' the conference to accept US 'demands' for labor and environment standards at the WTO." He was heartened by the fact, he wrote, that "developing nations refused to be cowed down—by street protests and demonstrations by US trade unions and some environmental groups, organized and encouraged by the US administration."[17]

Many in the developing world agreed with the antiglobalizers that global capitalism undermined national autonomy. The world economy was, they pointed out, dominated by the industrial countries, which ruled in a way that was autocratic and hypocritical. Autocratic, because the European Union, North America, and Japan wrote and rewrote the rules of the international economic game as they wished, with no input from the four-fifths of humanity living elsewhere. Hypocritical, because despite high-sounding rhetoric about open economies and free trade, the north imposed continuing obstacles to southern exports. Most egregiously, Americans, Europeans, and Japanese stepped up colossally expensive programs to protect and subsidize their own farmers, then preached the wonders of the marketplace to developing countries. Northern farm protection closed off markets to farmers elsewhere, while the dumping of surplus products on world markets drove world prices down. This was a cruel disaster for the hundreds of millions of developing country farmers whose hopes for economic advance rested on exporting agricultural products to the developed countries. Developing country advocates calculated that open northern markets for Third World farm products would bring in more money than all the economic aid the north provided, well more than the fifty billion dollars a year in development assistance.

Dissatisfaction with the world order was compounded by the fact that even in some of the more successful countries, the fruits of success were unevenly distributed. China was one of the world's fastest-growing economies, and poverty dropped rapidly in the Asian giant. Yet the gap between rich and poor—especially between the cities and the countryside—widened as the nation grew. By 2000 the average urban household had three times the income of the average rural household, a much greater multiple than in 1985. Shanghai was one of the world's great industrial and commercial centers, with more than half of the Fortune 500 companies present, but there are still nearly two hundred million

Chinese living in poverty. The sense that developing country governments had insufficient voice in global affairs was mirrored by the sense that the poor had insufficient voice in the affairs of developing countries.

Criticisms from northern activists and southern governments had little immediate impact on the structure of the international economic order, but they ratcheted upward debate over the nature of the international political economy. The Battle of Seattle was largely irrelevant to the actual business of the WTO ministerial meeting that was being protested; the meeting collapsed because of disagreements among member states, not because of street demonstrations. Nonetheless, the public furor indicated that global capitalism and the structure of its international institutions were now the target of global criticism and debates. There was sure to be conflict over international constraints on national aspirations. As the twenty-first century began, it could not be taken for granted that political winds would continue to favor globalization.

Global markets: ungoverned or unwanted?

Financial instability and political protest underscored tensions between the international and the national, the market and the social. Volatile international money and finance, with recurring currency and debt crises, led globalizers to call for effective global institutions to avoid further panic. Their buzzword was *governance*, new political institutions to manage difficulties in global markets. Antiglobalizers, for their part, accused the system of evading political responsibility and of savaging the prospects of poor nations. Their buzzword was *accountability*, new political institutions to allow the world's people to better control global markets.

The debates were reminiscent of the late nineteenth century, when the industrial countries developed into integrated national markets. Economies and companies had long been local, and local governments had regulated them. Over the course of the nineteenth century, as firms and economies became national, controversies erupted about the proper response. The new national businessmen wanted national governments to secure and supervise national markets; they got much of what they wanted from modern central government. Opposition movements, such as the socialists in Europe and the Populists in America, wanted national politics to control, not to monitor and enable, national corporations; they too got much of what they wanted from the modern welfare state. The growth of markets from local to national spurred demands for national governance, and national political accountability. Now, in the late twentieth century, the growth of markets from national to global spurred demands for global governance and global political accountability.

What could be done to alleviate the tensions between global capitalism and global politics? The system's supporters argued that the solution was to bring politics in line with markets. For example, international banking needed authoritative regulators and supervisors at the international level; cooperation among national governments was not enough. Global markets required global governance—if not global government, at least global economic institutions to allow the world economy to function smoothly.

Critics of globalization also focused on the divergence between global markets and politics, but they argued that globalization had gone too far and that politics needed to rein in, not empower, markets. The antiglobalizers charged that global capitalism had escaped social control. International economic institutions represented only the interests of northern corporations. National governments had ceded power to the WTO and the IMF or had had this power seized from them by international markets. The world economy needed to be brought back in line with political needs; national and global political structures must reflect the interests of the world's peoples and assert authority over global markets. Antiglobalizers wanted to limit and control international markets and take the edge off their effects.

Both supporters and critics of globalization identified a gap between international markets, on the one hand, and national politics, on the other. Both believed that worldwide economic problems required worldwide political solutions. But they favored different routes to resolve the conflict. Globalizers wanted international politics to facilitate the operation of the international economy. Antiglobalizers wanted international politics to restrict, counteract, or alleviate the effects of the international economy.

The century ended as it began: Capitalism was once again global, and the globe was once again capitalist. But despite the apparently triumphal march of global capitalism from continent to continent, challenges to globalization persisted. Some came from the operation of international markets themselves, such as when the volatile financial system threatened the pace and nature of economic integration. Some came from those outside the globalizing consensus, from labor, environmentalists, and other political activists. History showed that support for international economic integration depended on prosperity. If global capitalism ceased to deliver growth, its future would be in doubt.

Conclusion

Since 1850 the world economy has stimulated unprecedented economic growth and social change. It has hastened the spread of industrial society from a sliver of northwestern Europe to the rest of Europe and North America and in recent decades to much of East Asia and Latin America.

The international economy has transformed companies, countries, and whole regions. Nokia used access to world markets to remake itself from a small producer of rubber boots in rural Finland into the world's leading mobile telephone producer. South Korea and Taiwan in the 1950s were miserably poor countries whose very survival was in question; in the 1990s they graduated into the ranks of the world's advanced industrial nations. Thousands of companies rely on foreign customers and suppliers for their profits; millions of jobs depend on foreign business.

The international economy has enabled countries to develop, alleviate poverty, improve social conditions, lengthen life spans, and carry out social and political reform. The best hope for the impoverished masses of Asia and Africa is to gain access to the opportunities the world economy has to offer.

Yet there is another side of global capitalism. It can be seen at the site

473

of the Homestead steelworks, once a landmark of American industry. As many as twenty thousand people worked in this U.S. Steel plant a few miles from Pittsburgh, Pennsylvania, and the factory anchored a vast industrial complex that lined the Monongahela Valley. Today the vacant factory's shell is a shopping mall. The population of the town of Homestead, once over twenty thousand, is now about thirty-five hundred; the city of Pittsburgh's population is barely half what it was in its industrial heyday. The depressed region's main hope for the old mill is that the federal government will designate it a national historical site, helping attract tourists.

Foreign competition has shuttered tens of thousands of factories and done away with tens of millions of manufacturing jobs in Western Europe and North America. Industries in rich countries cannot compete with the manufactured products flooding out of Asia, Latin America, and Eastern Europe, where wages are one-tenth of American or European levels. White-collar jobs are going overseas too, as corporations hire Indians or Filipinos to write software, type documents, and answer telephones for customer complaints.

But developing nations have their own difficulties. They owe more than a trillion dollars to foreign creditors, and financial uncertainties have driven Thailand and Argentina, Indonesia and Brazil into deep crises. As they struggle to pay their debts, governments have fired public employees, sold off government assets, cut social spending, and raised taxes. Even the success stories, turning out clothing, furniture, and steel for world markets, wrestle with the effects of sweatshops, child labor, and demands for worker rights. In the greatest success story of all, China, the gap between rich and poor has grown even as the country has progressed.

The benefits of global capitalism come together with its costs. Companies borrow cheaply on international financial markets; this exposes them to the demands of foreign investors. Trade lets consumers buy inexpensive foreign products; this brings unwanted competition for domestic producers. Multinational corporations bring new technologies and methods; this drives domestic firms out of business. Foreign debt allows governments to spend more than they take in; this can lead to excruciating debt crises. Governments open their borders to the world economy and provide some citizens the potential for wealth and success; this can consign other citizens to hardship and distress.

There is no trade without competition, no finance without risk, no investment without obligation. There is no way to avoid the trade-offs inherent in global capitalism. And there is no generally accepted moral yardstick to weigh the suffering of a worker whose job was lost because of globalization against the benefits to a worker whose job depends on globalization.

Is global capitalism desirable? Will it last? Should it last? The history of the world economy in the twentieth century helps illuminate questions like these.

International economic integration generally expands economic opportunities and is good for society. The great alternatives to economic integration failed. Attempts to seal countries off from the rest of the world economy in the 1930s were ultimately disastrous. Germany, Italy, and Japan closed their economies and also turned toward dictatorship, war, and conquest. The poor countries and former colonies that created closed economies in the 1930s and 1940s collapsed into economic stagnation, social unrest, crisis, and military dictatorships in the 1970s and 1980s. Few countries have achieved economic progress without access to the international economy.

But an insistence on globalization at all cost is equally misguided. During the golden age of global capitalism before 1914, governments committed themselves to international economic integration and little else. Supporters of free trade, the gold standard, and international finance wanted governments to limit themselves to safeguarding these policies and their properties. But these governments ignored the concerns of many harmed by globalization. As the working and middle classes grew, so did their demands for social reforms to improve the lot of the unemployed, the poor, children, and the elderly. The clash between classical orthodoxy and these new social movements turned into bitter, often violent, conflicts, especially once the Depression hit. Attempts to maintain global capitalism without addressing those ill treated by world markets drove societies toward polarization and conflict.

After World War Two the new Bretton Woods order attempted to avoid the failures of autarky and of gold standard laissez-faire. The system's gold-dollar standard, gradual trade liberalization, and international institutions made compromises between economic integration and the welfare state. This allowed Western governments to combine moderate doses of social welfare policies with moderate degrees of international economic integration.

The rapid revival of the international economy eroded the Bretton Woods compromises. Freewheeling international markets and free-spending national governments conflicted, and the postwar economic order collapsed in the early 1970s. A decade and a half of inflation, budget deficits, and economic stagnation followed.

By the 1990s global capitalism was again in full flower. As before 1914, capitalism was global, and the globe was capitalist. The history of global capitalism from its earlier zenith, through its fall after 1914, to its gradual rise since 1970, illustrates the crucial tests that will determine the future of international economic integration. Before 1914 globalizers shunned social protection and reform, and that contributed to the system's ultimate collapse. Interwar governments spurned the world economy, and that led to their eventual downfall. Post-1945 Western nations chose a little bit of integration and a little bit of social reform, and that proved to be only a temporary solution.

The history of the modern world economy illustrates two points. First, economies work best when they are open to the world. Second, open economies work best when their governments address the sources of dissatisfaction with global capitalism.

The challenge of global capitalism in the twenty-first century is to combine international integration with politically responsive, socially responsible government. Contemporary ideologues of many stripes— pro- and antiglobalization, progressives and conservatives, marketeers and pamphleteers—argue that this combination is impossible or undesirable. But theory and history indicate that it is possible for globalization to coexist with policies committed to social advance. It remains for governments and people to put the possible into practice.

A Note on Data and Sources

Except where otherwise noted, all data are in U.S. dollars. When absolute numbers are given, they are typically in current dollars—that is, not correcting for inflation. However, when I use data for comparative purposes—as in growth rates, or relative sizes of economies, or relative income per person—I base the comparison on statistics expressed in constant-dollar purchasing power parity (PPP) terms. These calculations take into account inflation and differences in national price levels, in order to try to capture the actual purchasing power of different monetary values. The data used are almost all from the monumental enterprise of Angus Maddison and his colleagues at the OECD, as published in a series culminating in Maddison (2001).

I have cited sources only in English, to make them accessible to a more general English-speaking audience. Virtually every page could inspire a bibliographic essay, with works in many languages. I felt it more valuable to refer directly only to works that an interested reader might be able to consult.

Acknowledgments

Dozens of generous and talented people helped me write this book. Among them were the research assistants who catered to my incessant requests with good cheer and diligence. Elizabeth Foster, Geoffrey Hamilton, and Daniel Michalow did the bulk of the research assistance for the manuscript. Also valuable was the help of Danielle Buckley, Elizabeth Burden, Siyu Cheng, Larry Lee, Boris Nenchev, Jumana Poonawala, and Michael Spence.

A number of colleagues, friends, and family members were kind enough to read rough drafts of all or part of this work and to provide comments that helped me improve the manuscript. These include Brian A'Hearn, Jonathan Aurthur, Lawrence Broz, Marc Busch, Anabela Costa, Robert Dallek, John Ehrenberg, Barry Eichengreen, Nancy Frieden, Ken Frieden, Tom Frieden, Richard Grossman, Max Holland, Charles Kindleberger, Gary King, Susan Lilly, Harry Margolis, James Robinson, George Scialabba, Peter Temin, Harvey Teres, and Michael Wallerstein. My editor at W. W. Norton, Steve Forman, was a constant source of support and advice, not to speak of pressure to finish. Roby Harrington, also at W. W. Norton, gave me good counsel at crucial points in my work. The remaining flaws are, of course, my own responsibility.

Notes

Prologue: Into the Twentieth Century

1. Cited in Viner (1948).
2. Adam Smith (1937), Book Four.
3. Maddison (1995), p. 38. For an excellent survey of the period, see Marsh (1999).
4. Stamp (1979); Bairoch (1989), p. 56; Maddison (2001), p. 95.
5. O'Rourke and Williamson (1999), p. 209.
6. Calculated from Friedman and Schwartz (1982), pp. 122–37. The price indices are implicit price deflators.
7. Calculated from Gallman (1960), pp. 13–43; his Variant A is used for construction.
8. An essential set of readings on the gold standard is Eichengreen and Flandreau (1997).
9. The platform is in Hicks (1931), pp. 439–44.
10. Ibid., pp. 316–17 and p. 160.
11. Cain and Hopkins (1993a) provide an overview of the period.

Chapter 1: Global Capitalism Triumphant

1. The platform is in Hicks (1931), pp. 439–44.
2. *Times*, July 9, 1896.
3. Ibid.
4. *Times*, July 10, 1896.
5. *Times*, November 4, 1896.
6. All figures used here are in real terms—that is, they take into account differences in price levels both among countries and over time. Source for all: Maddison (2001).

479

7. Wilde (1985), p. 144.
8. See, for example, Estevadeordal et al. (2003) and López-Córdova and Meissner (2003).
9. Bordo and Rockoff (1996), pp. 389–428.
10. Eichengreen (1992); Eichengreen and Flandreau (1997). The presentation here is greatly simplified. Governments generally tried to manage their economies so as to avoid major gold flows. This could involve trying to retain gold by raising interest rates, which would tend to keep money at home in order to take advantage of the higher rate of return. Or it could involve trying to brake domestic wages, prices, and profits, so as to make exports more competitive. Nonetheless, these policies had their origin in the pressures that being on gold exerted on national economies and national governments.
11. Maddison (1995), p. 64.
12. O'Rourke and Williamson (1999), pp. 43–53. See also Capie (1983).
13. O'Rourke and Williamson (1999), pp. 208–12.
14. Lloyd Reynolds (1985), p. 87.
15. An outstanding study of the two wheat economies is Solberg (1987).
16. Bairoch (1975), pp. 52 and 15.
17. Adam Smith (1937), pp. 4–5.
18. Maddison (1995), pp. 36 and 249.

Chapter 2: Defenders of the Global Economy

1. Keynes (1920), pp. 11–12.
2. Ibid., p. 12.
3. A wonderful account of the process is in Irwin (1996), pp. 75–98.
4. John Nye questions even this, asserting that Britain simply used excise taxes on luxury goods to achieve the functional equivalent of trade protection. Nye (1996), pp. 90–112.
5. What follows is taken primarily from the classic study of the family, Niall Ferguson (1998). See also the essays in Heuberger (1994).
6. Strouse (1999), p. 173; Niall Ferguson (1998), pp. 872–73.
7. Niall Ferguson (1998), p. 866; the Barings crisis is covered on pp. 863–72. See also Cain and Hopkins (1993a), pp. 288–311, for the Argentine, Brazilian, and Chilean stories more generally.
8. *Economist* LXV (November 9, 1907), p. 1925.
9. Niall Ferguson (1998), pp. 927–29. The 1907 crisis is the subject of a substantial academic literature, on which see especially Eichengreen (1992).
10. Niall Ferguson (1998), p. 947.
11. On the Rothschilds in South Africa, see Niall Ferguson (1998), pp. 876–94, Cain and Hopkins (1993a), pp. 369–81, and Flint (1974).
12. Niall Ferguson (1998), p. 884.
13. Ibid., p. 892.
14. A classic statement, for a slightly earlier period, is Gourevitch (1977).
15. For an excellent survey, see Bairoch (1989), pp. 69–160.
16. Quotes taken from James and Lake (1989), pp. 18–21.
17. Cain and Hopkins (1993a), p. 178.
18. Mitchell (1998b) for the figures; Knudsen (1977) for a discussion.
19. Holtfrerich (1999).
20. Lake (1988), p. 76.
21. Davis and Huttenback (1986), pp. 81–88. The former figures are theirs, based on work by Michael Edelstein; the latter use Davis and Huttenback's sample of British firms. In

both cases, the comparison is between foreign nonempire investments and British investments. As Davis and Huttenback point out, rates of return inside the empire were typically not so high as in foreign countries. The original Edelstein data are in Edelstein (1982). Measurement of rates of return are confounded by many complex problems, which both books address in detail.

22. Cain and Hopkins (1993a), p. 178.
23. Cited ibid., p. 216.
24. Jeffrey Williamson (1995).
25. Cain and Hopkins (1993a), pp. 181–201, present a judicious summary of the debate.
26. Ibid., p. 217.
27. Feis (1930), p. 23, using Paish's contemporary estimates. Feis remains the best nontechnical source on European overseas investments in this period.
28. Goldin (1994).
29. O'Rourke and Williamson (1999), Tables 8.1 and 8.3.
30. Ibid.

Chapter 3: Success Stories of the Golden Age

1. Morand (1931), p. 74.
2. Ibid., p. 76.
3. Ibid., pp. 65–66.
4. Ibid., p. 75.
5. Mandell (1967), p. 111.
6. Morand (1931), p. 79.
7. Ibid., pp. 76–77.
8. Ibid., pp. 78–79.
9. Ibid., p. 79.
10. Mandell (1967), p. 84.
11. Morand (1931), p. 80.
12. Ibid.
13. Rostow (1978), pp. 52–53.
14. All had an output of manufactures per capita of above one-fifth of the American levels. Italy is borderline, with the north clearly industrialized but the south probably more backward than Spain or Portugal. W. Arthur Lewis (1978), p. 163.
15. The classic summary of the technological aspects of the process is Landes (1969), pp. 231–358.
16. A good summary is Falkus (1972), especially pp. 44–84, which surveys much of the available literature.
17. Rostow (1978), pp. 422–23.
18. Landes (1969), p. 241. By this year, according to Landes, Japanese yarn and cloth exports were greater than those of Germany and 40 percent of those of the United Kingdom.
19. Rostow (1978), pp. 196–97; p. 210 has the data used here.
20. Landes (1969), p. 300, on Germany; American data from Kerry Chase.
21. This was the argument made famous by Gerschenkron (1962). It remains controversial and is at best only partially right; but there is probably some truth to it.
22. Sandberg (1978, 1979).
23. Cited in Irwin (1996), p. 127.
24. Ibid., p. 126.

25. Ibid., p. 125.
26. Bairoch (1989), pp. 76 and 139.
27. Falkus (1972), pp. 44–84.
28. Bairoch (1989), p. 139.
29. Webb (1977, 1980).
30. Bairoch (1989), pp. 134–35.
31. Maddison (1995), p. 38, gives representative figures on exports as a share of GDP; Bairoch (1989), pp. 88–90, discusses the process more generally.
32. Western North America and southern Latin America were partial exceptions, although the preexisting social structures were too small and shallow to have much enduring impact. So too did the indigenous populations have nearly no effect.
33. Douglass North, as in his North (1989), pp. 1319–32, makes much of the North/South American–British/Iberian distinction and may be justified in doing so in comparative perspective. But the relevant differences on this dimension between Argentina and Canada pale in comparison to the differences between, say, Argentina and Indochina.
34. W. Arthur Lewis (1978), pp. 188–93, discusses the fact, which is at the center of his interpretation of subsequent development in tropical areas.
      The two features are related. The fact that indigenous populations were quite small in the areas of recent settlement was a function of prevailing patterns of agricultural productivity and agricultural production. Low levels of agricultural productivity in non-European temperate regions made them incapable of supporting dense populations. On the other hand, if the non-European populations had been substantially larger (as in Central America or West Africa, for example), it would have meant that the lands held more readily obvious riches, and they would have been exploited by Europeans much earlier.
35. Calculated from W. Arthur Lewis (1978), pp. 292–97; western Europe excludes Germany, which is more appropriately considered part of central or eastern Europe from the standpoint of agricultural production.
36. John Foster Fraser (1914), pp. 27 and 70.
37. The manufacturing output figure is from Rostow (1978), p. 496; data on textiles consumption are in David Reynolds (2000), p. 100; the per capita output figures are, like all others used here, from Maddison (1995).
38. Villela and Suzigan (1977), p. 294.
39. For a good survey of the political economy of the two countries' experiences, see Bates (1997), pp. 26–89.
40. Hopkins (1973) is the crucial source and convincingly shows the interaction of local and European economic interests in the colonial process.
41. David Reynolds (2000), p. 205.
42. Gerald K. Helleiner (1966), Hogerdorn (1975).
43. Reynolds (2000), p. 158.
44. Michael Adas, cited by Elson (1992), p. 144.
45. This is the central point of O'Rourke and Williamson (1999).

Chapter 4: Failures of Development

1. Phipps (2002), p. 164.
2. Maddison (2001), pp. 264–65.
3. Material here is from Hochschild (1998), Kennedy (2002), and Phipps (2002).
4. Phipps (2002), p. 21.

5. Cited ibid., p. 17.
6. Hochschild (1998), pp. 180–81.
7. Cited ibid., p. 164.
8. Ibid., p. 193.
9. Phipps (2002), p. 159.
10. Ibid., p. 162.
11. Quoted ibid., p. 171.
12. Zwick (1992).
13. Cited in Slinn (1971), p. 371.
14. The comparison with Uganda, where indigenous farmers were far more successful at growing cash crops for export, is instructive. Hickman (1970), pp. 178–97.
15. For a masterful treatment of the Irish and Algerian (and Israeli) experiences, see Lustick (1993).
16. W. Arthur Lewis (1978), p. 214.
17. Bairoch (1975), p. 160, provides estimates of sectoral employment.
18. Latham (1978), p. 20.
19. Mitchell (1998 a, b, c), passim.
20. David Reynolds (2000), p. 320.
21. The Ottoman Empire is difficult to categorize and measure. It included some relatively more advanced regions but overall was very underdeveloped. It was enormous, but what was and was not in the empire was open to debate. It probably had a population surpassed only by those of China and India, but we cannot be sure of this.
22. Tomlinson (1979), pp. 1–29, is an outstanding survey of the Indian experience.
23. Feuerwerker (1995a), p. 181. The detailed studies are on pp. 165–308. See also Feuerwerker (1995b) and Philip Richardson (1999). For a general overview, see Spence (1990). The more optimistic view of Waley-Cohen (1999) focuses on the more forward-looking views of reformers, while her own discussion makes clear that the implementation of policies informed by these views was typically blocked by powerful ruling groups.
24. This is an outgrowth of the staple theory developed by Canadian researchers, focusing on the principal product—staple—of the region. Schedvin (1990) is a useful survey, and the approach has been applied and extended by Engerman and Sokoloff (1997).
25. For example, De Graaff (1986).
26. Stover (1970) is a good summary of price and quantity movements in tropical exports over this period.
27. Norbury (1970), pp. 138–42.
28. Bates (1997), p. 56.
29. Stover (1970), p. 50.
30. Ibid., p. 57.
31. Nor was it quite so deterministic as presented here. Nugent and Robinson (1999) make a convincing case that political factors influenced the organization of coffee economies, showing that in El Salvador and Guatemala oligarchical regimes led to large-scale coffee farms, while in Costa Rica and Colombia more inclusive regimes led to smallholdings. The argument is about trends rather than certainties.

Chapter 5: Problems of the Global Economy

1. Kindleberger (1964), pp. 272–73.
2. Bairoch (1989), pp. 83–88; Cain and Hopkins (1993a), pp. 202–25. Marrison (1983) provides a useful analysis of industrial supporters and opponents of protection.

3. Quoted in Cain and Hopkins (1993a), p. 211.
4. The definitive analysis of the political economy of this election is Irwin (1994).
5. Cain and Hopkins (1993a), pp. 181–201, and Kindleberger (1996), pp. 125–48, provide brief surveys of the debates and evidence.
6. Kindleberger (1978), p. 224.
7. Cited in E. L. Jones (1996), p. 704.
8. Rogowski (1989) is an excellent presentation and application. The more common use of the Stolper-Samuelson theorem is to predict support for trade protection, but it also of course explains support for trade liberalization.
9. Przeworski (1980).
10. Cited in Hicks (1931), pp. 316–17.
11. Moreton Frewen, cited in Stanley Jones (1964), p. 14.

Chapter 6: "All That Is Solid Melts into Air . . ."

1. Evans and Geary (1987), p. 73; see also http://www.liv-coll.ac.uk/pa09/europetrip/brussels/kollwitz.htm
2. Carr (1939).
3. Noyes (1926), pp. 436–37.
4. Cooper (1976), p. 215.
5. Ibid., pp. 219–21.
6. Lamont (1915), p. 112.
7. Nearing and Freeman (1925), p. 273.
8. Carr (1939), p. 234.
9. The essential source is Feldman (1993); these data are from pp. 782–85. See also Aldcroft (1977), pp. 128 and 138.
10. Ernest Hemingway, "German Inflation, 19 September 1922," in *Eyewitness to History*, ed. John Carey (Cambridge: Harvard University Press, 1987), pp. 497–501.
11. Meyer (1970).
12. Eichengreen (1992), pp. 125–52, discusses the episode; see also Costigliola (1976).
13. Quoted in Feldman (1993), p. 855.
14. Ibid., p. 858.
15. Nove (1992), p. 94.
16. Aldcroft (1977), pp. 98 and 102.
17. Maddison (1995), pp. 238–39.
18. A classic study of the process is Maier (1975).
19. Cleona Lewis (1938), p. 341.
20. Frieden (1988), p. 66.
21. Cleona Lewis (1938), p. 377.
22. Aldcroft (1977), pp. 238–67; see also Kindleberger (1973), pp. 31–82.
23. Maddison (1995).
24. Villela and Suzigan (1977), p. 133.
25. This interpretation, while foreshadowed by others in the 1930s, was first presented in succinct form by Kindleberger (1973), pp. 291–308.
26. Eichengreen (1987). The fully formed presentation of this interpretation, set against the failures of the interwar gold standard, is Eichengreen (1992).
27. Flandreau (1997), p. 757. Although Flandreau argues against one variant of the cooperative view, the evidence he presents, especially for 1870–1914, indicates the centrality of international collaboration; see pp. 755–60.

28. Broz (1997).
29. Forbes (1981), p. 125.
30. Maltz (1963), pp. 204–5.
31. Feis (1950), p. 14.
32. Eichengreen (1989b); the quote is on p. 58.
33. Frieden (1988), p. 65.
34. The discussion here is based, except where noted, on the magisterial authoritative biography, Skidelsky (1983, 1992, 2000).
35. Skidelsky (1992), p. 181.
36. Skidelsky (1983), p. 239.
37. Ibid., p. 84.
38. Ibid., p. 227.
39. Ibid., p. 319.
40. Ibid., p. 370.
41. Ibid., p. 371.
42. Ibid., p. 391.
43. Skidelsky (1992), p. 205.
44. Ibid., p. 133.
45. Jensen (1989) and Sachs (1980) are two general discussions; a detailed cross-national study is Bernanke and Carey (1996).
46. Skidelsky (1992), p. 156.
47. Ibid., p. 192.
48. Ibid., p. 204.
49. Ibid., p. 194.

Chapter 7: The World of Tomorrow

1. Zim, Lerner, and Rolfes (1988), p. 71.
2. Edmund Gilligan, "Report of a Subway Explorer of His Trip to a Magic City," reproduced in Zim, Lerner, and Rolfes (1988); the quote is on p. 44.
3. Ibid., pp. 43–44.
4. Quoted in Rydell et al. (2000), p. 93.
5. Maddison (1995), p. 41; the measure used is simply GDP per hour worked.
6. Rostow (1978), p. 756.
7. Landes (1969), pp. 246–439. The wage figures are from Liesner (1989), p. 98.
8. Landes (1969), p. 443.
9. Chandler and Tedlow (1985), p. 408.
10. Figures from Kerry Chase.
11. Coffey and Layden (1996).
12. The classic history is Chandler (1977). See also Chandler (1969).
13. Mowery and Rosenberg (1989), pp. 59–97.
14. Calculated from ibid., pp. 68–69.
15. A good set of comparative articles is in Chandler and Daems (1980).
16. Daems (1980), p. 222.
17. Frieden (1988), p. 64.
18. Landes (1969), p. 446.
19. Poulson (1981), p. 525.
20. Sassoon (1996), pp. 27–82, provides an outstanding summary.

Chapter 8: The Established Order Collapses

1. Orwell (1958), pp. 85–86.
2. Watkins (1999), p. 57.
3. The first figures are from Kindleberger (1973), p. 71; the second from Eichengreen (1992), p. 224. Much of the account presented here is drawn from these two essential sources.
4. Temin (1989) develops this impulse propagation explanation of the relationship between the United States and the rest of the world.
5. Kindleberger (1973), pp. 143 and 188.
6. Farm products and building materials prices calculated from Warren and Pearson (1935), pp. 30–32; consumer durables from Shaw (1947), pp. 290–95.
7. Eichengreen (1992), p. 251.
8. Friedman and Schwartz (1963), p. 306.
9. Rostow (1978), p. 220.
10. Costigliola (1972) is an excellent overview.
11. Stögbauer and Komlos (2004) and van Riel and Schram (1992).
12. The issue is still controversial. See Eichengreen (1989a) for a rounded assessment.
13. Maddison (1995), p. 69.
14. Bernanke (1983), p. 260.
15. Ibid., p. 260; Alston (1983), p. 888; the 1928–1934 rate simply sums annual foreclosure rates, probably leading to slight overestimates because some farms may have been foreclosed more than once in the period.
16. As quoted in DeLong (1991), p. 11. To be fair, Robbins later repudiated his 1935 view as a "fundamental misconception." Temin (1989), p. xiii.
17. Quoted in DeLong (1991), p. 6.
18. Thomas Ferguson (1984) discusses differences within American industry; O'Brien (1989) argues for the consumption maintenance motive in nominal wage rigidity.
19. These figures are from Jensen (1989), pp. 558–59; somewhat different but comparable numbers are in Margo (1993), p. 43.
20. Bernanke and James (1991), pp. 51–53.
21. Henrik Ibsen, *The League of Youth* (1869), Act 4.
22. Bernanke (1983), p. 259.
23. Ibid.; Calomiris (1993).
24. Eichengreen and Temin (2000), p. 199.
25. Cited in Kindleberger (1973), p. 152.
26. Bernanke and James (1991), pp. 50–57; the figure for German foreign deposits is from Eichengreen (1992), p. 272.
27. Eichengreen and Temin (2000), page 201.
28. Ferguson and Temin (2003) present a summary and evaluation, emphasizing the currency component of the German crisis.
29. Kindleberger (1989), pp. 173–78; Cain and Hopkins (1993b), pp. 80–81.
30. Kindleberger (2000), pp. 15–31.
31. Rostow (1978), pp. 220–23.
32. Díaz Alejandro (1983), pp. 6–11.
33. Quoted in Temin (1989), p. 95.
34. Eichengreen (1992), pp. 294–96.
35. Calculated from Warren and Pearson (1935), pp. 30–32, and Shaw (1947), pp. 290–95.
36. Kindleberger (1973), p. 197.

37. Ibid., p. 219.
38. Ibid., p. 202.
39. Eichengreen (1992), p. xi.
40. Quoted in DeLong (1991), p. 12.
41. Keynes (1932).
42. Ibid.
43. Skidelsky (1992), p. 477.
44. Quoted in Eichengreen and Temin (2000), p. 202.
45. Blum (1970), p. 49.
46. U.S. Department of Agriculture (1949), p. 53; Kindleberger (1973), pp. 222–23.
47. Romer (1992), p. 759; Romer (1993), p. 35.
48. Bernanke and James (1991), pp. 35–45.

Chapter 9: The Turn to Autarky

1. Simpson (1969), p. 16.
2. Nurkse (1962), pp. 134–35.
3. Information in what follows is from Mühlen (1938), Peterson (1954), Schacht (1955), Simpson (1969), and Weitz (1997).
4. He was apparently still baffled at the time he wrote his memoir (Schacht [1955], p. 86), unable to understand that the examiner was trying to draw him out on the abstract attributes of material objects.
5. Ibid., p. 45.
6. Ibid., pp. 148–49.
7. Weitz (1997), p. 117.
8. Simpson (1969), p. 78.
9. Ibid., pp. 78–80.
10. Ibid., p. 80.
11. Weitz (1997), p. 139.
12. Ibid., pp. 135 and 197.
13. Schacht (1955), p. 303.
14. Hitler (1953), p. 350.
15. Overy (1982); Overy (1994), pp. 37–89; Karl Hardach (1980), pp. 56–64; James (1986), pp. 367–87.
16. Simpson (1969), p. 87.
17. Quoted in James (1986), p. 353.
18. Quoted in Feldman (1993), p. 855.
19. Kaiser (1980), pp. 325–27, and Neal (1979), p. 397; these are unweighted shares.
20. Overy (1994), p. 16; Overy (1982).
21. Simpson (1969), p. 131.
22. Ibid., p. 123.
23. Weitz (1997), p. 220.
24. Overy (1994), p. 57; James (1986), pp. 355–57.
25. Clough (1964), p. 383.
26. Nove (1992), p. 250.
27. Neal (1979).
28. The comparison (for doubling) is with the low point, usually 1932. Figures on manufacturing output are open to challenge, especially given the rapid price changes of the

period. These, which are intended only as illustrative, are from Overy (1982), p. 29; Rostow (1978), pp. 222–23; Díaz Alejandro (1983), p. 9; and Teichova (1985), p. 230.

29. In Blinkhorn (1990), p. 161 (retranslated by the author).
30. Stephen J. Lee (1987) and Berend and Ránki (1977), pp. 77–141, are excellent surveys.
31. Merkl (1980), p. 765.
32. The articles in Blinkhorn (1990) cover many aspects of the collaboration.
33. Sarti (1971), pp. 104–33; Gregor (1979), pp. 153–71; Ciocca and Toniolo (1984). Cohen (1988) convincingly debunks Gregor's claims that Italian fascism followed a methodical developmentalist plan but does not dispute the eventual importance of the state in the economy.
34. Teichova (1985), pp. 286 and 309.
35. Overy (1982), pp. 34 and 60.
36. Radice (1986), p. 31; Hauner (1985), p. 83.
37. Berend and Ránki (1977), pp. 94–95.
38. Nakamura (1983), Nakamura (1998), Lockwood (1968), G. C. Allen (1972), and Barnhart (1981).
39. Nove (1992), pp. 150 and 174.
40. These and all other figures used here (unless otherwise noted) are from the authoritative Davies, Harrison, and Wheatcroft (1994), p. 269 ff.
41. Nove (1992), p. 186.
42. Gregory and Stuart (1986), p. 115.
43. This system is very well summarized in Nove (1969), pp. 263–67; a more detailed discussion is in Gregory and Stuart (1990), pp. 155–265.
44. Nove (1969), p. 204.
45. All figures from Davies, Harrison, and Wheatcroft (1994).
46. Maddison (1995), pp. 194–200.
47. Robert C. Allen (1998).
48. Bairoch (1975), p. 124; Felix (1987), p. 23.
49. Bulmer-Thomas (1998), p. 77; see also Maddison (1989), p. 57.
50. Thorp (1984), p. 331; C. H. Lee (1969), p. 143.
51. Thorp and Londoño (1984), p. 94.
52. Elson (1992), pp. 186–91.
53. C. H. Lee (1969), pp. 152–53.
54. Owen and Pamuk (1999), pp. 38–44.
55. Kai-Ming and Barber (1936).
56. Feuerwerker (1983).
57. Villela and Suzigan (1977), pp. 138 and 356.
58. Owen and Pamuk (1999), pp. 16 and 244.
59. C. H. Lee (1969), p. 150.
60. Palma (1984), pp. 70–72.
61. Ocampo (1984), pp. 134 and 139.
62. Tomlinson (1979), p. 32. See also Dewey (1978).
63. Meredith (1975), p. 495.
64. Dixon (1999), pp. 61–67; Phongpaichit and Baker (1995), pp. 249–66.
65. Cain and Hopkins (1993b), pp. 188–94; A. D. Gordon (1978).
66. Tomlinson (1979), pp. 119–46.
67. Cited in Hopkins (1973), p. 267.
68. Elson (1992), p. 192.

Chapter 10: Building a Social Democracy

1. Keynes (1933).
2. Söderpalm (1975).
3. Cited in Berg and Jonung (1998), p. 11.
4. Carlson (1993), p. 174.
5. Ibid., p. 178.
6. Jorberg and Kranz (1989), p. 1082. See also Jonung (1981), pp. 302–3, and Esping-Andersen (1985), pp. 199–204.
7. Tilton (1990), p. 113.
8. Jorberg and Kranz (1989), pp. 1085–103.
9. Mabbett (1995), p. 87.
10. Benner (1997), p. 76.
11. Gourevitch (1986), p. 134.
12. Quoted in Poulson (1981), p. 610.
13. Wallis (1986); Harrington (1998), pp. 314–26. The Roosevelt quote is on p. 322.
14. Rucker and Alston (1987).
15. Troy (1965), pp. 1–2.
16. Wallis (1986), p. 18.
17. Esping-Andersen (1985), pp. 41–88.
18. Katzenstein (1985), pp. 136–90; Luebbert (1991), pp. 234–305.
19. Colton (1966), p. 93.
20. Ibid., pp. 92–197.
21. Keynes (1936), p. 383.
22. Ibid. On this interpretation—and it should be noted that interpretations of Keynes are still controversial—see especially Leijonhufvud (1968).
23. Keynes (1932).
24. Keynes (1936), p. 378.
25. Skidelsky (1992), p. 511.
26. Ibid., p. 507.
27. Ibid., pp. 573–74.
28. Laidler (1999) is a cogent example.
29. Barber (1996), pp. 83–85.
30. Skidelsky (1992), p. 506.
31. Barber (1996), p. 86.
32. The essays in Hall (1989) describe the influence of Keynesian ideas on several countries, typically after World War Two. They are decidedly agnostic on the independent impact of these ideas on policy.
33. Esping-Andersen (1985), p. 195.
34. Harrington (1998).
35. Ibid.
36. Tilton (1990), p. 131.
37. Troy (1965), pp. 1–2.
38. Cited in Swenson (1997), p. 80.
39. Ibid., p. 78.
40. Ibid., p. 72. These points are not uncontroversial. For more discussion, see Domhoff (1986), Colin Gordon (1994), and Thomas Ferguson (1984).
41. Swenson (1989), pp. 42–53.

42. Swenson (1997), p. 85.
43. Kindleberger (1989); Simmons (1994), pp. 174–274.
44. Eichengreen (1992), pp. 374–82; the quotation is from p. 380. See also Clarke (1977) and Kindleberger (1993), pp. 385–89.
45. Warren (1937), p. 71.
46. *Proceedings of the Academy of Political Science* 17 (1) (May 1936), p. 113.

Chapter 11: Reconstruction East and West

1. Leon Fraser (1940), pp. 56–57. On early wartime planning, see Oliver (1971), pp. 6–22, and Shoup and Minter (1977), pp. 117–87.
2. Richard Gardner (1980), p. 9. This classic study is the essential source for much of what follows.
3. Otto Maller, cited in Eckes (1975), p. 37.
4. Hull (1948), pp. 355–56.
5. Cited in Richard Gardner (1980), p. 19.
6. Ibid., pp. 40–68; the Welles quotes are on p. 49. See also Penrose (1953), pp. 11–31.
7. Cited in van Dormael (1978), pp. 93–94.
8. Ibid., p. 95.
9. Ibid., p. 255.
10. Cited in Eric Helleiner (1994), p. 164.
11. Feis (1930), p. 469.
12. Staley (1935), p. 495.
13. Eckes (1975), pp. 135–64; Richard Gardner (1980), pp. 110–44; van Dormael (1978), pp. 240–65.
14. *Financial Times,* March 15, 2003, p. Weekend: III.
15. Richard Gardner (1980), p. xvii.
16. Skidelsky (2000), p. 465.
17. Ansel Luxford, quoted in Richard Gardner (1980), p. xv.
18. General data from Maddison (1995), except for German industrial production, for which see Milward (1977), p. 335.
19. Milward (1977), p. 346. Milward also presents figures for the British Empire, which apparently includes the dominions.
20. DeLong and Eichengreen (1993).
21. Maddison (1995) and Mitchell (1998a, 1998b).
22. Irwin and Kroszner (1999) make and defend this case forcefully.
23. For biographical details on Acheson, see McLellan (1976) and Chace (1998).
24. Acheson (1969), pp. 267–75.
25. Quoted in Block (1977), p. 40.
26. Lloyd Gardner (1970), p. 219.
27. Richard Gardner (1980), p. 251; McLellan (1976), p. 94.
28. Chace (1998), p. 166.
29. Figures from Milward (1984), pp. 46–47, 96–97.
30. Ibid., pp. 224, 257, and 356; Gerd Hardach (1987); Karl Hardach (1980), pp. 90–109, 160–78.
31. DeLong and Eichengreen (1993).
32. Eichengreen (1993), pp. 44–53, finds that the impact of the devaluations on exports was substantial.

33. Acheson (1969), p. 727.
34. Sassoon (1996), pp. 83–136, provides an excellent overview.
35. David Reynolds (2000), pp. 13.
36. Linz (1985).
37. Radice (1986) and Brus (1986).
38. Ritschl (1996), pp. 508–11; Roesler (1991), pp. 47–51.
39. Notel (1986), pp. 230–36; Brus (1986), pp. 572–76.
40. Notel (1986), pp. 238–41. A nonillion in American and French terms is a quintillion in British terms; in either case they are ten followed by thirty zeros.
41. Brus (1986), pp. 608–41, is an excellent summary of the period.
42. Ibid., p. 626; figures in Maddison (1995), pp. 200–201, while somewhat more fragmentary, indicate a similar recovery by 1949–1951.

Chapter 12: The Bretton Woods System in Action

1. Monnet (1978), p. 228.
2. Maddison (1995).
3. The three exceptions that tested the rule (Spain, Portugal, and Greece) moved very rapidly in this direction over the course of the 1970s.
4. Boltho (1975), Hasegawa (1996), Nathan (1999), Morita (1986), Smith (1995), Tanaka (1991), Sakiya (1982), Togo (1993), Dower (1999), and Reingold (1999).
5. Maddison (1995); Western Europe includes Ireland, Spain, Portugal, and Greece but not Turkey. Overall rates of growth here as elsewhere, unless mentioned explicitly, refer to GDP per capita.
6. Maddison (1996), p. 36.
7. Van Ark (1996), p. 117. This point has been made forcefully by Temin (2000).
8. Branson (1980).
9. The information in this section is drawn from Monnet (1978), Duchêne (1994), and Moravcsik (1998), pp. 86–237.
10. Pruesssen (1982), p. 309.
11. Irwin (1995) is an excellent summary.
12. Jackson (1989), p. 53.
13. Maddison (1989), p. 32.
14. Rostow (1978), p. 669.
15. All figures calculated from Maddison (1995).
16. Ibid.
17. Bordo (1993) and Eckes (1975), pp. 211–71, are excellent surveys.
18. Data from Bordo (1993), pp. 7–11.
19. Wilkins (1974); Dunning (1983); Branson (1980); Lipsey (1988).
20. Bergsten, Horst, and Moran (1978); United Nations Commission on Transnational Corporations (1978).
21. United Nations Commission on Transnational Corporations (1978), pp. 263–73; Wilkins (1974), p. 403.
22. Lipsey (1988), p. 504.
23. Wilkins (1974), pp. 360–405; Rostow (1978), pp. 670–71; Hu (1973), pp. 19–29.
24. Hu (1973), pp. 28–38.
25. Sicsic and Wyplosz (1996), p. 235.
26. Hu (1973), p. 100.

27. Ruggie (1982), in an influential article, speaks of an integrated system he calls embedded liberalism, combining the two.
28. Kohl (1981), p. 310.
29. Olsson (1990), pp. 114–20.
30. Eichengreen (1993), p. 89.
31. Baldwin (1990), p. 138.
32. Cameron (1978) was probably the earliest explicit analysis of the relationship, which was developed in great detail in Katzenstein (1985).
33. Sassoon (1996), p. 140.
34. Baldwin (1990), p. 116.
35. Karl Hardach (1980), pp. 140–60.
36. Gallarotti (2000), pp. 26–27.
37. Atkinson (1999); see also Kraus (1981).

Chapter 13: Decolonization and Development

1. Bresser-Pereira (1984), pp. 2 and 74.
2. Maddison (1995), p. 38.
3. Kaufman (1990) summarizes the experience.
4. Frieden (1991), pp. 101 and 189; Villarreal (1977), p. 73. The numbers are for effective protection, which includes the impact of protection on inputs.
5. Baer (1989), p. 70.
6. Mitchell (1998a and 1998b); United Nations Centre for Human Settlements (1997).
7. Hong Kong might also qualify, but the British never claimed sovereignty over most of the city's territory. And although after 1965 Zimbabwe (then Rhodesia) was independent under white minority rule, this independence was not recognized by the international community until power was handed over to the black majority in 1980.
8. Kahler (1984), pp. 265–315, is an excellent survey.
9. Kunz (1991) is a detailed analysis.
10. Quoted in Love (1980), p. 52.
11. Prebisch also observed that manufacturing was typically unionized, so that wages were also less flexible, contributing to the rigidity of industrial prices.
12. Bates (1981) is the classic statement.
13. Quoted in Mukerjee (1986), p. 8.
14. Ibid.
15. Quoted in Audichya (1977), p. 111.
16. Tomlinson (1993), p. 184; this essay is an essential source on the period.
17. Johnson (1983), p. 136.
18. Khan (1989), p. 76.
19. Vaidyanathan (1983) is a good survey.
20. Tomlinson (1993), pp. 156–213; Johnson (1983), pp. 132–44.
21. Hassouna (1955), pp. 154–55.
22. All data from Maddison (1995).
23. Brown (1997), p. 67; Hossain, Islam, and Kibria (1999), p. 29.
24. Hansen (1991).
25. Fieldhouse (1986), pp. 152–53.
26. Hansen (1991), pp. 99 and 173; Owen and Pamuk (1999), pp. 244–51.
27. Owen and Pamuk (1999), p. 131; Fieldhouse (1986), p. 139.

Chapter 14: Socialism in Many Countries

1. The Soviet Union's Mongolian ally/satellite was a partial exception, although even the Soviets did not consider this country of two million nomads truly socialist.
2. Brus (1986), pp. 3–39.
3. Filtzer (1993).
4. Hutchings (1982), pp. 83–84.
5. Brus (1986), p. 64.
6. Nove (1992), pp. 303–11 and 342–48.
7. Millar (1971).
8. Brus (1986), pp. 131 and 79–82.
9. Goldman (1975), p. 39.
10. Gregory and Stuart (1990), pp. 146–51; Nove (1992), pp. 378–86; Keizer (1971), pp. 107–40; Goldman (1975).
11. Korbonski (1975), Lavigne (1975), Grossman (1966), Grossman (1968), Selucky (1972), Nove (1977), pp. 288–322, and Brus (1986), pp. 160–85.
12. Eckstein (1975); Perkins (1975).
13. This discussion of agriculture is drawn from Eckstein (1975), Chao (1970), and Perkins (1969).
14. Wheelwright and McFarlane (1970).
15. Cited in Spence (1990), p. 579.
16. Riskin (1988); Pyle (1997), pp. 41–45.
17. Crook (1975).
18. All data calculated from Maddison (1995).
19. Mesa-Lago (1974); Mesa-Lago (1981); Pérez (1988).
20. Lampe (1986); Turnock (1986).

Chapter 15: The End of Bretton Woods

1. Except where noted, the story presented here is from Safire (1975), pp. 509–28.
2. Quoted in Gowa (1983), p. 165.
3. Quoted ibid., p. 68.
4. Safire (1975), pp. 514–15.
5. Wells (1994), p. 73.
6. Quoted in Eckes (1975), p. 266.
7. The discussion here is based on Block (1977), pp. 139–202; Eckes (1975), pp. 236–71; Eichengreen and Kenen (1994); Garber (1993); Gowa (1983); and Solomon (1977).
8. Quoted in Eckes (1975), p. 250.
9. Cited in BARTLEBY.COM at http://www.bartleby.com/63/9/309.html.
10. G. C. Allen (1972), p. 170; Kindleberger (1996), pp. 196–99.
11. Servan-Schreiber (1968), pp. 3–7, 285, and 189.
12. Sigmund (1980).
13. Soskice (1978).
14. A good summary is Eliana Cardoso and Helwege (1992), pp. 84–99.
15. Díaz Alejandro (1965).
16. Bresser-Pereira (1984), p. 42; Baer (1989), pp. 317 and 355.
17. Taylor and Bacha (1976).
18. Baer (1989), p. 87; Urrutia (1991), pp. 51, 32, and 44–45.

19. All figures are from Maddison (1995).
20. Kaufman (1990), p. 130.
21. Nove (1977), pp. 161–71 and 188–90; Hutchings (1982), pp. 239–48; Gregory and Stuart (1990), pp. 402–17.

Chapter 16: Crisis and Change

1. Yergin (1991), pp. 615–17, 655, and 662–63.
2. Koopman et al. (1984).
3. Solomon (1977), p. 292; Koopman et al. (1984).
4. Sassoon (1996), pp. 707–13. This is an essential basic source of information on labor and Socialist politics in the period.
5. Henrekson, Jonung, and Stymne (1996), p. 269; van Ark, de Haan, and de Jong (1996), p. 318.
6. Eichengreen and Kenen (1994), p. 41. On the Latin American experience, see Frieden (1991).
7. Mussa (1994), p. 111; this essay is an excellent survey of the period.
8. *Economic Report of the President,* various issues. These are figures for average weekly earnings in constant dollars.
9. Volcker and Gyohten (1992), p. 181.
10. Díaz Alejandro (1984), Sachs (1985), and Sachs (1989) are among the many authoritative studies.
11. Eliana Cardoso and Helwege (1992).
12. Naughton (1995), Naughton (1996), Pyle (1997).
13. *Economic Report of the President,* various issues. These figures differ slightly from those given by Poterba (1994).
14. Volcker and Gyohten (1992).
15. Feldstein (1994), p. 270.
16. Frankel (1994) and J. David Richardson (1994) contain useful information on the episode, as do Destler and Henning (1989).
17. Gros and Thygesen (1998), pp. 95–101 and 191–236.
18. A good survey of the experience is Edwards and Naím (1997).
19. Stiglitz (2002), pp. 94–95.
20. Bank for International Settlements (various years); International Monetary Fund (various years); Corsetti, Pesenti, and Roubini (1999).

Chapter 17: Globalizers Victorious

1. *Foreign Policy Bulletin* 8, no. 5 (September–October 1997), p. 100.
2. *Foreign Policy Bulletin* 8, no. 6 (November–December 1997), pp. 26 and 24.
3. Ibid., p. 25.
4. *Wall Street Journal,* September 5, 1997, p. C1.
5. *Foreign Policy Bulletin* 8, no. 6 (November–December 1997), p. 24.
6. Ibid., p. 28.
7. Ibid., p. 27.
8. *Foreign Policy Bulletin* 8, no. 5 (September–October 1997), p. 100; *Foreign Policy Bulletin* 8, no. 6 (November–December 1997), p. 25.

9. DeLong (2000); Triplett (1999).
10. Strange (1986).
11. United Nations Development Program, *Human Development Report* (2001).
12. Data are from *The Merger Yearbook* (New York: Securities Data), various issues.
13. Evenett (2003).
14. John Williamson (1990).
15. Volcker and Gyohten (1992), pp. 167–68.
16. *Business Week* (February 7, 2000), p. 40. I include chemical production in manufacturing and petroleum services (equipment and exploration) in petroleum.
17. *Business Week* (January 22, 2001), pp. 66–72.
18. Cited in Frieden (1987), pp. 114–15.
19. What follows is taken from Slater (1996), as well as from articles in *Salon* (March 27, 2001), and the *New York Times*, December 6, 1998.
20. Stern (1977) is a classic account.
21. Mahathir is quoted at http://warisan_ku.tripod.com/pembohongan_pas.htm; the Ukrainian diatribe is by Lubomyr Prytulak and is in the Ukrainian Archive, http://www.ukar.org/.
22. Speech at World Forum on Democracy, Warsaw, June 25, 2000.
23. Ibid.
24. Lawrence (1991).

Chapter 18: Countries Catch Up

1. *The New Yorker* (May 27, 1961), pp. 49–50.
2. Lie (1998), p. 1.
3. Ibid., pp. 3–4.
4. Perry Anderson, "Diary," *London Review of Books* (October 17, 1996).
5. United Nations Development Program (1998), chapter 3.
6. Feenstra (1998).
7. Described ibid., pp. 35–36.
8. Data are from various issues of the International Iron and Steel Institute's *Steel Statistical Yearbook*.
9. *Financial Times*, August 10, 2001, p. 2.
10. See Goertzel (1999) for most of these biographical details.
11. Fernando Henrique Cardoso and Faletto (1979), p. xxiv.
12. Fernando Henrique Cardoso (1979), p. 55.
13. Fernando Henrique Cardoso and Faletto (1979), p. 210.
14. From Goertzel Web site, STILL A MARXIST.
15. Goertzel (1999), p. 94.
16. From Goertzel Web site, STILL A MARXIST.
17. Goertzel (1999), p. 160.
18. From Goertzel Web site, STILL A MARXIST.

Chapter 19: Countries Fall Behind

1. Chen and Ravallion (2001).
2. Maddison (2001), p. 129.

3. Chen and Ravallion (2001); World Bank (various years).
4. The most influential such arguments are by Jeffrey Sachs and his coauthors. See, for example, Sachs and Bloom (1998) and Sachs and Warner (2001).
5. An excellent survey of the Zambian experience is in Shafer (1994), pp. 49–93.
6. Kaunda (1988), p. 11.
7. The classic study of the foreign copper companies is Sklar (1975).
8. Quoted in Ihonvbere (1996), p. 52.
9. Kaunda (1988), p. ix.
10. Kaunda (1968), p. 37.
11. Kaunda (1988), pp. 41 and 65.
12. Bratton (1980), p. 259.
13. Mushingeh (1994).
14. Bratton (1980), p. 227.
15. On the country's economic and political crises, see Bates and Collier (1993) and Bratton (1994).
16. Pritchett (n.d.), p. 1.
17. "Nigeria confronts corruption." BBC News/World, November 11, 1999, available at http://news.bbc.co.uk/hi/english/world/africa/newsid_515000/515788.stm.
18. The data on Nigerian generators and Ghanaian public employment are from Collier and Gunning (1999), pp. 10–11.
19. Data for this section are from the United Nations Development Program's excellent annual *Human Development Report*.

Chapter 20: Global Capitalism Troubled

1. This account of the Seattle events is taken primarily from coverage in the *New York Times*, except where noted.
2. *Seattle Post-Intelligencer*, December 1, 1999.
3. *New York Times*, December 1, 1999.
4. *Seattle Post-Intelligencer*, December 2, 1999.
5. Ibid., December 1, 1999.
6. www.turnpoint.org.
7. *New York Times*, December 2, 1999.
8. *Business Week* (December 6, 2004), p. 104.
9. Freeman (1995), which remains an excellent survey of this voluminous literature.
10. http://www.aflcio.org/globaleconomy/index.htm.
11. http://www.aflcio.org/globaleconomy/meaning.htm.
12. From statements on "Global Monoculture" and "Invisible Government" from the Turning Point Project, on the Internet at www.turnpoint.org.
13. http://www.cleanclothes.org/intro.htm#7.
14. www.turnpoint.org.
15. Ibid.
16. http://www.uniteunion.org/sweatshops/action/action.html.
17. Chakravarthi Raghavan, "US, Moore Rebuffed, WTO Ministerial Ends in Failure," *SUNS: North-South Development Monitor*, December 7, 1999. Also at http://www.twn side.org.sg/title/rebuff-cn.htm.

References

Acheson, Dean. 1969. *Present at the Creation.* New York: Norton.

Aldcroft, Derek H. 1977. *From Versailles to Wall Street 1919–1929.* Berkeley: University of California Press.

Allen, G. C. 1972. *A Short Economic History of Modern Japan 1867–1937.* London: George Allen and Unwin.

Allen, Robert C. 1998. The Standard of Living in the Soviet Union, 1928–1940. *Journal of Economic History* 58 (4): pp. 1063–89.

Alston, Lee. 1983. Farm Foreclosures in the United States during the Interwar Period. *Journal of Economic History* 43 (4): pp. 885–903.

Atkinson, A. B. 1999. The Distribution of Income in the UK and OECD Countries in the Twentieth Century. *Oxford Review of Economic Policy* 15 (4): pp. 56–75.

Audichya, Janardan. 1977. *Economic Ideas of Jawaharlal Nehru.* Jodhpur: Jain Brothers.

Baer, Werner. 1989. *The Brazilian Economy: Growth and Development.* New York: Praeger.

Bairoch, Paul. 1975. *The Economic Development of the Third World since 1900.* Berkeley: University of California Press.

———. 1989. European Trade Policy, 1815–1914. In *The Cambridge Economic History of Europe,* vol. 8: *The Industrial Economies: The Development of Economic and Social Policies,* ed. Peter Mathias and Sidney Pollard, pp. 19–160. Cambridge: Cambridge University Press.

Baldwin, Peter. 1990. *The Politics of Social Solidarity: Class Bases of the European Welfare State, 1875–1975.* New York: Cambridge University Press.

Bank for International Settlements. Various years. *Annual Report.* Basel, Switzerland: Bank for International Settlements.

Barber, William. 1996. *Designs within Disorder: Franklin D. Roosevelt, the Economists, and the Shaping of American Economic Policy, 1933–1945*. Cambridge: Cambridge University Press.

Barnhart, Michael. 1981. Japan's Economic Security and the Origins of the Pacific War. *Journal of Strategic Studies* 4 (2): pp. 105–24.

Bates, Robert. 1981. *Markets and States in Tropical Africa*. Berkeley: University of California Press.

———. 1997. *Open-Economy Politics: The Political Economy of the World Coffee Trade*. Princeton: Princeton University Press.

———, and Paul Collier. 1993. The Politics and Economics of Policy Reform in Zambia. In *Political and Economics Interactions in Economic Policy Reform*, ed. Bates and Anne Krueger, pp. 387–443. Cambridge: Blackwell.

Benner, Mats. 1997. *The Politics of Growth: Economic Regulation in Sweden 1930–1994*. Lund: Arkiv förlag.

Berend, Iván, and György Ránki. 1977. *East Central Europe in the 19th and 20th Centuries*. Budapest: Akadémiai Kiadó.

Berg, Claes, and Lars Jonung. 1998. Pioneering Price Level Targeting: The Swedish Experience 1931–1937. SSE/EFI Economics and Finance Working Paper 290. Stockholm: Stockholm School of Economics.

Bergsten, C. Fred; Thomas Horst; and Theodore Moran. 1978. *American Multinationals and American Interests*. Washington, D.C.: Brookings Institution.

Bernanke, Ben. 1983. Nonmonetary Effects of the Financial Crisis in the Propagation of the Great Depression. *American Economic Review* 73 (3): pp. 257–76.

———. 1995. The Macroeconomics of the Great Depression: A Comparative Approach. *Journal of Money, Credit, and Banking* 27 (1): pp. 1–28.

———, and Harold James. 1991. The Gold Standard, Deflation, and Financial Crisis in the Great Depression: An International Comparison. In *Financial Markets and Financial Crises*, ed. R. Glenn Hubbard, pp. 33–68. Chicago: University of Chicago Press.

———, and Kevin Carey. 1996. Nominal Wage Stickiness and Aggregate Supply in the Great Depression. *Quarterly Journal of Economics* 111 (3): pp. 853–83.

Blinkhorn, Martin, ed. 1990. *Fascists and Conservatives: The Radical Right and the Establishment in Twentieth-Century Europe*. London: Unwin Hyman.

Block, Fred. 1977. *The Origins of International Economic Disorder*. Berkeley: University of California Press.

Blum, John Morton. 1970. *Roosevelt and Morgenthau*. Boston: Houghton Mifflin.

Boltho, Andrea. 1975. *Japan: An Economic Survey 1953–1973*. London: Oxford University Press.

Bordo, Michael. 1993. The Bretton Woods International Monetary System: A Historical Overview. In *A Retrospective on the Bretton Woods System*, ed. Michael Bordo and Barry Eichengreen, pp. 3–98. Chicago: University of Chicago Press.

———, and Hugh Rockoff. 1996. The Gold Standard as a Good Housekeeping Seal of Approval. *Journal of Economic History* 56 (3): pp. 389–428.

Branson, William. 1980. Trends in United States International Trade and Investment since World War II. In *The American Economy in Transition*, ed. Martin Feldstein, pp. 183–257. Chicago: University of Chicago Press.

Bratton, Michael. 1980. *The Local Politics of Rural Development: Peasant and Party-State in Zambia*. Hanover: University Press of New England.

———. 1994. Economic Crisis and Political Realignment in Zambia. In *Economic Change and Political Liberalization in Sub-Saharan Africa*, ed. Jennifer Widner, pp. 101–27. Baltimore: Johns Hopkins University Press.

Bresser-Pereira, Luiz Carlos. 1984. *Development and Crisis in Brazil 1930–1983*. Boulder: Westview.

Brown, Ian. 1997. *Economic Change in South-East Asia, c. 1830–1980.* Kuala Lumpur: Oxford University Press.

Broz, Lawrence. 1997. The Domestic Politics of International Monetary Order: The Gold Standard. In *Contested Social Orders and International Politics*, ed. David Skidmore, pp. 53–91. Nashville: Vanderbilt University Press.

Brus, Wlodzimierz. 1986. *The Economic History of Eastern Europe 1919–1975*, vol. 2, *Institutional Change within a Planned Economy*, ed. M. C. Kaser. Oxford: Clarendon Press.

Bulmer-Thomas, Victor. 1998. The Latin American Economies, 1929–1939. In *Latin America: Economy and Society since 1930*, ed. Leslie Bethell, pp. 65–114. Cambridge: Cambridge University Press.

Cain, P. J., and A. G. Hopkins. 1993a. *British Imperialism: Innovation and Expansion, 1688–1914*. London: Longman.

———— and ————. 1993b. *British Imperialism: Crisis and Deconstruction, 1914–1990*. London: Longman.

Calomiris, Charles. 1993. Financial Factors in the Great Depression. *Journal of Economic Perspectives* 7 (2): pp. 61–85.

Cameron, David. 1978. The Expansion of the Public Economy: A Comparative Analysis. *American Political Science Review* 72 (4): pp. 1243–61.

Capie, Forrest. 1983. Tariff Protection and Economic Performance in the Nineteenth Century. In *Policy and Performance in International Trade*, ed. John Black and L. Alan Winters. New York: St. Martin's Press.

Cardoso, Eliana, and Ann Helwege. 1992. *Latin America's Economy: Diversity, Trends, and Conflicts*. Cambridge: MIT Press.

Cardoso, Fernando Henrique. 1979. On the Characterization of Authoritarian Regimes in Latin America. In *The New Authoritarianism in Latin America*, ed. David Collier, pp. 33–57. Princeton: Princeton University Press.

————, and Enzo Faletto. 1979. *Dependency and Development in Latin America*. Berkeley: University of California Press.

Carlson, Benny. 1993. The Long Retreat: Gustav Cassel and Eli Heckscher on the "New Economics" of the 1930s. In *Swedish Economic Thought*, ed. Lars Jonung, pp. 156–94. London: Routledge.

Carr, E. H. 1939. *The Twenty Years' Crisis, 1919–1939*. London: Macmillan.

Chace, James. 1998. *Acheson: The Secretary of State Who Created the American World*. New York: Simon & Schuster.

Chandler, Alfred D. 1969. The Structure of American Industry in the Twentieth Century: A Historical Overview. *Business History Review* 43 (3): pp. 255–98.

————. 1977. *The Visible Hand: The Managerial Revolution in American Business*. Cambridge: Harvard University Press.

————, and Herman Daems, eds. 1980. *Managerial Hierarchies: Comparative Perspectives on the Rise of the Modern Industrial Enterprise*. Cambridge: Harvard University Press.

————, and Richard Tedlow. 1985. *The Coming of Managerial Capitalism*. Homewood: Richard D. Irwin.

Chao, Kang. 1970. *Agricultural Production in Communist China, 1949–1965*. Madison: University of Wisconsin Press.

Chen, Shaohua, and Martin Ravallion. 2001. How Did the World's Poorest Fare in the 1990s? Unpublished paper, World Bank, Washington, D.C.

Ciocca, Pierluigi, and Gianni Toniolo. 1984. Industry and Finance in Italy, 1918–1940. *Journal of European Economic History* 13 (2): pp. 113–36.

Clarke, Stephen V. O. 1977. Exchange Rate Stabilization in the Mid-1930s. *Princeton Studies in International Finance 41*. Princeton: International Finance Section, Department of Economics.

Clough, Shepard. 1964. *The Economic History of Modern Italy*. New York: Columbia University Press.

Coffey, Frank, and Joseph Layden. 1996. *America on Wheels: The First 100 Years, 1896–1996*. Los Angeles: General Publishing Group.

Cohen, Jon S. 1988. Was Italian Fascism a Developmental Dictatorship? Some Evidence to the Contrary. *Economic History Review* 41 (1): pp. 95–113.

Collier, Paul, and Jan Willem Gunning. 1999. Why Has Africa Grown Slowly? *Journal of Economic Perspectives* 13 (3): pp. 3–22.

Colton, Joel. 1966. *Léon Blum: Humanist in Politics*. New York: Alfred A. Knopf.

Cooper, John Milton. 1976. The Command of Gold Reversed. *Pacific Historical Review* 45 (2): pp. 209–30.

Corsetti, Giancarlo; Paolo Pesenti; and Nouriel Roubini. 1999. The Asian Crisis: An Overview of the Empirical Evidence and Policy Debate. In *The Asian Financial Crisis: Causes, Contagion and Consequences*, ed. Pierre Richard Agenor, Marcus Miller, David Vines, and Axel Weber. Cambridge: Cambridge University Press.

Costigliola, Frank. 1972. The Other Side of Isolationism: The Establishment of the First World Bank, 1929–1930. *Journal of American History* 59 (3): pp. 602–20.

———. 1976. The United States and the Reconstruction of Germany in the 1920s. *Business History Review* 50 (4): pp. 477–502.

Cox, Charles C. 1981. Monopoly Explanations of the Great Depression and Public Policies toward Business. In *The Great Depression Revisited*, ed. Karl Brunner, pp. 174–207. Boston: Kluwer-Nijhoff Publishing.

Crook, Frederick. 1975. The Commune System in the People's Republic of China, 1963–1974. In Joint Economic Committee before U.S. Congress on *China: A Reassessment of the Economy*, pp. 366–410. Washington, D.C.: U.S. Government Printing Office.

Daems, Herman. 1980. The Rise of the Modern Industrial Enterprise: A New Perspective. In *Managerial Hierarchies: Comparative Perspectives on the Rise of the Modern Industrial Enterprise*, ed. Alfred D. Chandler, Jr., and Herman Daems, pp. 203–23. Cambridge: Harvard University Press.

Davies, R. W.; Mark Harrison; and S. G. Wheatcroft. 1994. *The Economic Transformation of the Soviet Union, 1913–1945*. Cambridge: Cambridge University Press.

Davis, Lance E., and Robert A. Huttenback. 1986. *Mammon and the Pursuit of Empire: The Political Economy of British Imperialism, 1860–1912*. Cambridge: Cambridge University Press.

De Graaff, J. 1986. *The Economics of Coffee*. Wageningen: Pudoc.

DeLong, J. Bradford. 1991. "Liquidation" Cycles and the Great Depression. Unpublished paper.

———. 2000. What Went Right in the 1990's? Sources of American and Prospects for World Economic Growth. Unpublished paper.

———, and Barry Eichengreen. 1993. The Marshall Plan: History's Most Successful Structural Adjustment Programme. In *Postwar Economic Reconstruction and Lessons for the East Today,* ed. Rüdiger Dornbusch, Wilhelm Nölling, and Richard Layard, pp. 189–230. Cambridge: MIT Press.

Destler, I. M., and C. Randall Henning. 1989. *Dollar Politics: Exchange Rate Policymaking in the United States.* Washington, D.C.: Institute for International Economics.

Dewey, Clive. 1978. The End of the Imperialism of Free Trade: The Eclipse of the Lancashire Lobby and the Concession of Fiscal Autonomy to India. In *The Imperial Impact: Studies in the Economic History of Africa and India,* ed. Clive Dewey and A. G. Hopkins, pp. 35–67. London: Athlone Press.

Díaz Alejandro, Carlos. 1965. On the Import Intensity of Import Substitution. *Kyklos* 18 (3): pp. 495–511.

———. 1983. Stories of the 1930s for the 1980s. In *Financial Policies and the World Capital Market: The Problem of Latin American Countries,* ed. Pedro Aspe Armella, Rudiger Dornbusch, and Maurice Obstfeld, pp. 5–40. Chicago: University of Chicago Press.

———. 1984. Latin American Debt: I Don't Think We Are in Kansas Anymore. *Brookings Papers on Economic Activity* 1984: pp. 335–403.

Dixon, Chris. 1999. *The Thai Economy: Uneven Development and Internationalisation.* New York: Routledge.

Domhoff, G. William. 1986. Corporate-Liberal Theory and the Social Security Act. *Politics and Society* 15 (3): pp. 297–329.

———. 1987.The Wagner Act and Theories of the State. *Political Power and Social Theory* 6 (1987): pp. 159–85.

Dower, John. 1999. *Embracing Defeat: Japan in the Wake of World War II.* New York: Norton.

Duchêne, François. 1994. *Jean Monnet.* New York: Norton.

Dunning, John. 1983. Changes in the Level and Structure of International Production: The Last One Hundred Years. In *The Growth of International Business,* ed. Mark Casson, pp. 84–139. London: George Allen and Unwin.

Eckes, Alfred E. 1975. *A Search for Solvency: Bretton Woods and the International Monetary System, 1941–1971.* Austin: University of Texas Press.

Eckstein, Alexander. 1975. *China's Economic Development.* Ann Arbor: University of Michigan Press.

Economic Report of the President. Various dates. Washington, D.C.: U.S. Government Printing Office.

Edelstein, Michael. 1982. *Overseas Investment in the Age of High Imperialism: The United Kingdom 1850–1914.* New York: Columbia University Press.

Edwards, Sebastian, and Moisés Naím, eds. 1997. *Mexico 1994: Anatomy of an Emerging-Market Crash.* Washington, D.C.: Carnegie Endowment for International Peace.

Eichengreen, Barry. 1987. Conducting the International Orchestra: Bank of England Leadership under the Classical Gold Standard. *Journal of International Money and Finance* 6 (1): pp. 5–30.

———. 1989a. The Political Economy of the Smoot-Hawley Tariff. *Research in Economic History* 12: pp. 1–43.

———. 1989b. House Calls of the Money Doctor: The Kemmerer Missions to Latin America 1917–1931. In *Debt, Stabilization, and Development: Essays in Memory of Carlos Díaz-Alejandro,* ed. Guillermo Calvo, Ronald Findlay, Pentti Kouri, and Jorge Braga de Macedo, pp. 57–77. Cambridge: Blackwell.

———. 1992. *Golden Fetters: The Gold Standard and the Great Depression, 1919–1939.* New York: Oxford University Press.

————. 1993. *Reconstructing Europe's Trade and Payments: The European Payments Union.* Manchester: Manchester University Press.

————, and Marc Flandreau, eds. 1997. *The Gold Standard in Theory and History.* New York: Routledge.

————, and Peter Kenen. 1994. Managing the World Economy under the Bretton Woods System: An Overview. In *Managing the World Economy*, ed. Peter Kenen, pp. 3–57. Washington, D.C.: Institute for International Economics.

————, and Peter Temin. 2000. The Gold Standard and the Great Depression. *Contemporary European History* 9 (2): pp. 183–207.

Elson, Robert. 1992. International Commerce, the State, and Society: Economic and Social Change. In *The Cambridge History of Southeast Asia*, vol. 2: *The Nineteenth and Twentieth Centuries*, ed. Nicholas Tarling, pp. 131–95. New York: Cambridge University Press.

Engerman, Stanley, and Kenneth Sokoloff. 1997. Factor Endowments, Institutions, and Differential Paths of Growth among New World Economies. In *How Latin America Fell Behind: Essays on the Economic History of Brazil and Mexico, 1800–1914*, ed. Stephen Haber, pp. 260–304. Stanford: Stanford University Press.

Esping-Andersen, Gøsta. 1985. *Politics against Markets: The Social Democratic Road to Power.* Princeton: Princeton University Press.

Estevadeordal, A.; B. Frantz; and A. M. Taylor. May 2003. The Rise and Fall of World Trade, 1870–1939. *Quarterly Journal of Economics* 118: pp. 359–407.

Evans, Richard, and Dick Geary, eds. 1987. *The German Unemployed.* London: Croom Helm.

Evenett, Simon. 2003. The Cross Border Mergers and Acquisitions Wave of the Late 1990s. NBER Working Paper 9655. Cambridge: National Bureau of Economic Research.

Falkus, M. E. 1972. *The Industrialization of Russia 1700–1914.* London: Macmillan.

Feenstra, Robert C. 1998. Integration of Trade and Disintegration of Production in the Global Economy. *Journal of Economic Perspectives* 12 (4): pp. 31–50.

Feis, Herbert. 1930. *Europe the World's Banker 1870–1914.* New Haven: Yale University Press.

————. 1950. *The Diplomacy of the Dollar: First Era 1919–1932.* Baltimore: Johns Hopkins University Press.

Feldman, Gerald. 1993. *The Great Disorder: Politics, Economics, and Society in the German Inflation, 1914–1924.* New York: Oxford University Press.

Feldstein, Martin, ed. 1994. *American Economic Policy in the 1980s.* Chicago: University of Chicago Press.

Felix, David. 1987. Alternative Outcomes of the Latin American Debt Crisis: Lessons from the Past. *Latin American Research Review* 22 (2): pp. 3–46.

Ferguson, Niall. 1998. *The World's Banker: The History of the House of Rothschild.* London: Weidenfeld and Nicolson.

Ferguson, Thomas. 1984. From Normalcy to New Deal: Industrial Structure, Party Competition, and American Public Policy in the Great Depression. *International Organization* 38 (1): pp. 41–94.

————, and Peter Temin. 2003. Made in Germany: The German Currency Crisis of July 1931. *Research in Economic History* 21: pp. 1–53.

Feuerwerker, Albert. 1995a. *Studies in the Economic History of Late Imperial China.* Ann Arbor: Center for Chinese Studies, University of Michigan.

————. 1995b. *The Chinese Economy, 1870–1949.* Ann Arbor: Center for Chinese Studies, University of Michigan.

Fieldhouse, D. K. 1986. *Black Africa 1945–1980.* London: Allen and Unwin.

Filtzer, Donald. 1993. *The Khrushchev Era: De-Stalinisation and the Limits of Reform in the USSR, 1953–1964.* London: Macmillan.

Fischer, Stanley, and Ratna Sahay. 2000. Economies in Transition: Taking Stock. *Finance and Development* 37 (3): pp. 2–6.

Flandreau, Marc. 1997. Central Bank Cooperation in Historical Perspective: A Skeptical View. *Economic History Review* 50 (4): pp. 735–63.

Flint, John E. 1974. *Cecil Rhodes.* Boston: Little, Brown.

Forbes, John Douglas. 1981. *J. P. Morgan, Jr.* Charlottesville: University Press of Virginia.

Frankel, Jeffrey. 1994. The Making of Exchange Rate Policy in the 1980s. In *American Economic Policy in the 1980s,* ed. Martin Feldstein, pp. 293–341. Chicago: University of Chicago Press.

Fraser, John Foster. 1914. *The Amazing Argentine: A New Land of Enterprise.* London and New York: Funk and Wagnalls.

Fraser, Leon. 1940. Trade Barriers and World Peace. *Proceedings of the Academy of Political Science* 19 (1): pp. 56–57.

Freeman, Richard. 1995. Are Your Wages Set in Beijing? *Journal of Economic Perspectives* 9 (3): pp. 15–31.

————. 1998. Spurts in Union Growth: Defining Moments and Social Processes. In *The Defining Moment: The Great Depression and the American Economy in the Twentieth Century,* ed. Michael Bordo, Claudia Goldin, and Eugene White, pp. 265–95. Chicago: University of Chicago Press.

Frieden, Jeffry A. 1987. *Banking on the World: The Politics of American International Finance.* New York: Harper & Row.

————. 1988. Sectoral Conflict and U.S. Foreign Economic Policy, 1914–1940. *International Organization* 42 (1): pp. 59–90.

————. 1991. *Debt, Development, and Democracy: Modern Political Economy and Latin America, 1965–1985.* Princeton: Princeton University Press.

Friedman, Milton, and Anna Schwartz. 1963. *A Monetary History of the United States, 1867–1960.* Princeton: Princeton University Press.

————, and ————. 1982. *Monetary Trends in the United States and the United Kingdom.* Chicago: University of Chicago Press.

Fullerton, Don. 1994. Inputs to Tax Policy-Making: The Supply-Side, the Deficit, and the Level Playing Field. In *American Economic Policy in the 1980s,* ed. Martin Feldstein, pp. 165–208. Chicago: University of Chicago Press.

Gallarotti, Giulio. 2000. The Advent of the Prosperous Society: The Rise of the Guardian State and Structural Change in the World Economy. *Review of International Political Economy* 7 (1): pp. 1–52.

Gallman, Robert. 1960. Commodity Output, 1839–1899. In *Trends in the American Economy in the Nineteenth Century,* Studies in Income and Wealth, vol. 24, pp. 13–71. Princeton: Princeton University Press.

Garber, Peter. 1993. The Collapse of the Bretton Woods Fixed Exchange Rate System. In *A Retrospective on the Bretton Woods System,* ed. Michael Bordo and Barry Eichengreen, pp. 461–85. Chicago: University of Chicago Press.

Gardner, Lloyd. 1970. *Architects of Illusion.* Chicago: Quadrangle.

Gardner, Richard. 1980. *Sterling-Dollar Diplomacy in Current Perspective: The Origins and*

Prospects of Our International Economic Order (expanded ed.). New York: Columbia University Press.

Geary, Dick. 1991. *European Labour Politics from 1900 to the Depression*. Atlantic Highlands: Humanities Press.

Gerschenkron, Alexander. 1962. *Economic Backwardness in Historical Perspective*. Cambridge: Harvard University Press.

Goertzel, Ted. 1999. *Fernando Henrique Cardoso: Reinventing Democracy in Brazil*. London: Lynne Rienner.

Goldin, Claudia. 1994. The Political Economy of Immigration Restriction in the United States, 1890–1921. In *The Regulated Economy: A Historical Approach to Political Economy*, ed. Claudia Goldin and Gary Libecap, pp. 223–58. Chicago: University of Chicago Press.

Goldman, Marshall. 1975. *Détente and Dollars*. New York: Basic Books.

Gordon, A. D. 1978. Businessmen and Politics in Developing Colonial Economy: Bombay City, 1918–1933. In *The Imperial Impact: Studies in the Economic History of Africa and India*, ed. Clive Dewey and A. G. Hopkins. London: Athlone Press.

Gordon, Colin. 1994. *New Deals: Business, Labor, and Politics in America 1920–1935*. Cambridge: Cambridge University Press.

Gourevitch, Peter. 1986. *Politics in Hard Times: Comparative Responses to International Economic Crises*. Ithaca: Cornell University Press.

———. 1977. International Trade, Domestic Coalitions, and Liberty: Comparative Responses to the Crisis of 1873–1896. *Journal of Interdisciplinary History* 8 (2): pp. 281–313.

Gowa, Joanne. 1983. *Closing the Gold Window: Domestic Politics and the End of Bretton Woods*. Ithaca: Cornell University Press.

Gregor, A. James. 1979. *Italian Fascism and Developmental Dictatorship*. Princeton: Princeton University Press.

Gregory, Paul, and Robert Stuart. 1990. *Soviet Economic Structure and Performance*, 4th ed. New York: Harper and Row.

Gros, Daniel, and Niels Thygesen. 1998. *European Monetary Integration*, 2nd ed. Harlow: Longman.

Grossman, Gregory. 1966. Economic Reforms: A Balance Sheet. *Problems of Communism* 15 (6): pp. 43–55.

———. 1968. Economic Reform: The Interplay of Economics and Politics. In *The Future of Communism in Europe*, ed. R. V. Burks, pp. 105–40. Detroit: Wayne State University Press.

Hall, Peter, ed. 1989. *The Political Power of Economic Ideas: Keynesianism across Nations*. Princeton: Princeton University Press.

Hansen, Bent. 1991. *Egypt and Turkey*. Oxford: Oxford University Press for the World Bank.

Hardach, Gerd. 1987. The Marshall Plan in Germany, 1948–1952. *Journal of European Economic History* 16 (3): pp. 433–85.

Hardach, Karl. 1980. *The Political Economy of Germany in the Twentieth Century*. Berkeley: University of California Press.

Harrington, Michael. 1998. Trade and Social Insurance: The Development of National Unemployment Insurance in Advanced Industrial Democracies. Ph.D. dissertation, University of California, Los Angeles.

Hasegawa, Harukiyo. 1996. *The Steel Industry in Japan: A Comparison with Britain*. London: Routledge.

Hassouna, Mohamed Abdel Khalek. 1955. The First Asian-African Conference held at Bandung, Indonesia. Report submitted to the League of Arab States. Cairo: League of Arab States.

Hauner, M. 1985. Human Resources. In *The Economic History of Eastern Europe*

1919–1975, vol. 1: *Economic Structure and Performance between the Two Wars*, ed. M. C. Kaser and E. A. Radice, pp. 67–147. Oxford: Clarendon Press.

Helleiner, Eric. 1994. *States and the Reemergence of Global Finance: From Bretton Woods to the 1990s*. Ithaca: Cornell University Press.

Helleiner, Gerald K. 1966. *Peasant Agriculture, Government, and Economic Growth in Nigeria*. Homewood: Richard D. Irwin.

Henrekson, Magnus; Lars Jonung; and Joakim Stymne. 1996. Economic Growth and the Swedish Model. In *Economic Growth in Europe since 1945*, ed. Nicholas Crafts and Gianni Toniolo, pp. 240–89. Cambridge: Cambridge University Press.

Heuberger, Georg, ed. 1994. *The Rothschilds: Essays on the History of a European Family*. Rochester: Boydell and Brewer.

Hickman, Bryan D. 1970. Kenya and Uganda. In *Tropical Development 1880–1913*, ed. W. Arthur Lewis, pp. 178–97. London: George Allen and Unwin.

Hicks, John. 1931. *The Populist Revolt*. Minneapolis: University of Minnesota Press.

Hitler, Adolf. 1953. *Hitler's Secret Conversations 1941–44*. New York: Farrar, Straus, and Young.

Hochschild, Adam. 1998. *King Leopold's Ghost*. Boston: Houghton Mifflin.

Hogerdorn, Jan S. 1975. Economic Initiative and African Cash Farming. In *Colonialism in Africa 1870–1960*, vol. 4: *The Economics of Colonialism*, ed. Peter Duignan and L. H. Gann. Cambridge: Cambridge University Press.

Holtfrerich, Carl-Ludwig. 1999. *Frankfurt as a Financial Centre: From Medieval Trade Fair to European Banking Centre*. Munich: Beck.

Hopkins, A. G. 1973. *An Economic History of West Africa*. New York: Columbia University Press.

Hossain, Moazzem; Iyanatul Islam; and Reza Kibria. 1999. *South Asian Economic Development*. London: Routledge.

Hu, Y. S. 1973. *The Impact of U.S. Investment in Europe: A Case Study of the Automotive and Computer Industries*. New York: Praeger.

Hull, Cordell. 1948. *The Memoirs of Cordell Hull*. New York: Macmillan.

Hutchings, Raymond. 1982. *Soviet Economic Development*, 2nd ed. Oxford: Basil Blackwell.

Ihonvbere, Julius O. 1996. *Economic Crisis, Civil Society, and Democratization: The Case of Zambia*. Trenton: Africa World Press.

Internatioinal Monetary Fund. Various years. *World Economic Outlook*. Washington, D.C.: International Monetary Fund.

Irwin, Douglas A. 1994. The Political Economy of Free Trade: Voting in the British General Election of 1906. *Journal of Law and Economics* 37 (1): pp. 75–108.

———. 1995. The GATT's Contribution to Economic Recovery in Post-war Western Europe. In *Europe's Post-war Recovery*, ed. Barry Eichengreen, pp. 127–50. Cambridge: Cambridge University Press.

———. 1996. *Against the Tide: An Intellectual History of Free Trade*. Princeton: Princeton University Press.

———, and Randall S. Kroszner. 1999. Interests, Institutions, and Ideology in Securing Policy Change: The Republican Conversion to Trade Liberalization after Smoot-Hawley. *Journal of Law and Economics* 42 (2): pp. 643–73.

Jackson, John. 1989. *The World Trading System*. Cambridge: MIT Press.

James, Harold. 1986. *The German Slump: Politics and Economics 1924–1936*. Oxford: Clarendon Press.

James, Scott, and David Lake. 1989. The Second Face of Hegemony: Britain's Repeal of the Corn Laws and the American Walker Tariff of 1846. *International Organization* 43 (1): pp. 1–29.

Jensen, Richard J. 1989. The Causes and Cures of Unemployment in the Great Depression. *Journal of Interdisciplinary History* 29 (4): pp. 553–83.

Johnson, B. L. C. 1983. *Development in South Asia*. New York: Penguin Books.

Jones, E. L. 1996. Venetian Twilight: How Economies Fade. *Journal of Economic History* 56 (3): p. 704.

Jones, Stanley. 1964. *The Presidential Election of 1896*. Madison: University of Wisconsin Press.

Jonung, Lars. 1981. The Depression in Sweden and the United States: A Comparison of Causes and Policies. In *The Great Depression Revisited*, ed. Karl Brunner, pp. 286–315. Boston: Kluwer-Nijhoff.

Jorberg, Lennart, and Olle Kranz. 1989. Economic and Social Policy in Sweden, 1850–1939. In *The Cambridge Economic History of Europe*, vol. 8: *The Industrial Economies: The Development of Economic and Social Policies*, ed. Peter Mathias and Sidney Pollard, pp. 1048–1105. Cambridge: Cambridge University Press.

Kahler, Miles. 1984. *Decolonization in Britain and France*. Princeton: Princeton University Press.

Kai-Ming, Frank, and Alvin Barber. 1936. China's Tariff Autonomy, Fact or Myth. *Far Eastern Survey* 5 (12) (June): pp. 115–22.

Kaiser, David. 1980. *Economic Diplomacy and the Origins of the Second World War*. Princeton: Princeton University Press.

Kaser, M. C., and E. A. Radice, eds. 1986. *The Economic History of Eastern Europe 1919–1975*, vol. 2: *Interwar Policy, the War, and Reconstruction*. Oxford: Clarendon.

Katzenstein, Peter. 1985. *Small States in World Markets: Industrial Policy in Europe*. Ithaca: Cornell University Press.

Kaufman, Robert. 1990. How Societies Change Developmental Models or Keep Them: Reflections on the Latin American Experience in the 1930s and the Postwar World. In *Manufacturing Miracles: Paths of Industrialization in Latin America and East Asia*, ed. Gary Gereffi and Donald Wyman, pp. 110–38. Princeton: Princeton University Press.

Kaunda, Kenneth David. 1968. *Zambia's Guideline for the Next Decade*. Lusaka: Zambia Information Service.

———. 1988. *State of the Nation*. Lusaka: Kenneth Kaunda Foundation.

Keizer, Willem. 1971. *The Soviet Quest for Economic Rationality: The Conflict of Economic and Political Aims in the Soviet Economy 1953–1968*. Rotterdam: Rotterdam University Press.

Kennedy, Pagan. 2002. *Black Livingstone: A True Tale of Adventure in the Nineteenth-Century Congo*. New York: Viking.

Keynes, John Maynard. 1920. *The Economic Consequences of the Peace*. New York: Harcourt, Brace and Howe.

———. 1932. The World's Economic Outlook. *Atlantic* 1 (May): pp. 521–26.

———. 1933. National Self-Sufficiency. *Yale Review* 22 (4): pp. 755–69.

———. 1936. *The General Theory of Employment, Interest, and Money*. New York: Harcourt, Brace.

Khan, Mohammad Shibbir. 1989. *Jawaharlal Nehru: The Founder of Modern India*. New Delhi: Ashish Publishing House.

Kindleberger, Charles P. 1964. *Economic Growth in France and Britain: 1851–1950*. New York: Clarion.

————. 1973. *The World in Depression 1929–1939*. Berkeley: University of California Press.

————. 1978. *Economic Response: Comparative Studies in Trade, Finance, and Growth*. Cambridge: Harvard University Press.

————. 1989. Commercial Policy between the Wars. In *The Cambridge Economic History of Europe*, vol. 8, ed. P. Mathias and S. Pollard, pp. 161–96. Cambridge: Cambridge University Press.

————. 1993. *A Financial History of Western Europe*, 2nd ed. New York: Oxford University Press.

————. 1996. *World Economic Primacy 1500–1990*. New York: Oxford University Press.

————. 2000. *Comparative Political Economy: A Retrospective*. Cambridge: MIT Press.

Knudsen, P. H. 1977. *Agriculture in Denmark*. Copenhagen: Agricultural Council of Denmark.

Kohl, Jürgen. 1981. Trends and Problems in Postwar Public Expenditure Development in Western Europe and North America. In *The Development of Welfare States in Europe and America*, ed. Peter Flora and Arnold Heidenheimer, pp. 307–44. New Brunswick: Transaction Books.

Koopmann, Georg; Klaus Matthies; and Beate Reszat. 1984. *Oil and the International Economy*. Hamburg: Hamburg Institute of Economic Research.

Korbonski, Andrzej. 1975. Political Aspects of Economic Reforms in Eastern Europe. In *Economic Development in the Soviet Union and Eastern Europe*, vol. 1, ed. Zbigniew Fallenbuchl, pp. 8–41. New York: Praeger.

Kraus, Franz. 1981. The Historical Development of Income Inequality in Western Europe and the United States. In *The Development of Welfare States in Europe and America*, ed. Peter Flora and Arnold Heidenheimer, pp. 187–236. New Brunswick: Transaction Books.

Kunz, Diane. 1991. *The Economic Diplomacy of the Suez Crisis*. Chapel Hill: University of North Carolina Press.

Laidler, David. 1999. *Fabricating the Keynesian Revolution*. Cambridge: Cambridge University Press.

Lake, David. 1988. *Power, Protection, and Free Trade: International Sources of U.S. Commercial Strategy, 1887–1939*. Ithaca: Cornell University Press.

Lamont, Thomas. 1915. The Effect of the War on America's Financial Position. *Annals of the American Academy of Political and Social Science* 60 (July): pp. 106–12.

Lampe, John. 1986. *The Bulgarian Economy in the Twentieth Century*. London: Croom Helm.

Landes, David. 1969. *The Unbound Prometheus: Technological Change and Industrial Development in Western Europe from 1750 to the Present*. Cambridge: Cambridge University Press.

Latham, A. J. H. 1978. *The International Economy and the Undeveloped World 1865–1914*. London: Croom Helm.

Lavigne, Marie. 1975. Economic Reforms in Eastern Europe: Ten Years After. In *Economic Development in the Soviet Union and Eastern Europe*, vol. 1, ed. Zbigniew Fallenbuchl, pp. 42–64. New York: Praeger.

Lawrence, Robert Z. 1991. Emerging Regional Arrangements: Building Blocs or Stumbling Blocks? In *Finance and the International Economy 5: The AMEX Bank Review Prize Essays*, ed. Richard O'Brien, pp. 25–35. New York: Oxford University Press.

Lee, C. H. 1969. The Effects of the Depression on Primary Producing Countries. *Journal of Contemporary History* 4 (4): pp. 139–55.

Lee, Stephen J. 1987. *The European Dictatorships 1918–1945*. London: Routledge.

Leijonhufvud, Axel. 1968. *On Keynesian Economics and the Economics of Keynes.* New York: Oxford University Press.

Lewis, Cleona. 1938. *America's Stake in International Investments.* Washington, D.C.: Brookings Institution.

Lewis, W. Arthur, ed. 1970. *Tropical Development 1880–1913.* London: George Allen and Unwin.

———. 1978. *Growth and Fluctuations 1870–1913.* London: George Allen and Unwin.

Libecap, Gary. 1998. The Great Depression and the Regulating State: Federal Government Regulation of Agriculture, 1884–1970. In *The Defining Moment: The Great Depression and the American Economy in the Twentieth Century,* ed. Michael Bordo, Claudia Goldin, and Eugene White, pp. 181–224. Chicago: University of Chicago Press.

Lie, John. 1998. *Han Unbound: The Political Economy of South Korea.* Stanford: Stanford University Press.

Liesner, Thelma. 1989. *One Hundred Years of Economic Statistics.* London: Economist.

Linz, Susan. 1985. World War II and Soviet Economic Growth, 1940–1953. In *The Impact of World War Two on the Soviet Union,* ed. Susan Linz, pp. 11–38. Totowa: Rowman and Allanheld.

Lipsey, Robert E. 1988. Changing Patterns of International Investment in and by the United States. In *The United States in the World Economy,* ed. Martin Feldstein, pp. 475–545. Chicago: University of Chicago Press.

Lockwood, William. 1968. *The Economic Development of Japan.* Princeton: Princeton University Press.

López-Córdova, J. Ernesto, and Christopher M. Meissner. 2003. Exchange-Rate Regimes and International Trade: Evidence from the Classical Gold Standard Era. *American Economic Review* 93 (1): pp. 344–53.

Love, Joseph L. 1980. Raul Prebisch and the Origins of the Doctrine of Unequal Exchange. *Latin American Research Review* 15 (3): pp. 45–72.

Luebbert, Gregory. 1991. *Liberalism, Fascism, or Social Democracy: Social Classes and the Political Origins of Regimes in Interwar Europe.* New York: Oxford University Press.

Lustick, Ian. 1993. *Unsettled States, Disputed Lands: Britain and Ireland, France and Algeria, Israel and the West Bank.* New York: Cornell University Press.

Mabbett, Deborah. 1995. *Trade, Employment, and Welfare: A Comparative Study of Trade and Labour Market Policies in Sweden and New Zealand, 1880–1980.* Oxford: Clarendon.

Maddison, Angus. 1996. Macroeconomic Accounts for European Countries. In *Quantitative Aspects of Post-War European Economic Growth,* ed. Bart Van Ark and Nicholas Crafts, pp. 27–83. Cambridge: Cambridge University Press.

———. 1989. *The World Economy in the Twentieth Century.* Paris: OECD.

———. 1995. *Monitoring the World Economy 1820–1992.* Paris: OECD.

———. 2001. *The World Economy: A Millennial Perspective.* Paris: OECD.

Maier, Charles. 1975. *Recasting Bourgeois Europe: Stabilization in France, Germany and Italy in the Decade after World War I.* Princeton: Princeton University Press.

Maltz, Mary Jane. 1963. *The Many Lives of Otto Kahn.* New York: Macmillan.

Mandell, Richard D. 1967. *Paris 1900: The Great World's Fair.* Toronto: University of Toronto Press.

Margo, Robert A. 1993. Employment and Unemployment in the 1930s. *Journal of Economic Perspectives* 7: pp. 41–59.

Marrison, A. J. 1983. Businessmen, Industries, and Tariff Reform in Great Britain, 1903–1930. *Business History* 25 (2): pp. 148–78.

Marsh, Peter. 1999. *Bargaining on Europe: Britain and the First Common Market 1860–1892*. New Haven: Yale University Press.

McLellan, David S. 1976. *Dean Acheson: The State Department Years*. New York: Dodd, Mead.

Meredith, David. 1975. The British Government and Colonial Economic Policy, 1919–39. *Economic History Review* 28 (3): pp. 484–99.

Merkl, Peter. 1980. Comparing Fascist Movements. In *Who Were the Fascists: Social Roots of European Fascism*, ed. Stein Ugelvik Larsen, Bernt Hagtvet, and Jan Petter Myklebust, pp. 752–83. Bergen: Universitetsforlaget.

Mesa-Lago, Carmelo. 1974. *Cuba in the 1970s*. Albuquerque: University of New Mexico Press.

———. 1981. *The Economy of Socialist Cuba*. Albuquerque: University of New Mexico Press.

Meyer, Richard. 1970. *Banker's Diplomacy*. New York: Columbia University Press.

Millar, James, ed. 1971. *The Soviet Rural Community*. Urbana: University of Illinois Press.

Milward, Alan. 1977. *War, Economy and Society 1939–1945*. Berkeley: University of California Press.

———. 1984. *The Reconstruction of Western Europe 1945–1951*. London: Methuen.

Mitchell, B. R. 1998a. *International Historical Statistics: The Americas*, 1750–1993. London: Macmillan.

———. 1998b. *International Historical Statistics: Europe, 1750–1993*. London: Macmillan.

———. 1998c. *International Historical Statistics: Africa, Asia, and Oceania*, 1750–1993. London: Macmillan.

Monnet, Jean. 1978. *Memoirs*. Garden City: Doubleday.

Morand, Paul. 1931. *1900 A.D.* New York: W. F. Payson.

Moravcsik, Andrew. 1998. *The Choice for Europe*. Ithaca: Cornell University Press.

Morita, Akio. 1986. *Made in Japan: Akio Morita and Sony*. New York: Dutton.

Mowery, David, and Nathan Rosenberg. 1989. *Technology and the Pursuit of Economic Growth*. Cambridge: Cambridge University Press.

Mühlen, Norbert. 1938. *Hitler's Magician: Schacht*. London: George Routledge.

Mukerjee, Hiren. 1986. *The Gentle Colossus: A Study of Jawaharlal Nehru*. Delhi: Oxford University Press.

Mushingeh, Chiponde. 1994. Unrepresentative "Democracy": One-Party Rule in Zambia, 1973–1990. *Transafrican Journal of History* 23 (1994): pp. 117–41.

Mussa, Michael. 1994. U.S. Monetary Policy in the 1980s. In *American Economic Policy in the 1980s*, ed. Martin Feldstein, pp. 81–145. Chicago: University of Chicago Press.

Nakamura, Takafusa. 1983. *Economic Growth in Prewar Japan*. New Haven: Yale University Press.

———. 1998. Depression, Recovery, and War 1920–1945. In *Japanese Economic History 1600–1960*, ed. Michael Smitka. New York: Garland.

Nathan, John. 1999. *Sony: The Private Life*. Boston: Houghton Mifflin.

Naughton, Barry. 1995. *Growing out of the Plan: Chinese Economic Reform, 1978–1993*. Cambridge: Cambridge University Press.

———. 1996. Distinctive Features of Economic Reform in China and Vietnam. In *Reforming Asian Socialism*, ed. John McMillan and Barry Naughton, pp. 273–96. Ann Arbor: University of Michigan Press.

Neal, Larry. 1979. The Economics and Finance of Bilateral Clearing Arrangements: Germany, 1934–8. *The Economic History Review* 32 (3): pp. 391–404.

Nearing, Scott, and Joseph Freeman. 1925. *Dollar Diplomacy*. New York: B. W. Huebsch.

Norbury, Frederick. 1970. Venezuela. In *Tropical Development 1880–1913*, ed. Arthur W. Lewis, pp. 128–46. London: George Allen and Unwin.

North, Douglass C. 1989. Institutions and Economic Growth: An Historical Introduction. *World Development* 17 (9): pp. 1319–332.

Notel, R. 1986. International Credit and Finance. In *The Economic History of Eastern Europe, 1919–1975*, vol. 2, ed. M. C. Kaser, pp. 170–295. Oxford: Clarendon.

Nove, Alec. 1977. *The Soviet Economic System*. London: George Allen and Unwin.

———. 1992. *An Economic History of the USSR 1917–1991*. New York: Penguin.

Noyes, Alexander Dana. 1926. *The War Period of American Finance*. New York: Putnam.

Nugent, Jeffrey, and James Robinson. 1999. Are Endowments Fate? On the Political Economy of Comparative Institutional Development. Unpublished.

Nurkse, Ragnar. 1962. *Problems of Capital Formation in Underdeveloped Countries*. New York: Oxford University Press.

Nye, John. 1996. The Scale of Production in Western Economic Development: A Comparison of Official Industry Statistics in the United States, Britain, France, and Germany, 1905–1913. *Journal of Economic History* 56 (1): pp. 90–112.

O'Brien, Anthony Patrick. 1989. A Behavioral Explanation for Nominal Wage Rigidity during the Great Depression. *Quarterly Journal of Economics* 104 (4): pp. 719–36.

Ocampo, José Antonio. 1984. The Colombian Economy in the 1930s. In *Latin America in the 1930s: The Role of the Periphery in World Crisis,* ed. Rosemary Thorp, pp. 117–43. London: Macmillan.

Oliver, Robert W. 1971. *Early Plans for a World Bank*. Princeton Studies in International Finance 29. Princeton: International Finance Section, Department of Economics.

Olsson, Sven E. 1990. *Social Policy and Welfare State in Sweden*. Lund, Sweden: Arkiv.

O'Rourke, Kevin, and Jeffrey Williamson. 1999. *Globalization and History: The Evolution of a Nineteenth-Century Atlantic Economy*. Cambridge: MIT Press.

Orwell, George. 1958. *The Road to Wigan Pier*. New York: Harcourt, Brace.

Overy, R. J. 1982. *The Nazi Economic Recovery, 1932–1938*. London: Macmillan.

———. 1994. *War and Economy in the Third Reich*. Oxford: Clarendon.

Owen, Roger, and Sevket Pamuk. 1999. *A History of Middle East Economies in the Twentieth Century*. Cambridge: Harvard University Press.

Palma, Gabriel. 1984. From an Export-Led to an Import-Substituting Economy: Chile 1914–39. In *Latin America in the 1930s: The Role of the Periphery in World Crisis,* ed. Rosemary Thorp, pp. 50–80. London: Macmillan.

Penrose, E. F. 1953. *Economic Planning for the Peace*. Princeton: Princeton University Press.

Pérez, Louis. 1988. *Cuba: Between Reform and Revolution*. New York: Oxford University Press.

Perkins, Dwight. 1969. *Agricultural Development in China 1368–1968*. Chicago: Aldine.

———. 1975. Growth and Changing Stucture of China's Twentieth-Century Economy. In *China's Modern Economy in Historical Perspective,* ed. Dwight Perkins, pp. 115–65. Stanford: Stanford University Press.

Peterson, Edward Norman. 1954. *Hjalmar Schacht for and against Hitler: A Political-Economic Study of Germany 1923–1945*. Boston: Christopher Publishing.

Phipps, William. 2002. *William Sheppard: Congo's African American Livingstone*. Louisville: Geneva Press.

Phongpaichit, Pasuk, and Chris Baker. 1995. *Thailand: Economy and Politics*. Oxford: Oxford University Press.

Poterba, James. 1994. Federal Budget Policy in the 1980s. In *American Economic Policy in the 1980s*, ed. Martin Feldstein, pp. 235–70. Chicago: University of Chicago Press.

Poulson, Barry. 1981. *Economic History of the United States*. New York: Macmillan.

Pritchett, Lant. (No date.) The Tyranny of Concepts: CUDIE (Cumulated, Depreciated, Investment Effort) Is *Not* Capital. Unpublished working paper.

Pruessen, Ronald. 1982. *John Foster Dulles: The Road to Power*. New York: Free Press.

Przeworski, Joanne Fox. 1980. *The Decline of the Copper Industry in Chile and the Entrance of North American Capital, 1870–1916*. New York: Arno Press.

Pyle, David. 1997. *China's Economy: From Revolution to Reform*. London: Macmillan.

Radice, E. A. 1986. General Characteristics of the Region between the Wars. In *The Economic History of Eastern Europe 1919–1975*, vol. 1: *Economic Structure and Performance between the Two Wars*, ed. M. C. Kaser and E. A. Radice, pp. 23–65. Oxford: Clarendon.

Reingold, Edwin. 1999. *Toyota: People, Ideas, and the Challenge of the New*. New York: Penguin.

Reynolds, David. 2000. *One World Divisible: A Global History since 1945*. New York: Norton.

Reynolds, Lloyd. 1985. *Economic Growth in the Third World, 1850–1980*. New Haven: Yale University Press.

Richardson, J. David. 1994. U.S. Trade Policy in the 1980s: Turns—and Roads Not Taken. In *American Economic Policy in the 1980s*, ed. Martin Feldstein, pp. 627–58. Chicago: University of Chicago Press.

Richardson, Philip. 1999. *Economic Change in China, c. 1800–1950*. New York: Cambridge University Press.

Riskin, Carl. 1988. *China's Political Economy: The Quest for Development since 1949*. New York: Oxford University Press.

Ritschl, Albrecht. 1996. An Exercise in Futility: East German Economic Growth and Decline, 1945–89. In *Economic Growth in Europe since 1945*, ed. Nicholas Crafts and Gianni Toniolo, pp. 498–540. Cambridge: Cambridge University Press.

Roesler, Jörg. 1991. The Rise and Fall of the Planned Economy in the German Democratic Republic, 1945–89. *German History* 9 (1): pp. 46–61.

Rogowski, Ronald. 1989. *Commerce and Coalitions*. Princeton: Princeton University Press.

Romer, Christina. 1992. What Ended the Great Depression? *Journal of Economic History* 52 (4): pp. 757–84.

———. 1993. The Nation in Depression. *Journal of Economic Perspectives* 7 (2): pp. 19–39.

Rostow, W. W. 1978. *The World Economy: History and Prospect*. Austin: University of Texas Press.

Rucker, Randal, and Lee Alston. 1987. Farm Failures and Government Intervention: A Case Study of the 1930s. *American Economic Review* 77 (4): pp. 724–30.

Ruggie, John. 1982. International Regimes, Transactions, and Change: Embedded Liberalism in the Postwar Economic Order. *International Organization* 36 (2): pp. 379–415.

Rydell, Robert; John Findling; and Kimberly Pelle. 2000. *Fair America: World's Fairs in the United States*. Washington, D.C.: Smithsonian Institution Press.

Sachs, Jeffrey. 1980. The Changing Cyclical Behavior of Wages and Prices: 1890–1976. *American Economic Review* 70 (1): pp. 78–90.

———. 1985. External Debt and Macroeconomic Performance in Latin America and East Asia. *Brookings Papers on Economic Activity* 1985 (2): pp. 523–73.

———, ed. 1989. *Developing Country Debt and Economic Performance.* Chicago: University of Chicago Press.

———; David Bloom. 1998. Geography, Demography, and Economic Growth in Africa. *Brookings Papers on Economic Activity* 1998 (2): pp. 207–950.

———, and Andrew Warner. 2001. The Curse of Natural Resources. *European Economic Review* 45 (May): pp. 827–38.

Safire, William. 1975. *Before the Fall: An Inside View of the Pre-Watergate White House.* Garden City: Doubleday.

Sakiya, Tetsuo. 1982. *Honda Motor: The Men, the Management, the Machines.* Tokyo: Kodansha International.

Sandberg, Lars. 1978. Banking and Economic Growth in Sweden before World War I. *Journal of Economic History* 38 (3): pp. 650–80.

———. 1979. The Case of the Impoverished Sophisticate: Human Capital and Swedish Economic Growth before World War I. *Journal of Economic History* 39 (1): pp. 225–41.

Sarti, Roland. 1971. *Fascism and the Industrial Leadership in Italy, 1919–1940.* Berkeley: University of California Press.

Sassoon, Donald. 1996. *One Hundred Years of Socialism: The West European Left in the Twentieth Century.* New York: New Press.

Schacht, Hjalmar. 1955. *My First Seventy-six Years.* London: Allan Wingate.

Schedvin, C. B. 1990. Staples and Regions of Pax Britannica. *Economic History Review* 43 (4): pp. 533–59.

Selucky, Radoslav. 1972. *Economic Reforms in Eastern Europe: Political Background and Economic Significance.* New York: Praeger.

Serrin, William. 1993. *Homestead: The Glory and Tragedy of an American Steel Town.* New York: Vintage.

Servan-Schreiber, J. J. 1968. *The American Challenge.* With a foreword by Arthur Schlesinger, Jr. Translated from the French by Ronald Steel. New York: Atheneum.

Shafer, D. Michael. 1994. *Winners and Losers: How Sectors Shape the Developmental Prospects of States.* Ithaca: Cornell University Press.

Shaw, William. 1947. *Value of Commodity Output since 1869.* New York: National Bureau of Economic Research.

Shoup, Laurence, and William Minter. 1977. *Imperial Brain Trust: The Council on Foreign Relations and United States Foreign Policy.* New York: Monthly Review Press.

Sicsic, Pierre, and Charles Wyplosz. 1996. France, 1945–92. In *Economic Growth in Europe since 1945,* ed. Nicholas Crafts and Gianni Toniolo, pp. 210–39. Cambridge: Cambridge University Press.

Sigmund, Paul. 1980. *Multinationals in Latin America.* Madison: University of Wisconsin Press.

Simmons, Beth. 1994. *Who Adjusts? Domestic Sources of Foreign Economic Policy during the Interwar Years.* Princeton: Princeton University Press.

Simpson, Amos E. 1969. *Hjalmar Schacht in Perspective.* Paris: Mouton.

Skidelsky, Robert. 1983. *John Maynard Keynes,* vol. 1: *Hopes Betrayed 1883–1920.* New York: Penguin.

———. 1992. *John Maynard Keynes,* vol. 2: *The Economist as Savior 1920–1937.* New York: Penguin.

————. 2000. *John Maynard Keynes*, vol. 3: *Fighting for Freedom 1937–1946*. New York: Viking.

Sklar, Richard L. 1975. *Corporate Power in an African State: The Political Impact of Multinational Mining Companies in Zambia*. Berkeley: University of California Press.

Slater, Robert. 1996. *Soros: The Life, Times, and Trading Secrets of the World's Greatest Investor*. New York: Irvin Professional Publishing.

Slinn, Peter. 1971. Commercial Concessions and Politics during the Colonial Period. *African Affairs* 70 (281): pp. 365–84.

Smith, Adam. 1937 (1776). *An Inquiry into the Nature and Causes of the Wealth of Nations*. New York: Modern Library.

Smith, Dennis B. 1995. *Japan since 1945: The Rise of an Economic Superpower*. London: Macmillan.

Söderpalm, Sven Anders. 1975. The Crisis Agreement and the Social Democratic Road to Power. In *Sweden's Development from Poverty to Affluence, 1750–1970*, ed. Steven Koblik, pp. 258–78. Minneapolis: University of Minnesota Press.

Solberg, Carl. 1987. *The Prairies and the Pampas: Agrarian Policy in Canada and Argentina, 1880–1930*. Stanford: Stanford University Press.

Solomon, Robert. 1977. *The International Monetary System 1945–1976: An Insider's View*. New York: Harper and Row.

Soskice, David. 1978. Strike Waves and Wage Explosions, 1968–70: An Economic Interpretation. In *The Resurgence of Class Conflict in Western Europe*, vol. 2, ed. C. Crouch and A. Pizzorno, pp. 221–46. London: Macmillan.

Spence, Jonathan. 1990. *The Search for Modern China*. New York: Norton.

Staley, Eugene. 1935. *War and the Private Investor*. Garden City: Doubleday, Doran.

Stamp, A. H. 1979. *A Social and Economic History of England from 1700 to 1970*. London: Research Publishing Co.

Stern, Fritz Richard. 1977. *Gold and Iron: Bismarck, Bleichröder, and the Building of the German Empire*. New York: Alfred A. Knopf.

Stiglitz, Joseph. 2002. *Globalization and Its Discontents*. New York: Norton.

Stögbauer, Christian, and John Komlos. 2004. Averting the Nazi Seizure of Power: A Counterfactual Thought Experiment. *European Review of Economic History* 8 (2): pp. 173–99.

Stover, Charles C. 1970. Tropical Exports. In *Tropical Development 1880–1913*, ed. W. Arthur Lewis, pp. 46–63. London: George Allen and Unwin.

Strange, Susan. 1986. *Casino Capitalism*. Oxford: Blackwell.

Strouse, Jean. 1999. *Morgan*. New York: Random House.

Swenson, Peter. 1989. *Fair Shares: Unions, Pay, and Politics in Sweden and West Germany*. Ithaca: Cornell University Press.

————. 1997. Arranged Alliance: Business Interests in the New Deal. *Politics and Society* 25 (1): pp. 66–116.

Tanaka, Norihito. 1991. *The Postwar Economy of Japan*. Manila: De la Salle University Press.

Taylor, Lance, and Edmar Bacha. 1976. The Unequalizing Spiral: A First Growth Model for Belindia. *Quarterly Journal of Economics* 90 (2): pp. 197–218.

Teichova, Alice. 1985. Industry. In *The Economic History of Eastern Europe 1919–1975*, vol. 1: *Economic Structure and Performance between the Two Wars*, ed. M. C. Kaser and E. A. Radice, pp. 222–322. Oxford: Clarendon.

Temin, Peter. 1989. *Lessons from the Great Depression*. Cambridge: MIT Press.

————. 2000. The Golden Age of European Growth Reconsidered. Unpublished paper.

Thorp, Rosemary, ed. 1984. *Latin America in the 1930s: The Role of the Periphery in World Crisis*. London: Macmillan.

————, and Carlos Londoño. 1984. The Effect of the Great Depression on the Economies of Peru and Colombia. In *Latin America in the 1930s: The Role of the Periphery in World Crisis*, ed. Rosemary Thorp, pp. 81–116. London: Macmillan.

Tilton, Tim. 1990. *The Political Theory of Swedish Social Democracy*. Oxford: Clarendon.

Togo, Yukiyasu. 1993. *Against All Odds: The Story of the Toyota Motor Corporation and the Family that Created it*. New York: St. Martin's Press.

Tomlinson, B. R. 1979. *The Political Economy of the Raj 1914–1947*. London: Macmillan.

————. 1993. *The Economy of Modern India, 1860–1970*, vol. 3: *The New Cambridge History of India*. Cambridge: Cambridge University Press.

Triplett, J. E. 1999. *Computers and the Digital Economy*. Washington, D.C.: Brookings Institution.

Troy, Leo. 1965. Trade Union Membership, 1897–1962. NBER Occasional Paper 92. New York: National Bureau of Economic Research.

Turnock, David. 1986. *The Romanian Economy in the Twentieth Century*. London: Croom Helm.

Unger, Irwin. 1964. *The Greenback Era: A Social and Political History of American Finance, 1865–1879*. Princeton: Princeton University Press.

United Nations Centre for Human Settlements. 1997. *Human Settlements Basic Statistics*. Nairobi: United Nations.

United Nations Commission on Transnational Corporations. 1978. *Transnational Corporations in World Development: A Re-examination*. New York: United Nations.

United Nations Development Program. 1998. *Korean Human Development Report 1998*. Seoul: UNDP Korean Office.

————. Various years. *Human Development Report*. New York: UNDP.

United States Department of Agriculture. 1949. *Statistical Bulletin 85: Feed Statistics Including Wheat, Rye, Rice*. December.

Urrutia, Miguel. 1991. Twenty-five Years of Economic Growth and Social Progress, 1960–1985. In *Long-Term Trends in Latin American Economic Development*, ed. Miguel Urrutia, pp. 23–80. Washington, D.C.: Inter-American Development Bank.

Vaidyanathan, A. 1983. The Indian Economy since Independence. In *The Cambridge Economic History of India*, vol. 2, ed. Dharma Kumar, pp. 947–94. Cambridge: Cambridge University Press.

Van Ark, Bart. 1996. Sectoral Growth Accounting and Structural Change in Post-War Europe. In *Quantitative Aspects of Post-War European Economic Growth*, ed. Bart Van Ark and Nicholas Crafts, pp. 84–164. Cambridge: Cambridge University Press.

————; Jakob de Haan; and Herman de Jong. 1996. Characteristics of Economic Growth in the Netherlands during the Postwar Period. In *Economic Growth in Europe since 1945*, ed. Nicholas Crafts and Gianni Toniolo, pp. 290–328. Cambridge: Cambridge University Press.

————, and Nicholas Crafts, eds. 1996. *Quantitative Aspects of Post-War European Economic Growth*. Cambridge: Cambridge University Press.

Van Dormael, Armand. 1978. *Bretton Woods: Birth of a Monetary System*. New York: Holmes and Meier Publishers.

Van Riel, Arthur, and Arthur Schram. 1992. *Weimar Economic Decline, Nazi Economic*

Recovery and the Stabilization of Political Dictatorship: An Application of Public Choice Theory in Politico-economic History. Amsterdam: University of Amsterdam, Dept. of Economics.

Villarreal, René. 1977. The Policy of Import-Substituting Industrialization, 1929–1975. In *Authoritarianism in Mexico*, ed. José Luis Reyna and Richard S. Weinert, pp. 67–107. Philadelphia: Institute for the Study of Human Issues.

Villela, Annibal, and Wilson Suzigan. 1977. *Government Policy and the Economic Growth of Brazil, 1889–1945.* Rio de Janeiro: IPEA/INPES.

Viner, Jacob. 1948. Power versus Plenty as Objectives of Foreign Policy in the Seventeenth and Eighteenth Centuries. *World Politics* 1 (1): pp. 1–29.

Volcker, Paul, and Toyoo Gyohten. 1992. *Changing Fortunes.* New York: Times Books.

Waley-Cohen, Joanna. 1999. *The Sextants of Beijing.* New York: Norton.

Wallis, John Joseph. 1986. Why 1933? The Origins and Timing of National Government Growth, 1933–1940. In *The Emerging Modern Political Economy*, ed. Robert Higgs, pp. 1–51. Greenwich: JAI Press.

Warren, George, and Frank Pearson. 1935. *Gold and Prices.* New York: John Wiley and Sons.

Warren, Robert. 1937. The International Movement of Capital. *Proceedings of the Academy of Political Science* 17 (3): pp. 65–72.

Watkins, T. H. 1999. *The Hungry Years: A Narrative History of the Great Depression in America.* New York: Henry Holt.

Webb, Steven. 1977. Tariff Protection for Iron Industry, Cotton Textiles and Agriculture in Germany, 1879–1914. *Jahrbucher fur Nationalokonomie und Statistik* 192: pp. 336–57.

———. 1980. Tariffs, Cartels, Technology and Growth in the German Steel Industry, 1879 to 1914. *Journal of Economic History* 40 (2): pp. 309–29.

Weinstein, Michael M. 1981. Some Macroeconomic Impacts of the National Industrial Recovery Act, 1933–1935. In *The Great Depression Revisited*, ed. Karl Brunner, pp. 262–81. Boston: Kluwer-Nijhoff.

Weitz, John. 1997. *Hitler's Banker: Hjalmar Horace Greeley Schacht.* Boston: Little, Brown.

Wells, Wyatt C. 1994. *Economist in an Uncertain World: Arthur F. Burns and the Federal Reserve, 1970–78.* New York: Columbia University Press.

Wheelwright, E. L., and Bruce McFarlane. 1970. *The Chinese Road to Socialism.* New York: Monthly Review Press.

Whiting, Susan. 1996. Contract Incentives and Market Discipline in China's Rural Industrial Sector. In *Reforming Asian Socialism*, ed. John McMillan and Barry Naughton, pp. 63–110. Ann Arbor: University of Michigan Press.

Wilde, Oscar. 1985. *The Importance of Being Earnest and Other Plays.* New York: NAL Penguin.

Wilkins, Mira, 1974. *The Maturing of Multinational Enterprise: American Business Abroad from 1914 to 1970.* Cambridge: Harvard University Press.

———. and Frank Ernest Hill. 1964. *American Business Abroad: Ford on Six Continents.* Detroit: Wayne State University Press.

Williamson, Jeffrey. 1995. The Evolution of Global Labor Markets since 1830: Background Evidence and Hypotheses. *Explorations in Economic History* 32 (2): pp. 141–96.

Williamson, John. 1990. What Washington Means by Policy Reform. In *Latin American Adjustment: How Much Has Happened?*, ed. John Williamson, pp. 7–20. Washington, D.C.: Institute for International Economics.

Williamson, Oliver. 1981. The Modern Corporation: Origins, Evolution, Attributes. *Journal of Economic Literature* 19 (4): pp. 1537–68.

World Bank. Various years. *World Development Indicators*. Washington, D.C.: World Bank.

Yergin, Daniel. 1991. *The Prize: The Epic Quest for Oil, Money and Power.* New York: Simon & Schuster.

Zim, Larry; Melvin J. Lerner; and Herbert Rolfes. 1988. *The World of Tomorrow: The 1939 New York World's Fair.* New York: Harper and Row.

Zwick, Jim, ed. 1992. *Mark Twain's Weapons of Satire: Anti-Imperialist Writings on the Philippine-American War.* Syracuse: Syracuse University Press.

Index